A Half-Century of Greatness

A Half-Century of Greatness

The Creative Imagination of Europe, 1848–1884

Frederic Ewen

EDITED BY JEFFREY WOLLOCK

FOREWORD BY AARON KRAMER

New York University Press

NEW YORK AND LONDON

NEW YORK AND LONDON
www.nyupress.org

NYU Press gratefully acknowledges the generous support of Herbert Kurz
in making possible the publication of this work by Frederic Ewen.

Library of Congress Cataloging-in-Publication Data

Ewen, Frederic, 1899–1988
A half-century of greatness: the creative imagination of Europe,
1848–1884 / Frederic Ewen; edited by Jeffrey Wollock.
p.cm.
Continues: Heroic imagination.
Includes bibliographical references and index.
ISBN-13: 978-0-8147-2236-7 (cloth: alk. paper)
ISBN-10: 0-8147-2236-9 (cloth: alk. paper)
1. Europe—Intellectual life—19th century. 2. Romanticism—Europe. 3.
Europe—History—1848–1849. 4. Revolutions—Europe—History—19th century.
5. Europe—History—19th century. I. Wollock, Jeffrey L. II. Ewen,
Frederic, 1899- Heroic imagination. III. Title.
CB204.E938 2007
940.2'8–dc22
2006038469

10 9 8 7 6 5 4 3 2 1

Contents

Editor's Introduction

The work presented here, never previously published, is the second and concluding part of Frederic Ewen's *magnum opus* on the Romantic period of European literature in its social and political context. It gives central emphasis to the crucial influence exercised by the 1848 revolution, and its failure, on many Romantic and Victorian literary figures. Prof. Ewen seems to have begun work on this big project in the late 1960s, but the first volume, *Heroic Imagination*, was not published until 1984, and this companion volume has had to wait almost two decades after the author's death to appear in print.

Despite prior publication of *Heroic Imagination* both in the 1984 Citadel edition and in a 2004 reprint by NYU Press, it is only now, with the appearance of *A Half-Century of Greatness*, that the full scope of the project can be appreciated. Though each volume stands on its own, each gains by the other's company, and together they present a broad and striking panorama.

Ewen's orientation is Marxist, but not obtrusively so. He writes not as a theorist but a historian, allowing the reader to see the age in vivid perspective. In the light of more recent work, Ewen's approach is most akin to writers such as Marshall Berman (*Adventures in Marxism*, 1999), Richard Wolin (*Walter Benjamin: An Aesthetic of Redemption*, 1994), or Michael Löwy and Robert Sayre (*Romanticism Against the Tide of Modernity*, 2001). Like these writers, Ewen discovers the roots of Marxism in the fertile soil of Romanticism, an international movement with political as well as artistic dimensions. The approach is original in that Romanticism is territory conceded by scholars far more readily to the right than to the left of the political spectrum. Yet Ewen makes us think again, and in so doing, revises to a considerable extent the more familiar map of 19th-century intellectual history. He shows that what we think of today as "the Right" and "the Left" arose from the same revolutionary impulse, which Löwy and Sayre call "Romantic anticapitalism"—a term originally used by George Lukacs in a retrospective preface (1962) to his *Theory of the Novel* (1916) to describe his own pre-Marxist outlook. Ewen's dyptich can also be compared with E. P. Thompson's unfinished work on Wordsworth, Coleridge, Godwin, and Thelwall, *The Romantics: England in a Revolutionary Age* (1997)—itself a posthumous publication.[1]

The appearance of *A Half-Century of Greatness* thus not only demands a new hearing for *Heroic Imagination*, but also compliments recent research on Marxism and Romanticism and links it with earlier scholarship. Considering the period in which Ewen began this project, one may regard him as a bridge between the Old and the New Left (cf. Alexander 1999).

Ewen's erudition is evident throughout. His references include primary and secondary sources not only in English, but also in French, German, Russian, and Ukrainian. (Ewen was born in Lemberg, Galicia—now Lviv, Ukraine—and did not emigrate to the United States until he was 13 years old.)

* * *

While I am unable to provide a full history of the manuscript, it is clear that it began life as something called *Heroic Imagination*, covering European romantic literature from 1800 to 1880. This manuscript grew and grew until the author recognized that it could not be published as a single book. Instead he carved one book out of it, which, retaining the title *Heroic Imagination*, was published in 1984.

At the time of Prof. Ewen's death in October 1988, it was well known that he had been preparing a sequel to *Heroic Imagination*. Indeed, because his son Joel ran a printing business, Ewen enjoyed an advantage almost unknown in the days before the advent of desktop publishing. While still working on the book, he had galleys, and later page proofs set, section by section, using a then new but now obsolete phototype process that stored the information on magnetic tapes, allowing for easy changes. This went on over a long period of time, everything being done according to the author's exact instructions and under his supervision. Although an early title page bears the imprint "Helicon Press, Roanoke, Virginia," this was not an actual book production process; it simply allowed Prof. Ewen—without having to wait for the book's completion—to control the text and layout, making it easier for him to work on and, hopefully, easier to get published one day.

A Long Gestation

Prof. Ewen left a large number of papers and tapes of his writings and lectures. His widow, Miriam Gideon (1906–1996), a distinguished composer, did her best to collect and preserve his legacy. She set certain papers aside in the belief that they represented the last book that Prof. Ewen had been working on, and these were among the materials she gave to the Brooklyn College archives, where Ewen had taught from 1930 to 1952. The great majority of papers, however, remained to be sorted.

In the early 1990s, the author's grandson and executor, Alexander Ewen, gathered all the remaining papers together, and Veronica Farley sorted the pages that appeared to belong to the present book. While this was necessary, it was far from sufficient, because the papers represented an unknown number of different recensions, including some dating from before the original project had been separated into two different books. This initial sorting yielded what appeared to be the makings of a book, but it still was not clear how, or if, they could be fit together into a complete work.

At that time a large number of photographic page proofs and galleys were also discovered. As the phototypes were faded, some of them quite badly, photocopies were immediately made. (The magnetic tapes corresponding to the phototypes were never found.) One set of copies was sent in 1995 to the poet and translator Aaron Kramer, Professor Emeritus at Dowling College and a former student, friend, and colleague of

Prof. Ewen, on the basis of which he wrote a short foreword, included with this volume. Kramer passed away in April 1997. Meanwhile, owing to the vicissitudes of moving and storage, the proofs, along with the copies, went astray and were not rediscovered until several years later.

In 2003 a professional editor was engaged to see if a publishable book could be put together from the typescripts believed to belong to it. The attempt was not encouraging. Clearly there were sections missing, and the position of certain other sections was not clear.

In 2004 Alex Ewen, with whom I have collaborated on numerous writing and research projects over the years, asked me to see if it was possible to salvage the book. From what I had already heard, I was neither confident nor eager to undertake the task, but at Alex's urging, and with the generous support of the Kurz Foundation and the Solidarity Foundation, I agreed to attempt it.

Re-assembly of Ewen's Final Manuscript Recension

In retrospect, it can be seen that one of the main obstacles to previous attempts at reconstruction or reassembly of the manuscript was that the table of contents found among the Ewen papers did not correspond to the final version. Either it corresponded to some recension of the early, longer version of *Heroic Imagination*, or it was no more than an early outline, since there were no page numbers. For the preliminary sorting of papers it had been a useful guide, but in reconstructing the second book it now seemed more a source of confusion. Indeed, no table of contents matching the present text has ever turned up.

On the hypothesis that this "table of contents" might have outlived its usefulness, I abandoned it and set off on a different path. I began work on July 21, 2004 by reviewing the version put together by the previous editor. On July 26 I took an initial look at the papers in the four archival boxes from Brooklyn College held at the office of the Solidarity Foundation in New York.

On July 27 I collated the manuscripts to determine the final state in which Prof. Ewen left them; and in doing this I realized that many of the sections given to the previous editor were one or sometimes two versions prior to Ewen's final manuscript.

I also determined that the final recension is basically what the Brooklyn College archivist had labeled "Manuscript A" (i.e., first half of book) plus other sections (second half). Manuscript A is a typed manuscript, beginning with page number 5 (presumably pp.1–4 were front matter, now lost), put into continuous sequence by the Brooklyn College archivist. It was among the materials first given to Brooklyn College by Prof. Ewen's widow.[2]

"Manuscript A" ends with page 564, the end of the chapter on Wagner. Although the archivist could not have known this, to me there was no question that "Manuscript A" was an incomplete version of the sequel to *Heroic Imagination*, closely matching many parts already known. But clearly p. 564 was not the end of the book. The breakthrough soon came when I found the continuation of Manuscript A in the form of a typescript of the previous recension with its page numbers crossed out and new ones written in and not subsequently crossed out. These new handwritten page numbers, obviously the most recent, were found to continue directly the paging sequence of "Manuscript A" (i.e., with the chapter on Herzen, beginning on p. 565). Together these comprise the only manuscript of this book as a separate work *with its own pagination*, rather than as the second half of the uncut original *Heroic Imagination*, where the corresponding material begins somewhere around p. 700 and obviously represents earlier versions. As with any puzzle, I knew that if this was the right approach, the remaining pieces would fall into place rather easily—and they did. This continual pagination served as the "backbone" of the reconstructed "final recension."

On July 28 I searched through Section 5, Box 4, of the Frederic Ewen Papers at the Tamiment Library, New York University, to determine what was in folders 11–14, the only materials that seemed from the finding guide to be pertinent. On July 29 I reviewed my notes of the previous two days to further determine the manuscript's continuity; I also found a "missing" piece of Manuscript A (pp. 565–586, on Herzen) in another box.

The section on George Eliot (also among the Brooklyn College boxes) was separate and unpaginated; initially it was not clear to me (or to the previous editor) whether it was part of this book. I tentatively hypothesized that George Eliot was probably meant to come after the Brontës.

On July 30, 2004, in assembling the working manuscript, I discovered a fourteen-page gap (which later turned out to represent only eleven pages of text). These corresponded to the final page of the chapter on Carlyle followed by the first ten pages of the Dickens chapter. From the context it was clear that the end of the Carlyle chapter contained a quotation from Harriet Martineau. As for the Dickens pages, I expected on the basis of my Tamiment notes to find them in that archive, and indeed later that day I did. I did not find the last page of the Carlyle chapter. However, with the exception of that one page, I believed I now had pretty much the complete manuscript, although the status of the George Eliot section (part six) would remain under a question mark until the rest had been copyedited.

Due to other responsibilities, I was not able to begin the actual copyediting until February 2005. At its completion about the end of May, I prepared a detailed table of contents. Only while doing this did I realize, to my distress, that there was a forty-five page gap (pp. 413–458) in the manuscript corresponding to most of the second chapter of part three, except for the beginning of section one.

Fortunately, much of Ewen's final recension had turned out to be a repaginated and only lightly revised version of the previous one, and that was the case here: the corresponding forty-five pages from the previous recension (977–1022) fit the gap perfectly in both sequence and number. Any changes Ewen may have made in these missing forty-five pages would have been minor.

Significantly, the missing sections also correspond exactly to the running heads that Ewen designated in a note to the typesetters found among the papers—that sections 3 and 4 dealt with France, section 5 with Germany, and section 6 with Austria. (This portion also contains sections numbered 7 and 8, on the failure of the revolution.)* A likely explanation for the gap then was that the forty-five pages were given

---

* Section numbers in the present edition differ from those in the manuscript, due to the consolidation of certain sections.[Ed.]

to the typesetters and never found their way back to the manuscript. Corroborating this, the forty-five pages missing from the manuscript corresponded exactly to a gap in the proofs (which are, both preceding and following the gap, in the more preliminary state of galleys rather than page proofs).*

It is also interesting to note that in earlier versions of the huge work from which both *Heroic Imagination* and the present book were carved, the corresponding Part Three—there called Floodtide, 1848–1849—contained additional sections: 8 was on Grillparzer, 9 on Lenau, 10 also on Grillparzer, 11 on Hebbel, 12 on Nestroy, and 13 on the ballad and the *Lied*, treating of Eichendorf, Mörike, and Adalbert Stifter. What this tells us is that these portions were cut from the present work by Ewen himself, and they are not included in *Heroic Imagination* either. They exist in two different recensions, one containing sections 8 through 11, with pp. 1312–1313 missing; the other consisting of most of section 9 (except for the first one or two pages), part of section 10 on Grillparzer, and sections 12 and 13. The content of the two versions is similar, but the text differs considerably in wording. There are also a few pages from yet a third version.

Like the manuscript on George Eliot that now forms Part Six of this book, the whole of Part Five (England: Crystal Palace and Bleak House) in this final recension was also originally unpaginated (except for the first page, originally written in as 1376, then 670). But on the upper right hand were originally penciled in page numbers 1–71, then 1–28, then 1–30 (39 removed), five originally unnumbered pages, then 5/1 plus one unnumbered, 6a/1 plus two unnumbered, 7/3–7/15, one unnumbered, 7/17–7/19, and seventeen unnumbered pages (msp.776–793). All of this is evidence of an extensive rewriting and, mainly, great expansion, of this material (for example, the sequence 7/3–7/19 suggests a great expansion of an original p.7). Also, the Brontë chapter is roughly written and needed heavier editing—and no galleys or page proofs exist for this section, nor did the author specify running heads as he had in all previous sections.

These observations fit with what we know from plans of the earlier book that the Brontës and Eliot were originally conceived as going into a single concluding chapter. There are also no proofs or running heads for Part Six on George Eliot.

Rough writing and expansion is also seen in the section in Germany and the Poets (ms pp. 655–688), but this was evidently done somewhat earlier, since it exists in proofs.

To sum up: the manuscript on which this edition is based, what I call Ewen's last recension, is a substantially complete manuscript of slightly more than 900 pages. It is "unfinished," first, in the sense that the author was still evidently in the process of fine-tuning certain sections, or intending to. This is especially true of the chapter on the Brontës in Part Five, which had been revised but not yet retyped. As for the final section (Part Six: George Eliot), this existed only in an older, unpaginated manuscript that never received the final revision that most of the book underwent.

After preliminary editing of the rest of the manuscript, I turned to the George Eliot material. Ewen had placed this in a type of binder similar to those used for some other sections. But since it was unpaginated, I still was not sure whether it was actually part

---

* The missing pages, incorporating Ewen's last stylistic edits, were later found with the proofs. To the extent possible, these changes are reflected in the present text (pp. 220–255).

of the book or not. Fortunately, this did not remain a mystery for long. Numerous references to matters brought up in other parts of the manuscript prove that the Eliot not only belonged to the book, but was intended as a kind of summing up.

Over all, the editing was far more arduous than anticipated: on closer scrutiny much of the writing proved rougher than expected; also, through revision and retyping over the years, many corruptions had crept into both text and quotations.

The Proofs Again

When the missing page proofs were rediscovered in November 2005, it turned out that neither Parts Five and Six of the book, nor the endnotes and bibliography, were among them. This must have been one of the main reasons why the family believed that the work had never been completed. And they may have been correct in thinking that Ewen abandoned it after becoming discouraged that he would never be able to get it published. Whatever further light Joel Ewen might have been able to shed on this problem was precluded by his death just a few years after his father's, long before anyone had thought to investigate these questions.

Prior to the recovery of the proofs, I was able to consult only a photocopy of proofs of Chapter One found in the Tamiment archive. This includes a title page, and curiously, the title is given simply as *Heroic Imagination: The Creative Genius of Europe from Waterloo (1815) to the Revolution of 1848, volume II.* When the missing page proofs were found, it became clear that the Tamiment proof fragment was an earlier version.

Chapter One in the Tamiment fragment, however, was the same as in the later proofs—the only real difference was in the title of the book itself. According to a surviving table of contents of an early version of the larger project, the second part was already called "A Half-Century of Greatness: The Heroic Age of European Literature, 1830–1880." The Tamiment proof fragment calls it simply *Heroic Imagination*, vol. 2. The rediscovered proofs reveal that Ewen eventually changed the title back to its original form, but gave it a new subtitle: *The Creative Imagination of Europe, 1848–1883.*

Fortunately, the temporary disappearance of the proofs turned out to be no great disadvantage to the editing. The text of the proofs shows only minor differences from the manuscript recension that, on independent grounds, was identified as the final one and is the basis for the text edited here. This is because the proofs were set, at least for the most part, from that manuscript. Handwritten typesetters' codes can be seen on the upper left hand corner of many of the pages.

Not only do the proofs incorporate the author's handwritten changes to the final manuscript, but they also contain mistakes left uncorrected in that manuscript and add new typographical errors. So on the one hand they provide a "blind" confirmation of the text as reconstructed from our final recension, and on the other, they show that the manuscript was the better text.

In fact, the book could not have been reconstructed from the proofs. This is because parts five and six of the book are entirely lacking from the proofs, as are the reference citations. In the typescript these notes appear on the line following the corresponding superscript or close to it; but the fact that they do not appear as footnotes on the proof pages indicates that Ewen wanted them placed with the back matter as endnotes, and these too were never set in type.

The proofs nevertheless had their own value on a few specific points: (1) to ascertain Ewen's latest choice of title; (2) to restore the text of the final page of chapter 1—never found in ms.; and finally, (3) to serve as the ultimate authority on chapter subdivisions, titles, and running heads (specifically designated by the author for most of the book). Indeed a number of doubts and minor discrepancies were settled in favor of the proofs.

Philosophy of Editing

My goal was to reconstruct the author's latest intentions and, having done that, to treat the results as with any book submitted for editing, also bearing in mind that the author was still revising or intending to revise certain sections, especially parts five and six. Unfortunately he is no longer around to answer queries. Thus I did not treat the text as sacrosanct, but edited as lightly as possible, altering Ewen's prose only where I felt it necessary to add clarity or variety. Ewen was a stimulating and compelling writer, but like most writers he had certain recurrent stylistic quirks and in the last analysis English was not his native language. Among the most typical traits, he has what one might call a "shaggy" style, paratactic and somewhat Germanic; his sentences are often very long and often stray from parallel structure where it would be stylistically desirable and would be easier to follow, he almost never uses participial phrases, and so on. As noted also by Prof. Kramer in marginal comments, some sections of the book are particularly rough, because he did not finish revising.[3] (Kramer's incisive obervations were of great help to me throughout.)

These peculiarities are also consistent with what I learned anecdotally: that Ewen always composed directly and rapidly at the typewriter—and working with a typewriter (for those who do not know or no longer remember) is a very different experience from working with a word processor!

Thus I edited in such a way as to retain the author's style while clarifying the flow and connection of his thought. Ewen's punctuation is quite idiosyncratic. Among other things, he was what can only be described as "dash-happy." I reduced the number of dashes by perhaps 20 percent—substituting commas, colons, or parentheses. On the other hand, I actually inserted dashes on occasion where they helped to clarify the structure of some of his very long sentences. Although he almost never used participial phrases, there were sentences here and there that cried out for them.

I also gradually came to notice, after having edited quite a bit of the book, that at least one person other than Ewen had made edits. Thus, where I have indicated "author's deletion," this may include cuts by someone other than the author—but anyway not by me. Whatever cuts I made throughout the book are very few and very short. In a few instances I changed the position of a sentence in a paragraph. I inserted exactly one sentence (in the Eliot section) to remedy what I felt was a serious problem of continuity.

Bibliographical Apparatus

Ewen's reconstructed manuscript was found to contain almost all necessary reference notes. The problem was that most of them are given in short form—sometimes very short form—often with nothing more than a surname and page number. As it turns out, these surnames sometimes refer to an editor rather than an author, but the distinction is almost never indicated. I decided to leave these notes as the author left them (except to correct silently certain obvious errors), but they have been rendered functional by the provision of a bibliography. The reconstruction of the bibliography of cited sources on the basis of Ewen's notes was carried out mostly from July through November 2005 and in March 2006. While requiring much time and effort, the reconstruction was for the most part not too problematic, except for some of the cases where Ewen had not provided a title. These were eventually identified, but often not without considerable labor.

Even when a citation was identified, it was sometimes impossible to tell what edition Ewen had used. This was especially true of works printed in numerous editions—most of the Dickens titles and a few of the works by Carlyle and John Stuart Mill. Fortunately, the question is of little practical consequence. The same can be said of the choice between American and British editions, or exactly which reprint he might have used—it really makes little difference. In such "indifferent" cases, I tried to cite the more widely available editions. An inventory of Ewen's library, prepared after his death by Veronica Farley, proved to be of surprisingly limited value for the purpose, since very few of the titles cited by Ewen were found there.

It is a paradox of textual editing that, if the work is properly done, it should not be noticed. It will therefore be my greatest satisfaction if the effort that went into the preparation of this volume allows Prof. Ewen to speak directly to the reader as he intended.

Foreword

Aaron Kramer

Dedicating *Heroic Imagination* to his students was, of course, a most gracious act on the part of the author, but utterly in keeping, since it was to us, after all, that he had dedicated—through a shining life-span—his energies and his genius.

At the time, however, we hardly realized the uniqueness of our situation, assuming that every campus must have at least one Frederic Ewen. As for me, it was only later that the blessed subversiveness of my five Ewen semesters grew clear. America's English departments had long since fallen under the sway of the New Criticism—a tyranny from which they have even now not quite shaken loose. Cleanth Brooks, high priest of that sect, had made it his life's crusade "to stress the poem rather than the poet":

> So long as the emphasis is on the poet's personality rather than on his craftsmanship, on his sincerity rather than on his solution of an artistic problem, on the intensity of his emotions or his commitment to a cause rather than on the structure of meanings that he has realized in the poem, there is not likely to be much "close reading" as we now know it—though there may be a minute and even pedantic searching of his letters or autobiography.

Others subsequently trained me, and mostly I trained myself, in the areas of "craftsmanship, ... solution of an artistic problem, ... the structure of meanings," which are, of course, indispensable for a poet and a teacher of poetry. But if that had to be my total focus, as Cleanth Brooks and his apostles decreed, I would long ago have fled the sterile parishes of their aestheticist worship. More than anything else, the lessons of Frederic Ewen were vivifying; not only did he give life to every literary work by making it leap from the context of the author's epoch and personal situation, but—most remarkable of all—he made us forget we were in a classroom, exploring curricular materials. Whatever we studied, no matter its place or time of origin, spoke to our own turbulent place and time, illuminated our own developing young lives, and helped us live. What we received was a "close reading" of the human condition.

Opening the first volume in 1984 was like stepping into our professor's room again and, half a century later, renewing the grand experience of our youth, when each day's lecture whetted the appetite for more. Shakespeare said as much of Cleopatra: "she makes hungry Where most she satisfies."

In reviewing "this massive work and nearly unparalleled erudition," Lothar Kahn describes precisely the nature of our master's teaching, which into his eighties had lost none of its purity and vigor:

Ewen moves with remarkable facility from one national culture to another, from one genre to the next, one distinctive personality to a different one that was equally distinctive: tomes of vast scholarship often manage—without effort—to be quite dull. It appears that, just as effortlessly, Prof. Ewen has produced an extremely lively, colorful, even exciting account that is truly scholarship at its best.

And D.D. Murdoch, in his review, accurately characterizes the Ewen approach:

It is not statistical social science; it is narrative history with an emphasis on the personal lives and contributions of individual men and women of literary, artistic, and musical genius … Although essentially a "history of the spirit," the narrative documents the artists' involvement in social movements and their awareness of revolutionary economic and political developments … The book is written in a very personal style, with enthusiasm for its subject … The reader receives a sense of the ferment of the times.

Unswervingly defiant of the New Critics, Ewen had declared in an eloquent prologue what readers should expect: a "close reading" not so much of the poem as of its epoch. "This is a time when national genius transcends national boundaries, and spirits communicate across vast distances, affecting or being affected by those of other lands." His "close reading" was "concerned with the fruits of the interaction of the public 'collective consciousness' with the creative consciousness of the individual, the private creator."

The same two-fold synergy continues to be demonstrated in the period covered by the present volume, *A Half-Century of Greatness*, and it is cause for celebration that this astounding segment should at last be made available. Focused on the social and philosophic upsurges leading to 1848, and the bloody rage with which embattled tyranny crushed, city by city, every last spark of republicanism and revolution, the present book brings to thrilling, often appalling, life the episodes of that unprecedented time with the force of an epic poem. Thanks to both his sympathetic personal insights and his superb documentation, the outstanding figures of that moment move dynamically through Ewen's pages fully dimensionalized, liberated from the dull footnote entries of yellowing textbooks.

Everywhere fascinating bits of information leap out at the reader: John Stuart Mill accidentally throwing out as waste paper the manuscript of Carlyle's *French Revolution* … Dickens, in French, responding ecstatically to the February 1848 upheaval that he would henceforth write only in French … Wagner's second opera, *Das Liebesverbot*, inspired by *Measure For Measure* … The fiery battle-hymn "Il Canto degli Italiani," by Goffredo Mameli (who died in the defense of republican Rome), galvanizing Garibaldi—another of his hymns, "Suona la Tromba," set to music by Verdi … Lord George Gordon, leader of the infamous 1780 anti-Catholic riots, later converted to Orthodox Judaism and dying in jail as Israel bar Abraham Gordon … and on and on …

Embedded throughout are memorable scenes, unearthed by an indefatigable scholar from diaries, letters, news reports, memoirs: For four June days the leaderless insurrectionists man their barricades against an overwhelming force under Cavaignac … George Sand publicly denounces her country when it crushes the Parisian masses desperate for work and bread … Auguste Blanqui, on trial for "incendiary republicanism," turns accuser of his judges, like Dimitrov a century later … Turgenev recalls his history professor, Gogol, grotesque and pathetic in the classroom ... Vissarion Belinsky excoriates Gogol, formerly his idol, for betraying his genius and his ideals; the letter, though unpublishable at the time, is memorized by hundreds ... The Petrashevsky group are lined up before a firing-squad; at the last moment their death sentence is commuted; Grigoriev goes insane, Dostoevsky is reborn ... A letter to the Duke of Wellington from Cork's magistrate Nicholas Cummins during the potato famine, describes his visit to Skibbereen, a town of corpses and living corpses ... Taras Shevchenko, forbidden to write or sketch in his Siberian exile, smuggles into his boots bits of notepapers soon to blossom into splendid poems ... The Hunted Mikhail Bakunin suddenly materializes after Wagner's dress rehearsal of Beethoven's Ninth and declares: Should all music go up in flame in the coming world conflagration, this symphony must at all costs be preserved ... Petöfi at twenty-six sends a love-letter to his wife, asking her to wean their baby quickly and surprise him; two days later he dies a hero as 4,200 Hungarians face 18,000 crack Tsarist troops ... Defiantly, Viennese journalists Julius Becker and Herman Jellinek face Metternich's firing squad, along with Robert Blum, a beloved deputy in Frankfort's parliament, whose last letter to his wife lists the keepsakes each child is to have.

The reader who supposed himself well-versed in Robert Owen, the Chartist Movement, Hegelianism, Utilitarianism, Saint-Simonianism, Comte, Proudhon, Michelet, Herzen, etc., will come to know them truly, defined both in themselves and in their time. Harriet Taylor, hitherto mentioned as John Stuart Mill's already married companion and finally his wife, receives the long-overdue prominence she merits, not only for her emotional and psychological support, but for her profound influence on Mill's thinking and work.

Illuminating chapters are devoted to such titanic pioneers as Carlyle, John Stuart Mill, Ludwig Feuerbach, David Friedrich Strauss, Marx, Engels, and Wagner, whose lives and personalities are projected as spellbindingly as in a great novel, and whose works are explicated with immense sympathy and care, highlighted by beautifully chosen excerpts. The towering influence of Feuerbach and Strauss on such contemporaries as the youthful Marx and Engels, leads us to reconsider their masterpieces—*The Essence of Christianity* and *The Life of Jesus*—both of which a young George Eliot felt impelled to translate. Was it not to Feuerbach that Wagner dedicated his own most important philosophic work, publicly acknowledging his debt?

Judiciously selected passages of poetry, not dissected but dramatically offered—in their originals and in translation—bringing us close to the throbbing souls of Petöfi and Shevchenko, making it clear how these men, heirs of Shelley and Robert Burns, earned their status as the national poets of Hungary and Ukraine. Germany's revolutionary voices of the 1830s and 1840s—Büchner, Herwegh, Freiligrath, and Heine, among others less well known but finally given their due in this volume—are also heard at full force. For me, whose life began with the thunderous sonorities of *Rienzi*, perhaps the most spectacular discovery was "The Revolution," which Ewen calls Wagner's manifesto, an anonymously published 1849 prose-poem inspired by Bakunin.

As for the fiction, Ewen offers a feast of insightful commentary and sensitively chosen passages that unfold the essence of Gogol, Dickens, and early Dostoevsky—masterfully relating each story, each novel to its author and his epoch.

To relive the grand aspirations that culminated in 1848, and to share in their swift defeat, is a shattering experience for the reader. But Ewen lets us know that Hegel's dialectics were at work: thesis and antithesis inexorably leading to synthesis, destined to bring new struggles, even victories. If 1848 spelled the end of Romanticism, out of the ashes leaped Realism, its child. As for humanity's craving to be free, could it be stamped out by the hired boots of a Tsar, a Metternich, any more than Zeus could vanquish the flame of Prometheus?

A century later, when Senator McCarthy led a similar effort—temporarily successful—to suppress ideas, I ended each poetry reading with Whitman's "Europe: The 72nd and 73rd Years of These States," explaining 1848–49 as if I really knew those years and understood the huge throngs that hailed Kossuth in city after American city, thousands decked in the suddenly prevalent Kossuth hat. Only now, after absorbing the exhilaration and agony of these pages, do I fully comprehend the golden lines I memorized as a boy:

> Meanwhile corpses lie in new-made graves, bloody corpses of young men,
> The rope of the gibbet hangs heavily, the bullets of princes are flying, the
> creatures of power laugh aloud,
> And all these things bear fruit, and they are good.

> Those corpses of young men,
> Those martyrs that hang from the gibbets, those hearts pierc'd by the gray lead,
> Cold and motionless as they seem live elsewhere with unslaughter'd vitality.

> They live in other men O kings!
> They live in brothers again ready to defy you,
> They were purified by death, they were taught and exalted.

> Not a grave of the murder'd for freedom but grows seed for freedom, in its turn
> to bear seed,
> Which the winds carry afar and re-sow, and the rains and the snows nourish.

> Not a disembodied spirit can the weapons of tyrants let loose,
> But it stalks invisibly over the earth, whispering counseling, cautioning.

> Liberty, let others despair of you—I never despair of you.

> Is the house shut? Is the master away?
> Nevertheless, be ready, be not weary of watching,
> He will soon return, his messengers come anon.

Part One

England at the Great Divide

1830–1848

Chapter One

The Battle for Reform

Magnificent edifices, surpassing in number, value, usefulness, and ingenuity of construction, the boasted monuments of Asiatic, Egyptian and Roman despotism, have,
within the short period of fifty years, risen up in this
Kingdom, to show to what extent capital, industry, and
science may augment the resources of the state, while
they meliorate the condition of its citizens; such is the
factory system, replete with prodigies in mechanics and
political economy, which promises in its future growth
to become the great minister of civilization to the terraqueous globe, enabling this country, as its heart, to dif-
fuse along with its commerce the life-blood and religion
to myriads of people still lying 'in the region and shadow
of death.'
—Andrew Ure, *The Philosophy of Manufacture*, 1835

There is a King, and a ruthless King,
Not a King of the poet's dream;
But a tyrant fell, while slaves know him well,
And that ruthless King is Steam.
He hath an arm, an iron arm,
And tho' he hath but one,
In that mighty arm there is a charm,
That millions hath undone ...
—"King Steam," by Edward P. Mean, 1843

Though Victoria did not come to the throne of England until 1837, the "Age of Victoria"—a term which was coined somewhat later—actually commenced in 1830, with
the great struggles over the reform of Parliament. "Victorianism" has become a word
of many colors and patches, dyed and cut to many patterns. Each of these contains its
seed of truth, but such partial elements frequently tend to obscure the larger essence.
Though, for example, terms like "Victorian compromise," "propriety and discretion,"
"prudishness," "dilemma," all pinpoint certain aspects of the era, the central kernel of
the age may be succinctly described as a dual conflict: "Compromise" on one hand;
and an agonizing battle against it. The "Compromise" that triumphed was to be of the
greatest import both for Britain and the rest of the world. It was the accommodation

effected by the Tory landowning interests and the Whig industrial, commercial, and financial powers, enabling them together to rule England successfully throughout the century and extend her political and economic hegemony over a good portion of the earth. That there were to be internecine struggles between these two forces—representing "town and squire" respectively—did not prevent their conciliation, in times of crisis, when it came to addressing the ever-growing threats of a new enemy, the industrial and the agrarian worker.

The landowner exercised the dominant power. As Hobsbawm expressed it,

> The classical British solution produced a country in which perhaps 4,000 proprietors owned perhaps four-sevenths of the land which was cultivated—I take the 1851 figures—by a quarter of a million farmers (three-quarters of the acreage being in farms of from 50 to 50,000 acres), who employed about one and a quarter million of hired labourers and servants.[1]

This is the essence of the "Compromise": the successful creation of a highly developed capitalist structure uniting land, industry, commerce and finance, destined to become the cynosure, envy, object of hate, admiration, horror—and model for the rest of the world. For the landlords of other countries, the British landlord served as a model exhibiting the efficacy of the balance of power, the magnificence and influence of the House of Lords, and the methods of ruling one's tenants. For the rising bourgeoisie, the British could serve as prime examples of the miracles of industrialism and enrichment. For the socialists and liberals, the newly organized and fast-growing working classes and their political and social awareness would serve as encouragement and incentive for the organization of working-class elements in other countries. Not least, the rapid industrialization of Britain would unveil the true meaning of this staggering phenomenon—the obverse of the coin which featured on its other facet the enrichment of the few. This the brilliant Frenchman Alexis de Tocqueville noted when he visited Manchester in 1835:

> From this foul drain the greatest stream of human industry flows out to fertilize the whole world. From this filthy sewer pure gold flows. Here humanity attains its most complete development and its most brutish, here civilization works its miracles and civilized man is turned into a savage.[2]

"Gold" and "savagery"—could anyone have defined more vividly the presence of what Disraeli was to call the "two nations"—the antipodal phenomena of inexhaustible wealth and dire poverty? On the one hand the "miracles" of science, technology, and the prospect of a world of infinite possibilities for mankind, of progress almost God-decreed. On the other, horrors frightful to contemplate. How to reconcile this great contradiction? How to resolve it?

Perhaps it was after all a design of Heaven. In the blackest year of depression and unemployment, Lord Palmerston panegyrized Commerce:

> May [it] go freely forth, leading civilization with one hand, and peace with the other, to render mankind happier, wiser, better ... This is the dispensation of Providence.[3]

Or was it, as others believed, Nature's ineluctable ordinance? Or was it, perhaps, of mankind's own making? ...

Victorianism is also a drama—a drama of warring conscience. Victorianism is a crisis, reflecting what is sometimes called the "Victorian dilemma." Two battlefields stretch before us: the battlefield of the physical human beings ranged against one another, and the battlefield of morality, of the conscience, within the human being— "darkling plains" both ...

England was a changed land. Sixty years before, as Friedrich Engels described her in 1844,

> England was a country like every other, with small towns, few and simple industries, and a thin, but proportionally large agricultural population. Today, it is a country like *no other*, with a capital of 2½ million inhabitants, with vast manufacturing cities; with an industry that supplies, and produces almost everything by means of the most complex machinery; with an industrious, intelligent, dense population, of which ⅔ are employed in trade and commerce, and composed of classes wholly different; forming, in fact, with other customs and other needs, a different nation from the England of those days. The industrial revolution is of the same importance for England as the political revolution for France, and the philosophical revolution for Germany, and the difference between England in 1760, and in 1844 is at least as great as between France under the *ancien régime* and during the revolution of July. But the mightiest result of this industrial revolution is the English proletariat.[4]

At such moments, time-honored creeds begin falling by the wayside. Winds of doctrine blow hither and thither. Old moralities are shaken, religious beliefs challenged. The once solid bases of society are in danger of being uprooted.

*   *   *

The July Revolution of 1830 that had aroused so much consternation as well as hope outside of France did not leave England untouched. Not since 1789, or the time when Napoleon was about to invade that country, had England been so alarmed. British radicals rejoiced, as did portions of the populace. In Birmingham and in London the French tricolor was flaunted. In London, in December 1830, a thousand workers besieged the palace of St. James, waving the French flag. Hundreds attended meetings to express their sympathy with the French. Pilgrimages to Paris were organized. Delegations journeyed to France, including a number of distinguished Englishmen. Young John Stuart Mill was a member of one such delegation, which was received by Lafayette.

In Great Britain, grievances that had smouldered for many years now became articulate and explosive. Serious uprisings took place in various parts of the country, set off by the economic distress in factory and farm. Fires were set by discontented agrarian workers. Kent, Sussex, Hampshire, Wiltshire and other counties were actually up in arms. Numerous manifestos made their appearance, with inflammatory slogans. Such, for example, is one which was circulated in Hampshire in the year 1830:

> The flags of freedom and liberty are flying over the Churches and steeples on the continent. Rise Englishmen and assert your rights and pull down priest-craft and oppression. The Reform Bill is only a stepping-stone of our future advantages. Down with tithes! down with taxes! down with places! and down with pensions![5]

The ministry of Lord Grey proceeded to meet the insurgency with force. Lord Wellington described the then usual course of action:

> I induced the magistrates to put themselves on horseback, each at the head of his own servants and retainers, grooms, huntsmen, game-keepers, armed with horsewhips, pistols, fowling pieces and what they could get, and to attack in concert ... these mobs, disperse them, destroy them, and take and put in confinement those who could not escape ...[6]

Nine hundred arrests, three executions could not stem the tide of protest. The populace was in earnest. The reform of Parliament must be undertaken, suffrage widened, grievances attended to. The protests took the additional form of refusals to pay tithes, runs on banks, attacks on the clergy. They ranged all the way from the mines of Cornwall and Wales to the cotton manufactories of Manchester. Hitherto dormant political unions were resuscitated. The populace was angry.

Others were frightened—aghast. Sir William Napier wrote to his wife in January 1831 that he expected a revolution momentarily, for talk of sedition and rebellion was rampant everywhere.

> The first great man that steps forward will be sovereign of this country, or he will found a republic.[7]

Anger rose to fever pitch when the House of Lords continued obstructing the passage of a House of Commons reform bill. The Bishops were in the vanguard of the opposition. This was a diehard struggle, as the Lords, representing the vast landed interests, fought the new industrial and commercial powers. From many quarters came dire predictions and forebodings should a reform bill fail of passing. In the House of Commons, Thomas Babington Macaulay uttered his warning:

> ... If this Bill should be rejected, I pray to God that none of those who concur in rejecting it may ever remember their votes with unavailing remorse, amidst the wreck of laws, the confusion of ranks, the spoliation of property and the dissolution of social order ...[8]

Others, like the Rev. Thomas Arnold, father of Matthew Arnold, foresaw with the passage of the bill untold benefits and happiness: "I believe," [he wrote,] if it passes now, *felix saeclorum nascitur ordo*, "a happy new reign of ages will be born."[9]

And not least, the agrarian and manufacturing laborers—the working classes—without whose agitation, demonstrations, and sacrifices the bill would never have been passed, looked to its passage as promising them a better life.

A cynical politician remarked:

> The Tories prognosticate all sorts of dismal consequences, none of which will come to pass. *Nothing* will happen, because in this country *nothing* ever happens.[10]

But things did happen. The Lords finally yielded and the Reform Bill became law in June 1832. A historical necessity, propelled by popular action, a higher shrewdness that counseled the surrender of a small portion of their rights and parliamentary preponderance but served to preserve the major part of their political power, and in fact strengthen their economic hold, led to "compromise" on the part of the land-owning interests. A large number of "rotten" boroughs, which had no justification to be represented, were abolished, and sixty-three important cities, chiefly manufacturing, were given representation. Property qualifications for electors were moderately reduced or modified. But the loyal battle-companions, the working class, ever propertyless, were excluded. So were, of course, all women, who were forced to wait a full century before being granted the right to vote. It was a triumph for Whig and Tory. The manufacturer and trader came into their own. Their "alliance" with the "lower" classes had paid off. It was time now to cut whatever ties existed between the two. It was also time for Whig and Tory to join in stemming the tide of dissent, disaffection, and disenchantment among the laboring classes, and most important of all, disrupt and destroy any attempts at organization on their part.

The first Whig ministry to come to power since 1807 began, soon after its accession, to try to squelch what a contemporary economist called the "hydra of misrule"—the articulate and recalcitrant "lower" classes—using the machine in the process. "When capital enlists science in her service," Andrew Ure wrote, "the refractory hand of labour will always be taught docility."[11]

But the battle was far from over. Disenchantment among the working population was widespread. The burden of warfare against economic and political injustice would now have to be borne by the working classes themselves, with whatever aid they could attract and muster from liberals. The "shopocrat" franchise recently perpetrated was a fraud.

> The promoters of the Reform Bill, one of their spokesmen wrote, project it, not with a view to subvert or even remodel our aristocratic institutions, but to consolidate them by a reinforcement of sub-aristocracy from the middle classes ... The only difference between Whigs and Tories is this—the Whigs would give the shadow to preserve the substance; the Tories would not give the shadow, because stupid as they are, the millions would not stop at shadow but proceed onwards to realities.[12]

The "lower" orders were discovering a kind of "class" consciousness. It is here and now that the new movement that was to be called "Chartism" was born. It was a movement for a new Magna Carta, begun with the political defeats of 1833 and 1834, and the crushing of trade union organization. It was to make itself politically explicit in the proclamation of the "Six Points" of the Charter of 1838. Monster demonstrations took place, such as that in 1833, when colliers from Walsall, ironworkers from Wolverhampton, and other groups openly expressed

> a sentiment of common hatred to the parties who, having been mainly instrumental in forcing into power, they now assembled to express their disgust for the ... treachery which they had manifested.[13]

This meeting of May 1833 claimed an attendance of 180,000. There was a sense here of solidarity that extended not only to their own groups, but also to the Parisians of 1830, and to the insurgent Poles. These working people regarded themselves as "Men of the Great Family of Mankind."[14]

Revolutionary cries and slogans became rampant, such as for a need to "take over," "to swallow up the whole political power," "to abolish wages and become their own masters, and work for each other."[15]

Such was the growth of the people's collective consciousness. It harked back to the days of the Puritan Revolution, the Commonwealth, and to more recent history. It was all in the spirit of John Bunyan, of Thomas Paine, as well as that of William Cobbett and Robert Owen. One contemporary witness remarked on the gulf that existed in Manchester between the rich and poor,

> There is no town in the world where the distance between the rich and the poor is so great, the barrier between them so difficult to cross.[16]

Manchester, of course, was not the only example.

History and historians have unfortunately tended to overlook the hundreds upon hundreds of men and women, most of them destined to remain nameless, whose courage and participation in the activities made the victories of the commercial and manufacturing classes possible, and who paid dearly for betrayal at their hands. In 1834, in Tolpuddle, Dorsetshire, six leaders were arrested and transported to Botany Bay, Australia, for organizing a "union" of agricultural workers and "binding them by oath." One of these—George Loveless, a Methodist preacher—said on his return from deportation in 1836:

> I believe that nothing will ever be done to relieve the distress of the working classes unless they take it into their own hands: with these beliefs I lived in England, and with these views I am returned. Notwithstanding all that I have seen and felt, my sentiments on the subject are unchanged. Nothing but union can accomplish the great and important object, namely, the salvation of the world. Let the producers of wealth firmly and peacefully unite their energies and what can withstand them? The power and influence of the non-producers would sink into insignificance, the conquest is won, the victory is certain.[17]

Among the most effective weapons of repression in the hands of the government was control of the press. One such control was a law that imposed a four-penny tax on newspapers, the so-called "tax on knowledge." To counter this obstruction, there arose the "unstamped" journals, the so-called "Pauper Press." Astonishing as to number and circulation, these newspapers emanated for the most part from London, but they found distribution throughout the country. Not the least amazing phenomenon was their widespread readership. Copies passed from hand to hand, many of them being read aloud in taverns and other public houses. Their editors, printers, and vendors were subjected to prosecution, but they continued to defy the law and persisted so vigorously that they came to be regarded as formidable competition to the established press. Agitation for the lowering of the stamp tax became so intense, that it was finally, in 1836, reduced to one penny. The history of the nineteenth century, and of its working class, cannot be fully understood without reference to the literacy of the working-class supporters of the press, and the undaunted activities of the writers, editors, publishers, and distributors. The "Pauper Press" was in great measure instrumental in sharpening the awareness of its readers, as well as its many auditors who could not read, that the working class was an "excluded" class—excluded both from political life and economic power.[18]

The writers of these newspapers speak with pride, dignity, and fearlessness. "We begin this paper" says *The Cosmopolite* of 1832,

> in a spirit of warfare, and we are not to be scared by informations, or street arrests, or imprisonments. There is a sturdy band of us, not beggars, but sellers of cheap news and knowledge—who will not be beggars—who bid defiance to the hypocritical tyranny of whig malice ...[19]

Then there were such editors and writers as Richard Carlile—undaunted, more often in jail than out; Henry Hetherington, and James Bronterre O'Brien. Of course they were fighting an enemy who possessed all the advantages of the ruling powers— not least the force of personal influence, inexhaustible wealth, and innumerable organs of propaganda, in which they sought, through their own varied means of communication, to neutralize the physical and journalistic expression of the opposition and divert it into more manageable channels.

But they found no mean ideological opponent in Bronterre O'Brien, the editor of one of the most powerful of the "Pauper" journals, *The Poor Man's Guardian*. Here is one of O'Brien's instructive pieces:

> ... Since all wealth is the produce of industry, and as the privileged fraction produce nothing themselves, it is plain that they must live on the labours of the rest ... The 'property' people have all the law-making to themselves, make and maintain fraudulent institutions, by which they contrive (under false pretences) to transfer the wealth of the producers to themselves. All our institutions relating to *land* and *money* are of this kind. These institutions enable certain individuals, called "land-lords," to monopolize the soil, to the exclusion of the rest of society, who are thereby defrauded of this just and natural inheritance. To secure themselves in this monopoly, the landlords united with another band of conspirators called "capitalists," and from their union proceeds a *monied monopoly*, which is (if possible) a thousand times more baneful than the monopoly in land. From these two master monopolies proceed a thousand others ... all tending ... to the absorption of the annual produce of the country into the hands of the monopolists. One portion is absorbed under the name of *rent*, another under that of *tithes*, a third under that of *taxes*, a fourth under that of *tolls*, a fifth under that of *law* expenses, a sixth under that of *interest*, a seventh (which is by far the greatest) under that of *profits*, and so one with *commissions*, *agencies*, *brokerage*, etc., to the end of the chapter. These and the like are the pretences under which the useful classes are plundered for the benefit of the useless.[20]

To counter the agitations, the disturbances, the menace of working-class organization, the riots, demonstrations, and intermittent violence, the governing classes and their allies brought their own forces into the field in the twofold form of concessions along with more stringent coercive measures. The reforms included the repeal of religious restrictions on Catholics and the passage of various factory acts, such as limiting to eight or nine hours the labor of children under thirteen years of age, that of youngsters between thirteen and eighteen to no more than twelve hours. Children under nine were forbidden to work except in silk mills... Finally, in 1846, after an unprecedented series of agitations lasting many years, the Corn Laws, which had favored the landed interests by imposing exorbitant duties on the import of wheat, thus keeping up the price of bread, were repealed. On the ideological front, they encouraged the establishment of educational institutions for workers, such as the Mechanics Institute, and various societies for the "diffusion of knowledge." On the coercive side, there was the passage of the severe Irish Coercion Bill, the rejection of the Ten-Hour Working Bill, the incessant attacks on trade unions, and not least, the Poor Law Amendment Act of 1834, which established pauper workhouses for the unemployed and the disabled in conditions that led to violent protest and reactions.

Objections to limiting the hours of work for factory operatives ranged from that of Nassau Senior, who held that "all profit [is] made during the last half-hour of an eleven and a half-hour day,"[21] to that of Queen Victoria, who believed that the Ashley Ten-Hour Bill would deprive industry of seven weeks of child power a year, and thus damage England's productive position abroad.[22]

Entrenched power mustered its forces to prove that in the realm of political economy there were "inalienable laws"—almost natural laws—that forever determined that "whatever is, is right," and unchangeable. This held true of the level of wages, and it was shown by "Parson" Malthus that a rising subsistence level tended to increase population, with the result that wages simply had to decrease; and that it was necessary for the population to decline for wages to rise again to meet the competition for existing labor.

> The chief laws of political economy, the *Edinburgh Review* declared, however darkly they may lead to their result, are as unchangeable as those of nature; and it would be as possible to make the quicksilver in the thermometer expand beyond the temperature of its atmosphere as to fix wages at any other rate than that at which they would fix themselves, if undisturbed either by Unions or Acts of Parliament.[23]

Whether by divine decree or that of "Nature," the whole world could see that England was prospering! There was the production of over two million yards of cotton per year, fifty million tons of coal, more than half of the total pig iron of the world. There was the wide geographic expansion to the Near East, Far East, China, India, South Africa, Australia, New Zealand, Canada.

Yet for all these astounding successes, not all seemed to be well. For by 1842, there were almost one and a half million paupers in England and Wales, equal to one eleventh of the population. There was the condition of the agricultural workers, who, according to witnesses, were no better off than the paupers. How was one to console the laborer whose official standard of subsistence had dropped to a third below that calculated thirty-five years earlier as sufficient to sustain life? And what was to be the fate of the numerous class of handloom weavers, who in 1833 still outnumbered those in factories, when the irresistible factory system triumphed?

Nor can one omit from this dolorous chronicle of misery the condition of Ireland during the Potato Famine of 1845–1847, when about a million of Irish died of hunger and about a million fled overseas; or the wretchedness of those who sought and found employment in English factories.

It is in protest against these conditions that was born the most impressive, wide, and for a time the most vital element in the British labor movement—the "Chartists."

It would be useless to rehearse the drama of hunger, desolation, and misery that beset England and Ireland during the depressions and bad harvests, and the recurrent crises of 1837–1838, 1842, and 1848. It may be enough to recall that the epithet of the "Hungry Forties" was attached to that decade. In the 1830s it is recorded that weavers' families in Manchester were forced to subsist on one and a half pence a day, and that 50,000 were unemployed.

The movement for a new Magna Carta, a "People's Charter," was one of "fustian jackets, unshorn chins and blistered hands." It was a movement born of the later 1830s that produced fresh and vigorous leadership, such as that of the Irishman Feargus O'Connor, whose publication *The Northern Star* could in April 1839 boast the astonishing readership of 60,000; James Bronterre O'Brien of *The Poor Man's Guardian*; the remarkable Julian Harney, whose future career was to epitomize the more radical developments within British labor. There was the shoemaker Thomas Cooper, schoolmaster, people's poet, and editor of the Chartist *Midland Counties Illuminator*, who suffered a two-years' imprisonment in Stafford. There were also—no less memorable—William Lovett, Francis Place, and Henry Hetherington. There was also the brilliant pre-socialist theoretician and practical leader Francis Bray, author of the extraordinary treatise *Labor's Wrongs and Labor's Remedies*. And there were many others.

Naturally, Lancashire, which in 1840 had one quarter of a million operatives in the cotton industry, became the mainspring of the Chartist movement; though other industrial regions like the West Riding of Yorkshire were not far behind. The 1840s were to be the doom-years of the domestic weaving industry.

Despite legal obstructions and setbacks, the organization of labor had continued. The General Union of Carpenters, the Grand General Union of Cotton Spinners, the Operative Builders Union, the Miners Association of Great Britain, among others, supported the boast that England possessed the most advanced working class in the world.

And now in 1837 and 1838, having recovered from the disenchantment and demoralization of the previous years, the workers swung into action once more, to fill the succeeding decade with the most impressive agitations in nineteenth-century labor history. The struggle for the reform of the franchise attained its most powerful manifestation in the Chartist petitions. We cite one of these, the so-called "Petition Agreed to at the 'Crown and Anchor' Meeting, February 28, 1837," for its objective and highly dignified but damning presentation of the state of parliamentary representation, and for its demands:

… The intent and object of your petitioners—this is addressed to "the Honourable the Commons of Great Britain and Ireland"—are to present such facts before your Honourable House as will serve to convince you and the country at large that you do not represent the people of these realms …

Your Petitioners find, by returns ordered by your Honourable House, that the whole people of Great Britain and Ireland are about 24 millions, and that the males above 21 years of age are 6,023,752, who, in the opinion of your petitioners, are justly entitled to the elective right ... The number of registered electors, who have the power to vote for members of Parliament, are only 859,519 ...

... On an analysis of the constituency of the United Kingdom, your petitioners find the 331 members (being a majority of your Honourable House) are returned by one hundred and fifty-one thousand four hundred and ninety-two registered electors! ...

Your petitioners therefore respectfully submit to your Honourable House that these facts afford abundant proofs that you do not represent the numbers and interests of the millions; but that persons composing it have interests for the most part foreign or directly opposed to the true interest of the great body of the people ...

... Seeing all the elements of power wielded by your Honourable House as at present constituted, and fearing the consequences that may result if a thorough reform is not speedily had recourse to, your petitioners earnestly pray your Honourable House to enact the following as the law of the realms ...

Then follow the "Six Points" or demands: for equal representation of the people of Britain and Ireland, that is "universal male suffrage, annual parliaments, elimination of property qualification for members of Parliament, vote by ballot, and payment to elected members."[24]

Such were the demands that frightened the establishment, filled them with a fear of an approaching revolution, and roused them to a violent opposition.

Monster meetings, such as in Manchester in September 1838, confirmed support of the "People's Charter," and drew signatures amounting to 1,200,000. The Petition was presented to the House of Commons on June 14, 1839, and was rejected on a motion to consider. It was to be expected that disturbances would mark the agitations, and within the Chartist movement itself division began to appear between those who moved for more emphatic physical pressures, such as general strikes, and those who were content with the exercise of "moral" force.

The government brought "soldiers, bayonets, and cannon"—as one Methodist parson by name of Stephens described the opposition. Royal Dragoons dispersed the Manchester meeting, the 72d Highlanders those in Bolton. Force of arms triumphed, and the first Chartist Movement collapsed. Royal Commissions continued to investigate and describe the horrors prevalent in industrial towns and factories. A young German resident in England was about to describe the conditions and publish his classic work in 1846. This was Friedrich Engels, and his book, *The Condition of the Working Class in England.*

The 1840s, or as they were to be called, the "Hungry Forties," brought the Chartist Movement to the fore once again with its Second Petition, signed by over three million. Once more Parliament rejected, while the Duke of Wellington objurgated the petitioners, charging that

Plunder is the object. Plunder is likewise the means.[25]

But the battles were not over by any means. Chartism came forth once more—and for the last time—in the revolutionary year of 1848. Then it was to be bound up with world-shaking events which will be described in a later chapter of this book.

Chapter Two

The Battle for Minds and Secular Salvation
"Utopia" and "Utility"

1. "Utopia"

Community, the joyful sound,
That cheers the social band,
And spreads the holy zeal around,
To dwell upon the land.
—Owenite Hymn, No. 129

What other Utopians dreamed of, Robert Owen, son of a Welsh saddlemaker, tried to make reality. Undoubtedly a man of genius, he was a combination of the visionary and the realist. He had been moulded in the crucible of hard personal experience, had by his own efforts succeeded, achieved affluence, and thereafter had attempted to transform the lessons of that experience into broad social concepts, and these again into radical philanthropic experiments. That he ultimately failed was a great, even if predictable, tragedy, due as much to the unsoundness of his social premises, short-comings of his personality, and failure to understand the changing times and the tem-per of factory workers after 1834, as to the implacable hostility he aroused within the establishment when the full implications of his growing radicalism in politics and religion became apparent.

Genius is a mysterious thing. What are the forces at work when at a critical mo-ment it breaks through the cocoon of the past—traditions, customs, filiations—and emerges in its own independent originality? At what point did this young shop-assistant named Robert Owen, who had been sent out into the world to make his way, attain to that level of perception that resulted in an internal, personal revolution?

We do not know. Owen himself was incapable of giving us the clues.

Causes [he told his Lanark audience in 1816] over which I could have no control, re-moved in early days the bandage which covered my mental sight ... The causes which fashioned me in the womb ... these gave me a mind that could not rest satisfied without trying every possible expedient to relieve my fellow men from their wretched situation, and formed it of such a texture that obstacles of the most formidable nature served but to increase my ardor, and to fix within me a settled determination, either to overcome them, or to die in the attempt.[1]

He had risen fast when a very young man, and could have every incentive and temptation to enrich himself, like others, profiting from the interminable hours of labor of the children, women and men in the cotton factories. At eighteen he was already manager of a Manchester cotton enterprise, soon become a partner in it, and rapidly developed the reputation of one of the most enterprising and astute cotton mill administrators in England or Scotland. At twenty-nine he married the daughter of a Scottish mill-owner at New Lanark, and it was here and at Orbiston, close to Glasgow, that he projected the staggering experiments that were intended to reform the society of his day from top to bottom.

Owen was born in 1771 and died in 1858. He was thus the contemporary of what we may call two ages—the age of an expiring domestic industry and the age of the new triumphant industrialism. In his outlook he tried to assimilate both of them into the optimistic rationalism of the eighteenth century that permeated the thought of William Godwin and Shelley—namely, that Reason is an irresistible force for the elimination of the evils of society and for its re-creation once the veil of ignorance and superstition is lifted from the eyes of both the rulers and the ruled; and that there are immense possibilities inherent in the unprecedented productive powers unleashed by the new machines.

He came to the conclusion that

> society may be formed to exist without crime, without poverty, and with health improved, with little, if any misery, and with intelligence and happiness increased a hundred-fold; and no obstacle whatsoever intervenes, at this moment, except ignorance, to prevent such a state of society from becoming universal.[2]

He asked that the improvement of human beings—"vital machinery"—be placed on the same level as that which was "inanimate." For examples of what society should not be like, he needed to look no farther than the factory of his own father-in-law David Dale at New Lanark, with its two thousand workers, of whom one quarter were children brought from poorhouses and elsewhere, six years of age and upward, who labored alongside their seniors for fourteen to sixteen hours daily. Yet Mr. Dale was a devout and well-meaning Christian, who no doubt regarded the condition as part of an unchanging and unchangeable world order. For his son-in-law, however, it was these children that became his first care. Once he became part-owner of the factories, he began creating for them an environment that would favor their physical and mental growth. He originated the first infant school in England; he reformed the brutal primary schools and remade then into education institutions of humanity, kindliness and cooperation. His program was so advanced that it furnishes models even today.

With the same intensity, intelligence and sympathy, Owen worked to transform the entire community of Lanark into a truly habitable and comfortable place, with improved housing, sanitation, sites of recreation, and stores that would charge no more than the cost of the articles. He paid good wages, even at times when he was forced to keep his factories closed. He was, in other words, a model employer, and his town became a model town for all to come and see. And they came, great and small, to observe and marvel. Even Tsar Nicholas of Russia was an approving visitor ...

Owen's vision became more and more expansive. Why could not New Lanark become the model for the rest of the world? A new Garden of Eden with "superior habitations, surrounded by gardens, pleasure grounds, and scenery, far better designed and executed than have yet been possessed by the monarchs of the most powerful and wealthy empires."[3]

Why not a world in which the battlefields of competition would give way to "villages of co-operation," and the struggle between classes give way to a universal harmony of interests? If only manufacturers would practice some restraint on their profits, and like himself be satisfied with a profit, say, of 5%, and turn the surplus to the improvement of the workers' lot and environment. But he soon discovered that his own partners were not satisfied with such an arrangement, intended to destroy the "profit motive" so essential to modern enterprise, and Owen was forced to break with them. Gradually he moved toward a greater and greater radicalism; his anticapitalism took on fiercer tones, and he joined to it a persistent attack on religion and religious groups that estranged both the established and the dissenting religious bodies. From a well-meaning and somewhat eccentric "philanthropist," he had turned, it became clear to them, into an enemy of the establishment, an apocalyptic and fiery preacher of social upheaval. Sceptical of political reform, still hopeful of a peaceful transformation achieved by the triumph of Reason, he saw the New Jerusalem already in the making. Undauntedly he proclaimed that labor was the ultimate source of all wealth, and that since the invention of the steam engine and the spinning jenny, the latter had been appropriated by "a few ... who continue to absorb the wealth produced by the industry of many."

> The mass of the population are become the slaves to the ignorance and caprice of these monopolists, and are far more truly helpless and wretched than they were before the names of Watt and Arkwright were known ... Of this new wealth so created, the laborer who produces it, is justly entitled to his fair proportion; and the best interests of every community require that the producer should have a fair and fixed proportion of all the wealth he created.

Such were the sentiments he expressed in his celebrated "Report to the County of Lanark" in 1820. A year later he was ready to proclaim to the world "the commencement, on this day, of the promised millennium, founded on rational principles and consistent practice."[4]

He was not only a man of high-sounding word. He was also a man of deeds. Out of his own wealth he gave and gave toward the establishment of such cooperative villages, whether at Orbiston, or in America in the New Harmony colony of Indiana. He practically bankrupted himself in these enterprises; that they failed was undoubtedly due as much to the inevitable processes of history—the triumph of capitalism—as to the unrealistic vision of a future attainable without a class struggle.

But he swept the minds of thousands and thousands of workers, and left an indelible mark on the entire working-class movement of the period. He was a prime mover and the fashioner of the program of the mighty Grand National Consolidated Trades Union, founded in 1833, with a membership of near half a million, and one of the great forces in the spread of Britain's cooperative societies. Before long, he himself would witness the extent to which the very thing he had dreamt of avoiding, the inexorable clash of forces, became a reality, when, to meet the dark threat of the Grand

National Consolidated Trades Union, the powers of government and wealth set out to smash it, succeeding through a virtual lockout and the prosecution and transportation of a number of alleged "conspirators."

Perhaps the saddest and greatest tribute to Robert Owen was paid him by one of his followers, an architect named Welsh, a member of the Builders' Union—a tribute that no subsequent condescension toward Owen or disparagement of the Utopian dream can diminish:

> It is my impression that with your assistance and counsel we can plant a giant Tree the top whereof shall reach to Heaven and afford shelter to succeeding generations.[5]

2. "Utility" and "Happiness"

There may be a strong presumption that any aristocracy monopolizing the powers of government would not possess intellectual power in any very high perfection. Intellectual powers are the offspring of labor, but a hereditary aristocracy are deprived of the strongest motives to labor. The great part of them, will therefore, be defective in those mental powers.

—James Mill, "Essay on Government" 1814

The season of fictions is over.
—Jeremy Bentham

The new forces that now more cohesively and self-consciously marshalled their numbers to challenge the predominance of the Tory landlord establishment were the so-called "middle rank"—the middle classes—industrialists, financiers, the more affluent tradesmen, along with a number of intellectuals more and more vigorously asserting an identity of interests—in other words, a "class-consciousness." They were to become among the most formidable allies of the traditional party of "Whigs," who considered themselves the heirs of the "bloodless" Revolution of 1688, and drew a great measure of their support from the nonconformist religious sects, as well as the commercial and manufacturing segments of society.

Among them were to be found a self-styled group of "radicals," and among the most influential of these, the so-called "philosophical radicals"—the "Utilitarians"—established the ideological basis for middle-class activity and thought and laid the foundations of latter-day Victorian liberalism. They proved to be by far the most thoroughgoing of the middle-class reforming agents, and it was with their vigorous and articulate support and that of the working classes that the Whigs succeeded in carrying the great Reform Bill of 1832. The "Utilitarians" represented an astonishing phenomenon in the intellectual and political life of England; for aside from the extensive influence of their leaders, Jeremy Bentham, James Mill, and the latter's son, John Stuart Mill, they marked the first time in England's history that a British philosopher—to wit, Jeremy Bentham—had succeeded in founding not only a philosophical school, but a political party as well.

History—that is, time and place—proved a beneficent fostering mother to such a movement, for England was the motherland of the Industrial Revolution, and in this respect supreme in the whole world; the political and social situation in the country, the rising activities of the working classes, the mounting power of the "middle rank," the loosening hold of the Tory oligarchy over the country, were powerful historical elements favoring the Utilitarian cause.

Jeremy Bentham and his followers rose to the situation. Bentham was a bizarre, eccentric genius (unjustly belittled by Karl Marx), who lived from 1748 to 1832. In his long life he produced a staggering body of publications on legislation and ethics. He was the generous patron of both James Mill and John Stuart Mill. A wealthy bachelor, he became one of the partners in Robert Owen's New Lanark ventures. He was an open-handed, dedicated believer in the need for reform. It is gratifying to remember that he died in the year that the great Reform Bill was carried.

The Utilitarians grew in numbers and support. In 1824 they founded the *Westminster Review*, which set out to compete for influence with the *Edinburgh Review* and the *Quarterly Review*—the most conservative journals of the day. In 1828 they established University College, London (later to become the University of London), the first non-denominational institution of higher learning in England.

The general principles of the Utilitarian school go back in history as far as the seventeenth century. The doctrine of "utility" asserts that human conduct is morally good in so far as it promotes "the greatest happiness of the greatest number." What is of eminent significance for the nineteenth century is that the doctrine was not confined to moral and ethical speculation merely, but became a central element of, and was made the motive agent leading toward, "practice"—action. And that action was to be directed toward an alteration of things that were obstacles to the achievement of "human happiness"; in other words, reform of the *status quo*. It is for this reason that John Stuart Mill celebrates Jeremy Bentham as "the father of English innovation both in doctrines and institutions... He is the great subversive, or, in the language of continental philosophers, the great critical thinker of his age and country."[6]

Bentham was very much the offspring of the British and French Enlightenment; he was the heir of Locke and Hume and of the French *philosophes* of the eighteenth century. In many ways he was a kind of *philosophe* himself, thrust into a century of revolutionary upheaval and compelled to adapt his thinking to a new world of realities. He brought the tested weapons of the Enlightenment: a staunch belief in reason, common sense, experience, and fact. What could be more agreeable and welcome to the middle classes than the ethic of "enlightened selfishness"? What more easily comprehensible than Bentham's analysis of human nature?

> Nature, he wrote, has placed mankind under the governance of two sovereign masters, pain and pleasure. It is for these alone to point out what we ought to do as well as to determine what we shall do. On the one hand the standard of right and wrong, on the other hand the chains of causes and effects, are fastened to their throne.[7]

Or, as John Stuart Mill put it,

> The creed which accepts as the foundation of morals, Utility, or the Greatest Happiness Principle, holds that actions are right in proportion as they tend to promote happiness,

wrong as they tend to produce the reverse of happiness. By happiness is intended plea-sure, and absence of pain; by unhappiness, pain, and the privation of pleasure.[8]

Jeremy Bentham's was a computer mentality. His ambition was to reduce the feelings, pleasures and pains, and the human motives, to something approaching mathematical certainty. That was the so-called "hedonistic calculus" for which he was to be attacked so fiercely by those who felt that the highest human aspirations and qualities—virtue itself, honor, and duty—were being desecrated. To claim that the noblest characteristics of mankind, that its highest virtues, were to be reduced to a mere animal happiness! To assert that the moral sense was not inborn in man, but an acquired quality that could be developed by means of education! For education, the Utilitarians taught, and habitual practice, far from encouraging individual "selfishness," would tend to teach human beings to identify and reconcile their "selfish" interests with those of the community, which, like them, is concerned with the advancement of human happiness. Universal happiness is the product or sum of individual happinesses.

But Bentham was not unaware that there were "particular interests," "sinister inter-ests"—class interests—that were totally opposed to the "happiness" principle, so long as it subserved the interests of the majority. Hence Bentham advocated universal suf-frage—a franchise of equality, and a revision of the Constitution, which Bentham called, addressing himself to the Tory aristocracy,

> a collection of pretences under which, the written formulas in and by which you have been in the habit of carrying on incessant war for the sacrifice of the universal to your own particular interest—the carrying on in the most regular and commodious manner the work of oppression and depradation on the largest scale.[9]

In Bentham's mind industry and industrialism represented the irresistible liberat-ing forces of mankind, and he foresaw an almost idyllic Utopia in their continued advancement, marked by an ever-advancing benevolence. Every code of law, he claimed, that is to promote the greatest happiness, must aim to achieve "subsistence, abundance, security and equality."

The middle classes, then, in the eyes of the Utilitarians, were to be the props, main-stays, and propelling motive elements in advancing civilization. It is to them that the lower sectors of society would look for guidance and instruction. James Mill, intellec-tual son of Bentham, eloquently proclaimed that it was the "middle rank"

> which gives to science, to art, and to legislation itself their most distinguished orna-ments, and is the chief source of all that has exalted and refined human nature, (and) is that portion of the community of which, if the basis of representation were ever to be extended, the opinion would ultimately decide.[10]

This was written long before the Reform Bill of 1832 was to set the seal on middle-class ascendancy.

As for the laboring classes, the Utilitarians believed these would discover that their own interests coincided with those of the middle class, and that the ever-increasing fortunes of their masters would redound to their profit too. Seemingly conflicting "self-interests," becoming more and more "enlightened," would result in the achieve-ment of a joint "happiness" for all. Not that the Utilitarians were unaware of the sharpening intensity of the class struggle, for in 1821, James Mill wrote to the economist David Ricardo:

> It is very curious that almost everybody you meet with—whig and tory—agree in declaring their opinion of one thing—that a great struggle between the two orders, the rich and the poor, is in this country, commenced—and that the people must in the end prevail;—and yet that the classes of the rich act as if they were perfectly sure of the contrary … The old adage seemed to be true, that when God wants to destroy a set of men, he first makes them mad.[11]

The early Utilitarians never questioned the sanctity of private property, though they attacked without reservations the monopoly of the aristocracy and their immunity from taxation. Having a profound faith in education as a panacea for the ills of mankind, they labored in such organs as the *Westminster Review* for the reform of the franchise, for free trade, and in behalf of universal peace; and hoped to achieve a considerable extension of influence and knowledge through such organizations as the Mechanics Institutes and the associations for the diffusion of knowledge, which addressed themselves to the larger sections of the population. The University of London was to become one of the most influential centers for the diffusion of their ideas.

That they represented a very concrete threat to the established Tory order soon became apparent from the attacks to which they were subjected, as being "godless," as preaching "immoral" doctrines centered on the selfishness of human beings, as subjecting the finest emotions and aspirations of mankind to some kind of inhuman "calculation" and undermining long established traditions, beliefs, and practices. Their impact on contemporary literature very soon becomes discernible. When Bentham died in 1832, he could rest assured of a vigorous and active progeny, and would have smiled (perhaps triumphantly) over Thomas Carlyle's rage, expressed the year before in *Sartor Resartus*. With his customary exaggeration, Carlyle had written, that "Utilitarianism spreads like a dog-madness; till the whole World-kennel will be rabid."[12] And some years before, *Blackwood's Magazine* was sadly reflecting:

> In Mr. Brougham's pamphlet on the Education of the People, we think the terms servant and master are never used; it is constantly the working classes and their employers … Why are the good old English words—servant and master—to be struck out of our language?[13]

Chapter Three

Thomas Carlyle

Out of the "Nay" into the "Everlasting Yea"

Un peuple qui n'est pas heureux, n'a pas de patrie.

A people that is not happy has no fatherland.

—Saint-Just, 1792

What Act of Legislature was there that *thou* shouldst be Happy? A little while ago thou hadst no right to *be* at all. What if thou wert born and pre-destined not to be Happy, but to be Unhappy! Art thou nothing other than a Vulture, then, that fliest through the Universe seeking somewhat to *eat*, and shrieking dolefully because carrion enough is not given thee? Close thy Byron; open thy Goethe! …

—Thomas Carlyle

Amidst the clamors of protest, adjuration, warning and counsel, and the turmoils accompanying popular agitation for reform, there was also one voice that forcefully penetrated to the ears of the generation of the 1830s and the 1840s. It was the voice of a Scotsman who in June 1834 settled in London, and established himself at an address destined to become a celebrated landmark. Thomas Carlyle and his wife, Jane Welsh Carlyle, accompanied by their maid Bessie Barnett and a canary, took a lease on a house at 5, Cheyne Row, Chelsea. He was then approaching thirty—a tall, robust, large-boned man, shaggy-browed, with deeply-piercing eyes—a man of loud, raucous speech and laughter, and a writer with an unbridled, turbulent literary style that despite its "wildness" somehow fastened itself on the mind and the imagination of readers. Here was to be found the storm of the times articulate, the formal bonds of traditional speech broken into apostrophes, adjurations, personalia, and not least, into insights and perceptions that cast a new light on the times' needs. Jane Welsh was neither writer nor prophet, but she was highly intelligent and very beautiful—she was keen-minded and deep-feeling and brave. She had defied conventions, for as the daughter of a well-to-do physician who had left her extensive property, she had married a struggling writer, erstwhile teacher and candidate for the ministry, and ventured with him on a very hazardous future. He had been her tutor, and they had fallen in love.

Her hopes were not unfounded, nor her confidence in him. Already he was making a name for himself as the prime interpreter of German letters, here outdistancing even his predecessor Coleridge. Here he had produced brilliant periodical essays, an epoch-making life of Friedrich Schiller, and a magnificent translation of Goethe's *Wilhelm Meister*. He had brought to the attention of his readers many of the German unknowns, notably such figures as Jean Paul Richter, Novalis, and other representatives of German Romanticism.

For the Victorians—and these included some of the greatest—he was to epitomize a great moral crisis and its transcendence. For the younger generation he was to stand forth as a "seer" who had emerged from the Hell (or as he called it, the Hebrew "Tophet") of doubt and nullity, into a heaven of spiritual affirmations. He had sought new guides, and had found them.

In Goethe, he had found his Moses, in Goethe's *Wilhelm Meister* his new Tables of the Law. Goethe, in turn, had recognized in Carlyle a "moral force," and had entered into a prolonged correspondence with him, one of the very few Britishers to be so honored.

In the eyes of many of his admirers he stood forth as something of a "hero." He had fought a hard battle with poverty and physical infirmities. He was the son of a stonemason. He had had the courage to break with the formal Calvinism of his forebears, but the essence of his Presbyterian upbringing persisted within him in a surrogate, secular Calvinism—metaphysical and nonreligious, but retaining the old character of the Scottish "kirk." A stern and inexorable Jehovah remained with him, though without angelic choirs. For his new creed he had amalgamated secular versions of predestination, original sin, and special grace, having also adapted to his purposes something of German idealistic philosophy and—above all—the works and thought of Goethe. He was the self-ordained prophet, or as he was to describe himself, a "missionary to the British heathen."

Though more closely fettered than any other portion of Britain to a theocratic Presbyterian "kirk," Scotland had not escaped the new waves of ideas emanating from the continent. It had its own tradition of scepticism in the great philosopher David Hume. Robert Burns testifies to the struggles between the conservative "auld lichts" and the more radical "new lichts." Carlyle read prodigiously in literature as well as the physical sciences, especially mineralogy. He fell with eagerness on Newton's *Principia*. It was then, as he later confessed to William Allingham, that "I ... first clearly saw that Christianity was not true."[1] In 1819 he began to study German. A year later he was reading Goethe's *Faust* in the original.

In Goethe he found his new "religion"—a religion for what he called "these hard, unbelieving utilitarian days," a religion that wedded "clear Knowledge."[2] It was a bold thing to try to transform the image of Goethe that prevailed in the literate English mind up to that point. For the English at large, and the Scots as well, the outstanding representative of German letters was Friedrich Schiller. Coleridge went into raptures over Schiller's *Robbers*, and succeeding generations found in the German poet and dramatist a high moral idealism that, in their minds, contrasted sharply with what they deemed the amoral paganism of Goethe.[3]

In Goethe, Carlyle saw a grander replica of himself in the journey from unbelief to belief:

"At one time, we found him in darkness, and now he is in light; he was once an Unbeliever, and now he is a Believer ... How has this man, to whom the world once offered nothing but blackness, denial and despair, attained to that better vision which now shews it to him, not tolerable only but full of solemnity and loveliness? ..." The long passage from *The Sorrows of Werther* to *Wilhelm Meisters Wanderjahre* and the second part of *Faust*, was it not the prototype of his own tortured winding way from an "everlasting Nay" to an "everlasting Yea"? ...

Carlyle was to depict his own agonies of desolation and his emergence therefrom in the unforgettable words of his veiled autobiography *Sartor Resartus*. From those moments in 1821 when the Great Doubt befell him, to the moment of Salvation, he passed through an ordeal of fire. And it is not without significance that the image of the phoenix was to occur in his works with such frequency. The desolation he had experienced—when his poor physical health, his bare worldly prospects, his tormented mind and outlook all combined to form one vast chaos—brought him to the verge of suicide, from which he recoiled only because there were some last swatches, or as he called it, an "after-glow," of religious feelings left.

He lay in the uneasy torpor of a sick young man. He searched feverishly for a replacement of his "absentee God." At that moment he might have envied the sure faith of his reticent father, the uncompromising belief of his mother. The feelings of internal dismemberment were accentuated by the turmoil in the outside world. The times were beckoning for significant speech and action. He was well aware of the sad economic plight of the Scottish farmer and worker. He had seen the inside of factories, and had been appalled. He had been amazed at the advances in technology—and affrighted at the sight of the workers. In 1824 he had visited Birmingham.

> I was one day thro' the iron and coal works of this neighborhood—a half-frightful scene! A space perhaps 30 square miles to the north of us, covered with furnaces, rolling mills, steam-engines and sooty men. A dense cloud of pestilential smoke hangs over it forever, blackening even the grain that grows upon it; and at night the whole region burns like a volcano spitting fire from a thousand tubes of brick. But oh the wretched hundred and fifty-thousand mortals that grin out their destiny there! In the coal-mines they were literally naked ... black as ravens; plashing about among dripping caverns ... In the iron-mills it was little better; blast-furnaces were roaring like the voice of many whirlwinds all around; the fiery metal was hissing thro' its moulds, or sparkling and spurting under hammers of a monstrous size, which felt like so many earthquakes ... It is in a spot like this that one sees the sources of British power. The skill of man combining these coals and that iron ore (till forty years ago—iron was smelted with charcoal only) has gathered three or four hundred thousand human beings round this spot, who send the products of their industry to all ends of the Earth.[4]

It was in the hours of his great despair that Germany and the German writers came to his rescue and opened a new world for him.

To explain them best, I can only think of the revelation, for I call it no other, that these men meant to me. It was like the rising of a light in the darkness, which lay around and threatened to swallow me up. I was then in the very midst of Wertherism—the blackness and darkness of Death. There was one thing in particular which struck me in Goethe. It is in his *Wilhelm Meister*. He had been describing an association to receive petitions and give responses. A number of applications for advice were daily made and answered. *But many people wrote in particular for recipes for happiness.* All that was laid on the shelf and not answered at all. "What!" I said, "is it not the *recipe* of happiness that I have been seeking all my life? And is it not precisely because I have failed in finding it that I am now miserable and discontented?"[5]

No! Happiness was not the answer to his own and the world's distresses. In a world beset by mischiefs and falsehood, oppressions and tyrannies, misled by Wertherism, Byronism, Benthamism, Utilitarianism, eighteenth-century rationalism—all of these sceptical, cynical, "mud-gods" preaching selfishness, acquisitiveness, a dismal *laissez-faire* of political economists—what was required was new thinkers, poets, prophets, indeed altogether new "heroes," new "saints," and, one might add, new "bibles."

For Carlyle, Goethe fulfilled such functions. The first part of *Faust* had already become a portion of the intellectual life of the Romantic world—appropriated, as we well know, by poets, musicians, and painters. *Wilhelm Meister* was practically unknown in England before Carlyle. Both *Faust* and the two novels concerned with Wilhelm Meister occupy a special place in Goethe's life and development, for they might be said to have been well-nigh lifetime preoccupations. All together, *Wilhelm Meisters Lehrjahre* (the *Apprenticeship*) and *Wilhelm Meisters Wanderjahre* (*Travels*) took fifty years to complete, from the 1770s to the 1820s; Goethe finished the second part of *Faust* a year before his death in 1832, which with the first part spanned almost sixty years. Thus both works represent a lifetime of experience, poetic and intellectual development, and innumerable mutations. Together they may also be said to epitomize the cultural history of Germany between 1770 and 1830.

The two *Wilhelm Meisters* became the fountainheads of the so-called *Bildungsroman*—studies in narrative form of the "self-development" of an individual personality in his search for a harmonious existence. They bore the stamp of their times no less than of their point of origin, the little duchy of Weimar, a patriarchal and preindustrial community governed by an autocratic ruler—an enclave, one might say, in a world of storms and upheavals. Wilhelm Meister is the son of a bourgeois merchant who sets out to fashion his life into a work of art—to become a *Lebenskünstler*. To adapt the philosophy of such a novel to the new world of industry and commerce that England represented in the 1820s and the 1830s required on Carlyle's part a particular sort of legerdemain, considering his own moral and spiritual predispositions and background. Such a task involved turning the "pagan" and life-loving Goethe into a moralizing Scottish Jeremiah. In translating *Wilhelm Meisters Lehrjahre*, we have no doubt, Carlyle had to overcome numerous reservations and personal sentiments, particularly such as violated a certain prudishness on his part, not to mention certain moral ambiguities of the German original.

To fashion his own life not according to the vacuous tenets of the petty bourgois—to fight the "philistines" of his day that glorified and worshipped a "materialistic" existence of the business-counter—to develop his inner predilections and talents no matter where that led—that was the goal Wilhelm Meister set himself. With repugnance he turns away from the ideal of a business career in order to nourish his own great passion—the theatre. In the process he encounters life in its many and varied manifestations, meets a great many people, falls in love with and is loved by numerous women, some of them of "easy virtue." Wilhelm becomes the protector of the strange Italian girl, Mignon, and befriends her mysterious companion the Harpist. He associates freely with actors and actresses and learns something of their exciting but precarious existence. Wilhelm's friend Werner, the thoroughgoing Philistine, and a bourgeois merchant, adjures him to turn to a settled career. But he scoffs at the idea: "*Was hilft es mir,*" he asks,

> *gutes Eisen zu fabrizieren, wenn mein eigenes inneres voller Schlacken ist? und was ein Landgut in Ordnung bringe, wenn ich mit mir selber uneins bin?*

> Of what use is it for me to manufacture iron, when my inner self is full of slag? And of what use is it to bring order to an estate, when I am at odds with myself?[6]

He is horrified at being treated by his friend as if he were a piece of merchandise.

> You cannot of course deny your character ... You meet your friend after a long absence and all you see in him is some goods with which to speculate and make money.[7]

But unbeknownst to himself, there are watchful eyes upon Wilhelm. There is the Society of the Tower—*Gesellschaft vom Turm*—a kind of aristocratic Freemasonry, of which he eventually becomes aware and under whose guidance he finally becomes convinced that neither by character nor talent is he fitted for the theatrical profession. He is exhorted to turn from such dilettantism to an education which will serve to make him socially useful. He becomes Mignon's guardian, and the educator of his illegitimate son Felix by the actress Marianne. His own training has in truth begun, and like Goethe himself he sets off for Italy.

It is in *Wilhelm Meisters Wanderjahre* that Goethe draws up a complete program for the education of the soul, the mind, and the heart of both Wilhelm and Felix. Wilhelm has drawn away from the circle of lower-class actors, and now associates primarily, like Goethe, with aristocrats. It is they who set the stamp of true development upon him. And now they turn his eyes on the need for perfection of some particular skill or talent, founded upon true dedication to a handicraft. His son Felix is being educated according to a new system housed in the *Pädagogische Provinz*—the Pedagogic Province. Here he is instructed in the principles of a new morality based upon manual labor, which is regarded as conducive to the full unfolding of the personality. Wilhelm too is made aware of new religious concepts that govern the institution, concepts based upon the idea of "Reverence." "No religion that is founded on fear is respected here," he is told.

"Reverence" has a three-fold aspect—it is Reverence "for that which is above us"; Reverence "for that which is our equal"; and Reverence "for that which is below us, which is Christian ... the consummation of that which Humanity must and can achieve."

In a beautifully moving passage Goethe describes the nature of this third Reverence, one that takes cognizance of "lowliness and poverty, mockery and contempt, disgrace and wretchedness, suffering and death, and conceives of them as divine; yes," one that even looks upon sin and crime with understanding and compassion, as "furthering that which is holy."

The most Ancient of the Three Guardians addresses Wilhelm:

"I invite you to come back in a year to see how far your son has progressed. Then you will be initiated into the Sanctuary of Sorrow."[8]

In the end, we obtain a summary statement of the ideal goal of this *Bildung*—the "cultivation of the self."

Thought and Action, Action and Thought, this is the sum-total of human wisdom ... Both move in life like the inhalation and the exhalation of breath, like question and answer. Whoever makes a law unto himself of that which the Genius of Human Understanding secretly whispers into the ear of each newborn—namely, that Action must be tested by Thought, and Thought by Action—he cannot err, and if he should, he will soon find the right way."[9]

Yet, the *Wanderjahre* is not only a book of high didactic declarations. It is filled with evidence of a devotion to actual manual labor undertaken in the spirit already described, such labor including mining and mineralogy, as well as cotton-spinning. It is interesting to observe that Goethe selects as his locale of industry the still undeveloped manufacturing site of Switzerland. He is disposed to emphasize domestic rather than factory industry, and in particular, landed property.

This is a far remove from Manchester or Birmingham, though it is likely that such primitivism would have appealed strongly to Carlyle. In the end, Wilhelm Meister dedicates himself to medicine and is thus enabled to save his own son's life...

One more element deserves attention: Goethe subtitled the *Wanderjahre* as *die Entsagenden*—"the Renouncers." For one of the most important aspects of "education," so far as Wilhelm Meister himself and the other characters in the book are concerned, is the need for self-limitation—the development and nourishing of one's particular aptitude or talent, as against self-dispersion and dilettantism; the supreme importance of that order of self-discipline that recognizes inner and outer organization as prerequisites of a creative life. Goethe's own ideal was the *Kulturstaat*, a state that concentrated on culture, inner and outward, but remained indifferent to the political or social structure in which the individual was to find his personal fulfilment.

Carlyle was particularly attracted by the element of *Entsagen*—renunciation—and proceeded to redefine it in quasi-theological terms. Goethe's goal of an aesthetic perfection is turned into a moral imperative of an almost ascetic renunciation of Happiness. With this notion, Carlyle also conjoined, as particularly attractive, the notion of "Sorrow"—endowing the "Worship of Sorrow" with a special Carlylean, Calvinistic dourness.

Goethe did not achieve canonization easily at Carlyle's hands. While he was translating *Wilhelm Meister's Apprenticeship*, he fumed, fussed and stormed; he was frequently outraged, admiration and repulsion constantly warred within him. There it was—a book with "touches of the very highest, most ethereal genius in it, but diluted with floods of inspidity, which even I would not have written for the world. I sit down to it every night at six, with the ferocity of a hyena." And he had his own moral tussles with the "players and libidinous actresses and their sorry pasteboard apparatus for beautifying and enlivening the 'moral world.'"[10]

Wilhelm Meister was to have a powerful influence on many writers during the nineteenth and even the twentieth century. Carlyle himself ventured on a *Bildungsro-man—Wotton Reinfred—*in 1827. After completing seven chapters, he wisely abandoned the work, which did not appear in print until after his death. While the imprint of *Werther* and *Wilhelm Meister* is only too obvious, the characters are lifeless. But direct and indirect influences of *Wilhelm Meister* were to play upon the English novel from the time of Bulwer-Lytton to Meredith and beyond. In that movement, Carlyle's role as initiator cannot be minimized...[11]

* * *

But England was no Weimar. The country was in a state of ferment, and Carlyle anticipated the worst when in 1831 the Lords again blocked the passage of the Reform Bill, and political and social disturbances broke out in Coventry, Worcester, and Bristol; there was the threat of a march from Manchester; and not least, the ravages of cholera. All these events seemed to bode the end of the world; or, at the least, another revolution like that in France. Almost in despair, Carlyle cried out,

> ... there is nowhere any tie remaining among men. Everywhere, in court and cathedral, brazen falsehood now stands convicted of a lie, and famishing Ignorance cries, Away with her, away with her! God deliver us![12]

There was the example of the 1830 Revolution in France. Would Reform Bills be of any help? Carlyle had little faith that reform of the parliamentary structure would solve any of the crucial problems.

> The whole frame of society is rotten, he wrote in his *Note Books*, and must go for fuel-wood, and *where* is the new frame to come from? I know not, and no man knows.[13]

In 1829, he had launched in the pages of the *Edinburgh Review* a formidable attack on the spirit of the age, entitled "Signs of the Times." Self-interest, he exclaimed, was the sole rule of this world; we are living for the sake of the "purse" rather than for "conscience." The dominant religion today consists in "Expediency, and Utility ... and Profit." Would England take note of many warning signs from abroad? There was the Carbonari movement in Italy, and ominous tumults in Spain, Portugal, and Greece. All of society is being racked by a grinding collision of "the new and the Old." The revolution inaugurated by France in 1789 is far from accomplished. "The final issue," he wrote, "was not unfolded in that country; nay, it is not yet anywhere unfolded." That revolution which has as its object political freedom is not enough. There is a higher freedom "than mere freedom from oppression by his fellow-mortals."

> To reform a world, to reform a nation, no wise man will undertake; and all but foolish men know, that the only solid, though a far slower reformation, is what each begins and perfects on himself.[14]

Strangely enough, the strident voice emanating from far-off Scottish Craigenput-tock found echoes and responses in France. "Signs of the Times" was reprinted in the

Paris *Revue Britannique*, and came to the attention of the Saint-Simonians, whose critique of the essay, while laudatory, sharply censured the writer's failure to note the saving powers of association and unity. In July 1830, one of the Saint-Simonians' leading missionaries, Gustave d'Eichthal, sent Carlyle a packet of Saint-Simonian literature, a critique of his essay, and Saint-Simon's important *Le Nouveau Christianisme*. This was a warming recognition for one who seemed unheard in his own land, and Carlyle, though not converted to the new "religion," found in it sufficient support for his own ideas, as well as some highly impressive and stimulating new ones. Here was a call to social as well as moral response. Carlyle noted that "*la classe la plus pauvre*" of the Saint-Simonians was rising from its "present deepest abasement." He noted the disparity existing between rich and poor, when "a man with £200,000 a years eats the whole fruit of 6,666 men's labour the year" and "private individuals" earn wages equal to the "wages of seven or eight hundred thousand other individuals."

> What do these highly beneficed individuals *do* to society for their wages? *Kill partridges! Can this last?* No, by the soul that is in man it cannot, and will not and shall not![15]

As he did in other cases, he translated the Saint-Simonian cyclical theory of history—the alternation of periods of dismemberment and organic reconstruction—into his own terms as periods of "Denial, Irreligion and Destruction" and periods of "Affirmation, of Religion."[16] The present was of course a time of dismemberment.

He is reported to have prepared a translation of *Le Nouveau Christianisme*, with an Introduction, which remained unpublished and seems to have disappeared. But even meetings with two prominent Saint-Simonians in London—the Eichthal brothers— did not serve to keep his interest in the Saint-Simonian doctrines at full heat, and by 1832 it had almost petered out.

For he was already deep in the transcendentalism of his "Clothes" philosophy, soon to take shape as *Sartor Resartus*. Though he was not to forego the ideas of Progress, Change, History as Process, the mystic was to triumph over the rationalist, and he suffused even these ideas with his own brand of supernaturalism. But he was heartened that in so irreligious (as he thought then) nation as France there was an emergent "religion," the Saint-Simonian, that preached a gospel that "Man is still Man."[17]

There was scarcely another voice in England—in 1831—that spoke with such fervor to the conscience of the middle and upper classes, addressing himself to what he believed were their better qualities. He became, so to speak, the conscience of the bourgeois that fought the bourgeois morality of acquisitiveness and selfishness; and also the Tory conscience as it warred against the threatening bourgeois dominance. Both elements dreaded the prospect of violence on the part of the "lower" classes; both sought for some moral alleviation of their troubled souls. Here was an eloquent voice that fought clear of advocating "materialism" and "atheism," yet affirmed the notion of Progress, the necessity of Change, while at the same time assuaging theological and clerical misgivings by proposing the invisible workings of a Providence. Yet he was also anticipating indirectly some elements of a later socialism, almost pre-envisioning the dialectic of Karl Marx.

> In change [he wrote in "Characteristics"] ... is nothing terrible ... On the contrary, it lies in the very essence of our log and life in this world ... Change, indeed, is painful yet ever needful ... Nay, if we look well into it, what is all Derangement, and necessity of great Change, in itself such an evil, but the product of *increased resources*, which the *old methods* can no longer administer; of new wealth which the old coffers will no longer contain: What is it, for example, that in our own day bursts asunder the bonds of ancient Political Systems, and perplexes all Europe with the fear of Change, but even this: the increase of social resources, which the old social methods will no longer sufficiently administer?

At the same time he lightened disturbed hearts with his affirmation of a "clear ascertainment that we are in Progress," noting how Paganism gave way to Christianity, Tyranny to Monarchy, and Feudalism to Representative Government. He comforted himself and others by claiming that Scepticism and Materialism had disappeared, and a "Faith in Religion is again possible and inevitable for the scientific method ..."

But he was not unaware—and made others aware—of the ever-widening gulf between rich and poor, exposing what was later to be called the "contradictions" within society—the anomaly of Progress and Poverty:

How was it, he asked, that though

> Labour's thousand arms, of sinew and metal, all concurring everywhere, from the tops of the mountains to the depths of mine and caverns of the sea, ply unweariedly for the service of man: yet man remains unserved; he has subdued this Planet, his happiness and inheritance; yet reaps no profit from the victory. Sad to look upon: in the highest stage of civilization, nine tenths of mankind have to struggle in the lowest battle of savage or even animal man, the battle against Famine. Countries are rich, prosperous in all manner of increase, beyond example; but the Men of those countries are poor, needier than ever of all sustenance outward and inward: of Belief, of Knowledge, of Money, of Food ... So that Society, were it not by nature immortal, and its death ever a new-birth, might appear, as it does in the eyes of some, to be sick to dissolution, and even now writhing in its last agony.[18]

He had larger works in mind with which to medicine the world and help restore an "absentee God." The first of these, necessarily, was a sort of confessional—his own spiritual pilgrimage, the soul's migration out of the chaos of Doubt into the delectable valleys of Affirmation—a metaphysical *Lehr-* and *Wanderjahre.* It was *Sartor Resartus.* ...

* * *

He had Goethe in mind (and himself too) when he wrote in *Sartor Resartus:*

> What too are all Poets and moral Teachers, but a species of Metaphorical Tailors? Touching which high Guild the greatest Guild-brother has triumphantly asked us: "Nay, if thou will have it, who but the Poet first made Gods for men; brought them down to us; and raised us up to them?"[19]

A tailor to repatch the world! especially his own dear England! The idea was high and worthy, but its realization meant, first of all, repatching himself. The idea of writing a veiled autobiography of his spirit took root in 1830, when Carlyle's material resources were low indeed, his reputation as a writer, despite his translations, the important *Life of Schiller*, and numerous periodical contributions, yet in the balance. He was still deep in the valleys of self-doubt. But this, his new work, was to be the theoretical manifesto of a new Credo, as seven years later, under more favorable circumstances, his second major achievement, *The French Revolution*, was to be the practical exposition and exemplification of his ideas as reflected on the stage of world history.

Both labors were to be accompanied by staggering fatalities and accidents, though differing in kind. *Sartor Resartus* had begun as a fantasy on the subject of Clothes and soon widened into a full-sized philosophical or metaphysical tract. High in hopes, Carlyle sent it forth from Craigenputtock, still in partial form, to the publisher Fraser in London, in November 1830. Its title then was *Thoughts on Clothes*. It was rejected. Undeterred, Carlyle continued working on it, completing it in July 1831. Then, on a borrowed fifty pounds, he set off for London. Eluded by success, he returned to Scotland, and in May of 1833 broke the book up into "strips," which he sent once more to Fraser for serial publication in *Fraser's Magazine*. Rechristened *Sartor Resartus*, it ran there from November 1833 to August 1834.

In Britain, the work met with almost unanimous disapproval or indifference. But in America it received warm recognition, and here it was published in book form in 1836. Ralph Waldo Emerson, principal instigator of the publication, also wrote a preface for it, left unsigned. It was not until 1838, Carlyle's *French Revolution* having now taken England by storm, that Fraser ventured to issue *Sartor Resartus* in book form and it came into its own.

There were good reasons for the failure of *Sartor Resartus* on its first appearance. Its style struck out recklessly, full of rhetorical heresies. Taking advantage of the disguise he assumed in the book as the putative editor of the German Professor Diogenes Teufelsdröck's treatise on clothes, Carlyle gave vent to his inner anarchism, as if declaring war on traditional classical English prose. In his own rebel style he fused dithyramb with the disconnected explosiveness of the German Romantics, the style of Jean Paul Friedrich Richter and others; the humor, sentimentality, and designed incoherences of Laurence Sterne; and the brilliant coruscating clothes symbolism of Jonathan Swift's *Tale of a Tub*. Frequent apostrophes, fusillades—many of them in German—strikingly new metaphors, and above all the high tension of the at times ecstatic locutions, strike the reader with the insistence of kettle-drums. ... At such moments, it might almost have seemed that we were seeing not our Carlyle, but a type of German university professor—some *Professor extraordinarius* in some German university town redolent of Teutonic *Gemütlichkeit*—in the company of philosophical pundits, scholars, students, and in an atmosphere of *Rauchtabak* in one of the town's favorite inns—a Carlyle matching his own biting, sardonic, Scottish wit and raucous laugh against those of his German confrères, far, far away from the sepulchral quietism of Oxford or Cambridge, or the Bentham-ridden new London University, or the parochialism of Edinburgh!

Carlyle's German professor is named Diogenes Teufelsdröck—that is, "Diogenes Devils'-dung." He is Professor of Allerlei-Wissenschaft (All Sorts of Knowledge), at Weissnichtwo (I Know Not Where);—he resides in the Wahngasse (Vanity Street), and is a nightly visitor at the good tavern of The Green Goose. He is the author of a redoubtable book, *Die Kleider, ihr Werden und Wirken*—"Clothes, Their Origin and

Influence." Through some good fortune the book had fallen into the hands of the "Editor," who, with the generous assistance of Hofrath Heuschrecke (Court Councillor Grasshopper), a source of some additional biographical material, is enabled to round out the volume.

From his perch in that attic apartment in Vanity Street, Teufelsdröck looks down on the world of Weissnichtwo—his microcosm. Apparently something of a political radical, he is also unconventional so far as philosophical and moral ideas are concerned. As he sits there, he reflects: These human beings passing down below, what are they? Who are they? In their various vestments, ranging from the opulent apparel of the visiting Baron, down to the drab garb of the poor widow—each of them, the Professor states, is an Apparition. This confidence he communicates to the only two persons admitted to his retreat, the Editor and the Court Councillor. Each "apparition," he insists, is a "living link in that tissue of History, which interweaves all Being." Each is a portion of Eternity...

Strange Professor Teufelsdröck! He never lectures at the University, for though there is a chair there, it has not been endowed. Stranger still are his origins, for no one knows where he came from. As a child, he was deposited at the home of a very respectable couple and brought up by them.

Our Professor's spiritual and moral pilgrimage through life has not been an easy one. Only in the course of mortal anguish and struggle had he reached the point where he was enabled to penetrate beyond the external vestures of Man and Nature, and discover the true Vesture—the Mystery of Man... "To the eye of vulgar Logic," he writes

> ... what is man: An omnivorous Biped that wears Breeches. To the eyes of Pure Reason what is he? A Soul, a Spirit, and divine Apparition...

Not Logic, nor merely rational thought, but only "Pure Reason"—which is Intuition—could bring one to see the true nature of existence, the true nature of Man and the World.

But to achieve the true vision requires much labor and anguish. Teufelsdröck wanders widely, like another Wilhelm Meister; he suffers the torments of unfulfilled love; he is frustrated by the differences existing between classes and is overcome by a sense of futility, nullity, chaos and despair. Thus he has reached the Everlasting No!—the conviction that there is no fixed moral order in this universe; that necessity, evil, human limitations, suffering and death are the only true realities. All else is illusion. The world is a neutral, if indeed not hostile, machine. Human life is ringed by Necessity. There is no Freedom. Man lives in the "hot fever of anarchy and misery," shut off from all hope.

> Well might he exclaim, in his wild way, 'Is there no God, then; but at best an absentee God, sitting idle, ever since the first Sabbath, at the outside of his Universe, and seeing it go?'

> A feeble unit in the middle of a threatening Infinitude [Teufelsdröck continues], I seemed to have nothing given me but eyes, whereby to discern my own wretchedness.

The universe seemed "one huge, dead, immeasurable Steam-engine," to grind him "limb from limb..." a "vast gloomy Golgotha, the Mill of Death!"[20]

Utterly shattered, Teufelsdröck wanders through the "dirty little street of Saint-Thomas d'Enfer"—just as Carlyle had in Leith Walk, Edinburgh—when suddenly he is struck by a startling question:

> What *art* thou afraid of? … Despicable biped! what is the sum-total of the worst that lies before thee? Death? Well, Death; and say pangs of Tophet too, and all that the Devil and Man may, will or can do against thee! Hast thou not a heart; canst thou not suffer whatsoever it be; and, as a Child of Freedom, though outcast, trample Tophet itself under thy feet, while it consume thee? Let it come, then; I will meet and defy it!"

Such was the beginning of Teufelsdröck's "Spiritual New-birth."

Follows a period of torpor, the "Center of Indifference." He has discovered the "Me" but not yet found his new view of the universe. The Ego must transcend itself, pass through the purgatory of self-annihilation—the *Selbst-tötung*—before its eyes can be unsealed, and its hands "ungyved." He begins to be aware of his fellow human beings and their plight. The "sacred gates" of the "Sanctuary of Sorrow" are about to open for him. He discovers the meaning of Goethe's *Entsagen* (Renunciation), that is, the renunciation of Happiness.

> What Act of Legislature was there that *thou* shouldst be Happy? … There is in man a higher than Love of Happiness… Love not Pleasure; love God. This is the Everlasting Yea, wherein all contradiction is solved… Be no longer a Chaos, but a World, or even Worldkin. Produce! Were it but the pitifullest infinitesimal fraction of a Product, produce it, in God's name… Work while it is called Today, for the Night cometh, wherein no man can work.[21]

He has now discovered that the world is Symbol, and Man, too—both Symbols of God; all of these, "embodiment and revelation of the Infinite." Thus he has overcome the great Negations, the "mud-gods" of "our Logical, Mensurative faculty," and now affirms that it is our Imagination which is "King over us." Thought is master of the world, the great magician, who through the mouth of poets and prophets "makes and unmakes the whole world." And Thought is "father of the Act." Thus an idea in the mind of James Watt transmuted into the steam engine is "rapidly enough overturning the whole old system of Society," to wit, Feudalism, and preparing us for Industrialism and "the Government of the Wisest."

Then came the staggering news from France, the "three glorious days" of the July 1830 Revolution. At the tavern of the Goose, where everything was bustle and buzzing with the news, Professor Teufelsdröck sat and spoke not a word for a whole week, "except once these three: *Es geht an* (It is beginning)…" He (like his Editor) had not been untouched by Saint-Simonian ideas, and when their publications reached the tavern, to be subjected to "one vast cackle of laughter, lamentation, and astonishment, our Sage sat mute; and at the end of the third evening said merely: Here also are men who have discovered not without amazement, that Man is still Man," and was heard to quote the celebrated Saint-Simonian dictum that the "golden age, which a blind tradition has thitherto placed in the Past, is before us."

Then the Professor disappears. He had apparently been in correspondence with the Saint-Simonians! Was he in Paris? Or was he, as the Editor is inclined to conjecture, actually in London?

But he had left his Clothes Testament to the world. Here was his acid critique of contemporary society:

> Call ye that a Society ... where there is no longer any Social idea extant; not so much as the Idea of a common Home, but only of a common over-crowded Lodging-house? Where each, isolated, regardless of his neighbour, turned against his neighbour, clutches what he can get, and cries "Mine!" and calls it Peace, because in the cut-purse and cut-throat Scramble, no steel knives, but only a far cunninger sort, can be employed? Where Friendship, Communion, has become an incredible tradition; and your holiest Sacramental Supper is a smoking Tavern Dinner, with Cook for Evangelist? Where your Priest has no tongue but for plate-licking: and your high Guides and Governors cannot guide; but on all hands hear it passionately proclaimed: *Laissez-faire*, Leave us alone of *your* guidance, such light is darker than darkness; eat you your wages and sleep![22]

Such, then, the alienation of modern man and woman. How then to restore or recreate those "organic filaments" that bind all things together in this world? How to attain the "higher Freedom"? Neither Saint-Simon nor the ballot can be instruments in their achievement. What is needed is to cast off the veil that shrouds the eye from the perception of the Miracles that are around us and in us—the miracles of Creation, of Nature, of Past and Present—the miracle that is Man, and the miracle that lies in the fact that one "can stretch forth" one's hand at all! What wonders await us once we transcend the chains of "blind Custom, and become Transcendental"! The whole world is a book of Revelations!

But who is there to open that Book? Carlyle replies: the Hero—the Great Man! Heroes are

> the inspired (speaking and acting) Texts of that Divine Book of Revelation, whereof a Chapter is completed from epoch to epoch, and by some named HISTORY.[23]

Such is the intoxicated book that Carlyle was offering to this generation of the 1830s as a new bible. Here was a dilution of German idealistic transcendental philosophy that saw all Creation as Spirit—*Geist*—and asked of it to cast off its worldly integuments—materialism—and perceive its kinship with the Godhead. Aside from these mystical adjurations there was also the eloquent call to become aware of the miseries—actual miseries, both moral and physical—besetting this new world of industry and machines. And not least, the call to translate thought into action.

But what Action? Carlyle leaves us in total doubt. The new temples of regeneration he envisions would house a joint participation in the heroic suffering of Man, but the fitting medicine for its assuagement is left unnamed. To the well-meaning and deeply troubled he advanced a gospel of the heroic—of "self-annihilation," of "renunciation." To a society deep in the morass of "materialism" he offered an ethic of labor, abjuration of the worth of happiness, the need for obedience and reverence toward that which is "higher." To all, the prospect of a regenerating Hero, God-sent, who in the person of Poet, Prophet, Legislator, or "King" would help reweave the tattered "organic filaments"—the human tie. But all in all, Carlyle's was an invocation to search one's soul, and there was nothing the Victorian needed more urgently.

Carlyle was now prepared to translate a metaphysic into a philosophy of History and enter upon the second stage of his development with the query: What can History teach us of the ways of God and Man?

* * *

Now in London, the Carlyles loved their new home in Cheyne Row. Old friendships were revived, new friendships formed. Carlyle's name was becoming known more and more widely, and men and women were being drawn to Cheyne Row not merely by Carlyle's intellect, but also by the beauty and brain of his wife: John Stuart Mill and Harriet Taylor; Leigh Hunt, veteran of many literary and journalistic battles; young John Sterling; Robert Browning and Tennyson; Ralph Waldo Emerson; French Saint-Simonians, and foreign liberals fleeing the repressions of the July Monarchy; somewhat later, Giuseppe Mazzini, Italy's apostle of national liberation. After the publication of Carlyle's *French Revolution* the stream of visitors and admirers widened, and on one occasion Frédéric Chopin agreed to touch the none-too-workable pianoforte for Jane's delectation. Carlyle remained as ever deaf to music as he had been, and was, deaf to poetry.

But he was always at work. Already in September 1834, barely three months after settling in London, he commenced the first chapter of his great historic work on the French Revolution. Friends came to his aid with the needed but not easily procurable materials—especially John Stuart Mill, who was the most helpful. Jane Carlyle, to the outward eye a perfect Victorian mate, bore with her husband's difficult temperament—his explosions, her own isolation while he worked, and unfortunately other marital dissatisfactions that Victorians were not prone to mention or think about. Her dedication to her husband's great work was complete, but its progress was accompanied by a notable disaster.

The incident is well known but bears repetition, revealing Carlyle at his spiritual best. He completed the first part of the *French Revolution* in January 1835. Some time later John Stuart Mill, who was then already emotionally involved with Harriet Taylor, had taken it to read in her company, as well as for review. The rest of the story is told by Carlyle himself in a letter written March 23, 1835 to Dr. John Carlyle (his younger brother), then living in Rome:

> … Well, one night about three weeks ago, we sat at tea, and Mill's short rap was heard at the door; Jane rose to welcome him; but he stood there unresponsive, pale, the very picture of despair; said half-despairingly gasping, that she must go down to speak to "Mrs. Taylor." … After some considerable additional gasping, I learned from Mill this fact: that my poor Manuscript, all except four tattered leaves, was *annihilated!* He had left it out (too carelessly); it had been taken for waste-paper; and so five months as tough labour as I could remember of, were as good as finished, gone like a whiff of smoke.—There never in my life had come upon me any other Accident of much moment; but this I could but feel a sore one. The thing was *lost*, and perhaps worse; for I had not only forgotten all the structure of it, but the spirit it was with was past; only the general impression seemed to remain, and the recollection that I was on the whole well satisfied with that, and could hardly hope to equal it…
>
> …And so, I began at the beginning…[24]

"And so, I began at the beginning."

The mind is staggered at these words—an immensity of labor undertaken anew. And brought to completion! On January 12, 1837 it was finished, and six months later published. It met with instant acclaim. Mill and Thackeray reviewed it enthusiastically. Robert Southey, it is reported, "read it six times over."[25] Thousands of others read it at least once. For Carlyle's generation and its successors the book represented an epochal revelation.

For, it must be remembered, not a few of the readers of Carlyle's book had lived during the days of the French Revolution (take Wordsworth, for example), its aftermath, Napoleon, Waterloo, the Restoration, and even just a few years before, the Paris Revolution of July. The staggering historical changes were not a matter of fantasy— they were there, right before them, inescapable realities. History was being made at an unprecedented pace of change, and change was of course the mark of the nineteenth century. The century was to feel as if Eternities and Infinities were unfolding before its gaze. Those hieroglyphics of Nature that Carlyle spoke of as symbols were in very fact now being deciphered by the Champollions and the Grotefends. The no longer symbolic fossils embedded in the earth's crust or in the ocean's depths pointed to an incalculable past history. And would Man's own antiquity not soon be set back millions of years, his own emergence be made a portion of the rocks, the oceans and the mountains? There had been no century like this before. Nothing fixed, everything in motion. Nothing frozen, everything a Process! What was the nature of these processes? What, if any, were the Laws of History? What the motive forces that directed the course and the life of nations?

Friedrich Schiller had shown that History was philosophy "teaching by experience." "World history is the world-court of law."

And what could offer greater challenge to the philosophical and moral imagination of the historian than the outstanding single event of modern times, the French Revolution? It was a daring thing that Carlyle had undertaken, and successor historians have not been slow in finding flaw with Carlyle's work. But Carlyle was working with still inadequate source material, mostly with memoirs and letters; he had no access to the historical archives of France, which were not opened until 1860. For all its shortcomings, Carlyle's *French Revolution* still amazes with the sweep of its style, its pace, vividness, and occasional grandeur. For his contemporaries the book proved a revelation. It gave them a dramatic spectacle of a revolution, a sense that they were themselves living in a revolutionary age whose end was still indeterminate. As Carlyle himself indicated in speaking of the Revolution as "*the* event of these modern ages," this was an "unfinished" revolution: Find the right key to the understanding of the Revolution in France and you may have the key to the understanding of History itself. And might that not lead to a discovery of means of obviating or avoiding our own revolution? As he was to write in his pamphlet on "Chartism,"

> Since the year 1789, there is now half a century complete; and a French Revolution not yet complete! Whosoever will look at that enormous Phenomenon may find many meanings in it, but this meaning as the ground of all: That it was a revolt of the oppressed lower classes against the oppressing or neglecting upper classes; not a French revolt only; no, a European one; full of stern monition to all countries of Europe. These

Chartisms, Radicalisms, Reform Bill ... and jargon that there is yet to be, are *our* French Revolution; God grant that, we, with our better methods, may be able to transact it by argument alone.

It may be hard for our generation, so much more sophisticated in matters of history, fully to understand the profound influence of this and other works of Carlyle on his contemporaries. Let us remember that there had been nothing like his *French Revolution*—addressing itself, as we have seen, not only to a historical event, but to all the most serious concerns of the Victorian age. Carlyle was actually writing a "drama," evoking the past as if it were present. He gave them the feeling of participating in the march of history, and he unrolled that vast panorama with his own special rhetoric, irony, satire, personal objurgation and laudation, apostrophes, questions, all marked by an intoxicated sense of the prophetic. At such moments he was himself the prophet as he envisioned the finger of God and His "celestial sanctions" operating in the rise and fall of men, parties, movements.

Thus he celebrates May 4, 1789 as the "baptism-day of Democracy ... The extreme-unction of Feudalism! A superannuated System of Society ... is now to die; and so, with death-throes and birth-throes, a new one is to be born." "The age of Miracles has come back!"

Yet Carlyle is no friend of Democracy, and he steers his way skilfully between the exaltation of Feudalism of an Edmund Burke, and an exaltation of the Revolution of a Thomas Paine. But he is writing a "drama," so to speak; and a "drama" centers on personalities. And here there are Actors, whether great heroes or great sinners, or endowed with portions of both the heroic and the sinful. Here also is an Actor of magnitude, the "mob." A "mob" may mean Anarchy! But Anarchy itself is a necessary in the progression of Mankind—a flame needed to burn away the prevailing and baleful imposture of the age.

This mob or *canaille* is twenty-five million screaming out their grievances against their oppressors. It consists of "units," and "every unit of these masses is a miraculous Man." "The plebeian heart too has red life." "A new Unknown of Democracy was coming into being."

> Down in those dark dens, in those dark heads and hungry hearts, who knows what strange figure the new Political Evangel may have shaped itself; what miraculous 'Communion of Drudges' may be getting formed?[26]

They too, like the great individual Actors, are working out God's purposes, perhaps unknowingly. For the Revolution is fit punishment for the sins of France, "the parent of misery," the "long despotism tempered by epigrams."

The old Adam of radicalism in Carlyle overcomes him at times, as he appears to be participating in the breathtaking events. Thus when the Third Estate declares itself the National Assembly on the eve of the taking of the Bastille, the author explodes: "Forward, ye maddened sons of France; be it towards this destiny or that! Around you is but starvation, falsehood, corruption, and the clam of death. Where ye are is no abiding ... They who would make grass be eaten do now eat grass." "Fear not Sansculottism ... it too came from God: for has it not *been*?"

And now for the grand Actors: Marat, Danton, Camille Desmoulins, Mirabeau, Robespierre:

> Jean Paul Marat of Neufchâtel! O Marat! Renovator of Human Science, Lecturer on Optics; O thou remarkablest Horseleech ... as thy bleared soul looks forth, through thy bleared, dull-acrid, woe-stricken face, what sees it in all this?

And Danton, with his "black brows, and rude flattened face..." and Mirabeau, "the world compeller,"

> with the thick black locks ... through whose shaggy beetle-brows, and rough-hewn, seamed, carbuncled face, there look natural ugliness, small-pox, incontinence, bankruptcy—and burning fire of genius ...

and Robespierre:

> ... that anxious, slight, ineffectual-looking man, under thirty, in spectacles; his eyes (were the glasses off) troubled, careful; with upturned face, snuffing dimly the uncertain future time ...[27]

Few novelists could have excelled Carlyle in his descriptions of the royal family's flight to Varennes, and their capture and return to Paris. No less vivid is the recital of the arming of the counterrevolutionary coalition and the preparations of Brunswick to march against France. But Carlyle's own feelings break out rapturously when he comes to write about the heroic men marching from Marseilles to defend the Republic "from foreign despots":

> But to our minds, the notablest of all these moving phenomena is that of Barbaroux's "Six hundred Marseillese who know how to die." ... These Marseillese remain inarticulate, undistinguishable in feature; a blackbrowed Mass, full of grim fire, who wend there, in the hot, sultry weather: very singular to contemplate ... Fate and Feudal Europe, having decided, come girdling in from without; they, having also decided, do march within ... The Thought, which works voiceless in this blackbrowed mass, an inspired Tyrtaean Colonel, Rouget de Lisle ... has translated into the grim melody and rhythm; into his *Hymn* or *March of the Marseillese*. The sound of which will make the blood tingle in men's veins; and whole Armies and Assemblages will sing it, with eyes weeping and burning, with hearts defiant of Death, Despot and Devil ...[28]

On January 21, 1793, Louis XVI is executed. France becomes a divided land. From without, the Great Coalition of Austria, England and Prussia threatens the destruction of the new state. From within, civil war: the "respectable washed Middle Classes" against the hunger-screams of twenty-five millions near the point of starvation. And then the so-called "Reign of Terror." Behold, within this seeming Chaos, the French armies perform miracles against their foreign enemies.

Well, what about that "Reign of Terror"? What is the truth and what is the legend?

> History, Carlyle writes, ... confesses mournfully that there is no period to be met with, in which the general Twenty-five Millions of France suffered *less* than in this period which they name the Reign of Terror! But it was not the Dumb Millions that suffered here; it was the Speaking Thousands, and Hundreds and Units; who shrieked and published, and made the world ring with their wail ...

This Terror, Carlyle admits, was a frightful thing. How many perished in it? Enemies of the Revolution claim two thousand? Even four thousand? How compare that number with the thousands sacrificed on fields of battle, such, for example, as in the Seven Years War?

Let all take this as a warning:

> If the gods of this lower world will sit on their glittering thrones, indolent as Epicurus' gods, with the living Chaos of Ignorance and Hunger weltering uncared-for at their feet, and smooth Parasites preaching, 'Peace, peace,' when there is no peace, then the dark Chaos, it would seem will rise;—has risen, and, O Heavens! has it not tanned their skins into breeches for itself? That there be no second Sansculottism in our Earth for a thousand years, let us understand well what the first was; and let Rich and Poor of us go and do *otherwise* ...[29]

And so, the confused wreck of a "Republic of the Poverties" ends in the Reign of Terror, and is given its *coup de grâce* by the Napoleonic grapeshot ... And now, what follows? What of today? What are the new rulers who have succeed the former despots?

> Aristocracy of Feudal Parchment has passed away with a mighty rushing; and now, by a natural course, we arrive at Aristocracy of the Moneybag. It is the course through which all European Societies are at this hour travelling. Apparently a still baser sort of Aristocracy? And infintely baser; the basest yet known.[30]

Carlyle had tried to do partial justice to the "masses." In that respect he contrasts significantly with Edmund Burke's depiction of them as a "band of cruel ruffians and assassins, reeking with .... blood," or Hippolyte Taine's description of them, forty years after Carlyle, as "smugglers," dealers in contraband salt, poachers, vagabonds, beggars, old offenders ... society's dregs come to the surface.[31] But Carlyle did not understand the importance of the French Revolution as a "bourgeois" revolution, or the heroic role of the bourgeoisie within it. Once again the mystic and the realist are at war within him; he is apocalyptic as he traces the finger of the Lord in its workings in the revolutionary phenomenon; realistic in his appraisal of the role of poverty and despotic oppression as causes of the Revolution, and in his warnings to his own contemporaries. But he blunts the sharp barbs of his exhortations by denouncing Democracy, Constitutions, Ballot-boxes and franchise reforms as illusions, thus appeasing the fears of both Whig and Tory, neither of whom minded his attacks on greed and materialism (these being always not their own, but someone else's).

Others of his contemporaries, more radical than Carlyle himself, saw more clearly the implications of an "unfinished" revolution: Bronterre O'Brien, the Chartist, who saw such revolutions as "begin in the upper regions ... till they reach ... the classes who live by buying and selling," as doomed to failure; and as for the bourgeois, having attained his goal against the aristocracy, he "flings off his old auxiliaries (the lower classes), and to keep them down, unites with their former oppressors."[32]

* * *

Carlyle was famous. He undertook popular lectures on Literature as well as on Heroes, and more and more spoke with the accents of a Hebrew prophet. Yet he would not be a true Victorian if he did not harbor within himself serious contradictions. On the one hand he was obsessed with the "Condition of England Question," a critic of his age aghast at the brutality, injustices, wretchedness and oppressions he saw around him. With unexampled fervor, even fury, he delivers the infamy of his times. Up to 1848, one could say, the element which predominated in his thought, writing and speeches, and which brought him closest to many of his gifted and sensitive contemporaries, was his sharp, incisive appraisal of the nature of the changed world in which both he and they were living. In the "Hungry Forties" he unweariedly kept before his readers and audiences the glaring contrast between an England "full of wealth, of multifarious produce" and an England "dying of inanition"; the horrifying situation of the needy and the unemployed, the shame and terror of the "Workhouses, Poor-law Prisons," those "Bastilles"—the one million and a half paupers. He lashes out at the "Unworking Aristocracy," that is, the landed gentry, for having surrendered their true responsibilities of "guidance and government" of England; he is equally severe on the powerful new bourgeoisie, "the Working Aristocracy, Mill-owners, Manufacturers, Commanders of Working Men," servitors of the "Gospel of Mammon," imploring, exhorting, and frothing at them to "reform their own selves from top to bottom ... England will not be habitable long, unreformed."[33]

> Behold! Supply-and-Demand is not the one Law of Nature; Cash-payment is not the sole nexus of man with man,—how far from it! Deep, far deeper than Supply-and-demand, are Laws, Obligations sacred as Man's Life itself.[34]

In *Past and Present* another element comes to the fore, which we may call Carlyle's "Tory Romanticism." It proved attractive to many diverse spirits. Here was a glorification of the Middle Ages and Medievalism that combined a moral, spiritual, religious and economic critique (already in a smaller compass adumbrated in the pamphlet on Chartism). Here Carlyle established a vivid contrast between human relations as they subsisted in the Middle Ages and as they manifested themselves at present. That which distinguished the social polity of those times and bound together kings, lords, and subjects was a degree of unity, morality, humaneness that has since almost disappeared. Of course there was also less poverty, less misery and wretchedness. Because,

> ... in one word, *Cash-Payment* had not then grown to be the universal sole nexus of man to man; it was something other than money that the high expected from the low, and could not live without getting from the low. Not as buyer and seller alone, of land or what else it might be, but in many senses still as soldier and captain, as clansman and head, as loyal subject and guiding king, was the low related to the high. With the supreme triumph of Cash, a changed time entered; there must a changed Aristocracy enter.[35]

Past and Present delineated this contrast brilliantly. Carlyle was drawing upon a medieval chronicle of Jocelin of Brakelond and the latter's picture of twelfth-century St. Edmundsbury as illustrating the moral and spiritual qualities of the Middle Ages and its remarkable leader-figure, the Lord Abbot Samson. An idealized picture, it presented a vision of dedicated sanctity, especially the sanctity of Work. *Laborare est orare.* Relationships among the various estates, fixed as they were, were founded on responsibility and duty. A serf, though tied to the soil in perpetuity, was always assured of subsistence. ...

How wretched by contrast is our own age—Chaos of Selfhood and Greed, domain of Midas and Mannon! ...

Strange and varied was the company that drew sustenance from *Past and Present.* Such a romantic Medievalism—so different from that of Shelley and Byron—was likely to appeal strongly even to Tories, who could overlook Carlyle's attacks on them and find solace and even joy in his glorification of medieval paternalism, medieval feudalism, and his exaltation of the more humane relationships between lord and serf. This was the very gospel embraced by the so-called Young Tory movement, and its prophet Benjamin Disraeli ... If Tory Romanticism dreamt of some kind of a neo-medieval political and religious Restoration—not unlike their German Romantic counterparts (Novalis, for example)—others were to draw more radical conclusions from Carlyle's protestations and, focusing on the magnificent artistic contributions of the Middle Ages, spark far-reaching questioning, as in John Ruskin and William Morris, as to the relations of Art and Society. Carlyle's identification of the "cash-nexus" as the terrifying element of kinship in modern society was to find epoch making expansion in Karl Marx's *Das Kapital.* Friedrich Engels wrote appreciatively of Carlyle, who without doubt had considerable impact on his own celebrated work, *The Condition of the Working Class in England.*

Yet even before 1848, certain ominous notes become audible in Carlyle's writings that to a keen ear were anticipatory of a later full-fledged retreat from his "radicalism" of the 1830s and 1840s. "Democracy ... means despair of finding any Heroes to govern you," he wrote in *Past and Present.* It is in that remarkable and very militant essay, "Chartism," that he advances the notorious tenet that Might is Right:

> Might and Right do differ frightfully from hour to hour; but give them centuries to try it in, they are found to be identical. Whose land *was* this of Britain? God's who made it, His and no other's it was and is. Who of God's creatures had the right to live in it? The wolves and the bisons? Yes, they; till one with better right showed himself. The Celt, "aboriginal savage of Europe," as a snarling antiquary names him, arrived, pretending to have a better right; and did accordingly, not without pain to the bisons, make good the same. He had a better right to that piece of God's land; namely a better might to turn it to use ... The bisons disappeared; the Celts took possession, and tilled. Forever, was it to be? Alas, *Forever* is not a category that can establish itself in this world of *Time* ... No property is eternal but God's, the Maker's; whom Heaven permits to take possession, his is the right ... nothing more can be said ... By the same great law do Roman Empires establish themselves, Christian Religions promulgate themselves, and all extant Powers bear rule. The strong thing is the just thing: this thou wilt find throughout in our world;—as indeed was God and Truth the Maker of our world, or was Satan and Falsehood?

If this is the case, one cannot help wondering why Carlyle—having already insisted that "labor" was the laboring man's "property" as sure as forests and fields and lands were that of the Aristocracy—censures the latter for appropriating that of the laboring man. And with one stroke of the pen, guided by what he calls "the miraculous breath of Life" in him, Carlyle destroys the very physical character of "property," transmogrifying it into Spirit! Addressing himself to his "unhappy brother, most poor insolvent brother," who like Carlyle himself is often possessed of an empty purse, he instructs him that he has a property worth far more: "the miraculous breath of Life," and rights "stretching into Immensity, far into Eternity!" "... Fifteen pence a day; three-and-sixpence a day; eight hundred pounds and odd a day, dost thou call that my property?"[36]

By 1850 he was already writing that

> Slave or free is settled in Heaven for a man ... Slaves are in a tremendous majority every-where and the voting of them—not to be got rid of just yet—is a nuisance in proportion ... The free man is he who is *loyal* to the *Laws* of the Universe; who in his heart sees and knows, across all contradictions, that injustice *cannot* befall him here. The first symptom of such a man is not that he resists and rebels, but that he obeys.[37]

It would be a useless task, and a sad one, to trace in detail the course of the moral and social petrification of Carlyle's thought, from his early "radicalism" to his delivery of a gospel of despotism. Recent scholarship has tried forcefully to rehabilitate Carlyle, insisting that he was a continuing "permanent" revolutionary to the end of his days;[38] but it founders on the brute facts of his later writings and actions.

For all that, one need not minimize Carlyle's prodigious services in exposing eloquently the miseries, the shams, the injustices of the times, with their perpetrators and victims. The mystic in him appeals to such vaporous, undefined ethereal forces as "the great deep law of Nature," "the great fact of existence," "the law of the whole," "God-like reality," never defining or clarifying with the precision he was able to bring to his descriptions of the actual conditions existing in his England. His deep social passion, his critical self, however, was transmitted to others, like Dickens and George Eliot.

But he is incapable of developing any positive "revolutionary" theory that does not center on some "Hero" like Cromwell or Frederick the Great.

His prejudices ran deep; his hatred of Jews was intense. He called Disraeli "a su-perlative Hebrew Conjuror." Even more intense was his revulsion from Negroes. In 1849 he contributed an article to *Fraser's Magazine* entitled "Occasional Discourse on the Nigger Question," on the subject of Jamaican Blacks. And he addresses himself to them as follows:

> ... Decidedly you will have to be servant to those are born wiser than you, that are born lords of you; servant to the Whites, if they *are* (as to what mortal can doubt they are?) born wiser than you. That, you may depend on it, my obscure Black friends, is and was always the Law of the World, for you and for all men.

And he applied the Master–Servant relationship to his own household, especially as it concerned the role of woman:

> "The man should bear rule in the house, and not the woman." This is an eternal axiom, the law of nature, which no mortal departs from, unpunished ... I must not, and I can-not, live in a house of which I am not the head.[39]

This was, of course, standard Victorian doctrine, though there was many a wife who bridled against it, even revolted, or for want of proper outlet submitted but

frequently took to illness, neurosis, and hysteria. And so far as "sex" was concerned—
let us call it "Love"—he held that it was "utterly damnable" that love

> be represented as spreading itself over our whole existence, and constituting one of the
> grand interests of it; whereas love—*the thing people call love*—is confined to a very few
> years of a man's life; in fact, a quite insignificant fraction of it, and even then is one thing
> to be attended to among many infinitely more important things.[40]

It is best, then, to remember Carlyle for what he did achieve, rather than for his
failures; acting in the first half of the nineteenth century as a spur to the conscience of
the Victorians, and as one who extended Englishmen's knowledge and understanding
of German literature, and of Goethe in particular, immeasurably. It is best to remember him in the words of Harriet Martineau:

> If I am warranted in believing that the society I am bidding farewell to is a vast improve-
> ment upon that which I was born into, I am confident that the blessed change is attrib-
> utable to Carlyle more than to any single influence besides.[41]

Or those of G. H. Lewes, the author of the first comprehensive English life of Goethe:

> I sat at your feet when my mind was first awakened; and I have honored and loved you
> since both as teacher and friend.[42]

Chapter Four

Charles Dickens

The Novel in "The Battle of Life"

"I believe" … said Alfred, "there are victories and struggles, great sacrifices of self, and noble acts of heroism …
not less difficult to achieve, because they have no earthly
chronicle or audience—done every day in nooks and
corners, and in little households, and in men's and
women's hearts—any one of which might reconcile the
sternest man to such a world, and fill him with belief
and hope in it, though three-fourths of its people were at
war, and another fourth at law, and that's a bold word."
—Charles Dickens, "The Battle of Life"

"The Child is father of the Man."
—William Wordsworth, "My Heart Leaps Up"

The year is 1833—an embattled year, as we have seen, rampant with auguries, good and
evil, for the state of England, battered by conflicting winds of doctrine and threats of
violence, even though the Great Reform Bill had been passed the year before. Disenchantment was already setting in, as the greater mass of England's population was still
left disfranchised. An anonymous ballad of the day expressed the feelings of the working classes:

'Tis twelve months past, just yesterday, since earth and sky and sea
And rock and glen and horse and men rang loud with jubilee;
The beacons blazed, and cannons fired, and roared each plain and hill
With the Bill—the glorious Bill and nothing but the Bill!

But each now holds his hands up in horror and disgust
At this same document—once termed the people's trust
That at last was to bring grist to all the nation's mill.
Oh, curse the Bill, ye rogues, the Bill, and nothing but the Bill! …[1]

On a December day in 1833, a young man strolling through the Strand there
bought a copy of the *Monthly Magazine*. Through tear-stained eyes he saw his first
published work—unsigned, but unmistakably there! Though unsupported by any
form of remuneration, the experience was undoubtedly one familiar to many a writer
whose firstling effort appears in print, an event thereafter held second only to one's

first reciprocated love. No doubt Charles Dickens read his own piece, "A Dinner at Poplar Walk," innumerable times. But he could scarcely have been aware that a career was about to open before him that would bring him thousands upon thousands of readers. More sketches (still unpaid for) would follow the first, soon signed "Boz." Transferring his contributions to the newly established *Evening Chronicle*, an offshoot of the *Morning Chronicle* at which he worked as a reporter, Dickens now began to be paid for them. In 1836 his collected efforts appeared in two volumes under the title *Sketches by Boz.*

Genius is the sensing and realizing of "possibilities." The popularity of Dickens' *Sketches by Boz* was itself one of the unmistakable "signs of the times." With that assurance that was always to characterize him, Dickens had put his finger upon the pulse of the age. His propitious gods had decreed this to be the right moment, the right place, and himself the right man. London had been written about before with affection, tenderness and humor—notably by Charles Lamb and Leigh Hunt. But here was an eye and an ear that had penetrated into other corners of the vast city—had ferreted out a "shabby-genteel" domain of characters, boarding houses, prisons, a great deal of nondescript life—and yet had brought all that to readers as a living presence, with understanding, whimsy, sympathy, and humor. Here a family is being distrained for nonpayment of rent; yonder is Doctors' Common, and its courts with its legal squabbles as well as its marriage licenses; here is the still romantic hackney coach and coachman; and so on ...

Where had that young genius been schooled to observe so keenly, to amalgamate his observations, to endow them with novelty and freshness? Not from the sparse and intermittent education that his family's variant fortunes permitted, but from the drastic experiences of childhood and youth. He learned the elements of political economy not from the treatises of Adam Smith and James Mill, but from the live household in which he had been brought up and the occupations into which he had been thrust as a very young boy, as well as those he undertook as a young man. He did not need to read Carlyle (whom he was to admire exceedingly) to understand the meaning of money and the "cash-nexus." He had studied them first hand, for debts and debtor-prisons had been a part of his family life! He had learned a great deal about child psychology in the same way—he needed no textbook to understand the meaning of disfranchised childhood, of the tragedy in a household where affection and care of children disappear; where a mother is constantly occupied with child-bearing, household duties, and holding things together; a household in which the father's cavalier improvidence frequently ends in the seclusion of a debtor's cell. Charles Dickens' childhood drudgery in Warren's blacking establishment was squalid enough; but not so destructive as the gruesome reality of his parents' indifference to his feelings and his plight, his deprivation of schooling, and the devastating sense of abandonment. To the natural fears and dreads of childhood were superadded the menaces of London, transfigured as claws of destruction reaching out after innocence and inexperience. Evil is rampant everywhere, but especially in the mephitic and malignant slums. Salvation therefore takes the form of money—in the person of some beneficent deity, present providentially at times, a fatherly deity—to rescue, to salvage orphan childhood ...

Dickens knew the pangs of hunger; later, in his better years, he would compensate for such deprivations by reveling both in person and in his books in food and drink, much to the horror of his more abstemious readers. He came to understand the complex drama of money, class and love on his rejection as a wooer by Maria Beadnell, probably under pressure of her status-conscious parents.

And what he suffered, he never forgot—neither his rejection as a child nor as a lover.

Dickens was middle-class consciousness personified. He long kept secret his employment as a drudge in the blacking factory. He felt déclassé, degraded to own that his mother had behaved like other mothers of the lower classes. He could scarcely have been consoled by statistics of the year 1835 showing practically fifty thousand children between the ages of eight and thirteen employed in the English cotton-spinning industry alone. It was taken for granted that working-class children were there to eke out the sparse incomes of their families, to be readily replaced as "commodities" when the high mortality rate, abetted by cholera, reduced the child-labor market ...

Yet he was indomitable. He lived (as Bacon once said) as if "the mould of his fortunes" was in his hands. He braved Adversity; he challenged Fate. He became a law clerk; and having mastered shorthand, the best of parliamentary reporters. As a newspaper man he was adventurous and indefatigable. His memory was prodigious; his brain chronicled everything. His contempt for Parliament, its mentality and procedures, dated from the time of the Reform agitation and persisted thereafter. He saw how ruthlessly and unscrupulously Tory agitation and political electioneering were being conducted. He heard cases in court, got to know law and lawyers, judges and magistrates. The lower depths of life were already well known to him. And now the once shabby factory hand became the dandy. He loved the theatre, was himself an accomplished actor. Though unsuccessful as a playwright, he brought to his novels and stories scenes, characters, and dialogue that would find no equal on the British stage until Bernard Shaw. His energies rivaled those of Balzac. Under his hand enterprises and undertakings proliferated, as they did with the great Frenchman. But unlike Balzac, Dickens would never know the complete fulfilment of love.

* * *

While the *Sketches by Boz* were still in progress, the publishers Chapman and Hall invited Dickens to write a series to illustrate the sporting engravings of Robert Seymour. But being Dickens, he soon made the illustrations subserve his text, and thus, on March 31, 1836, was launched the first of the monthly installments of *The Posthumous Papers of the Pickwick Club*. Seymour committed suicide before the second number appeared, and was succeeded as illustrator by "Phiz"—Hablôt Knight Browne. The first four issues moved slowly; but thereafter sales mounted, soon reaching an unprecedented number of forty thousand.

And thus was born a new "hero," Mr. Samuel Pickwick, a rotund and sentimental bachelor, destined to join, in his bespectacled middle age, the great comic figures of literature—the merry company of Falstaff, Don Quixote, Parson Adams, the heroes of Rabelais and of the English humorists of the preceding century. Mr. Pickwick and his crew of unforgettable companions captured the hearts of his own age and kept them in thrall forever after.

Though the scenes are set presumably in the England of 1827, we are really thrust back into the preceding century. There are no factory smokestacks to blur the rustic landscape, and no railroads as yet. The stagecoach is still a roaring fast conveyance, sometimes harrowing and perilous as it rumbles and shudders over impassable roads. It is still a magic chariot, for who can foretell what might befall passengers on the highways and byways of the country? The highways, like the city of London itself, were Dickens's domain. He knew them at first hand, moving as a child between Portsmouth, Rochester, Chatham, and London, and later as a wily reporter hastening to anticipate a rival and "scoop" him with some tidbit, parliamentary or otherwise. It is in such a coach that the Pickwick Club, under the leadership of its president Mr. Pickwick, and with his three jolly companions, Mr. Tupman, Mr. Winkle, and Mr. Snodgrass, set out on their adventurous "researches." Mr. Pickwick will fill his note-books with novel entries, for in addition to unpredictable adventures, there is the grand prospect of meeting and making new acquaintances like the squire Wardle and the fascinating Mr. Jingle, he of the stenographic rhetoric, charmer and scamp! We feel as if we were back in the days of Addison and Steele, Fielding and Smollett, the days of Sir Roger de Coverley. Mr. Pickwick could surely have come out of the pages of *The Spectator*: see him now, the very epitome of benevolence, a benign squire in his old-fashioned gaiters, gazing out through his spectacles. "General benevolence was one of the leading features of the Pickwickian theory." Mr. Pickwick's notebook "is blotted with tears of sympathizing humanity."[2]

But the true "drama" of the *Pickwick Papers* commences in London's White Hart Inn, whither Mr. Pickwick and his cohorts had rushed to frustrate the nefarious schemes of Mr. Jingle, who had eloped with Squire Wardle's maiden sister. For it is here that they also encounter Mr. Sam Weller, the "boots"—while he is engaged polishing boots and shoes with all the earnestness and conviction that, says Dickens, "would have struck envy to the soul of the amiable Mr. Warren." (Oh, that memory of Mr. Warren's blacking establishment!)

If it is true, as some biographers insist, that with the appearance of Sam Weller and his father Tony Weller the fortune of the *Pickwick Papers* was made doubly sure, it is, in fact, no wonder. For Sam Weller is not just another character in these papers, he is a portentous event. In creating him, and the older Mr. Tony Weller, Dickens had found his own true voice.

For through this means, that which had been an "idyl" of another age is suddenly transformed into a portrait of present reality. Through this means Mr. Pickwick, nature's child, sentimental and guileless, brimful of good feelings toward the world at large, is brought into a world that was to tax his benevolence as well as his innocence. Not that he will be corrupted (Heaven forfend!)—he will be "educated," and his teacher will be none other than Samuel Weller, "boots" of the White Hart Inn, but now that Mr. Pickwick has hired him, a gentleman's servant.

Don Quixote had his Sancho Panza; Mr. Pickwick has Sam Weller. Sam Weller is, as Mr. Pickwick soon recognizes, a philosopher, of a very deep school. The "sunbeam of placid benevolence" that is Mr. Pickwick has now met the sharp crystal of Mr. Sam Weller's mind and deep experience, and is soon diffracted. Master and servant will change roles, and the servant will become his master's teacher.

In Sam Weller, language becomes character, just as his character becomes language—aphoristic, epigrammatic and wise—with its own special dialect and intonation. Such is Dickens' special gift, that we often think of his characters and remember them at first for their speech. What two strange backgrounds now coalesce in the confrontations of Mr. Pickwick and his servant! Of Mr. Pickwick's background we know practically nothing (this will be true of many of Dickens' benefactors). What need is there? He is like one of those gods, demigods, or celestial messengers sent down to earth by an Almighty Power to see how the world fares, and to amend things wherever possible. Only this one is somewhat stoutish, middle-class in outlook and temperament. He likes to drink, and is fond of a good meal. His heart is warm and human, but like most angels he is somewhat naive. Here are Sam Weller and Mr. Pickwick—both looking at the country landscape:

"Delightful prospect, Sam," said Mr. Pickwick.

"Beats the chimbley-pots, sir," replied Mr. Weller, touching his hat.

"I suppose you have hardly seen anything but chimney-pots and bricks and mortar all your life, Sam," said Mr. Pickwick, smiling

"I worn't always boots, sir," said Mr. Weller, with a shake of the head. "I wos a vagginer's boy, once."

"When was that?" inquired Mr. Pickwick.

"When I wos first pitched neck and crop into the world to play at leap-frog with its troubles," replied Sam. "I wos a carrier's boy at startin', then a vagginer's, then a helper, then a boots. Now I'm a gen'lm'n's servant. I shall be a gen'lm'n myself one of these days, perhaps, with a pipe in my mouth and a summer-house in the back-garden. Who knows? I shouldn't be surprised for once."

"You are quite a philosopher, Sam," said Mr. Pickwick.

"It runs in the family, I b'lieve, sir," replied Mr. Weller. "My father's very much in that line now. If my mother-in-law [i.e. stepmother] blows him up, he whistles. She flies in a passion and breaks his pipe; he steps out and gets another. Then she screams very loud and falls into 'isterics; and he smokes very comfortably till she comes to agin. That's philosophy, sir, an't it?"

"A very good substitute for it, at all events," replied Mr. Pickwick, laughing. "It must have been of great service to you in the course of your rambling life, Sam."

"Service, sir," exclaimed Sam. "You may say that. After I run away from the carrier, and afore I took up with the waggi/ner, I had unfurnished lodgin's for a fortnight."

"Unfurnished lodgings?" said Mr. Pickwick.

"Yes—the dry arches of Waterloo Bridge. Fine sleeping-place—within ten minutes' walk of all the public offices—only if there is any objection to it, it is that the sitivation's *rayther* too airy. I see some queer sights there."

"Ah, I suppose you did," said Mr. Pickwick with an air of considerable interest.

"Sights, sir," resumed Mr. Weller, "as 'ud penetrate your benevolent heart and come out on the other side. You don't see the reg'lar wagrants there; trust 'em, they knows better than that. Young beggars, male and female, as hasn't made a rise in their profession, takes up their quarters there sometimes; but it's generally the worn-out, starving, houseless creeturs as rolls themselves in the dark corners o' them lonesome place—poor creeturs as an't up to the twopenny rope."

"And pray, Sam, what is the twopenny rope?" inquired Mr. Pickwick.

"The twopenny rope, sir," replied Mr. Weller, "is just a cheap lodgin'-house where the beds is twopence a night."[3]

Innocence and Experience ... How Innocence is transmogrified into Experience is soon demonstrated when Mr. Pickwick, in announcing his intention of hiring a servant to his landlady, Mrs. Bardell, and asking, "Do you think it is a much greater expense to keep two people than to keep one?"—finds her precipitating herself into his arms, and him into a breach-of-promise lawsuit, into the hands of pettyfogging lawyers, into court cases and juries, and eventually, when he refuses to accept the verdict against him, into jail! What he sees in prison is enough to make him exclaim, "I have seen enough ... My head aches with these scenes, and my heart too."[4]

Tears of benevolent sympathy alternate with scenes of broad comedy. Who is likely to forget Tony Weller, Sam's father? Father and son meet by accident in a London tavern, not having seen each other for "a year and better." The conversation naturally turns to the elder Weller's second marriage to a widow, the mistress of a public house in Dorking. The "widder" becomes Sam's stepmother, or as she was called in Victorian days, his "mother-in-law."

> "Vy, I'll tell you what, Sammy," said Mr. Weller senior with much solemnity in his manner; "there never was a nicer woman as a widder than that 'ere second wentur o' mine— a sweet creetur she was, Sammy; all I can say on her now is that as she was such an uncommon pleasant widder, it's a great pity she ever changed her condition. She don't act as a vife, Sammy ... I've done it once too often, Sammy: I've done it once too often. Take example by your father, my boy, and be wery careful o' widders all your life, 'specially if they've kept a public-house."[5]

Yes, his cup overfloweth, but not with joy, for in addition, "mother-in-law" is "gettin' rayther in the Methodistical order lately." Having come under the influence of a religious fourflusher, she now tries to convert her husband. Stiggins—that is his name—is ever on the look-out for "wessels of wrath" (like Tony Weller) and is always in the public house, imbibing liberally under the indulgent eyes of the erstwhile "widder." Dickens hated hypocrisy, wherever it might appear, and he and the Weller practice just retribution upon the mealy-mouthed bibber. ...

We linger long over the book, not solely because, as Gilbert K. Chesterton insists in his beautiful study of Dickens, it is one of the author's greatest works, but also because it contains *in ovo* the major themes of his subsequent productions—both the lights and the shadows. True, the vision will grow more somber at times, the elements of conflict more sharply delineated, the humor more biting. For the *Pickwick Papers* must remain for us Dickens's "Pastoral Symphony": the landscape is fresh and clear; we're in the unspoiled country, as it were. There is of course the brief summer squall, soon followed by a wonderful clearing announced by the shepherd's pipe. In the end, all is well. And as we leave the scene, we can envision Mr. Pickwick, Mr. Sam Weller, Mr. Tony Weller and some others slowly fading into immortality, to a coda of Dickens's parting words:

There are dark shadows on earth, but its lights are stronger in the contrast. Some men, like bats and owls, have better eyes for the darkness than for the light. We, who have no such optical powers, are better pleased to take our last parting look at the visionary companions of many solitary hours when the brief sunshine of the world is blazing upon them.[6]

＊ ＊ ＊

"Dark shadows" and "light" now alternate in his works, or are juxtaposed, and the world around him makes a sharp contrast with rustic innocence and an idyllic past. The world was "too much with him," and his own deepest experiences too overwhelming, to allow him to escape mandates of action. He was a child of the 1830s, and in England. Here there was no room for a romantic *Weltschmerz*, or a *mal du siècle*, no room for that self-enclosement of the ego that was beating its wings in a void. He understood what it meant to "fall upon the thorns of life." He had succeeded in raising himself upright, but did not overlook those who had failed or been unable to do so; he strove to raise them.

He would never cease to rehabilitate innocence, but would seek the sources of its perversion in the modern age. There could be no more vivid symbol of innocence than childhood, nor a more scarifying testament to its perversion than the treatment of children at the hands of society.

Romanticism had looked at childhood anew. Rousseau had called for a "natural" education; Wordsworth had endowed the child at its birth with "intimations of immortality," trailing "clouds of glory" that the ever-narrowing prison house of life gradually darkened and sometimes extinguished. In Blake, the glories and distresses of childhood had been sounded more eloquently than ever before. Dickens, too, was deeply aware of the "prison-house" that distorted the young, but, concerned as he was for the child's soul, was eminently preoccupied with the child not as it emerged from Eternity, but as surrounded by the dark and dire forests of the Present.

From the whimper of a disfranchised orphan child named Oliver Twist in the poor-house, to the scalding sorrows of an alienated David Copperfield, the cry of the abandoned, the unloved, the misunderstood and the maltreated young sounds with persistence. It speaks out of the workhouses where at the time nearly 43,000 pauper children were being "cared" for; it is heard in the schoolrooms into which young Nicholas Nickleby is thrust as a tutor to witness the sadistic performances of Squeers; it is heard, though in other tones, in the premature adulthood of Little Nell, no less than in the brutalized beginnings of Barnaby Rudge and the illegitimate Hugh in *Barnaby Rudge*; it speaks as movingly in the pathetic efforts of poor Florence Dombey to win the affections of her father. It is there in the premature death of young Paul Dombey.

Societies take various forms of brutality for granted. We have lived through too much in our own day to be unaware of how much can be taken as a "matter of course." The increased pauperization of the agricultural laborer in England during the first half of the nineteenth century, the migration of the farmworker into the cities and their factories, the invasion of Irish labor, the fluctuations of employment, had raised the problem of relief to an unprecedented level. It had been customary until 1834 to supplement the fixed wages of the agricultural worker with a minimum dole; but the new "free" economy, in order to make relieved pauperism as unattractive as possible, spawned the Poor Law Amendment Bill of 1834. This eliminated "out-door" relief for the able-bodied, and compelled paupers (as in the days of Queen Elizabeth) to earn their relief in workhouses, where conditions would be made less desirable than those of the poorest laborer who was not on relief. Recipients were separated from their families and were pressured in every way to enter the "free" labor market. "Our object," wrote one of the Commissioners of the time, "is to establish therein a discipline so severe and repulsive as to make them a terror to the poor and prevent them from entering."[7]

Setting aside the usual conditions of filth, disease, and demoralization, one of the most execrable devices was the starvation diet on which the pauper was made to subsist. As for the children, to the ordinary terrors of childhood were added personal brutality, abuse, and of course hunger. Oliver's plea in the workhouse, "Please, sir, I want some more," echoed in the cries of thousands of such children as well as adults, and became reflected in the serious anti-Poor-Law agitations of 1836 and 1837.

It is no small portion of Dickens' genius that he was able to etch such horrors in the grotesqueries of character and speech. Just as the Russian Gogol's may be called a "tragic grotesque," so Dickens' may be termed "ironic grotesque."

Here is the canting beadle, Mr. Bumble, discanting on the evils of meat, and its influence on Oliver:

> "Meat, ma'am, meat," replied Bumble with stern emphasis. "You've overfed him, ma'am. You've raised an artificial soul and spirit in him, ma'am, unbecoming a person of his condition … What have paupers to do with soul and spirit? It's quite enough that we let 'em have live bodies. If you had kept the boy on gruel, ma'am, this would never have happened."[8]

Mr. Wackford Squeers, in *Nicholas Nickleby*, is also an authority on the relation of morals to food:

> "Conquer your passions, boy, and don't be eager after vittles … Subdue your appeties, my dears, and you've conquered human nature."[9]

But hunger is not the worst of evils besetting childhood. Worse are physical cruelty, moral humiliation, and deprivation of affection and understanding. Here it is not only such "Bastilles" as the workhouses or schools that are the culprits; the family itself, parents and guardians, can also serve as the prime agents of childhood distortion, for they are the crucial formative influences directing the child's future growth. Even where overt physical brutality is absent, as in the more fashionable educational institutions, subtler ways of undermining the character and mind of a child can still prevail. Fragile and sensitive Paul Dombey becomes such a victim at the hands of Mrs. Pipchin, and subsequently of Dr. Blimber. As for Mrs. Pipchin,

> She was generally spoken of as a great manager of children; and the secret of her management was to give them everything that they didn't like, and nothing that they did— which was found to sweeten their dispositions very much … It being a part of Mrs. Pipchin's system not to encourage a child's mind to develop and expand itself like a young flower, but to open it by force like an oyster, the moral of these lessons was usually of a violent and stunning character; the hero—a naughty boy—seldom, in the mildest catastrophe, being finished off by anything less than a lion or a bear.[10]

This is not the overt brutality of the Squeers establishment, but the more insidious brutality of the mechanized mind. How could the Mrs. Pipchins and all the Blimbers have understood the tender and sensitive character of dreamy young Paul Dombey, a child already incapable of coping with the world and doomed to an early death? How could his own father, Mr. Dombey, an "establishment" man—with money and status writ large over all his thoughts and doings, transforming all around him into "Property"—how could such a man understand and deal with this strange phenomenon in his own household?

The problem becomes only more acute in a world no longer that of Mr. Pickwick. The stagecoach has given way to the menace and speed of the railway, the smoke of the city factories penetrates more and more insistently even into the countryside, and prophets like Mr. Carlyle are now crying, Doom! and exhorting England to find a replacement for an absentee God. How to bring coherence into a seemingly incoherent world? That is a problem also for Dickens. If God is justice and benevolence, he must also triumph in this world. The struggle of Good and Evil are not taking place in some translunary universe, but are manifesting themselves more clearly than ever in our quotidian existence, in people, in institutions, within our own very selves. How is Innocence to assert itself? Evil is no metaphysical concept—it bears a human face and a name. Now it is Greed. Now it is sheer impenetrable malevolence. It has its own Hell, but that Hell is a visible geographical entity in the very heart of London: It is Whitechapel, Jacob's Island, or some other mephitic region of London's netherworld. That Hell reaches out its tentacles, ever ready to snatch at the innocent, ever ready to corrupt. Evil is Fagin, lord of petty thieves, a powerful descendant of medieval anti-semitic demonology acceptable even in the nineteenth century, and by Dickens underscored through the generic title of "the Jew." The terrifying grotesquerie of his appearance, language, and behavior—he is described as being "like some loathsome reptile"—only accentuates the type. He is a degraded Satan; for he is the mentor of a gang of thieves and prostitutes, even if Victorian reticence will bar open naming of members of the oldest profession, as it will also moderate the character of underworld speech. Innocence is Oliver Twist, sucked into hell.

Luckily there is an absentee God who reveals himself now in the guise of Mr. Brownlow, a substitute father whose benevolence gives Oliver a home and restores to him his rightful inheritance. Was Dickens aware that he was himself something of a god, whose wishes fathered lucky accidents, coincidences, and moral and physical reimbursements, and kept wide-eyed innocence, in such figures as Oliver Twist, miraculously untainted by the filth and evil of Hell?

With the *Pickwick Papers* and *Oliver Twist*, Dickens was launched on the broad highway of fame, success, and money. Seemingly indefatigable and inexhaustible, he continued month after month in unremitting output. Practically each succeeding year after 1836 saw the appearance of a new work, *Oliver Twist, Nicholas Nickleby, The Old Curiosity Shop, Barnaby Rudge, Martin Chuzzlewit, Dombey and Son*, and *David Copperfield*—and this only up to 1849, aside from various journalistic stints, theatrical enterprises, acting—and, of course, living! This busy life also included a visit to the United States in 1841.

But his own personal life was not free from severe emotional shocks. In 1837 his sister-in-law, the seventeen-year-old Mary Hogarth, died suddenly of a heart attack. She had adored him, and he was undoubtedly in love with her. When in love, Dickens became obsessed, and along with Maria Beadnell, Mary Hogarth became the personification of unattainable desires. Life with his wife Catherine was unsatisfying. Poor woman, she was incapable of coping with genius, domestic duties, and the births of ten children. Even had she had the time, she would scarcely have had the energy or talent for keeping up with the feverish pace of her husband's life. His was an erotic nature, and he fulfilled his marital duties punctiliously. But he was never to know a full mature relationship with a mature partner; his imagination turned to young girls, virginal, beautiful, and spiritual, but sufficiently maternal to satisfy his own lack of a mother and a wife. After his separation from Catherine in 1858, it was his other sister-in-law who stepped in to take her place as housekeeper and manager—a surrogate for the dead Mary Hogarth.

The humanitarian benevolence Dickens preached and projected in his picture of the world as he saw it, or imagined it, struck his readers deeply, touched their sentimental nerve. They were moved to tears at his characters' woes, to laughter at their eccentricities, to rage at their villainies. But they found their prime satisfaction in the sense of a universe that meted out justice to the oppressor and the oppressed, and in a benign deity that would always emerge to restore a just balance. Perhaps, also, their troubled conscience, perhaps even a fear of vengeance at the hands of the abused, was appeased by the thought of someone ready to appear with a well-filled purse and the right amount of benevolence to redeem the downtrodden and the suffering. Dickens himself shared this fear of violent upheavals. Hence so many of his troubled young characters are passive figures to whom things are done—recipients rather that actors. They do not change in the process of living; they are at the end what they were at the beginning. Where there is a change in character, it comes by way of a moralistic fiat at the author's command. There are many deathbed conversions. Triumphs of nature, morality, and goodness are asserted, not proved. And the benevolent deities do not appear to effect any changes in the general conditions which they have come to relieve. Light and darkness are opposed; but the penumbral, the transitional, which is Life itself, with its confusions and mixtures of elements, is absent.

Dickens's own consciousness of the world around him was itself in the process of growth. Here and there, even now, his questioning mind stops to ask, "Why must this be?"—without as yet finding the answer. Hence, the excesses of anger, even violence in him. In defiance of his affected readers who pleaded for a living Nell, he insisted that little Nell must die, good human being though she was—just as Mary Hogarth had to die. But by whose edict? And by what right?

The world was celebrating him as the painter of the human heart. Douglas Jerrold's *Shilling Magazine* hailed him in a "Sonnet to Charles Dickens" in 1845:

> Oh, potent wizard! painter of great skill!
>   Blending with life's realities the hues
>   Of a rich fancy; sweetest of all singers!
> Charming the public ear, and at thy will
>   Searching the soul of him thou dost amuse,

> And the warm heart's recess ...
> And every blessed feeling, which the world
>   Had frozen or repressed with its stern apathy
> For human suffering. ...[11]

He was discovering a world more complex than even he had imagined it, with large forces at work which individual benevolence and good feelings were too weak to combat. There were the Hungry Forties, and in that same decade a great speculating mania in railway stocks, and a crash.

But even before that, in *Nicholas Nickleby*, the broad comedy and farce is shadowed by a sense of darkness, as Dickens notes the ramifications of Greed reaching out to despoil and degrade human ties through the "cash-nexus." Nicholas Nickleby himself is about to fall victim to that malignant force, for the young woman he loves is being coerced into marriage with the horrible old Mr. Gride, with her father's connivance. He is brought to reflect on the nature of the world in which he is living:

> Last night, the sacrifice of a young, affectionate, and beautiful creature to such a wretch, and in such a cause, had seemed a thing too monstrous to succeed; and the warmer he grew, the more confident he felt that some interposition must save her from his clutches. But now, when he thought how regularly things went on, from day to day, in the same unvarying round; how youth and beauty died, and ugly griping age lived tottering on; how crafty avarice grew rich, and manly honest hearts were poor and sad; how few they were who tenanted the stately houses, and how many those who lay in noisome pens, or rose each day and laid them down each night, and lived and died, father and son, mother and child, race upon race, generation upon generation, without a home to shelter them or the energies of one single man directed to their aid ..., how ignorance was punished and never taught; how jail-doors gaped and gallows loomed, for thousands urged towards them by circumstances darkly curtaining their very cradles' heads ..., how much injustice, misery, and wrong there was, and yet how the world rolled on from year to year, alike careless and indifferent, and no man seeking to remedy or redress it; when he thought of all this, and selected from the mass one slight case on which his thoughts were bent, he felt, indeed, that there was little ground for hope, and little reason why it should not form an atom in the huge aggregate of distress and sorrow, and add one small and unimportant unit to swell the great amount.[12]

Here, already, the glass mirroring the naive simplicities of life is misted over by Doubt, almost Despair. But here too, evil is frustrated not by the actions of the hero, but by the fortunate intervention of philanthropic benevolence in the persons of the impossible but well-to-do twins, the Cheeryble brothers. Once more the wish is father to the impossible.

But alas! the impossible, the dream of a redeemed and balanced universe, was always bedeviled for Dickens by the urgencies of reality. And his conscience was never at rest. He was ridden by internal ambivalences. He was fearful of violence—and yet there was the great Chartist agitation threatening to explode at any moment; and, he felt, for good reason.

> I went [he wrote in 1838] some weeks ago to Manchester, and saw the *worst* cotton mill. And then I saw the *best*. *Ex uno disce omnes*. There was no great difference between them ... But on the 11th of next month I am going down again, only for three days, and then

into the enemy's camp and the very headquarters of the factory system advocates ... What I have seen has disgusted me and astonished me beyond all measure. I mean to strike the heaviest blow in my power for these unfortunate creatures, but whether I shall do so in 'Nickleby', or wait some other opportunity, I have not yet determined.[13]

Nor was he taken in by the Tory image of "good old England," and he indited a savage parody of "The Fine Old English Gentleman," as fierce as any Corn Law Rhyme:

I'll sing you a new ballad, and I'll warrant it first-rate,
Of the days of that old gentleman who had that old estate;
When they spent public money at a bountiful old rate
On ev'ry mistress, pimp, and scamp, at ev'ry noble gate,
   In the fine old English Tory times;
   Soon may they come again! ...

The good old laws were garnished well with gibbets, whips and chains,
With fine old English penalties, and fine old English pains,
With rebel heads and seas of blood once hot in rebel veins:
For all these things were requisite to guard the rich old gains
   Of the fine old English Tory times;
   Soon may they come again! ...

The bright old day now dawns again; the cry runs through the land,
In England there shall be—dear bread! in Ireland—sword and brand!
And poverty, and ignorance shall swell the rich and grand,
So rally round the rulers with the gentle iron hand ...[14]

"Among the false book-backs with which he decorated his study at Gad's Hill was a set called 'The Wisdom of our Ancestors'—I. Ignorance. II. Superstition. III. The Block. IV. The Stake. V. The Rack. VI. Dirt. VII. Disease."[15]

Such was the rage that smouldered within him, and yet—

In *The Old Curiosity Shop* Little Nell and her grandfather are fleeing from the dire machinations of the evil Quilp, and in their journey north come upon factories in the Staffordshire district. Here both of them are witnesses of the desolations wrought by the factory system, the unemployment, the misery of men, women, and children, who "wan in their looks and ragged in attire ... begged upon the road, or scowled half-naked from the doorless houses."

But the night-time in this dreadful spot! ... when people near them looked wilder and more savage; when bands of unemployed labourers paraded in the roads, or clustered by torch-light round their leaders, who told them in stern language of their wrongs, and urged them on to frightful cries and threats; when maddened men, armed with sword and firebrand, spurning the tears and prayers of women who would restrain them, rushed forth on errands of terror and destruction, to work no ruin half so surely as their own—night, when carts came rumbling by, filled with rude coffins (for contagious disease and death had been busy with the living crops) ... night, which, unlike the night that Heaven sends on earth, brought with it no peace, nor quiet, nor signs of blessed sleep—who shall tell the terrors of the night to that young wandering child![16]

Yes, Dickens' sympathies went wide and deep. Unlike Carlyle, he had friendly feelings for the persecuted Chartists; unlike Carlyle he was willing to help them. But the larger issues of those struggles escaped him. For the individual victim of oppression, barbarity, and poverty he has a large-hearted compassion; and for his oppressor an equally large-hearted hatred. But he is fearful of the mass, and its potential explosiveness. There are instances when he is able to depict the "insulted and injured" with a pathos and directness that might well rival the skill of a Dostoevsky, as for example in the character of the little slavey in the employ of the lawyer Brass, in *The Old Curiosity Shop*. Here the bare presentation of a situation—this time again the horror of hunger—is worth pages of eloquent exhortation.

The schism between those of the Chartists who preached the use of "moral force" in the attainment of their objectives, and those who preached "physical force," troubled him. The deformations of character he saw emerging from the mould of injustice, bad food and brutality roused him to internal anger, and he at times allowed his characters to recriminate with physical violence—watching the victims' discomfitures with glee. But in the face of mass violence real and potential, Dickens recoiled. Such was the dilemma that produced his first historical novel, *Barnaby Rudge*, published in 1841. It was written under the influence of Carlyle's *French Revolution*, and though set in the eighteenth century, was in its picture of mob-violence and its suppression an indirect commentary on the Chartist agitation of his own day. The idea of *Barnaby Rudge* had been with him for some time. Carlyle had shown him the way: history could be made dramatic. Carlyle had shown him history in motion—with the masses moving, making a revolution. Carlyle's book, too, had been written with the author's own times in mind.

The so-called "Gordon Riots" took place in London in 1780, presumably directed against Catholics, and assumed to have been fomented by Lord George Gordon. The riots took place against the background of a lost war against the American Colonies, economic strains and tensions, and a general hostility to the King and his ministers. The immediate and ostensible occasion was the parliamentary attempt to encourage Catholics to join the armed forces by easing some of their disabilities, without re-pealing the major ones, through a harmless Catholic Relief Bill. But the uprising also released a number of hidden forces within the populace of London, among them longstanding grievances against current abuses, courts of justice, the competition of Irish Catholic laborers, a challenge to the already low wage-scale of Protestant workers. Protestant fury turned against not only Catholic chapels and the houses of well-to-do Catholics, but soon enough against wealthy and powerful Protestants, venting itself most intensely upon the prisons—Newgate, the "British Bastille," in particular. For that prison housed numerous inmates destined under the laws of the day for hanging—petty thieves and such, but soon also those immured for the recent rioting. The alleged leader of the insurgent movement, Lord George Gordon, was a mixture of madness and extraordinary philanthropic proclivities, a figure that often makes fiction a feeble replica of reality. Strongly anti-Catholic (he was the leader of the so-called Protestant Associations), Gordon had democratic sentiments, was opposed to capital punishment, and was in general a "friend of the people." In Parliament he was a thorn in the flesh of both Tories and Whigs. After the carnage of the Gordon Riots—almost five hundred either killed or wounded by the military—he was tried, but acquitted of High Treason. Soon, however, trapped by the publication of a "libellous" attack on the French queen Marie Antoinette, he was convicted and sentenced. He managed to escape abroad; then, returning to England, became a convert to Orthodox Judaism. Once again apprehended, Gordon spent the rest of his life in jail, where he held court like some major East European Rabbi and Savant, gave audience to high and low, and crowned his career with the aura of a Messiah. He who had been Lord George Gordon lived his last years as Israel bar Abraham Gordon!

But it is in the subordinate figures that Dickens sought to reveal as best he could the character of the uprising, and extract historical meaning. As in Carlyle, the movement takes on the character of some "natural" force, embodied in human beings, themselves a kind of natural force, to work out their vengeance on an oppressive world. These are "primitives"—Barnaby Rudge, and Hugh, an illegitimate son of an aristocrat, John Chester. Barnaby is an "idiot" boy, son of a murderer. He is innocence betrayed, endowed with deep feelings and innate perceptions. Hugh, on the other hand, is an "animal," more at home with dogs and beasts of the field than with human beings, a thing traduced and abandoned. Barnaby's constant companion is the crow Grip, almost human; Hugh's is a dog. Along with many others, but more like poetic symbols of the lurking violence within the world itself, these two are sucked into the almost irresistible surge of hate and vengeance, deeper potentials of revolution. Elemental chaos threatens to dissolve Authority, and Order armed by Authority triumphs, soon wreaking its vengeance, chiefly on blind scapegoats. Barnaby barely escapes execution; Hugh is hanged.

It is in the character and actions of Hugh, the "natural," the "primitive," that Dickens salvages whatever social meaning he can draw out of these dire events. As he is led to the scaffold to be hanged, Hugh becomes humanity's spokesman. He arraigns those who have made him the brute he is; he becomes the voice of the dumb inheritors of the earth's transgressions, crying out against "this hardened, cruel, unrelenting place."

> Upon these human shambles, I, who never raised his hand in prayer till now, call down the wrath of God. On that black tree, of which I am the ripened fruit, I do invoke the curse of all its victims, past, present, and to come. On the head of that man who, in his conscience owns me for his son, I leave the wish that he may never sicken on his bed of down, but die a violent death as I do now, and have the nightwind for his only mourner. To this I say, Amen, amen![17]

No reader could miss the parallel between the events of *Barnaby Rudge* and the Chartist agitations. That Dickens should even have imagined such a parallel, points to his still inadequate understanding of the great historic changes that had taken place between 1780 and 1840. Two momentous revolutions on the continent had intervened. That which was so inchoate and confused in the former period, had acquired doctrine and programs of action. The forces that had participated in 1789 and 1830 had become well defined as classes. In 1780, it seemed to Dickens and many others, it was the "mob" against the authorities. The book attains to its climactic fortissimo in the horrifying description of the invasion by the hordes of men and women of the distillery owned by a Catholic, and the near-orgy as they drink themselves to death in the gutters of the city. The central representatives of society's outrages, agents and victims, are embodied in such figures as the sadistic hangman Dennis (symbolic of "justice");

Hugh, the eruptive volcano of hatred, the alienated symbol of disintegrated family ties (he is a bastard, and his mother, victim of a seduction, had been executed); and Barnaby Rudge himself, the imbecile offspring of crime. They are all of them indictments of a blind and cruel society, not merely Freudian or Jungian archetypes. They can be best understood as Nicholas Nickleby, in another context and another book, understands the spiritually and physically stunted Smike, when someone looking at him remarks, "So odd, isn't he?, and Nicholas replies, "God help him, and those who made him so, he is indeed.."[18]

But Chartism in the 1840s, at the height of its agitation, was the response to the disappointments of 1832 and the Reform Bill. Chartism again clamored for universal suffrage and a place for the people in the seats of power. Lord Russell had then exclaimed, "No more Reform!" and such moderate Whig liberals as Macaulay had said,

> My firm conviction is that, in our country, universal suffrage is incompatible, not with this or that form of government, but with all forms of government, and with everything for the sake of which forms of government exist; that it is incompatible with property, and that it is consequently incompatible with civilization.[19]

Both Whigs and Tories were affrighted by the specter of "democracy," bearing the threat to private property. A perspicacious contemporary of the 1780 riots, Mrs. Elizabeth Montagu, saw more clearly than Dickens the implications of that upheaval, and the importance of its suppression. Writing after the arrest of Lord George Gordon, she almost thanked him for having "precipitated" the riots.

> I believe Lord George Gordon has prevented infinitely more mischief than he has done. I look upon him as a Political conductor, he has brought down the electrical matter which threatened our whole state ... His Lordship has wonderfully purged the ill-humour of his fellow-subjects and I hope in a great degree cured the epidemical democratick madness. The word petition now obtains nowhere, the word association cannot assemble a dozen people. We are coming to our right senses ... The gathering storm which threatened our strongest, noblest and most venerable edifices has by him been brought down and sunk into the earth before it burst on our heads, he had indeed buried it under the gallows.[20]

In Dickens's day the fear of "democracy" was in some circles intensifed by the alarm: Was the tyranny of absolute monarchy to be replaced by the "tyranny of the majority"? There was the warning contained in the brilliant book by Alexis de Tocqueville, *Democracy in America*, the first volume of which had been available to English readers since 1835. There was Carlyle's high-pitched voice pronouncing anathemas on Reform, Parliament and the Franchise ...

Dickens set out for America with high hopes. What he brought back in 1842 was the memory of an overwhelmingly friendly reception for himself, and a shock of exasperation. Dickens had come to America already hailed as a democrat, "a kind of embodied protest against what was believed to be worst in the institutions of England."[21]

In New England he had been impressed with the extraordinary economic well-being of the population—everyone possessing a "blazing fire," and enjoying "a meat dinner every day ..."[22] There were no beggars in the streets, and no charity uniforms in children's institutions. He experienced his first major and disagreeable shock at the reception accorded his plea for more stringent copyright protection for British authors, victims of unconscionable piracies on the part of American publishers. American writers had been no less subject to such depredations. Dickens was attacked in the press and in anonymous letters. And he wrote bitterly,

> I believe there is no country, on the face of the earth, where there is less freedom of opinion on any subject in reference to which there is a broad difference of opinion than in this ... I write the words with reluctance, disappointment, and sorrow ...[23]

His travels in the American South and Midwest only strengthened a number of unpleasant impressions. He was outraged by the treatment of Negro slaves and the sanctimonious defense of slavery offered by many; he was shocked by the absence of social graces among the generality of Americans he met—the spitting, the tobacco-chewing, the indifference to personal cleanliness, the boastfulness and arrogance; the contempt for and ignorance of British institutions. But he was particularly aroused by what seemed to him to be the paramount concern for money. For all that, he noted an affectionate temper, generosity and hospitality among other Americans. He was, however, aghast at the intolerance shown in public matters.

> This is not the republic I came to see; this is not the republic of my imagination. I see a press more mean and paltry, and silly than in any country I ever knew ... I speak of Bancroft, and am advised to be silent on that subject, for he is a "black-sheep—a democrat." I speak of Bryant, and am entreated to be more careful—for the same reason. I speak of international copyright, and am implored not to ruin myself outright.[24]

These and other personal impressions he published in his *American Notes* in October 1842, and in the novel *Martin Chuzzlewit* the following year. Both works met with pronounced hostility on American soil. On his side, Dickens insisted that he had been candid, that he had tried to speak the truth. And he could claim, with justice, that he had been more sharp in his treatment of England than of America. If like young Martin Chuzzlewit he had brought back from across the Atlantic a somewhat tarnished image of the American Eagle, he had, with this character, also tried to face and relentlessly portray the common scourge in both countries, the drastic phenomenon of the "cash-nexus" in the modern world. In the novel, old Martin Chuzzlewit's wealth is the golden fleece that attracts a covey of appetent would-be heirs, who strive to win the favors of the old man and labor to undo the prospects of young Martin. Here, too, Dickens has succeeded in creating an epic figure—that of Hypocrisy—in the person of Pecksniff, the Tartuffe of the modern age, the age of finance and speculation. He is the personification of mealy-mouthed repectability. Pecksniff masks his planned depredations with humility and forgiveness. At a meeting in Pecksniff's home, called to discuss possible strategies designed to bring old Martin Chuzzlewit around, another Chuzzlewit, namely Anthony, himself no mean predator, scents out Mr. Pecksniff.

> "Pecksniff," said Anthony, who had been watching the whole party with peculiar keenness from the first: "don't you be a hypocrite."
> "A what, my good sir?"
> "A hypocrite."

Pecksniff forthwith turns to one of his two daughters:

"Charity, my dear," said Mr. Pecksniff, "when I take my chamber candlestick to-night, remind me to be more than usually particular in praying for Mr. Anthony Chuzzlewit, who has done me an injustice."[25]

We are thrown into a nest of cormorants, with Pecksniff as the master buzzard. He is sanctimony, hypocrisy, greed, and wile. He is also the personification of British "cant." "For myself," he says, "my conscience is my bank." And it is obvious, of course, that the reverse is the truth. A master of intrigue, he is, however, outwitted by the even more consummate and adroit, though attractive, rascal Tigg Montague, who soon shows the true nature of his genius as he rises from being a sly applicant for a hand-out, to preside over the Anglo-Bengalee Loan and Life Assurance Company—a gigantic fraud decked out with offices of eye-dazzling splendor. Even old Martin Chuzzlewit, cynic though he is, understands the miasma of acquisitiveness. "Oh ... self, self, self," he exclaims. "Every man for himself and no creature for me."[26]

Greed acquires epic magnitude. It sows its corruption very deep, to the point where one of old Martin's nephews plots the death of his own father. And young Martin, a victim of these intrigues, and also of his grandfather's displeasure, seeks to escape, carrying with him his primal innocence as well as a disappointment in love. In America he finds no better world, and is glad to return to England, leaving to Dickens the task of directing his destiny to its proper happy ending. But his American adventure has not been all disaster. Young Martin achieves a sort of self-discovery: his own selfishness contrasts sharply with the generosity and devotion of his traveling companion Mark Tapley, which he is finally able to estimate at its worth.

The world is not all impenetrable darkness. There are, as ever in Dickens, avenging angels. Wickedness is relieved by incomparable humor. The edges of evil are blunted in those unsurpassable characters Mr. Pecksniff and, in an even greater measure, the cruel, garrulous, bibulous, but unforgettable Mrs. Gamp. She too is epic humor, presiding like some mighty and hilarious goddess as midwife at births, and as nurse at the laying out of the dead. She adds to birth and death the benign qualities of the grotesque. Out of her imagination, she has invented a Mrs. Harris, with whom she holds conversations that benefit her hearers with verbal testimony to Mrs. Gamp's none-too-modest attainments. Once again we come across a figure in whom language is made body, and body, language. Called upon by Pecksniff to lay out the body of the deceased Anthony Chuzzlewit, brother of old Martin, she discourses, or better, monologizes in Pecksniff's presence:

... "If it wasn't for the nerve a little sip of liquor gives me (I never was able to do more than taste it), I never could go through with what I sometimes has to do. 'Mrs. Harris,' I says, at the very last case as ever I acted in, which it was but a young person, 'Mrs. Harris,' I says, 'leave the bottle on the chimley-piece, and don't ask me to take none, but let me put my lips to it when I am so dispoged, and then I will do what I'm engaged to do, according to the best of my ability. 'Mrs. Gamp,' she says, in answer, 'if ever there was a sober creetur to be got at eighteen pence a day for working people, and three and six for gentlefolks—night watching,'" said Mrs. Gamp with emphasis, "being a extra charge—you are that inwallable person.' 'Mrs. Harris,' I says to her, 'don't name the charge, for if I could afford to lay out all my feller creeturs out for nothink, I would gladly do it, sich is the love I bear 'em. But what I always says to them as has management of matters, Mrs. Harris"—here she kept her eye on Mr. Pecksniff—"be they gents or be they ladies—is, don't ask me whether I won't take none, or whether I will, but leave the bottle on the chimley-piece, and let me put my pips to it when I am so dispoged.'"[27]

In the light of such behavior, such speech, and such delight, we are inclined to forgive her her cruelty, her appetence, and her sly bibulousness. She, too, is stamped with immortality.

* * *

He was restlessness and fever personified. Yet he was irrepressible. He seemed never to be at peace with himself. In these years of the 1840s, his activities continued unabated. Neither continental trip, a sojourn in Italy, nor a visit to Paris brought him much alleviation. But he savored his fame, for Europeans came to recognize and acclaim him as England's great novelist. No British writer aside from Shakespeare, Byron, and Sir Walter Scott, had received such appreciation from abroad. His contact with France's most notable men and women of letters and their warm welcome bolstered his sense of a writer's stature and broadened his view of society. He was struck by the responsiveness of the French to social problems—greater, he felt, than in his own country.

But away from London, away from England, Dickens' creative impulses languished. He was Londoner through and through, and like the giant Antaeus, felt the need of physical contact with England so as to recover his creative strength. If only for a brief stay, he felt he must return, even if only to read to his friends—Carlyle among them—his Christmas tale *The Chimes*.

Money, which plays such an outstanding role in his books, played no less a role in his life. His needs were great—he was supporting a large family, his parents, helping out his brothers, and not very sparing of his own expenses. What he missed as a younger man, ownership of property, now became a necessity. He felt that Chapman and Hall, his publishers, did not sufficiently appreciate his success and popularity, and he turned to other publishers. But he was most generous in his own philanthropic deeds, and luckily found an affluent coadjutor in the wealthy Angela Burdett-Coutts to help him in such undertakings as the "Ragged Schools," volunteer institutions for the education of deprived children, as well as sundry other charitable benefactions such as reformatories for prostitutes.

His visionary horizon was expanding rapidly. If his mind was not that of a formal philosopher, if he did not possess broad metaphysical concepts, he thought deeply as he sought to achieve both an inner coherence and a view that would enable him to unravel the world's incoherence. Transcendentalism meant as little to him as did Utilitarianism; they seemed to him either murky streams of thought or veiled and dangerous expressions of selfhood and selfishness. He anchored his ideas on concrete things, events, human beings, and observed their interactions. Not in vain had he been a first-class journalist. Centering on the world around him, he came more and more to see the insidious relations of Property and Power. Unlike Carlyle, whom he continued to admire to the end of his life, he was not concerned with seeking out the "world-soul" or any other transcendental "spirit." It was the concrete soul Dickens sought to define, embodied in the physical human beings around him, in their alienations, their spiritual and physical hungers, their quotidian aspirations toward a good life, their defeats, and their occasional victories. It was this ever-deepening sense of people that moved him to try to understand the lives and activities of the striking working men of Preston. It was in the forties for the first time that the figure of a Chartist appears in his stories; notably in the person of Fern in *The Chimes*. And it is significant that his *Christmas Stories*, intended for a time of rejoicing, present stark pictures of misery and wretchedness and resound with stern warnings to the nation at large ...

The dimensions of Dickens' growth as an artist may be gauged by another central element. Disturbed and unsettled as was his internal life—unsatisfied as he was in the love of woman—he yet achieved a major victory in these years that enabled him to create masterpieces. He now found it possible to translate his own personal history— the shamefulness he felt at his early experiences in the blacking factory as a boy, the humiliation of a son in the face of an ever-improvident father, the sense of desertion by a mother, the lack of a formal education, the struggle for a career, the bitterness of a rejected lover—into the triumphant poetry of his novels, and make of his personal griefs and humiliations, epics of the universal human. It is from these new heights that he was able to bring forth *David Copperfield* and *Dombey and Son*.

* * *

Mr. Dombey is traveling to Leamington, in the company of Major Bagstock, shortly after the death of his young son Paul. He is traveling by railroad. Not so long ago he would have gone by coach. The railroad has taken over. Juggernaut or blessing?

> ... All day and night, throbbing currents rushed and returned incessantly ... Crowds of people and mountains of goods, departing and arriving scores upon scores of times in every four-and-twenty hours, produced a fermentation in the place that was always in action ... Night and day the conquering engines rumbled at their distant work, or, advancing smoothly to their journey's end, and gliding like tame dragons into the allotted corner grooved out to the inch for their reception, stood bubbling and trembling there, making the walls quake, as if they were dilating with the secret knowledge of great power yet unsuspected in them, and strong purposes not yet achieved.[28]

Even the powerful Mr. Dombey is abashed at the new phenomenon. For this new monster, tearing along at a hitherto unimaginable speed, is also roaring its way into the future—tearing down the past, clearing away the old, churning up the earth, and annihilating time. In what now seemed the blinking of an eye, it could carry the coal or the iron ore to the factory or to the smelting furnace; it could move crowds apace, and not least, in due time, it could carry the military with their equipment at such speed as to change the character and fate not only of people but of whole nations ...

It is against this background of a rapidly changing world that the drama of *Dombey and Son* takes place, a drama that might well have been entitled "The Greatness and Decline of the Firm of Dombey and Son." For Dombey and Son stands for a powerful mercantile house of an older lineage; the name had been handed down from generation to generation, and would now, so the elder Dombey had hoped, be handed down to the newly-born Paul. In the tradition, then so well rooted throughout the world, the son would be the heir. There is already a girl in the family, six years old. But she does not represent future "capital"—nor does her dying mother. The mother, Fanny, is merely the instrument that brought forth an heir to the house; the daughter, Florence, is supernumerary.

The Dombey view of life was all-embracing.

The earth was made for Dombey and Son to trade in, and the sun and moon were made to give them light ...[29]

Dickens is writing the first great English novel of capitalism. For Dombey is Power. Dombey is Money. Dombey is Possession of human beings, as well as things. For the Dombey mind turns all of Nature into things—human beings too, of course. Florence, being a girl, is a Thing—almost a No-Thing. Affections and Feelings have become—to use a more noble term than Thing—"reified." Things, living or inanimate, are there to be manipulated, altered. Little Paul Dombey is there, a long-awaited object, to be transformed into another Mr. Dombey, and what begins in the cradle will be continued in school, whether that of Mrs. Pipchin or of Doctor Blimber.

There is only one obstacle in the way of a successful transformation of a human being into a "Thing." Little Paul Dombey defies the Dombey nature. He is one of those "delicate children of Life"—later a favorite subject of Thomas Mann's stories—whose rampant and beautiful innocence, child-honesty, and strange thinking and musings, mark him out for an early doom. His blind teachers misname him "old-fashioned"—somehow not fitting into their modern world. His is the poetry of childhood; his is the inchoate artist nature; his too is, unfortunately, the poetry of death. He is a child-visionary, hearing the music of the waters, and seeing fantasy-images on the room's walls. Within him is the prescience of early demise, as well as the doom of that which alienates him—Power, Property, Money, Possession. He is the vulnerable and destructible element that these forces pervert and destroy. Into the psychic self of Paul, Dickens has penetrated with a superb sensitiveness and poetry that would serve that other master-novelist and student of the bourgeois mentality in depicting the musician-artist Hanno Buddenbrook.

Young Paul Dombey, then, is true Nature at war with Nature raped, distorted, warped. His is a brooding precocity, ancient with premonitory wisdom.

"Papa! what's money?"

The abrupt question had such immediate reference to the subject of Mr. Dombey's thought that Mr. Dombey was quite disconcerted.

"What is money, Paul?" he answered.

"Yes ... what is money? ... I mean, Papa, what can it do?" ... Mr. Dombey drew his chair back to its former place, and patted him on the head.

"You'll know better by-the-by, my man," he said. "Money, Paul, can do anything..."

"Anything means everything, don't it, Papa? ... Why didn't money save my mama?" returned the child. "It isn't cruel, is it?"

"Cruel!" said Mr. Dombey, settling his neckcloth, and seeming to resent the idea. "No. A good thing can't be cruel ..."[30]

Mammon is God. He is Nature. He is inexorable and he can be destructive. Before his blasting influence the "delicate" must perish. Paul Dombey withers away and dies before he is eight. With the approach of night and darkness, in the nearness of his own death, he sees and hears the river in his mind...

> His fancy had a strange tendency to wander to the river, which he knew was flowing through the great city; and now he thought how black it was, and how deep it would look, reflecting the hosts of stars—and more than all, how steadily it rolled away to meet the sea...[31]

Mighty as he is and deems himself, Mr. Dombey is powerless against death. Enraged, he turns his wrath upon human beings—and most of all against the living relict and reminder of his impotence, his daughter Florence. Not yet fourteen at her brother's death, she had already learned the meaning of thwarted affection and love and the desolations of loneliness. Like so many of Dickens' girl-mother figures, she too, herself motherless and fatherless, becomes mother to the dying boy. For, as Dickens puts it, she is "in the capital of the House's name and dignity ... merely a piece of base coin that couldn't be invested."[32] And now, more than ever, she is an ever-present monition of the approaching end of the male line of Dombey and Son. The strong fund of feelings on which she draws is wasted on her father, until she at last realizes her bankruptcy in that direction. Yet not all the characters are caught up in the maelstrom of "power" and "possession." While Mr. Dombey is at war with feelings, both in himself and others, there are those possessed of a natural goodness—Paul's nurse, Polly, Toodle, her railroad stoker husband; the maid Susan Nipper, and a whole body of Dickensian eccentrics like Captain Cuttle, old Solomon Gills, proprietor of an anachronistic nautical shop "The Midshipman," the ever-amusing Toots ... These form a small enclave of salvation in the vast sea of selfhood and price and power.

Paradoxically enough, it is the power that believes it can buy everything and everyone that eventually brings Mr. Dombey to his knees. He buys a wife—the purchase and sale being forthright, crass and direct—beauty and aristocratic distinction being marketable items for those with the means to buy them. There are traders ready to sell—like mothers. It is through this commonplace of life—a daughter for sale, a rich man ready to buy—that Dickens embarks upon his first mature treatment of marriage as a function of the commodity market. Here it is the beautiful and proud Mrs. Edith Granger, a widow, an alienated and self-alienated woman, who sells herself into marriage. She is fulfilling the dearest wish and hope of her mother, Mrs. Cleopatra Skewton, a ghoulish, crippled near-carrion, a painted-over image of Death, who had once before succeeded in selling her daughter into a loveless and disastrous marriage. All that the daughter can now offer in the market is her dead heart, her beauty and her rank. She is poisoned by anger and hatred. She has reached the depths of self-abasement, and her candor is frightening. She will not lure, but she will accept. To her mother she says,

> "... Who takes me, refuse that I am, and as I well deserve to be ... shall take me, as this man does, with no art of mine put forth to lure him. He sees me at auction, and he thinks it well to buy me. Let him! ... He has considered his bargain; he has shown it to

his friend; he is even rather proud of it; he thinks it will suit him, and be had sufficiently cheap; and he will buy to-morrow..."[33]

The bought article must be made to submit, to bend to the superior force of a husband. She is proud and must be brought low. It is full submission Mr. Dombey demands, such as he exacts from "connexions and dependents." He finds a way of striking at Edith through his daughter Florence, toward whom Edith has opened her arms and to whom she extends affection and understanding. He will force their separation, and when this device fails to sway her, she in turn demands her own separation from her husband.

> "Good Heaven, Mrs. Dombey!" said her husband, with supreme amazement, "do you imagine it possible that I could even listen to such a proposition? Do you know who I am, Madam? Do you know what I represent? Did you ever hear of Dombey and Son? People to say that Mr. Dombey—Mr. Dombey!—was separated from his wife! Common people to talk of Mr. Dombey and his domestic affairs! Do you seriously think, Mrs. Dombey, that I would permit my name to be handed about in such connexion? Pooh, pooh, madam! Fie for shame! You're absurd."[34]

There is nothing for her to do but escape. Her hatred knows no bounds, nor even wisdom. She allows Carker, Mr. Dombey's manager, to assist in her flight; and though she fears and hates him, she allows him to join her in France. In the meantime, Carker has been manipulating Mr. Dombey's affairs to such a point of over-expansion that the House of Dombey is ruined. Carker, in turn, falls a victim to condign punishment, as, pursued by Mr. Dombey, he falls to his death before an oncoming train. Mr. Dombey, bankrupt, betrayed, abandoned and undone, is redeemed by the love of his daughter Florence, now wife and mother. Edith Dombey, too, saddened and wiser, comes back to live out her life alone, hopeful of eventual forgiveness and compassion for both herself and her hapless husband, aware that there can never be a reunion … In Mr. Dombey's life, and in keeping with Dickens' penchant, she is replaced by Florence, another of Dickens' favored young mother-figures.

One would have been happier had Dickens, in an excess of benefactions and retributions, not been so generous a divinity; had he not yielded so easily to his predilection for the sensational, or to the unofficial censorship or pressure of a vast readership, Mudie's Lending Library, and his own inner censor. Carker, the Manager, is evil enough without the need of another Nemesis in the form of a girl he had seduced. And his death in the path of a train jars our sense of the probable.

But on the other and weightier side stand the eminent excellences of the great novel. Dickens had seized here upon the central operative forces within his society and artistically integrated them into narrative and characters. He had made Carlyle's "cash-nexus" a live element, with the reality and convictions of a human character. He had exposed the roots of Alienation—though the term had not yet become current in England—an alienation brought about by the conversion of human beings and human values into market commodities. He had mercilessly exposed the marriage of convenience and had shown its brutal consequences. He had delineated the corrosion of family life and family relationships, the demolition of natural instincts and feelings, the desecration of "Nature." And he had mirrored his own times—the technological revolution, represented by the railroad, and the rising power of Capital.

But perhaps chiefest of all, he had managed to combine all these elements with a profound psychological insight. Little Paul Dombey is a masterpiece of objective and subjective depiction; the delicate analysis of his mental processes is a prose-poem assimilating realistic descriptions of the outer life, one of the finest depictions of child life in Victorian literature. His sister Florence's obsessional attachment to her father appears in all its intensity, with fine psychological insight. Perhaps most shattering of all is the denaturalization of a worthy human being depicted in the devastated figure of Edith, intelligent and beautiful, turned into a piece of merchandise.

For many years, before the publication of *David Copperfield*, Dickens had been thinking of writing an autobiography, but he found the reminiscences so utterly painful that he could not continue it. A fragment published by Forster after Dickens' death is sufficient revelation of his agonies:

> … How much I suffered, it is … utterly beyond my power to tell. No man's imagination can overstep the reality … For many years, when I came near to Robert Warren's in the Strand, I crossed over to the opposite side of the way, to avoid a certain smell of the cement they put upon the blacking-corks, which reminded me of what I was once.[35]

This and other harrowing experiences of his early life—not least his unhappy love for Maria Beadnell, and much else—he eventually found the courage (and this was no mean triumph) to embody in the novel *David Copperfield*. Yet *Copperfield* is much more than autobiography. Enriched by the recollective imagination, expanded by the sum of new experiences, it is universalized, one might say, in the creation of another world, touched with all the great and deep emotions of sorrow, pain, aloneness, but also lightened by joys of love—unfulfilled in the writer, vicariously fulfilled in his hero. The world of David Copperfield is a world of wish-fulfilments. But what a rich world of living characters Dickens has created! In David Copperfield, the young boy and the young man in his *Lehrjahre*—the years of his apprenticeship to life—Dickens managed to present (as he had previously in Paul Dombey) one of the first truly sensitive depictions of the meaning of a child's life in the English novel, to be equalled, only some years later, in George Eliot's *The Mill on the Floss*. He was thus enabled to universalize the child for his Victorian readers; for David could as well have stood for the children enslaved in the cotton manufactories, or in the mines, or, like Dickens himself, in a blacking establishment. In another sense, *David Copperfield* represents a triumphant achievement for the novelist, in his ability to transcend his earlier repugnance for his own experiences, to objectify them, while still preserving their initial reality. But the Victorian taboos that loured over his genius—like his own self-imposed taboos—foreclosed a commensurate expression of more mature love-relationships— of intimate love. A child-wife is scarcely allowed to grow up into sexual awareness; a young man's sensuality is suppressed and converted to a platonic eroticism—as if in the age of Victoria, Adam and Eve had never eaten of the forbidden tree, never consummated their love, and never really attained to what the Book of Genesis called "knowledge." But where such a relation involved horror or terrifying frustration, as in the case of Edith Dombey in her abhorrence of both her husband and Carker, Dickens is near his best. Dickens is equally the master in depicting the erosion or extinction of the emotional life, as of the struggle against such an enormity: David Copperfield against his stepfather Murdstone; Florence Dombey *vis-à-vis* the elder Dombey, with the latter magnificently and succinctly typified in the daughter's eyes by "the blue coat and stiff white cravat, which, with a pair of creaking boots and a very loud ticking watch, embodied her idea of a father," as well as by the door to his room, which she finally penetrates only to discover her father's absolute hatred of her.

It is a rich world of characters through which David Copperfield moves: characters like the ambiguous Steerforth, the worshipped hero of David's schooldays; the simple Peggotys, nobility shod in wooden clogs; Barkis, who is "willin"; little Em'ly; the sadistic stepfather Murdstone and his equally horrible sister; the wonderful aunt Betsy Trotwood; and, at the summit of Dickens' profound humor touched by sadness, Mr. and Mrs. Micawber, making a kind of mythical greatness of his own father and mother—sharply critical and yet understanding, mingling laughter and pity—and finally, the monolithic hypocrite, "umble" Uriah Heap.

The grandeur of Dickens, despite his many shortcomings, consists in his success in revealing the multiform, life-bursting world around him. His most notable humorous characters are not merely monochromes, as in the so-called comedies of "humors," in which one trait predominates and rounded character never emerges. In Dickens, even the relatively monochromatic characters become human beings, ever memorable. Dickens has made them "real," inhabitants of a real world. In this, his "realism" is not unlike that of Gogol—a multifaceted mirror, but a miraculous one behind which stands a creative consciousness that directs the shapes and their movements. Always that consciousness is aware of the wide world beyond, and is penetrated by it. Dombey senior, self-immured, traveling on the railroad train, may not be aware of the full meaning of the outside world that appears through the carriage window as he approaches the industrial towns of the north, now rapidly laid bare by the fast-moving train—but Dickens is:

> There are dark pools of water, muddy lanes, and miserable habitations far below. There are jagged walls and falling houses close at hand, and through the battered roofs and broken windows, wretched rooms are seen, where want and fever hide themselves in many wretched shapes, while smoke and crowded gables, and distorted chimneys, and deformity of brick and water penning up deformity of mind and body, choke the murky distance ...[36]

Dombey is self-immured. Dickens is not. His experience is ever widening, the mirror of his artistic consciousness becomes ever more revealing. And if, after 1848, the world is reflected in deeper shadow, it is only a greater knowledge, wisdom, and understanding reflecting the objects all the more clearly.

On the outbreak of the February Revolution in France, in 1848, Dickens was beside himself. To his friend and future biographer John Forster he wrote a letter in French:

> *Mon ami, je trouve que j'aime tant la République, qu'il me faut renoncer ma langue et écrire seulement le langage da la République de France...*

> My Friend: I find I love the Republic so much that I must renounce my own language and write solely in the language of the French Republic, the language of gods and angels,

the language, in short, of the French ... Long live the glory of France! Long live the Republic! Long live the People! No more Royalty! No more Bourbons! No more Guizot! Death to the traitors! Let us shed our blood for Liberty, Justice, and the Cause of the People!

Citizen Charles Dickens.[37]

He had not yet penned David Copperfield's words to Uriah Heap, but he might almost be envisioning the approach of a new age in this great event of the falling Tyranny:

"It is you who have been, in your greed and cunning, against all the world. It may be profitable to you to reflect, in future, that there never were greed and cunning in the world yet, that did not do too much, and overreach themselves. It is as certain as death."[38]

Chapter Five

John Stuart Mill

The Majesty of Reason

> Yet no one whose opinion deserves a moment's consideration can doubt that most of the great positive evils of the world are in themselves removable, and will, if human affairs continue to improve, be in the end reduced within narrow limits. Poverty in any sense implying suffering, may be completely extinguished by the wisdom of society, combined with the good sense and providence of individuals. Even the most intractable of enemies, disease, may be indefinitely reduced in dimensions by good physical and moral education, and proper control of noxious influences; while the progress of science holds out a promise for the future of still more direct conquests over this detestable foe ... All the great sources, in short, of human suffering are in a great degree, many of them almost entirely, conquerable by human care and effort.
>
> —J. S. Mill, *Utilitarianism*

It would no doubt have shocked those two remarkable Utilitarians, both religious sceptics—Jeremy Bentham and James Mill—if they had been told that the latter's brilliant son, John Stuart Mill, was being brought up like one of those Old Testament youths ultimately to be dedicated to the priesthood, or to a prophet's mission. In this instance, the dedication would be to the gospel of "Philosophical Radicalism," or "Utilitarianism."

When John Stuart Mill was born in 1806, Jeremy Bentham was already fifty-five years old and renowned throughout England and the Continent for his works on legislation, and as the founder of a new political party challenging both Whigs and Tories. James Mill was then thirty-three, no less well endowed in mind, but much less so in worldly fortunes. Jeremy Bentham was rich and generous, and James Mill was lucky to have him as a patron. Between them grew up a strong and devoted friendship, now more firmly cemented by the presence of that remarkable boy—"a successor worthy of both of us," as James Mill wrote to Bentham when, in a humorous letter full of sincere conviction, he bequeathed young John to Bentham's keeping in case of his own prior death.[1]

John was indeed a prodigy. As is often noted, he began the study of Greek at the age of three. In a letter written to Bentham's brother when he was thirteen, he boasted that by the time he was eight he had read "Thucydides, Anacreon, and *I believe* the *Electra* of Sophocles, the *Phoenissae* of Euripides, and the *Plutus* and the *Clouds* of Aristophanes."[2] And how much more!

The story is well known, and since the publication of Mill's *Autobiography* in 1873, has been the subject of extensive commentary and analysis. It casts a sharp light not only on the psychic life of one individual, but on the overall problems of Victorian childhood, education, family and parental relations.

An outsider looking in on the Mill household, or present at one of Jeremy Bentham's many social gatherings, could not but have been convinced that here was a young boy living in an ideal environment and destined for great happiness. In Mr. James Mill's study he might have spied young John construing Greek grammar, or imbibing the elements of Political Economy, Logic, and Psychology, while the elder Mill was preoccupied in preparing his monumental history of India or composing an article for the *Edinburgh Review*. Or, if he was a visitor at Ford Abbey, Bentham's country estate, he would find young John in the company of such eminent worthies as the political economist David Ricardo; Sir Samuel Romilly, law reformer; Francis Place, the famous master-tailor and philosophical radical—all minds of extraordinary keenness and daring. Here too was young John, almost an equal among equals, equipped to understand, to enquire, even to argue. It is not recorded that John's mother was ever present at these high colloquies; if anywhere in the vicinity, she was ever in the background—ever, with her husband's assistance, procreative—mother, eventually, of eight more children, and caretaker of the busy household. The marriage was not a happy one. Mrs. Mill, who had brought her husband some substance, rarely enjoyed his company, and in her son's *Autobiography* scarcely figures as an influence in his life except in somewhat condescending remarks of the mature man, with whatever fondness he might once have had for her barely remembered.

Had he been less of a genius, devoid of his own internal creative and moral strength in the ever-monitory and directing presence and influence of his two towering mentors Bentham and James Mill, the "crisis" John Mill was destined to undergo at the age of twenty might have proved utterly disastrous for his growth. Child prodigies are sufficiently problematic in their own right; the pressures of ambitious though well-meaning elders are scarcely unmixed blessings. John had not one, but two solicitous fathers. And though one may admire James Mill's patience, perseverance, and the unremittent concern he bestowed upon his son while himself one of the busiest of men, his attentions were fixed only on the development of his son's intellect—to the subtler and more essential needs of the young man he was utterly blind. John was to be, his mentors felt, the shining heir and apostle of Utilitarianism. And the young man proved highly responsive.

He was ready for an all-encompassing philosophy of life, and in Bentham he felt he had found the key. Like Keats encountering a copy of Chapman's Elizabethan translation of Homer, he fell upon Bentham's *Traité de Legislation*:

> The reading of this book was an event in my life; one of the turning points of my mental history.

The principle of the "greatest happiness for the greatest number" was a revelation.

> (It) burst on me with all the force of novelty ... The feeling rushed upon me that all pre-vious moralists were superseded, and that here indeed was the commencement of a new era ... When I laid down the last volume of the *Traité*, I was a different being. The prin-ciple of utility, understood as Bentham understood it, and applied in the manner in which he applied it through these three volumes, fell exactly into its place as the keystone which held together the detached and fragmentary portions of my knowledge. It gave unity to my conceptions of things. I now had opinions; a creed, a doctrine, a philosophy; in one (and the best) sense of the word, a religion; the inculcation and diffusion of which could be made the principal outward aim of a life. And I had a grand conception laid before me of changes to be made in the condition of mankind by that doctrine.[3]

He accepted his father's creed, with its two central tenets: representative govern-ment and complete freedom of discussion. Human nature could be changed, and the most effective instrument to that end was education.

At the age of fourteen, John Stuart Mill was privileged to spend half a year in France with the redoubtable Sir Samuel Bentham, Jeremy's brother—man of the world, naval architect and engineer, brigadier-general in the service of Russia, and for-mer Commissioner of the British navy. Here was a man with the aura of new worlds. The Bentham family lived in the south of France, and John Mill saw Provence, the Pyrenees, and Toulouse. He attended the University of Montpellier. He came in con-tact with a new civilization. The boy, hitherto so repressed, came to life and blos-somed forth: he botanized; he learned to write a fluent French. Years later in a letter to Auguste Comte, he called it "The six happiest months of my youth"—"*Les six mois les plus heureux de ma jeunesse, ceux de l'hiver 1820-1821.*"[4] He also obtained his first sight of Paris. Here he met the eminent political economist J.-B. Say, and at the latter's house caught a glimpse of the impoverished but celebrated Count Saint-Simon. France was to prove of seminal influence in John Mill's intellectual development.

When John Mill was seventeen, his father, since 1809 assistant examiner in the East India Company, obtained for him a junior clerkship in the same office. Like his father, he was in due time to rise to the important office of Examiner.

His duties at the India Office were none too onerous, allowing him time for many other activities and projects. His biographer thus summarized his life in the single year 1825:

> ... When he was nineteen, John Mill set out to edit Bentham, founded the Debating Society, discussed Political Economy three hours a week at Grote's house in Thread-needle Street, wound up the Utilitarian Society, contributed major articles to the *West-minster Review*, went for long country walks with Graham and Roebuck, carried out his mounting duties at the India House with conspicuous success, and continued to be solely responsible for the education of his brothers and sisters.[5]

At the same time he was studying German with Sarah Austin, wife of the promi-nent juridical philosopher John Austin.

A year later he broke down ...

Mill's account of his mental crisis of 1826 is, along with John Henry Newman's *Apologia*, one of the most famous contributions to Victorian autobiography. What

John Mill's crisis revealed, aside from many other important elements, was the struggle of a young and original mind to free itself from an authority that he felt threatened to cripple him mentally and emotionally. He sensed the presence of a serious malady in his personality that none of the high-minded values and goals set by his elders—neither their lofty ethic of service to mankind through a rational education, nor his own education—was in a position to cure. Such crises, which arise frequently in the lives of gifted young people, are aggravated by an absence of confidence in or communication with one's peers or elders. In the case of John Mill, the situation was compounded by the presence of a highly endowed and powerful father, and the absence of a mother. James Mill was planning an imposing work on human psychology, but he had apparently overlooked the psychological nature and needs of the still unformed human being sitting beside him, whose emotional demands could no longer be satisfied by abstract theories, questions, and purely rational answers. To put it plainly, John Mill wanted someone to love and to love him. His own deep feelings found no outlet or corresponding understanding. Crucial passages in an early draft of his *Autobiography*, rejected or modified in the published version, throw a sharp light not only on this particular case, but on the generality of Victorian family life and its problems. This is what John Mill wrote:

> Personally I believe my father to have had much greater capacities of feeling than were ever developed in him. He resembled almost all Englishmen in being ashamed of the signs of feeling, & by the absence of demonstration, starving the feelings themselves. In an atmosphere of tenderness & affection he would have been tender & affectionate; but his ill assorted marriage & his asperities of temper disabled him from making such an atmosphere ... It must be mentioned ... that my father's children neither loved him, nor, with any warmth of affection, any one else. I do not mean that things were worse in this respect than they are in most English families; in which genuine affection is altogether exceptional; what is usually found being more or less of an attachment of mere habit, like that to inanimate objects, & a few conventional proprieties of phrase & demonstration. I believe there is less personal affection in England than in any other country of which I know anything ... That rarity in England, a really warm hearted mother, would in the first place have made my father a totally different being, & in the second would have made the children grow up loving & being loved. But my mother with the very best intentions, only knew how to pass her time in drudging for them ... I thus grew up in the absence of love & in the presence of fear ... Without knowing or believing that I was reserved, I grew up with an instinct of closeness.

Modern psychology will scarcely have trouble in translating his father's role into that of the superego:

> I was so much accustomed to expect to be told what to do, either in the form of direct command or of rebuke for not doing it, that I acquired a habit of leaving my responsibility as a moral agent to rest on my father, my conscience never speaking to me except by his voice ... The things I ought *not* to do were mostly provided by his precepts, rigorously enforced whenever violated, but the things I *ought* to do I hardly ever did of my own mere motion, but waited till he told me to do them ...[6]

He reached a point of depression in which he could not extract an iota of happiness from contemplating the realization of his social hopes for beneficent changes in institutions. "The whole foundation on which my life was constructed fell down … I seemed to have nothing left to live for."[7]

Like Coleridge in another context, Mill came to the conclusion that the desiccation of his emotional life was due to the habit of "analysis," with its "tendency to wear away the feelings." Like Coleridge, John Mill experienced what might be called a "death of the heart," due, each of them believed, to the inability to "feel." One need scarcely observe that such simplifications scarcely go to the root of the problem.

And then suddenly, in John Mill's case, came the release. One day, he broke down in tears on reading in the Frenchman Marmontel's *Memoirs* how the young boy felt on the death of his father. "The oppression that all feeling was dead within me," Mill wrote later, "was gone." The re-education of his heart and mind now commenced. Of course, the processes by which Mill attained to this salvation are veiled for us, as they must have been for him, for he was himself probably unaware of the secret movements within his own being, the processes of growth that, working subtly, began revealing to him the central needs of which he was being deprived—contact with others, release of repressed feelings, love. What happened in the end was that the apparent dichotomy of mind and feeling was resolved, and as the feelings were released, his very mental processes enlarged. Poetry and music came to his aid. Wordsworth, in particular, showed him how Nature, Feeling, Thought, and human sympathies, could all be reconciled; that high emotion could also be rational, and high reason could be bound up with feelings; that the greatest art was not in fact a disseverance of Emotion and Reason, but a creative fusion of both. The poets now supplied that "culture of feelings" which Mill had been seeking, by presenting him not with "mere outward beauty, but states of feeling, and of thought coloured by feeling, under the excitement of beauty."[8] He reached out for aesthetic satisfactions of which he had been hitherto deprived; for many of the Utilitarians, Bentham among them, looked with suspicion on poetry as "fiction," a feeder of illusions. John Mill now enjoyed the music of the Romantic composer Carl Maria von Weber; he discovered a kindred spirit in the poet Coleridge, and must have relished and been saddened by the latter's poem, "Dejection, an Ode," in which Coleridge tried to explain his own—never to be conquered—poetic sterility, also attributing it to his passion for philosophy:

> And haply by abstruse research to steal
> From my own nature all the natural man—
> Till that which suits a part infects the whole,
> And now is almost grown the habit of my soul.

Of course poetry and music could only be gateways to greater discoveries for Mill (such as Coleridge was never destined to find), namely, emotional fulfilment through the love of a woman. Soon he was to enter into a relationship that would prove epochal for himself, his mind and his emotional life, and set him on the road to greater intellectual creativeness with a concomitant sense of a new freedom.

* * *

Of course there could be no total break with the past. But there was a reassessment intellectually of his mentors, Bentham and James Mill, in the light of his new probings and experiences. He was now prepared to reconstruct the "ruined fabric of happiness" on the basis of his newborn convictions, to bring the past and present into some sort of harmony. In that spirit, he wrote,

> If I am asked, what system of political philosophy I substituted for that which, as a philosophy, I had abandoned, I answer, No system: only a conviction that the true system was something more complex and many-sided than I had previously had any idea of, and that its office was to supply, not a set of model institutions, but principles from which the institutions suitable to any given circumstances might be deduced.[9]

He now believed that he had freed himself from the incubus of the Necessitarian philosophy, the notion that he was the "helpless slave of antecedent circumstances," and that the character of a person was formed by agencies beyond his control and powers. In the past, he had been sure that human beings were formed by outside circumstances, and such belief had, during the period of his severe depression, exercised a paralyzing effect upon him. But now,

> I saw that though our character is formed by circumstances, our own desires can do much to shape those circumstances ... that we have real power over the formation of our own character; that our will, by influencing some of our circumstances, can modify our future habits or capabilities of willing.

By 1828 Mill was, as he put it, no longer a "well-equipped ship and rudder, but no sail." Now he was ready to launch forth upon new seas of experience. He had not abandoned his radical political principles. "I was as much as ever a Radical and Democrat for Europe, and especially for England." But he had acquired the "sail," and could now, with assurance, chart a secure course ...

He sought out new shores, new sources for the enlargement of his mind. German thought—with the possible exception of Goethe—was to remain a closed land, immunized as he was by Utilitarianism against all sorts of transcendentalism. The philosophical revolution that had produced Hegel and the post-Hegelian thinkers remained his *terra incognita*. It was almost natural that France should prove the most attractive terrain, with its revolutionary spirit still very much alive and at that moment approaching an explosive realization. England, too, with its high excitement attendant upon the reform agitations, and its new "radicalism," seemed ready for profound changes. It was at one of the meetings of the so-called Debating Society, in which Mill was a leading figure, that a young Frenchman, Gustave d'Eichthal, a fervent Saint-Simonian, became deeply impressed with young John Mill both as speaker and thinker, and sensing a potential convert, on his return to France sent him several numbers of the *Producteur* and a copy of an early work by Auguste Comte, the *Système de politique positive*. If one adds to these the book by Alexis de Tocqueville, *Democracy in America*, which Mill was to read in 1835, we have practically an abstract of the French influence that was to determine a great part of his thinking during the succeeding years.

He was fascinated with the Saint-Simonians and their doctrine. A new vision of history rose before him. "Progress," in which he, like the other Utilitarians, had always believed, now acquired a more precise meaning. He was particularly struck by the

Saint-Simonian success in presenting a "connected view of the natural order of human progress," with its division of history into "organic" and "critical" periods. He now saw his own times as a "critical" period, a "period of criticism and negation" in which there was an erosion of old convictions, "except the conviction that the old was false." His faith in the future was greatly strengthened, "a future which shall unite the best qualities of the organic periods: unchecked liberty of thought, unbounded freedom of individual action, in all modes not hurtful to others,"

> but also, convictions as to what is right and wrong, useful and pernicious, deeply engraven on the feelings by early education and general unanimity of sentiment, and so firmly grounded in reason and in the true exigencies of life, that they shall not, like all former and present creeds, religious, ethical, political require to be periodically thrown off and replaced by others.[10]

There was for him also a kind of exhilarating shock in the Saint-Simonian critique of private property and the laws of inheritance. For "security" and "property" were the keystones of Utilitarian social doctrine, in so far as they pertained to the interests of the manufacturing and commercial classes, though property of the landed aristocracy was excluded from their protective sanctities as being "unearned"—not the product of their labor. Above all, Mill was struck by the boldness with which the Saint-Simonians approached the subjects of woman and family, proclaiming "the perfect equality of men and women"—in his view "an entirely new order of things in regard to their relations with one another."

He was also deeply exercised over and absorbed by Auguste Comte's doctrine of historical development, the so-called law of the "three stages" of human history. For Comte believed that he had found the "fundamental law, to which human intelligence in its diverse spheres of activity was subject"—the law that "every one of our principal conceptions, every branch of knowledge, passes through three different theoretical stages: the theological, or fictive; the metaphysical, or the abstract; the scientific, or the positive stage."

It was this last stage that more than any of the others impressed Mill. For in this "positive" or "scientific" stage, which was still to come, the human mind was seen as once and for all abandoning the attempt to achieve absolute knowledge, and the fruitless aim of seeking to discover the origin or destination of the universe. By means of reason and observation it will discover the laws of nature and man, the *lois naturelles invariables*—the "natural and invariable laws" governing the world—and these will be reduced to the smallest possible number.

And Comte proclaimed,

> Now that the human mind has established celestial physics, terrestrial physics, whether mechanical or chemical; organic physics—vegetable, or animal—it behooves him now to conclude the system of scientific observation by establishing social physics.[11]

In other words, establishing "Sociology." Human beings were shaped by history and society. The law of "progress" will enable us to predict future events ...

John Mill's widening view of history did not prevent him from even more sharply criticizing contemporary English society. He moderated d'Eichthal's effervescent enthusiasm for the productive and industrial as well as commercial contributions of the British and warned him of the evil inherent in them and only too rampant among the general population—the tendency or "disposition to sacrifice every thing to accumulation." He took issue with the Saint-Simonian design to place the business of government in the hands of the *industriels*, the *savants*, and artists.

> I do not know, he wrote to d'Eichthal, how it may be in France, but I know that in England these three are the very classes of persons you would pick out as the most remarkable for a narrow & bigoted understanding, & a sordid & contracted disposition as respects all things wider than their business or families.[12]

Yet amid the excitement over his new intellectual discoveries, he could not forbear complaining of his sense of loneliness, which he felt to be his "future lot." He lacked, he said, the presence of someone who would give him the "feeling of being engaged in the pursuit of a common object and mutually cheering one another on, and helping one another in an arduous task ... There is now no human being (with whom I can associate on terms of equality) who acknowledges a common object with me ..."[13]

Two events occurred in the following year which were to change his feelings radically. In the summer of 1830 he met Mrs. Harriet Taylor. In July of the same year a revolution broke out in France. These two events, though outwardly seemingly unrelated, were to make another stage in John Mill's *Bildung*. His *Wanderjahre* would be over ...

*   *   *

It was apparent even before July 1830 that things were moving toward an explosion. Spain was in upheaval, and her plight found ardent sympathy in many an English heart. A number of Englishmen conceived a fantastic plan for launching an invasion of that country in support of Spain's insurgent patriots. Among these supporters and sympathizers were John Sterling, friend of Carlyle and John Mill, and young Alfred Tennyson. Under the leadership of the Spaniard Torrijos and the Irishman Boyd, an army of fifty was recruited, which soon set out. Forewarned by spies, the Spanish authorities captured the would-be invaders at Malaga and executed their leaders, Torrijos and Boyd among them. One can well imagine the dismay of their English supporters.

But very soon the news from France served to alleviate their grief. English liberals greeted reports of the July Revolution with joy. And a number of them, including John Mill, John Graham, and Roebuck, journeyed to France to share in the triumphs. Early in August they were in Paris, where they were received by Lafayette. They were amazed by the discipline displayed by the populace, especially the working classes, and Mill extolled their "simplicity of character" and their deep conviction of the "morality and lawfulness of their resistance." From Paris he wrote,

> The inconceivable purity and singleness of purpose, almost amounting to *naiveté* ... has given me a greater love for them than I thought myself capable of feeling for so large a collection of human beings, and the more exhilarating views which it opens of human nature will have a beneficial effect on the whole of my future life.[14]

Mill was present at the opera when the newly inducted Citizen-King. Louis-Philippe, greeted his fellow citizens. He met with the Saint-Simonians Enfantin and

Bazard, and was introduced into the Society of *Aide-Toi*. But he soon became disenchanted with the course the new French leadership was taking and complained that there was "not a Radical among them except Dupont de l'Eure," nothing but placehunters; and that even Thiers manifested nothing but "weakness and pusillanimity."[15] In the *Examiner* he began publishing three letters on "The State of the Public Mind and Affairs at Paris," unsigned. On January 6, 1831 appeared the first of his articles on "The Spirit of the Age," also unsigned. It was this series that caught the attention and interest of Thomas Carlyle and initiated a new friendship that proved of significant influence in the life of John Mill.

The influence of France on Mill cannot be overestimated. Whatever the vicissitudes of that country's fortunes or his own particular estimates of her politics and social philosophies, France remained the center of his interests and left a permanent mark on his outlook. Not even the presence of Carlyle and the latter's German preoccupations could divert him from France.

The pace of Mill's radicalization was now accelerated. The rejection of the Reform Bill by the House of Lords on October 8 roused him to fury. He was particularly incensed by the overwhelming opposition of the Bishops, only two of whom favored the Bill. "You may consider," Mill wrote to John Sterling in the same month, "the fate of the Church as sealed." He foresaw a populace aroused against the recalcitrant Peers, ready to call a national convention by universal suffrage.

> If there were but a few dozens of persons safe (whom you & I could select) to be missionaries of the great truths in which alone there is any well-being for mankind individually or collectively, I should not care though a revolution were to exterminate every person in Great Britain and Ireland who has £500 a year.[16]

And in the *Examiner* he wrote that in order that "man may achieve his destiny... there must be a moral and social revolution, which shall, indeed, take away no man's lives or property, but which shall leave no man a fraction of unearned distinction or unearned importance."[17]

The phrase "Spirit of the Age," seemed to echo Carlyle's "Signs of the Times"— both an echo of the German *Zeitgeist*. Carlyle found much in Mill's articles to sympathize with: the indictment of the times, the sense that these were in a "transitional" stage, the need of an adequate new leadership. Mill was writing, "The superior capacity of the higher ranks for the exercise of worldly power is now a broken spell." The times called for a new leadership, for which the men of "wealth" were altogether unfitted. How was an ill-informed mass of the people filled with so much "fallacious and visionary" ideas to be guided, and by whom? Naturally, what was needed was a new heroism—a heroic élite!

> It is, therefore, one of the necessary conditions of humanity [so Mill had written] that the majority must either have wrong opinions, or no fixed opinions, or must place the degree of reliance warranted by reason, in the authority of those who have made moral and social philosophy their peculiar study.[18]

It is as if the fiery radicalism of John Mill, expressed in his private letters, were giving way to a public elitist philosophy that tried to fuse Coleridge's now conservative call for a rule by a "clerisy"—a new church leadership—and secularize it; along with a dose of Saint-Simonianism and Comtism, with its call for a ruling hierarchy of brain and science.

Carlyle liked Mill, for here was an intelligence that compensated him, with its admiration and capacities, for the isolation that had been his lot in Scotland and which he felt even now in London. Mrs. Carlyle liked him too. He was, in Carlyle's words, "slender, rather tall and elegant ... with small Roman-nosed face, two small earnestly-smiling eyes; modest, remarkably gifted with precision of utterance, enthusiastic, yet lucid, calm ... The youth," Carlyle continued, "walked home with me almost to the door; seemed to profess, almost as plainly as modesty would allow, that he had been converted by the head of the Mystic School, to whom personally he testified very hearty-looking regard." As the self-proclaimed "head of the Mystic School," Carlyle felt highly flattered. Mill, too, was flattered—but respectful, even reverential. It was a happy occasion for both, brought about by Mrs. Sarah Austin, writer and translator, and wife of a famous jurist. The young man had found a new teacher; the older man (for some time to come), a devoted disciple ...

* * *

May 1834, Thomas Carlyle writing about John Stuart Mill:

> Mrs. Austin had a tragical story of his having fallen *desperately in love* with some young philosophic beauty (yet with the innocence of two sucking doves), and being lost to all his friends and himself, and what not; but I traced nothing of this in poor Mill; and even incline to think that what truth there is or was in the adventure may have done him good.[19]

July 22, 1834:

> Our most interesting new friend is a Mrs. Taylor, who came here for the first time yesterday, and stayed long. She is a living romance heroine, of the clearest insight, of the royalest volition, very interesting, of questionable destiny, not above twenty-five. Jane is to go and pass a day with her soon, being greatly taken with her.[20]

January 12, 1835. Jane Welsh Carlyle to Dr. John Carlyle:

> There is a Mrs. Taylor whom I could really love, if it were safe and she were willing; but she is a dangerous looking woman and engrossed with a dangerous passion, and no useful relation can spring up between us.[21]

In 1834, Harriet Taylor was twenty-seven years old, eight years married, and the mother of two sons and a daughter. She had been brought up a Unitarian, and her husband John Taylor was one of the pillars of the London Unitarian community, with its remarkable minister William Johnson Fox. Carlyle thought the husband "an innocent dull good young man." But he was also somewhat out of the ordinary run of men, for being well to do (partner in the wholesale druggist firm of David Taylor & Sons), he was also a convinced liberal, a member of the Reform Club, and probably one of the supporters of the University of London. Political exiles from abroad found his and Harriet's home a haven. She was eighteen when she married, he eleven years older. In the summer of 1830 (possibly the fall) William James Fox, editor of the

Unitarian journal the *Monthly Repository*, brought John Stuart Mill to the Taylor establishment. John Mill and Harriet Taylor fell in love. Romantic fiction demands tragedy as an ending, for there is no doubt that like Paolo and Francesca they read books together and talked philosophy, morality, Utilitarianism, and other things young people talk of. Whatever strong winds that blew them about succeeded only in bringing them into each other's arms. The love drama of Mill and Harriet, filled as it was to be with moments of sadness and difficulties, found a happy consummation after some years in marriage and continued love, a happiness marred only by her premature death. . . .

Harriet Taylor brought the love he had been seeking, and more. Subsequent biographers, psychohistorians and scholars of both sexes, with their retroactive passports into the human unconscious, have cast doubts on the authenticity of John Mill's numerous attestations of debt to Harriet, and of the extent of the influence she had upon his life and thinking. She was, it is true, no genius. She had beauty and brains—to some admirers of John Mill, already a suspect combination. They find it incredible that a "lesser" woman could not only inspire in such a genius a profound love, but also help in deepening his thought, help in extending his emotional as well as his intellectual horizon.[22]

She helped to free him. Harriet Taylor came from a Unitarian environment, and the Unitarians had a long and painful history in their struggle for the emancipation of the human mind. Of the dissenting Protestant sects, they were far to the left in their theology, denying the divinity of Christ and insisting on the "unipersonality" of the Godhead. Among their ancestors were innumerable martyrs burned in England during the sixteenth century. At the time of the French Revolution they were among its most articulate defenders in England, and one of them, Richard Price, delivered the inflammatory sermon that spurred Edmund Burke to the composition of his celebrated retort, *Reflections on the Revolution in France* (1790). Joseph Priestley was one of them; and young Coleridge and young Southey, in the heyday of their Pantisocratic radicalism, held Unitarian views, some of which Coleridge expressed in his sermons. Eventually the Unitarians won a measure of tolerance, but they remained faithful to their radicalism. Among the outstanding Unitarians of the early nineteenth century, William James Fox was eminent as preacher and writer. It was for him that supporters built a new Finsbury Unitarian chapel. In time he grew more and more radical, politically as well as theologically, and as editor and owner of the *Monthly Repository* after 1831, assisted by a crew of hardy coadjutors, espoused liberal causes of reform. The emancipation of women—their right to the vote—became one of their most fervent activities. Fox's views of marriage and divorce went far beyond the most extreme views of his day. In his private life he scandalized society by separating from his wife and establishing a household in the company of the much younger Eliza Flower who, along with her sister Sarah, had been his ward. Undaunted by adverse gossip and public slur (even the London *Times* did not disdain to glance at "Fox and the Flower"), Fox continued indefatigably as journalist and preacher, lecturing to working men and women, attacking the Corn Laws, supporting the Utilitarians, agitating for compulsory secular education. He was elected to Parliament and died in 1864 at the age of 78.

He it was who gave young Robert Browning his first favorable review, in the *Monthly Repository*, and it was no secret that the poet was in love with Eliza Flower.

It was in such an atmosphere that Harriet Taylor had grown up. She was a rebel in some respects more radical than John Mill. On the subject of woman and marriage they were in agreement. She was more demonstrative than he; militantly against the bondage of conformity, whether religious, political, moral, or social. "What is called the opinion of Society," she wrote

> is ... a combination of the many weak, against the few strong; and association of the mentally listless to punish any manifestation of mental independence. The remedy is, to make all strong enough to stand alone; and whoever has once known the pleasure of self-dependence, will be in no danger of relapsing into subserviency.

On the subject of marriage and divorce she was no less explicit:

> Women are educated for one single object, to gain their living by marrying—(some poor souls get it without the churchgoing. It's the same way—they do not seem to be a bit worse than their honoured sisters.) To be married is the object of their existence and that object being gained they do really cease to exist as to anything worth calling life or any useful purpose. One observes very few marriages where there is any real sympathy or enjoyment or companionship between the parties ... Would not the best plan be divorce which could be attained by any *without any reason assigned*, and at small expence, but which could only be pronounced after a long period? ... In the present system of habits & opinions, girls enter into what is called a contract perfectly ignorant of the conditions of it, and that they should be so is considered absolutely essential to their fitness for it![23]

What role George Sand played in the diffusion of like ideas is hard to gauge; but beginning with 1833, her name and her works became bywords for a daring feminism, and in the following decade she was the most widely read, lauded and stigmatized French writer in England. Jane Carlyle read her works, much to the disgruntlement of her husband (who did not spare objurgations); as did Elizabeth Barrett and many others, like George Eliot, G. H. Lewes, and throughout his life her most devoted admirer, Matthew Arnold.

John Mill was now emboldened to defy the world, to "part company"—as he put it—"with the opinion of the world." And she, being a woman, knew fully to what gossip and malicious imputations she would be exposed—and not least, to what severe social ostracism. Today it is hard to believe that they kept to a covenant and avoided sexual relations so long as John Taylor was alive. She became free in 1849, and they were married in 1851. But during their long "courtship" the world whispered, mocked, and did not believe; though the husband behaved with dignity, he was derided as a cuckold, and she objurgated as a wanton. Carlyle commiserated with John Mill, who, as he believed, was "far above all that"—by which he meant all those Unitarian goings-on, "with their strange conceptions of 'duty'," "and all of them indignant at marriage."[24]

The reluctance to consider Harriet Taylor (now Harriet Mill) a thinking being extended even to doubts as to her authorship of an important article in the *Westminster Review* of 1851 on "The Enfranchisement of Women." Here, Harriet indicated how the demoralization of woman in an unhappy marriage demoralizes the man too—how her status of inferiority makes for an inferiority in him; how both partners become "servile-minded." "There is no inherent reason or necessity," she wrote, "that all women should voluntarily choose to devote their lives to one animal function and its consequences." Women must obtain admission to all social privileges; they do not ask for some sort of "sentimental priesthood."[25] If, as some assert, Mill guided the pen, is it too far-fetched to assume that an intelligent woman, brought up in a Unitarian environment whose journal, the *Monthly Repository*, was among the first to do full justice to the works of George Sand, could also have some radical thoughts on the woman question? Or that she might even have guided the mind and thought of John Mill? At any rate, it is doubtful whether Mill could have written the most important manifesto on the rights of woman—his own *The Subjection of Women*, published some eighteen years later—with the same fervor and clarity, absent Harriet's prior essay, or her influence.

In some respects, her social views outdistanced his—as on the question of Socialism. She incited him to a closer study of the subject which, though it never proved exhaustive, was sufficient to move him to significant changes in later editions of his *Principles of Political Economy*, to the great distress of a number of his admirers.

Must we then distrust Mill himself in his assessment of her valuable contributions to his development as a full human being? That in the hopes and labors, which they both shared, for the "radical amendment" of human life, she supplied the double stimulus of a critical mind that balanced in the "region of ultimate aims, the constituents of the highest ideal of human life, with that of the immediately useful and practically attainable"? That it was to her he owed his "wise scepticism"?[26] Must we then believe that in the high tribute he paid his deceased wife in his *Autobiography* he was deceiving both himself and all others?

* * *

Gladstone called him the "Saint of Rationalism." With even greater justice might he be called the "Paladin of Liberalism." To assimilate the many doctrines into one whole; to reconcile opposites; to mediate between them and effectually produce new moderating doctrine—this was no easy task. He was too much a child of his century not to crave some infallible system. Like so many Victorians, he was himself full of contradictions; and these are as important for an understanding of the man and his age as his actual positive contributions. The questions he asked but could not always satisfactorily answer were, under other circumstances and in other forms of social organization, destined to bedevil the next century as well.

Like all creative intellects he was at pains to free himself, at the proper moment, from his teachers, while at the same time striving to retain what was best in them and assimilate it into his maturing thought. Thus he sought to amalgamate within himself the best of Bentham and of the Utilitarian doctrine (while abandoning the less valid or satisfying elements), as well as the aesthetic and emotional content of Wordsworth and Coleridge, seeking a balance between Reason and Feeling, and a place for poetry; to steer a judicious course through the doctrines of the Saint-Simonians and the Comteans in confronting the new world of industry and capital, as well as that of the vast mass of the laboring, now seemingly more than ever embattled. And there also loomed the whole problem of Democracy. What was it? Portent, terror, prophecy, or promise?

Thus liberalism moved between Scylla and Charybdis—terrfying predicaments. Anarchy and Order, Equality and Liberty, Society and the Individual, the Mass and the One, Progress and Poverty, Art and Science, Reason and Feeling, the Elite and the People, Laissez-faire and Control, Woman and Man, Private Property and Socialism, Freedom and Necessity—where in all these opposites to find reconcilement?

There was yet another contradiction that Mill was scarcely aware of, an inner one. He was an important official of the East India Company, one of the most powerful arms of British imperialism. Was he himself caught up in the deftly woven net that constituted the "interests"? What else could account for his affirmation that such dependencies as Ireland and India needed "despotism" to keep them under control? But such aberrations, so far as Ireland was concerned, were only momentary, for in 1848 he attacked Carlyle for advocating the reduction of Ireland "into slavery ... will it or not."[27]

Gradually he drew away from Carlyle. That which had once attracted him earlier in life—the rhetoric of outrage at an age bound by ties of a "cash-nexus"—grew less and less satisfying as the fuller implications of Carlyle's former radical transcendentalism crystallized into concrete reactionary formulas. As Mill put it, still tactfully, he found Carlyle's dicta about "mystery" and "infinitude ... in the universe" repeated too often for his taste. This criticism appeared in his predominently favorable review of Carlyle's French Revolution. Three years later, in 1840, Mill could no longer brook Carlyle's attacks on Bentham in his lectures on Heroes and Hero-Worship. The 1840s, as we have seen, were the testing-ground of beliefs and adherences. Carlyle's "Occasional Discourse on the Nigger Question" in Fraser's Magazine of 1849, and Mill's response, "The Negro Question" in the same review, mark the wider points of departure; and the differences became ultimately unreconcilable when a few years later they opposed one another in the case of General Eyre and his alleged atrocities in the West Indies. In his article of 1850, Mill took Carlyle to task for his doctrine that Might is Right.

> The author issues his opinions, or rather ordinances, under imposing auspices; no less than those of the "immortal gods" ... This so-called "eternal act of Parliament" is no new law, but the old law of the strongest—a law against which the great teachers of mankind have in all ages protested: it is the law of force and cunning; the law that whoever is more than another is "born Lord" of that other, and other being his "servant" ... I see nothing divine in this injunction. If "the gods" will this, it is the first duty of human beings to resist such gods ... The history of human improvement is the record of a struggle by which inch after inch of ground has been wrung from the maleficent powers, and more and more of human life rescued from the iniquitous dominion of the law of might.[28]

Earlier differences between the two had been marked by a reproach addressed to Carlyle for speaking of Madame Roland as being almost rather a man than a woman. "Is there really" he asked, "any distinction between the highest masculine and the highest feminine character?" In January 1834, he wrote to Carlyle, "Our differences are indeed of the first importance." "I have only what appears to you much the same thing as, or even worse than, no God at all, namely a probable God." "Another of our differences is, that I am still, and am likely to remain, a utilitarian."[29] He also confessed to doubts about the immortality of the soul.

They remained friends, however, for some time to come. But Mill's deep involvement with Harriet, amid the spoken and unspoken reservations of friends and acquaintances, could not but chill the atmosphere around them. In the fall of 1833, John Taylor agreed to an experimental separation of six months from his wife; she left for Paris, where John Mill joined her in October.

One of the major tasks he set himself was to break down what appeared to him the barriers of English insularity; to bring the English into the general stream of European thought, especially that of France. For France, he claimed, was now producing "not only among the profoundest thinkers, but the clearest and most popular writers of their age." It had produced Saint-Simon and Comte. And now, in 1835, Mill was trumpeting the extraordinary merits of Alexis de Tocqueville's *Democracy in America*. In the two parts of Tocqueville's seminal work, published respectively in 1835 and 1840, and immediately translated, Mill found startling counterparts to his own thinking and a rich source of new ideas from which he could draw enrichment for his own later breviaries of liberalism, such as the essays "On Liberty" and "Representative Government."

Tocqueville was an aristocrat and a Catholic, a man possessed of a penetrating and logical mind much like Mill's, and like the latter bent on discovering the fundamental laws of human conduct in an age of advancing "democracy." Unlike Mill, however, Tocqueville was a devout believer. For him history was the revelation of Providence and His intentions. Within these intentions, Tocqueville contended, lay the ultimate triumph of democracy. America was the testing-ground of that new sweeping and irresistible movement. It was therefore most important to determine what was good and what was deleterious within American democracy and the great egalitarian wave; how to advance the good that was in it and eschew that which might prove destructive.

Mill found such an appeal to practical experience and observation, combined with brilliant generalities, extremely fascinating. For both were in search of the laws of history. Though he might differ with the Frenchman on a number of details, Tocqueville's essential evaluations of the benefits and shortcomings of democracy carried compelling conviction; and the popularity of the book, variously interpreted by Whig and Tory, suggested its importance for contemporaries.

Like Carlyle—but oh! how differently—Tocqueville saw the hand of God at work in advancing democracy in the world. This was an "irresistible revolution"—"the gradual development of the equality of conditions"—a phenomenon manifesting itself "throughout Christendom."

> The gradual development of the equality of conditions is ... a providential fact, and it possesses all the characteristics of a Divine decree; it is universal, it is durable, it constantly eludes all human interference, and all events as well as all men contribute to its progress. Would it, then, be wise to imagine that a social impulse which dates from so far back can be checked by the efforts of a generation? Is it credible that the democracy which has annihilated the feudal system and vanquished kings will respect the citizen and the capitalist? Will it stop now that it has grown so strong and its adversaries so

weak? None can say which way we are going for all terms of comparison are wanting ...
The attempt to check democracy would be ... to resist the will of God; and the nations
would ... be constrained to make the best of the social lot awarded to them by Providence.[30]

What is our first duty? he asks. It is to "educate democracy," and for that, a "new
science of politics is indispensable." It was to profit his own country, where he felt the
ideals of the Revolution had remained unfulfilled except in the "material parts of
society," that he had turned his attention to America, where what he called the "great
revolution" had already reached its "natural limits." Here, he said, was the first nation
to have escaped the domination of absolute power, and to have established and maintained the sovereignty of the people. The soil of America is "opposed to a territorial
aristocracy."

> The government of democracy brings the notion of political rights to the level of the
> humblest citizens, just as the dissemination of wealth brings the notion of property
> within the reach of all the members of the community; and I confess that, to my mind,
> this is one of its greatest advantages.[31]

Brilliantly, Tocqueville proceeds to enlarge upon the advantages and disadvantages
of American democracy. Among the great advantages, he found these: it promotes the
welfare of the greatest possible number; it is able to commit faults which it can afterwards remedy; the governed are more enlightened and attentive to their interests—
they are vigilant; the interests of the governors do not differ from those of the
community at large; there are no complaints against property; there are no paupers;
no class of persons that does not exercise the elective franchise; and the lower orders,
by participating in public business, become educated in the democratic process. A democratic society concerns itself chiefly, he held, with prosperity, "the greatest degree
of enjoyment and the least degree of misery."

But it fails in many important respects. It is deficient in the selection of exceptional
men to govern it, or in finding them out; it exhibits feelings of envy and a propensity
to reject the most deserving and distinguished as governors; unlike an aristocratic society it scorns the "embellishments" of manners; it is indifferent to the advancement
of the arts and to renown, and does not sufficiently scorn temporal advantages. It is
not devoted to the "virtues of heroism."

But the greatest danger in a democratic society like that of America lies in the unlimited power of the majority, and the "inadequate securities which exist against
tyranny."

> The majority possesses a power which is physical and moral at the same time; it acts
> upon the will as well as upon the actions of men, and it represses not only all contest,
> but all controversy. I know of no country in which there is so little true independence of
> mind and freedom of discussion as in America.[32]

In America, in a democratic republic, public opinion is the executioner. Here the
dissident is eventually forced into silence by the "slights and persecutions of daily
obloquy." "If ever the free institutions of America are destroyed, that event may be attributed to the unlimited authority of the majority, which may at some future time

urge the minorities to desperation, and oblige them to have recourse to physical force."[33] He notes with regret that American democracy is exclusively involved in "commercial habits," not inclined toward cultural pursuits. In trade and manufacture it has certainly exhibited extraordinary progress. What he fears is the emergence of a new "despotism"—the despotism of a degraded egalitarianism, and the governing despotism of a tutelary power which will spare the vast mass "all care of thinking and all the trouble of living," while providing them with "the petty and paltry pleasures" with which to glut their lives. And the warning is such as to find an echo even today:

> ... The will of man is not shattered, but softened, bent, and guided: men are seldom forced to act, but they are constantly restrained from acting; such a power does not destroy, but it prevents existence; it does not tyrannize, but it compresses, enervates, extinguishes, and stupefies a people, till each nation is reduced to be nothing better than a flock of timid and industrious animals, of which the government is the shepherd ...[34]

But Tocqueville does not despair. If a state of equality is perhaps "less elevated," it is more just: "and its justice constitutes its greatness and beauty." And he concludes the entire work with mighty words:

> I am full of apprehensions and hopes. I perceive mighty dangers which it is possible to ward off—mighty evils which may be avoided or alleviated; and I cling with a firmer hold to the belief that for democratic nations to be virtuous and prosperous they require but to will it ... The nations of our time cannot prevent the conditions of men from becoming equal; but it depends upon themselves whether the principle of equality is to lead them to servitude or freedom, to knowledge or barbarism, to prosperity or wretchedness.[35]

To these sentiments, opinions, and general conclusions John Stuart Mill responded with an impassioned heartiness that found expression in two reviews, each dedicated to the individual parts. But an even greater tribute was the one he paid Tocqueville by assimilating and expanding the latter's ideas in his own most important works.

To Tocqueville he wrote:

> You have accomplished a great achievement; you have changed the face of political philosophy, you have carried on the discussions respecting the tendencies of modern society. ... into a region both of height & depth, which no one before you had entered ... There is no living man in Europe whom I esteem more highly or of whose friendship I should be more proud than I am of yours ...[36]

The two reviews of Tocqueville's book appeared in the *London and Westminster Review* in 1835 and in the *Edinburgh Review* in 1840. He agreed with the Frenchman on the perils that adhere to democratic institutions, the threats of destruction of individuality, the suppression of minority opinion, and the danger of stagnation and immobility inherent in greater and greater centralization. At the same time he made his readers aware of the limitations of Tocqueville's analysis, particularly the latter's overestimation of the character and role of an aristocracy. Whatever the qualities of aristocratic governments of France, Mill insisted that England's aristocracy failed to reveal characteristics of "prudence and steadiness." The only steadiness he saw revealed here was the tenacity with which it clung to its own privileges.[37] It would be difficult, he wrote, for democracy to exhibit less of a willingness to place itself under the "guidance of the wisest ... than has been shown by the English aristocracy in all periods of their history, or less than is shown by them at this moment." He denied Tocqueville's contention of the overall extension of the "passion for equality," particularly so far as England was concerned. Here,

> the inequalities of property are apparently greater than in any former period of history. Nearly all the land is parcelled out in great estates, among comparatively few families; and it is not the large but the small properties which are in the process of extinction. An hereditary and titled nobility, more potent by their possessions than by their social precedency, are constitutionally and really one of the great powers in the state ... The passion for equality, of which M. de Tocqueville speaks almost as if it were the great moral lever of modern times, is hardly known in this country even by name ... Of all countries in a state of progressive commercial civilization, Great Britain is that in which the equalization of conditions has made least progress. The extremes of wealth and poverty are wider apart, and there is a more numerous body of persons at each extreme, than in any other commercial community.[38]

Actually, Mill asked, does not American society resemble "any thing so much as an exaggeration of our own middle class"? Is not the "competitiveness," "the treading upon the heels of one another," as true of British as of American civilization today? The significant contrast between England and America lies solely in the fact that in the former, great fortunes are continually accumulated but "seldom distributed," whereas in America the transfer of wealth is much more frequent and fluid. Nearly all the moral and social influences, Mill concludes, which Tocqueville enumerates with respect to America are "shown to be in full operation in aristocratic England." The class that is now truly in power in England at this time is the Middle Class, which is the "arbiter of fortune and success."

The dangers that inhere in Democracy and Egalitarianism, the "tyranny of the majority" or of the "mass," can be obviated,

> ... if the superior spirits would but join with each other in considering the instruction of democracy, and not patching of the old worn-out machinery of the aristocracy, the proper object henceforth of all rational exertion.[39]

Auguste Comte was another of the forceful influences in the thinking of John Mill. But Mill was never to be a blind disciple and follower. Though profoundly impressed by the positive philosophy, so far as its emphasis on science as a liberating force and on its interpretation of the necessary laws of history and historical development, Mill took issue with the Frenchman on the nature of woman and the role of marriage. Mill began a correspondence with Comte in 1841. Acknowledging his *grandes obligations intellectuelles*, since 1818, to the French philosopher and his *Course of Positive Philosophy*, Mill was all for a philosophy that would replace the idea of God with one rooted in humanity. But on the subject of property and marriage, he differed with his French mentor. "While plainly recognizing ... the necessity of such fundamental institutions as property and marriage," he wrote

> ..., I am inclined to believe that these two institutions may be destined to undergo more serious modifications than you seem to think, although I feel totally unable to foresee

what they will be. I have already mentioned to you that the question of divorce is still an open one to me, despite the powerful argument advanced in your fourth volume, and I am guilty of an even more fundamental heresy, for I do not admit, in principle, the necessary subordination of one sex to another.[40]

Comte countered with the assertion that biology sufficiently established a hierarchy of the sexes, showing that the anatomical and physiological organization of the female in all the animal world constituted a kind of "radical infancy." Mill began giving ground, and even granted that the smaller brain size in woman made her less capable of continued and prolonged intellectual labors. She was better fitted, he granted, for poetry and for practical life than for science. On the other hand, he added, one must take account of the influence of "circumstances" in making woman what she was. He would not entrust the government of society solely to women, but would society not be better managed if both sexes took part in directing its interests?

Not at all! Comte replied. Women are incapable of abstract thought; they are unable to subdue passion to reason, and hence unfitted for science, philosophy, aesthetics, practical life, industry, the military, commerce; no good as directors or executors, but good enough as persons to be consulted ...[41]

One need not be a psychologist or a psychohistorian to recreate Harriet Taylor's reactions to the Comtean attitude. She reproached John Mill for his indecisiveness, pointing out the dangers inherent in such views, allegedly based on biology and phrenology.[42]

More clearly than Mill, she seemed to sense the implication of Comte's philosophy for the whole hierarchical structure of the Positivist society. All too soon, Comte was to justify both their fears, so that by 1848, John Mill was to state that Auguste Comte's political writings (apart from his admirable historical views) were "likely to be mischievous rather than useful."[43]

How truly "mischievous" Comte's ideas might appear to the liberal mind can be gauged from the following passage from the *Positive Philosophy*:

> It is only by the positive polity that the revolutionary spirit can be restrained ... Under the rule of the positive spirit ... all the difficult and delicate questions which now keep up a perpetual irritation in the bosom of society, and which can never be settled while mere political solutions are proposed, will be scientifically estimated, to the great furtherance of social peace. At the same time it will be teaching society that, in the present state of their ideas, no political change can be of supreme importance ... Again, the positive spirit tends to consolidate order, by the rational development of a wise resignation to incurable political evils ... A true resignation—that is, a permanent disposition to endure, can proceed only from a deep sense of the connection of all kinds of natural phenomena with natural laws ... Human nature suffers in its relations with the astronomical world, and the physical, chemical, and biological, as well as the political. How is it that we turbulently resist in the last case, while, in the others we are calm and resigned ...[44]

Yet on the positive side, John Mill acknowledged his debt to Comte (among others) for solidifying his faith in History and the historical process, and in the potential creation of a "Social Physics" which, with the aid of Science, would enable mankind to create a science of society with all the predictive possibilities inherent in the natural sciences. Mankind then would be able to transfer its ideas of Volition from metaphysical and supernatural forces to Man himself. Ceasing to speculate on ultimate causes and concentrating on the immediate problems facing him would enable him to labor toward the amelioration of human conditions. History, Mill boasted, "has been made a science of causes and effects," affording "the only means of predicting and guiding the future, by unfolding the agencies which have produced and still maintain the Present."[45]

* * *

The 1830s were crucial years for Mill. In 1830 he met Harriet Taylor. Jeremy Bentham died in 1832; James Mill, John's father, in 1836. Saddened as he was at the loss of his two great mentors, he could not escape the feeling that he was at the same time being liberated from the sternness that, throughout these many years of intellectual obligations, had inhibited a full expression of his differences and dissents. He had kept his inner revolution a secret from both; and of his love for Harriet his father knew practically nothing, despite the fact that by the time of his father's death he had known her for six years! To that tide of intellectual liberation was added the torrent of his released feelings for Harriet. He felt he had grown and that he was now in a position to do justice to both his father's and Bentham's contribution without having to hesitate in also expressing reservations. In the same spirit, he could now acknowledge the worth and importance of the Romantic poets and thinkers like Wordsworth and Coleridge.

On one crucial issue he was departing from Bentham. While acknowledging that Bentham liberated English law from feudal shackles by expelling its mystical elements, Mill at the same time rejected his advocacy of the rights to a franchise of the "numerical majority." In his eyes, Bentham had failed to take note of the actual and potential "despotism of public opinion."[46]

Mill defined "radicalism"—it must be remembered that the Utilitarians called themselves "philosophical radicals"—as the "claim of pre-eminence for personal qualities above conventional and accidental advantages." The "radical," he wrote,

> believing the government of this country to be in the main a selfish oligarchy, carried on for the personal benefit of the ruling classes ... [and] not Utopian enough to address himself to the reason of his rulers ... endeavours to attain his object by taking away their power.

Mill's "radicalism" included a time-honored reverence for property and a diehard abhorrence of universal suffrage. He is staggered by the anticipated preponderance and "mass of brutish ignorance ... of the barbarians whom Universal Suffrage will let in ... of the depraved habits of a large proportion of the well-paid artisans," no less than by the debased condition of the agricultural laborers. And he does not wonder that the "middle classes, who know all these things ..., should tremble at the idea of entrusting political power to such hands."[47]

At this point—in 1839—he is still aroused by the failure of the Reform Bill of 1832 which, he saw, instead of weakening the hold the landed oligarchy exercised over the country, had in fact strengthened it. "They are the government," he wrote. As for the more radical labor theoreticians, he has no more use for them than for the oligarchic cliques.

They believe they are ground down by the capitalist. They believe that his superiority of means, and power of holding out longer than they can, enables him virtually to fix wages. They ascribe the lowness of those wages, not, as is the truth, to the *over*-competition produced by their own excessive numbers, but to competition itself; that state of things inevitable so long as the two classes exist separate—so long as the distinction is kept up between Capitalist and Labourer. These notions are in fact Owenism... but Owenism does not necessarily, it does not in the mind of its benevolent founder, imply any war against property. What is hoped for is, not violently to subvert, but quietly to supersede the present arrangements for the employment of capital and labour.[48]

The best course for labor is to put itself in the hands of the middle classes—"the motto of a Radical politician should be: Government *by means of the middle* for the working classes."

The 1840s, soon called the "Hungry Forties," presented a sufficient number of problems to perplex, terrify, harass, and depress the Victorian conscience. There was the hysterical railway boom, the frenzied speculation and building of railway lines—true of Europe no less than of Great Britain—with its eventual collapse. There was the even more serious potato blight, which destroyed the crops not only in Ireland, but also in Great Britain, Belgium, and Germany. The wheat crop had also suffered. Along with these afflictions, the prohibitive Corn Laws still prevailed, to the profit and enjoyment of the landed interests. John Mill was aroused by the torpor and indifference that seemed to dominate British society, and he excoriated the upper classes for their deficient intellect, will, and character.

He even allowed himself a few dangerous ideas. Thus, he wrote in 1847:

In England... I often think that a violent revolution is very much needed, in order to give that general shake-up to the torpid mind of the nation which the French Revolution gave to Continental Europe. England has never had any general break-up of old associations & hence the extreme difficulty of getting any ideas into its stupid head. After all, what country in Europe can be compared with France in the adaptation of its social state to the benefit of the great mass of its people, freed as they are from any tyranny which comes home to the greater number, with justice easily accessible, & and strongest inducements to personal prudence & forethought? And would this have been the case without the great changes in the state of property which, even supposing good intentions in the Government, could hardly have been produced by anything less than a Revolution?[49]

Then came the news of the February Revolution in France. Harriet and John rejoiced. A French republic established! He could not contain his enthusiasm:

I am hardly yet out of breath from the reading and thinking about it. Nothing can possibly exceed the importance of it to the world or the immensity of the interests which are at stake on its success... The republicans have succeeded... Communism has now for the first time a deep root, and has spread widely in France, and a large part of the republican strength is more or less imbued with it. ... If France succeds in establishing a republic and a reasonable republican government, all the rest of Europe, except England and Russia, will be republicanized in ten years and England itself probably before we die. There never was a time when so great a drama was being played out in one generation. ...[50]

He was outraged by John Austin's expressed horror at what was happening in France, an event which in Mill's eyes had "broken the fetters of all Europe"; and even more so by Lord Brougham, who had called the Revolution in France the "work of some half-dozen artisans, who met in a printing office…, a handful of armed ruffians, headed by a shoemaker and a sub-editor."[51] Mill was particularly irked by Brougham's failure to understand that the new government of France was creating productive employment, encouraging cooperative associations, and at the same time protecting private property.

Mill could not pretend to, nor did he claim to, possess a thorough understanding of the vast meaning of the events of 1848. Aside from the overshadowing historical revolutions throughout Europe, 1848 was also, it must be remembered, the year of publication of both Mill's *Principles of Political Economy* and Marx and Engels's *Communist Manifesto*. Both works dramatically symbolize the epochal polarization that was taking place in the realm of theory, while the historic events of that and the following years were to inscribe that polarization in blood. Firmly anchored as Mill was in bourgeois political and economic thought, he could not escape the impress of the new events on his own thinking. He recognized that Socialism (or Communism) was on the agenda of history. Subsequent editions of his *Political Economy* would reveal to what extent he was ready to modify his views in the light of the historic events and changes and under the influence of Harriet Taylor.

He had begun by regarding private enterprise as superior to any other even "in ideal circumstances," and communal ownership as "too chimerical to be reasoned against." Nothing was so much in harmony with the requirements of human nature as that mode of distribution of the produce of industry, which allows a share of each individual to depend on that individual's own energies and exertions. "It is not the subversion of the system of individual property that should be aimed at, but the improvement of it." He rejected, as he had always done, the right of private property in land, and declared himself for a peasant ownership. In his theory of labor, he was still tied to the so-called wage-fund theory, which held that only a fixed sum of capital was available for labor, that the remedy for labor's ills lay in family planning, and that no activity by the workers themselves, such as strikes, combinations or legislation by government, would be of any help or use. Under Harriet's promptings, he was willing to grant that the "poor have come out of leading strings," that they should be treated as equals, and that their future depended on "the degree in which they could be made rational beings."

On the whole, Harriet appeared to be more aware of the nature and power of upper-class interests than Mill. In the midst of the disturbances of 1848, when Irish unrest was being savagely repressed and the Habeas Corpus was suspended, she pointed out to him how differently the upper classes reacted to the old bugaboo of "government interference" when it affected their own interests; but how indifferently they reacted when the government invoked repressive legislation against the poor. Harriet was in her way a convert to Socialism, and while she did not succeed in bringing him around to her views, she elicited certain concessions which he made public in the 1852 edition of his *Principles of Political Economy*.

If, therefore, the choice were to be made between Communism with all its chances, and the present state of society, with all its sufferings and injustices; if the institution of private property necessarily carried with it as a consequence, that the produce of labour should be apportioned as we now see it, almost in an inverse ratio to the labour—the largest portions to those who have never worked at all... the remuneration dwindling as the work grows harder and more disagreeable, until the most fatiguing and exhausting bodily labour cannot count with certainty on being able to earn even the necessaries of life; if this or Communism were the alternative, all the difficulties, great or small, of Communism would be but as dust in the balance. But to make the comparison more applicable, we must compare Communism at its best, with the régime of individual property, not as it is, but as it might be made. The principle of private property has never yet had a fair trial in any country; and less so, perhaps, in this country than in some other.[52]

He never threw off those fears he harbored of the "tyranny of the majority"—the fears of universal suffrage. If all were to have the vote, he insisted, then there must be provisions for giving some "greater weight" to the suffrage of those of the "more educated" ... "the more intrisically valuable" members of society, those "more competent for the general affairs of life." "A person who cannot read is not as good, for the purpose of human life, as one who can."[53]

It did not occur to him that the "educated" voter might himself represent a special "class" interest, even if unconsciously. The experience of the American Civil War in its repercussions in England showed him that at times the lower orders were more capable of noble impulses, of unselfishness, than their social superiors. For in this instance it was the operatives in the British cotton mills who, to their own economic disadvantage, supported the cause of the American North by boycotting Southern cotton, while their upper-class (and presumably more "educated") masters placed their own interests above all moral considerations—in this case the matter of black slavery.

But John Stuart Mill was not one to put self-interest ahead of moral principles. John Taylor died in 1849, leaving to Harriet a life interest in his entire property. Before marrying Harriet, John Mill made a formal declaration renouncing any rights to such property were they to be married. The marriage took place on April 21, 1851. Their happiness was marred only by their troubled health. Both suffered from consumption, but hers was more advanced. That she was to die in the very year of his retirement, when his pension and the income from his books would have enabled both of them to enjoy the leisure and luxury of joint creation, was indeed tragic. Her death occurred on November 3, 1858 in Avignon, France, and she was buried in the local cemetery of the suburban St.-Véran. There Mill bought a small house, in which he was to spend the greater part of his life. At the Hermitage de Monloisier, his stepdaughter Helen took over the cares of the household as well as secretarial duties, proving an invaluable support to Mill for the rest of his life. Though for a time shattered by Harriet's death, he kept his promise to her to continue what he considered their joint efforts, publishing "On Liberty" in 1859, and "The Subjection of Women" in 1861. In his brief term as a member of Parliament, he moved, during the debate on the Reform Bill in 1867, that the word "man" be replaced by "person." Though voted down, he at least had the satisfaction that one third of the scant attendance supported him. He was fervent in championing the interests of the North during the American

Civil War, and hailed the Emancipation. He died in Avignon on May 7, 1873, and was buried beside Harriet.

Though his longer works, such as the *Political Economy* and the *Logic*, would remain academic texts for many years, and in both the Scandinavian countries and Russia (along with his "Utilitarianism") became breviaries for advanced liberals, it is his *Autobiography*, and his essays "On Liberty" and "The Subjection of Women," that have the most profound meaning for our own generations. The *Autobiography* remains a penetrating, moving psychological document. The two essays are complementary, both concerned with the problems of equality and individuality. Both deal with forms of enslavement and the possibilities of emancipation—and both were to acquire additional importance with the times, as the issues gained wider significance. For they both address the disaster that can befall a society when it rejects or suppresses valuable minority ideas and opinions; and with the tragic loss it risks by repressing the productive capacities of a good portion of its members. Debasement and crippling inhere in such enslavement not only to the enslaved, but to the enslaver as well. Tyranny distills within itself a destructive poison, whether it be that of the social mass or of the individual within a family. Mill attacks the tyranny of custom, when it is raised to the level of the "natural" and achieves the rank of "universality," becoming a "right." Such a custom accepts slavery and force as natural phenomena—not jarring "with modern civilization, any more than domestic slavery among the Greeks jarred with their notion as a free people."

The irrational or anti-rational, disguised euphemistically as "instinct," becomes identified with the "intention of Nature and the ordinance of God." They become particularly potent elements in any discussion of the "nature" of woman and her position in the family and in society, her "rights" and "duties."

Mill's "The Subjection of Women" was (and is) not merely a manifesto, eloquent and moving, of woman's rights, or an appeal for justice, but in a broader sense a universal manifesto of human rights the world over, embracing all minorities.

The subjection of woman in modern society, Mill holds, is based on the right of the stronger over the weaker. It is also based on a total ignorance of the "nature" of woman, the understanding being obscured by the very character of her relation to man in our present society. Restricted as she is by the common demand of what Mill calls the "hot-house and stove cultivation," she is bound to remain a secret—her life a secret—the secret of an inferior who cannot afford to be sincere or open toward someone she must "look up to." And the secret will not be revealed "until women themselves have told all they have to tell"—that is, until they reach a state of equality. Dependent as she is on her husband for her subsistence, woman is doubly a bond-slave by virtue of the law—the marriage contract that not only makes her the property of her spouse, but makes her own property her husband's—so that "what is mine (the woman is speaking) is yours, but what is yours is not mine." The morality of submission engenders in the male—in many, many instances—brutality, selfishness, and self-indulgence. Wife and family are considered "belongings." The family turns into a school of despotism, when it should be a school of virtue and freedom.

By reason of such arrangements, society excludes one half of mankind from occupations and functions which are arrogated as a monopoly by the stronger sex, giving preference to males of lesser mental equipment merely by virtue of their birth as males, in preference to women of indisputably higher intelligence and capacities. In the same way, woman is enjoined from participating in public affairs, from having a voice in the choice of those who are to govern her in the public domain.

So far as women's capacities are concerned, Mill insists that "it cannot now be known how much of the existing mental differences between men and women is natural, and how much artificial; whether there are any natural differences at all..."[54]

> We do not know whether they could produce a Homer or Aristotle; but we do know that they could produce and have produced a Deborah, or a Joan of Arc. We do know that they have produced remarkable works of fiction—such as those of Madame de Staël and George Sand. [Mill might have added some names closer to home, such as those of the Brontës and Mrs. Gaskell.]

But not the least loss entailed by the exclusion of women from active life in society—aside from the reduction by one half of the "mental faculties available for the higher services of humanity"—is the loss to woman herself, the impoverishment of her own inner and outer life; in fact, her dehumanization, her depersonalization.

> There is nothing after disease, indigence and guilt so fatal to the pleasurable enjoyment of life as the want of a worthy outlet for the active faculties.[55]

And he concludes:

> What in unenlightened societies, colour, race, religion, or in the case of a conquered country, nationality, are to some men, sex is to all women; a peremptory exclusion from almost all honourable occupations, but either such as cannot be fulfilled by others, or such as those others do not think worthy of their acceptance... When we consider the positive evil caused to the disqualified half of the human race by their disqualification— first in the loss of the most inspiring and elevating kind of personal enjoyment, and next in the weariness, disappointment, and profound dissatisfaction with life, which are so often the substitute for it; one feels that among all the lessons which men require for carrying on the struggle against the inevitable imperfections of their lot on earth, there is no lesson which they more need, than not to add to the evils which nature inflicts, by their jealous and prejudiced restrictions on one another. Their vain fears only substitute other and worse evils for those which they are idly apprehensive of: while every restraint on the freedom of conduct of any of their human fellow-creatures (otherwise than by making them responsible for any evil actually caused by it), dries up *pro tanto* the principal fountain of human happiness, and leaves the species less rich, to an inappreciable degree, in all that makes life valuable to the individual being.[56]

In the breadth of his conception, in the sweep of his humanism, Mill was addressing not only his own century, which long remained not even partially persuaded by his argument—but *a fortiori* also the twentieth. While pleading for the humanization of a whole sex, he was at the same time pleading for the humanization of any minority—whether racial or religious. In his essay "On Liberty" he is no less fervently concerned with the preservation of the human element in the individual within a society dominated by the sway of the majority. He is interested in and concerned with the "interests of a man as a progressive being." Once more he is pleading the cause of a "minority"—pitted against a society whose general tendency is "to render mediocrity the ascendant power among mankind," where, as in England, the middle class acts as a "collective mediocrity." What is essential in such a society as ours, Mill contends, is the safeguarding of individuality within those portions of the body politic that affect only the individual himself: liberty of conscience, of thought and feeling; the freedom of one's opinions and the right to their expression. Truth is after all a "question of reconciling and combining opposites." The incubus of conformity is upon us; we are living in an age of conformity where there is "scarcely any outlet for energy… except business." We are once more, as in the battle for sexual equality, engaged in the "war of truths," and the suppression of a potential truth, though it smack of heresy, is bound to debase the oppressor as well.

> It is not the minds of heretics that are deteriorated most by the ban placed on all inquiry, which does not end in the orthodox conclusions. The greatest harm done is to those who are not heretics, and whose whole mental development is cramped, and their reason cowed, by the fear of heresy.[57]

In the "present low state of the human mind"—as Mill puts it—no government, whether aristocratic or democratic, can rise above mediocrity, "except as the sovereign Many have let themselves be guided… by the counsels and influence of a more highly gifted and instructed One or Few."[58]

> The initiation of all wise or noble things comes and must come from individuals; generally at first from some one individual. The honour and glory of the average man is that he is capable of following that initiative…

It is such individuals who may be the bearers of the truth; even if only, at times, of a partial truth. And even if the "received opinion" be the whole truth, such truth, unless challenged, may degenerate into nothing more than a blind prejudice, and the "dogma" become merely a mechanical or formal profession "inefficacious for good."

Even "eccentricity" is to be commended in an age such as ours, in order to break through the "tyranny of opinion." "The amount of eccentricity in a society has generally been proportional to the amount of genius, mental vigour, and moral courage it contains."[59]

Much as he was opposed to the tyranny of the "collective mediocrity" evidenced by the middle classes, Mill was no less critical of government interference in the lives and activities of its citizens—particularly suspicious of a dominant bureaucracy. (Not that he was unaware that "collective mediocrity" and government might not represent identical special interests.) Every extension of the powers of the government, he averred, "causes its influence over hopes and fear to be more widely diffused, and converts, more and more, the active and ambitious part of the public into hangers-on of the government, or some party which aims at becoming the government."[60]

And he concludes his essay "On Liberty":

> The worth of a State, in the long run, is the worth of the individuals composing it … A State which dwarfs its men, in order that they may be more docile instruments in its hand even for beneficial purposes—will find that with small men no great thing can be accomplished; and that the perfection of machinery to which it has sacrificed everything

will in the end avail it nothing, for want of vital power, which, in order that the machine might work more smoothly, it has preferred to banish.

Here was one of Victorian England's most luminous minds struggling with what was to prove the appalling dilemma of Victorian society. He was the apostle of Reason, with whose power he was hopeful of "reconciling opposites"—conflicting interests and ideologies. He was certain that the domination of an oligarchy of the landed interests (which he regarded as "sinister"), which to him represented the real government, had to be or was about to be broken. But here was another oligarchy, no less ominous, but pretty certain of eventual triumph—the thriving capitalism—that was unloosing new problems no less threatening to the "conscience" of the thoughtful bourgeois.

The bourgeois conscience was doubly challenged. Here was the phenomenon of apparent injustices and exactions perpetrated by their own class; here were also the importunities and pressures of the lower orders demanding "justice." And here also was the threat to the sanctity of their own individualities—assimilation to mass, to mediocrity. The sanctity of an individualism now in danger of being violated, if not extinguished, forced upon them a new struggle for "freedom." This was their form of "alienation." The superior moral values which they represented, they imagined, could not only resist the pressures of conformity and mediocrity, but might even serve as the sources of adjudication, arbitration, and mediation among the many conflicting groups and ideas, reconciling these in the name of an even higher morality. Such a superior morality might now serve as a surrogate for religion, which seemed equally vulnerable in the chaos of the new social order.

But triumphant Empire, Commerce, Industry, and Finance found a new secular religion in its own right. It will be remembered that Mill's "On Liberty" appeared in 1859, the same year as Darwin's *Origin of Species*. And that was a significant but fateful coincidence. In Darwin's evolutionary theory the potential middle class saw the emergence of a god which, even more powerfully than that of Bentham, James Mill, or John Stuart Mill, proved the superterrestrial dogma that *laissez-faire* was a law of Nature. Here was a new dogma built on solid scientific ground! As Malthus had opened the eyes of Darwin with his "iron law of wages," so now Malthus and Darwin, combined, presented the capitalist world with a new theology, confirming the rights of Empire, and political, social, and economic expansion and domination, by analogies with such natural phenomena as "the survival of the fittest" and "the struggle for existence." The God of Competition and the "survival of the strongest" were built into God's universal process from time immemorial.

The influence of John Stuart Mill gradually diminished with the years. So far as the working classes were concerned, after 1848 they sought new forms of organization, and found social and political theories designed to forge a new consciousness of themselves as a "class." Here too, John Stuart Mill had nothing to offer them.

Yet the questions and problems he left as a heritage to a tortured Liberalism would not only bedevil the whole of the nineteenth century, but would prove very provocative even to the twentieth. Reconciliation of the demands of Individuality and the Mass, the Individual and the State, the right of Dissent and the supreme Social Good, are problems still unresolved. They are still crucial problems even for those societies whose birth and growth Mill could scarcely have anticipated, where new social forms and relationships, if the future is to be theirs, demand the resolutions of these antinomies, the reconciliation of Equality, Liberty, and Individuality, as well as Criticism and Dissent.

Part Two

Russia: Dark Laughter and Siberia

Nikolay Gogol and Young Dostoevsky

NOTE: In our transliteration from the Russian, *zh* is to be pronounced like the French *j* in *bonjour*; *dzh* like the English *j* in *just*; *kh* like the *ch* in the German *ach!*

Chapter One

The Dark Laughter of Nikolay Gogol

Russia! Oh Russia! From an enchanted far-off haven I
see you now ... Boundless as you are, are you not the
land destined to bring forth geniuses boundless as yourself? Are you not the land fated to breed heroes, you who
can offer them scope and terrain in which to realize their
powers? ... Oh Russia! land of glittering and sublime
horizons, of which the world is utterly ignorant! ...

—Gogol, *Dead Souls*

Strange are the anomalies that at times occur in what appears to be a predictable universe. Such, for example, as happened when Tsar Nicholas I of Russia extended his
imperial permission for the production and performance of a comedy, *The Inspector
General*, composed by Nikolay Gogol. The play opened at the Aleksandrinsky Theatre
in St. Petersburg on May 1, 1836, in the presence of the Tsar and his august entourage.

Certainly, we may guess that scarcely one person in the audience could have suspected he was present at a major theatrical event—that the play before him was not
only to inaugurate a new era in the Russian theatre, but would also stir up passions
and controversy for years to come. In extending his permission, the present Tsar was
acting more kindly than his father, Alexander I. The latter's censors had been keeping
a strict eye on the theatre, wary of anything that might smack of pointed satire or
criticism of the authorities—even the slightest. Thus the dramatist Aleksandr Griboedov, the most brilliant playwright of that era, had been subjected to irreparable harassment, and his most notable comedy, *Wit Works Woe*—a mild, if provocative, satire
of contemporary gentry society—was banned from production during the author's
lifetime.

But here, before an audience including the highest of the land, Gogol was presenting a side of Russian life scarcely anyone had dared exhibit before. The audience was
stunned, baffled, intrigued, amused, or outraged—and it would take years before they
would fully assimilate the import of *The Inspector General*.

The plot of the comedy is simple. The mayor of a provincial Russian town, also in
fact a kind of prefect of the police, is informed through a friend's letter that an Inspector General is about to arrive incognito with a view to investigating conditions.
Appalled at the prospect, he calls a meeting of the other officials to consider a suitable
"strategy." The district judge, the welfare commissioner, the superintendent of
schools, the postmaster, the hospital's German doctor—all arrive and begin to share

in the general consternation. For it appears at once that there is something "rotten" in the way the town has been run.

A lightning-like series of exchanges soon throws a glaring beam on the several derelictions of these officials, ranging from peccadilloes like the postmaster's irrepressible relish in reading the mail entrusted to him, to the welfare commissioner's super-efficient management of the hospital, where patients are cured in "Nature's way"—that is, those who are destined to die, die; those destined to live, live; patients are cured like "flies," and the doctor does not even speak Russian. But the master craftsman of malfeasance is the Mayor himself, an amalgam of brutality, greed, arrogance, and genius for extortion, not averse to administering a flogging or two when necessity commands.

Soon two potbellied town gossips rush in—Bobchinsky and Dobchinsky—breathless with the news that there is a young man staying at the inn who does not pay his bills and refuses to go away. Surely this is —. Appalled, the Mayor sets off for the inn to pay the stranger a visit. . . .

In fact, there is a young man staying at the inn. His name is Khlestakov, and he is a very ordinary young man, a petty government clerk, more interested in gambling than in his official duties or advancement, but extremely adroit in spending his father's money. He has lost heavily at cards, and is now on his way back to the family estate. Penniless, he has been staying at the inn, living on credit reluctantly granted him by the landlord, and is now in fear of immediate arrest. He is accompanied by his servant Ossip, whose homely comments about his master serve to round out the unflattering picture of the ne'er-do-well.

The Mayor of course figures that this must be the Government Inspector in disguise. A terrified Mayor confronts an equally terrified Khlestakov. What a surprise for both: The Mayor invites Khlestakov to stay in his house. Khlestakov accepts, and from that moment on, his fortunes change. Having become a person of grand importance, he soon begins to take advantage of his mistaken identity. He makes "loans" from the attending officials; he extracts sums from toadying merchants come to lodge complaints against the Mayor. He captures the hearts of both the Mayor's wife and his daughter, proposes to the latter, and fills the Mayor's heart with pride, joy, and expectations.

Had Khlestakov only hearkened to the advice of wise Ossip, his servant, all would have been well. But the foolish young man, instead of skipping, as Ossip advises, confides his successes in a letter to a friend in Petersburg; which letter, as we may rightly surmise, is inspected by the Postmaster, and its contents revealed to the entire covey of town scoundrels. Khlestakov escapes, but in the midst of all this, lightning strikes the panic-stricken coterie: a gendarme appears, announcing the arrival of the real Inspector General and summoning all of them to the inn . . .

If, at first glance, the theme of the play might seem commonplace—a case of mistaken identity, and local skulduggery—the brilliance with which Gogol manipulates the action, the rapidity of incident, and the wit he manifests through the individual characters are truly amazing. But seen additionally in the context of the time and the place, the play grows in a double stature. The brush-strokes are rapid, few, and telling.

The interplay among the several rascals confronted by an unavoidable catastrophe has all the freshness of high comedy and sharp satire.

Take for example the scene in which they begin accusing one another. The district judge confesses to a "sin"—he has been taking wolfhound puppies as "gifts." The Mayor (himself no mean sinner) berates him:

> The Mayor: Wolfhounds, or anything else. They're bribes all the same, aren't they?
>
> District Judge: Oh, no, Anton Antonovich. If a man takes, for example, a fur coat worth 500 rubles and a shawl for his wife—
>
> Mayor: OK! OK!—So you take only wolfhounds … But … You don't believe in God, and you never go to church. Now I—I'm religious, I go to church every Sunday. But you—I know you. When you begin to talk of the creation of the world, it makes one's hair stand on end …

Well—it takes a thief to catch a thief … But the thieves also have their sense of status, as exhibited when the Mayor castigates one of his menial subordinates:

> See here. You'd better look out. I know your sort! You work hand in glove with all kind of people … You slip silver spoons into your boots … Look out. I've got sharp ears. What did you grab from the merchant Chernayev the other day? He gave you two yards of cloth for your uniform, and you pinched the whole piece. Take care! I warn you! For this sort of thing—remember you're still small potatoes. You grab more than someone in your station is entitled to. And now, get going! …

And now, this shrewd Mayor—so conscious of his rank and, of course, his shrewdness, who has outwitted half the town, skinned the merchants and helped the merchants cheat the government—has allowed himself to be duped by a nondescript ninny like Khlestakov! Before the final bombshell falls and the arrival of the true Inspector General is announced, he castigates himself:

> And I am—oh what an idiot! I deserve every bit of it! What an ass I've shown myself! Thirty years in the service, and not one dog of a merchant of building contracts had had the better of me. I've outwitted every rogue in creation. I've taken the measure of cheats and scoundrels who could fleece the whole world. I've hoodwinked three governors. But what are governors, after all!

And he turns to the audience:

> Come, come, all you good Christians, take a good look at me. See what an ass I've turned out to be. A petty windbag like that, a shred of rags, and I mistook him for a person of consequence! Now he will spread the story all over the world, and some scribbler will come along and put me into a comedy, and the whole world will grin and clap … What are *you* laughing at? Why, you're laughing at yourselves! …

De te fabula, dear audience!

The young wastrel, Khlestakov, also undergoes a preternatural inflation of his ego as a result of his vast and easy successes at extortion. Caught up in his own fabrication, he magnetizes his astounded audience of lickspittles and misled admirers:

> Perhaps you imagine I'm nothing but a copying clerk. Not by a long shot! I'm on the most intimate footing with my section head … I spend only a minute or two in the

office, just enough to say, "Do this" or "Do that" ... I'm acquainted with pretty actresses ... and I'm on friendly terms with Pushkin. When we meet, I say, "Hello Pushkin my boy, how goes it?" "So—so, my friend, thanks ... So—so ..." He's a quiet character, that Pushkin ... I'm the author of lots and lots of works—*The Marriage of Figaro, Robert le Diable, Norma*. Bless me if I can remember all the titles ... On my table, for example, there is a watermelon that cost seven hundred rubles. The soup I serve is brought in a casserole by steamer straight from Paris. You raise the lid and Heavens! what an aroma—there's nothing like it in the world! As for my whist parties—the Foreign Minister, the French ambassador, the German ambassador—and me! ... Then I rush home and climb to the fourth floor, and can barely say to my cook, "Mavrush, take my overcoat"—but what am I saying?—I forgot I live on the first floor. In the morning you'd be surprised what my waiting-room looks like—counts and princes ... humming like a swarm of bumblebees—bz ... bz ... bz ... (The Mayor and the other are overcome with awe, and rise from their seats.)

According to one report, the Tsar laughed and laughed, and said, "Everyone has caught it, but I've caught it more than anyone else." He must have been particularly struck by the final tableau—the "frozen petrification"—demanded in the stage directions, in which the actors were required to remain glued for a minute or two in their places, and in characteristic poses, absolutely motionless and dumb—until the fall of the curtain. Was this meant to be a picture of petrification—of a petrified society, come to be judged? The Tsar did not draw such conclusion, but others did ...

The Tsar laughed, so did the Tsarina, the heir to the throne, and various duchesses and grand duchesses. The Tsar, it is reported, ordered his ministers to see the play. This from Aleksandr Nikitenko, among the more liberal of the government's censors, who records in his diary for April 28, 1836 (Old Style):

Gogol's comedy *The Inspector General* has created quite a sensation. It is performed continuously almost every other day ... I saw the third performance ... In front of me, in the stalls, sat Prince Chernyshev and Count Kankrin. The former expressed his utter delight; the latter said only: "Was it worth going to see such a stupid farce?" Many people feel that the government should not approve a play in which it is so harshly censured. I saw Gogol yesterday. He wears the expression of a great man tormented by a wounded pride. Gogol, however, has really performed a great service. The impression produced by his comedy adds substantially to what we are coming to realize about the existing order of things in our country.[1]

Thus, two divergent camps faced each other in opposition. The old diehards saw in *The Inspector General* a libel on the Russian people. On the other side, Pushkin, Prince Viazemsky in *The Contemporary*, and somewhat later the critic Vissarion Belinsky, defended the play vigorously. Belinsky hailed Gogol as the "poet of reality."

But Gogol himself was unhappy. He felt the world had turned against him.

Elderly and respectable civil servants are shouting [he wrote] that, having dared to speak like that about civil servants, I hold nothing sacred. The policemen are against me, the merchants are against me, the literary clique is against me. They abuse me and go to see my play; all the tickets for the fourth performance are sold out ...[2]

With what eagerness he had worked on this play and how he had looked forward to its production! Upon completing it, he had written to Pogodin in jubilation:

Now let us laugh, let us laugh as much as possible, Long live Comedy![3]

What sweat and energy in order to break down the objections of the censors—and it was only through the steps taken by Zhukovsky and Aleksandra Smirnova, lady-in-waiting to the Empress, that he had finally succeeded in breaching the barricades of opposition. He had already before this abandoned a satire on bureaucracy, *The Vladimir Cross*, in which an ambitious but empty-headed government official aspires to this honor with such a fanatic intensity that he dreams of being turned into the Cross. Instead he had composed a harmless though highly amusing comedy of middle-class life, *The Marriage*, a subject at which, he said, "even the police commissioner would not be offended." "But what good is a comedy devoid of truth and malice?"[4] "Malice, laughter, and salt," were not these the necessary ingredients? In desperation he had turned to Pushkin,

> Give me [he implored] anything for a subject and I will compose a comedy in five acts, I swear, that it will be funnier than the very devil.[5]

Pushkin may indeed have suggested the subject of *The Government Inspector*, out of his own similar experience, but the theme of mistaken identity has innumerable analogues in literature, and it is very likely that Gogol drew on many other sources for hints that he amalgamated into his own original version. Yet few of these ante-cedents could have supplied the genius which went into Gogol's composition. One merely has to compare Gogol's comedy with one of its archetypes, undoubtedly familiar to the Russian writer, *Die deutschen Kleinstädter* (*German Provincials*), by that most prolific, popular, and mediocre German dramatist Kotzebue, to note what genius can achieve.[6]

Gogol had undoubtedly struck home. He had lanced that most cankerous sore in Russian society—its general corruption. How prevalent it was—how generally accepted as a common *modus vivendi*—may be judged from the attitude of Gogol's mother, a simple, generous and well-intentioned person, who entertained high hopes of her son's enrichment in the Civil Service from the concomitant perquisites derived from bribes! Even university professors were not immune to such temptations in grading civil service examinations![7]

Among the pack of rascals and adventurers he was satirizing, Gogol insisted there was one "honest, noble character there ... Laughter." "Laughter that deepens every-thing ... without whose penetrating force man would be aghast at the emptiness and pettiness of existence."[8] Thus Gogol sanctified Laughter. He had hoped through its agency to cleanse the moral atmosphere. He had miscalculated. He could not have foreseen, of course, its ultimate effect on succeeding generations. The radical writer Chernyshevsky was to epitomize its impact by saying that Gogol had "awakened our self-consciousness."

In looking back on his literary career in St. Petersburg, Gogol did not have much cause for complaint. He had arrived there in 1818 at the age of twenty, a "raw youth" in quest of a government position but already obsessed by his literary ambi-tions. In 1831 he leaped into fame as the author of a series of Ukrainian folk tales, *Evenings on a Farm near Dikanka*, and had received acclaim and won the friendship of Zhukovsky and Pushkin. With pride he could inform his boyhood friend, Danilevsky,[9]

> Almost every evening we gathered together: Zhukovsky, Pushkin and I. Oh, if you only knew how much that is delightful flows from the pen of these men!

The succeeding five years had been almost continuously productive, as he published another of the *Dikanka* tales, remarkable short stories in a collection called *Arabesques*, a historical novelette "Taras Bulba," a story collection *Mirgorod*, and a series of comedies.

What young writer embarking on a writing career would not have relished the kind of reception young Gogol experienced at the hands of the greatest poet, himself no mean storyteller, when *Evenings on a Farm near Dikanka* appeared? For this is what Pushkin wrote in August 1831 in a letter to the magazine, *Russky Invalid*:

> I have just read Evenings by the Dikanka. It astonished me. Here is real gaiety, which is sincere, unforced, without affectation, without pomposity. And in places what poetry! What sensitivity! All that is so unusual for our contemporary literature that I have not yet come to my senses … For God's sake take his side, if the reviewers in their customary manner attack the *indecency* of his expressions, the *mauvais ton* etc. It is high time that we laughed *les précieuses ridicules* of our literature to scorn, those people who are for ever talking of their "fair readers," which they have never had, of the highest social circles, to which they are not invited.[10]

Such was the enviable tribute extended to the raw youth from the Ukrainian province of Poltava, the scion of a lesser-gentry Cossack family. His father, a sickly man with literary pretensions, died when the boy was sixteen, By that time his mother, who had married at the age of fourteen, had borne twelve children, few of whom survived. She was a simple, unsophisticated and very superstitious woman, who, after her husband's death, proved far from an efficient manager of the family's estate at Vasilyevka. Nikolay Gogol, her son, was the apple of her eye: upon him she lavished her affection and in him she placed her hopes. Deeply religious, she filled her children's imaginations with pictures of otherworldly bliss attendant upon a good life here on earth, and horrifying visions of the tortures to which sinners were exposed in the eternal flames of hell. High-strung, sensitive, Nikolay never outgrew this kind of "education." Whatever his own psychological and physical disposition, there can be little doubt that the terrors described with such vividness impressed themselves forcefully upon his imagination and in later years formed a part of his obsessional character. He dreamt of St. Petersburg and a literary career. His mother dreamt of the high offices that would fall to her precocious son, despite a mediocre school record that could at best win him an inferior rank in the official hierarchy of government clerks.

St. Petersburg at first proved far from the hospitable haven and heaven he had imagined. Believing himself to be a poet, he had composed an "idyl" entitled *Hans Küchelgarten* and had it printed in St. Petersburg at his own expense under the pseudonym of V. Alov. But he soon suffered a traumatic shock. The few reviews that deigned to notice the poem were devastating. The young would-be poet bought up the bookseller's remaining copies and burned them. This was a very perspicacious stroke of self-criticism: Gogol realized he was no poet.

The "idyl" in "eighteen pictures" was no worse than hundreds of such idyls and pastorals that had flourished during the preceding century, most of them inspired by a celebrated poem, *Luise*, by the German poet J. H. Voss. Gogol's German hero, a true German romantic, has his allotment of *Weltschmerz*—that indefinite cosmic yearning swelled by vaporous aspirations and restlessness. Like his predecessors he must "wander" abroad. Roaming as far as Greece but never finding the world he is seeking, he finally settles down to a constructive and peaceful domesticity, in secure *Gemütlichkeit*, a cozy bourgeois existence, with his ever-patient beloved. The only element in common between Hans and Nikolay Gogol, so far as this poem is concerned, is the *Wanderlust*—his need to "get away"—which was to be one of Gogol's lifelong obsessions.

But his literary *auto-da-fé* did not deter Gogol from pursuing literary ambitions. He turned to prose fiction, and in the process of realizing himself in that medium, he, along with Pushkin, inaugurated a new era of prose in Russian literature. For Pushkin was publishing his remarkable prose tales at practically the same time. Both Pushkin and Gogol were, in their way, responding to the needs and requirements of a growing readership eager for new ideas, new forms, presented in imaginative terms and less susceptible to the strictures and vagaries of censorship. And what was even more remarkable, Gogol was presenting life—but life spiced with such laughter as to astonish readers who, in Pushkin's estimation, hadn't laughed like that in many years.[11]

The laughter of which Pushkin speaks was to resound often, and with deeper notes, as Gogol's horizon expanded artistically through a widening life-experience. But these folk-tales of Ukrainian life, the *Dikanka* tales, with their rich colloquial sensuousness, with their earthiness, catch the full savor of Ukrainian village communities, their inhabitants and their superstitions. Despite the surrounding laughter, many of these tales are actually ridden with terror, full of witchcraft and Satanic incursions. Such terrors, witches and devils were not—as they might have been for E. T. A. Hoffmann and his successors in provincial but sophisticated Germany, or for the British, or French—an aesthetic game, brilliantly enacted but none the less not to be taken too seriously. Among the impoverished peasant and serf populations of the Russian village, and even the Russian town, they were realities; even among the isolated landowners as well as the more worldly Cossack settlements, the hold of the supernatural was strong indeed. That which one's own efforts could not attain to—riches, love, a husband or wife—appeals to the Devil and his cohorts might achieve. And how delightful, too, if one could at times outwit those infernal spirits and pay them back for the frights they engendered! In one of the stories, the beautiful but haughty Oksana must have the Tsarina's shoes before she will consent to accept the burly, handsome but poor blacksmith Vakula. Vakula succeeds in obtaining mastery of the Devil and wins not only the Tsarina's shoes, but Oksana as well. But the tales that boast of successes over Satan are balanced by those accompanied by frightful consequences. Thus, the peasant Petro, alas! too poor to marry the girl he loves, falls into the clutches of Satan's alter ego, is lured to search for a hidden treasure, and murders an innocent child. A daughter, in another tale, discovers that her new, very beautiful stepmother is actually a witch, and drowns herself. But the full acme of terror and tragedy is reached in "A Terrible Vengeance," which mingles horror with incest, when an Antichrist figure, burdened with an inherited curse, brings destruction on his own daughter, her husband, and himself.[12]

There was also another world, not ridden, it is true, by witches and devils of a supernatural order, but no less filled with darkness and terror—the world of one's interior, with one's own Satanic spirits, one's own devils, one's own panics and nightmares. Already in *Dikanka* Gogol had included such stories as that of "Ivan Shponka," a simple, naive and withdrawn ex-lieutenant, whose only joy in life consisted in attending to his duties. On retiring and taking over his family estate, he is persuaded by his aunt to court a neighboring lady. The prospect of such a step triggers a trauma:

> Ivan Fyodorovich stood as though thunderstruck. It was true that Marya Grigoryevna was a very nice-looking young lady, but to get married! It seemed to him so strange, so peculiar, he couldn't think of it without horror. Living with a wife! Unthinkable! He would not be alone in his own room, but they would always have to be two together! ...

And then he has a grotesque dream.

> ... He was running and running, as fast as his legs could carry him. Now he was at his last gasp. All at once someone caught him by the ear. "Ouch! Who is it?" "It's me, your wife!" a voice resounded loudly in his ear, and he woke up. Then he imagined he was married, that everything in their little house was so peculiar, so strange: a double bed stood in his room instead of a single one; his wife was sitting on a chair. He felt queer: he did not know how to approach her, what to say to her, and then he noticed that she had the face of a goose. He happened to turn aside and saw another wife, also with the face of a goose. Turning again, he saw yet another wife; and behind him a fourth... Then he suddenly dreamed that a wife was not a human being at all, but a sort of woollen material; then he went into a shop in Mogilyov. "What sort of stuff would you like?" asked the shopkeeper. "You had better take a wife, that is the most fashionable material! It wears well! Everyone is having coats made of it now." The shopkeeper measured and cut off a wife. Iven Fyodorovich put her under his arm and went off to a Jewish tailor. "No," said the Jew, "that is poor material. No one has coats made of that now."[13]

One need not be a specialist in the workings of the human mind to note at once the very significant and peculiar elements in this narrative. What they meant so far as the writer himself was concerned will become more apparent when his later works are examined. At this point one may merely indicate a few guideposts: evasion and flight—in this case from a close relationship with a woman; the transformation of the woman in the nightmare into a creature of the animal world, or into an object—what might be called the "reification" of the human element and an alienation from it. A later comedy, *Marriage*, presents a more realistic treatment of the same theme: the protagonist-suitor jumps out of a window at a critical moment in order to escape commitment. As in the story, so in the play, the grotesquerie of the situation is brilliantly merged with seriousness—anxiety and terror. We may add, also, that in Gogol's supernatural stories the devils are frequently playful fellows, the witches, on the other hand, invariably baneful.

The years between 1831 and 1836 were for Gogol notably creative ones. St. Petersburg inspired his genius and offered him the characters and background for his most celebrated short stories, especially those concerned with the "little nobodies"—the civil servants—ample material for satire, the grotesque, as well as the pathetic. It was at this time that he composed "The Nose," and "The Diary of a Madman." His interest in the Ukraine, Ukrainian history and Cossack life found lively realization in the short prose-epic of "Taras Bulba," lusty, bloody, broad and brutal. He resigned his official government position and turned teacher, first at a girls' institute, later as lecturer in history at the University of St. Petersburg. Totally unfitted for an academic career, he concluded it after what he called "sixteen inglorious months of … humiliation," with a resounding fiasco. He was not a professional historian, he was not made to be a teacher, and he was a poor judge of his own abilities. Young Ivan Turgenev, one of students, testifies to this "tragi-comedy":

> I attended Gogol's lectures in 1835 when he was teaching history at St. Peterburg University. To tell the truth, this "teaching" was carried on in a peculiar manner. First of all, Gogol was sure to miss two lectures out of three; secondly, even when he did appear on the rostrum, he didn't speak, but whispered something rather incoherent, showed us little etchings with views of Palestine and other oriental countries, and was extremely embarrassed throughout the whole period… During the final examination in his subject, he sat there with a kerchief tied around his head, allegedly because he was suffering from a toothache, with an expression of utter despondency on his face, and didn't even open his mouth… As if it were today, I see his lean, long-nosed figure before me, with the two ends of a black silk kerchief sticking up high above his head, looking like ears…[14]

In May 1836, the year of *The Inspector General*, he wrote to his friend Pogodin:

> A modern writer, a comic writer, a writer of memoirs, must be as far away from his homeland as possible.[15]

This was written a month after his departure from Russia in the company of his good friend Danilevsky. Except for two brief sojourns in his fatherland, he was to remain away from 1836 to 1848. He was taking with him a few chapters of a new novel which he had begun in 1835. It is hard to enter into Gogol's feelings at this time—but there is no question that there was an upsetting turmoil within him, a restlessness, a fever that was to drive him from place to place and take him to Paris, to Rome, even to Jerusalem. At the same time he was also in high spirits. To Zhukovsky he wrote,

> I swear that I shall do something that no ordinary man could do. I feel a lion's strength in my soul and I can almost feel the transition from childhood, spent in school exercises, to manhood.[16]

Whatever it is that he was fleeing from or fleeing towards, he felt that he was under the special guidance of Heaven, and in the same letter to Zhukovsky insisted:

> My present withdrawal from my fatherland has been decreed from above by the same great Providence sent for my education. This is the great turning point, a great epoch of my life. I will not return soon for anything in the world. I shall stay abroad as long as I can.

He roamed the cities of the continent. Now he was in Paris, where he sought out Adam Mickiewicz, attracted no doubt by his messianic mysticism, but scarcely out of a concurrence in Mickiewicz's political radicalism; he went to Baden-Baden for a cure (he was becoming more and more a hypochondriac); and then to Rome, his only semi-permanent resting place. Rome was to be his refuge from the terrors that haunted him, the terrors within him, but also from that terror he would later call "the horrors and terrors of Russia." Sporadically he recognized that that there was no such thing as flight from oneself or from one's land, as he confessed in 1846 in reply to a troubled letter from one of his women correspondents:

> What you report to me in secret, is only a small part of the story. Were I to tell you all that I know (and I doubtless do not know all), your spirits would be darkened, and your sight blinded, and you would think of only one thing: How can I flee from Russia? But where should one flee? That is the question. The situation in Europe is even more difficult than that of Russia.[17]

The tragic death of Pushkin served further to unsettle him and reinforce his decision. Urged by his friend Pogodin to return to Russia, Gogol asks, "What for? To repeat the fate of poets in my homeland?"

In Rome he felt most at ease. Here was an almost paradisiacal haven. Here he felt safe when he returned from his various feverish excursions. He could not savor enough of the air, the monuments, the atmosphere of Rome's medieval antiquity. Here he shut himself off from the political stirrings that were agitating Italy. In the cloistered medievalism of the Papal domains he worked, at times with fierce intensity, to complete his prose "poem"—as he called it—the novel *Dead Souls*, which he had brought with him. Italy and the novel were now his obsessions. Italy, he wrote to Zhukovsky, was "his." "No one in the world will take her away from me. I was born here." He feasted on her magnificent beauty, and shouted with exuberance, "Life, life, a little more of life!"[18]

It was with the same febrile intensity, once the spirit moved him, that he would turn to writing the novel. Pavel Annenkov, who has left us one of the most vivid chronicles describing his contemporaries, graphically depicts Gogol in Rome, entirely shut off from the world outside. Just as in Paris he had remained indifferent to political events, believing it was not the business of a poet to "intrude into the world's market-place," so in the Papal States he scarcely took note of the stirs and tensions in the political arena.

During his European stay, Gogol tended more and more to associate himself with Russian aristocratic families, among them that of Princess Smirnova, the Balabins, and the Volkonskys. The Princess Volkonsky tried to convert him to Roman Catholicism, to which she herself adhered. He was already something of a celebrity as a writer, greatly admired for his stories and welcomed in many of the prominent households both in Russia and abroad. Flattered, and listened to with interest, he began developing a tendency to consider himself a kind of bard-prophet, whose "pure, spotless soul speaks only to God." There were, of course, those who admired him genuinely for his great literary talent and saw in him the natural heir of Pushkin. Others tended to see him as a useful and gifted as well as highly articulate pillar of their own conservative, even reactionary, political, social, and religious convictions. Such associations were to exert a serious influence on Gogol's own spiritual and ideological direction.

The writing of *Dead Souls* did not always prove easy. Often Gogol felt barren. Then, suddenly, unexpectedly, in strange places, inspiration came upon him, and he would begin writing... And he would write and write.

On his second return to Russia in the fall of 1841, he brought with him the completed first part of *Dead Souls*. The Moscow censors proved obdurate and refused to pass the book for publication. He was more fortunate in St. Petersburg, where the friendship of Zhukovsky availed much, aided by the good sense of censor Aleksandr Nikitenko. Gogol acquiesced in certain of the required modifications, and the book appeared at the beginning of June 1842.

Gogol described his tribulations with the Moscow censor in his own humorous way: "The committee" of censors, he wrote, received the book

> as though they had been prepared for it, and were attuned to playing a comedy. For all their objections were without exception farcical to the highest degree. As soon as the chairman of the committee, Golokhvastov, heard the title, *Dead Souls*, he cried in the voice of an ancient Roman: "No, this I shall never allow. A soul is immortal. There cannot be a dead soul. The author is taking up arms against immortality."[19]

There were other brain-athletes who saw in the book an attack on the institution of serfdom. However, the book did appear, with the slightly modified title of *The Adventures of Chichikov, or, Dead Souls*.

* * *

Seven years before the publication of *Dead Souls*, Gogol had written to Pushkin, who had vaguely suggested the theme:

> I have begun writing *Dead Souls*. The subject has already expanded into a very long novel and I think it's going to be very funny. But now I have stopped in the third chapter. I am looking for a good slanderer with whom I might get acquainted. In this novel I should like to show the whole of Russia, even if only from one side.[20]

By the time Gogol completed the first part of *Dead Souls*, he had found not only the slanderer but many other characters and situations to fill out the vast canvas he was projecting. In the process of creating, Gogol changed much, and as happens so often in the career of great writers, the work became enlarged not only physically, but also in richness and depth. It was the heir of a host of literary traditions and literary works, styles, manners, subjects—as happens with any grand masterpiece—but the addendum of that magic element called genius crystallized it into something new and unique. In searching for antecedents and analogues of *Dead Souls* one can easily trace the impress of Homer, Cervantes, Laurence Sterne; the picturesque elements of the "picaro" or "rogue" romances; and, not least, Russian folklore and folk life.

Gogol called his novel a *Poema*—a "Poem"—meaning thereby an epic, a term frequently employed for a prose novel of some extent. In place of a grand Homeric hero, however, we are presented with Russia's grand "anti-hero," Pavel Ivan Chichikov. And we are introduced to him at once:

> *V vorota gostinnitsi gubernskovo goroda NN. ...*

> A rather smart little chaise on springs—such as is favored by bachelors, half-pay lieutenant-colonels, staff captains, and landowners with about a hundred serfs—in

short, all such as are spoken of as "gentlemen of a middling sort,"—drove through the gates of an inn in the provincial town of NN. In the chaise sat a gentleman, who could be called neither handsome, nor homely, not too stout, but not too thin; it could not be said that he was old—nor was he very young either...[21]

What would this Pavel Ivanovich be doing in the provincial town of NN? We are soon told: He is buying serfs. But strangely enough, he is buying not live serfs; for that, he is not rich enough. It is dead serfs—"dead souls"—that he is after. Serfs in that day were taxable property, and a government census was taken every ten years. Serfs who had died in the interim remained on the tax-rolls, a liability on the landowners. One day our "hero" had the brilliant idea—while at work in a government office and at his wits' end as to how to re-establish himself financially—of buying up such "dead souls," and (since serfs could be mortgaged to the State Treasury for considerable sums) mortgaging them, enriching himself, and leading a good life. At the same time he would be relieving the seller of a burdensome debt.

Chichikov—to carry forward the epic analogue—is Gogol's Ulysses. In his chariot he will course the Russian provinces in quest of his new self, and wealth. This may indeed be a purpose more mundane than that of Ulysses; but then, the world that Chichikov is exploring is so different from that of Ulysses's day. But like Ulysses—in Tennyson's poem—Chichikov too must explore "manners, climates, councils, governments." Like any modern shrewd trader, he must explore the "territory" so as to gauge the possibilities of success. He must make the acquaintance of the foremost citizens of the provincial town—the local governor, the district judge, the postmaster, the police commissioner, and, of course, the landowners who might be willing to cooperate in his strange enterprise...

Chichikov is astute and engaging. The local gentry take to him; he is invited to dinners, at which his inquiries seem matters of course: How many serfs has so-and-so? Have there been any epidemics in the vicinity? Many deaths among the serfs?

And now we meet them, one by one—the gallery of landowners, a most remarkable collection. There's Manilov, the embodiment of a feudal *laissez-faire*. Nothing in his house is ever finished; the book he is reading is always open to page 14. He is even willing to give Chichikov his "dead souls" for nothing! Chichikov capers with delight. For, mind you, this fellow Chichikov is a great actor. Though his own career has been checkered by not a few peccadilloes and minor transgressions, he manages to put on the act of someone who has suffered innumerable persecutions. "What have I not suffered ... for having followed the path of justice," he cries, almost in tears, and for "being true to my conscience!"

Then we meet Madame Korobochka, herself an astute trader, who acquiesces once Chichikov promises her other "government contracts." There is Nozdrev, a fantastic scapegrace of a landlord, a liar, a gambler, a backbiter, a tale-bearer, a master at insults, a cheat out of a sheer love of cheating, who grows very angry when exposed. Chichikov barely escapes with his skin intact, but without any serfs...

And Sobakevich (as in all other instances in Gogol's story, each name has a meaning, and *sobaka* means "dog") has a face "broad and round as a Moldavian pumpkin," while his wife's is "long and narrow as a cucumber, crowned with a cap." It seems that nature, in shaping Sobakevich's face had eschewed using such fine tools as a file or gimlet, but had rough-hewn him with an axe, and formed his eyes with a drill. But he is no slouch of a trader himself. "'You are in need of dead souls,' Sobakievich inquired with simplicity, without a show of surprise, as if they were talking about bread." He had penetrated Chichikov's soul. And he asks the astonishing price of a hundred rubles apiece.

Long before the term "black humor" was invented, Gogol had mastered it. The scene with Sobakevich is one of the many supreme examples. When he is faced by an outraged Chichikov, Sobakevich is amazed. "Why," he explains, "they are all craftsmen and sturdy peasants," and he retails their particular aptitudes, skills, and virtues! He grows eloquent. When Chichikov counters that they are dead, Sobakevich retorts, "You're trying to buy them, so that means they are worth something. They are wanted." He finally sells the serfs at two and a half rubles apiece...

We are in the realm of the epic grotesque. Homeric laughter turned into the macabre of the modern market.

There is more, much more. There is still Plyushkin, the epic miser, owner of a thousand serfs, possessor of a neglected estate fallen into decay, yet whose granaries and storehouses are filled to the bursting point. For Plyushkin saves everything, and all around him is colossal disorder. Unlike other landowners, he is gaunt, and his chin is so prominent that he is forced to cover it with a handkerchief whenever he spits. His eyes scurry like mice, and are as watchful. Chichikov's heart bounds with delight when he learns that a fever has killed off many of Plyushkin's peasants, and that since the last census there are some one hundred and twenty "dead souls." There is one more touch in this particular scene that will serve for hundreds of potential descriptions of Plyushkin's miserliness. He summons his little thirteen-year-old servant Proshka, who appears "wearing such large boots that he seemed to be stepping out of them as he walked." For Plyushkin keeps only one pair of boots for all his servants, and this lone pair stands in the hallway ready to accommodate any of the serfs who are to make their entrance.

Now Chichikov is the owner of hundreds of "souls." Among them are also "live" ones—that is, serfs who have run away. If he mortgages all of them he will be worth hundreds of thousands of rubles, he will marry and have heirs and become an honored and respectable member of society. Is he a rogue and a scoundrel? And what of the others?

The grotesque is a secular form of exorcism. It has its origin in the urges of defiance: defiance of the horror or terror of life, defiance with twisted laughter. It is recrimination against powers, agencies, forces, natural or supernatural, that threaten human existence, while at the same time it is a form of self-affirmation and affirmation of human power to defy such threats. It is in its way a distortion of sublimity. In the gargoyle it is plastic incantation—fear and broad laughter mingling, a juxtaposition of two contrasting, conflicting elements. In the modern artist it is the unquenchable need to protest against destructive realities by "estranging" them for the spectator, to use a Brechtian term. It recalls such realities by hunting them out of their terrestrial heights or hells—just as the medieval artist sought them out in the trans-terrestrial spheres. Caricature enlarges upon one feature of a phenomenon; the grotesque embraces a totality of experiences.

In Gogol the grotesque is likewise an "exorcism" of the "horror and terror" of the world, this time of Russia. For him the center of his grotesque lies in the juxtaposition of Life and Death. Such a grotesque can assume many forms; it can range from the gentle to the savage; from the ridiculous to the sardonic; from the pathetic to the tragic; from the eerie to the macabre. Gogol's overall mastery of the grotesque is revealed in the drama of the figurative "exhumation" of already dead serfs, who even during their lifetime of wretchedness and misery were scarcely living creatures, and who are not allowed to rest even in their graves. Traded while they were alive, they are still traded when dead.

They do come to life, these peasant serfs, if only for a brief moment. Back in his hotel room, Chichikov begins to go over the rolls of his "acquisitions." As he reads over the names and the crafts of the "souls," Chichikov reflects:

> Goodness, dear chaps! How many of you are crowded in here! And what did you do, dear souls, in your lifetime? How did you manage to get along? Accidentally his eyes rested on one name. It was that of Pyotr Savelyev, nicknamed "You've put your foot in it," an ancient serf belonging to Madame Korobochka. And again he could not refrain from saying, "My, how lanky he is! He stretches across the whole line!" Were you a crafts-man or just a common muzhik? And what sort of death did you die? Was it in a tavern brawl, or did some clumsy wagon run you over in your sleep? An you, Stepan Probka, Stepan "the Cork," carpenter, and model of sobriety! Ah, Stepan Probka, carpenter, and model of sobriety! Giant of a man, fit to join the Guards! How you must have trudged the provinces, axe in belt, boots slung over the shoulder, eating a kopeck's worth of bread and two kopecks worth of dried fish, though I wager you carried home a hundred or so rubles in silver in your bag each time, or a note sewed up in your hempen breeches or stuck in your boot! Where did you meet your death? Did you climb up the church steeple, or perhaps even try to reach the cross, and did you slip down from the cross-beam, and strike the ground with a thud, and some Uncle Mikhey, who was standing by, scratched the back of his neck, and said, "Ekh, Vanya, this time you've really done it!" And tying a rope around him, began climbing in your place? …
>
> And what about you dear chappies? he went on, casting his eyes on the list on which Plyushkin's runaway serfs were inscribed. You're still alive, but what's the good? You might as well be dead. Where have your nimble legs carried you? Were you so badly off with Plyushkin? Or are you roaming and scouring the highways? Are you in jail, or have you found new masters for whom you plough the land?[22]

It is a piece of triumphant irony on the part of Gogol to bring Chichikov into human contact with peasant-serfs who are dead and gone, and even bring him to ex-press some feeling about them, when during his whole lifetime he probably hadn't given a moment's thought or attention to their plight while they were alive! Chichikov, like Gogol himself, takes serfdom for granted, as if it had been deliberately designed by God.

Chichikov's star is at its apogee. He has become a legend in the district. The popu-lation endows him with qualities unnoted before. The ladies buzz about him. But he is not aware that he is teetering on the brink of disaster. Yes, the official transactions (aided by some subtle bribery) have all gone well. But alas! who could have predicted that at a public ball, at which he is the center, and where he pays court to the governor's lovely daughter, a bomb would fall and wreck his putative fortunes! A drunken Nozdrev makes his appearance and unmasks Chichikov not as the "millionaire" he is presumed to be, but as a buyer of dead souls! The jig is up and it is time to run.

Gogol had known all along that he was treading on dangerous ground. But what Russian writer was not? As early as 1836, he had written to Zhukovsky, while he was at work on the novel:

> Immensely great is my work, and its end is still far off. New classes of the population and many more people will rise up against me, but I'm afraid that cannot be helped. It is my lot to be in conflict with my fellow-countrymen. *Patience!* an invisible someone is writing before me with a mighty sceptre. I know that my name after me will be luckier than I and that the descendants of these self-same countrymen of mine will perhaps utter words of reconciliation to my shade with eyes moist with tears.[23]

In one of the chapters of *Dead Souls*, Gogol digresses to defend his novel and its hero. There are novelists, he states, who never stoop from their heights to touch the earth and mingle with their "poor, insignificant fellow-creatures, but continue to dedicate themselves to their remote and elevated images." These achieve ready fame, glory, and applause. But how different is the fate of the writer who has the temerity to present to the readers' eyes the "horrid slime of trivialities in which our lives are sunk, the inner depths of those cold, petty everyday characters who swarm on our bitter and dreary life's way." What critics, Gogol continues, recognize that the "telescope that brings the sun close to us, and the microscope that makes visible for us the movements of unnoticed insects," are equally wonderful?

"The time has come to harness the rogue." The microscope that Gogol has turned upon Russian humanity, has eschewed the "poor, virtuous hero" favored by other writers—another example of the hypocrisy of the times.

Who is this "rogue" Chichikov? Simply "a proprietary and acquisitive man." Why then is he "repulsive"? The very people who will turn from him aghast when he appears in a novel, will not disdain to dine with him and pass the time in his company! Is Chichikov any worse than, say, — ? And turning to the reader:

> You even guffaw over Chichikov, perhaps you will even praise the author, and say, "My— you must admit, once or twice he really hits the mark. He must be a jolly good fellow! After that, with a double measure of smugness and a smile of self-satisfaction, you add: "One must admit that in certain of our provinces you will find some bizarre and odd characters, a couple of whom might even turn out to be scoundrels!" But how many of you have enough Christian humility to search your conscience in private, and ask yourselves this question: "Don't I, too, have something of Chichikov in me?" Not one of you, I believe! But should an acquaintance of yours pass by, one, you understand, of middling rank, who of you will refrain from nudging your neighbor, and guffawing: "Look, there goes Chichikov!" and like a youngster, forgetful of the respect due his elders, you will run after him, and tease him: "Chichikov! Chichikov! Chichikov!"[24]

Early in June 1842, two days after the appearance of *Dead Souls*, Gogol was off again, bound for the Continent. His collected works in four volumes were to appear toward the end of that year, and among other published and unpublished pieces, contained the comedy "The Marriage", and Gogol's most celebrated short story "The

Overcoat." As usual, he was practically without funds, and henceforth would live on and off his friends, borrowing liberally and boarding with them. In both respects he was very fortunate. In their admiration for the writer, though too frequently taxed by his personal eccentricities and demands, they opened both their purses and their houses. Once again he was headed for Rome.

* * *

The year 1842 marks the end of one major epoch in Gogol's life and the beginning of another. He had reached his apogee as a creative artist. In his mind, however, there were innumerable plans, not the least being a continuation of *Dead Souls*.

In *Dead Souls* and in *The Inspector General* he had given us a picture of the middle gentry—a class mired in banality and dreariness, mediocrity and philistinism. But there was also a nether world, the world of the petty bureaucrat, the world, we might add, "of all of us," to which he had been and was drawn—a world too of nullities, of victims. Here there is no room for Homeric parodies; here we have little epics of degradation of which an earlier story, "The Diary of a Madman" (which had appeared in the collection *Arabesques*), the narrative of "Captain Kopeikin" (included as the postmaster's story in *Dead Souls*), and "The Overcoat" (published in 1842), may be taken as the prime exemplars.

In the drab figure of the *chinovnik*, the government clerk of low degree, Gogol embodied the tragi-comedy of *poshlost*—the platitude, banality and humdrum, even hopelessness of life, with its failed search for some illusory dream-fulfilment—the creation of an imaginary "double" that might in some measure justify a mean existence. Such a character is Poprishchin in "The Diary of a Madman," a government clerk gone mad, who finds escape in the insane illusion that he is the Spanish King Ferdinand VII, and understands the language of dogs, and can read their correspondence. He has his own "holy grail"—his eyes are fixed on the unattainable daughter of his Director, the destined bride of a Court Chamberlain. Poprishchin is forty-five years old, forever tethered to his inferior clerk's office, contemned by his immediate superior, his "chief." He finds his deepest joy in sharpening the quills of the Director and in catching a glimpse of the "Beatrice" of his aspirations.

The *chinovnik* is Gogol's Everyman, the ignoble forerunner of that long line of the "insulted and injured" destined to wend their way through Russian literature and unmoor the consciousness and conscience of innumerable readers. Of course, Gogol's "little man" is not a newcomer to Russian literature. He had a number of predecessors, notably in Pushkin's *The Brazen Horseman*.[25] But no one before Gogol had so deeply imprinted the character on Russian literature, as Dostoevsky was to testify. Neither French nor British literature has created his equal. Dickens' "Shabby-Genteel Man," of the *Sketches by Boz*, is Poprishchin's bourgeois British counterpart, but he never experiences the feeling of degradation and the self-torment of the Russian while he sits thumbing through books in the British Museum.

How could a Poprishchin and hundreds of his fellows ever hope to liberate themselves? How ever climb up that spiraling stair that runs from the lowest grade of collegiate councillor to titular councillor, collegiate assessor, and up, up to the empyrean heaven of General, Privy Councillor, and beyond? The heavy boot on the rung above presses hard on the shoulder of one below. How could one ever dare turn one's face and head so as to be able to look into the frozen face above? And every rank meek and groveling before a superior! Sometimes one can stand it no longer, and momentarily one rebels. Poprishchin obliterates this horror of nonexistence in the fantasy of a kingship, and ends in a madhouse where he is beaten. A shrieking *Miserere* breaks from him:

> No, I can't stand it any longer. My God! what are they trying to do to me?! They pour cold water on my head! They won't listen to me; they won't see me; they won't hear me! What have I done to them? Why do they torment me? What do they want from me, poor creature than I am? What can I give them? … Save me! Take me away! Give me a troika with speedy horses, that will fly like the whirlwind! Take your seat, driver, ring out, ring out my little bell, hasten forward my steeds, and carry me far away from this world! Farther, still farther away, so that nothing can be seen, nothing at all …

The episode of Captain Kopeikin in *Dead Souls* contains a suggestion of direct rebellion, unfortunately softened and modified by the collaboration of Gogol and the censor. It is a story of bureaucratic ineptitude and heartlessness. This time the victim is a veteran of the wars of 1812, who had lost an arm and a leg defending his Russian fatherland. He returns to Russia and finds himself without any means. He appeals directly to a high official in St. Petersburg, then to a commission, but is put off time and again, until driven to desperation. Furiously he turns upon the members of the commission:

> You … you … are … you don't even know your own duties … You pedlars of the law! …

He is admonished by a very high official, "You must help yourself. Find your own means," and forcibly escorted out of the building. Placed in a cart, he mutters to himself, "Find your own means? Yes, I will."

In deference to the censor's wishes, Gogol changed the character of Kopeikin and turned him into a greedy epicure who makes excessive demands for "cutlets, French wines, and theatre!" Kopeikin squanders the money a high official gives him. But even in the censored version enough came through to make Gogol's point. What means Kopeikin eventually found is not, of course, made clear. Perhaps, like the hero of Pushkin's story "Dubrovsky," he became a brigand …

Gogol's most triumphant depiction of the *chinovnik* is without doubt to be found in "The Overcoat." Here is a small epic of alienation and degradation. Here Gogol struck the full ground-notes of the "little man's" agonies. Even his name speaks of nothingness. He is called Akaky Akakievich Bashmachkin. The given patronymics are scatological; and the surname stands for "shoe." His own colleagues (themselves objects of contempt and persecution by their superiors) heap insults upon him. He earns a bare 400 rubles, and is the perennial titular councillor. Life offers him scant joys, but there is one that is incomparable: He loves to copy documents, and even takes his work home with him (he has no family), in order to continue and complete it. But Petersburg winters are severe; his coat is old and frayed, and can no longer be repaired. He must have a new one made. He will eat less, be careful about the way he walks so as not to wear out his shoes; he will save as much as he can.

Now he dreams his dream: the new overcoat! And he realizes it. With the acquisition of this magnificent garment he becomes a person. Even his colleagues now pay attention to him, and invite him to a party. Thoughts that had slumbered within him now come to the fore—even erotic ones! Unfortunately, going home after the party, in the dark night, he is assaulted by two thieves who rob him of his coat and beat him to the ground. He embarks on a vain search to recover his treasure. To whom shall he turn? First to the police commissioner, then to the Person of Consequence—and in both cases he suffers nothing but arrogance, humiliation and insults. Now, this Person of Consequence had only recently been a Person of No Consequence, and he reprimands Akaky Akakievich for his insolence in not having proceeded through "proper channels" before making his appearance in the grandee's chambers. Akaky Akakievich staggers out into the cold streets, into the snowstorm, catches cold, and within a few days, dies ...

What follows is transcendental phantasy. Rumors spread all over St. Petersburg that a corpse looking much like a government clerk is haunting one of the city's quarters looking for a stolen overcoat, and in the process stripping coats from passers-by. One of these is none other than the very important Person of Consequence. "So here you are," the clerk shouts, "at last I've got you, and it's your overcoat I'm taking." Thereafter the apparition ceases to haunt the city.

As for Akaky—well, he was dead, he had died the death of a "nobody," and as Gogol put it, "Petersburg carried on without him." What of the overcoat? That acquired a personality, a life. For can Akaky Akakievich be said to have really lived before he acquired the overcoat? This was his *alter ego*—his *Doppelgänger*, his unrealized self come to life. Akaky is what he appears—the overcoat. For a short moment he has broken out of the cage of nonbeing, becomes human, and is recognized as a human being. The fetishism of things has changed him into a human entity, just as it often changes a person into a thing ...

In "The Overcoat" we move from the lucid realms of Pushkin into dark corners, the "underside" of human consciousness. We have come upon the "underground" man, who for a moment emerges from the dismal cellars of nothingness into the light of elementary "being." And for a brief moment, Gogol, who had not customarily given way to this anguish of existence of the No-man, raises a sob-freighted cry through the lips of his madman and utters the muted whimper of Akaky Akakievich, a "creature vanished and departed." For a moment the frozen hell in which its inhabitants lie congealed is thawed, and a human being emerges ...

For Gogol Russia remained a mystery, and, as he believed, would remain a mystery to the rest of the world. An apostrophe included in *Dead Souls* evokes that mystery:

Nye tak li i ti, Rus, shto boiikaya neobroneemaya troika, neseshsya?

Are you not like that too, Russia, as you speed along like a spirited troika, not to be overtaken? Underneath you, the road smokes, the bridges thunder, all is overtaken and left behind. The passer-by stands amazed, as if struck by a miracle from heaven. May not this be a lightning bolt from heaven? What is the meaning of this terrifying onrush? What mysterious power is it that resides in these horses, unknown to the world? Ekh, your horses! And what horses! Are whirlwinds secreted in your manes? Is there some sharp

ear in every one of your veins? … Russia, where are you flying? Answer! She does not answer. The bells tinkle enchantingly; the air is torn to shreds, and whirls like the wind.
Everything on earth is flying past you; and askance the other nations and peoples draw
aside and make way for her.[26]

Thus Gogol apostrophizes Russia at the conclusion of the first part of *Dead Souls*,
at the moment when Chichikov is racing away from the town of NN. toward his future destiny. Gogol, too, was on his way to face his destiny, but away from Russia.

Dead Souls met with the same divided reception as *The Inspector General*. Whatever
the interpretations later generations would put on the novel, when academics and
others would subject both *Dead Souls* and "The Overcoat" to various investigations
ranging from the mystagogical and allegorical to the psychographic, for Gogol's contemporaries the meaning of his writing about Russia was clear enough. Gogol was describing the Russia of his day. The censors led the way of interpretation by expunging
or having expunged passages that they believed to be incriminating. Critics of the
conservative wing had no doubts either: the Bulgarins and their cohorts meted out
abuse to *Dead Souls* with a generosity only too common among critics of all times,
sparing neither venom nor vocabulary. In their eyes the novel was the epitome of vulgarity, obscenity, and vilification. Russia, in their opinion, had never before suffered
such grievous defamation as now. On the other side, Russian liberals likewise agreed
that Gogol's book had Russia herself in view. For them, the novel was a superlative
creation, particularly valuable for its exposure of the *poshlost*—the vulgarity, meanness, banality—of Russian gentry life. Vissarion Belinsky proclaimed Gogol the leader
of the new "natural" school of fiction. Konstantin Aksakov crowned Gogol another
Homer. The so-called "younger" generation, that of the 1840s and 1850s, saw in him a
guiding light in the war on oppression, hypocrisy, and exploitation, and his novel and
stories as the foundation stone of a new social aesthetic.

It is instructive to turn from his critics and interpreters to Gogol himself, when he
spoke in his own defense of the life he had depicted in *Dead Souls* and of his own talent to depict it:

This gift is revealed most forcibly in *Dead Souls*. If it frightened Russia and produced
such an outcry, it is not because it revealed her wounds, her sicknesses, or even because it
showed vice triumphant and virtue persecuted. Not at all! My heroes are far from being
criminals. All I had to do was to give one of them some sympathetic trait to reconcile my
readers with all the characters. But what frightened my public was the overall banality,
the fact that my heroes are all of them flat, and that the reader does not find one consoling picture, not the least occasion to rest or breathe easily, so that when he is through
with the book, he feels as if he had emerged from some underground basement. I would
have been pardoned had I drawn some picturesque monster, but the banality was unfor-
giveable. The Russian reader is more terrified of his nullity than of his weaknesses and
vices.[27]

He became recognized as posterity's spokesman. In 1851, Alexander Herzen wrote,

… *Dead Souls* shook the whole of Russia. It is a picture of her disease, painted by a master hand. Gogol's art is like a cry of shame and terror on the part of a man who has been
degraded by the vulgarity of existence and has suddenly perceived in a mirror his

animal-like features. But in order to release such a cry from one's breast, one must possess some healthy portions of a body as well, and a great capacity for restoring one's health.[28]

And Vissarion Belinsky, in 1847:

> Gogol's influence on Russian literature was tremendous. Not only all the young talents hastened along the path he had indicated, but some writers of repute abandoned the path which they had hitherto trodden to follow the new one. Hence the appearance of a school which its opponents thought to belittle by calling it the natural school ... His school alone now holds the literary scene.[29]

Gogol was not aware, of course, that with the publication of *Dead Souls* and the four-volume edition of his *Collected Works*, his purely literary career was over. He was to live on another ten years, for six of these still a "pilgrim," but the sources of creation seemed to have dried up, and the storms that racked his depths cast up no new pearls. It was not that he did not struggle. He strove for the rest of his life to complete his epic of *Dead Souls*, he tried to redefine his life and his life's work and clarify his mission. He sought also—and this proved most harrowing—to exorcise the sins he believed were in him, and cleanse his soul through prayer and deed. He was obsessed by the Satan he believed resided within him. In the end he succeeded in this task of self-discipline and self-mortification by killing his body. Trammeled by a sense of guilt that now embraced his published works, seared by penitence, he believed he would achieve redemption through new writings. But there was no retrieval. All the *mea culpas*, all the *peccavis* proved ineffectual in loosening the bonds that fettered his creation. The peace of mind and soul that he believed he could attain, not even a pilgrimage to the Holy Sepulchre in Jerusalem could achieve. He felt forsaken by God and saw the desiccation of his talents as a punishment from above.

All genius is obsessive; but its obsessions are creative, crystallizing in works of art or science or philosophy. Gogol was now beset as never before, but his obsessions were destructive, contradictory: his self-effacing humility warred with a megalomaniacal arrogance. Now he was down in the dust; now he was proclaiming his mission as prophet to the Russian people—guide, teacher, and prophet, specially designated by God. His masochism knew no bounds. He oscillated between a pathological submissiveness and an equally pathological need to dominate. Whatever his earlier "sins"—whether of carnal onanism or latent homosexuality—he turned them now into incitements to moralistic and spiritual self-flagellation.[30]

His life became a series of immolations. Just as in his early years he had tried to burn all available copies of *Hans Küchelgarten*, he destroyed in 1845 the completed portions of the second part of *Dead Souls*; and in 1852, the year of his death, he again burned a new version of the same work. He then completed his soul's and body's immolation by literally starving himself to death.

When the prophetic or apocalyptic urges were upon him he spoke as if the mantle of Elijah had descended upon him. A "wonderful work," he felt, was perfecting itself within him. He was a "precious vase"—though one still full of cracks, but filled with a treasure. "Oh, believe my words! From now on my word is clothed with the highest power. Everything can disappoint, deceive, betray, but my word will not betray."[31]

His friends and associations abroad tended to heighten this mystical fervor. There was the religious Russian painter Ivanov; in Rome, also, the leader of the German Nazarene painters, Friedrich Johann Overbeck; the Catholic Princess Aenaida Volkonskaya; Polish exiles strongly tinged with messianic mysticism; the recently deceased young Count Vielgorsky, whom Gogol had tended with almost a lover's devotion in his last illness; and not least, the ever-present Aleksandra Smirnova. The women found in Gogol a particularly persuasive teacher, whose prestige no doubt would also make for converts.

He began soon, if not to abjure his earlier works, to reinterpret them in the light of his own new visions. Rarely has a great writer so virulently disparaged and derogated his creations. "I do not like my works that have been written or published till now, especially *Dead Souls*," he wrote to Smirnova, after he had burned the new chapters of the book. He warned her not to be taken in superficially by the overt themes of the novel. The work, he now protested, had nothing to do with Russian provincial life or with a few monstrous landowners. It contained a "secret" which would be revealed in succeeding volumes.[32] It is possible that he was saying this out of his new-born honesty. But less pleasing are his remarks to the notorious minister Uvarov, who had reproached him with the tendencies to be found in his novels and stories. Gogol promised to reform, and to compose a work far more useful than his former "scribblings," for which, he said, Uvarov would be grateful, and much closer to Uvarov's own "convictions."[33]

He would now make clear to people how they had misinterpreted the intention and meaning of his previous works, and reveal their true secret significance by producing a new book that would at once astonish, electrify them, and disclose an altogether new Gogol ...

He proceeded to allegorize *The Inspector General* by unfolding its "secret." Of course, such a town as depicted in the play does not really exist. Well, he continues, what

> if this town is really our spiritual town, and is to be found in every one of us? ... Say what you will, but the government inspector who is waiting for us at the entrance of the grave is terrifying indeed. Why pretend? This government inspector is our awakening conscience, which forces us suddenly to take a good look at ourselves. From this government inspector nothing will be hidden, because he is sent by the Almighty ... Khlestakov is ... our frivolous, earthly conscience ... Through him we will never uncover anything in our soul ...[34]

Is it any wonder that recent critics, having been granted this passport and visa and freedom to allegorize Gogol, have allowed their own predilections and bents free play, even if at total variance with what Gogol himself had once stated? Thus one noted scholar transforms "The Overcoat" into Gogol's reprobation of the passion for earthly goods (i.e., an overcoat), and a parable on the need for self-denial and the consequences of a failure to devote oneself to one's soul.[35] Another well-known authority, Vladimir Nabokov, sees in our friend Chichikov a kind of "ill-paid representative of the Devil, a traveling salesman from Hades."[36]

To prove that he was actually "atoning for the uselessness of everything I have published until now," he set about writing a work containing "thoughts more needful to men than in my works." This was the *Selected Passages from Correspondence with Friends*, which appeared early in January, 1847. It was to be both a *confessio fidei* and a handy manual for the moral, political, religious, and social guidance of Russians, high and low. Governors of provinces as well as their wives are addressed with magisterial authority on how to conduct themselves and their affairs, and they and others are counseled on how best to bring about a restoration of the moral, political, religious and social order.

The recipe may be summed up as a recall to a "patriarchal" society as of yore, under the tutelage of the Russian Church, an absolute monarch and a "noble" aristocracy.

> This Church, which since the time of the Apostles has preserved her pristine purity, like a chaste virgin, this Church, with her profound teachings and her minutest external ceremonies, descended directly from Heaven for the sake of the Russian people, is capable of resolving all doubts and questions. In the face of all of Europe, she is capable of the greatest and most unheard of miracles—for she can induce all estates, offices and occupations to keep within their assigned limits, without shaking or overturning the State, she can make Russia great and powerful, and astonish the entire world through a well-framed harmonious order of an organism. ...[37]

Like the Church, so too the Russian Tsar is an agent "ordained, anointed by the Lord for the enlightenment of the people" who, though not responsible to any one at all, yet carries the awe of responsibility within him; who "perhaps sheds bitter tears in secret of suffering and anguish."

Having vindicated Orthodoxy and Absolutism, Gogol turned his attention to the landowner, whom he addresses as follows:

> Call all your peasants together, and explain to them what you are and what they are. That you are their landowner, because you were born a landowner, and because you will have to answer to God if you give up this calling for another. That everyone must serve God in *that* station in which he has been placed, and not in another. So they, the peasants, having been born under the authority of the landowner, must obey this authority, because there is no authority which is not from God. You must show them the New Testament, so that they will be convinced. Furthermore, you must tell them that you are making them work not because you need money for your pleasures and enjoyments, and to prove this, burn a few banknotes in their presence—and do it so, that they are convinced that money means nothing to you. Say to them that you are having them work because it is the will of God. God has commanded man to earn his bread by labor and by the sweat of his brow ... To teach a peasant to read, to enable him to read all those vapid books which the European humanitarians issue for the common people, is sheer nonsense. The peasant has not time for it anyway. The village priest can tell the peasant more of what is needful to him than all this book-rubbish ... Actually they must not know that there are other books in the world aside from the Holy Bible ...[38]

The peasant should be told that if he works diligently for "a year or so," he can become "as rich as Croesus" ...

As for the aristocracy, Gogol characterizes them as "the flower of our people," remarkable for their "moral nobility," a gift of God, and destined for the education of "all of Russia," especially the peasantry, who could become the models for all of

Europe. This Letter, addressed to a "Personage in High Office," was censored, perhaps because it also contained some sombre reflections on the moral condition of Russia, where, as Gogol put it, it is "difficult to govern," because of the numerous abuses prevalent. "There is not a single man in our country who is not to some extent guilty, so that it is impossible to say at first who is more guilty than another."[39]

Interspersed with these letters were others of an autobiographical nature, mostly apologies for the writer's failure to complete the second part of *Dead Souls*, and for the destruction of what had already been written—all ordained by the Lord, along with promises that out of these destructions a new work, like a "phoenix out of its ashes," would arise, purified and transfigured. "My task is the Soul ... When the proper hour strikes, that upon which I have labored painfully for five years, will see completion within a few weeks."[40]

That hour was never to strike. But Gogol was soon to learn what it is to feel all the anguish of a humbled pride. With the publication of *Selected Passages* he had expected at least to be recognized as Russia's prime writer-pedagogue, if not writer-prophet. What he received, was, in his own words, "a slap in the face." With very few exceptions, most of his friend were infuriated and outraged. Sergei Aksakov accused Gogol of insulting "God and humanity."[41]

Gogol felt as if his prophet's mantle had been rent and trod in the dust. "I am broken," he wrote.[42] But, as so often before, he consoled himself that it was all from God, and all for the best, a punishment for his arrogance. "I needed such a public slap in the face ... God suddenly has spread before me such a heap of treasures."[43] In addition, he prepared a public *apologia pro vita sua, An Author's Confession*, a prime example of humility and expostulation. He had hoped, he said, with his book to bring about reconciliation and harmony into the lives of Russians, but instead had only aroused strife and reproaches.

Now he was about to suffer the gravest blow of all.

Vissarion Belinsky, who had once proclaimed the coming of a "Gogol era" and of a new "natural school of literature" with Gogol as its leader, was outraged by the *Selected Passages*. In a review of it published in *The Contemporary*, he lashed out against Gogol's horrifying reactionary proclamations, particularly those that concerned the role of the Russian Church, the education of the peasantry, and the disparagement of the journalistic activities of the Belinsky group and their preoccupation with contemporary letters. The review found its target in the now vulnerable author. Gogol took the attack very personally and replied in a letter in which he asserted that he could not understand Belinsky's anger, for he had always believed that Belinsky was a good human being, free of malice.

Vissarion Belinsky was then at an Austrian spa, in Salzbrunn, when Gogol's letter was forwarded to him. He was already mortally ill of tuberculosis. (He would die in 1848.) He wrote a reply to Gogol, which, though it was not published until some years later, was circulated in manuscript and copies and almost immediately memorized. It would become one of the most celebrated manifestos—political and literary—of the generation of the forties and the fifties.

> Yes [Belinsky wrote], I loved you with all the passion with which a man, bound by ties of
> blood to his native country, can love its hopes, its glory ... on its path of consciousness,

development and progress. You have been accustomed for so many years to look at Russia from your *beautiful far-away*, ... you live in and within yourself or with a circle of the same mentality as your own, which is powerless to resist your influence on it. Therefore you failed to realize that Russia sees her salvation not in mysticism, asceticism, nor pietism, but in the successes of civilization, enlightenment and humanity.

What Russia needed, Belinsky continued, was not sermons or prayers, but an awakened sense of human dignity, rights and laws conforming with common sense and justice.

Instead of which she presents the dire spectacle of a country where men traffic in men, without even the excuse so insidiously exploited by the American plantation owners who claim that the Negro is not a human being.

At a time when

the most vital of national problems in Russia ... are the abolition of serfdom and corporal punishment,

Russia's "great writer," who had enabled her in the past to look at herself as though in a "mirror," comes out with a book teaching barbarian landowners how to make still greater profits out of their peasants! Had Gogol really been inspired by the "truth of Christ and not by the teachings of the Devil," he would have instructed the landowner that

since his peasants are his brethren in Christ, and since a brother cannot be slave to his brother, he should either give them their freedom or at least allow them to enjoy the fruits of their own labor to their greatest possible benefit ...

But this Gogol did not do. What right did he have to mix up Christ in his preachments, and laud the Orthodox Church and base his teachings on her, a Church "which has ever been the servant of despotism"! Gogol speaks of his spiritual conversion and of going on a pilgrimage to Jerusalem:

He who is capable of suffering at the sight of other people's oppression bears Christ within his bosom and has no need to make a pilgrimage to Jerusalem.

Proponent of the knout, apostle of ignorance, champion of obscurantism and Stygian darkness, panegyrist of Tatar morals—what are you about! Look beneath your feet—you are standing on the brink of an abyss! ...

If you have had the misfortune of disowning with proud humility your truly great works, you should disown with sincere humility your last book, and atone for the dire sin of its publication by new creations which would be reminiscent of your old ones.[44]

The impact of Belinsky's letter, even in its underground circulation, as it passed from hand to hand, was such that L. V. Dubelt, superintendent of the secret police—the "Third Section," as it was called—regretted that he was not able to make its author "rot in prison" for that document. I. S. Aksakov wrote to his father, almost ten years after the letter's appearance, that the name of Belinsky was known "to every one who longs for a breath of fresh air amid the stinking quagmire of provincial life. There is not a single high-school teacher in the *gubernia* who does not know Belinsky's letter by heart."[45] In its own way it was to affect hundreds upon hundreds of Russians, and according to Herzen, it became Belinsky's revolutionary testament to his generation. Among those deeply impressed by the document was young Fyodor Dostoevsky.

* * *

As for Gogol himself, the rest of his life was to be a sort of tragic epilogue. It was as if he were being pursued by the hounds of hell, and fleeing to retrieve his soul. The agony persisted until the moment of his death. It was as if he, like many Russians, were living in anticipation of the coming of Antichrist, in which even the Tsar himself believed. Many years before, in 1835, Gogol described what might seem a prevision of the feelings he was to experience more than ten years later. It was in an early version of a story, "The Portrait."

> For long years the Antichrist has craved to be born ... He is choosing man himself for his dwelling-place, and appearing in those persons whose angel seems to have abandoned them at their very birth and who are branded with the terrible hatred towards men and everything that is the work of the Creator ... Marvel ... at the terrible power of the devil. He strives to make his way into everything; into our deeds, into our thoughts, and even into the inspiration of the artist ... It is the same black spirit which forces itself upon us even in moments of the purest and holiest meditations.[46]

He who had once felt he had access to special illuminations now stood like one utterly forsaken by God, who, in his words, "has withdrawn from me for a long time the capacity for literary creation." He began to wonder whether he had not lost faith. Nothing seemed to help. Beleaguered by demons, he thought a pilgrimage to Jerusalem might purify and restore him, and early in February 1848 he left Russia. His disrupted state of mind can hardly be described. He had been staying at the house of his fanatical friend Count A. P. Tolstoy, who had put him in touch with the man who was to become Gogol's spiritual mentor—the priest Matvey Konstantinovsky, destined also to be Gogol's *homme fatal*, the whipping rod of Gogol's conscience and the goad to his self-destruction. On the eve of his departure for Palestine, Gogol had written to him:

> Oh, my friend, my confessor, sent me by God! I burn with shame, and do not know where to hide me from the infinite multitude of weaknesses and vices, which I did not even suspect existed ... It even seems to me that I have no religion. I confess the God-Man in Christ, but it is my reason, and not my faith that commands it ... *I only wish to believe*, and in spite of this I now dare to go on a pilgrimage to our Savior's Tomb! Oh, pray for me![47]

But even at the Holy Sepulchre his heart did not "know how to pray." And on his return he felt no better. He was now almost totally the possession of Father Matvey, a powerful fanatic from Rzhev, rabid persecutor of dissenters, filled also with a hatred of secular culture. Whether in his presence in Moscow, or at a remove from him, Gogol was always made aware how close he was to being immersed in a "pool of iniquities."

Yet he persevered in the composition of *Dead Souls*, and even read a few of the new chapters to his friends. How far he had gone by the end of 1851 it is hard to say. We do know that he had completed at least eleven chapters. To what extent Father Matvey was responsible for Gogol's final decision to destroy his work can only be conjectured. Such decisions require profound psychic collaboration. Gogol's internal panics, his fear of damnation, proved only part of the motives for such destruction. From the few surving chapters of Part Two of *Dead Souls*, dating from around 1845, we can perceive that there might have been a basic reason for the action. Alas! the sap of creation was drained; the imagination had withered; here and there only a sad hint of the greatness of a past day; the rest is all dead branches.

He had dreamt of a kind of Dantesque *Commedia*—the soul's pilgrimage and ultimate redemption. Chichikov was to be reformed, redeemed, and was to see the light of Heaven. But what steps Chichikov actually takes toward such an approach to *Paradiso!* He desires to own a vast estate with hundreds of serfs, to amass a fortune, and settle down to the comfortable existence of a landowner. In his progress he does not hesitate to participate in the forgery of a will; he is discovered, punished, and rescued by a good Samaritan, and admonished to good behavior in the future. Gone the broad rich humor, and hearty laughter and satire, the opulent imagery of the first part. How much more human was the "rogue" then!

Gogol was living with Count A. P. Tolstoy in Moscow, when, on a fateful night in February 1852, he decided to burn his works. At three in the morning he called his young servant, and together they consummated the last immolation.

> When all the papers were destroyed, he crossed himself, and went back to his room, kissed the boy, lay down on a couch, and broke into tears ...[48]

Now all that remained was to die ... The body that had been racked by illness was now subjected to deliberate starvation. The ineptness of his medical counsellors helped him on his last pilgrimage out of this world. Ten days after he had burned his life's unfulfilled fruits, soul and body of the tortured genius finally achieved peace. He died March 3, 1852.

Gogol's truly creative life had come to an end ten years before, in 1842. What he had been saying and writing up to then had made the human spirit live and the heart respond. What he was saying in 1847, a new generation no longer understood or wished to hearken to. At the end he was addressing himself to a past, a decaying past, and idealizing it, writing in the spirit of de Maistre and Bonald, such pillars of the Restoration as Metternich and Adam Miller, and Russians like the Benckendorffs and the Uvarovs. Works like the *Selected Passages from the Correspondence* fill one with tragic sadness. They are dead. But the *Government Inspector*, "The Overcoat," *Dead Souls*, and many of the other tales remain ineffaceable.

The government, always wary of writers, even dead ones, did its best to suppress obituaries. Ivan Turgenev wrote one such: "Gogol is dead!" he wrote.

> What Russian heart will not be deeply moved by these words. He is dead ... the man whom we now have the right—a bitter right conferred on us by death, to call great.

And he had the added temerity to name Gogol in the same breath as Pushkin, Lermontov, and Griboedov—each of whom had died a violent death, as if this was the due fate of genius in Russia. Turgenev later recalled that, having sent the article to one of the Petersburg journals, he waited in vain for its publication.

> Running across the editor of the journal in the street, I asked him why he did not publish it. "You see the sort of climate it is," he replied allegorically. "I'm afraid it can't be done." "But," I observed, "my article is a most innocent one." "Innocent or not," the editor replies, "the point is that we've been forbidden to mention Gogol's name."

The obituary was finally published in the *Moscow News* later in March 1852. Turgenev was forthwith arrested, imprisoned for a month for breaking censorship rules, then banished to his country estate.[49]

With the death of Gogol ends the first great era of Russia's literary genius. With Pushkin he was to exercise a mighty power over the century and beyond. Gogol belongs with the great satirists of all ages and countries, a brother to Aristophanes, Rabelais, and Swift. He set afoot and inspired the great stream of Russian realism, for despite their grotesque character, Gogol's novels and stories penetrated into the very core and center of the Russian character and the Russian land and brought an understanding of the "real" or true forces moving both the individual characters and their society. Realism has many mirrors with which to reflect the outward and inward world of human beings and their surroundings, their motivations, and their conflicts. Gogol used the mirror of distortion to achieve his objective—to discover the nexus of forces operative within the world in which he was living, which he was observing, and which—it must be added—like all true artists, he saw with fresh eyes. But the operative forces act not only upon the "outside" reality, they act upon the artist himself. He is product and producer; recipient and innovator. Realism then is the artistic consciousness alerted to the new relations within its world, able to translate them into comprehensible and apprehensible terms. A work is no less realistic if it makes use of forms that do not "mirror" reality with objective detail. True realism consists in the search for and uncovering of the nexus of forces acting upon the lives and actions of characters, giving these characters human depth and variety—fusing, so to speak, the artist's "I"—his genius, knowledge and insights,—with the "other"—the world outside in its multifaceted plenitude. Myth, symbol, the grotesque may be equally valid as instruments with which to convey the "reality"—the true relations within the world freshly perceived and imaginatively transformed so as to give the reader a new experience of "reality."

Such too is Gogol's great achievement, the enlargement and deepening of our consciousness and emotional experience through the grotesque. At the height of his powers he gave Russia the rich creation that inspired others to emerge, so to speak, from "under his Overcoat" and made possible that grand procession of novelists and short-story writers unequalled in any other land. In the tragic dismemberment of his later life he also anticipates that flight into the enclaves of the irrational, the mystical, the obscurantist and fanatical that was itself a mark of Russia's confusion and convulsion, eventually to culminate in the Rasputinism of a decayed autocracy, and its ultimate effacement.

Chapter Two

Young Dostoevsky

The Road to Siberia

Oh, may it come quickly
   The time when the peasant
Will make some distinction
   Between book and book,
Between picture and picture;
   Will bring from the market,
Not the picture of Blücher,
   Not a stupid "Milord,"
But Belinsky and Gogol!
   Oh, say, Russian people,
These names—have you heard them?
   They're great. They were borne
By your champions, who loved you,
   Who strove in your cause,
'Tis *their* little portraits
   Should be in your houses!
Nekrasov, "Who Can Be Happy in Russia?"

Farewell Russia, my unwashed land,
Land of serfs, land of masters,
Farewell, gendarmes in handsome blue,
My people, their victims, farewell!
Perhaps the steep crags of the Caucasus
Will save me from your pashahs,
Their ever watchful, ever wakeful eye,
And ears that the least sound alerts. ...
         —Mikhail Lermontov

No imperial lightning rods established by Tsar Nicholas I and his agents after the Decembrist uprising of 1825 were sufficiently effective to deflect the flow of new ideas or the mental unrest of a part of the younger generations. The powerful and populous armies of the Tsar, "the gendarme of Europe," might stand ready on the borders of Poland in anticipation of another uprising, or, at the call of a harassed ally, be prepared to rush to his aid; at home, the censorship, the knout, Siberia, and the ever-watchful political police, the "Third Section," directed by Count Benckendorff, or later by Prince Orlov, might be perpetual monitions to good behavior, right thinking and speaking—still, young brains continued working; ideas knew no customs barriers; books in amazing numbers kept on being imported from abroad, often smuggled into the country. And restless youth kept on thinking, recalling, and reading—even speaking …

Such indeed was the situation that prevailed among the students and some teachers at the universities of Moscow and St. Petersburg during the 1830s. In his vivid *Memoirs*, Alexander Herzen, himself a member of that generation, has left us a lucid picture of the era:

> … In our second year at the university—that is in the autumn of 1831—in the lecture room of the Faculty of Physics and Mathematics, Ogarev and I met among our new comrades two with whom we became particularly intimate. Our friendships, our sympathies and antipathies, were all derived from the same source. We were young men and we were fanatics: learning, art, connections, home, social position, everything was subordinated to one idea and one religion. Wherever there was an opening to convert, to preach, there we were on the spot with all our heart and mind, persistent, importunate, unsparing of time, work and even blandishments. We went into the lecture-room with the firm purpose of founding in it the nucleus of a society in the image and semblance of the Decembrists, and therefore we sought proselytes and adherents. … The day on which we sat side by side on a bench in the amphitheatre, looked at each other with the consciousness of our dedication, our league, our secret, our readiness to perish, our faith in the sacredness of our cause—and looked with loving pride at the multitude of handsome young heads about us, as at a band of brothers—was a great day in our lives. We gave each other our hand and *à la lettre* went out to preach freedom and struggle in all the four quarters of our youthful "universe," like the four deacons who go on Easter Day with the Four Gospels in their hands. We preached in every place at all times … exactly what it was we preached it is hard to say. Our ideas were vague: we preached the Decembrists and the French Revolution, then we preached Saint-Simonism and the same Revolution; we preached a constitution and a republic, the reading of political books and the concentration of forces in one society. Most of all we preached hatred for every form of violence, for every sort of arbitrary tyranny practised by governments. Our society in reality was never formed; but our propaganda sent down deep roots in all the faculties, and extended far beyond the walls of the university.[1]

Herzen and Ogarev were students in Moscow. What he was describing was equally true at the university in St. Petersburg. The memory of the Decembrists the executions, the exiles and their equally heroic wives, remained unobliterated, though it peered, like some dim sunlight, through the murky miasmatic atmosphere of the day. Yet in what seemed an almost static, swamp-like quietude, the years between 1825 and 1849, and particularly those after 1835, began to exhibit some remarkable changes both in the country, and in the mentality of its forward-looking citizenry. Russia was, of course, far behind the West in the matter of industrialization; nevertheless, that too was proceeding sporadically but none the less firmly, especially in household industries. Though predominantly in the hands of the nobility, factories—particularly those making cloth—were also gradually becoming the property of liberated serfs, who had managed to buy their freedom, and graduated from being supervisors to being proprietors.

Industrialization demands the free movement of labor; and the inevitable process of transforming part of a peasant population into an industrial proletariat was to take place eventually here as it had in the more advanced western countries. But capitalist development in Russia was as yet so small that it was to play but a minor role in the eventual emancipation of the serfs in 1861. What actually was to move the landowners toward acceptance of emancipation was the agricultural changes that were taking place under the impact of more efficient farming methods, derived from the example of the English; so that in the more highly fertile "black-soil" country it would profit the landowner to recover the land used by the peasants for their subsistence; in the less fertile regions, where the landowner derived revenues from the industrial occupations of the peasant, he would welcome emancipation but would expect to be compensated for any land surrendered.

Thus the peasant problem remained for some time the central moral as well as politico-social problem of the land, in a country where they represented practically ninety percent of the population. Yet it must not be overlooked that between 1825 and 1850 the number of factories doubled; and the industrial population rose from about 100,000 to practically half a million.

Peasant reform was in the air; peasant disturbances began mounting between 1825 and 1849; in 1846 alone there were over fifty uprisings—suppressed, of course. The number of landlords murdered by their serfs increased markedly after 1840, rising to almost two hundred between 1845 and 1849. In the industrial regions strikes were known to occur, the most disturbing being that in Kazan in 1834.[2]

To allay the ferment, to seek out dissident ideas to meet any disturbances, the government of the Tsar knew only one method: brute force. Its instrument of inquisition was the political police, the so-called "Third Section," organized in 1826 as a part of His Majesty's Own Chancery. Its spies were everywhere, and its particular field, the educated few. Minister of Education Uvarov's words served as the gospel for educational leaders:

> It should be the purpose of the government gradually to win the minds of the young and lead them imperceptibly to that essential state at which the solid scientific learning indispensable to our age is united with a deep faith in the profoundly Russian principles that are the guardians of Orthodoxy, Autocracy and the idea of the Nation, which constitute our sole anchor and the measure of our country's strength and greatness.[3]

To abet and achieve such goals, the censorship offered its own invaluable aid. Articles and books were scrutinized for hidden meanings, and hidden meanings were, of course, found. Thus Benckendorff observed that in an article by Kireevsky on "The Nineteenth Century" in 1832, His Majesty the Tsar had with his special astuteness "discovered" that "the word enlightenment" meant "liberty"; "the mind's activity," "revolution"; and "the skilfully contrived middle ground," "nothing but 'constitution'"; hence permission to print the article was itself an indefensible violation on the part of the censor. So the censor was fined and the journal closed down.[4]

As for writers of Russian history, Benckendorff asserted, they must keep in mind that

Russia's past has been admirable; her present is more than magnificent; as to her future, it is beyond the power of the boldest imagination to portray ... There ... is the point of view from which Russian history should be conceived and written.[5]

Such was the dream of the autocracy. The problem was how to persuade the people, particularly students, teachers, writers, and others of influence, to accept that dream. There, indeed, was the rub!. ... For many of them had their own dream, and in the process of trying to express it among their fellows they were often bound to fall afoul of Benckendorff, Prince Orlov, his henchman and successor Dubelt—all destined to acquire an immortal notoriety. Like their predecessors, the young men of the thirties began their idealistic education by absorbing the poems and plays of Schiller, as well as his philosophical essays. In this respect they were sharing in the particular exultation felt by all of romantic Europe. Young Coleridge had exclaimed with ecstasy on coming upon *The Robbers*; he had himself translated the great series of plays around Wallenstein. The Russian youth likewise drank in the humanitarian idealism of the German poet, but they went beyond him, retaining with the rest of the world what was permanent—a high dedication—but demanding something beyond that. The Marquis Posa of *Don Carlos* embodied one portion of his ideal—total involvement in a friendship and a high concern for "freedom." But the alembic in which the new ideas were being precipitated out could hold even stronger elements, which at first were drawn from the German treasure-trove of transcendental idealism. University professors like Pavlov, though themselves lecturing on science, did not shy away from introducing the overwhelming concepts emanating from Schelling. For him, as for his audience, the drama that depicted the whole universe as one organism, saw spirit in nature—though unconscious of itself—evolving ever higher until it reached its noblest and loftiest manifestation in the self-consciousness of Man, made of the dream a transcendental reality. It is as if the process that was being described was being realized in actuality within the consciousness of the young audience. And when, to cap the drama, that very human consciousness was conceived as a creative one, a portion of the vaster activity that emanated from God himself; and when man's noblest realization of himself was envisioned to be that of the artist; what more entrancing vision could have been vouchsafed? They too were artists, or would soon be such; they would write, create—they were visionaries waiting to reveal the true nature of the world. Had not the great Friedrich Schiller proclaimed that whatever could not be achieved in the everyday world of actuality, the artist could attain in the realm of the imagination? And had not Schelling joined him in depicting history as a constant progression of Spirit working through matter—unconsciously—moving ever upward and onward, constantly enlarging Nature's and Man's scope? For the time being at least, the crude world of matter—Tsar, police, censor, prison, the oppressive air, a sordid and degraded world—disappeared, dissolved in the cloudless heavens of idealism. Theirs was the living word that would re-create the world. If practical activity was for the time being denied them, they would swing aloft on the pinions of song, words, discussions, plans. God was on their side; for all forms of nature, as Schelling taught, were "objectifications of the infinite in the finite." Here, in the regions of art, was true freedom.

They had teachers invisible in the halls of the universities. They went to school with the Germans: Schelling, then Hegel, thereafter the Young Hegelians: Feuerbach and Strauss. And then came the French. ...

True, Saint-Simon and Utopian Socialist ideas had already come in with the Decembrists, and the Saint-Simonian doctrines had not all disappeared with their departure. But along with the Saint-Simonians, new names and new books now appeared—those of Fourier, Considérant, and, somewhat later, Proudhon. Even the Englishman Robert Owen was acquiring notoriety. It was indeed remarkable. Things that could not be read in Russian could be found in foreign journals, which somehow passed the customs barrier, and in innumerable foreign books, German and French, that made their appearance on the shelves of booksellers. Furthermore, students and teachers coming back from their sojourn in the West, especially from Berlin, brought with them tales and ideas of new philosophical movements, which they proceeded to advance and even to adapt and adopt. Such was indeed the experience of the most eminent historian of the day, Granovsky. Such was the experience of the brilliant but unfortunately short-lived Stankevich, who on his return became the intoxicated high-priest of Hegelianism.

What could not be read openly or discussed in the halls of the universities was read and discussed and argued in intimate "circles." To these came others, interested outsiders. What happened more openly in the cafés of Berlin or Paris took place in the close apartments of St. Petersburg or Moscow, and sometimes on the more comfortable country estates of affluent enthusiasts. Russian periodicals were read, digested, torn apart or acclaimed; searched carefully for hidden ideas, meanings, suggestions, intimations. Since all ideas except those proclaimed by the government were considered *ipso facto* "dangerous," here, in these intimacies, "dangerous" ideas were harbored and even expressed. For in the world outside stalked the enemy, ever alert. To the thrill of discovery of fresh ideas was added the ever-present threat of apprehension; there was scarcely as yet even a suggestion of putting these ideas to the test of direct action, but thinking thoughts was itself a kind of subversive activity. ...

Yes, the dangers were real, ever present, and many a member of these "circles" was destined to pay heavily for his participation in what might today appear harmless talk. They knew the hazards and they were ready to accept the consequences. There were some among them, it is true, who talked for talk's sake, spoke loftily and grandly, shaped immoderate schemes, and came to nothing. For this the heavy weight of op-pression and fear was as much responsible as their own characters. But there were others whose presence, intelligence, wide range of vision, and commitment made them centers from which radiated ideas that were to have consequences for many years to come. Here indeed was the incubation of many plans and discoveries in the realm of philosophy and social and political thought that were to bear very practical offspring in the years following the Emancipation down to the Russian Revolution of 1905. It was they who prepared philosophy for a descent from the heavens to the earth; but to their credit be it also added that they personally helped her on the journey. As these young men and women of the so-called "generation of the 1840s" imagined themselves the "sons and daughters of the Decembrists," so, in fact, did the later generations of Russian writers and reformers, as well as revolutionaries, look upon themselves as the direct heirs of the "forties."

It was this education, begun in the 1830s and continued into the next decade, that complemented rather than replaced Hegelianism, orthodox and left, with French socialist ideas, fused the enthusiasm for Schiller with an equally fervent assimilation of the novels of George Sand, and made of the years 1840 to 1849 an "extraordinary" decade, as Annenkov was to describe it. It was out of the "circles" and their intellectual leaders—such men as Alexander Herzen, Vissarion Belinsky, Mikhail Bakunin, and the youthful N. V. Stankevich—that impulses and ideas were diffused which took practical form in the creation of a new literature.

This was the new "intelligentsia" that came into being (the term itself was to achieve currency somewhat later), groups of intellectuals recruited now not only from the educated nobility and sons of landowners but also from the bourgeois and plebeian elements. All of them, whether "repentant" noblemen, or persons of a lower order, were marked by an inordinate curiosity, intellectual and moral, about new ideas, along with a growing preoccupation with the social and political problems besetting their country. They searched for solutions. Many of them, of course, looked to the West for answers; some looked to the Russian past, Russian history, and Russian traditions. Already it became evident that two schools of thought and action were being born, although as yet not too sharply divided—the "Slavophiles" and the "Westernizers." Their philosophical, social ideas were necessarily cloaked in an aesthetic garb; hence the seemingly inordinate preoccupation with aesthetics and *belles-lettres*, with story and poetry taking the place of overt ideology. Journals as well as their readership, limited of course when judged by the standards of Paris or London—grew in number, always subject to the mercies of the censor, appearing and disappearing with frightful rapidity, then reappearing in another vestment. One never knew when or for what reason the axe would fall; when this or that writer of an article or story, editor of a journal, or member or visitor of a "circle" would be summoned by the Third Section. Sometimes the pressures seemed to ease, as in the few years before 1848; but the preceding years had taken their toll of a number of hardy spirits. It was not only from Hegel and the Hegelians that these men learned of the law of contradictions; exile and prison proved a no less enlightening school.

In 1836, a year before Pushkin's death and a year after young Herzen was sent into exile, Pyotr Chaadaev published the first of his "Philosophical Letters" in *The Telescope*. As a result, its editor Nadezhdin was exiled for a year, the magazine suspended, and Chaadaev officially declared mad by the government. What was it this time that proved so abhorrent to the status-quo? Chaadaev had attacked Russia as backward! Russia had been bypassed by history, he claimed; she was outside of the circle of "great human families," belonging neither to the West nor to the East. Unlike Europe, Russia had no "common physiognomy." "We are nothing but a gap in the intellectual order." "We have given nothing to the world, we have learned nothing from it … whatever we have absorbed from the world's progress, we have disfigured." He even set Western Catholicism above Russian Orthodoxy: "Though we were Christians, the fruit of Christianity did not mature for us."[6]

This was the first major blast in the East–West war, and its repercussions spread far and wide. In far-off Viatka, the exiled Herzen's heart warmed on reading the essay. Though he had no sympathy with Chaadaev's religious views, he was at one with him in his Westernism. ...

How quickly new ideas were assimilated! Young Stankevich—he would die in 1840 at the age of 27—the Moscow mentor in Hegelianism to Belinsky, Bakunin, and Granovsky among many others, fresh from Berlin, where young Ivan Turgenev also had come under his sway—was already translating the Hegelian dialectic into a philosophy of action. Speaking of the Young Hegelian, August Cieszkowski—whose *Prolegomena zur Historiographie* became a call to "doing," not merely thinking, and who had divided history into three periods, Art, Science and Action—Stankevich remarked:

> This division is false, because it is not based on history. But this last thought—that Science must turn into Action, must melt in it—is correct ... We now feel the need to bind these categories more closely together, to combine philosophy and feeling not only in the head but in the blood, the body, the whole being.[7]

Of course, action, at this point, could mean writing and talking; but also a search for and discovery of sympathetic and talented brother-spirits. And in this respect, the "extraordinary" decade proved more than an idle boast. It was not only that, under the influence of the leaders of these "circles," young and unpublished genius and talent had its first public demonstration; but that the whole domain of letters was given a new course, and its meaning interpreted in new terms. It is in the periodicals of this *avant-garde* that the first major efforts of Fyodor Dostoevsky, Ivan Turgenev, Ivan Goncharov, Nikolai Nekrasov, and Alexander Herzen make their appearance; and here Vissarion Belinsky emerges not only as a prime discoverer and encourager of new talent, but also as the consummate critic of the new era, and its interpreter.

It is hard for a later generation to reconstruct fully, or even fully sense, the air of exhilaration that prevailed in the early forties. Annenkov is once more a contemporary witness of the changed atmosphere, particularly as evidenced in St. Petersburg:

> ... When I arrived back in Petersburg in the fall of 1843 ... I was far from done with Paris, but instead found at home reflections of many aspects of her intellectual life of the time. Proudhon's book, *De la propriété*, by then almost out of date; Cabet's *Icarie*, little read in France itself except by a small circle of poor worker-dreamers; the far from widespread and popular system of Fourier—all these things served as objects of study, of impassioned discussions, of questions and expectations of every sort ... Whole phalanxes of Russians followed them there, overjoyed at the chance to change over from abstract, speculative thought without real content to just the same kind of abstract thought but now with a seemingly real content ... Among such inflammatory materials, one must include. ... Feuerbach's famous book [*The Essence of Christianity*], which was then in everybody's hands. It could be said that Feuerbach's book had nowhere produced so powerful an impression as it did in our "Western" circle, and nowhere did it so rapidly obliterate the remnants of all preceding outlooks ... Herzen, needless to say, was a fervent expositor of its propositions and conclusions; among other things, he connected the upheaval it revealed in the realm of metaphysical ideas with the political upheaval heralded by the socialists, in which respect Herzen once again coincided with Belinsky.[8]

What all these new conceptions engendered was the feeling that, despite the seemingly static nature of the Russia of their day, the heavy hand of authority holding back all progress, here in these thinkers was the electrifying conviction that the world *was* changing, here was an unfolding of ideas, men, movements; the world was an organism, of which the individual, himself another organism, was an essential part, interacting with it and with other individuals, thus making history. Saltykov-Shchedrin, another writer, reported:

> From France—of course not from the France of Louis-Philippe, or Guizot, but from the France of Saint-Simon, Cabet, Fourier, Louis Blanc, and especially George Sand—there flowed into us a *belief in humanity,* from which there shone forth for us a conviction that the golden age was not behind us but before us.[9]

And Herzen's closest friend, Ogarev, like the former an aristocrat, and destined for a hard life in behalf of his ideals, recalled those days:

> I remember the room, ten by ten,
> The bed and the chair, and the table with the tallow candle,
> And us three, sons of the Decembrists,
> Pupils of the new world
> Of Fourier and Saint-Simon.
> We swore to devote all our lives
> To the people and its liberation.
> The foundation we set was Socialism.
> And to achieve our sacred ends
> We had to create a secret society
> And spread it secretly, step by step.[10]

* * *

It is well to remember that in all the endless vastness of Russia, St. Petersburg and Moscow represented the two central enclaves of culture. Now and then, in some outlying town or district like Kazan and Kiev, forbidden or suspect works made their way, even into a theological seminary. The city of Odessa too might be cited as an exception. On a number of the estates could be found well-stocked libraries, many of them filled with the works of eighteenth-century writers, in which the growing mind could find nourishment, though not always of an unequivocal kind. But for the less favored children of indigent or moderately circumstanced parents, the road of intellectual development and freedom inevitably led to one or the other of the great cities. Here they might find a career, and perhaps achieve some measure of independence. But if their eyes were set on literary success and not on a post in the civil service, they were most frequently destined for hardships and deprivations. If they had the talent and were fortunate enough to have it discovered, they might be welcomed in the circles of the intelligentsia, where class distinctions were ignored and intellect honored.

It was the good fortune of Vissarion Belinsky not only to have his own talent discovered and honored, but to become himself the principal discoverer of the talents of others.

He was of what might be called "plebeian" origin. His father was a naval surgeon. In his brief, hectic, intense life Belinsky represented an abridgement of the revolutionary education in which a number of his contemporaries participated. He was in turn recipient, giver, and transformer. As a "plebeian" member of the various circles, he reflected the social fluidity of the intelligentsia; as a mentor, the mutation of letters and thought taking place between 1840 and 1848. He was reared for rebellion. An unhappy childhood and a brutal father prepared the way for that revolt that among the young found imaginary and imaginative outlet in the reading of Schiller. As Alexander Herzen put it, referring to the impact of the Schillerian rebels and dissidents in *The Robbers, Don Carlos, Wallenstein*, and *Cabal and Love*, "Schiller was exactly the right author for our students. Posa and Max (Piccolomini), Karl Moor and Ferdinand were students, robber-students; it is all the protest of the first dawn, of the first indignation."[11]

What the romantic brigands began, Moscow University and the Stankevich "circle" completed. Schiller played a prominent part, it seems, in cutting short Belinsky's academic career. The insurrectionary reverberations of Schiller's *Robbers* (possibly also, of Goethe's *Götz von Berlichingen*) resounded in Belinsky's youthful drama, *Dmitri Kalinin*, where he arraigns the injustices of the social order. Here, Kalinin, the illegitimate son of a noble, becomes the proponent of freedom, personal and social, and falls prey to the oppressive forces of Russian society. It seems probable that it was this work, which was rejected by the censor, rather than his failure as a student, that was responsible for his expulsion from the university. The Stankevich circle in Moscow rounded out his primary education. Here he was in the midst of equally ardent students of Hegel, such as Mikhail Bakunin, whose later revolutionary career was to outdo the wildest fantasies conceivable by the young members of the group. In the pages of the literary supplement of the ill-fated Moscow *Telescope* Belinsky made his public debut as critic, when his reviews of contemporary literature, particularly of Gogol and Pushkin, ignited the literary landscape with a call for a literature expressive of the spirit of the "people" and their inner life. Already he sensed that, to be truly reflective of its age, this literature would and must be one of "prose," as Pushkin's, for its own day, was one of poetry. For all that, Belinsky and his confrères were still swimming in the deep seas of German idealism—Schelling and Fichte. Like a diver entranced with the aqueous beauties around him, he was so far removed from the *terra firma* of reality that he spurned all contact with it. No German Romantic could then have outdone him in his contempt for what he called "political economy and statistics"—that sort of "partial knowledge" that "vulgarizes a person." "Most of all," he wrote in a letter of 1837, "leave politics alone and oppose every political influence upon your manner of thinking … All hope of Russia lies in enlightenment and not in revolt, not in a revolution and not in a constitution."[12] It is not therefore surprising that when, under Stankevich's preachments, Bakunin and he came upon Hegel, both of them (like so many other Hegelians) should have adapted that philosopher's "What is rational is real, what is real is rational" to an utterly reactionary outlook, and to a justification, indeed glorification, of the Tsarist status quo! The brew, concocted of undigested, mostly of second-hand ingredients, worked like a first-class champagne. They mistook inebriation for vision … Here is Belinsky writing to Stankevich two years later, describing that episode:

I arrive in Moscow; Bakunin arrives; we live together. That summer he had been looking over Hegel's philosophy of religion and law. A new world opened up before us. "Might is right and right is might." No. I cannot describe to you with what emotion I heard those words; it was a liberation. I understood the meaning of the downfall of empires, the legitimacy of conquerors; I understood that there is no crude material force nor conquest by swords and bayonet, nothing arbitrary, nothing accidental. ...[13]

Alexander Herzen, himself a close student of Hegel, was shocked both by this sort of interpretation, and even more so by its undemocratic application. He was later to set Belinsky right; and when they met again in St. Petersburg toward the end of 1839, Belinsky's process of reeducation began, and the so-called "reconciliation with reality" was bound to give way. Belinsky was soon to undergo a new crisis of thought when he entered upon his association with the prominent St. Petersburg journal *Notes of the Fatherland*. The diver into the deeps of transcendentalism now came up for air—the air of the Hegelian Left, of Feuerbach and Strauss, the same air breathed by Herzen and Ogarev. Belinsky's "theocratic theism" began to dissolve; Herzen introduced him to the biological materialism of the German Karl Vogt. A new view of the nature of man rose before him. As T. G. Masaryk put it, "Belinsky played the part of John the Baptist to Herzen and Herzen provided the organic continuation of Belinsky's work."[14] Belinsky's earlier condescension, verging on contempt, for the French was now replaced by a vivid interest in the ideas of French socialists. In him, as in his contemporaries, the revolution in thought was meteoric ... He began soon to apply his new principles to his literary and aesthetic criticism, as well as his entire *Weltanschauung*.

What he termed the "struggle against the actual" began in earnest. "Negation is my god." He began looking around him more closely, and exclaimed, "And this is society, existing on rational principles, the manifestation of reality! ... And after this, does a *man* have the right to forget himself in art, in science! ..." "What is it to me that the universal exists when the individual suffers?"[15] The Feuerbachian in him now cries out that in the words God and religion he sees "obscurity, darkness, the chain and the knout."[16]

Germany and German thought begin to recede. France moves to the fore. The names on his lips are now those of Fourier, Cabet, Proudhon and Louis Blanc—and not least—that of George Sand, "the Joan of Arc of our times, the star of salvation and the prophetess of a great future."[17] "The French are a great people." He is beginning to understand the great French Revolution. Annenkov records Belinsky's virtual intoxication with Louis Blanc's *Histoire de dix ans*. To V.P. Botkin he wrote in 1841:

> ... And so, I am now at a new extreme, which is the idea of *socialism*, that has become for me the idea of ideas, the being of beings, the question of questions, the alpha and omega of belief and knowledge. ... It is the question and the solution. It has for me engulfed history and religion and philosophy. ... Reality springs from a soil, and the soil of all reality is society ... The source of interests, purposes, and activity is the substance of social life... Seeking a way out we rushed avidly into the alluring sphere of German contemplation and thought we could create for ourselves a charming inner world bathed in light and warmth outside the surrounding reality. We did not understand that this intrinsic contemplative subjectiveness constituted the objective interest of the German nationality,

is for Germans what sociality is for the French. ... Sociality, sociality, or death! ... What care I if genius on earth lives in heaven when the crowd is wallowing in the dirt?. ... My heart bleeds and shudders when I view the crowd and its representatives. Grief, poignant grief overcomes me at the sight of the barefooted little boys playing knucklebones in the street, of tattered beggars, of the drunken coachmen, of the soldier returning from sentinel duty, ... [There will come a time when] Woman will not be the slave of society and man, but, like man, will freely follow her inclinations without losing her good name, that monstrosity of conventional ideas. There will be neither rich nor poor, neither kings nor subjects, there will be brethren, there will be men, and, at the word of the apostle Paul, Christ will pass his power to the Father, and Father-Reason will hold sway once more, but this time in a new heaven and above a new world. ..."[18]

Dangerous, daring words! They could not of course be put into his criticism in these very terms. But journalism was full of circumlocutions, and readers would understand. It was in this spirit that he wrote glowingly of Gogol, and *Dead Souls*, calling attention to its importance as a "Russian national creation" in its depiction of the life of the people. The artist must be the voice of human protest!

It was in this spirit, indeed, that Belinsky wrote the first truly incisive and perceptive appreciations of the place of Lermontov, Pushkin, and Gogol in Russian literature. It was in this spirit that he lent the first critical support to new writers like Turgenev, Goncharov, and Dostoevsky. He was writing, or better rewriting, literary history—setting it in new terms and in a new context—that of society, and the historic moment. He was also previsioning its main direction. It was he who transformed the poet Nekrasov's attitude and understanding of the nature of poetry. The "natural school" of which Belinsky spoke, that is, the school of the new "realism," was equally valid, he saw, for the new prose. It was out of these beginnings that Nekrasov eventually became the foremost representative of the new poetry, and the author of the noblest realistic epic of this period, "Who Can Be Happy in Russia?"

In the eyes of a number of his contemporaries Belinsky had the soul of a giant, housed in the fragile, ungainly body of an already tubercular and doomed man, with a voice at once weak and husky, but never without animation or excitement. He was in their view the epitome of honesty and dedication, with almost the simplicity of childhood. Ivan Turgenev, the novelist, recalled him as he was in 1843:

> No one who saw him only in the street, when, in his warm cap, his old threadbare raccoon overcoat and down-at-heel goloshes, he made his way hurriedly and falteringly along the walls, looking round him with the timid sternness peculiar to nervous people—no one could form any impression of what he was really like ... Belinsky, which is so rare with us—was a truly passionate and truly sincere man, capable of selfless enthusiasm but devoted entirely to truth, irritable but not egoistic, who knew how to love and to hate disinterestedly.

In constant search, even torment to find the Truth, he remained an "inquiring spirit" to the end of his life. Indefatigable in discussion, he could sometimes be unwittingly amusing. Here is Turgenev's description once more:

> Coughing continuously, and with a pulse of one hundred a minute and a hectic flush on his cheeks, he would begin his conversation at the point where we had left off the day

before... It was not easy to cope with a man like Belinsky. "We haven't yet decided the question of the existence of God" he said to me once with a bitter reproach, "and you want to eat!"[19]

Belinsky was irrepressibly excited when he came upon a new literary talent. And it was in this respect that he became involved momentously with the career of Fyodor Dostoevsky—with the latter's literary beginnings and, in an equally fateful way, in 1849—although by that time, Belinsky was no longer alive.

* * *

At one of my visits to Belinsky, before dinnertime, when he used to rest from his morning writing, I saw him from the courtyard of his house standing at his parlor window and holding a large copybook in his hands, his face showing all the signs of excitement. He noticed me, too, and shouted: "Come up quickly, I have something new to tell you about." "You see this manuscript?" he continued, after we shook hands. "I haven't been able to tear myself away from it almost two days now. It's a new novel by a beginner, a new talent; what this gentleman looks like and what his mental capacity is I do not know as yet, but his novel reveals such secrets of life and characters in Russia as no one before him even dreamed of. Just think of it—it's the first attempt at a social novel we've had, and done, moreover, in the way artists usually do their work. I mean, without themselves suspecting what will come out of it. The matter in it is simple: it concerns some good-hearted folk who assume that to love the whole world is an extraordinary pleasure and duty for every one. They cannot comprehend a thing when the wheel of life with all its rules and regulations runs over them and fractures their limbs and bones without a word. That's all there is—but what drama, what types! I forget to tell you, the artist's name is Dostoevsky."

This is the way that Annenkov recalled his and Belinsky's first encounter with a work of Fyodor Dostoevsky.[20]

It was no mean triumph for a young man of twenty-two. The novelette was entitled *Poor People*. It was completed in 1845, published early in 1846 in the *Petersburg Almanac* edited by Nekrasov, and subsequently hailed in articles by Belinsky in *Notes of the Fatherland*. Had a new young Gogol arisen? And was he destined in time to repeat, if not outdo, the miracle of *Dead Souls*? Of the young man's attainments there could be no doubt; nor even that the spirit of Gogol had hovered over him while he was composing his tale of the pitiful middle-aged government copying clerk and his love for his distant young relative Varenka.

For the remarkable decade of 1840 had been inaugurated, tragically, with the premature death in 1841 of the poet-novelist Lermontov; and auspiciously, in 1842, with the publication of Gogol's *Dead Souls*. A new era in literature had begun, and the prospect of a new type of literary creation was hailed by the critic Belinsky. "The natural school," as he called it, was already launched. And here was a story, obviously coming "from under 'The Overcoat,'" that appeared to promise an extension and a deepening of the "natural" or "realistic" school of fiction, and what was to be preeminently an age of prose.

Actually, both in form and content, *Poor People* is old-fashioned, even if judged by then prevalent standards. It is an "epistolary" novel in the eighteenth-century tradition of Samuel Richardson and Rousseau, or of Goethe's *Werther*. It is also a novel of "sentiment." Its two principal characters, the forty-eight year old minor government clerk and his distant young relative, an orphan girl, correspond, though they live within a window's sight of each other on the same courtyard. They pour out their sad lives' experiences in their letters. It is indeed a story of two "poor people," abjectly and desperately seeking liberation from a morass of poverty and humiliation. It was these very elements—the cries of loneliness, despair, hope, hopelessness, the longing for happiness, the search for understanding—that so took that generation by storm and swept its author into celebrity, at the same time overwhelming his readers with paroxysms of tears. All this was capped by the double tragedy, the surrender of the girl to an inevitable but loveless marriage to a well-to-do suitor, and the concurrent extinction in the clerk of the little beam of light that had guided him. From this moment he is doomed to an endlessly hapless existence. Dostoevsky had concentrated within the walls of two lackluster dwellings drabness, banality, temptation, humiliation, and a struggle to assert some claim to life, dignity and happiness—all this made human, touching, and real through compassion and understanding.

Again, we are in the presence of "little" people of "no account": Makar Devushkin, living in malodorous squalor, trying with his exhausted means to help the impoverished and helpless Varenka. He is a petty copying-clerk, a timid, oppressed and humiliated character, never destined to rise; the butt of his fellow-workers, eternally living in dread of his superiors. His life is one of unreal hopes and illusions. A naive personality, his living quarters are an epitome of his whole existence—a miserable, partitioned-off corner of a kitchen—a "corner" of a lonely, human life that in years to come Dostoevsky was to lift to epic heights.

And the girl? Varvara (or Varenka) Alexeyevna, too, is a "victim"—a poor seamstress, whom a distant relative, the well-to-do but high-class bawd Anna Fyodorovna, is trying to seduce to an easier, more luxurious, but equivocal existence. The power and magnetism of money are evident throughout. The affluent Mr. Bykov, thwarted in his attempts to win Varenka for a mistress, capitulates, and wins her as the wife of a brutal, authoritarian master. Of course, there are other wretched characters in the story; the tutor, who dies before Varenka's eyes; the tutor's decayed father, a hopeless, hapless, useless but lovable man …

Where Gogol had poured all the bitterness of genius for the grotesque on a government clerk and his obsession with a garment, Dostoevsky lavishes sentiment, sometimes maudlin, on his characters. But there is in his narrative at least one episode worthy to stand beside Gogol's masterpiece. That is the incident that occurs between Makar and his superior, "His Excellency," when the poor clerk is being called in to account for some copying infraction. His clothes are shabby; a number of buttons on his jacket are loose and about to come off.

> "What is the meaning of this?" he began angrily. "Why are you not more careful? It was an urgent document and you have spoilt it!" His Excellency now turned to Yevstafy Ivanovich and I could hear only snatches of what he said. "Such negligence … Extra trouble …" Several times I opened my mouth—to apologize, but no sound came. I should have liked to run away, but dared not. And then came the worst, something so awful, my darling, that my pen trembles for shame! A button on my coat, the devil take

it, a button that was hanging by a single thread suddenly broke off and hopped and skipped, jingling and rolling to the very feet of His Excellency. And this amid the general silence. This was what came of an apology. This was my only answer to His Excellency. The consequences are too horrible to describe. His Excellency turned his eyes upon me, noting the details of my figure and my dress. I remembered what I had seen in the mirror and—stooped to capture that button. What possessed me to do it! I snatched at it, but the thing kept rolling and spinning; and so you see, I also distinguished myself by my gracefulness. I felt my senses leaving me. All was lost: my reputation and all, irretrievably lost! In the jumble of my mind I could somehow hear the shrieks and shouting, and the gossip of a thousand tongues. Finally, I overtook the button, arose and stiffened. I should have stood perfectly still with my hands at my sides. But no! I had to fiddle with that button, push it on the broken threads as though it could stick on again. And all the time I was smiling. Yes, just smiling …[21]

To Makar Devushkin's great amazement, His Excellency proves kindly. Having dismissed the others who were present, left alone with Devushkin, His Excellency draws a wallet from his pocket and presses a hundred-ruble note into Makar's hand; takes the latter's "unworthy hand" into his own and shakes it like an "equal." And now Makar is again enabled to help Varenka.

The psychic, emotional, intellectual needs of one age frequently remain a puzzle, even a mystery, to its successors; and we continue to marvel at the exaggerated or inadequate responses to an event, whether historic or intellectual, that strike us so differently. But whatever the time or the land, psychic or emotional impulses, long repressed for whatever reasons or as a result of whatever causes, tend to break out, frequently in response to influences not always easily evaluated by posterity. Feelings, as we have remarked, also have a social history; and a part in history, for they often determine the course of objective events and actions. The fervent response to Dostoevsky's *Poor People* is only one such instance of an event, literary in character, that corresponds to the immediate needs, emotional or mental (for the moment let us divide the two), of the time, in turn affecting the course of history. But the continuity of great letters, of great thought, that which sometimes is called its "universal" character, consists in very specific elements and, whatever the degree of response, rests upon certain deeply-rooted elements of the human character. The response itself, no less than its revealed source, is socially conditioned, historically determined. What is taken for granted in one age, or in one social group, becomes a source of amazement, horror, or delight in another. Brutality is such an instance. It is scarcely necessary to detail changes in attitude that developed with respect to this particular form of behavior in the course of history. We no longer—at least in common practice—manacle and beat insane people. Military organizations, whatever their other brutalities may be, no longer punish the common soldier by laying him across a bench, exposing his buttocks, and flogging him without mercy. Revolutions of feelings are a part of social and political revolutions. It is with this in mind that we must appreciate the Russians' reaction to the publication of *Poor People*, Belinsky's enthusiasm, and Nekrasov's emotional outbursts.

Belinsky wrote:

Honor and glory to the young poet whose Muse loves those who live in garrets and basements, and speaks of them to the inhabitants of gilded halls, saying: "These also are men and your brothers."[22]

Dostoevsky's fellow student, D. V. Grigorovich, who was sharing the writer's apartment at the time of the writing of the story, was one of the first to read it:

> ... I tore the manuscript from him by force, and took it to Nekrasov forthwith. ... I myself read the work aloud. At the last scene, when Devushkin takes leave of Varenka, I could no longer control myself and broke into sobs. I saw that Nekrasov was also weeping.[23]

Neither Varenka nor Makar is a rebel. Makar, in fact, accepts his fate as almost a part of the divine order of the universe; his place in the world has been preordained, and only very, very rarely does he indulge in "dangerous" thoughts—but then almost immediately recants them and repents. In moments of deep resentment at Varenka's deprivations, he writes her:

> Why is it that you are so unhappy, Varenka? My dearest angel, in what way are you worse than the others? You are so kind, beautiful and learned. Why should your lot in life be so hard? Why should a good man live in need and neglect, while happiness comes to the others uninvited? Of course, my darling, I know that I should not have such thoughts because it savors of free thought. But in all fairness, why is it that fate should smile upon one while he is still in the womb and croak at another only because he was born an orphan ... It is sinful of course to think this way ...[24]

It is the common denominators of brutality, humiliation, injustice, and self-abasement that now stand out in lurid visibility. It is the element of loneliness of the human being that is being brought home. It is the persistent sense of "shame" that is disclosed—reputations tarnished and blackened; disrepute of appearance; perpetual anxieties that gnaw at one's innards; self-abasement so that one feels like a "dish-clout"; and the humiliations of physical outrage—like being thrown downstairs by some supercilious lackey at the behest of some arrogant master; the outrage to one's honor, which one is not able to avenge; the feelings of utter helplessness in the face of brute force. Such were the feelings that now made themselves pervasively felt, and resented. Brutalization, be it added, at the hands of one's superiors in rank—easily understandable; but worse than that is brutalization at the hands of your own equals, your own co-workers, your fellows. How could the "insulted and injured" little man understand that this too was a manifestation of the frustrated, humiliated being, avenging himself, because helpless, on victims near him?

And worst of all—the emptiness of life! The rat-like sameness of one's meaningless occupation, copying, copying, and copying ... That is why "corners" are so wonderfully hospitable, beds are sanctuaries from distresses. That is why Makar's final words pierce with such acid penetration, when Varenka goes off with her husband to a life that will mean security but assure her nothing else. There will be no one now to whom he can write. "My style," he writes in his last letter to her, "is just taking shape now ... What style? I hardly know what I am saying and what I am writing about, and it doesn't matter as long as I keep on writing and writing ... My little dove, my one and only one—my darling!"

Young Fyodor Dostoevsky was floating on clouds of glory, inebriated with success. He left a meeting with Belinsky—so he recalled many years later—with the latter's words ringing in his ears: "To you as an artist, truth is revealed and declared; it came to you as a gift. Treasure, then, your gift, be faithful to it, and you will become a great writer!" And here is Dostoévsky reminiscing:

> All this he was telling me then. All this he later told about me also to many others who are still living and who can corroborate my account. In a state of ecstasy I left him. I stopped at the corner of his house, looked at the sky, at the bright day, at passers-by, and with my whole being I felt that a solemn moment had occurred in my life, a break forever; that something altogether new had begun, something I had not anticipated even in my most impassioned dreams ... This was the most delightful minute in my whole life ...[25]

When Dostoevsky came to write his first full-length novel, *The Insulted and Injured*, some fifteen years later, he could not forbear making that event an episode in the novel.

But who could blame him? In his mood of egocentric exhilaration he writes to his brother Mikhail of the way in which he is being courted by notables like Prince Odoevsky, by Count Sologub, the distinguished Panaev family, especially by the hostess Avdotya Panaeva (Nekrasov's beloved); even by that rising aristocrat and literary star Ivan Turgenev!

He could scarcely believe his good fortune. Were the hardships, the tribulations, the terrors of the past really over? There were matters he would gladly forget, if forgetfulness could be commanded. But it did seem that he was achieving freedom. Here he was at the age of twenty-four and already a celebrated man of letters! If only his mother were alive! And his father? He had better not think of him. Dead, too—murdered by his own serfs in 1839—only one year after young Dostoevsky's admission to the St. Petersburg School of Engineering. His father had accompanied him to the capital, and this was the last time Dostoevsky was to see him. The retired army doctor, Mikhail Andreyevich Dostoevsky, had not been noted for kindliness to his serfs on his modest estate in Dorovoye and Cheremashnaya, about one hundred miles from Moscow. Perhaps he was no worse than most of the gentry; probably he was as brutal as they, and assuaged the painful boredom, the vacuity, his frustrated ambitions, and recent widowhood with whoring, drinking, beatings, and seductions of his young servants. And one day in June 1839—Fyodor was then seventeen—a number of his father's peasants avenged whatever horrors their master had perpetrated, and murdered him. Such was their court of justice—they knew no other; at least they knew that whatever justice was officially administered would never favor them. In the case of such violent murders against landowners, the latter's self-interest dictated a quietus, lest the law deport not only the presumed perpetrators, but sometimes entire villages. In the case of the Dostoevskys, it was deemed best to claim death by a "seizure."

Though the doctor had never beaten his children, he was by nature a tyrant and a martinet, and gave them little affection. Young Dostoevsky did not love him; more likely he hated him. In his last letters written to his father from St. Petersburg, Dostoevsky mingled humble, somewhat hypocritical, attestations of affection, with insistent requests for money.

Whatever his feelings on his father's death—and he did not speak of them openly—the murder remained deeply engraved on his mind and body. It may well have been this incident that once more activated or intensified the epileptic fits from which he was to suffer for the rest of his life, and which had occurred, so a number of his biographers believe, as early as his seventh year.[26]

Readers of Dostoevsky's novels need scarcely be reminded that parricide plays a most crucial role in *The Brothers Karamazov*. But a tyrannizing father makes his appearance in Varenka's story in *Poor People*, and in the unfinished novel of the late 1840s, *Netochka Nezvanova*.

His boastful letters to his brother belie his own deeper feelings. Far from being so utterly blasé in the presence of prominent persons who were, in his notions, wooing him, he was shy, retiring, uneasy, and terribly sensitive to anything that touched his self-esteem. As a child and young boy in Moscow, he had early shown a disposition to silence, obstinacy, and retirement; a brooding disposition, an active imagination, a passion for reading. Daily prayers, pilgrimages, church sermons, saintly lessons were the order of the day—no less than the stern tutoring of his father. His youthful imagination was also fed by the proximity of his father's hospital, and the pitiful sight of the patients—no less than by the religious services, the sight of the poor church attendants, and not least, during summers on the estates, the experiences with serfs—euphemistically referred to as "souls"—and their masters.

He had not liked the engineering school and the army discipline it involved, or the customary feral barbarism of the student body. Here too he displayed an independence and retiring disposition that attracted attention. Not long after graduation he resigned from the service to devote himself to what he believed was his true vocation, authorship. Already he was notoriously in need of money; and when he obtained some, he played the spendthrift—a habit he would retain to the end of his life.

He had begun writing early, and his literary efforts—like all literary efforts of young writers—were deeply affected by his wide reading. Into the boiling cauldron of his early creations he poured reminiscences and impulses derived from his favorite, Schiller; the Gothic novels his mother loved to read aloud; the marvels and weird fantasies gathered from E. T. A. Hoffmann; Sir Walter Scott, and, of course, Pushkin and Gogol. Somewhat later he added Balzac, and even Dickens, to his repertory. Balzac had visited Russia in 1843; and Dostoevsky set about making a free translation of *Eugénie Grandet*, which a journal published. Soon George Sand too was to impress him deeply.

But the genius—though still obviously tentative, and in many places derivative—was his own. Within himself he already harbored "secrets" he would reveal only indirectly. What, for example, did he mean, when in recalling his early experiences with Belinsky, he wrote, "And if only Belinsky knew what nasty, shameful thoughts dwell within me"?[27]

When he was eighteen he wrote in a letter:

> My soul is now inaccessible to the raging squalls that used to shake it. In it, all is at peace as in the heart of a man who harbors a deep secret …

and the year before,

The atmosphere of a man's soul consists in a fusion of heaven with earth; and man is a kind of illegitimate child … It seems to me that our world is a purgatory for heavenly spirits who have been saddened by a sinful thought …[28]

Was it a pose when, speaking of his favorite, E. T. A. Hoffmann, he said,

I have a project to go mad. Let people rage, try to cure me, let them try to bring me to reason …[29]

He was wont to dramatize himself; but even such potential posing conceals elements of reality. Whence came that incomparable ability, exhibited in the depiction of Makar Devushkin, to paint "shame" and "shamefulness" and all their companion feelings? Shadowed by the ample wings of Gogol and Hoffmann, the young writer struggles to reveal inner depths, hesitatingly and sometimes clumsily, while at the same time trying to conceal their personal appositeness and aspects of self-revelation.

If Belinsky had hoped to establish Dostoevsky as the new Gogol, the risen star of the "natural" school, with a social direction, he was soon disenchanted. For in the wake of *Poor People*, with the feeling that his talents were now being given a free flow, and his ambitions and hopes still high, Dostoevsky embarked on a number of stories in which he revealed that his writing and thinking were also taking another direction. It was not clear to his critics at the time that this too was destined to be "new," but it shocked by its obvious derivation (some critics thought it "shameless") from Gogol—but also by its unprecedented deviation into strange regions. … For with somewhat unsteady hand, but unquestioned talent, Dostoevsky was uncovering, laying bare, inside layers of the mind and soul, reaching deeply into troublesome and disturbing psychological states—exploring "dangerous" areas of human behavior …

In discussing *Poor People*, Belinsky had written,

His talent belongs to the order of those which are not at once appreciated and acknowledged. During the course of his career many talents which will be set up against him will appear, but in the end they will be forgotten by the time he achieves the apogee of his fame.[30]

Now in quick succession Dostoevsky published a number of stories, among them "Mr. Prokharchin," "The Landlady," and *The Double*. In these and other stories of this period it became obvious to the literary critic—or at least it seemed to him—that Dostoevsky was abandoning "realism," as well as humanitarianism, in favor of melodramatic elements. Relations between Dostoevsky on the one hand, and Belinsky and Nekrasov, began to cool.

Belinsky, of course, could not have foreseen to what lengths Dostoevsky was to carry his methods and procedures in years to come, when he developed these particular insights to their fullest in his longer masterpieces. Belinsky died in 1848, a year before the critical turning point in Dostoevsky's life. But a certain element of prophetical prevision in him told him that the path the novelist was now entering upon would lead in directions directly antipodal to his own conceptions. He could not of course have anticipated, from these rough beginnings, that Dostoevsky was to revolutionize the novel in his own way.

Nor could he have appreciated how clearly these new tendencies of Dostoevsky reflected the essential cleavages of the writer's character and life, and were in fact objectifications of those contradictions. And certainly he could not have foreseen that the recurrent themes of these early works were to represent leitmotifs of all the great works of years to come, orchestrated and enlarged with all the matured insights of the writer, and refined in the crucible of fiery experiences such as few artists had undergone or were destined to undergo.

It was indeed a strange series of characters, situations, and events that Dostoevsky now set himself to portray. Though his individual characters are in most cases ordinary people, mostly minor government clerks, they are marked by striking mental characteristics. They appear to live in an unreal world—the world outside; inside them is the world of reality. They are in fact "outsiders," marginal characters, whose daily battles to survive are fought out with unnatural intensity within them. Already they appear in a few instances as "underground" beings, who emerge from their shabby retreats, their "corners" both physical and psychic, as lonesome people, never truly at home in the real world, glad to retreat into their own hiding places, mental and physical.

Such, for example, is the pathetic elderly government clerk, a miser, who goes by the name of Mr. Prokharchin in a story by the same name. He is an alien member in a boarding establishment. His fellow boarders are a hostile world, and look with suspicion upon this creature living behind a screen, who denies himself the simplest necessities on the pretext of supporting a "sister-in-law." He is the butt of their jests and practical jokes, which he takes seriously, and which arouse panic fears within him. He begins to behave strangely at home and, what is worse, in the office. At home he has a battered trunk under his bed, probably, so his fellows feel, filled with old rags. In one of his paranoid attacks, he disappears for days and is brought back apparently stricken with some kind of "fit." He lives out his last days in a delirium filled with frightful images of retribution and persecution, which his fellows observe with partial sympathy. They cannot understand him—his fears, his nightmares, his ravings. They do not understand how a frivolous word could drive him into a distracted panic...

> And what was he frightened about? It would have been all very well if he had had a good post, had had a wife, a lot of children; it would have been excusable if he were being hauled up before the court on some charge or other; but he was a man utterly insignificant, with nothing but a trunk and a German lock; he had been lying more than twenty years behind his screen, saying nothing, knowing nothing of the world nor of trouble, saving his half-pence, and now at a frivolous idle word the man had actually gone off his head, was utterly panic-stricken at the thought he might have had a hard time of it...[31]

Mr. Prokharchin dies. The "personage of gentlemanly demeanor, with a severe and displeased-looking face"—that is, a representative of the government office—makes his appearance, is assured of the death, and departs, while the rest of the boarders and the landlady begin to examine the dead man's belonging, feverishly in search of what wealth he may have stored up. The trunk reveals nothing but rags; but the mattress, when slit open, discloses stores of roubles! Exactly 2,497 roubles and a half! And the corpse? It lay there.

He seemed … to have grown shrewder, his right eye was, as it were, slyly screwed up. Semyon Ivanovitch seemed wanting to say something, to make some very important, communication and explanation and without loss of time, because things were complicated and there was not a minute to lose…And it seemed as though they could hear him.

The death of a nobody; the death of an "outsider." One whose life was beset by incomprehensible fears; one who creeps out of his corner to look at life and runs back into it to die there. Outside, a hostile world, full of threats and insecurities. Inside him, a delirious imagination, guilt-ridden. Over what and why? A tormented victim—but wasn't there a suggestion that the author was somewhat enjoying the torment, somewhat too comically commenting on the poor man's end? Was it this element Belinsky observed, and found repellent? The superimposition upon Gogolian satire of a layer of cruelty?

Whatever this additive, one thing emerges clearly: the specific character of the "outsiders"—lonely, unwomaned, shy, prematurely broken; subordinate clerks, afraid of the world, often humiliated, and even more frequently "ashamed," filled with impenetrable guilt feelings, and time and again cleft in two. Now and then they are "malicious"—and being downtrodden and insignificant, devoid of a future, they live out a life of fantasy, which often turns to schizophrenia and madness. They create another "self" for themselves, to compensate for their own deficient one. And when their conflicts become insoluble, they lose their mind.

Such is Yakov Petrovich Golyadkin, the "hero" of *The Double*. The story, somewhat amorphous, repetitious, and longwinded—obviously fathered by Gogol's "The Nose"—still contains elements of startling intensity and insights. It is the antecedent of the innumerable "doubles" that will appear in Dostoevsky's more mature works, products of a more profound understanding of the hidden nooks of the human mind, culminating in the superb epitome of Ivan Karamazov.

Once again we are with a government clerk, one more affluent than Mr. Prokharchin; more ambitious, more active, more malicious—and more aware of the world to which he is opposed, and which opposes him. There is the whole body of his fellow-clerks, and above them the hierarchy of his superiors, from his chief, Andrey Filippovich, to the empyrean His Excellency—a world of terror and aspiration. His character combines elements of opposition—that dualism which in the later Dostoevsky will give rise to the amazing development of an "interior dialectic" of the human personality. Golyadkin is "timid," for his heart "had the habit of beating feverishly on all other people's staircases"; he is "humble," for he knows himself to be a "simple person," an "unimportant person." He has "enemies"—"I have malignant enemies who have sworn to ruin me." His abject self-consciousness is almost attractive, as is his self-conscious abjectness: "Being scared is our special line… To be abject on every occasion is our line." He aspires to the hand of an upper-class woman who is destined for a more successful rival; and he alternates between bouts of self-appreciation and self-denigration. Like so many characters in Dostoevsky, he is shown the door, more or less unceremoniously; and in the same way, he manages to create "scandals." Refused admittance to the ball given by his "patron and benefactor" in honor of his daughter (Golyadkin's cynosure), he worms himself into the reception through the

back stairs, and amazes by his shameless behavior. He flees into the night, and then encounters the other Golyadkin, Golyadkin Jr.—his other self. All that he is *not*, the
other Golyadkin *is*. All that Golyadkin Sr. desires to be, the other succeeds in being—
sly, adept, shrewd, unscrupulous, daring, calculating, sharp, stronger, and altogether
too well informed about his senior partner, especially his more shameful actions of
the past. Golyadkin finds his junior installed in his office without attracting any particular astonishment from the others; he is there with His Excellency, on good terms;
he is up to innumerable tricks at Senior's expense; he has a habit of arraigning the
other; and he finds the other revolting! He must be gotten rid of at any cost! One
cannot go on living like that. "I'm not a rag," he exclaims. "I'm not a rag, sir!" And
speaking of his Junior, "He's such a toady! He's such a lickspittle. He's such a Golyadkin!"
he complains. There is no end to the humiliations to which he is exposed. The romantic elopement he has dreamed up, turns to burlesque tragi-comedy, and ends in the
inevitable. Golyadkin is led off to an insane asylum. ...

Though Golyadkin is no Akaky Akakievich of "The Overcoat"—after all, he has a
valet and even sports a hired carriage—he too must flee from his reality: his own impossible self and his meaningless occupation, his comrades, his superiors, his own
meanness and "nastiness"—in fact, his nothingness. He flees into a schizophrenia,
creating another Golyadkin to complement his inadequate self. It is his only way of
temporary survival, against the successes of another, against his foiled courtship,
against his constant paranoia and the presence of enemies, against his own lack of
daring and dignity. But there is another, very significant and trenchant manner in
which Golyadkin differs from his Gogolian predecessor: There is no pity for Golyadkin in Dostoevsky's heart. His is a cruel story, and the rollicking humor that swells
into laughter at certain episodes only accentuates the pathos of the derangement.
There is an atmosphere of reptilism about Golyadkin in his constant insinuations into
places and situations which he is aware will only bring about his further abasement
and humiliation. Though we are aware there is some tyranny against which Golyadkin is struggling, it is never clearly set forth; and the destruction of Golyadkin
through his self-created satanic "other" leaves no heartache in the reader. The faceless,
nonentity that is Golyadkin, the cipher, is after all one of those hundreds, devoured by
the bureaucratic machinery, who need another personality. In his reptilism, Golyadkin becomes one of the innumerable prototypes of the self-abasing buffoon that will
populate Dostoevsky's later novels.

The young writer is reaching out in numerous directions, exploring the field of
psychic conflicts, without as yet arriving at a unifying center. He is preoccupied with
unusual states of the "soul" of individuals, whether with satirical or ironic intent, or
with a sense of emotional identification. There are stories of this period—written before 1849—deeply poignant, in which the distresses of the mind are set forth with
understanding and even compassion. Others, also deeply moving, leave one with a
feeling of confusion, as if the intent outran the possibility of consummation, or as if
the author wished to conceal more than he wished to reveal. "A Faint Heart" is a story
of the latter kind, a study of the disintegration of a personality, again a humdrum, impoverished copying clerk, through a traumatic—to us a seemingly commonplace—
experience. The slightly deformed Vasya Shumkov announces to his friend and

roommate, the much stronger, forceful. Arkady Ivanovich Nefedevich, that he proposes to marry. At the same time, to eke out a bare income, he has taken on extra
copying work. Vasya is one of Dostoevsky's febrile, overexcited, fragile creatures,
whose heart overflows with a yearning for happiness, for himself and others, but who
feels himself unworthy of it. His excitement knows no bounds: he is proud in the
promise of a dear girl, and in the possession of an equally dear friend. He is haunted
by his obligation to his superior to complete the assigned work. Under the triple
strain of his betrothal, his imminent parting from Arkady (though in typical Dosto-
evskyan pattern, the three plan to live together!), and the weight of his work obligation, Vasya's overtaxed frame cracks. He is led off to a hospital, under the paranoid
fear that he is to be sent for a soldier.

For Vasya is one of Dostoevsky's "dreamers"—or "tortoises"—defined by one of
the principal characters in another of these stories, "White Nights."

> Listen Nastenka... Let me tell you that in these corners live strange people—dreamers.
> The dreamer—if you want an exact definition—is not a human being, but a creature of
> an intermediate sort. For the most part he settles in some inaccessible corner, as though
> hiding from the light of day; once he slips into his corner, he grows to it like a snail, or,
> anyway, he is in that respect very much like that remarkable creature, which is an animal
> and a house both at once, and is called a tortoise. Why do you suppose he is so fond of
> his four walls, which are invariably painted green, grimy and reeking unpardonably of
> tobacco smoke?[32]

Such dreamers, as we have seen, are beset by attacks of anxiety, or perhaps more
exactly, are subject to almost constant anxiety neuroses. The terror that prevails in
their social environment—the "reality"—that filters down from the Tsar on high to
the meanest little clerk in the government bureau, becomes intensified to the point of
destruction in the fear-ridden mind of the "little man." Vasya is crippled both in body
and in mind—his emotional tides tend to drown out his reasoning faculties; he is
overpowered by them and by a sick imagination that is fed by what he believes to be
authority, and by the guilt within him, for failing to live up to his "responsibilities." He
needs a stronger will to lean on, and here the modern reader will sense elements of
the relationship between himself and the more aggressive Arkady that might explain
the disastrous resolution of the conflicts within Vasya—perhaps a conflict of choices,
attachment to his friend, love for the girl, and the obligation to authority. It is suggested, but never fully disclosed, that the destructive element lies in Arkady's triumphant possessiveness toward the weaker Vasya.

"White Nights," too, sets the stage for a less drastic, but none the less moving little
drama of loneliness. Here the unhappy tortoise—also a government clerk—emerges
into the streets of St. Petersburg (the entire drama takes place outdoors) in search of
some companionship, where he meets another lonely character, a girl equally miserable but awaiting the return of the man she has fallen in love with, and for a few days
experiences the warmth of human exchange and understanding. The eerie white light
of the Petersburg nights serves as background for the brief, heartrending encounter.
The girl's lover really returns, as he had promised, and the "tortoise," left alone once
more, retreats into his carapace.

The isolation of the character is further underlined by the presence in his room of a spider that his slovenly housekeeper never takes the trouble to remove, doing so only when his little life's interlude of communication is already over. Readers of *The Possessed* will scarcely need to be reminded of the symbolic meaning of the same insect in that novel, composed many years later...

Dostoevsky is the "poet" of St. Petersburg, the laureate of its middle and lower-class quarters, and may be said to have inaugurated the literary cult of that city. But this is not the St. Petersburg of Pushkin's "Bronze Horseman," the city of palaces and monuments, the city of magnificence. Dostoevsky's is a city of mists, snows, rain, a city of drab streets, strange corners and nooks, sometimes made mysterious by the curtain of fog but most frequently a maze, filled with scurrying strangers butting against sharp winds and seeking the warmth of some "corner" called home. We are more often inside the houses than outside, or in courtyards, on stairways. Only very occasionally and rarely is there splendor, light, and joy. St. Petersburg too is alien—frequently the "enemy." ...

Anyone seeking clues to the later Dostoevsky in these early works of the 1840s will not have far to look. Certain thematic materials—though not, of course fully developed or even clarified—that will appear and reappear in full openness with almost obsessive insistence in the works following Dostoevsky's exile, are already in evidence. At the center of such themes, which become almost central leitmotifs, is self-division, the dichotomy within an individual's soul, along with humiliation and self-abasement, shame, human isolation and alienation, and not least, anxiety. Fantasy also plays an important role. Less directly indicated, though clearly enough suggested, are other forms of "forbidden" feelings, thoughts and actions such as parricide or matricide, real or imagined; types of eroticism; and—to use more modern terminology—intimations of sadism, masochism and paranoia; as well as, in at least two instances, types of homosexuality. Manifestations of schizophrenia are more patently exposed. The treatment is frequently crude, sometimes so vague as to suggest deliberate concealment; the artistry is at times gauche. But the young Dostoevsky is groping toward an understanding of both himself and his fellow men and women; and the tentacles of his powerful if still unschooled imagination strike out to embrace more of the complex world than they can actually hold on to.[33]

Belinsky was outraged by *The Double* as well as "The Landlady." "In our time," he wrote, "the fantastic has its place only in insane asylums and not in literature, and is to be found in the care of physicians and not of poets."[34]

Dostoevsky, who worshipped Belinsky, felt devastated by this criticism. Having floated on clouds of glory, he now felt betrayed and rejected. Belinsky had occupied a special place in his life as advocate and teacher. When Dostoevsky heard of Belinsky's death in 1848, he was seized with another epileptic fit. It was not to be expected that Belinsky should have looked deeply into Dostoevsky's heart, where he would have been amazed to find turmoil, insecurity, doubts—in short, the tortures of a "malignant demon." He saw only what appeared to him as the asocial side of the stories. The element of rebellion against an oppressive social order or society was absent, he felt. But there was also another Dostoevsky, a storm-bird, whose preoccupations were to plunge him into a major cataclysm. When that great crisis occurred, Belinsky had already been dead one year. He could not then have known that he himself had a considerable part in bringing it about ...

* * *

Dostoevsky was "thrall to rebel powers" within him that craved outlet. The stories only partially revealed the storms that were raging. He was in feverish search, and a portion of the turmoil within him found expression in his stories: the feelings of humiliation and deprivation, and, not least, tormenting anxieties. His characters suffer from often undisclosed tyrannies. In his own life he found release in "dangerous" activities. He associated himself with one or another of the "circles"—the *kruzhki*—dedicated to the discussion of contemporary issues, with politics to the fore. The best-known of these was headed by M. V. Petrashevsky, an employee of the Ministry of Foreign Affairs, already since 1844 "under surveillance." Petrashevsky's apartment in Pokrov Square became the gathering place on Friday evenings from 1845 to April 1849. He was one of those not infrequent Russian intellectuals, a member of the gentry, who while still at the Lyceum had become imbued with the generative ideas of the 1830s, and whose insatiable curiosity led him into unusual pathways. A selfless preoccuation with social and philosophical thought marked him throughout, and a certain excusable fanaticism, once he was persuaded, clung to him till the day of his death in exile. A genial moderation kept him from violent agitation or action, but his fervor knew no bounds. With his own means he bought and established a library of Western literature, which he lent out to all his associates and friends and which included in good measure the advanced thought of France. He was the editor and writer of a *Dictionary of Foreign Words*, in whose seemingly innocent pages and definitions he disseminated radical ideas. Harmless catchwords concealed dangerous notions. Thus "Negrophile" attacked serfdom, "Opposition" was a defense of civil rights, "Odalisque" an apology for women's rights. More daringly, an article "Owenism" set forth that Englishman's program.

Among his intellectual demigods there was none equal to the French utopian, Fourier.

> When I read his works for the first time, [he wrote], I seemed to be reborn. I bowed down in front of the greatness of his genius. Just as if I had previously been not a Christian but a pagan, I destroyed all my other idols, and made him my only god.[35]

And his confrères, though they differed on many other matters, shared those feelings. He was especially taken with Fourier's psychology of the emotions, and even more so with the idea of the Phalanstery, Fourier's ideal community, for which he kept on agitating even when in exile. "To read his critical analysis of the life of society," Petrashevsky continued in the same vein, "is the same as to be born anew."[36]

He was opposed to violent measures and, like most of his group, favored the emancipation of the serfs as well as reform of the system of justice. Petrashevsky himself, however, under the persuasive influence of Tocqueville's book, favored the establishment of a republic on the American model.

The range of his and his group's reading makes one wonder about the efficiency of the Tsarist censorship and watchfulness: Fourier, of course; but also Lamennais,

Michelet, Proudhon, the Christian socialists, Louis Blanc, Cabet, as well as the Saint-Simonians. Even more surprising is the appearance of Ludwig Feuerbach's *Essence of Christianity*, which Petrashevsky utilized for his article on "Naturalism" in his *Dictionary*, and David Friedrich Strauss's *Life of Jesus*. And most surprising, Karl Marx's *La Misère de la Philosophie*, and Friedrich Engels' *Condition of the Working Class in England*.

In such an atmosphere one needed neither headier wines nor Lucullan viands to warm one's insides, make the heart beat faster and the head swim. Argument clashed with argument, words flew, the smoky room was aquiver with the thunderbolts of ideas; sometimes bolder words than was meet were shouted forth, hopefully to be buried in the bosoms of those present as eternal secrets. For there was one bond that united all in that quarter—their hatred of the Tsar Nicholas I. The poet A. N. Pleshcheyev wrote of such meetings:

> I sit surrounded by a noisy crew.
> At a great feast, I hear the sound of chains;
> And there appears far in the distance, like a vision before me,
> Crucified upon a cross, the Great Nazarene.[37]

More intemperately, another member of the group read a paper entitled "The Foundation of Rome and the Reign of Romulus." The reader, N. Mombelli, introduced the following sentence:

> No, the emperor Nicholas is not a human being, but a monster, a beast; he is that Antichrist of whom the Apocalypse speaks ... How strangely the world is organized: one loathsome man and how much evil he can do, and according to what right?[38]

Though some of the visitors were more or less religious, and a number of them might be called Christian socialists, there was no lack of atheists; Petrashevsky had not read Feuerbach in vain.

Petrashevsky's *Dictionary* supplied a sufficient amount of ammunition for frequent detonation. In the innocuously titled article on "Oratory" one could read a vitriolic condemnation of Russia's backwardness:

> Would it not be strange to search for reason, for discoveries, for improvements and inventions useful to the whole of mankind where every demonstration of reason, every innovation, is something illegal, immoral: where justice itself has never been fair; where the high court of society is nothing but an organ of preservation of every falsehood? Where, as it were, everything, both man and nature, has been covered by a mold of stagnation and inactivity ... where one set way, monotony, and lack of sense and more lack of sense is the law of social life ... as is the case in Turkey and China.[39]

What more appropriate than to celebrate the birthday of patron saint Fourier, as was done at a dinner on April 7, 1849, where speaker after speaker rose, heated no doubt by the occasion as well as the toasts, and where one of those present, Khanykov, uttered heartwarming words:

> Greetings to thee, Genius, to thee my feeble words, but pronounced from the heart, in an inspired manner! Oh, how I desire at this moment to unite with thee—in thought, in feeling!. ...[40]

Fyodor Dostoevsky was not one of those present at that dinner. But he had been attending the Petrashevsky "Fridays" since 1847, bringing with him his own stores of thought and feeling and also profiting from the intellectual stimulus offered by the participants and the books that were so freely lent. He had always been a voracious reader, and now, armed with the ideas he had found in Belinsky and his associates, he sharpened them on these new whetstones. We may be sure he listened intently as Ensign Konstantin Timkovsky expounded and read from Lamennais' *Paroles d'un croyant*; Petrashevsky urged the advantages of a socialist phalanstery for Russia; another preached the need and the benefit of dividing the world into two polities, one Fourierist and the other Communist, in what might be called "socialist competition."

It was all done in high spirits, but in good fun; it was discussion and nothing more—and these gatherings acquired a celebrity throughout the city, becoming, among other sights and events, one of the "attractions" of St. Petersburg. Thus one visitor, Petrov, cited the main pleasures to be obtained there as "the opera, the circus, the theatre, the sermons of Nilson, the articles by Pleshcheyev, and the propaganda of Petrashevsky."[41]

Another participant recalled the "Fridays" with relish:

> We did not have an organized club, no general plan of activity, but once a week there were meetings at Petrashevsky's, at which the same people did not always attend; some came frequently, others rarely, and it was always possible to meet new people there. It was an interesting kaleidoscope of the most varied opinions concerning contemporary events, government decrees, and the latest literature in various branches of knowledge. The city's news was brought there, and one spoke loudly about everything, without any inhibition. Sometimes, one of the specialists delivered a communication in the form of a lecture … At these gatherings, no specific projects or plots were worked out, but judgments of the existing order were expressed, jokes, laments of the present state of things … Our small circle which concentrated around Petrashevsky at the end of the forties carried within itself the germ of all the reforms of the sixties …[42]

And he added that there were a few "desperate" people among the other, more moderate, members of the group.

That was true.

There were those who felt that there was too much talk but too little action; those who bridled at what seemed a certain passiveness that left crucial matters hanging high in a cloud-cuckoo land, when all around the hand of oppression and fear lay heavy. While Petrashevsky and a few of the others felt that one should proceed slowly; that, for example, before one could demand the liberation of the serfs, one should fight for a reform of the juridical system—there were those who proposed more radical measures, even suggesting the need for an "uprising." A dissident group split off from the *Petrashevchi* under the leadership of Sergey Durov and Nikolay Speshnev. That was in the fall of 1848. Revolutions had swept the European continent, and Russia too was shaken. Tsar Nicholas proclaimed: "Revolution is at the gates of Russia, but I swear it shall not enter as long as I have a breath of life left within me."[43] In March of that year, in anticipation of troubles from Poland, he had ordered mobilization and the return of Russians from abroad. Russian troops occupied Poland,

suppressed some minor uprisings in the Baltic provinces and some peasant disturbances around Kiev. The terror that had seemed somewhat relaxed in the few years
before 1848 was now intensified. In the circle that now met at Durov's or at Speshnev's, political tempers grew more heated.

Dostoevsky joined the Durov group. The excitement of historic events, the heightened climate of discussions and plans, somewhat alleviated the depression he had
been feeling over his own creative work. The year 1847 had been a lean one—productive only of "The Landlady" and the inconsiderable "A Novel in Nine Letters." The following year had been better: he had written four stories. But his mood was low. He
was in constant monetary distress; he felt the drudgery of writing to order and kept
on pressing his editor Kraevsky for larger and larger advances. He had not recovered
from Belinsky's critical displeasure. He lacked direction. At least here at Durov's was
an escape valve for his explosive emotions and thoughts. And here too was one person
who appeared an adequate replacement for the seemingly irreplaceable Belinsky. He
needed someone strong to lean on. Belinsky had freed him intellectually and artistically; Belinsky had also liberated him from the bondage of religion. Belinsky had
turned him into an unbeliever—an atheist! This was his own testimony, made many
years later. Belinsky "knew that the revolution must necessarily begin with atheism ...
During the last year of his life I did not visit him. He took a dislike to me, but then I
had passionately embraced his teaching."[44]

But Belinsky's circle was not primarily a political one. Durov's was. And here,
Speshnev dominated. All who knew him or came in contact with him testified to his
magnetic personality. Handsome, eloquent, somewhat dissolute, brilliant, and well
educated, he had been to Germany, where he had become acquainted with the
Hegelian and post-Hegelian philosophies. He was probably the only member of those
circles who knew Karl Marx's *Misère de la Philosophie* and the *Communist Manifesto*.
He was an ardent Feuerbachian. A man of wealth, he had been to Paris, Vienna, Dresden, and Switzerland. In Paris, the socialist Leroux was so thoroughly impressed with
him that he invited him to collaborate on the *Revue Indépendante*. He was reputed to
be the author of a book on socialism, which apparently disappeared. He called himself
a "communist," and there could be no doubt that his range of acquaintance with radicals in Paris was quite wide. He clearly saw the direction that philosophy was taking,
and in 1847 wrote to the Polish émigré K. E. Chojecki:

> You are right—all German idealism of the nineteenth century—the "great" German
> philosophy beginning with Fichte ... drives only towards anthropotheism, to the point
> where, having reached its summit in the person of its latest standard-bearer and leading
> figure, Feuerbach, it calls things by their right name and exclaims with him: *Homo
> homini Deus est*—man is God unto man ... This is the second assumption of the God-
> Man, or the Man-God, who, according to legend, takes his body with him to heaven.[45]

He was unsympathetic to Fourier's gradualism. He was an advocate of activism
and conspiratorial organization. He regarded peasant revolts in the manner of Puga-
chev as the only means of revolution. The revolution in Russia would come soon, the
land would be nationalized, and the new government would control both agriculture
and industry.

Dostoevsky fell under this man's spell. In 1854 he wrote about him: "The wondrous fate of that man; wherever and however he makes his appearance, the most unconstrained, the most impervious people immediately surround him, with devotion and respect."[46] He was indeed regarded by those who met him as a "most remarkable personality." For Dostoevsky, the person and the activities and thoughts of Speshnev had a kind of demonic attractiveness. His handsome appearance was matched by brilliance of mind; but he was also a rebel. Dostoevsky's troubled and unsure soul responded to the assurance and mastery of Speshnev. And within the group he found a corresponding rebelliousness and radicalism of thought—now allied to practice—Thought leading to Action. Here were men of daring, ready to engage in what seemed dangerous enterprises. The watchwords were "revolution," "uprising," "insurrection." Members of the secret group were presumably bound to secrecy and loyalty by a "threat of death in case of treason."[47]

Among intemperates, it was reported that Dostoevsky was not in the rear. The writer Grigoriev had prepared a brochure that was to be distributed among soldiers urging upon them rebellion against the Tsar. What was needed was a secret press, and Speshnev and Dostoevsky and five others were commissioned to buy the necessary parts. Parts of the machine were actually bought and lodged at the house of a fellow-conspirator. This was no puny act. The press was, it appears, actually assembled in the fateful month of April 1849.

Thus Dostoevsky expressed his defiance. Speshnev was generous; he had loaned Dostoevsky some five hundred rubles. Speshnev towered. Speshnev was Belinsky's surrogate, but also a man of action. Dostoevsky was now imbibing ideas, experiences; encountering personalities and situations that would serve him as a writer for many years. Had he pledged himself along with the others "to take part openly and fully in the uprising and fight, when the Committee has decided that the time for rebellion had arrived?"[48] He was to have prepared an essay on socialism to be read before the group. (He never did.) And now he was engaged in the printing-press enterprise, which, in the eyes of the government, was a most heinous offense. Fortunately, when the blow fell, the press was never discovered.

The demoniac struggles which were henceforth to rack him had already begun. Whatever faith he had had was by this time undermined. He was an unbeliever, tortured by his unbelief. There can be little doubt that one of Petrashevsky's articles in his *Dictionary*, which under the guise of "optimism" actually discussed atheism, stuck in his mind for many years to come and was to form the basis of one of the most celebrated dialectical exchanges in *The Brothers Karamazov*.

Atheism [Petrashevsky had written] .... the teaching which denies the existence of God and the presence of omnipotent divine providence, bases itself on facts which it thinks are directly opposed to the idea of the divine, such as the death of children in the wombs of their mothers, death of anybody at all prior to his full physical and mental development, and, in one word, the perishing of any being before it had reached its normal development. ... These facts, as well as other similar facts, have constantly remained the stumbling block and the temptation for thinkers who have tried to reconcile evil with eternal goodness, the foreknowledge of the Creator with the freedom of the will.[49]

Thus, too, his relationship to Speshnev was to form the seedbed for future conflicts, projected onto his great novels. He was at once exhilarated and tormented by
the other man—in his own mind feeling a hold upon him he could not free himself
from. Whatever he may have given up in giving up religion, he had not surrendered
the Devil. The reader of Dostoevsky's later novels will not long need to speculate
about the causes for the mental and physical distresses Dostoevsky experienced at this
time. His friend Dr. Yanovsky recalled—and the reminiscence may not be too accu-
rate—that Dostoevsky in those days became "rather apathetic, more irritable, more
easily offended and prone to find fault with the most insignificant trifles, began especially often to complain of dizzy spells." The reason for this, according to Dostoevsky's
own admission, was his familiarity with Speshnev, or to put it more exactly, "a loan
which he had made from him." Dostoevsky is reported to have told the doctor: "No, it
will not pass ... Now I am with him and his. And I'll never be in a position to recoup
this sum, but then he wouldn't even take the money back; that's the individual he is.
Do you understand that from now on I have my own Mephistopheles?"[50]

The account sounds authentic, and is probably true. But the explanation hardly
satisfies. Dostoevsky owed money to many others and was not particularly anguished
by that fact. Undoubtedly, his relationship to Speshnev had certain aspects that were
not clear even to himself, and which he could not have explained to Dr. Yanovsky—
and would not have, had he understood them. When the time came, he was to be
more explicit. The demoniacal obsessions and guilts he was probing would eventually
finds expression in such figures as Stavrogin and Pyotr Verkhovensky of *The Possessed*,
and the unresolved dualism within his own character, in the celebrated colloquy of
Ivan Karamazov and the Devil. While in exile, he wrote to the wife of the Decembrist
Fonvizin: "I will tell you regarding myself that I am a child of the age, a child of non-
belief and doubt, up till now and even (I know it) until my coffin closes."[51]

And now, in April 1849, when his soul was in revolt and he was aching for action,
his life was to be disrupted by an event that was to bring about such changes in him as
have rarely occurred in the life of a human being. Here, once more, Vissarion Belinsky
was to play an unwitting but critical role.

* * *

Events taking place in the other parts of Europe did not go without profound effect in
Russia. Nicholas I might boast in 1848:

> Let the peoples of the West look for happiness in revolution! Russia contemplates these
> movements with serenity ...

and to the King of Prussia he announced,

> This is a solemn moment that I have been predicting for eighteen years; revolution has
> risen out of its ashes and an unavoidable peril threatens our joint existence.[52]

Whatever the degree of the Tsar's serenity, he was taking no chances. The redoubtable General Paskevich was readied, and was soon to make his way toward
Poland and Hungary. Internally, panic swept the authorities.

The Petrashevsky group had been under surveillance since March of 1848. For
already in January of that year a lithographed sheet had come to the attention of the

Ministry of the Interior. It was addressed to the St. Petersburg Assembly of the Nobility, "On the Means of Increasing the Value of Populated or Gentry Estates," recommending that merchants purchase serf land in order to raise its value. Ivan Petrovich Liprandi, an employee of the Ministry, was ordered to investigate, and he in turn found in P. D. Antonelli, son of an academician, a willing agent to penetrate the radical circles and bring in compromising information. What both Liprandi and Antonelli immediately discovered was that, in contradistinction to the Decembrist groups, which were constituted exclusively of gentry and army officers, these groups included, "along with Guards officers and officials of the Ministry of Foreign Affairs, … non-matriculated students, petty artisans, dealers, and even tobacco sellers."[53]

Antonelli fulfilled his assignments efficiently. What he heard, or what he alleged he heard, was dynamite enough. The Third Section could not but rejoice to hear that the Petrashevsky and the other groups had vowed to follow the "executive committee's" orders "to openly participate … in all struggles and risings," having provided themselves "with fire-arms or steel"; or that Petrashevsky himself had said at one meeting, "We have condemned to death today's society. Now it behooves us to execute the verdict."[54]

What occurred in the secret discussions of the Durov group was never revealed by any of its members. What the more radical members of the Petrashevsky group were talking about, Liprandi reported, was the need to arouse the country, especially the peasants, against the government; the need to undermine religion and to spread their insurrectionist propaganda throughout Russia.

The spy Antonelli reported on a meeting at Petrashevsky's in 1849:

> At the meeting of April 15 Dostoevsky read Gogol's correspondence with Belinsky, and notably Belinsky's letter to Gogol.[55] This letter summoned a considerable amount of enthusiastic approval from the society, in particular.… at that point where Belinsky says that religion has no basis among the Russian people. It was proposed that this letter be distributed in several copies.[56]

As a matter of fact, Dostoevsky read the letter three times, twice at Petrashevsky's and once at Durov's. In addition to the attack on the Church, and the supposed myth that the Russian people were truly religious, the informer might also have reported Belinsky's contemptuous reference to the alleged love of the Russian people for the Tsar, and the "round paunches of the Russian priests."

When Count Orlov was certain that his file was complete, he submitted it to the Tsar, who wrote down on the margin:

> I have read everything; this is a serious affair. Even if all of it were only chatter, it is nevertheless criminal and intolerable. They must be arrested, as you recommend. Go to it, in the name of God, and let His will be done.[57]

His Majesty's orders were obeyed, and Orlov reported:

> I have the honor to inform Your Majesty that the arrests have been made and that thirty-four persons with their papers have been handed over to the Third Section.[58]

The rest of the story can best be told in Dostoevsky's own words:

The 22nd or better to say the 23rd of April, I returned some time around four o'clock from N.P. Grigoryev's, lay down in bed, and immediately fell asleep. Not more than an hour passed when I felt, as though in a dream, that some strange and suspicious persons had entered my room. ... With effort I open my eyes and hear a soft, sympathetic voice: "Get up!" I look: there is a quarter or district superintendent of police with a handsome pair of side whiskers. But it was not he who had spoken; the gentleman who spoke was dressed in light blue, wearing a lieutenant-colonel's epaulettes. "What's happened?" I asked, raising myself in bed. "At the command of ..." I look: it actually was "at the command ..." At the door a soldier was standing, also in blue. It was then his saber that had rattled.[59]

Confined along with the others in the Peter-Paul Fortress, Dostoyevsky was forbidden to write or receive mail. Some of the prisoners became demoralized; one went insane, another planned suicide. In the meantime, investigations and interrogations went on. The first commission brought in a verdict of not guilty, but was immediately superseded by a military commission which sentenced fifteen of the prisoners to be shot, six to be deported, six to be released. However, the Tsar transferred the case to a third commission, the so-called Auditoriat-General, which at first extended the death sentence to all, but recommended commutation to hard labor. Dostoevsky was sentenced to eight years of hard labor in Siberia, but the Tsar changed the sentence to "four years, the rest as a soldier."

The story of what followed is well known, but bears repetition. The prisoners, instead of being taken out, as they thought, to hear the verdicts, were herded into carriages and taken to the Semyonovsky parade grounds. It was freezing weather. And now was enacted a macabre "comedy" devised by that supreme engineer of cruelty, His Majesty Tsar Nicholas I. All was in readiness here: the scaffold, the stakes, the soldiers with fixed bayonets, even the priest to read St. Paul and hold up the crucifix to be kissed. There was also the "executioner" mantling the condemned in white robes. All was set for the executioner and the execution, down to the loading of the guns. ... Petrashevsky, Mombelli and Grigoriev were already tied to the posts. ... Dostoevsky was sixth in line and soon his turn would come too. ... The verdict of death was pronounced ...

Such was the scenario carefully prepared by the Tsar and his advisers, with all the precision of a stage director.

And then, suddenly, retreat was sounded, and the sentence of commutation was read: "The defendants, who deserved the death penalty in accordance with the law, are pardoned by the infinite clemency of His Majesty the Emperor." Grigoriev went insane. He had seen death, and he died—the death of the mind. Dostoevsky had seen death, and he lived, never to be the same thereafter. He was alive, and he rejoiced. Siberia seemed little enough to bear after such an ordeal. But that moment of near-death would never be obliterated. This was an end. And this was also a beginning.

On the same day, December 22, 1849, Dostoevsky wrote to his brother Mikhail:

Brother, I'm not depressed and haven't lost spirit. Life everywhere is life, life is in ourselves and not in the external. There will be people near me, and to be a human being among human beings, and remain one forever, no matter what misfortune befall, not to become depressed, and not to falter—that is what life is, herein lies its task ... Now, upon changing my life, I am being born again in a new form. Brother! I swear to you I will not lose hope and will preserve my spirit and my heart in purity. I'll be reborn the better. This is my entire hope, all my consolation![60]

Precisely at midnight on December 14th, Fyodor Dostoevsky celebrated the birth of the Savior in an unforgettable manner. He was put in irons, placed in an open sleigh with a gendarme beside him. Another sleigh with Durov was standing near. On January 9, 1850, Dostoevsky and his escort reached Tobolsk. Some days later they were in Omsk. For four years he was to remain in this Siberian prison-house—a convict, in a home he was later to immortalize as the "House of the Dead."

Thus ended the first act of the drama that was Dostoevsky's life. What happened on that December day when he faced a firing squad, what happened on Christmas eve, then in prison and exile, was to form the second act and a new epoch in that drama.

Part Three

Europe: Revolution 1848–1849

Chapter One

The Lightning of Ideas

Reason and Revolution 1835–1848

> The insight then to which. ... philosophy is to lead us, is that the real world is as it ought to be—that the truly good—the universal divine reason—is not a mere abstraction, but a vital principle capable of realizing itself. This *Good*, this *Reason*, in its most concrete form, is God. God governs the world; the actual working of his government—the carrying out of his plan—is the History of the World. ... Before the pure light of this divine Idea— which is no mere Ideal—the phantom of a world whose events are an incoherent concourse of fortuitous circumstances, utterly vanishes.
>
> —Hegel, *The Philosophy of History*

> German philosophy is a serious matter, of concern to all mankind. Our remotest descendants alone will be able to judge whether we are to be blamed or praised for having first produced our philosophy and then our revolution. But it seems to me that a methodical people like the Germans had to commence with the Reformation. Thereafter they could occupy themselves with philosophy, and only when they had completed that task, were they in a position to pass on to political revolution. I find this sequence very reasonable. The heads which philosophy used for reflection could later be chopped off by the revolution, for its own purposes. But philosophy could never have used these heads if the revolution had first chopped them off.
>
> —Heinrich Heine

> Until now philosophers have only interpreted the world in various ways; the point is to change it.
>
> —Karl Marx

While Britain was roaming the high seas, sending its goods and its culture far and wide—and from its factories, teeming treasures of linens, cottons and woollens, coal and iron—a revolution was taking place in Germany that was to shake the world as profoundly, though in an altogether different manner, as the industrial revolution in England. This revolution, now in the making, had as yet no terrestrial abode except in the minds of philosophers—who had, as one wit remarked, taken heaven for their empire as the English had taken the earth. Had these philosophers remained in their celestial regions all might have been well, or at least quiescent, on earth. But Thought is a restless thing, even when it is transcendental and ideal. Once it descends from its empyrean lodgments, finds a congenial home and the right moment, and turns to Action—the consequences may be far-reaching.

1. G.W.F. Hegel

Georg Wilhelm Friedrich Hegel died of cholera in 1831, in his sixty-first year. Johann Wolfgang von Goethe died in the fullness of his eighty-two years in 1832. Two mighty phenomena, they epitomize the end of a great era: Hegel the last of the philosophic encyclopedists, Goethe the last of the poet-pansophists. Of both it might be said, as Bacon said of himself, that they had "taken all knowledge to be their province." Both constructed vast theodicies, cosmic in character, and secular, though mantled in quasi-religious garb: Hegel translating God into the ideal forms of Reason and Logic, which irresistibly, as Creator, objectified themselves in an ever-developing universe, moving toward the attainment of absolute Freedom; protean Goethe, who had completed his *Faust* in the year of his death, objectified the cosmic process in the titanic figure of an *Übermensch*, a superman, Faust, and synthesized the world's major intellectual experiences in that scholar's journeyings through microcosm and macrocosm. In Goethe's work are concentrated *Sturm und Drang*, classical and Christian heaven and hell, medievalism and Romanticism, and the achievement, through activity, of ultimate salvation. Faust is the last embodiment of a cosmopolitan *Humanitätsideal*, the last evidence of that Olympianism that bridged two centuries and saw the advent of its own disintegration. Hegel, too, synthesized a world of thought and experiences, marking out an upward path toward a secular salvation. Each of them was to experience, if not personally, certainly in his creations, the questionings of a young opposition, characteristically in one case, *Jung Deutschland*—Young Germany; in the other, the *Jung-Hegelianer*—Young Hegelians. The Young Germans saw in Goethe the last representative of what Heine called the "Art Epoch" in German literature; a figure standing "above the battle," grand in his own right but unfitted now to guide a new generation in its intellectual, political and social warfare against absolutism. A wing of the *Young Hegelians* will begin to batter down the mighty fortress built by the master, and attempt new structures from its huge fragments ... It is not often that history materializes a portentous symbolism of an epoch, as it did when it brought three world-historic figures together within the compass of the minuscule area of a world map: Napoleon, Goethe, and Hegel—Hegel in Jena in 1806; Goethe in Weimar at the moment when the reality and fiction of a Holy Roman Empire was being shattered at the Battle of Jena. Goethe confronted Napoleon as an equal, his Jovian calm unruffled by the course of history. Hegel, philosopher-professor, wandered through Jena, carrying the completed version of his *Phenomenology of Mind* to his printers, probably still unaware of the meaning of the cannonade. If he saw Napoleon but at a distance, he was no less reverent toward him than Goethe. ...

It is not carrying the simile too far to see in Hegel a Faustian character. But what Faust strove to but could never realize, it seemed the philosopher achieved. Faust had cried out in an agony of frustration his need to discover what it was that held the world together:

> *Dass ich nicht mehr mit saurem Schweiss,*
> *Zu sagen brauche, was ich nicht weiss;*
> *Dass ich erkenne, was die Welt,*
> *Im Innersten zusammen hält,*
> *Schau' alle Wirkenskraft und Samen. ...*

> That I no more with sour sweat
> Need speak of things I know naught of,
> That I might know what mortise binds
> The world's most inmost being,
> And see its seedbed and its workings. ...

Like Faust, Hegel sought to grasp and hold "infinite Nature"—*die unendliche Natur*. It might seem heretical to speak of Romanticism in these connections, but is it not true that here the two greatest Romantics of the age meet on common ground— that Faustian romantic aspiration finds its most consummate realization in the seemingly cold abstraction of a triumphant World Reason? Both wish to raise the veil that hides "ultimate" Reality. Hegel felt that he had finally done so in piercing the unknowability of Kant's *Ding an sich*, "The Thing in Itself." The absolute idealist was now to display the structure and movement of the universe in its totality. In an age that included such remarkable polymaths as Herder and Alexander von Humboldt, this did not seem a superhuman objective ...

It was not only Hegel, but his students and colleagues too, who felt that something mighty and ultimate had been attained in his work. He was the Aristotle of modern times, and after him—what? Could there be philosophy after him? So a very young student of his in Heidelberg meditated in 1818:

> A terrifying gulf seemed to open up, a long sleep like that which lasted throughout the Middle Ages. Would Hegel fare like Aristotle? Would there be nothing but mechanical repetition of what he had been saying?[1]

Here, in Hegel, was the last expression of that cultural idealism which had been striving to achieve Freedom and thought it had found it in the realms of the mind, precluded as it was from realizing it—as yet—in the realms of action. At last, it seemed, that dichotomy which had been the nightmare of German philosophers, that of Mind and external Reality, Mind and Matter, was to be resolved. The hegemony of Mind would be preserved; but its triumphant course would be manifested in Activity. A new Unity would now emerge ...

After his appointment to the University of Berlin in 1818, where he remained until his death, he dominated the philosophical horizon. He gathered around him a notable group of students and followers, some of whom were to remain faithful to the last word of the Master, with others more faithful to his memory than to his word. For the dialectical process of which he was the supreme exponent had a way of continuing to operate in forms that no doubt would have brought Hegel consternation had he been alive to see its ultimate working-out in his successors. ...

He was far from an eloquent speaker. Yet soon students listened and were entranced. He spoke in a dry, hesitant, rasping manner; at times he seemed scarcely aware of his audience; he leafed unintermittently through innumerable papers before him, drawing out his mighty sentences with difficulty. He seemed to be in another world. Yet at times, flashes of inspired rhetoric, a poetic analogy, a reference, an allusion, a metaphor emerged. The hard and very special terminology acquired clarity. Posterity was to note among his hearers notable names-to-be: Heinrich Heine, Ludwig Feuerbach, Eduard Gans the legal philosopher, David Friedrich Strauss. Another young student describes his feelings:

> ... The most wonderful streams of thought wound themselves, pressed forward, and struggled, now singly, now jointly, hesitatingly here and there, and then rushing forward in spasms, but ahead, irresistibly. ... Then the voice rose, the eyes shone, sharply scanning the assembled auditors, and the words flowed easily, seizing upon the heights and depths of the soul. All now seemed so clear and exhaustive, of such simple persuasion, that those who could grasp it felt as if they themselves had thought it and found it ...[2]

To some it seemed as if they were present at some primal act of creation. Hegel appeared like some mighty demiurge brooding over the "abyss" and "making it pregnant." With his daring genius he was unfolding the March of Mind in the process of achieving "self-consciousness"—"self-realization"—which he said was also the March of Freedom. ...

* * *

God the Creator was Mind, Reason, Spirit. Restless, a driving force, moving with the inexorable necessity of Logic, Reason objectified itself and manifested itself in determinate Nature and its highest product, Man. Reason was the Absolute, itself changeless yet exhibiting itself in constant Change, a continuing process of Activity whose goal was the attainment of total Self-Consciousness—Freedom. Reason's march was toward Perfectibility. It transcended the dualism of form and content, mind and matter, self and community, the individual and the world. It realized itself in History. Reason subsumed all realms of being—the inorganic as well as the organic, Nature, Society. ... It represented universal unity. The world was its arena of action, and its progression was towards Absolute Truth. Its center was Man, the thinking subject. Its instrument, Change. Constant change was the means by which the living being unfolded his potentialities, developing and expanding them in a continuous process of self-knowledge, knowledge of the world. The world of history was the living theatre of this change of the potential into the actual. Such a cosmic process meant a constant struggle for mastery, as the human mind reached out for greater and greater freedom, and moved from elementary sense-certainty toward the higher stage of perception, from perception to understanding, and then to self-certainty. This ultimate stage was the Truth of Reason.

The world, then, was a purposive one. Though in constant movement, constantly changing—as was the mind of man—it was not a meaningless chaos. For its movement was of a special kind. It was a *dialectical movement*—a movement through inner contradiction.

For Being means Becoming. Nothing in the universe is ever at rest. Everything is in process of change. A stone changes, but the stone is not conscious that it is changing. The plant changes as it emerges from the seed, and flowers. Here the potential has become the actual; what was in the seed is potentially the ultimate flower. The change that has taken place is different from that which the stone undergoes. But the plant too has no consciousness of the process. Only man has this consciousness. Within him that consciousness is the resultant of a long process, a slow process. Only Man is conscious of the nature of change. Only he is conscious of being changed, of a changing world, or of changing the world—of the translation of the potential into the actual. He is the highest realization of Reason as Activity.

Dialectics means inner contradiction. It means that a content can be unfolded only through passing into its opposite. It is in this process of opposition and interaction that important changes take place. Something new emerges, something qualitatively new. Some of the elements of the old are still preserved; others are eliminated. All finite things contain within themselves this contradictory element. This element is "Negativity," the "No" which is within the "Yes" of any element, which is its undoing, and its motive force of change. It is, in Hegel's words, "the innermost source of all activity, of living and spiritual self-movement." It is all-pervasive. It takes a triadic form of Thesis—that which is the given, the finite object or thought; its opposite, already contained within it, the Antithesis—this is the "Negative," the destructive; and finally the higher, which emerges, the Synthesis. Such is the "untamed restlessness"—the *haltungslose Unruhe*—"the unrest of self-movement," of Being, Non-Being, and Becoming. Dialectics is Reason actualizing itself in Man's thinking. It has something godlike about it, at once terrifying and awesome, as well as exhilarating. Transformation taking place is an an ever-richer progression, ever wider, ever more creative ...

Life is Death, as Death is Life. In a finite world—and finitude is an inherent quality of the world—things can develop their potentialities only by perishing and passing into another form of being. As Hegel put it,

> The finite does not only change ... It perishes, and its perishing is not merely contingent, so that it could be without perishing. It is rather the very being of finite things that they contain the seeds of perishing as their own Being-in-Self (*Insichsein*), and the hour of their birth is the hour of their death. ... The highest maturity or state which any Something can reach is that in which it begins to perish.[3]

So that,

> Negation is just as much Affirmation as Negation, or ... what is self-contradictory resolves itself not into nullity, into abstract Nothingness, but essentially only into the negation of its *particular* content.[4]

Such is "Pan-logism," the movement of Thought in its contradictions. Such too, the "terrorism" of Thought—its destructiveness and its creativeness. Hegel speaks in dramatic terms of the "seriousness, the suffering, the patience and the labor of the negative,"[5] and the "portentous power of the Negative," in its progress towards Universality.

Time, too, is such a "destroyer and preserver." In a beautiful retelling of the myth, Hegel gives us the central kernel of his idea:

It was first Chronos—Time—that ruled the Golden Age, without moral products; and what was produced—the offspring of Chronos—was devoured by it. It was Jupiter—from whose head Minerva sprang, and to whose circle of divinities belong Apollo and the Muses—that first put a constraint upon Time, and set a bound to its principle of decadence. He is the Political god, who produced a moral work—the State. ... Zeus, therefore, who is represented as having put a limit to the devouring agency of Time, and stayed this transiency by having established something inherently and independently durable—Zeus and his race are themselves swallowed up, and that by the very power that produced them—the principle of thought, perception, reasoning, insight derived from rational grounds, and the requirement of such ground.[6]

Man's self-conscious activity, therefore, "annuls reality, the permanence of what is, but at the same time it gains, on the other side, the essence, the notion, the universal." Hence the march of Spirit is a progressive one. Change is its essence and agent. Change imports dissolution; but it also brings new life. "While death is the issue of life, life is also the issue of death." But the new life is not merely a resurrection or a rejuvenescence of the old. Spirit now comes forth "exalted, glorified, a purer spirit." It is not merely changed Spirit, but "Spirit manifesting, developing and perfecting itself in every direction which its manifold nature can follow."[7] Mind is moving toward an ever-growing comprehension of itself and the world, and what holds it "together." Its movement is toward Universality.

Spirit's field of activity is History. Hegel now spreads out a vast canvas in which the World Spirit marches like a triumphant God—or might it be a Napoleon?—in constant process of self-development and self-consciousness, an ascent toward Freedom. Growth and decay alternate in each historic epoch or stage, each implicit in its predecessor. Here is no repetition. Here is process and progress. In this majestic advance, Reason objectifies itself in Man and in his actions. It moves with inexorable Logic toward its higher purposes. Here individuality matters not at all. What operates is the Cunning of Reason, *die List der Vernunft*. The human individual is the unwitting agent of a force he does not comprehend, a force that works the ultimate good. The individual may fall by the wayside. So may the political state. To the superficial eye, History may even appear as the "slaughter-bench" of happiness. It does not matter. The "Cunning of Reason" uses them as means to something higher.

The History of the World is not the theatre of happiness. Periods of happiness are blank pages in it, for they are periods of harmony—periods when the antithesis is in abeyance.[8]

The larger issues which the World Spirit wills become manifest and are realized in world-historic figures, the Heroes. They too are unconscious of those higher purposes. They are bearers of the Idea, while prosecuting their own aims. They are agents, rather than independent actors. But they possess insight into "the requirements of the time." They are "thinking men," and understand what it is that is ripe for development in their age. Driven by an irresistible passion, they fulfil their particular missions, ignorant of the fact that they are all a part of a great plan. Neither for them, nor for those innumerable lesser others, need there be "litanies of lamentation."

What then are the stages of progress of the World Spirit and the World Will as they move through the finite and determinate world of ours? The history of the world is the "theatre," the "possession," the "sphere of realization," of the World Spirit. ...

> Spirit begins with a germ of infinite possibility, but *only* possibility—containing its substantial existence in an undeveloped form, as the object and goal which it reaches only in its resultant—full reality. In actual existence Progress appears as an advancing from the imperfect to the more perfect; but the former must not be understood abstractly as *only* the imperfect, but as something which involves the very opposite of itself—the so-called perfect—as a *germ* or impulse. So—reflectively, at least—possibility points to something destined to become actual. ... Thus, the imperfect, as involving its opposite, is a contradiction, which certainly exists, but which is continually annulled and solved; the instinctive movement—the inherent impulse in the life of the soul—to break through the rind of mere nature, sensuousness, and that which is alien to it, and to attain to the light of consciousness, *i.e.* to itself.[9]

Now, every step in this process has its "determinate principle." In history it is the "idiosyncracy of Spirit"—that is, the peculiar national genius which in turn exhibits itself in its polity, its ethics, legislation, science, art.

Now let us further follow the World Spirit as it actualizes itself from the past to the present:

> It may be said of Universal History, that it is the exhibition of Spirit in the process of working out the knowledge of that which it is potentially. ... The Orientals have not attained the knowledge that Spirit—Man as *such*—is free; and because they do not know this, they are not free. They only know that *one is free*. ... That one is therefore only a Despot; not a *free man*. The consciousness of Freedom first arose among the Greeks, and therefore they were free; but they, and the Romans likewise, knew only that *some* are free—not Man as such. ... The Greeks, therefore, had slaves ... The German nations, under the influence of Christianity, were the first to obtain the consciousness, that man, as man, is free; that is the *freedom* of Spirit which constitutes its essence.[10]

Conformant to the three phases of the development of Freedom are the particular state forms: for the Orient, despotism; for Greece, democracy; for the German world (the present), monarchy.

It may come as a shock—certainly as a seeming paradox—that the forward sweep of the *Weltgeist*, "World-Spirit," toward Freedom, which had reached the realization that "Man as Man" is free, should find its objective realization in a State, with a Monarch as ruler—actually, the Prussian State and its King. But this is in fact Hegel's logical deduction from the course of history and the historic process that brought the new concept of Freedom into being. For with the German Reformation came "the first successful attempt to introduce the principle of subjectivity into changing political relations. It placed some responsibility for his deeds on the free subject and challenged the traditional system of authority and privilege in the name of Christian freedom and equality."[11] This subjectivity was recognized, as Hegel put it, "as that which can and ought to come into the possession of the truth; and this subjectivity is the common property of *all mankind*. ... In the proclamation of these principles is unfurled the new, the latest standard round which the peoples rally—the banner of

Free Spirit, independent, thought finding its life in the Truth, and enjoying independence by it ... This is the essence of the Reformation: Man in his very nature destined to be free."[12]

The French Revolution thought to realize this *essential* Freedom, but it failed because it had not yet found the Truth. It released a "self-destructive" freedom; man had not yet discovered his "true interest"—"he did not place himself under laws that secure his own freedom and that of the whole."[13]

What followed, to put it briefly, was the anarchy of modern society in the emergence of the bourgeois state, a society in which individual interests clashed, in which the "universal" was lost sight of in the appetences and struggles of the "subjective," the individual. This is our "civil society," which reflects the conflict between the right of the whole and that of the individual. Private property clashes with common property. Accumulation of wealth posits the "growing impoverishment of the working class." The particular, not the universal, prevails. Some other element is needed, superior to civil society, which is concerned with securing and protecting property and personal freedom, and yet bringing them under control and harmonizing the diverse interests in the name of some higher authority. It is the "universal." This new higher element is the State. The State is here to harmonize the specific and the general interest. The State is "an autonomous and independent power"; the State is "the march of God in the world."

What the State is to Civil Society, the Monarch is to the State. He is "outside" civil society, "exalted above all that is particular and conditional." He is "pure ego." Absolute, autonomous, bound by no particularity of social ties or class, he stands "above the battle." The sovereign State is likewise autonomous, unbound by any higher law than its own. It stands in relation to other states, equally sovereign, exposed to "continuous struggle." These states "maintain and procure their rights through their own power and must as a matter of necessity plunge into war."[14]

It seems that the anarchy which Hegel had curbed within the State, explodes the moment it confronts another state! Such then is the March of Reason, as it culminates politically in the absolute state, the monarchy. Within the state man finds his true freedom. It is not as yet absolute freedom. Since Philosophy does not predict, but only surveys what is and has been, the further unfolding of Reason toward Freedom is as yet unrevealed.

> Philosophy comes too late to teach the world what it should be. ... When it paints its grey upon grey, a form of life has already become old: and in grey and grey it can no longer be made young again but only understood. The Owl of Minerva begins its flight when the shades of twilight have already fallen.[15]

No matter. The Owl of Minerva has flown over vast stretches of world history and experience, even if in the twilight air. It has shown us how the abstract determinations of Logic have realized themselves through a dialectic moving through all the domains of Thought and Action—History, Art, Religion, and Philosophy itself. It has shown the upward ascent of Reason in human activities and achievements. An unceasing unrest, a *haltungslose Unruhe*, has characterized the irresistible flow of history. Faust's hunger to embrace the totality of experience has been conjoined with the

Mephistophelean spirit of "denial," for was not Mephistopheles the spirit that always denied, *der Geist der stets verneint*, Hegel's "Negativity"? With this principal difference, that Mephistopheles "wills evil, but creates good." But Negativity is free of such moral coercions. It is one of the principles of creation ...

Was there really no predictability in all this, save a general dialectical potentiality and actuality? Certainly the dialectic would never stop, like Joshua's sun in Gibeon, at some fiat! Hegel might preach the Prussian State, Christianity as the ultimate religion. What if Hegelianism itself was only a moment in history—as was shown of other moments—and carried within itself the germ of its own dissolution into something higher? This Dialectic was indeed a terrible thing! Hegel might see the Prussian State as the highest embodiment of Reason and the Actual, but that too had its own Negativity. And what of the ever-unfolding of the idea of Freedom bred of the Reformation, the Freedom of "Man as Man"? Such thoughts would soon arise in Berlin not long after Hegel's death.

But for the time being Hegel reigned as the official Prussian state philosopher, a kind of philosophical dictator. Yet he himself was not free of certain inner psychological contradictions, as more intimate students or associates observed. Now and then he would invite one or two of them to share a cup, and toast the Fall of the Bastille on the anniversary of July 14, 1789. He had not, apparently, forgotten those days at the Tübingen Seminary when, along with his fellow-students Schelling and Friedrich Hölderlin, he danced around the Tree of Liberty on the outbreak of the French Revolution. Nor perhaps those radical writings of his youth (not to be published until long after his death), in which he excoriated Christianity as a destructive force that had done away with the naturalness, homogeneity, and the social and political character of the Greek religion, and had substituted fantasies derived from a people "whose climate, whose law, whose culture, whose interest are alien to us, whose history has not the slightest connection with us."[16] But now none but himself was aware of these youthful indiscretions. How certain Young Hegelians would have rejoiced to have had these as additional ammunition to add to the Hegelian dialectic in their warfare on authority! ...

Now, in Berlin, God had made his reappearance in that great secular theodicy—but *God* none the less, God as Reason, God as the State, God as Logic. True, he became a triadic God: as God of Christianity, he became Spirit that created its own opposite and in turn became the return of the opposite unto itself. The Triad ruled: Spirit, and its antithesis, the Son of God; Spirit "reduced to limited and particular conception... the World-Nature and Finite Spirit. Finite Spirit itself is therefore posited as a constituent element in the Divine Being. Man himself therefore is comprehended in the Idea of God. ..."[17] Christ is Man who is God, and God who is Man.

This element, then, the sharing in the Spirit on the part of Nature and Man, will be turned to good uses by Hegel's followers; nor was it to save Hegel himself from the suspicion of atheism ...

But the magic of Hegelian doctrine reached out far and wide, in and beyond the halls of the university, in fascinating and strange adaptations and transformations. It reached into Russia, Italy, France, the Scandinavian countries, spread throughout the German lands; though it was not to invade England until much later. It would meet with merciless criticism, often vituperation, like that of Schopenhauer and Kierkegaard. It would be made the instrument of conservatism and radicalism. No domain of knowledge would be free of its influence. It would enter literature, especially the drama, and indirectly affect Henrik Ibsen, among others. In this fashion Hegelianism nourished divergent schools and divergent interests. As the official philosopher of Prussia, he outraged liberal colleagues by his reactionary political opinions, such men as Alexander von Humboldt and the great biblical scholar de Wette (whose views cost him his chair at the university). His attack on his fellow-philosopher Jakob Friedrich Fries for the latter's unorthodox political activities would not soon be forgotten. Conservative students were gratified by Hegel's deification of Reason. In a number of them he appeared to encourage a sort of quietism, even cynicism. Thus one young enthusiast wrote to his parents in 1819:

> Hegel has unified my views, and has done me a great service thereby. ... Hegel has given me views concerning the State, and now I know what is to be done, and what left alone. I know that a Republic, the Franchise, equality of goods, etc. are of no use at all ...[18]

But such students as Heinrich Heine, David Friedrich Strauss, and Ludwig Feuerbach would not be deterred from drawing other conclusions when their time came. Hegel offered enough riches for them to take what they wanted and needed ... They would acknowledge their debt and go beyond their teacher in their speculations. But here, too, Hegel's figure cast its immense shadow. ...

Friedrich Engels was too young to have attended Hegel's lectures, but he studied his works and understood them. His own debt and that of posterity he acknowledged in a tribute that combines the reverence of a disciple and the understanding of an opponent, and crystallizes the nature of that influence:

> The newer German philosophy [he wrote] culminated in the Hegelian system, in which, for the first time—and this is its great merit—the whole natural, historical and spiritual world was presented as a process, that is, as in constant motion, change, transformation and development. From this standpoint the history of mankind no longer appeared as a confused whirl of senseless deeds of violence, all equally condemnable before the judgment seat of the now matured philosophic reason, and best forgotten as soon as possible, but as a process of development of humanity itself. It now became the task of thought to follow out the gradual stages of this process through all its devious ways, and to trace out the inner regularities running through all its apparently fortuitous phenomena.[19]

∗ ∗ ∗

In an obituary tribute to his teacher Hegel, the legal philosopher Eduard Gans said:

> Philosophy has now come full circle; its progress is only to be considered as the thoughtful working over of its material in the manner which the lately departed has so clearly and precisely indicated.[20]

He was wrong and unjust, if not to Hegel, who believed that his own philosophy was the "absolute reality of the Idea of Philosophy," then at least to Hegel's *Weltgeist*, the "World-Spirit" that stubbornly persisted in actualizing itself in a number of critical historic and intellectual phenomena, and even in Hegel's last years insisted on materializing itself in an eruptive July Revolution, with repercussions all over the Continent. The July Revolution of Paris displeased the great philosopher and upset him. It also materialized itself, and was to do so with increasing vigor, in the economic transformation of the German states over the following years, no less than in the repressive actions of the various German governments, once more affrighted by the specter of revolution and intensifying their persecution of dissidents, especially writers and thinkers. That loosely joined group of writers known as "Young Germany" soon fell victim to authority, suffering imprisonment or exile or making its peace through early recantations. Enjoined from political activity, the younger intellectuals turned to philosophy, the philosophy that reigned supreme, the Hegelian. This surely was safer ground, they thought—and it was, for the moment.

Hegel had said:

To apprehend what is, is the task of philosophy, because what is, is Reason. As for the individual, every one is the son of his time; so philosophy also is its time apprehended in thought. It is just as foolish to fancy that any philosophy can transcend its present moment, as that an individual could leap out of his time or jump over Rhodes. If a theory transgresses its time, and builds up a world as it ought to be, it has existence merely in the unstable element of opinion which gives room to every wandering fancy.[21]

Hegel had said:

"What is rational is actual; and what is actual is rational."

It is out of the interpretation of these two statements that the progeny of Hegel split into two wings, soon named by David Friedrich Strauss the Right Hegelians and the Left Hegelians.

The right wing continued to expound the Master's word in orthodox fashion, defended him passionately against the charge of atheism, or pantheism, and proceeded to prepare an edition of his works. They underscored the second half of the sentence above, "what is actual is rational," to support that which was, the *status-quo*. For them, Hegel had said the last word.

The Left Hegelians based themselves on the Master's word that philosophy too, like any individual, was a child of its time. If so, was this not true also of the Master's thought? Was it not also the content of an inexorable dialectic, in which the "negativity" was already becoming apparent? And they took the first part of that celebrated sentence and underscored it: "What is rational is actual," they said. Which they interpreted as meaning: Whatever can be shown to be rationally valid, will ultimately be realized. The world must and can be shaped to correspond to Reason!

In and around the University of Berlin these left-wing Hegelians met and argued. To Berlin came those from the outside to study Hegel. Here they proceeded to radicalize Hegelianism with results that would soon startle, appall, electrify the world, and revolutionize the form and content of European and world thought. Few periods in European intellectual history have compressed so much change in so short a span of time. Few could have suspected that already not too far off one could be dimly aware of what the Germans would call the *Götterdämmerung des deutschen Idealismus*— "German Idealism's twilight of the Gods." Few could have perceived in the soaring cloud above, in the philosophies of subjective idealism, absolute idealism, etc., the gathering storm—thunder and lightning of ideas—that would shake the foundations not only of Christianity itself, but of all Religion—and soon, too, of the political state, and society in general. Within the brief compass of less than fifteen years, what another young Hegelian, Moses Hess, called the "bridge to bring us back from heaven to earth," was completed. The historic progression from Hegel to Strauss, and thereafter to Feuerbach, Marx, Engels, and Bakunin (to name only the most important), itself marks the accelerated convulsiveness of the philosophic transformation—from 1835, when David Friedrich Strauss's *Life of Jesus* appeared, to 1848, the *Communist Manifesto*. Such was the unpredictable March of the Idea, as Theory became translated into Practice, and Thought into Action. Such was the lightning of Reason!

2. David Friedrich Strauss

Berlin, November 15, 1831.

To whom should I be writing that Hegel is dead, if not to you of whom I have been thinking constantly, as long as I was enabled to see and hear the living one? ... Imagine, how I found out. I could not get to see Schleiermacher until this morning. Naturally he inquired whether the cholera had not deterred me from coming; I replied that the reports were encouraging, and it seems it was coming to an end. "Yes," he said, "but it has claimed a great sacrifice. Professor Hegel died of the cholera last night." Imagine what I felt! My first thought was to leave. What would you be doing here without Hegel? But soon I bethought myself: ... I have come here; I have no desire to undertake another journey. True, Hegel died here; but he is not extinct. I rejoice that I have listened to and seen the great Master before his end. I attended both lecture series of his: the History of Philosophy, and the Philosophy of Right. ... Friday he still held both of his sessions; ... Monday it was announced that because of a sudden illness he would be away; but that he hoped to continue on Thursday. ... The Thursday before I visited him. When I gave him my name and my birthplace, he said at once: "Ah, From Württemberg!" And he showed his genuine pleasure. ... He asked me to come and visit him often ... Well, tomorrow ... he will be buried. ...[22]

Thus wrote David Friedrich Strauss, very recently arrived in Berlin in pursuit of his theological and philosophical education. He was twenty-three years old; like Hegel he was a Suabian; like Hegel he had studied in Tübingen. Sharply aware of the philosophical and theological currents of the time, swept along with the tide of transcendental idealism and the theological ideas of Schleiermacher, the young theological student was finally converted by the *Phenomenology* to Hegelianism. It was an almost blinding experience, this synthesis that Hegel offered. "Universal history unrolled before one's eyes in a new light. Art and religion, in their varied forms, emerged in their place, and all this rich manifestation proceeded from consciousness and returned there anew, testifying to its omnipotence."[23] As a curate, he had already undergone the ordeal of self-division between his more recent beliefs and his duties to his congregation. In Berlin from 1831 to 1832 his Hegelianism was confirmed; but he was already beginning to modify it as he began planning his most important work, the *Life of Jesus*, at the beginning of 1832. His very close friend in Berlin, Johann Karl Wilhelm Vatke, was at work on his epochal book on the Old Testament, *Die Religion des Alten Testaments*, practically as fundamental for the newer criticism of the Bible as Strauss's book was to be for Christology. Both books were published in 1835.

It has been remarked that the first significant transformations of Hegelianism into a radical criticism took the form of a critique of religion. This is indeed the case, and comprehensible. On the one hand, the historical examination of the Old and New Testaments was a part that great movement of research and reappraisal abetted and indeed made possible by the excavations, discoveries and decipherment of Egyptian and Assyrian and Babylonian inscriptions; by the examination of historical documents, the creation of historical archives, the studies of comparative civilizations, especially religions; in short, by the vast accumulation of new knowledge, including geologic, anthropologic, biologic history, that made the nineteenth century the greatest of epochs in historical research. Such an expansion of historical knowledge and questions was bound to have notable repercussions in all other fields of human activity, especially the political and social. Time-honored authorities, if not toppled, appeared shaken. Religion and religious institutions, the bulwarks of state power, were now subjected to such critical inquiry. In states, like those of Germany, where absolutism precluded political and social action, the religious establishment, traditions, and sacred texts represented the outer fortifications of power which, if taken, might open the way to vaster assaults. To scrutinize the holy texts, to assess them in the light of history, to question their authorship, and, not least, to question the historicity of events and characters in them, was indeed a first step toward an unsettling of all authority. German Protestant theologians led the way in what was to be known as the "Higher Criticism" of the Bible, in dismembering the texts and assigning them to various authors, a procedure not without its immediate dangers to their propounders, as both the great de Wette and Vatke found to their distress. It stands to reason that a similar application of criticism to the New Testament would also concentrate on the historic role, presence, and even existence—the "historicity"—of Jesus Christ.

David Friedrich Strauss was not the first to raise the question of the historicity of Christ, but his book *Das Leben Jesu—The Life of Jesus*—which appeared in 1835–1836, was the most sensational of its day, and the most widely influential throughout Europe and America. Its impact may be judged by the number of adversaries and replies it generated no less than by the number of converts it made. In the major religious crisis that England was soon to undergo it played an important role, particularly when it appeared in George Eliot's translation. Without Strauss, the most widely known and popular *Life of Jesus*, that of Ernest Renan, would never have come to be.

It was a daring thing for a young theologian like Strauss, who aspired to a professorship at a university and was himself a preacher, to attack the historicity of the Gospels and eventually to annul the very existence of the Savior. But the Hegelian wine was very heady—the intellectual atmosphere was tense with new ideas and the political climate made for great heat in other than political discussion. The young Hegelians were ready to take chances, some of them prepared to cut themselves off from intellectual careers and security in quest of what they believed to be the truth.

They were soon to recognize that the political authorities were well aware of the danger hidden in their seemingly philosophical dismemberment of religion in the name of a Hegelian dialectic; aware too of the danger of a continuing Hegelianism at the universities. In the early forties they imported old Schelling to undo the work of Hegel and bring a measure of supernaturalism into the philosophical *aulae* of Berlin. Hadn't farsighted Metternich warned the French, even before 1830, of the hazards in allowing atheistic literature such wide distribution in that country?

The heavy guns of Hegelian dialectic were now turned on Christianity. In fourteen hundred pages of close analysis of the Gospels, buttressed by a thorough knowledge and scholarship of the sources and of history, Strauss began demolishing the physical reality of Christ. He was not out to destroy Christianity; he wished to purge it of its contradictions, inconsistencies, superstitions. He wished, in a Hegelian sense, to raise it to the intellectual and philosophical level it deserved to inhabit. He wished to prove that the Christ tradition, denuded of its impossible miracles, produced a Christ who was the creator of a new religion of humanity. Christ *was* Humanity.

Hegel had shown the way, but only partly. For Hegel, religion and philosophy were identical in essence, for they both were revelations of God; it was *form* that separated them. Religion reveals in symbols the rational content of philosophy. Thus the whole system of the Creation was symbolic: what Hegel called a *Vorstellung*—a figurative thought. God as Creator was Idea, and the creation is the externalization of this Idea in—again!—triadic form. The Idea externalizes itself in the World. The Universe—the Father—puts forth the "particular"—the Son; Son is the finite world of Nature, and man—the "other." The incarnation and the history of Christ are the unity of Man and the Eternal. Such is the eternal timeless process. This is the transition from Logic to Nature. Thus the Hegelian Idea is God the Trinity, and Christianity represents the Kingdom of the Father, the Kingdom of the Son, and the Kingdom of the Spirit—the God-Man, materialized in the Church. "If the Kingdom of the Father was the logical Idea, God before the Creation of the world; if the Kingdom of the Son was the Idea in its Otherness—Nature; the Kingdom of the Spirit, as the third moment, is the unity of the foregoing, Church is the Kingdom of God on the earth."[24]

The masses, who cannot as yet "support the startling light of pure logic," must be satisfied with the highest kind of thinking of which they are capable, that is, figurative thought. For pure abstract thought is beyond them. Religion offers them these concrete symbols in Father, Son, Creation, Heaven and the Fall. The philosophic mind will understand these symbols as the representations of the eternal triadic Idea, with God as the Absolute Idea, and the Trinity as the symbol of the triadic dialectic movement realizing the unity of contraries. The Redemption then was the Spirit that surmounted the dualism and the contradiction, that attained to the full consciousness of itself, and thus to Eternal Truth. ... Philosophy, therefore, is also a divine service, but serves God in a special way. ... With this mighty stroke, Hegel both preserved and destroyed Christianity.

This was enough of a springboard for Strauss. Not symbol, not *Vorstellung*—but "Myth" was the essence of Christianity and Christ. The story of Jesus was "myth."

What is "Myth" or "Mythus"?

Myth is the creation of a fact out of an idea ... A people, a religious community, finds itself in a certain condition or round of institutions of which the spirit, the idea, lives and acts within it. But the mind, following a natural impulse, desires to gain a complete representation of that existing condition, and to know its origin. The origin, however, is buried in oblivion, or is too indistinctly discernible to satisfy present feelings and ideas. Consequently an image of that origin, colored by the light of existing ideas, is cast upon the dark wall of the past, which image is, however, but a magnified reflection of existing influences ...[25]

Myth is the garment, the outer vestment—the historical vesture of primitive Christianity. It arose not out of an individual consciousness, but out of the collective unconscious of a people, spontaneously. It is a "naive" creation. Strauss speaks of myth as the unconscious, artless, spontaneous creation of the imagination. Myth requires distance of time for its creation. So there is a gap of at least thirty-one years between the death of Jesus and the origin of our Gospels.

Subjecting the gospels to a critical examination, Strauss concluded that neither a supernaturalistic interpretation nor a rationalistic one satisfies, particularly in reference to the miracles. The figure and the life and activities of Christ were born out of a popular imagination that drew the figure of a Messiah in the image of that conceived by the Jews. A historic character named Jesus produced upon his disciples such an impression that they took him for the Messiah, and attributed to him all the characteristic, acts, and behavior of such a figure. A myth embodies the hopes, needs, thoughts of a people in a particular period. It embodies the Idea. It actualizes a dream, which finds expression in this "collective" imagined personality. Now the Idea that is here embodied is not of an individual person—a Savior—but a Savior who stands for Humanity, for humankind. The Godhead is not One—not Jesus of Nazareth. The Godhead is Humanity.

It is out of the Hegelian system that Strauss distills his radical idea of the unity of opposites as it is manifested in the universal aspect of Christ as Man-God, which is Humanity:

Humanity is the union of two Natures—God become man, the Infinite manifests itself in the finite, the finite Spirit remembering its Infinitude. It is a child of the visible Mother and the invisible Father, Nature and Spirit; it is the worker of miracles, in so far as in the course of human history, the spirit more and more completely subjects nature, both within and around man, until it lies before him as the inert matter on which he exercises his active power; it is the sinless existence, for the course of its development is a blameless one, pollution cleaves to the individual, and does not touch the race or its history, It is humanity that dies, rises and ascends to heaven, for from the negation of its phenomenal life there ever proceeds a spiritual higher life, from the separation of its mortality as a personal, national, and terrestrial spirit, arises its union with the infinite spirit of the heavens. By faith in this Christ, especially in his death and resurrection, man is justified before God: that is, by the kindling within him of the idea of Humanity, the individual man participates in the divinely human life of the species.[26]

For just as Plato's God created the world in contemplating the Ideas, the community drew the portrait of Christ, and in doing so, unconsciously kept before its eyes the Idea of Humanity in its relation to Divinity. Here are resolved the contradictions which the Church was unable to reconcile because it regarded Christ as the individual, a God-man. In the human race, these contradictions are reconciled—the finite and the infinite.

It is in this sense that Strauss sees the universality of the Idea represented by the Idea of Christ.

> Shall we interest ourselves, he asks, more in the cure of some sick people in Galilee, than in the miracles of intellectual and moral life belonging to the history of the world—in the increasing, the almost incredible, dominion of man over nature—in the irresistible force of ideas, to which no unintelligent matter, whatever its magnitude, can oppose any enduring resistance? Shall isolated incidents, in themselves trivial, be more to us than the universal order of events, simply because in the latter we presuppose, if we do not perceive, a natural cause, in the former the contrary?[27]

And in a memorable and eloquent passage, Strauss reiterates this central idea of the universality of the God-Man and the Idea in manifesting itself not once, but in the manifold context of the generality—Man.

> This is indeed not the mode in which the Idea realized itself; it is not wont to lavish all its fulness on one exemplar, and be niggardly towards all others—to express itself perfectly in that one individual, and imperfectly in all the rest; it rather loves to distribute its riches among multiplicity of exemplars which reciprocally complete each other—in the alternate appearance and suppression of a series of individuals. And is this no true realization of the idea? Is not the idea of the unity of the divine and human nature a real one in a far higher sense, when I regard the whole race of mankind as such a realization? Is not an incarnation of God from eternity, a truer one than an incarnation limited to a particular point of time?[28]

Such is indeed Strauss's "apotheosis of the species." He had enlarged the Hegelian Idea and made it manifest in the world of human beings. He had translated what appeared an individual transterrestrial event into a continuity, embodied in the "species" (*Gattung*) that is humanity. He had established a new kind of eternity in the ascendant mastery of Nature by man, and humanized the miracles by transplanting them into activities of the human being in achieving such mastery. Strauss had naturalized the Godhead Ideal. He had undermined a number of theories, beliefs and convictions by specifically casting doubt on the credibility of the Gospel narratives as contemporary testimonies to Christ's workings. The philosophic consciousness found itself exhilarated by this exaltation of the Christ-idea to the sphere of the universal myth and a portion of the progressive advance of both the Idea and of Mankind. Rudolph Haym, Hegel's biographer and severe critic, recalled how Strauss's book had affected him upon its appearance:

> It was Strauss's *Das Leben Jesu* that both filled me and a number of my companions with Hegelian attitudes and also made us more and more disillusioned with theology. The spell that this book exercised over one was indescribable; I never read any book with so much pleasure and thoroughness ... It was as though the scales fell from my eyes and a great light was shed on my path.[29]

Haym and his fellows saw the positive, the progressive contribution that Strauss was making. The spirit of the time made them receptive to his ideas, particularly such as explored the collective character of religion, as it expressed its aspirations, its hopes, its feelings and ideas in "myth"; society and humanity acquired the character of something divinely ordained, something in a constant state of progress. Humanity was given miraculous powers in triumphing over nature, in ordering and mastering matter, and also itself playing out the drama of the Ascension. The true life of the individual lay in his participation in the work of humanity, sharing the divine character of the species, and thus achieving union with Infinite Spirit. Far from being a destruction of faith, as many claimed, these adherents saw in this a restoration of faith. Strauss had done all this by using modern historico-critical methods, and had profoundly deepened the meaning of "myth" as a product of a people's collective consciousness or unconscious. He had shown that Christianity could resolve the dualism of the human and the divine in the Man-God. History and historical development lay in the hands of the "species." It is here on earth that the "divinity" of man is revealed. What Strauss was proclaiming, that to which he was to give greater precision five years later, is expressed in his paean to the earthly-divine:

> The earth is no longer a vale of tears through which we journey towards a goal existing in a future heaven. The treasures of the divine life are to be realised here and now, for every moment of our earthly life pulses within the womb of the divine.[30]

But there were many more on the other side, who fell upon Strauss with vehemence and without pity. There were more than sixty replies in opposition, and it was these latter who triumphed by scotching Strauss's university expectations and aspirations. A chair in a German university was out of the question. Switzerland seemed a likely refuge, since it had undergone radical political changes and liberalism appeared in the ascendant. He was accepted as professor of theology at the university of Zurich, but the hue and cry raised by a rabid conservative party consisting of the moneyed interests and like-minded clerics, succeeded in intimidating Strauss's supporters into a repudiation. Strauss was forced to withdraw, but accepted a pension. His career as teacher and preacher was over.

His book was more fortunate. It fell into many hands, at critical moments in the lives of its readers, and formed a strong element in the intellectual current of the time that was carrying many a person on to new terrains. For example, a young man of nineteen from the Rhineland, brought up in a Calvinist household, was reading *Das Leben Jesu* in 1839. He was then in Bremen, sent by his merchant father to prepare himself for a career in business. This is what Friedrich Engels wrote to his friend Wilhelm Graeber:

> Oh, William, William! ... I am now an out and out Straussian! ... I, poor poet, am now crawling under the wing of the gifted David Friedrich Strauss. What a chap! ... Here he comes along like a young god, and brings chaos out of darkness into the light and— *Adios* Religion! It's as full of holes as a sponge. ... If you can disprove Strauss, I'll turn pietist again ...[31]

3. Ludwig Feuerbach

It is hard for us today to appreciate or understand the feverish excitement and heated involvement that attended philosophical controversy in Germany—and particularly in Berlin—during the years of and following Hegel's lifetime, and particularly during the 1840s. Of course, philosophical, and more particularly theological, discussions were the valves by means of which the discussants found relief for their pent-up thoughts and feelings in an atmosphere of intellectual and political repression. Yet they lived in a time astir with new ideas, movements, and exciting news from abroad. Even more surprising is it to find with what eagerness youth turned to philosophy instead of the more substantial rewards that careers such as law and theology promised. A number of them even gave up successful occupations in favor of philosophic studies. And this despite the knowledge that such preoccupations might entail hazards both personal and economic, and even worse.

It was therefore with relief, and even jubilation, that the younger spirits hailed the accession of the new king of Prussia, Frederick William IV, in 1840. Though already known as a "romantic," a pious Christian, an ardent supporter of the Restoration governments and monarchs, a bitter opponent of the Enlightenment and the French Revolution, and a ruler convinced of his divine mission to teach and guide his nation, he began his reign in a rainbow aureole of promise. His first actions seemed to justify high hopes. He amnestied political prisoners and called for meetings of the provincial diets every second year. In the Rhenish provinces, always the most advanced of the Prussian states, the new regime was hailed as progressive. It was in this heady atmosphere that the *Rheinische Zeitung* was founded. It spoke for the more liberal and industrial elements and was soon to become the organ of the Hegelian school, drawing upon its more radical exponents.

Alas! the honeymoon was soon over. The new King showed his true colors almost immediately, and proved as uncompromising as his predecessor. The heavy hand of oppression once more bore down on the young hopefuls, and their elders.

Disenchanted, they discovered what a hazardous vocation philosophy could prove —as dangerous as politics, as dangerous as theology. Intensified censorship soon took care of the press; the police and the government authorities took care of too advanced teachers by depriving them of the right to teach.

Yet it is interesting to observe that as the government moved more and more to the right, the philosophers (at least one important group) moved more and more to the left.

Philosophy was a menace. The scandal over Strauss's *Life of Jesus* was very much alive, and Strauss had gained influence and disciples. As a matter of fact, theological students were already transcending Strauss. Witness Bruno Bauer, who had begun as a right Hegelian, and was soon publishing daring but scholarly critiques of the Gospels that actually denied even the historicity of Christ, and devastated the "myth" theory of Strauss as itself the construction of another mystical religion. Removed from Berlin to Bonn, he soon was deprived of the latter chair, and proceeded to become one of the most outspoken and radical critics of both religion and society ...

Yes, there was good reason to be concerned for and over these philosophers. It was urgent to counter the subversive teachings that prevailed in Berlin, and in the words of the Monarch, to extirpate the "dragon-seed of Hegelianism." And so the aged philosopher Friedrich Wilhelm Joseph von Schelling was imported into Berlin, and in November 1841 commenced his lectures on the Philosophy of Revelation. Curiosity, enthusiasm, expectancy, and other motives led to a lively attendance. Among the strongly variegated audience could be discerned the eager faces of Bakunin, Friedrich Engels, and Kierkegaard! …

In that same year, 1841, had appeared a book that was destined to dominate the thinking of a great many writers and philosophers for years to come. Another Hegelian was to do honor to his master by subverting him. This was Ludwig Feuerbach, and the book, his *Essence of Christianity*. It was a book that was to reach out far and wide. In England, it profoundly affected the thinking of George Eliot (who translated the work) and her circle; it was to make an even deeper impression in Russia, where a generation of thinkers was also undergoing a rite of passage from Hegel to his successors; it was to change the life and thought of many continental writers, among them the greatest of the novelists writing in German, the Swiss Gottfried Keller; and it was to revolutionize—at least for a time—the life and thought of Richard Wagner. Not the least of those affected were Karl Marx and Friedrich Engels. It was a book that, when rediscovered in the twentieth century, was to sound forth modern notes bearing fruitfully upon contemporary theology, philosophy, and psychology.

It is not therefore in a tone of levity that one can speak of a "dramatic" element present in the course of thought that now is taking place. Here is a drama of three mighty acts, the first of which was David Friedrich Strauss and *The Life of Jesus*; and the second, now, Ludwig Feuerbach and *The Essence of Christianity*. The third was to follow soon in a climactic fortissimo. Hegel's Absolute Idea, roaming on high, must have been startled, if not appalled, by the transformed externalizations of Itself in its progress; and Hegel himself, from the heavenly retreat allotted to philosophers, might have watched with a wry smile his brainchild, the great Dialectic, playing unforeseen, diabolical tricks. For a number of his disciples were now contending that there were actually two Hegels, one the "exoteric," the public Hegel; the other, the "esoteric," the "hidden" Hegel, who was in fact an atheist!

The drama now being enacted on the stage of philosophy had many brilliant actors, to whom it would be impossible to do justice in a brief compass, for in their disparate and sometimes contradictory ways they contributed to the fervid controversies of the time: figures such as Arnold Ruge, Moses Hess; the anarchist thinkers Max Stirner and Bakunin; Bruno Bauer and his brother Edgar. Though divergent, their work in fact coalesces into a kind of turbulent unity predictive of an explosion. One may with some justice call this drama "The Descent of the Absolute Idea from Heaven to Earth," the humanization of the Absolute, the transfiguration of Absolute Consciousness into the concrete consciousness of Man.

Among the most influential of these actors was Ludwig Feuerbach, and we may well call his achievement the second act of the "drama."

He belonged to a family of extraordinary intellectual and artistic endowments. His father was an outstanding jurist, and another member of the family, Anselm Feuerbach, one of Germany's most distinguished painters. Ludwig Feuerbach began, like so many of his contemporaries, as a student of theology, matriculating at the University of Heidelberg. But soon falling under the spell of Hegelianism, he went to Berlin. Like Hegel's other disciples he felt this sense of immediacy, of urgency, and knew that Hegel would offer him satisfactory answers to many of the problems that troubled him and his generation. Like all good students of great teachers, Ludwig Feuerbach paid his master the tribute of courageous disagreement with an expansion of the Hegelian doctrines.

Writing to his father in 1825, he described his feelings: He could no longer study theology, which was like a beautiful, faded flower ...

> I desire to press nature to my heart, from whose depths the frightened theologian shies away; and Man, the whole man, not man as dealt with by the theologian, anatomist, or lawyer, but as object of philosophy.[32]

For two years, 1824 to 1826, he was in Berlin. What Hegel meant to him we have in Feuerbach's own words: his brief sojourn had acquired a significance for "eternity" and become "a turning point of his entire life, making Berlin into a Bethlehem of the new world."

> I stood in a more intimate and influential relation toward Hegel than to any other of our spiritual forebears; for I knew him personally. For two years I attended his lectures, and listened to him with total dedication, attention, and enthusiasm. I did not know what I wanted or should do, I was so confused and divided when I came to Berlin. But I had listened to him for barely six months, when my head and heart were set to rights. I knew what I should do and what I wanted to do: Not theology, but philosophy! Not drivel and ravings, but study! Not to believe, but to think! It was in him I came to a consciousness of myself and of the world. It was him I called my second father, even as I then called Berlin my spiritual birthplace.[33]

The die was cast. He had made his choice. He received his doctorate from the university of Erlangen (to which city his father had removed), and was appointed to a lecturing post there in 1829. His academic career was not to be long-lived. In 1830 he published anonymously his *Thoughts on Death and Immortality*, in which he denied personality immortality, insisting only on the immortality of the spirit. Instead of seeking immortal men, he said, we should ask for spiritually and physically healthy human beings; for physical health was of greater importance than immortality. True religion must manifest itself in deeds here on earth. The authorship of the book soon was made manifest; the censorship went into action. With every chance of advancement closed off, Feuerbach became a freelance philosopher and writer. Marriage into a well-to-do family made it possible for him to pursue these vocations in comfort and dedicate himself to the clarification of his ideas on the nature of religion. Like a number of other Young Hegelians, he too saw religious criticism as a gateway to politics.

> I remain firm in my opinion: in Germany theology is the only practical vehicle for politics, the only vehicle likely to lead to success, at least in the near future.[34]

And again,

> The Protestant is a *religious* republican. ... When Protestantism is dissolved ... it leads to political republicanism.[35]

It was thus necessary to take the outer bastions constituted by religious institutions before the inner citadel of the State could be assaulted.

> Palestine is too narrow for me [he had written his father in 1825]. I must, I must go out into the wide, wide world, and only the philosopher carries this world on his shoulders.[36]

He proved true to his word. He had broken with Hegelianism in 1839, and in 1841 he published *Das Wesen des Christentums*—*The Essence of Christianity*—which was to make its way into "the wide, wide world" in a very brief time.

> Religion is the dream of the human mind. But even in dreams we do not find ourselves in emptiness or in heaven, but on earth, in the realm of reality: we only see real things in the entrancing splendor of imagination and caprice, instead of in the simple daylight of reality and necessity. Hence I do nothing more to religion—and to speculative philosophy and theology also—than to open its eyes, or rather to turn its gaze from the internal towards the external, *i.e.*, I change the object as it is in the imagination into the object as it is in reality.[37]

Homo homini Deus. "Man is God to Man."

It is this dictum that serves as the center of all of Feuerbach's speculation concerning Man, his Religion, and his God. For Man is the center of Feuerbach's world, or as he himself put it, "God was my first thought; Reason my second; Man my third and last thought."[38]

And the theme of the *Essence of Christianity* may be said to be the Alienation of Man in Religion, and his reconstitution as Man and member of his Species through an understanding and transcendence of the sources of that Alienation. And at the same time the book is intended to restore Nature to its rightful place and role as an important element in the development of human consciousness, and not merely as some degraded element, product of an "alienating" Idea. Nature, too, was to have its own, independent existence. The primacy was therefore assigned to Nature and Man.

Theology must be changed into anthropology. The doctrine of otherworldliness and of God must be turned into the doctrine of Man. Hegel had pointed the way, but only in part: Hegel too must be demystified, demythologized, for though he had transformed theology into Logic, theology remained imbedded in the concepts of Absolute Idea, Reason, and *his* Logic. They were there—eternal, absolute, necessary. They existed apart from Man and Nature, both of which were but externalizations of the Absolute Idea. They were not the creations of human consciousness, but its creator. Nature was something derived from the structure and movement of Absolute Thought. It was time, Feuerbach held, to reverse the process, in the name of truth; to recognize that Thought was a second reality, but Nature was the primary reality. Absolute Idea, Absolute Consciousness, Logic were the creations of the concrete human Mind. Being is an abstraction of concrete human being.

Hegel's absolute mind—was that anything but the "finite" mind, enlarged and possessed of infinite potentiality? And its self-externalization as matter—was that not truly a kind of "incarnation"? Spirit become flesh?

Yes, Hegel's system, Feuerbach contended, was theology: Nature, Reality were to Hegel but realizations of the Idea. Material substance was created by an immaterial substance—abstracted substance. Art, religion, philosophy were, accordingly, manifestations of the absolute spirit, they were the loftiest that we can know of Spirit. But, Feuerbach asked, can one separate art and religion from sensations, fantasy, perceptions of man; can one sever philosophy from human thinking, separate absolute spirit from the nature of man?

No. *Being is subject, and Thinking is the predicate*, not the reverse, as in Hegel. Thought rises out of being, not being out of Thought.

"Nothing is unquestionably and immediately certain except the object of the senses, of perception, and sensation. ... The object in its true meaning is given only by the senses."[39]

> The essence of speculative philosophy is nothing but the rationalized, realized essence of God, brought into our presence. Speculative philosophy is the true, consistent rational theology. . . . He who does not give up Hegelian philosophy does not give up theology. The Hegelian teaching that nature, reality, is posited by the Idea is only the rational expression of the theological teaching that nature is created by God, that material being is created by an immaterial, i.e., abstract being.[40]

> It is *Man* who thinks, not the Self, not Reason. ... When the old philosophy therefore says *only the reasonable is the true and real*, the new philosophy responds, *only the human is the true and real*, for only what is human can be reasonable. *Man is the measure of reason.*[41]

Man, along with other animals, possesses "consciousness." But man's consciousness is different from that of the animal. It determines his nature as Man. He is conscious of himself not only as an individual, but also as a member of the human species. He is a "species-being," a *Gattungswesen*. He is conscious of himself as a member of the human species, apprehending in other men the "human essence" that is his. It is this relation to his "species," this ability to conceive of "species," that is fundamental in his power of reasoning. Logical truths are the fruits of Man as "species being," the results of the concrete nature and activities of man. Truth is social in origin and in its nature. The individual human consciousness is as much a product of Nature as it is of other individual consciousnesses; and its perceptions and truths are the results of social relations and processes.

It is with these presuppositions that Feuerbach approaches the central problem of the nature of religion. Here again he differs with the Hegelian interpretation of the character of religion. The Hegelians contended that in *content* religion and philosophy were the same; they differed only in form. What has happened to the Hegelian insistence that content and form were one? The latter is true, Feuerbach affirms: *Yes, content and form of religion are one:* "The basic dogmas of Christianity are the fulfilled wishes of mankind."

Hegel had only given a "critical" analysis of thought. Feuerbach proposes to give a "genetic-critical" analysis. *The Essence of Christianity* sets out to examine the origins and sources of man's religious thought. It takes its point of departure from Man. ... Not Man in isolation, however, but Man who is such by virtue of his "two-fold life," because "Man is himself at once an I and Thou." "Man is nothing without an object." It is through the contemplation of the "object" that man becomes acquainted with himself. "Consciousness of the objective is the self-consciousness of man." So that in affirming anything at all, we are at the same time affirming ourselves. As Man, a species-creature, we cannot get outside our species, and whatever we predicate about others is always drawn from our own nature—projections of ourselves.[42]

Hence consciousness of God is also Self, and knowledge of God is self-knowledge. Historically, then, what has been happening is that what in earlier religions had been regarded as "objective," is now recognized as "subjective," "what was formerly worshipped as God is now perceived to be something human." Religion, then, and more specifically, the Divine Being, are projections, objectifications of humanity's profoundest, dearest wishes and its highest qualities.

> The divine being is nothing else than the human being, or rather, the human nature purified, free from the limits of the individual man, made objective—i.e., contemplated and revered as another, a distinct being. All the attributes of the divine nature, are, therefore, attributes of human nature. ... Thou believest in love as a divine attribute because thou thyself lovest; thou believest that God is a wise, benevolent being because thou knowest nothing better in thyself than benevolence and wisdom; and thou believest that God exists, that therefore he is a subject—whatever exists is a subject, whether it be defined as substance, person, essence, or otherwise—because thou thyself existest, art thyself a subject.[43]

Does it then follow that because the existence of God is a "chimaera," the best of human qualities and attributes, "goodness, justice, wisdom," are also chimaeras? Not at all. A quality is divine not because God possesses it, but He possesses it because it is itself divine, and without this quality, God would be a "defective being." "Man in religion—in his relation to God—is in relation to his own nature."

> The mystery of the inexhaustible fulness of the divine predicates [of God] is therefore nothing else than the mystery of human nature considered as infinitely varied, infinitely modifiable, but, consequently, phenomenal being. Only in the realm of the senses, only in space and time does there exist a being of really infinite qualities or predicates.[44]

In proportion, therefore, in which Man has attributed to his Godhead the highest virtues, capacities, attributes, he has diminished them in himself. But what Man has taken from himself is not lost; "it is preserved in God."

> To enrich God, man must become poor; that God may be all, man must be nothing. ... What man withdraws from himself, what he renounces in himself, he only enjoys in an incomparably higher and fuller measure in God.[45]

But not only the best of qualities has Man transferred to God; all that Man denies in himself, human dignity, the human *ego*, egoism—and goodness as a quality of human nature—all these become God's. Man is declared to be corrupt; he finds in God all the goodness he desires. But Man does not as yet observe that all these attributions are human; that what man declares concerning God he is declaring concerning himself. So it is with human activity—what he thinks he cannot do with his own strength, what he cannot achieve of himself, he once again transfers to his God. But he does not as yet realize that

He who makes God act humanly, declares human activity to be divine.

Thus man has made himself an "object" of the very image of himself he has projected, an object to God. "God is, *per se*, his relinquished self."

We have reached a crucial point. We have come to see how Religion is the "disuniting of man from himself; he sets God before him as the antithesis of himself." In Religion man contemplates his own latent nature. It must be shown that this "differencing of God and man," with which religion begins, is a "differencing of man with his own nature." What do we affirm when we say "God"? We affirm our highest idea, our highest power of thought, that God is "the sum of all realities."

"To deny man is to deny religion."

Hence, the vital elements of religion are those only which make man an object to man. Man posits the moral perfection of God—hence he is also positing his own imperfection. He is conscious of Sin. He is at disunion with himself. He is alienated from himself. How is he to overcome this inner disunity? How is he to liberate himself from this consciousness of Sin? From the "distressing sense of his own nothingness?"

> Only by this; that he is conscious of *love* as the highest, the absolute power and truth, that he regards the Divine Being not only as a law, as a moral being, as a being of the understanding; but also as a loving, tender, even subjective human being (that is, as having sympathy with individual man).[46] ... Love is the middle term, the substantial bond, the principle of reconciliation between the perfect and the imperfect, the sinless and sinful being, the universal and the individual, the divine and the human. Love is God himself, and apart from it there is no God.[47]

Love is also the true unity of spirit and nature. Love is materialism. "Immaterial love is a chimaera." Love is a thing of flesh and blood. "Not abstract beings no! only sensuous, living beings are merciful. Mercy is the justice of the sensuous life. ... It is only his human blood that makes God merciful, allays his anger; that is, our sins are forgiven us because we are not abstract beings, but creatures of flesh and blood."

This is rehabilitation of the flesh, rehabilitation of matter ... Hence the Incarnation is the "practical, material manifestation of the human nature of God." And in a beautiful image, Feuerbach describes the Incarnation as "a tear of the divine compassion, and hence. ... only the visible advent of a Being having human feelings, and therefore essentially human."[48] Here the divine significance of man's nature becomes evident to him. And, in God, he learns to love man. In the Passion, he learns that "love attests itself by suffering."

And the Trinity? The Trinity is the symbolic projection of the relationship of the "I", the "Thou" and the idea of Community. "We can think alone," Feuerbach asserts, "but we can love only with another."

> God the Father is *I*, God the Son *Thou*. The *I* is understanding, the *Thou* love. But love with understanding and understanding with love is mind, and mind is the totality of man as such—the total man. ... The third Person in the Trinity expresses nothing

further than the love of the two divine Persons towards each other; it is the unity of the Son and the Father, the idea of community …[49]

And thus the secret of the Trinity lies in the fulfilment of a participated and participating life, which is "alone the true, self-satisfying, divine life." The Virgin Mary rounds out the element of participation by adding the maternal principle. The feminine principle is also divine. "The Father is a truth only where the Mother is a truth." For herein—in the feminine and maternal principle—do we encounter the deepest love, the love within living nature, the "holy necessity and depth of Nature." Herein, then, in our conception of the Trinity we find the projection of the deepest needs and wants of human nature. Herein also is the summation and the possibility of transcendence:

> The triune God has a substantial meaning only where there is an abstraction from the substance of real life. The more empty life is, the fuller, the more concrete is God. The impoverishing of the real world and the enriching of God is one act. Only the poor man has a rich God. God springs out of the feeling of a want; what man is in need of, whether this be a definite and therefore conscious, or an unconscious need—that is God. Thus the disconsolate feeling of a void, of loneliness, needed a God in whom there is society, a union of beings fervently loving each other.[50]

In a brilliant derivation from, and expansion of, the Hegelian symbolization of the Trinity, in which Hegel had God objectify himself in his "opposite" and thus achieve a consciousness of himself, i.e., "self-consciousness," knowing another than himself—an act of creation—Feuerbach describes the parallel process in the human being, translating it into an important psychological as well as social thesis: the transition within Man from consciousness, to self-consciousness, then to consciousness of another—the "I", the "Thou," and the "Other." In the discovery of the "Other," his fellow man, Man also discovers the bond that ties him to the world. Thus is broken that "isolation" that also explains his former need of Heaven.

> The *ego*, then, attains to consciousness of the world through consciousness of the *thou*. Thus man is the God to man. That he is, he has to thank Nature; that he is man, he has to thank man; spiritually as well as physically he can achieve nothing without his fellowman. Four hands can do more than two, but also four eyes can see more than two. And this combined power is distinguished not only in quantity but also in quality from that which is solitary. In isolation human power is limited, in combination it is infinite. The knowledge of a single man is limited, but reason, science, is unlimited, for it is a common act of mankind; and it is so, not only because innumerable men co-operate in the construction of science, but also in the more profound sense, that the scientific genius of a particular age comprehends in itself the thinking powers of the preceding age, though it modifies them in accordance with its own special characteristics. Wit, acumen, imagination, feeling as distinguished from sensation, reason as a subjective faculty—all these so-called powers of the soul are powers of humanity, not of man as an individual; they are products of culture, products of human society. … Only where man suns and warms himself in the proximity of man arise feeling and imagination.[51]

Having now established this basic relation of consciousness and its development to society, Feuerbach proceeded to expand this relationship to that between Man and

Nature, Intelligence and Matter. And here the break with Hegelian doctrine is both final and fundamental, and the foundations laid for a materialist theory of the universe. How, he asks, if traditional idealistic and theological notions are assumed to be true, can one explain Nature, considered hitherto "impure"—"confused, dark, desolate, immoral, or. ... unmoral"—as originating in the pure spirit of God? How to assign a "divine origin to Nature?" Only, he answers, by positing this impurity, this darkness in God, God as possessing within Himself both the principle of light and of darkness. But since Nature is presumed to be irrational, material, how can it be explained as a result of intelligence?

> On the contrary, it is the basis of intelligence, the basis of personality, without itself having any basis; spirit without Nature is an unreal abstraction; consciousness develops itself only out of Nature.[52]

In the same way, personality, individuality, consciousness are nothing without Nature. Nature is nothing without body. A body does not exist without flesh and blood, and flesh and blood is nothing "without the oxygen of sexual distinction." "If God is not polluted by Nature, neither is he polluted by being associated with the idea of sex."

The individual is limited; the species unlimited. The individual dies; hence he longs for the assurance of some sort of immortality. He posits the Resurrection, and thus satisfies this longing for an immediate certainty of his personal survival after death. Let him now see that though his life is bound to a limited time, that of humanity is not. For the history of mankind represents the continuous and progressive conquest of limits, and in its progress reveals that the alleged or apparent limits were limits only of individuals. Consider the history of philosophy and science! "The species is unlimited; the individual alone is limited."

> He therefore who lives in the consciousness of the species as a reality, regards his existence for others, his relation to society, his utility to the public, as that existence which is one with the existence of his own essence—as his immortal existence. He lives with his whole soul, with his whole heart, for humanity. How can he hold in reserve a special existence for himself, how can he separate himself from mankind? How shall he deny in death what he has enforced in life? And in life his faith is: *Nec sibi sed toti genitum se credere mundo.*[53]

"Born not for himself, but for the whole world." "The beginning, middle and end of religion is Man."

> *Homo homini Deus est:* this is the great practical principle—this is the axis on which revolves the history of the world. The relations of child and parent, of husband and wife, of brother and friend—in general, of man to man—in short, all the moral relations, are *per se* religious. Life as a whole is, in its essential, substantial relations, throughout of a divine nature. Its religious consecration is not first conferred by the blessing of the priest ... Let friendship be sacred to thee, property sacred, marriage sacred—sacred the wellbeing of every man; but let them be sacred *in and by themselves.* ... It needs only that the ordinary course of things be interrupted in order to vindicate to common things an uncommon significance, *to life, as such, a religious import.* Therefore let bread be sacred for us, let wine be sacred, and also let water be sacred! Amen.[54]

With these words, Feuerbach concluded his epoch-making book. It rang forth like a battle-cry, a call to arms; it acted also as a new Book of Revelations. The "I" now saw in the "Thou" the world itself, and knew itself only through that world.

Not many books have had such an immediate impact. David Friedrich Strauss, from whose views those of Feuerbach represented so sharp a departure, wrote: "Today, and perhaps for some time to come, the field belongs to him. His theory is the truth for this age."[55] Friedrich Engels was no less excited:

> Then came Feuerbach's *Essence of Christianity*. ... One must himself have experienced the liberating effect of this book to get an idea of it. Enthusiasm was general; we all became Feuerbachians. ...[56]

And Karl Marx himself, writing in 1842:

> To you, speculative theologians and philosophers, I give this advice: free yourselves from the concepts and prejudices of previous speculative philosophy if you wish really to discover things as they are, that is, if you wish to discover the truth. And there is no other way to truth and freedom than through the "river of fire." Feuerbach is the purgatory of the present time.[57]

The impress of Feuerbach as thinker can be gauged from Engels' essay, written years later, in which he deplores Feuerbach's geographical isolation in the years following the *Essence of Christianity* in a small Bavarian town far removed from the main currents of thought, particularly the revolutionary contributions of science. But for these deficits, his influence and importance might have been even greater and more permanent.

Yet the implications of the *Essence of Christianity* were far-ranging for the thinkers of Feuerbach's day. They transcended the province of religion and extended to a critique of society as a whole. They exposed the dangers and falseness of man's unconscious creations, especially so far as the sanctities of state and the social organism were concerned. If the "beginning, middle and end of religion is Man," is he not also those things, say, for the State, or for Society in general? And if, as Feuerbach held, productive activity is the "positive essence of one's personality," then how better to realize that productive activity than in the effort fully to realize Man as Man?

It was therefore with some justice that Karl Marx wrote in his *Critique of Hegel's Philosophy of Right*, with Feuerbach in mind:

> The criticism of religion ends in the teaching that man is the highest being for man, it ends, that is, with the categorical imperative to overthrow all conditions in which man is a debased, enslaved, forsaken, contemptible being.[58]

> *Durch Himmel und durch Hölle deinen Gang*
> *Hast du gemacht, wie jener grosse Dante.*
> *Von göttlicher Komödie sprach man lang,*
> *Bis sie als menschliche dein Blick erkannte.*

> Through Heaven and Hell you made your way,
> In the wake of the great Dante.
> Long men spoke of his Comedy as Divine,
> Until as Human your keep eye perceived it.

Thus the German poet Georg Herwegh, on Feuerbach's death in 1872.[59]

But Feuerbach wrote his own best epitaph in 1846:

> Enjoy the good things of life, and reduce, so far as you are able, the evils thereof. Believe that things can be better on earth than they are, and they will really be better. Do not expect that the best will come from death, nor from an imagined immortality, only from yourselves! Those evils that are eradicable—evils that have their roots in the indolence, badness, and ignorance of men—these are evils that are the most terrible. Death that is conformable to nature, death that is a culmination of the fullest development of a lifetime, is no evil. But Death that results from necessity, from vice, from crime, from ignorance—that is the Death that you must abhor.[60]

4. Karl Marx

The third act of our philosophical drama also opens with a letter to a father. It was dated Berlin, November 10, 1837, and was written by a student of law and jurisprudence at the university there:

> Dear Father: There are moments in one's life that represent a border-line of the past, and at the same time clearly indicate a new direction. In such a period of transition we feel ourselves compelled to consider the past and the present with the eagle eye of thought, in order to realize our true position. Indeed, History itself loves such retrospect and self-inspection, which often gives her the appearance of standing still or going backwards, while she is merely throwing herself into an armchair, in order to understand herself and penetrate into her own mental processes.[61]

Karl Marx was then nineteen. He had left his native town of Trier, spent a year at the University of Bonn, and was now in Berlin. He had become secretly engaged to the lovely Jenny von Westphalen, was deeply in love, and unhappy at the separation. But he was also deep in his studies of law at the celebrated institution whose juridical stars were Friedrich Carl von Savigny, who represented the "historical" school of law, and Eduard Gans, the Hegelian. Like so many young Germans in love, Marx was also composing sentimental lyrics, in the style, but not with the genius, of Heine. In philosophy, he had already left Kant and Fichte behind, and at first had shied from Hegel's "grotesque crag-like melodies." But then, when his strenuous studies were taking their toll, he was advised to rest.

> During my illness, I got to know Hegel from beginning to end, along with most of his disciples. Through several gatherings with friends in Stralow I obtained entry into a doctorate club. ... In the discussions here many contradictory views became manifest, and I became more and more attached to the current philosophy that I had thought to escape ...

He was still compliant with his father's wishes that he follow a legal career, but felt himself more fitted for jurisprudence than for public administration. At the same time, philosophy became more and more enticing. ...

The letter was intended to reassure his father that this need "to come to grips with philosophy" was a necessary concomitant of, and prerequisite to, his mastery of the philosophy of law. A voracious reader and indefatigable student, he also impressed his companions and teachers with his sharp intellect. The atmosphere of the *Doktorenklub*, which met in a café, was exhilarating; for here, among other bright intellectuals, was also the redoubtable Bruno Bauer, teacher, theologian and Hegelian, who was soon to shock with his radical interpretations of the New Testament. More and more, Marx's eyes were turning toward a university career, as the letter to his father hinted; and the latter, himself an eminent lawyer in Trier, was without doubt disturbed by this radical suggestion of a detour. But Heinrich Marx died in 1838, an overwhelming loss to Karl, who was deeply attached to him; and while his father's death freed him from a professional commitment, it also exposed him to the worry of sustaining himself and, should he marry, his future wife. Bruno Bauer had accepted a university post at Bonn and was soon urging Karl Marx to complete his doctoral dissertation and join him. Aside from a brilliant young philosopher, Bauer needed also a courageous and liberal supporter in the battles he was anticipating. And so in 1841, Marx went to Bonn; he was twenty-three, hopeful, vigorous, eager, and anxious to establish himself. Bauer's admiration was equalled by others who met him at this time. Moses Hess, whose *Sacred History of Mankind* (one of the very first socialist books published in Germany) had appeared in 1837, was even more extravagant in his praise. He was writing to his friend, the novelist Berthold Auerbach:

> This man has made a most extraordinary impression. … the greatest, the only true philosopher now living, who, on public appearance, will attract the eyes of all of Germany. He surpasses. … D. F. Strauss, and even Feuerbach, which is saying a great deal. He will deliver the *coup de grâce* to religion and medieval politics.

In short, he continues, Marx is an amalgam of Rousseau, Voltaire, Holbach, Lessing, Heine and Hegel![62]

And all this about a very young man who only recently achieved his doctorate at Jena with a dissertation on "The Difference between the Democritean and Epicurean Natural Philosophy"!

But Bruno Bauer, as a result of his works critical of Christianity, soon lost his post at the University of Bonn, and Marx, too, realized that an academic career was closed to him. He began to engage in politics.

Marx's first political article was to appear in 1842 in the *Deutsche Jahrbücher* edited by Arnold Ruge. It contained a sharp criticism of the newly promulgated censorship laws of Frederick William IV. His own intellectual world had been undergoing a constant change. Ludwig Feuerbach now loomed large as an influence; and though he was never to replace Hegel, he became an important element in rounding out Marx's development. It was on Hegel and Feuerbach that Marx was now sharpening his mind, gradually also removing himself from most of the Young Hegelians (who now called themselves *Die Freien*, "The Free Ones" and, from Berlin, were promulgating highly romantic, frantic, and unrealistically militant theories, but seemed as far away as possible from concrete political engagement). The ferment that was within Marx led him more and more to an incisive examination of politics and immediate political situations, while at the same time he was enlarging his theoretical vision. Since we are now in possession of many of his writings unpublished or believed lost during his lifetime, we can follow the astonishing growth he underwent in the course of the few years preceding the events of 1848.

Two elements contributed to this unprecedented efflorence: an insatiable appetite for knowledge, and an incessant application and genius for combining the theoretical and the practical. These were conjoined with an uncompromising capacity for self-criticism, which accounts for his suppression of many of his most illuminating writings until he felt himself ready to publish them. He was forever testing his insights, ever on the alert to support them critically and factually. He possessed a thorough classical training, and his interest in literature was wide. As a polemicist he would soon have few equals. There seemed no limit to the energies he was ready to expend in the fulfilment of a task he deemed important—whether in the study of books in the British Museum, or in humdrum but necessary labors of organization. He was the embodiment of his own worldview, the fusion of Theory and Practice.

To himself, however, his growth must have seemed slow, as he continued gathering his forces. Personal insecurity beset him on all sides: his mother was reluctant to support what she deemed a vagrant career; Jenny suffered untold difficulties at home, for though her father, Ludwig von Westphalen, favored Marx, other members of the family regarded her unwavering attachment as an aberration, considering her superior social position. But she remained steadfast in her attachment.

As for Marx himself, he possessed the essential quality of genius—daring. He was in love and beloved. But he was under no illusions that his journalistic career on which he was embarking would be an easy one. The political situation in the Rhenish provinces was tense; censorship was on the watch. He would be a marked man. Already Arnold Ruge was unable to publish Marx's article on the Prussian censorship in his *Hallesche Jahrbücher*, and was forced to transfer it to another publication, the *Anekdota*, in Switzerland, where it appeared in 1843.

* * *

Marx was now embarking on his hazardous course of political involvement, with its constant risks of persecution, or banishment—a life of wandering. He was fortunate in the devoted companionship and support of his wife Jenny. It was a life filled with incessant economic hardships—in short, a life that would draw upon all the inner strength he and Jenny could muster.

The stages of Marx's growth toward achieving a "synthesis" can be clearly mapped, a growth that persisted throughout his life to the very end, when so much of what he had planned still remained unfulfilled. The elements of the ideas and activities that would find their consummation in *Das Kapital*, in 1867, and in the "First International" of 1864, are all to be found *in ovo* before 1848.

He drew intellectual nourishment from innumerable sources—and was glad to acknowledge them; but the richest of them are represented progressively by Hegel, thereafter Feuerbach, and finally the early socialists and the bourgeois economists—though such a sketch is unjust to many other important though lesser tributaries. Not less significant and determinant was the changing history of his own times, of Europe, of the Continent and of England; and, after 1844, the lifelong association and friendship of Friedrich Engels, whose practical experience and interest in economics inspired a more profound study of that subject in Karl Marx. Thus the journey took him from abstract philosophy to politics, and then into economics—all of which he absorbed into his projected synthesis and eventually transformed.

Hegel was his touchstone and his mind's whetstone. On the dialectical method, on the Logic, on Hegel's philosophy of history, of law and of the state, Marx sharpened his own theories, setting down his own critique item by item. His devotion and reverence for Hegel never wavered, though he was to prove his sharpest critic; as would also be the case for Feuerbach, whom he regarded, after Hegel, as the outstanding influence in his early development. From Feuerbach, Marx took the critique of religion; Feuerbach's partial materialism; and his view of Man as a "species-being." Unlike Strauss and Feuerbach, unlike even Engels, Marx was not preeminently concerned with religion as such. Though he came of a family which on both sides was descended from distinguished Jewish savants and rabbis, his father belonged to that group of post-Napoleonic Jews who had severed their religious ties with Judaism, and in the face of the renascent oppressions and persecutions of the Restoration, threw in their lot with either Protestantism or Catholicism. Heinrich Marx, a disciple of Voltaire and the Enlightenment and a worshipper of Kant, indifferent to religious dogma and threatened with professional ostracism, entered the Prussian official church. By the time Marx began a serious study of society, he already considered the critique of religion as over and done with.

A number of his predecessors among the Young Hegelians had already begun to withdraw from Hegelian abstract idealism and its consummation in the Hegelian philosophy of state. In view of the challenging political situation in Germany, they demanded a conversion of theory to practice. But with few exceptions, such "practice" remained purely abstract, impractical, and merely noisy and vapid. It remained moored to an abstract discussion of "consciousness," without bringing that consciousness to bear upon direct political or social action.

Even Feuerbach, brilliant as were his insights, had gone no farther than his critique of religion, although more than any other of the post-Hegelians he had penetrated into the social nature of consciousness and its manifestations in religious projections and sublimations. Yet Marx no doubt read with approval Feuerbach's statement, made in a letter to Arnold Ruge:

> What is theory, what is practice? Wherein lies their difference? Theoretical is that which is hidden in my head only, practical is that which is spooking in many heads. What unites many heads, creates a mass, extends itself and thus finds its place in the world. If it is possible to create a new organ for the new principle, then this is a *praxis* which should never be missed.[63]

Practical knowledge and practical experience in politics and economics were enlarged for Marx when he became a contributor to, then editor of, the *Rheinische Zeitung* during 1842 and 1843. This was the organ of the more enlightened industrialists and commercial interests of the Rhineland, who sought to obtain greater influence and more viable economic and political concessions from the Prussian government to which they were subject. As already noted, this preeminently Catholic section of Prussia was industrially the most advanced of the German states and at variance with the more backward attitudes and policies of Prussia. For a time, Marx found in the *Rheinische Zeitung*, issued in Cologne, a particularly appropriate forum for his already brilliant polemics—directed now against the Prussian state and its censorship laws, and the hypocrisy of the provincial diets, whose constitution by the upper classes was in blatant contradiction to its representative pretensions. More and more he became aware of the interrelations of economic and political power, and of the plight of the lower classes. The official censorship counterattacked by suppressing a number of his articles. The rival and conservative *Kölnische Zeitung* smelled out Young Hegelian blasphemies and radicalism, giving Marx the occasion for an eloquent defense of philosophy as against religion. Philosophy, he contended, was not something divorced from the world; it was the bone and marrow of social, economic and political life and had played, and was playing, an important role in the progress of a society. At the same time, as editor, Marx began paying attention to the social problems of the Rhineland; attacked the Rhenish Parliament on its proposal to rescind the right of the populace to collect fallen timber and to punish offenders severely; he called attention to the economic plight of the Moselle wine-growers. At this moment he was warding off polemical attacks on the part of the Berlin *Freien* and was still embroiled in troubles at home. But worse was in the offing.

The *Rheinische Zeitung* had by now doubled its subscription readership and was no longer a negligible thorn in the side of the authorities. King Frederick William IV by this time had second thoughts on his quasi-liberal attitude toward the press, which in his eyes was now becoming more and more rampantly offensive. He struck out at the editors of newspapers in Mannheim and Königsberg, ordering his provincial authorities to look closely at their local publications. The President of the Rhineland province took the instructions to heart and found ready pretext at hand for action: the article by Marx on the theft of wood, and a subsequent one dealing with divorce, the more liberal laws of which the King was secretly planning to restrict. There was a brief quietus, and then the conditions became intolerable for Marx, who was regarded as a *bête noire*. On March 18, 1843 he published a declaration in the newspaper that he was retiring from the conduct of the *Rheinische Zeitung*. He had before this begun to plan residence abroad. The newspaper ceased publication on March 31, concluding its valiant existence with a poetic flourish depicting the brave sailors with heads unbowed, promising to sail other vessels. ...

The "sailing" would also have to be in other waters. In Germany there was no prospect of free expression. One after another, reviews and journals fell under the censor's axe. Arnold Ruge's *Jahrbücher* was one of the victims, and it seemed prudent to transplant it to Switzerland. Julius Froebel, a distinguished Swiss professor of mineralogy and a publisher of great courage and liberalism, was interested in bringing Marx to Zurich. In the end Marx and Ruge agreed on a new publication which would represent the best that France and Germany could offer in conjoint liberal thought, the *Deutsch-Französische Jahrbücher—Franco-German Annals*. It would appear in Paris ...

On June 12, 1843 Karl Marx and Jenny von Westphalen were married at Kreuznach, where she was then living. They had waited seven years ... On to fresh fields and fresh enterprises! Assured of financial support from Ruge and his associates for the proposed publication of the *Deutsch-Französische Jahrbücher*, and of such gifted collaborators as Ruge, Moses Hess, Karl Froebel, and the poet Georg Herwegh; hopeful of attracting leading French socialists, and such liberals as Lamennais and Lamartine; Marx and Jenny set off for Paris, where they arrived in October 1843 and settled in the rue Vanneau 38. Jenny was already pregnant.

Here they were, in Paris, smithy of revolutions! Winds of controversy blew hard and fast; the cauldrons of ideas were ever a-boiling; doctrine clashed with doctrine; the barricades of 1830 had not been forgotten; storms were in the offing ... Socialist and even more radical ideas found full expression; the names of Saint-Simon, Fourier, Considérant, Louis Blanc, Blanqui, Proudhon became battle cries ... Paris was the asylum of political exiles from all over, even from Russia. Paris was the city of organizations, of societies, of "clubs"—like the German "League of the Just." Here literature was politics and politics was literature. Here lived Germany's greatest poet, Heinrich Heine. Here had lived and died Germany's foremost journalist, Ludwig Börne. In Heine, Marx soon found another contributor to the *Deutsch-Französische Jahrbücher*.

What a change from the stagnant apathy that prevailed in the German lands!

Here Marx rounded out the first stages of his education—the attainment of that "reform of consciousness" (a term of his invention) which was to represent a strong leap forward into new regions of thought and action ...

In the roster of contributions to the first issue of the journal was one from Friedrich Engels, sent from England, forging the first links in that chain of association which was to prove epochal not only for the lives of both men, but for history. They had met casually two years before in Cologne, but without establishing a bond. Paris brought them together in a lifetime friendship, association and collaboration.

The *Deutsch-Französische Jahrbücher* appeared in a double number in March 1844. Alas! this was its first and last appearance. It had not secured the cooperation of the French socialists; Froebel withdrew his support after the first issue, Ruge was in disagreement with its radical policies and articles, and the Prussian government brought representations upon French minister Guizot to suppress it and, failing that, took measures to bar the journal from German territories, confiscated a number of issues, and publicly declared Ruge, Marx, Heine and others guilty of high treason and subject to immediate arrest upon crossing the border. The remarkable first and last issue had contained Heine's bitterly satirical poems on King Ludwig of Bavaria; the important essay by Marx, the "Critique of Hegel's *Philosophy of Right*"; Engels' article on Political Economy, and his review of Carlyle's *Past and Present*.

Though deprived of this particular source of income, Marx was not left destitute. Friends in Cologne rallied and contributed to his support. Jenny had given birth to a daughter in May 1844, and soon thereafter had returned to Germany with the child to visit her family.

Marx's studies were now, if anything, intensified. The charged atmosphere of Paris proved a mighty auxiliary in his development: the presence of a strong and active working class, an advanced economy, and not least, the ineradicable revolutionary tradition of France. He began a thorough study of the French Revolution, as well as of the bourgeois economists, spurred on to the latter by Engels' profound investigations of British capitalism. The tempo of his intellectual progress and understanding may be gauged by the fact that Paris marked the crucial, revolutionary stage of his development:

his total break with the Young Hegelians. By the time he left the city in 1845, he had not only completed his studies of Hegel (and achieved a break with and a critique of that philosopher), but was also working out his ideas in the remarkable series called the "Paris Manuscripts of 1844." He culminated that period with *The Holy Family*, in collaboration with Engels, and elaborated his theories of dialectical materialism.

Before leaving for Paris, Marx had written to Ruge in September 1843:

> Our slogan, therefore, must be: Reform of consciousness, not through dogmas, but through an analysis of the mystical consciousness that is unclear about itself, whether in religion or politics. It will then become evident that the world had long dreamed of something, of which it only must become conscious in order to possess it in actuality. It will become evident that there is no big gap between the past and the future, but rather a matter of carrying out the thought of the past. It will be evident, finally, that mankind does not begin any new work, but accomplishes its old work consciously.[64]

In Paris, he labored to flesh out that slogan. The tasks that were on the current agenda of Humanity had been set for some time by History. "If our business is not building the future and its perfection for all time to come, what we do have to accomplish now is all the more certain: I mean the relentless critique of all that exists, relentless in the sense that the critique is neither afraid of its own results nor of coming into conflict with the powers that be."[65]

Yet if it was a "relentless" or "reckless" critique of the "existing," it was also a critique that produced, gradually, a fresh and new "synthesis" centering upon Man and Mankind. This was "historical materialism." Many elements went into its making, but what emerged was something new. The element that fused all the discrete materials into one "totality" came from the combined genius of Marx and Engels. The stages of progress that led to the final achievement might be marked out as Philosophy, Anthropology, and Economics. Hegel's dialectical method, his historical view of "process," was now appropriated, as was Feuerbach's anthropology and his theory of "alienation," and their full light was turned upon the activities of the human being as a productive being, in relation to the forces that make up society. The starting point was now not the Absolute Idea, Absolute Reason, Spirit as it externalized itself in determinate Nature, Man, and Man's consciousness, but *concrete* Man and *his* consciousness, man as a productive being, man as a product also of the varied forces that made up society and history.

For Marx, too, as for Hegel, the goal was Freedom; but freedom as actualized in the rehabilitation of man as man, man as member of society, man as the creative being, whose expanding "consciousness" was such as to make him ever more aware of his own powers to master nature and his environment and to attain to an understanding and knowledge of the laws of nature and society so as to "universalize" his humanness. Hegel had seen the consummation of Freedom as achieved in the present political State; in Marx's view, this was only epitomizing the nature and character of the bourgeois society of Hegel's time. Marxian critique had now to be directed toward examining the basis of that state, and of that society, in an effort to discover their internal contradictions as they revealed the potentialities for the next steps in the attainment of Freedom.

Relentlessly, Marx proceeded to a critique of present society, beginning with that of Germany and proceeding thereafter to a more general critique of all of bourgeois society. Like the other Young Hegelians he recognized the role a critique of religion had played as prologue to a subsequent critique of the state and the social order. It was necessary now to proceed to a reclamation of Man as Man by freeing him from illusions induced by his failure thus far to recognize that an "inverted world" had produced within him an "inverted" view of reality. That which man had "alienated" from himself—the qualities of "universal" humanity—and attributed to transterrestrial powers, must be restored to him. But how?

> For Germany [Marx wrote], the criticism of religion has been essentially completed; and the criticism of religion is the premise of all criticism ... Man, who has found in the fantastic reality of heaven, where he sought a superhuman being, only a reflection of his own self, will no longer be inclined to find only a semblance of himself—a non-human being—where he seeks and must seek his true reality.

But Man is not an abstract being, outside of this world. He is the "human world, the state, society." Man makes religion; religion does not make man. Religion is the "fantastic realization" of man, because the human being does not possess the true reality. But religion is at the same time an expression of real suffering and a protest against real suffering. Here occurs that celebrated (or notorious) epithet, which, taken out of its true context, has done so much to distort Marx's true meaning:

> Religion is the sigh of the oppressed creature, the feeling of a heartless world, as much as it is the soul of soulless conditions. It is the opium of the people.

Religion, then, is itself the evidence for and an implicit critique of a world that makes for human misery. It is now the task of history, and its auxiliary, philosophy, to unmask this unreal world and the self-alienation of man in its "secular" form, now that it has been unmasked in its "sacred" form.[66] The backwardness of Germany politically is in sharp contrast to its forward position in speculative philosophy. And this critical, speculative philosophy of right leads on to tasks which can only be solved "by means of practical activity."

The problem then is not merely of raising Germany to the "official level"—political and social—of modern nations, but also to the "human level, which will be the immediate future of those nations." Can Germany be capable of such a revolution, imbedded as she is in an *ancien régime*? Theoretically she has reached that stage; but practically? Materially?

> Material force can only be overthrown by material force; but theory itself becomes a material force when it has seized the masses. Theory is capable of seizing the masses when it demonstrates *ad hominem*, and it demonstrates *ad hominem* as soon as it becomes radical. To be radical is to grasp things by their root. But for man the root is man himself.

Germany has exhibited its radicalism in theory in it its criticism of religion, and beginning with the "resolute positive abolition of religion," it has moved toward the doctrine that "man is the supreme being for man."

It ends, therefore, with the categorical imperative to overthrow all those conditions in which man is an abased, enslaved, abandoned, contemptible being. ...

But who, indeed, is to be the bearer of this revolutionary idea, who is to represent this revolutionary force? Which is the class capable of undertaking a general emancipation of society? Such a class as can arouse in itself and in the masses the enthusiasm and sentiment so that it is recognized as "the general representative of that society"? In other words, a class that "universalizes" its sufferings into universal suffering or wrongs? A class that can speak for all?

Thus is announced the world-emancipating role of the proletariat. ...

Where is there, then, the real possibility of a German emancipation? We reply: In the formation of a class with radical chains, a class in civil society that is not a class of civil society; an "estate"which is the dissolution of all estates, a sphere of society which has a universal character because of its universal sufferings, and which does not lay claim to a particular right, because the injustice it suffers is no particular injustice, but injustice in general. A sphere of society which does not lay claim to a historical status, but only a human status ... a sphere, finally, which cannot emancipate itself without emancipating itself from all the other spheres of society, without, also, emancipating all other spheres of society, which in a word, is a total loss of humanity and which can only recover itself through a total redemption of humanity. This dissolution of society, as a particular class, is the proletariat.[67]

And Marx concludes: "The emancipation of Germany will be the emancipation of Man. Philosophy is the head of this emancipation, the proletariat its heart. Philosophy cannot be realized without the dissolution of the proletariat, the proletariat can only be abolished by the realization of philosophy. When all inner conditions are fulfilled, the day of German resurrection will be heralded by the crowing of the Gallic cock."

* * *

We have thus, with Marx, passed beyond Hegel as well as Feuerbach in the conversion of theory into practice. Practice is made tangible by its application to the masses of mankind, under the leadership of the most oppressed class. Alienated man has thus abolished alienation, and restored himself to himself, in his universal action of emancipation.

But what, in truth, is Alienation? And who is he who is the greatest sufferer of it in our society? Marx asks. Obviously, looking at modern industry, the worker. He is the proletarian; that is, he lives without capital or rent, solely from labor. Traditional political economy treats him solely as a worker, so that, like a horse, he must receive just as much "as will enable him to work." It does not deal with him as a human being, as one with free time, but "leaves that aspect to the criminal law, doctors, religion, statistical tables, politics and the work-house beadle." The impoverishment of the contemporary worker is an open book to anyone capable of reading it. And this phenomenon is all the more striking as it shows itself in the fact that he becomes poorer and poorer the more wealth he produces for others. In proportion as the value of the things he makes increases, his own human world is devalued. And so we are faced with this particular reality: The worker has not only produced goods; he has produced himself as a *commodity*, as well as his labor.

In considering the various aspects of Alienation as reflected in the capitalist society of his day, Marx, as a matter of fact, is exposing a central problem for the modern world, with its manifold implications for psychology, sociology, ethics and morality; a situation particularly aggravated since Marx's time by the amazing technological advances on the one hand, and the greater concentration of economic power in giant monolithic enterprises on the other; a situation foreseen and analyzed by him. For the first time, he was enabled to establish the nexus between a contradictory society and the process of dehumanization and atomization of the individual member as a resultant of the social forces at work. In our computerized, automated world his conclusions strike out with particular force and pathos.

In a commodity economy, the worker has become a commodity. As producer he has become a product; a product as inanimate as the product he has produced. And his product has become something alien to him (multiply this by division of labor, mechanization, speed-up). His product is no longer a "part of his nature," his creation, his self-fulfilment, his means to a higher consciousness of himself and the world. It has become a "means" for the satisfaction of other needs—it has become forced labor. As a producer and as a product he has now been appropriated. *He is owned.* And in the process, he is dehumanized as a civilized being—"free" only in his animal functions and pleasures, so called, not because these are not genuinely human in themselves, but because they are dissociated from other human functions that contribute to a total fulfilment of the self. Isolated, dehumanized, alienated from himself, he is also alienated from his fellows. Appropriated by his owners, the owners of his labor, he is also alienated from "property," which comes to be something outside of himself. That which his hands have made, his product, acquires a character of independence and, instead of appearing as a product, now appears as an ominous force, a power. But it is not only the expropriated producer that is dehumanized; he who buys labor is also distorted as human being. Human beings as well as objects are turned into objects of "egoistic" possession and acquisition. Thus all social relations of individuals are transformed into commodities, into their value, into functions of money. In religion, God was conceived as the author of the historical process; now it is money that maneuvers and moves Man around as object. Money is man's alienated self. Money reduces all human qualities to interchangeable quantities and values.

What then of property? Hegel had maintained that property was the realization of the human personality through objectification in the "external, phenomenal world." Property represented human freedom. Lack of property inhibits man's participation in the universality represented by the State, therefore in the universality of Reason. "If property constitutes the first endowment of a free person, the proletariat is neither free nor a person, for he possesses no property."[68] In like manner, he is severed from art, religion, philosophy—hence from man's very essence—and therefore he represents the "complete loss of man." Such then is the contradiction which the unpropertied class reflects in bourgeois society; a revelation of how the mode of labor on which it is founded totally vitiates it, and "represents a total negativity" (in Hegelian terms) challenging the reality of Reason, of Truth. Thus, too, history and social reality "negate" speculative philosophy, which can no longer be the instrument of a critique of society. Such a task falls to "socio-historical practice."[69]

What, according to Marx, does history reveal about "Spirit," "Consciousness," "Reason"? History reveals that "Spirit" is not antecedent to history, but that its emergence represents a late stage in the evolution of man. "It is a product of the power of development immanent in the 'species life,' generated and impelled by man's life in society, the development which accounts for constant growth and ever new achievement."[70] Consciousness is therefore not a static thing:—it is an ever-growing, ever-developing attribute of Man, the resultant of Man's interaction with Nature and with other members of the species through Practice—Activity. And since History begins with Production and the Process of Production, Production is the defining characteristic of Man. It causally brings about History and (to invert the Hegelian idea), as Practice, becomes revolution "actualizing the idea of Reason."[71] Practice changes consciousness, raises it to a new level of comprehension, so that it is thus enabled to change reality and ultimately achieve true Freedom.

> Men have always freed themselves to the extent to which not their ideal of humanity, but the existing forces of production, prescribed and permitted. All previous liberations have been based upon limited forces of production, whose products, insufficient for the whole of society, made development possible only by some satisfying their needs at the expense of others, and consequently, the former, the minority, obtained the monopoly of the development, while the others, the majority, through the continued struggle for the satisfaction of their urgent needs, for the time being—that is, till the creation of new revolutionary forces of production—were shut out from all development. So society has hitherto always developed within an opposition, which, among the ancients was that of freemen and slaves, in the middle ages, between nobles and serfs, in modern times, of bourgeoisie and proletariat.[72]

The "reform of consciousness," so far as the proletariat and (through the proletariat) the world at large is concerned, will be achieved when, through *praxis*, the former develops a new consciousness that comprehends that, under the existing form of production (capitalism), he is degraded to a mere object, a commodity. With the attainment of this comprehension the worker ceases to be an object, a commodity, and becomes a "subject." Instead of being a passive recipient, he becomes an active agent. Through understanding the theory, he has been enabled to proceed to revolutionary practice. Bringing to an end the alienated experience, he emerges as the complete, free man, a "universal" being with the readiness to fulfil all his potentialities. History is the history of class struggles, and in abolishing private property and its system, he has also abolished his class. He has abolished Alienation.

With the abolition of this society, what Marx calls the pre-history of mankind will come to an end. Man's actual history will commence. ...

In one of his very few predictive passages on the nature of a future devoid of present-day forces of alienation, Marx speculated:

> Suppose we had produced things as human beings; in his production each one of us would have twice affirmed himself and the other. (1) In my production, I would have objectified my individuality, and its particularity, and during this activity, I would have enjoyed an individual life, for in viewing the object I would have experienced the individual joy of knowing my personality as an objective, sensuously perceptible, and

indubitable and exalted power. (2) In your satisfaction and your use of my product I would have had the direct and conscious satisfaction that my work satisfied a human need, that it objectified human nature, and that it provided an appropriate object for another human being. (3) I would have been the mediator between you and the species, and for you, therefore, a completion of your own nature and a necessary part of yourself. And I would have been affirmed in your thought as well as in your love. (4) In my individual life's activity, I would also have created your life's activity, and realized my true human and social nature. ... My labor then would be a free manifestation of life, and an enjoyment of life. ... imposed upon me not by external and accidental necessity, but by an internal and determined necessity.[73]

We have here, in brief, an epitome of the new ethics, aesthetics, psychology of the fulfilled individual and an unalienated society. The abolition of the present system, through an abolition of private property—that is, through "communism"—therefore represents the "real appropriation of human nature through and for man." Communism "is the solution of the riddle of history and knows itself to be this solution."[74]

5. Friedrich Engels

Nothing could have been farther apart from the quietness of Trier—its agrarian vineyard environs, and the family life into which Karl Marx was born—than the surroundings and life that fell to the lot of Friedrich Engels. The small town of Barmen also belonged to the Rhineland, but it lay in the valley of the Wupper, in the heart of Germany's industrial region.

Two years younger than Marx, Engels, who was born in 1820, was brought up in a highly comfortable cotton manufacturer's family; in a household that, like a great part of the Barmen community and the adjoining manufacturing town of Elberfeld, was penetrated by a deeply religious pietism. In Engels' home prevailed a strict Calvinism, ascetic in character; and its devotions were almost evenly divided between the formal pieties of home and church, and the more secular pieties of business and work. It was to be expected that the bright offspring of such a family would, after a preliminary general education, enter upon the same career as was so prominently blazoned forth in the firm names of Engels in Barmen, and "Engels and Ermen" in Manchester, England. Barmen proudly called itself the Manchester of Germany, as displayed in its less populous but none the less busy life, its fuliginous chimney stacks, its factory workers, children included, its long working hours, its frequent inebrieties and occasional violence, its poverty, as well as its Sunday devotions, punctuated by no less frequent admonitory sermons—all the evidences of advanced industrialism and its triumphs. Thus unlike Marx, young Engels was brought early into direct contact with the conditions and effects of the modern factory system. Also unlike Marx, he began the battle for mental emancipation and personal self-realization with a religious crisis, before he could enter upon the more secular philosophical pilgrimage and achieve intellectual freedom.

He received a thorough preparatory education in Barmen and at the gymnasium in Elberfeld, the latter, unfortunately, terminated at the behest of his father before graduation. But not even dreary provincial Barmen, and the slightly less provincial Elberfeld, were immune to intellectual disturbances from abroad; in fact, Elberfeld workers had on one occasion during Friedrich's boyhood vented their fury and frustrations in highly alarming riots. Neither town could establish a *cordon sanitaire* against ideas. Young Engels wanted to be a poet and sought to satisfy the cravings of his imagination by composing poems and plunging into a reading of heroic literature. His preferred heroes were Siegfried, Faust, and the Wandering Jew. An intransigent and unsympathetic father watched these aberrations with suspicion, then with resentment, especially as the young man began to show strange religious leanings and an evident reluctance to follow his father's steps as a life's vocation. None the less, Engels acquiesced for a time. He could hardly have anticipated to what uses he would eventually put the lessons he learned, first in his father's offices, then in the offices of the export firm of Heinrich Leupold in the shipping center of Bremen. Actually, he was already living two lives: the practical life of a future manufacturer and the private life of imagination and intellect that had already turned from pietism to a kind of vague agnosticism. He read widely; he had even begun a minor journalistic career. He knew himself to be a writer (for the time at least). Though his formal education had been interrupted, he continued educating himself indefatigably and relentlessly. He became a linguist, got to know French, Italian, English, Spanish, even Portuguese—Latin and Greek of course, even a little Hebrew. He read Strauss's *Life of Jesus* and was converted. From Strauss it was natural then to go to Hegel and the Young Hegelians, Feuerbach among them. Already his eyes were turned toward Berlin.

In literature he became a disciple and admirer of the writers of the Young Germany school: of the still radical novelist Karl Gutzkow, of Heinrich Heine, and especially of Ludwig Börne, whose political liberalism and republicanism he admired. Under the name "Friedrich Oswald," Engels acquired a local reputation through a number of vivid sketches in Gutzkow's *Telegraph* depicting life in the Wupperthal. When the military claimed him, he volunteered and was thus enabled to choose a locale for his activities. He joined the artillery, was stationed in Berlin, and here began developing an interest in military science that was to remain with him and serve him well in his later analyses of the tactics and strategies of European and American armies.

He was in Berlin from September 1841 to August 1842. There he attended lectures at the university as auditor, became a frequenter of the Young Hegelian *Doktorenklub*, and began to contribute to the *Rheinische Zeitung*. What Strauss had begun, Moses Hess completed. Under his influence, Engels was converted to socialism. Hess envisioned the approach of revolution as emanating from the converging influences of three countries: England and its economics; France and its political radicalism; and Germany with its philosophy. In fact, Engels was soon to find himself in the role of mediator between philosophy and economics. To the English he would very soon try to clarify the meaning of German philosophical radicalism; to the Germans, the nature of economics as revealed in what was taking place in England. In his knowledge and understanding of the true nature of industrialism and capitalism he was, of course, far ahead of any of his associates in Berlin, as well as of Marx himself at this stage. A brief meeting in Cologne in 1842 did not begin their partnership; it took two years, and Paris, to make for the beginning of a lifelong association. For the present,

Engels was off to England—to Manchester. The most crucial, critical, and productive part of his education was about to commence.

England was to be very close to him. He had taken Shelley and his poetry to heart. Poets were for him the great missionaries of human emancipation and salvation; Shelley was the poet as revolutionary. He, too, felt himself one of "the free singers."

Like other young intellects of the time, he was astir with the new thoughts and movements within and outside of the country. "*Ich kann des Nachts nicht schlafen vor lauter Ideen des Jahrhunderts.*" "The ideas of the century keep me from sleeping nights."[75] He was always to be intoxicated by new ideas. He felt that way when he came upon Hegel's philosophy, especially Hegel's notion of God, and in his twentieth year interpreted it in the light of a pantheism. It was an electrifying experience:

> When the God-idea of the last of philosophers first became manifest to me—this giant-idea of the nineteenth century …, then the depths of speculation lay before me like an impenetrable ocean, from whose very bottom the eye cannot avert its eager gaze … We felt that all around us and we ourselves are suffused with God.[76]

He had also been present at the Berlin lectures of Schelling on Revelation, which that philosopher directed against Hegel and his followers. Engels then published a diatribe against Schelling and at the same time affirmed his faith in the future opened up for him by his master Hegel:

> The world that had seemed like a prison, now revealed itself in its true aspect, as a magnificent palace, open now to all of us, to enter and to leave, for rich and poor, for high and low … This belief in the omnipotence of the Idea, in the victory of eternal Truth, this firm assurance that it can never waver or yield, even though the whole world stood up against her, this is the true religion of a true philosopher, this is the basis of the positive philosophy, the philosophy of world history.[77]

His boldness was greater than his knowledge, for he was scarcely competent as yet to judge Schelling; nor was he advanced in his understanding of Hegel. The fervor of the *Doktorenklub* was upon him. Marx, who had left Berlin shortly before Engels' arrival, was no longer there to set him right; but Engels made up in zeal what he still lacked in learning. History was also a valuable teacher, especially that of his own day, for many important things were happening in France and England. News had come of the unsuccessful insurrectionary attempt on the part of the radical Frenchman Blanqui in Paris in May 1839; there was the Chartist agitation in England, especially the great strike in the textile industry of 1842. The contemporary novels of Dickens, George Sand, and Eugène Sue were read, discussed, and admired for their pronounced social declarations. All these and many other influences now affected him and helped form him as he prepared to join his father's firm in Manchester. Here he was to find a "university," not bound by classrooms or lecture halls, but no less enlightening and formative than Berlin with its university and its *Doktorenklub*. He had already made the acquaintance of Karl Marx's critique of Hegel's *Philosophy of Right*. He was prepared to test his theoretical knowledge against the practical experiences and observations derived from the economic realities of the greatest workshop in the world. Many years later he described what he had learned there:

While in Manchester, I was forcibly brought to realize that economic facts, which have so far played no role or only a contemptible one in the writing of history, are, at least in the modern world, a decisive historical force; that they form the basis for the origin of the present-day class antagonisms; that these antagonisms, in the countries where they have become fully developed, thanks to large-scale industry, especially therefore in England, are in their turn the basis of the formation of political parties and of party struggles, and thus of all political history.[78]

From Manchester he conveyed his newly acquired knowledge and observations to Marx through his contributions to the *Rheinische Zeitung* and the *Deutsch-Französische Jahrbücher.*

In England originated or were brought to completion some of the most significant of Engels' works, based upon his experiences in that country: *Letters from England,* "The Condition of England," *Outlines of a Critique of National Economy,* a review of Carlyle's *Past and Present* and, of the greatest moment, the volume on *The Condition of the Working Class of England in 1844,* published in 1845. In addition, he contributed articles to the Owenite journal *The New Moral World,* and entered into close relations with the Chartist leader and editor George Julian Harney. As we have noted, Engels was the bridge that linked Continental socialist movements with those of the English working class. He became deeply involved in the appalling plight of the Irish workers in England. He wrote glowingly of their courage.

> Whoever has not seen the Irish, cannot know them. Give me 200,000 Irishmen, and I won't give the whole of the British Monarchy much of a chance.[79]

Here, in England, he claimed, was the most advanced, the best-organized working-class movement in the world. Here the social conditions glaringly displayed the misery, the deprivation, the degradations of millions of beings. Here were man and women schooled in the bitter lessons of proletarian conflict, defeats, and ever-continuing counterattack—intelligent, enlightened masses, eager to learn the truth and act upon it. Unfortunately they were bogged down in their efforts because they relied on political action to solve their social problems. If only they could master the theories of class-struggle and revolution! For Engels believed that England was on the verge of a mighty revolution. It seemed to him that the necessary forces were present there already.

He was deeply impressed with Thomas Carlyle's writings and recognized in their author a moral force of great importance and influence. Somewhat recklessly he called him the only English writer worthy of being read. It was therefore with a respectful though critical spirit that he reviewed Carlyle's *Past and Present.* He understood that in his political ideas Carlyle was more Tory than Whig. "This is certain," Engels wrote. "A Whig could never have written a book half so human as *Past and Present.*" In his review, which was to be published in the *Deutsch-Französische Jahrbücher,* Engels fully approved of Carlyle's violent rage against a society that worshipped Mammon and was bound only by the "nexus" of cash; against an aristocracy that was lazy and indifferent, as well as inefficient; against manufacturers and traders concerned solely with their profits. He was all sympathy with Carlyle's outrage at the poverty and misery only too prevalent in England. But he rejected Carlyle's attempted solutions to these problems; raised severe objection to his idealization of a medieval society, with its alleged greater cohesion and humanity, and particularly to his demand for a return to religion. Carlyle, Engels stated, who knew so much about German literature, had failed to see its completion and its consummation in German philosophy, particularly that of Feuerbach and Bruno Bauer, about whom he seemed to have no knowledge. Had Carlyle searched more deeply into the causes of the great crisis of the day, he surely would have found them in the state of religion itself. He would have perceived that though the question hitherto had been "What is God?"—German philosophy had resolved it in its discovery that God is Mankind. "We see in history not the revelation of God, but of man, and only of man." Carlyle was seeking "heroes" to guide mankind; had he truly conceived of man in his infinity, in his totality, he would not have fallen back upon an ignoble conception that divided mankind into sheep and goats, ruler and ruled, aristocrat and mob. He would not have clung so closely to the notion that property was sacred. Like Carlyle, Engels added, "we carry on a battle to the death," with all the evils of the day, "but we have a greater chance of success than he, for we know what we want."[80]

It was a Feuerbachian still speaking. Engels' sojourn in England from the end of 1842 till August 1844 gave him an unequalled opportunity to extend both his knowledge and his understanding of the British economy and polity. With a fine scalpel he began removing the outer layers of English political and social life to bare its true insides. For the German newspaper *Vorwärts*, published in Paris, he wrote a series of brilliant analyses of the "Condition of England," bringing to light some of the illusions he believed surrounded the idea of the British Constitution, and the alleged "democracy" inherent in British institutions. In substance, he asserted, all these concealed the true rulers of England: the House of Commons, the real organ and instrument of the conquering manufacturers and commercial interests. All the powers of "the Constitution, the Crown, the House of Lords, the House of Commons" were "deceptions," the masks of privilege. "The democracy that will triumph in England is a *social* democracy. Simple democracy is incapable of curing social evils. Democratic equality is a chimaera, and the struggle between the poor against the rich cannot be resolved by means of political democracy. This represents only a transitory phase, whence will be born a new element—a principle that will transcend every political element—the principle of socialism."[81]

In even fiercer terms Engels excoriated the hypocrisy of the British bourgeoisie, with its claim that it had destroyed the "barbarism of monopoly, and carried civilization to the farthest corners of the world, and enlarged the brotherhood of man, and diminished wars." Yes, Engels said, addressing himself to such pious braggarts,

> You have destroyed the little monopolies, in order to allow the greater and basic monopoly, property, to act more freely and without restraints. You have civilized the corners of the world, in order to win new territories for the better expansion of your abysmal greed; you have brought brotherhood to peoples, a brotherhood of thieves; you have diminished wars, in order to obtain the greater gains of peace, in order to push the enmity of the individual—the dishonorable war of competition—to its highest point ... Where have you ever been virtuous, without advancing your own interests, without concealing your immoral, egoistical motives?[82]

6. Marx and Engels

Major turning points in history are not always signaled by articulated fanfare, or even observed at the time. The ten-day meeting of Engels and Marx in Paris in August 1844, when Engels was returning home, passed practically unnoticed except by a number of their associates. Yet it marked a most significant moment in the history of socialist thought and action, an affirmation of intellectual identity on the part of the two thinkers; the beginning of actual collaboration that set forth and clarified the theoretical elements and joined them to practical realization. In their own ideas they achieved that "reform of consciousness" that transcended absolute idealism and brought forth historical and dialectical materialism both as theory and practice. Granted that the theories were true, and substantiated by history and fact, they were useless unless translated into practice—that is, the creation of a movement. In the unpublished manuscripts of 1844, the so-called "Paris" manuscripts, Marx had already seen the need of these ideas to catch hold of the masses, who, through their "reformed" or "heightened" consciousness, would turn them into concrete realities—that is, bring about a revolution.

It would be futile and meaningless here to enter upon a discussion as to which of the two was the greater or the more original genius, which contributed most, and which originated this or that particular idea or notion. Both men were geniuses of a high order, and each contributed in accordance with the richness of his own particular powers and in the interchange through which they drew upon one another's resources. Genius, is, after all, just such a "reform of consciousness," a new perception of fundamental relationships in whatever world it deals with: science, art, philosophy. It is a leap forward in creation, made possible by the springboard of the times and its antecedents. In turn it affords an expansion of consciousness on the part of the recipient—an *expansion* that may take different forms, depending upon the particular cultural form. The full impact of such innovations may not become apparent until some time after their appearance or proclamation. It is a fact that the most influential of all the Young Hegelians between 1840 and 1848 was not Marx, nor Engels, but Ludwig Feuerbach, who in turn represented historically one of the preliminary stages of preparation for the ideas of Marx and Engels.

One might say that what now emerged as theory and practice was in fact a fulfilment of Moses Hess's anticipation. Three elements had been fused: German philosophy, French revolutionary political thought and revolutionary tradition, and England's industrial triumphs—England as economic fact, Germany as theory, and France as revolutionary practice. To his collaboration with Marx, Engels brought his practical experience in industry and his vast knowledge of economics; Marx on his side contributed his philosophical acumen, wide knowledge of history, and extraordinary theoretical insights.

Let us remember too that Marx and Engels labored under severe pressures and urgencies. The political horizon was clouded, and a storm, many felt, was imminent. In this approaching explosion what was needed was theoretic clarity, particularly when so many clashing doctrines were in the air and acrimonies raged far and wide. Polemics were sharp and, to modern ears, unusually raucous and intolerant at times.

Much of the argumentation directed by Marx and Engels against Proudhon, Bakunin, German Utopians, German idealists, messianic socialists, appears outdated today, but at the time seemed of paramount importance, when the task was not only to counter intellectual opposition, but also to convey viable ideas to the working classes in order to move them to fruitful activity. The astounding fact was that such work *was* productive, both theoretically and practically. The almost inexhaustible energies spent upon it did bear epoch-making fruit: a political and social manifesto of unequaled importance for that and the following century, and an organization that was destined in one form or another to effect untold radical changes in the entire world. It must also not be forgotten that such works were undertaken, begun and completed in an atmosphere of uncertainty: at any moment an order might be issued by the government that would mean expulsion for its proponents and removal to a new and strange home ...

And indeed it happened to Marx. Engels went back to Barmen to carry on political activity and education—in the end to find himself in difficulties with the police (not to mention his father). Marx had become an important contributor to the German newspaper *Vorwärts* appearing in Paris. He and Heinrich Heine had become intimate, and it was under Marx's influence, and for that newspaper, that the poet composed some of his most trenchant and moving political poems and prose works—notably the poem "The Weavers," aroused by the revolt of the Silesian workers in 1844. Engels' contributions on England had also appeared in that journal. *Vorwärts*, under the editorship of Bernays, had become an outspoken radical organ with a number of left-wing contributors. An indiscreet article concerning the attempted murder of King Frederick William IV by a certain Burgomaster Tschech inspired the Prussian government to ask France for the prosecution of editor Bernays. Guizot took advantage of Bernays' failure to post the required security demanded of newspapers, and had him jailed and fined. The other editors of *Vorwärts* thereupon changed the journal into a monthly, which was not subject to such restrictions. In response, Guizot ordered the Minister of the Interior to proceed and expel editors and contributors Heinrich Heine, Bernays, Karl Marx, Mikhail Bakunin, Ruge, and others. The order was issued on January 26, 1845, and of these only Marx and Bakunin suffered final expulsion. Marx left Paris on February 1, 1845 and arrived in Brussels on the ninth. Another critical but even more fruitful period was to commence. He was joined by his wife and daughter, and settled in a Brussels suburb. He was not to be alone, for in addition to his family there were friends he knew in Brussels already. Soon others would arrive, like himself either involuntary or voluntary exiles. Here Marx was to remain until 1848, except for a brief stay in England in the company of Engels.

In Barmen Engels carried on political agitation, along with Moses Hess; made speeches, and organized meetings which were well attended by members of the middle class, though workmen stayed away. Enthusiastic over their reception, Engels and Hess tended to overestimate the practical effects of these meetings and the proximity of political action. Patiently speakers explained the meaning of "communism," but revolution was toned down. Engels' father was outraged. The son, on the other hand, still bound to the counting-house, felt himself to be an exploiter. He was happy only when he was out in Elberfeld or beyond, spreading the new doctrine, or when adding another chapter to his book on the *Condition of the Working Class in England.* Early in

February 1845, the local authorities became seriously concerned and forbade further gatherings. Unhappy at home and apprehensive of further trouble, Engels betook himself to Brussels in April.

In the light of our later knowledge, it is impossible to overrate the significance of the Brussels period, and the interdependent relationship of Marx and Engels. It was marked in 1845 by the publication of Engels' *Condition of the Working Class*, and by the collaboration of both Engels and Marx on what was to be called the theory of historical materialism. Unfortunately the work in which these ideas were developed at the time, *The German Ideology*, was not to see the light of day until 1932. Its authors regarded it as a personal working-out of their thoughts, though on the basis of their conclusions they proceeded to put these thoughts into practice. Both thinkers now set out to act upon Marx's celebrated statement in his *Theses on Feuerbach*: "Philosophers have hitherto interpreted the world in various ways; the point, however, is to change it." It was time to begin to organize like-minded radical groups, scattered and fragmented as they were, into some unity, and to make them the practical arm of socialist theory.

The fundamental theory of historical materialism, as set forth in *The German Ideology*, was precisely and eloquently summarized as follows:

> In direct contrast to German philosophy, which descends from heaven to earth, we here ascend from earth to heaven ... We set forth from real, active men, and on the basis of their real life-process we demonstrate the development of the ideological reflexes and echoes of this life-process. The phantoms formed in the human brain are also, necessarily, sublimates of their material life-process, which is empirically verifiable, and bound to material premises. Morality, religion, metaphysics, and all the rest of ideology, and their corresponding forms of consciousness, thus no longer retain their semblance of independence. They have no history, no development; but men, developing their material production and their material intercourse, alter along with their existence, their thinking and the products of their thinking. Life is not determined by consciousness, but consciousness by life.[83]

> In the way individuals manifest their lives, such they are. What they are coincides therefore with their production, with what they produce as well as how they produce. What individuals are depends on the material conditions of their production.[84]

Man is the basic, primary element of history. What he produces and how he produces is what makes history. The satisfaction of his basic needs, and the creation of modes of production to satisfy them, in turn create new needs—hence new instruments of production. Concomitantly, his social relations develop and change and are enlarged. He stands in relation to Nature and to Society. The reciprocal transformation that takes place—between the individual, changing and changed Nature, and the social milieu (for in transforming Nature man also transforms himself)—represents the essential content of history. He cannot satisfy his growing needs individually, hence he must enter into relations with other human beings; enter, so to speak, into social relations of productions. The development of the forces of production determines, as it also transforms the social relationships, man's consciousness and thought. Consciousness and language are social products. The resultant change in the consciousness of man is the product of its interaction with Nature and Society, a response to the changes in the forces and modes of production. The course of history is the result of a dialectical process, for as the forces and means of production change to meet new needs, prevalent social relationships become a clog on the new forces of production and must be replaced by newer social relationships. This contradiction between the forces of production and social relations is the source and origin of political and social struggles, which constitute the motor of history. Such transformations do not take place automatically, nor does replacement of one form by another occur immediately. The old will persist by the side of the new: water-powered machinery by the side of steam-powered machinery. The same is true of ideas, modes of conduct, mores, etc. Domestic industry will persist for a time side by side with the factory, feudal systems side by side with a triumphant bourgeois economy. The central element in all these transformations is struggle—struggle carried on by human beings—a struggle of classes. It is a struggle of possessors and non-possessors. Often these struggles are masked in religious or political forms, thus concealing their essentially social character, but they are class struggles none the less. The dominant class creates in the state and its political organs means to subserve its own interests, hence every ascendant class must perforce appropriate the state, *i.e.*, its army, police force, its legal and judicial apparatus. The modern state takes form at a time when private property has become capital. The domination extends not only to the physical or material elements of society, but also to its very ideas and thinking.

> The thoughts of the ruling class are in every period the ruling thought, *i.e.*, the class that is the ruling material power of society, also is the ruling spiritual and intellectual power … The ruling thoughts are but the ideal expression of the ruling material relations … The division of labor, which we have already found to be one of the principal forces of history to date, also expresses itself in the ruling class as division of the spiritual and material labor, so that within this class one part comes forward as the thinkers of that class (the active conceptual ideologues thereof)… while the others behave towards these thoughts and illusions more passively and receptively, because they are in reality the active members of that class, and have less time to form illusions and thoughts about themselves.[85]

Hence, the proletariat has no chance of making a successful revolution until it frees itself totally from the illusions and mystifications by means of which the bourgeoisie seeks to divert it from struggle, and until it is guided solely by its own class interest. But that class interest, as we have seen, is according to Marx and Engels a "universal" interest. The principal condition for revolutionary success lies in the total development of the capitalist system, which will permit the proletariat to appropriate the totality of the productive forces arrived at the highest degree of their development, and to become by their employment of it universal men, and give communism a universal character corresponding to that which capitalism had taken on.[86]

Such were the conclusions at which Marx and Engels had arrived by 1845–1846.

For Engels, the experiences of Manchester had been paramount in determining his conception of history. So that his comprehensive work, *The Condition of the Working Class of England in 1844* was, in fact, the factual complement of the theories Marx had been developing. Engels' book was based on a first-hand acquaintance with the situation he was describing, as well as a thorough study of published sources and official documents. It was projected not only as a description of the effects of the triumphant industrial revolution and of capitalism in the most advanced country in the world, but also as supporting and justifying socialist theory. For the German socialists it was especially important to know the reality of modern capitalism in its most highly developed form. For it was only in Great Britain, and England in particular, that the conditions appeared in their "classical" form and were there consummated. Interest in the conditions of the laboring classes ran high in those days, particularly stimulated by the recent revolt of the Silesian weavers, as well as by numerous studies of English industrial life by foreigners and Englishmen. Engels' book went beyond those of other observers in not merely providing a graphic description of factual conditions, but also drawing practical conclusions from them. Here was exhibited how the changes in the forces and modes of production that had taken place, not only in industry but in agriculture as well, had effected changes in human relations in every sector of the society and, in many instances, in other parts of the world. Here were exhibited the evidences of sharpening differences between the classes. The wretched condition of the industrial worker in Lancashire was matched by the wretchedness of the agricultural worker. Pauperism, starvation, slums, disease, moral, physical and spiritual degradation of the masses, depopulation of Ireland—these were only a portion of the effects. A new form of slavery had come into being. But it was far from a passive form. A new class had been created which was becoming conscious of itself as a class, and in the process of asserting itself, as against the makers of their condition. Its two arms were trade unions and socialism. Its strength had already become manifest, even in the signal Chartist defeat of 1842, for it had not been destroyed. What it lacked was a theoretical understanding of its own historic role and how to act upon it. But it was potentially a revolutionary class, which, through its "reformed consciousness," would be enabled to change the structure of society. A great crisis was in the making: Engels predicted it for the years 1846–1847—when it did, in fact, take place. Such crises were bound to occur with greater and greater frequency, particularly as other nations (America, for example), entered into competition with Great Britain. Thereafter, a revolution would take place that would make that of France look like child's play. Engels expressed the hope that by that time communist thought and communism would have sufficiently penetrated the working classes to enable them to make the revolution without bloodshed.

That a major crisis was imminent was apparent not merely to radical thinkers, but to conservative and liberal thinkers as well. Reactions, of course, differed greatly. One merely has to compare Carlyle's "Signs of the Times" and *Past and Present* with Engels' utterances, to see how antipodal interpretations and conclusions could be. No less diverse were the opinions and theories of the various schools of socialism, anarchism, liberalism, and other movements of reform.

Isolated as they were in Brussels, with few companions of a like mind, Marx and Engels realized that their primary duty was to bring some measure of unity and cohesion to the various groups generally sympathetic to their socialist ideas, though not by any means in accord with them. Looked at from any perspective, what they finally achieved before 1848 was no less prodigious. A great deal of bitterness and heartache, but also an incalculable amount of energy and effort, were expended in the process, but both men and their associates worked tirelessly. Both of them possessed immense reparative capacities, so that neither change of locale nor occasional setbacks could divert them from their projected goals.

They began to establish firmer contacts with various groups of the "League of the Just." This organization of German artisans and workingmen of Paris had succeeded in establishing branches in Germany and Switzerland, especially under the leadership of Wilhelm Weitling. A tailor whose apocalyptic socialist vision drew many to him, Weitling was the author of a number of very influential works such as *Humanity as It Is and Should Be, Guarantees of Harmony and Freedom*, and *The Evangel of a Poor Sinner*. Along with his own personal fervor and persuasiveness, these found unusual response. The London branch of the League was particularly strong, and sympathetic to the call for unity. Engels had already formed a close association with the British Chartists and such of its leaders as Harney and Watts.

Marx and Engels had formed a Correspondence Committee in Brussels which brought them into contact with various other groups. In August 1846 Engels settled in Paris to carry on the work of propaganda and organization. What emerged from these efforts of contact, association, and correspondence was, in fact, a kind of international workers' movement—the first of its kind. The London branch of the "League of the Just," which had begun to free itself from Weitling's influence, was very active, open to new ideas, and ready for cooperation. Thus Paris, London, Brussels, and other cities were joined in a common exchange of ideas, opinions and plans. When the Paris groups were subjected to police persecution, the headquarters of the "League of the Just" shifted to London. It was here, at the suggestion of the Brussels Correspondence Society, that an international congress of communists was called for May 1847. The times were urgent, and the needs were pressing. Marx and Engels joined the League, and Engels went to London to attend the congress, which was actually held between June 2 and 7, 1847. The name of the organization was now changed to *Der Bund der Kommunisten*—"The League of Communists." For the first time the slogan of "Proletarians of All Countries Unite!" appeared in the statutes of the congress. The key words were no longer "love for humanity, but organization; no longer equality, but solidarity."[87] With the consciousness of growing strength based on the existence of militant groups in London, Marseilles, Lyons, Brussels, Berlin, Hamburg, Bremen, Munich, Leipzig, and other cities, there came the call for a second congress in London for the end of 1847. Marx and Engels were present, and the program of the League was promulgated. Karl Marx, entrusted with the responsibility of drawing up a "confession of faith," returned to Brussels and, basing himself upon an earlier draft by Engels, set about perfecting a work that was completed in February 1848. The manuscript was printed in London in German. Called *Manifest der Kommunistischen Partei*, it is now known as *The Communist Manifesto*. Rarely has such a seminal document appeared at such a historic moment. A few days after its publication, the February Revolution broke out in France.

The pamphlet's appearance was overshadowed by mighty historic events; it was not to have its true effect until many years after, until an international socialist and working-class movement came into being. Thereafter it was to become the *vade-mecum* of socialism around the world, and translated into all the world languages.

In its eloquent brevity, appositeness and clarity, it set forth concisely the principles of socialism, the role of the working class, and historical relations in political economy and society that made the revolutionary triumph of the working classes not only necessary but inevitable in view of the accentuated crises of bourgeois society. History was to amend its predictions—sometimes tragically—as it was to amend the ideas and theories of its authors in years to come, though it would never alter its essential value as theory and description of society as constituted, nor of the need for radical change. Nor was it ever to shake the confidence of its authors in the potential future fulfilment of its prophecies. Its celebrated slogans were to re-echo year after year as the unintermittent battle of classes continued, ultimately embracing East and West, eventually to change the face of the world. Its succinct formulations became axiomatic battle-cries, from its initial statement:

> A specter is haunting Europe—the specter of Communism. All the Powers of old Europe have entered into a holy alliance to exorcise this specter: Pope and Tsar, Metternich and Guizot, French Radicals and German police spies,

to its first section:

> The history of all hitherto existing society is the history of class struggles,

and on to

> The bourgeoisie, wherever it has got the upper hand … has left remaining no other nexus between man and man than naked self-interest, than callous "cash payment."

(Thus is Carlyle put to new uses!) And

> Not only has the bourgeoisie forged the weapons that bring death to itself; it has called into existence the men who are to wield those weapons—the modern working class, the proletariat.

And,

> The workingmen have no country. …

down to the celebrated conclusion:

> The proletarians have nothing to lose but their chains. They have a world to win. Working men of all countries, unite!

In this pamphlet are embodied many ideas derived from previous socialist thinkers, men like Saint-Simon and Babeuf, as well as others; and Marx never claimed to have invented all of them.

> As far as I am concerned [Marx wrote to Weydemeyer in 1852], I cannot claim the honor of having discovered the existence either of classes in modern society or of the struggle between them. Bourgeois historians a long time before me established the historical development of this class struggle, and bourgeois economists its economic anatomy.[88]

But he did lay claim to certain important contributions: To wit, "that the existence of classes is bound to definite historical phases of the development of production, that class struggle leads to the dictatorship of the proletariat, and that this dictatorship is itself only a transition to the abolition of all classes and leads to a classless society."[89]

The *Manifesto*, then, constituted a brief compendium of the history of society to the point of bourgeois triumph through modern industrial transformations, the emergent crises and anarchy, as well as its insoluble problems, which it believes it can solve by such means, among others, as the conquest of new markets, and more thorough exploitation of old ones. They thus forge new weapons of their own destruction, and also have "called into existence the men who are to wield those weapons."

> The immediate aim of the Communists is the same as that of all other proletarian parties: the formation of the proletariat into a class, overthrow of the bourgeois supremacy, conquest of political power by the proletariat.[90]

The first step then is "to win the battle of democracy." And the immediate measures proposed include, among others, the "abolition of property in land and application of all rents of land to public purposes; a heavy progressive or graduated income tax; abolition of all right of inheritance; centralization of credit in the hands of the State; centralization of the means of communication and transport in the State; equal liability of all to labor; combination of agriculture with manufacturing industries; free education for all children in public schools; abolition of children's factory labor in its present form …"

Then follows a critique of contemporary and past socialist theories and movements. The Manifesto concludes with the expectation of a proximate bourgeois revolution in Germany which "will be but the prelude to an immediately following proletarian revolution." The Communists, it is made clear, fight for the attainment of the immediate aims and interests of the working class; hence, without losing sight of the ultimate objectives, they support whatever progressive movements there are that are struggling for political, national, or economic and social emancipation.

Revolution: 1848–1849

Eighteen-hundred-forty-eight
Bringer of the morning star
Peoples, earth are now awakened!
Night is fled; and Day is here.
Red the cheeks,
Dawn's red splendor
Spreads beside the dusky light
Over grove and plain
Showing—blood, and shame, and fury
In awakened nations' eye. . . .

Great the times!
Holy now the words made flesh:
"One flock only and one shepherd"—
Only one religion reigns:
"Freedom!"
Gods are falling,
From their rubble
A new temple we will build,
Great and glorious, none so mighty,
Roof—the sky's great brilliant tent—
And for altar's light—the sun!
—Sándor Petöfi, 1848

Progress has settled on the barricades . . . It advances with
giant steps, and covers great distances on the wings of
electricity. The telegraph turns to the left to tell us that
freedom arrived at Brussels; it turns to the right and we
learn that liberty has reached London and Berlin. . . .
Long live the European republic!. . . . In a year, long live
the universal republic!
—François Vincent Raspail, 1848

For those who could read, hear, or see, there were auguries, portents, and forewarnings of an imminent explosion. They were there in the writings of journalists, in the speeches of politicians and statesmen, but most unmistakably in the actions and faces of men, women, and children. The "Hungry Forties" spoke out more forcibly than any other voices. Of these years, those between 1846 and 1848 were probably the worst

Europe had ever seen. While not the sole example, the "Great Hunger" of Ireland that stalked that land from 1845 on was not only the most glaring but also the most symbolic aspect of the current state of public misery and human decimation.

For even as late as 1851 a Census Report described the situation in Ireland in the following terms:

> The starving people lived upon the carcasses of diseased cattle, upon dogs, and dead horses, but principally upon the herbs of the field, nettle tops, wild mustard, and water cresses. In some places dead bodies were found with grass in their mouths.[1]

Such was the consequence of the potato blight that struck all of Europe (and America as well) in 1845. The misery and depopulation of Ireland, of course, had no equal anywhere else, compounded as it was by the indifference of the British government, with its traditional antipathy toward the Irish Catholics, by a religious devotion to the operation of "natural causes," as well as the "cash-nexus" that prohibited the violation of the Corn Law tariff and interference with private trading enterprise—a complex of attitudes abetted by a touch of genocidal intent. "God sent the blight," the Irish said, "but the English landlords sent the Famine!"[2]

Conditions in the rest of Europe were only slightly less disastrous. The world had entered upon its cycle of economic crises, and industry as well as agriculture felt the impact. Since England was the prince of economic powers, what happened there had almost immediate international repercussions. The general commercial and industrial crisis in England,

> already heralded in the autumn of 1845 by the wholesale reverses of the speculators in railway shares, delayed during 1846 by a number of incidents such as the impending abolition of the corn duties, in the autumn of 1847 ... finally burst forth with the bankruptcy of the London banks and the closing of the factories in the English industrial districts. The after-effect of this crisis on the Continent had not yet spent itself when the February Revolution broke out.[3]

The great depression of the 1840s swept all of Europe, producing large armies of unemployed who became dependent upon public and private relief. As if the additional scourge of the potato blight—which destroyed the entire potato crop of Ireland, Belgium, the Netherlands, and Germany—were not enough, a disastrously poor grain harvest followed in 1846. There were food shortages in Western and Central Europe beginning with 1847. Wheat and bread prices rose by over 100%; in a number of regions the price of potatoes went up by almost 600%. Added to starvation came eruptions of cholera, typhus, dysentery. It might have seemed that once again the ten Egyptian plagues were rampant ...

In Flanders the populace fed on roots and carrion. Belgium alone was forced to extend relief to 700,000. Bread and potato riots occurred in many localities, and frequently troops were called out to quell them. In Berlin and Vienna barricades came into evidence.

In Ireland, thousands of poor tenants, unable to pay their rent, were dispossessed and cast adrift. Nations have different ways of starving, some with greater, others with lesser gentility. The Irish defied all decencies both in the mortality figures and their manner of dying ...

Nicholas Cummins, magistrate of Cork, after visiting the Irish town of Skibbereen, wrote a letter to the Duke of Wellington which he also had published in the *Times* of December 24, 1846:

> My Lord Duke ... Being aware that I should have to witness scenes of frightful hunger, I provided myself with as much bread as five men could carry, and on reaching the spot I was surprised to find the wretched hamlet apparently deserted. I entered some of the hovels to ascertain the cause, and the scenes which presented themselves were such as no tongue or pen can convey the slightest idea of. In the first, six famished and ghastly skeletons, to all appearances dead, were huddled in a corner on some filthy straw, their sole covering what seemed a ragged horsecloth, their wretched legs hanging about, naked above the knees. I approached with horror, and found by a low moaning they were alive— they were in fever, four children, a woman and what had once been a man. It is impossible to go through detail. Suffice it to say, that in a few minutes I was surrounded by at least 200 such phantoms, such frightful spectres as no words can describe, either from famine or fever. Their demoniac yells are still ringing in my ears, and their horrible images are fixed upon my brain ... In another case, decency would forbid what follows, but it must be told. My clothes were nearly torn off in my endeavour to escape from the throng of pestilence around, when my neckcloth was seized from behind by a grip which compelled me to turn, I found myself grasped by a woman with an infant just born in her arms and the remains of a filthy sack across her loins—the sole covering of herself and the baby. The same morning the police opened a house on the adjoining lands, which was observed shut for many days, and two frozen corpses were found, lying upon the mud floor, half devoured by rats. A mother, herself in fever, was seen the same day to drag out the corpse of her child, a girl of twelve, perfectly naked, and leave it half covered with stones ...[4]

And a few months before this, Lord Brougham, not the worst of men, spoke in the House on the subject of the evictions of impoverished Irish tenants:

> Undoubtedly it was the landlord's right to do as he pleased, and if he abstained he conferred a favour and was doing an act of kindness. If on the other hand he chose to stand on his right, the tenants must be taught by the strong arm of the law that they had no power to oppose or resist. ... Property would be valueless and capital would no longer be invested in cultivation of land if it were not acknowledged that it was the landlord's undoubted, indefeasible and most sacred right to deal with his property as he list.[5]

Hand in hand with the economic crisis—the rising misery, the poverty, and hunger—and not disjointed from it—was the corrosion of the political power of the old régimes. What had been left of the Holy Alliance and its succession was beginning to crumble. In Galicia, the Polish region of Austria, a new uprising took place. It was very soon turned by the adroit manipulations of the Austrian governors into a massacre of Polish landlords by their peasantry, and resulted, through the intervention of Russia, in the absorption of the hitherto semi-independent Cracow into the Austrian empire. In Italy, the election in 1846 of the allegedly "liberal" Pope Pius IX promised a new era of long-anticipated freedoms. The triumph of the Swiss liberals over the separatist Catholic *Sonderbund* in 1847, and the resultant greater democratization and centralization of the country, proved another alarming portent to the Metternichs and their allies. Once more it seemed as if that drowsy giant—the masses of Europe— was rousing himself.

Indeed, the tocsin of revolution—of the Revolutions of 1848 and 1849—was first sounded, strangely enough, in Sicilian Palermo, on January 12, 1848. "*All' armi! Viva Pio Nono! Viva l'Italia!*" A frightened King Ferdinand made haste to promise a constitution, soon followed by King Charles Albert of Piedmont.

On the 22nd of February, Paris rose up against Louis-Philippe. The revolution in France was the powderkeg that set off explosions and conflagrations everywhere else.

Nothing like this had happened before—not in the same degree. The incendiary sweep moved with a celerity that soon embraced every state on the Continent, England and Ireland as well. It moved into the states of the German Confederation. In March it was in Vienna, in Berlin, in Bavaria, in Rome, in Milan. In April it swept England; somewhat later, Ireland. Soon it arrived in Hungary and Bohemia.

Monarchs, princes and prime ministers raced to find shelter in ever-hospitable England. Prince Metternich ran, Louis-Philippe ran, so did Prince William of Prussia and Minister Guizot of France. England was never so poor as to turn away a fugitive king or statesman.

The revolutionary storm lasted from January 1848 to September 1849—to the moment when Hungary was finally crushed. When it was over—the initial vertiginous hopes, the heroism, then the sorrow, the bloodshed and the final butchery—Europe was scarcely aware that she was entering upon a new era, opening a window, in fact, on the succeeding century.

1. France

La République, cette reine
Qui donne des leçons aux rois,
En trois tours d'horloge, a sans peine
Ressuscité tous nos vieux droits. ...

Que la terre entonne un cantique!
Gloire au peuple, joie en tout lieu!
Jurons par l'eau, l'air et le feu
De conserver cette relique:
La République vient de Dieu,
   Vive la République!

The Republic, that majestic queen
The teacher of Kings,
In three days, without pain
Has reconquered our ancient rights ...

Let the earth sound forth her psalms!
Glory to the People! Joy in the world!
Let us swear by fire, air and water
To hold fast by that sacred shrine:
The Republic is from God.
   Long live the Republic!
—Pierre Dupont, "*La Républicaine*," 25 February, 1848

François Pierre Guillaume Guizot had been minister of France from 1840 on, and the prime architect of the policies of the *juste milieu* reign of Louis-Philippe. A brilliant writer and historian, particularly of revolutions, he did not see a revolution brewing directly under his very eyes. For him the era of social upheavals was over; and so it seemed to many souls, satisfied with the fact that out of a population of about thirty-five millions there were no more than 200,000 electors eligible to vote. In their eyes, as in Guizot's and the King's, all seemed right with the world, and anything that was not could be amended either by prohibition or by force. With Guizot they thanked God and their own good sense, and echoed Guizot's words:

> Today, thanks to the victory of the good cause and to God, who gave it to us, situations and interests are changed. No more war from those below against those above; no more motive for raising the standard of the many against the few; no more obstacle for the mass of the ascending movement; except all those natural obstacles, inherent in the condition of man, such as God has made it, ever laborious, often hard and sad. God has destined man to exertions, though his exertions do not always meet with reward here below.[6]

Society was in his view divided into *mangeurs* and *mangés*—the eaters and the eaten. "Get rich and you will also get the vote," was his celebrated dictum. All you had to have is the 200 francs in taxes. "The movement of ascension is nowhere stopped." And it was true that many had "ascended" and become wealthy. There were the railroads and railroad stock; there were the huge loans floated by the government from which a number could draw large interest. The House of Rothschild alone controlled ten percent of the total investment in French railways. There were emoluments, perquisites, and offices to be bought and sold, as in all governments; and there were scandals.

But the fact remained that the greatest part of France was bereft of political power. For rule lay in the hands of the small segment of the finance aristocracy, the bankers, the stock exchange, the railway kings, the owners of coal and iron works, and a number of landed proprietors, while the industrial middle class was barely represented, and the petty bourgeoisie, the peasantry and the working classes not at all. It was this isolation of the *haute bourgeoisie* from their economic inferiors, the *petite bourgeoisie*—this unmasking of the special advantages derived from the former's political control of the country and its economy, to the disadvantage of trade, industry, agriculture—that stimulated the union of the artisans and the proletariat with the petty bourgeoisie, and engendered its revolutionary vitality. For it was not only the radicals or revolutionaries who recognized the true nature of the régime.

What the liberal-minded but careful Alexis de Tocqueville said in his *Recollections*:

> In 1830 the triumph of the middle class had been so complete and final that all political power, every franchise, every prerogative, the whole government of the country, were enclosed, and so to speak, piled up inside the narrow limits of that class. Not only was it the sole ruler of society, but it may be said, it became the farmer of society.

the more radical Karl Marx would state more emphatically:

The July Monarchy was nothing other than a joint stock company for the exploitation of French national wealth, the dividends of which were divided among ministers, Chambers, 240,000 voters and their adherents. Louis-Philippe was the director of this company. ... The bourgeoisie in the July days had inscribed on its banner: *gouvernement à bon marché*—"cheap government."[7]

With Balzac's tradesman Crevel, in *Cousin Betty*, they could have said that, in addition to fearing God, "I am of my own time, and I honor money!" He was lucky: he both honored money, and had it. But there were many hundreds of thousands that had none to honor or to possess. And there were many too who, having a little, wanted more.

In 1846 the Prefect of the Seine reported that there were in that district over six hundred thousand distressed inhabitants, and that almost 70% of the population of Paris were living in conditions of poverty. Diseases were rife in the lower segments of the cities, causing in some cases the extinction of large segments of the population. In certain cities of France, 50% of the children of the working classes died before the age of five. Statistics are dreary things; and those of poverty and mortality drab commonplaces, wearing repetitions. Suffice it to say that France too was a country caught up in the crises of the 1840s; that in 1847 there were in Paris alone over a million persons receiving public assistance; that in the city of Roubaix, 8,000 of the 13,000 workers were unemployed.

"We are dancing on a volcano," Heinrich Heine wrote in 1842, "but we are dancing."[8]

What Guizot in his self-confidence did not perceive was that the Revolution was far from over. The social implications and aspirations of the first French Revolution still simmered, even boiled, below the surface. And what was even more serious, he had failed to note clearly enough that these unsatisfied demands had become those of a new class—a proletariat, even if not as yet sufficiently unified to achieve leadership. But the rumblings could be heard, sometimes very distinctly, as, for example, in the song of the Lyons silk-weavers, the so-called *canuts*:

> *Pour gouverner il faut avoir*
> *Manteaux ou rubans en sautoir ...*

For the rulers, mantles, and ribbons spread crosswise—these we weave, oh, great ones of the world; but we stay naked, and are buried without shroud.

> But once our reign arrives,
> And once our reign is over,
> We will weave the old world's shroud
> For you can hear the groans of revolt
>   It is we, the *canuts*
> Naked no more. . . . . .
>
> *C'est nous les canuts*
> *Nous n'irons plus tout nus. ...*[9]

A song that was to echo in Heine's ear when he came to write his own Silesian weavers' hymn.

It was heard in the worker-poet Pierre Dupont's "*Chant des Ouvriers*" of 1846, a poem Charles Baudelaire greatly loved:

> Mal vêtus, logés dans des trous,
> Sous les combles, dans les décombres. ...

In tattered rags, living in holes, in garrets, midst offal. ... while the red blood boiling in our veins longs for the bright sun and the branches of oak-trees. ....

It could be heard also in the more commonplace prosaic plaint of the ordinary working man of Lille:

> I am a textile-worker earning 2 francs a day, the maximum wage for a weaver. My wife is a lace-worker, working at home, and earning 15 centimes a day. We have four children, the eldest is ten ... Meat is too dear, we can afford offal, three times a week at 25 centimes ... We are living like beggars ...

He, too, has to live on exiguous charity and handouts. For his minimal living expenses amount to 12 fr. 63 sous a week.[10]

About the same city, Lille, the contemporary Dr. Gasset could report that "... Before the age of five, in the rue Royale one out of three children died; and in the rue des Étaques alone, 46 out of 48. So much for the talk about equality in death."[11]

Was it a wonder that the parents of these children, and of their ilk in other industrial and commercial cities—Lyons, Paris, Marseilles—when they began to strike out in desperation, represented an invasion of "barbarism" more frightful than that which was to engulf Rome? The conservative *Journal des Débats*, speaking of the insurrection of 1831, uttered a dire warning:

> The Lyons revolt has laid bare a grave secret: that of the struggle of the class with possessions and the class without. The barbarians who are threatening society are not in the Caucasus or on the steppes of Tartary; they are in the suburbs of our manufacturing towns. It is not a question of the Republic, or of the Monarchy, but of the safety of Society.[12]

Clairvoyant Heine, living in Paris, was not taken in by the deceptive quietus of the 1840s so greatly extolled by Guizot. Again, writing in 1842:

> The greatest calm is prevailing at the present time. An exhausted, drowsy, yawning peace. All is quiet as in a snow-laden winter night. Only there is a slow, monotonous dripping sound. These are the interest rates that continue to trickle down on the funds, which are constantly swelling. And in between, the sobs of poverty. Sometimes too, one hears a clatter as of knives being sharpened.[13]

For despite intensified repressions and restrictions, republican, revolutionary and socialist ideas had not been extinguished, nor their exponents altogether shackled. True, those two firebrands of insurrection Armand Barbès and Auguste Blanqui had been jailed after an ill-timed and ill-advised attempt at an uprising; but their sentence of death had to be commuted as a result of a popular uproar. Underground societies such as the "Society of the Seasons" continued their perilous existence, and the words of Blanqui continued to resound from behind the bars. The "League of the Just," precursor of the Communist League, was no less persistent. Once again Heine, who was no stranger to these groups, describes the underground ferment. One must remember that the terms Communist and Socialist were still used interchangeably. Speaking of the impending election of June 29, 1842, he calls attention to a hidden antagonist:

This antagonist still preserves his terrifying incognito, and resides like a needy pretender on the ground floor of official society, in those catacombs, where amid death and decay, a new life is germinating and flowering. Communism is the secret name of this terrible antagonist, who opposes the present régime of the bourgeoisie with the sovereign rule of the proletariat in all its consequences. There will be a fearful duel. How will it end? Only the gods and the goddesses know it—they, who know what the future holds in store. We know only this much: Communism, although it is little spoken of today and is loitering in the obscure garrets on its wretched straw pallet, is the sombre hero, destined for a great, though transient role in modern tragedy, waiting only for its cue to enter upon the stage.[14]

For most Frenchmen, the revolutionary days of 1789, 1793, and 1830 represented living realities. The urgencies of the necessary and unfulfilled promises were with them all the time. Living survivors of the first Revolution brought home to them the idealism, the *élan*, the passion that actuated the deeds of those years, contrasting so luridly and graphically with the grasping selfishness and appetence of the *juste milieu*. There was the living presence of Filippo Buonarroti, the intellectual tutor of Auguste Blanqui, the companion and associate of the unforgotten Gracchus Babeuf, leader of the insurrection of 1796. That tragic and memorable event Buonarroti recalled for all to read in his own *La Conspiration des Égaux—The Conspiracy for Equality*—a book that was being read by the cabinet makers and the locksmiths in the *faubourgs* of St.-Denis and St.-Martin. These were the aristocrats of the laboring classes, who were to play a significant role within a few years in the revolutionary uprisings. For them, Robespierre still shone as the "saint" of the Great Revolution. But they too had been denied the vote in 1830 and were likewise the sufferers in the economic crises of the 1840s. The more radical and more proletarian "mechanics"—mostly railway workers in the industrial suburb of La Chapelle—found in the ultra left-wing societies—the "Seasons" and the "Rights of Man"—more closely-knit links with the radical history of the French Revolution.

It is not, therefore, surprising that the stirring memories of the French Revolution represented the most sought-for intellectual nourishment of the French population. For "revolution" was in every mouth, on all lips—whether in the conservative extollment by Guizot of the English Revolution of 1688 as the ultimate achievement of political sagacity, or the more moderate but none the less vivid French revolutionary histories of Adolphe Thiers, or the sensationally popular and remunerative *History of the Girondins* of the poet-politician Alphonse de Lamartine. Readers craved to be reminded of, and to relive, those stirring days, and while these historical works did not cause, they did in fact serve as an emotional stimulant to, the revolutionary activities that were soon to erupt.

On all sides Frenchmen were reminded of their glorious responsibilities as the beacon lights of freedom. The presence in Paris of ever so many refugees from other, less enlightened lands, their activities and publications, their organizations—even if kept within bounds and soon to be seriously curtailed—still kept France and Paris alive as an international center of ceaseless political controversy. Russians, Germans, Poles, Italians—were these not the living symbols of what France stood for and had been standing for during a half-century? The cries of the oppressed of the world found ready sympathy and response in France. France, the liberator of mankind!

> *Sur un Caucase ardent les nations gémissent;*
> *J'ai vu des peuples rois qu'on liait au rocher.*
> *Quand sera le vauteur, sous qui les coeurs périssent,*
> *Immolé par l'archer?*
>
> On a burning Caucasus the nations groan;
> I have seen regal peoples nailed to the rock.
> When will that vulture, feasting on human hearts,
> Perish at the hands of the archer?

Thus Edgar Quinet, poet and philosopher, in the poem *Prométhée*.[15]

The march of democracy was irresistible—so the aristocrat Alexis de Tocqueville had asserted, even if with trepidation—such was God's way and decree. The old was bound to fall before its onward march, just as the *ancien régime* had fallen in 1789. France had led the way.

> It is not because the French have changed their former opinions and altered their former manners that they have convulsed the world, but because they were the first to generalize and bring to light a philosophical method by the aid of which it became easy to attack all that was old and to open a path to all that was new.[16]

France spoke to the generality of mankind, to Man; and in his early days Tocqueville foresaw the whole world as eventually becoming "one people."[17]

Even many years later, in a period of intense disenchantment, he still recalled the ecstasy of 1789, expressing feelings that were common to many of his contemporaries, and not only Frenchmen:

> I think that no epoch of history has ever witnessed so large a number, so passionately devoted to the public good, so honestly forgetful of themselves; so absorbed in the contemplation of the common interest, so resolved to risk everything they cherished in their private lives, so willing to overcome the small sentiments of their hearts ... The spectacle was short, but it was one of incomparable grandeur. It will never be effaced from the memory of mankind. All foreign nations witnessed it, applauded it, were moved by it ... I venture to say that there is but one people on this earth which could have staged such a spectacle. I know my nation—I know but too well her errors, her faults, her foibles, and her sins. But I also know of what she is capable. There are enterprises which only the French nation can conceive; there are magnanimous resolutions which this nation alone dares to take. She alone will suddenly embrace the common cause of humanity, willing to fight for it; and if she be subject to awful reverses, she has also sublime moments which sweep her to heights which no other people will ever reach.[18]

For Tocqueville, too, had divined both the nature of the "continuing revolution," or as he called it, the "one" revolution, "which has remained always the same in the face of varying fortunes, of which our fathers witnessed the beginning, and of which we in all probability, shall not live to see the end,"[19] but also the different character of the participants now becoming more and more apparent. On the eve of the February Revolution of 1848, in fact, only a fortnight or so before its outbreak, he delivered his celebrated speech in the Chamber of Deputies, in which he asserted: "I believe we are at the moment sleeping on a volcano." He was warning against the delusion of a continuing peacefulness, and was pointing to the changes in the mentality of the "working classes."

> No doubt they are not disturbed by political passions, properly so called, to the same extent as they have been; but can you not see that their passions, instead of political, have become social? Do you not see that they are gradually forming opinions and ideas which are destined not only to upset this or that law, ministry, or even form of government, but society itself, until it totters upon the foundations on which it rests today? ... Do you not hear them repeating unceasingly that all that is above them is incapable and unworthy of governing them; that the distribution of goods prevalent until now throughout the world is unjust—that property rests on a foundation which is not an equitable one? And do you not realize that when such opinions take root, when they spread in an almost universal manner, when they sink deeply into the masses, they are bound to bring with them sooner or later, I know not when or how, a most formidable revolution?[20]

But the writer who most closely sensed the spirit of the decade in interpreting history, and that of the French Revolution in particular, was also France's greatest historian—Jules Michelet. In an era that produced grand, generous, courageous men and women—and this age had no lack of them—who in the name of honor and principle underwent untold privations, and even imprisonment, Jules Michelet does not suffer by comparison. Born and brought up in poverty, son of a destitute printer, and a printer himself at an early age, Michelet possessed one of those inordinately curious minds that consumed knowledge unceasingly. The abnegation of his parents assured him an education; but most of what he learned he acquired on his own. A chance encounter with the *Scienza Nuova* of the great eighteenth-century polymath Giambattista Vico opened for him the vast possibilities of an organic synthesis of history, embracing all aspects of knowledge and experience. J. G. Herder and the German historical school reinforced his philosophical speculations, particularly as to theories of progress. An appointment in the governmental historical archives completed his preliminary education. Here he painstakingly scrutinized original documents of French history as few French historians had done before him. He began work on a universal history and completed a few portions. But soon he embarked on his *History of France*, a work which was to engage him for the rest of his life. He interrupted that work when he reached the Middle Ages in order to begin the story of the French Revolution, the first two volumes of which he completed in 1847. He brought his vision and boldness into his classroom, and along with Edgar Quinet and Adam Mickiewicz became one of the most inspiring and courageous teachers at the Collège de France. His attacks on the Jesuits and all religious bigotry (he was himself a Catholic) soon brought down on him the wrath of the theological hierarchy.

For Michelet, too, the French Revolution was the culminating point in the history of mankind, a landmark in the emergence of the modern world. Unlike other historians, who had concentrated on the "heroic" figures of the Revolution as its makers, Michelet saw and made the "people" its heroes and makers. He thus revolutionized the interpretation of that epochal phenomenon—not to the prejudice of individual personalities, for he had a genius that could bring them to life as few others. But he also had the vision of a poet that embraced all that was around the figures he was describing: the landscape, the earth, the city, the country. It was "the people," however, that always occupied center stage. In his own words,

> Another thing which this History will clearly establish and which holds true in every connection, is that the people were usually more important than the leaders. The deeper I excavated, the more surely I have satisfied myself that the best was underneath, in the obscure depths, and I have realized that it is quite wrong to take these brilliant and powerful talkers, who expressed the thoughts of the masses, for the sole actors in the drama. They were given the impulse by others much more than they gave it themselves. The principal actor is the people. To find the people again and put them back in the proper role, I have been obliged to reduce to their proportions the ambitious marionettes whose strings they manipulated and in whom hitherto we have looked for and thought to see the secret play of history.[21]

In 1846 Michelet published a personal social manifesto, *Le Peuple—The People*, in which he described the condition of France in his day: the state of the peasant, now become serf to usurer and moneylender; of the factory worker turned into an *homme-machine*—"machine-man"—laboring in "the Hell of boredom," *enfer de l'ennui*. He also examined the other social strata. Here was a startling picture of "alienation," engendered, as he believed, by an ever-mounting mechanization. Desiccation of feeling, he noted, was especially glaring among intellectuals, as compared with the "inferior" classes. He noted the inability of intellectuals to engage in action, and their propensity for talk, gossip, and recriminations.

> The classes we call inferior, are more prone to follow their natural instincts, and are therefore more capable of action—and always ready for it. We, on the other hand, the cultured gentry, we chatter, dispute, we expend our energies in words ... We race from book to book, and let them engage in bitter battles. We turn our lofty indignation on petty objects ... We do nothing. We accomplish nothing. They, on the contrary, do not talk so much; they do not get hoarse throats from screaming, like our learned sages and grey-beards. But when the occasion arises, they take advantage of it, without noise. They act with vigor. Their economy of words enhances the energy of their actions. ... The outstanding, the capital trait I have been struck by in my extensive study of the people, is that amidst the disorders of destitution, the vices of wretchedness, I have discovered a wealth of feeling, a goodness of heart, very rare among those better off. The whole world saw how during the outbreak of the cholera—who was it that adopted the orphans? The poor.[22]

If there is a kind of mystical idealism in this conception of the people, and if Michelet's proposed solution of the ills of alienation and mechanization through the power of Love smacks of a certain naïveté, nevertheless his overall view of the motive forces of history, magnificently developed in his massive work with all the poetry and drama of an ardent scholar and the scholarship of a dedicated and inspired visionary, did much to illumine for his readers a new view of history and its actors, indeed of the historic process and its meaning, that was bound to transform historical scholarship in France. Movement in history is not the revelation of some absolute Fatality. Movement in history is movement of people. As man incessantly shapes his earth and his heaven, so he shapes events. There is the mystery! Man is the shaper of Man; "man is man's environment."

It was in this spirit that, in 1842, he suddenly interrupted his work on the Middle Ages and turned to a consideration of the French Revolution, mother of the present age. Like Lamennais in search of a new kind of Christianity, Michelet saw as the two principal actors in modern history—the *deux grands faits*—*le Christianisme et la Révolution*. "It was incumbent on God that he have his second epoch, that he appear on earth as the incarnation of 1789."[23]

How he came to write his *French Revolution* he described in his own inimitable way:

> By way of my study of Louis XI, I was about to enter upon the centuries of the monarchy. I was embarking on that venture, when chance brought me up sharply. One day, passing through Rheims, I saw in great detail its magnificent cathedral, the marvelous chapel of the coronation.

He climbs up to the uppermost belfry.

> Here a strange spectacle faced me. The round tower was decorated with a garland of criminals. Here one with a rope around his neck. There one has lost an ear. The mutilated were more wretched-looking than the dead. With good reason! What horrifying contrast. What! The church of festivities!

For here was performed the rite of crowning, when Church and King were united in mystic wedlock.

> What a lugubrious bridal necklace this! This pillory of the people right above the altar! And could not these tears ... fall upon the head of the Kings? Dreadful unction of the Revolution, of the Lord's wrath! "I will never understand the centuries of monarchy, if at once, before all else, I do not set up within me—the heart and faith of the people." This I said to myself, and after Louis XI, I wrote the *French Revolution*.[24]

But the historians, great and lesser, supplied only a small segment of the impulse that pushed toward the explosiveness of 1848. The forces that Heine recognized as restlessly fermenting "below," readying for action, found their spokesmen and ideologists best represented in the radical thinkers, ranging from the relics of Saint-Simonianism and the Utopians like Étienne Cabet—whose popular representation of an ideal commonwealth, *Icarie*, and its attempted realization in America, formed the epigonal analogue to Robert Owen's generous dreams—to the more revolutionary and influential activities of Buonarroti, Louis Blanc, Proudhon, and Blanqui. There were many women who participated in the movements and agitations of the 1840s, such as George Sand, with her novels and journalistic writings, and the astonishing Flora Tristan, one of the earliest projectors of an international association of workers, who unfortunately did not live long enough to experience February 1848. Nor were men like Fourier and Pierre Leroux without their coteries and influence.

Each group of workers—from the skilled artisans and craftsmen to the mechanicals and proletarians—had its journals: the conservative *bonnetiers*, the hosiers, read *Le National* or *Le Siècle*; stout republicans and radicals, the *ébonistes*—the cabinet makers—adherents of Cabet and Robespierre, read *La Réforme* and followed Louis Blanc; the mechanics of the workshops, most radical of all, looked to Blanqui and Barbès for leadership.

Whatever their tendencies, and their often far-fetched dreams and schemes and projects, the ideologues of this period—men and women—displayed an inexhaustible dedication to their ideas, courage in the face of repressions, readiness to accept social and political responsibilities at extreme risk to life and livelihood, equalled only by the devotion of their numerous followers. Together, despite their internecine animosities and differences, they fill us with a sense of the historic importance of their age, of its greatness and its demands, so that even in their errors and defeats and failings they impart a transcendent feeling of power, of human selflessness. It was this feeling that made it possible for adherents and followers, when moments of great stress and crisis arose and leaders of name were lacking, to create their own leadership and fight independently.

With the notable exception of Proudhon, the majority of revolutionary leaders and ideologues were not "sons of the people." Louis Blanc was the son of Joseph Bonaparte's inspector-general of finance in Madrid; Blanqui, the offspring of a sub-prefect. Pierre-Joseph Proudhon's father, on the other hand, was a peasant-proletarian of Besançon.

Louis Blanc was on his mother's side related to the aristocratic and powerful conservative diplomat Count Pozzo di Borgo. Inspired by the July Revolution, Blanc came to Paris, suffered hardships, and engaged in journalism. Here, from 1834 on, he became associated with the cause of the working class, and in their interest developed his major program, which he expounded in 1840 in his *De L'organisation du Travail—On the Organization of Labor*. Put into partial practice after February 1848, its ideas were to play a critical role in the Revolution and its aftermath. Blanc was an opponent of class war, and his principles were moderate. He was hopeful of revolution by consent. He advocated a sort of producers' cooperative, financed by the state, and hoped that eventually through "saintly" competition with private enterprise it would succeed in eliminating the latter. The state was to guarantee to every working man "the right to work." This was a slogan apparently coined by Blanc, and became a battle-cry of the workers of 1848. "From each according to his capacity, to each according to his need!"—that was to be the ultimate achievement of social planning.

The state would thus be the "banker of the poor" and aid in establishing a social republic ruled by God. With the abolition of competition and human exploitation, a moral revolution would follow. "It is not force that governs the world," he held; "it is thought." Universal suffrage would enable the workers to gain control of the state, which in turn would establish the social workshops; and these, while self-governing, would still remain under the guidance and tutelary authority of the beneficent state. Such a state will eventually disappear, with the disappearance of class distinctions. "The seedbed of socialism can be fertilized only by the wind of politics." In this spirit of trusting benevolence, Blanc addressed himself to the wealthy:

O, rich men, you are deceived when you become aroused against those who dedicate their waking hours to the calm and peaceful solution of social problems. Yes, the sacred cause of the poor man is your cause too. A solidarity of heavenly origin binds you to their misery through fear and links you by your own interest to their future deliverance. Only their emancipation is capable of opening up to you the real treasure, that of tranquil joy, which you have not known as yet; the virtue of the principle of fraternity is precisely that, as it lessens the sorrows of the poor, it adds to your joys ... No, rest assured, violence is to be feared only where discussion is not permitted. Order has no better protection than study. Thank heaven, people today understand that, if anger sometimes chastises evil, it is nevertheless incapable of bringing about good, that a blind and ferocious impatience would only pile up ruins under which the seeds of the ideas of justice and love would smother to death. It is not a question of taking wealth away; it is a question of fertilizing it so that it becomes universal. It is a question of raising the level of humanity for the good of all, without exception.[25]

Blanc was to learn, in time to come, the bitter lesson of this trusting benevolence, when even the slogan of "the right to work"—weak and meaningless as it was—was deemed too incendiary and was made to yield to the "right to obedience."

At the same time he was preparing a study of contemporary history—*Histoire de dix ans, 1830–1840—A History of Ten Years*—a critical appraisal of the *juste milieu* of Louis Philippe's first decade. For Frenchmen of the 1840s he recalled year by year the aggravating contrast between ruling France and the condition of the people, the ignominy of the self-enrichment of the few, headed by the King—"*par caractère et par position ... le premier bourgeois de son royaume*"—"by character and position ... the first bourgeois of the realm"—and the shameful persecution of republicans, their courageous opposition during the many trials, and the disgraceful massacre of the rue Transnonain. Once more he recalled the role of France as the international voice of European emancipation; and on Minister Périer's failure to vote for intervention in favor of the oppressed Italians on the score that "French blood belongs in France," Blanc exclaimed: "Impious words! Blasphemy born of ignorance and incapacity! The genius of France had always been rooted in her cosmopolitanism and her devotion, imposed upon her by God as an element of her power and a condition of her life."[26]

What is Socialism? he had asked. And he answered: "It is the Bible in action."[27]

Yet of all these ideologues, none approached Auguste Blanqui in the price exacted from him for his socialist activities. He became known in later years as the "prisoner"—*l'enfermé*—for he spent over thirty-three years of his life, practically one half of it, in jail; and forty-four years under persecution. He was in truth a "son of the Revolution," for his father had been a member of the revolutionary Convention of 1792. The Revolution of 1830 determined his career—republican, radical, revolutionary, and socialist—but above all he became a dedicated activist. Romain Rolland named him the "immortal hero of the French proletariat"; Karl Marx, "the head and the heart of the proletarian party in France."[28] He was the martyr-idol of the lower classes. Heinrich Heine attended a meeting of the republican "Society of the Friends of the People"—*Les Amis du Peuple*—on February 2, 1832, of which Raspail, Blanqui, and Godefroy Cavaignac were the shining lights. There were over fifteen hundred in the audience, young, middle-aged and old, men and women. Blanqui was then awaiting imprisonment for one of his numerous activities—this time, his unconventional behavior at the Trial of the Fifteen for incendiary republicanism. The crowded assembly listened to him as, in Heine's words, he excoriated

> the bourgeoisie, the shopkeepers, who had chosen Louis-Philippe, himself "la boutique incarnée"—incarnation of the shop—for their king, solely in their own interest, certainly not in that of the people, which "had no share in this shameful usurpation.". ... A dignified seriousness marked the attitude of both old and young in the assembly, characteristic of people who have powerful feelings. Only their eyes lit up, and at times they cried out, "That's it. That's true!" .... Robespierre's last speech before the Eighth of Thermidor is their gospel.[29]

At the trial, distinguished by many notable speeches of the accused, Raspail's among them, Blanqui too had made a programmatic address in a forthright statement of the objectives of the "Society of the Friends of the People" and of his own principles and views. It was here that he made clear his understanding of, and belief in, an unmitigated class war as an outstanding element of the social structure of the *juste milieu*, and graphically outlined the nature of that society.

In the interrogation he had been asked his profession, and he, who had been a teacher, studied law and medicine, and was a journalist of some note, replied, *Proletaire*, upon which the president of the court countered, "That is not a profession." "If it is not a profession," Blanqui retorted, "then I am without any." And again, "What! not a profession! Why, it is the profession of thirty million Frenchmen, living by their labor and deprived of their political rights.!"[30]

He turned accuser of the court as the enemy of his class, and of himself.

> I am not [he said] in the presence of judges, but of enemies. ... As a proletarian ... I deny the competence of this tribunal, composed as it is of the privileged who are not my peers ... Yes, Messieurs, this is a war between the rich and the poor; the rich have willed it, for they are the aggressors; only they have found it displeasurable that the poor offer resistance. ... They never cease to denounce the proletariat as "thieves" ready to hurl themselves and seize their property. Why? Because the latter complain that they are being crushed by taxes imposed for the benefit of the privileged. ... Who are these "thieves" deserving of such anathemas and punishments? Thirty million Frenchmen who pay imposts of a billion and a half, and an almost equal sum to the privileged. And the possessors, sheltered by the powers of the society, are only two or three hundred thousand idlers who peacefully devour the billions paid by the "thieves." It seems to me we have here in a new guise, and with other adversaries, the war of the feudal barons and the merchants they robbed on the highways ... The organs of the ministry repeat with complacence that there are ways open for airing the proletarians' grievances ... That is a joke ... The people do not write in the newspapers; they do not send petitions to the Chambers. That would be a waste of time. On the other hand, the voices that find an echo in the political arena ... are those of the privileged. None of them is that of the people. They are mute ... We demand that the thirty million Frenchmen choose a form of government which is theirs, and nominate, through universal suffrage, true representatives, to make the laws. ... So that the taxes, instead of being taken from the poor and given the rich, will be taken from the superfluity of the idlers and distributed among the masses of the indigent ... They will strike at the unproductive consumers, and enrich the sources of production. ... This, Messieurs, is the way we understand the republic.[31]

He had early been enrolled among the French *carbonari*. Secret societies were his life's food and drink. As the repression of the régime became intensified and secret societies came under a ban, he formed close association with such groups as the "Society of the Families" and the "Society of the Seasons," eventually becoming the leading influence of the latter. Pledged to absolute secrecy, small in number, strongly disciplined, and save for the usual complement of informers and *agents provocateurs*, thoroughly dedicated to armed insurrection, the members were prepared for whatever fortune might be in store for them. They listened reverently as their leader instructed initiates:

Each member has the mission of spreading, by whatever means, republican doctrines ... Later, when the hour strikes, we will take up arms and overturn a government that is traitor to the fatherland. Will you be with us on that day? Reflect well, it will be a dangerous enterprise. Our enemies are powerful; they have an army, the means, the support of foreign kings, they rule by terror. We, poor proletarians, we have nothing but our courage and our righteous cause. Are you ready to brave the danger? When the alarm sounds, are you resolved to die, arms in your hand, for humanity's sake? ...

I swear not to reveal to anyone, not even to those closest to me, that which is said among us; I swear to obey the laws of the association, to pursue with hate and vengeance the traitors who glide into our ranks, to love and succor my brothers and to sacrifice my life and my liberty for the triumph of our sacred cause ...

Have you arms, munitions? Each member, upon entering the association, furnishes a quantity of powder, in accordance with his means ... During the combat, the members must obey their leaders in accordance with all the severity of military discipline ...[32]

"To work for the deliverance of the people and of the human race"—*pour travailler à la délivrance du peuple et du genre humain*—such was their aim. Not political, but social revolution. ...

An unregenerate revolutionary, Blanqui was no sooner out of captivity than he was again involved in agitation. Indefatigable, indestructible (or so it seemed at the time), wherever there was discontent or incipient insurrection, he was there. He was undersized; for most of his life in ill health, aggravated by his prison experiences; but the electric current of intense activity, restlessness, and anger at what he felt to be the betrayal of the people never diminished. He excoriated black slavery in the colonies. He fulminated against white slavery in France:

For that matter, he wrote, there is less difference than meets the eye between the social condition of the colonies and that in our own country ... Servitude, in effect, does not consist solely in being a man's chattel or a serf attached to a plot of ground. A person is not free when he is deprived of the instruments of labor and must remain at the mercy of those privileged persons who detain him. It is this kind of monopolizing, and not one political constitution or another, that makes the masses into serfs. Hereditary transmission of the soil and of capital places the citizen under the yoke of the property-owners. The citizens have no freedom but that of choosing their masters ... The facts have their own eloquence; they prove that there is a duel going on, a duel between profit and wage. Who will succumb?[33]

He was brave, frequently intemperate and foolhardy. In 1839, Blanqui, Barbès and associates believed the moment had come for a *coup d'état*. Though well organized and planned in many respects by the "Society of the Seasons," the insurrection of May 12, 1839 was a disaster. Blanqui and other leaders had made fatal miscalculations. They believed the people would rise once again and follow them. They would establish a republic under a dictatorship. But the people did not rise. In the bloody scuffle that ensued, Barbès was badly wounded. Many others died. The leaders were captured. Blanqui, after evading pursuit for a number of days, was taken. Both Blanqui and Barbès were condemned to death; then their sentences were commuted to life imprisonment. Blanqui was consigned to the fortress-prison of Mont-Saint Michel, where he remained till 1844. Thereafter, for reasons of health, he was transferred to Tours, and subsequently put under police surveillance in Blois. It was here that the news of the February Revolution reached him. He hastened back to Paris, weak of body but unbroken in spirit, in hope, in mind, and at once took his rightful place among the insurgents. He organized the "Société républicaine centrale."

Count Alexis de Tocqueville was a member of the republican assembly amidst the revolutionary turmoil. Fastidious as ever, he contemplated the tumult and the confusion around him, when one of the speakers attracted his attention.

> It was then that I saw appear, in his turn in the tribune, a man whom I have never seen since, but the recollection of whom has always filled me with horror and disgust. He had wan, emaciated cheeks, white lips, a sickly, wicked and repulsive expression, a dirty pallor, the appearance of a mouldy corpse; he wore no visible linen; an old black frock-coat tightly covered his lean, withered limbs; he seemed to have passed his life in a sewer and to have just left it. I was told it was Blanqui.[34]

It *was* Blanqui.

He had returned after an imprisonment of eight years. Now he stood there, pleading the cause of embattled Poland and calling for vengeance on the perpetrators of a massacre of working men and women of Rouen that had recently taken place. ...

He was a part of the tornado of doctrines that swirled unceasingly, gathering for and presaging upheavals.

Christian Socialists, such as Lamennais, P. J. B. Buchez, and Pierre Leroux, mentor of George Sand, preached a revitalized Christianity.

More strident, more powerful were the voices of anti-theism, even of atheism, among which that of Pierre-Joseph Proudhon, social anarchist, was the most eloquent. The doctrine he was pleading was called "Mutualism."

* * *

Proudhon came of peasant-artisan stock from the vicinity of Besançon, birthplace also of Victor Hugo and Charles Fourier. Except for a brief schooling in that city, he was almost totally self-educated. He was a genius, pertinacious and self-assured, and he amazed with the vast store of knowledge and information he succeeded in acquiring—diverse, somewhat disorganized—ranging from Hebrew and comparative philology to the Fathers of the Church and the social sciences.

Never dismayed by poverty or want—of which his experience was manifold—Proudhon was in turn printer, accountant, employee of a large transport firm, and ever the restless journalist. He was indefatigable in competing for prizes, and even won a number of them. And he shocked their donors by his outrageous radicalism. For lack of prizes, he struggled along as he best could, never concealing his views.

In a competition for a Besançon Academy prize on the theme of the usefulness of Sunday, he proclaimed slogans that were to become world-famous or notorious, such as,

> What is Royalty—we ask—a myth? What is religion—a dream of the Spirit? What is God—the eternal X? What is property—theft?[35]

With this essay he won only a bronze medal. He printed his work on his own press in Besançon. In 1838 he obtained a pension from the Besançon Academy for a serious work and went to Paris to pursue his studies. He was, in fact, preparing a bombshell. It fell soon enough when, in 1840, he presented an essay with the provocative title, *What is Property?* and with the even more provocative answer: "Property is theft!"

> If I were asked to answer the following question: *What is slavery?* and I should answer in one word; *It is murder*, my meaning would be understood at once. No extended argument would be required to show that the power to take from a man his thought, his will, his personality, is a power of life and death; and that to enslave a man, is to kill him. Why, then, to this other question: *What is property?* may I not likewise answer, *It is theft*, without the certainty of being misunderstood? ... *Property is theft!* That is the war-cry of '93! That is the signal of revolutions! Reader, calm yourself: I am no agent of discord, no firebrand of sedition. I anticipate history by a few days; I disclose a truth whose development we may try in vain to arrest; I write the preamble to our future constitution. ...

Having come into contact indirectly with the ideas of Hegel, as sifted through many strainers, Proudhon arrived at his own "Hegelian formula." He was ever after to employ what he believed to be a Hegelian dialectic with a *sang-froid*, born of a diluted understanding, that was to prove the despair and horror of Engels and Marx. He now applied it to the theory of property:

> To express this idea by a Hegelian formula, I will say: Communism—the first expression of the social nature—is the first term of social development—the *thesis*; property, the reverse of communism, is the second term, the *antithesis*. When we have discovered the third term, the *synthesis*, we shall have the required solution ... The third term of society, the synthesis of communism and property, we will call *liberty*. . . . . Politics is the science of liberty. The government of man by man (under whatever name it be disguised) is oppression. Society finds its highest perfection in the union of order with anarchy. ...

In the same way, the exploitation of labor is theft, for labor alone is the basis of value. What the capitalist appropriates is not only the labor of the individual worker, but the vast heritage of past installations, accumulated techniques, and cooperation. This is the true "surplus value" appropriated, which is never paid. It is theft of "collective" work. Property is incompatible with Justice.

What are the solutions? For all forms of regulative systems of social improvement, such as the socialisms of the Saint-Simonians, of Fourier, or for the communism of such ideologues as Cabet and others, Proudhon has no use at all. In one form or another, they disguise the principle of property. For what is the difference, if instead of the individual, the community becomes the owner not only of the property, such as land and factory, but also of the person himself, his labor, his talents, his faculties, to use them for the common good? Absolute equality and liberty are incompatible with a state, no matter what its character.

> As man seeks justice in equality, so society seeks order in anarchy. Anarchy—the absence of a master, of a sovereign—such is the form of government to which we are every day approximating.

It is obvious that Proudhon, in his advocacy of "anarchist individualism," is still thinking of an agrarian society such as he was brought up in, rather than of a highly developed industrial entity. The "synthesis" that is to represent the resolution of contradictions, and which he terms "mutuality," sees in the independent workshops a replacement for the state—an establishment of individual communes, consisting of small landowners who are masters of their fields.

> What then is the government of the future? I hear some of my readers reply: "Why, how can you ask such a question? You are a republican." "A republican? Yes, but that word specifies nothing. *Res publica*, that is, the public thing. Now, whoever is interested in public affairs—no matter under what form of government, may call himself a republican. Even kings are republicans." "Well, you are a democrat." "No.". ... "Then what are you?" "I am an anarchist.!"[36]

It can be readily understood that with an "anarchist" attitude like this, and also with an already defined antagonism to "class-war" and overt action, he should have come into conflict with Marx and his followers. Karl Marx had been very appreciative of Proudhon's *What Is Property?*—particularly the latter's analysis of the nature of "surplus value"—anticipations, in fact, of his own more elaborate labor theory of value. He regarded Proudhon's essay as a penetrating work and as having an exceptional importance for the times. Before Marx was expelled from Paris in December 1845, he had had occasion to discuss matters with Proudhon, for Proudhon was then already in contact with the German expatriates like Ruge, Heine, Marx himself, and other socialists, as well as the Russian, Mikhail Bakunin. From Brussels, Marx wrote Proudhon, inviting him to join in the effort to establish a corresponding society in various countries, that would put sympathizers and adherents in touch with each other, and make for a potential international organization. Proudhon agreed, but with such ideological reservations as to make further communication between Marx and himself utterly impossible. The differences become obvious in the letter or reply that Proudhon addressed to Marx:

> ... I have also some observations to make on this phrase of your letter: *at the moment of action*. Perhaps you still retain the opinion that no reform is at present possible without a *coup de main*, without what was formerly called a revolution and is really nothing but a shock. That opinion, which I understand, which I excuse and would willingly discuss, having myself shared it for a long time, my most recent studies have made me completely abandon. I believe we have no need of it in order to succeed; and that consequently we should not put forward *revolutionary action* as a means of social reform, because that pretended means would simply be an appeal to force, to arbitrariness, in brief, a contradiction. I myself put the problem in this way: to bring about the return to

society, by an economic combination, of the wealth which was withdrawn from society by another economic combination. In other words, through Political Economy to turn the theory of Property against Property in such a way as to engender what you German socialists call *community* and what I will limit myself for the moment to calling *liberty* or *equality*. But I believe that I know the means of solving this problem with only a short delay. I would therefore prefer to burn Property by a slow fire, rather than give it new strength by making a St. Bartholomew's night of the proprietors.[37]

Here, certainly, there was no reconciliation of "opposites." Proudhon disbelieved in the class struggle, disbelieved in revolution. He disbelieved in political action. "The social revolution is seriously compromised if it comes through a political revolution." The small, independent farm holding and the workshop were for him the focal centers for the education toward a new order. Yet while he pleads, "No hatred, no hatred. Eliminate by principle," he also states that "the new socialist movement will begin with the war of the workshops."[38]

His dream was of "Association," a community of worker-producers, drawing upon a People's Bank for credit and exchange. These would eventually push out the exploiters and the owners of capitalist means of production and of land. His hostility to all other forms of socialism did not prevent him from anticipating that they too would be drawn into these associations, even the Communists, and "by 1860, the globe will be overrun by the Association."[39]

So strongly individualist was he that he took on God almost singlehandedly, as he fulminated against Him.

Actually, his dialectic, far from subsuming a "synthesis" born out of "conflict," was an effort at balancing out the "good" and "evil" in each of the opposing elements and bringing about a "reconciliation." His small proprietor, eventually to establish himself as part of similar proprietors in voluntary federations, now has not "property" but "possession."

> Not only is no government and no authority compatible with the principle of mutuality, but no authority can aid in the work of reform ... For this moment we must live to ourselves and to ourselves alone.[40]

Proudhon's "mutualism," based as it was on a rejection and eventual elimination of government authority or authority of any kind except that growing out of an individualist morality, was to find far-echoing sounding boards, adherences, and practical applications in such divergent figures and movements as Mikhail Bakunin, Leo Tolstoy, Prince Peter Kropotkin, and the "syndicalist" labor organizations.

His publication in 1846 of *The System of Economic Contradictions, or, the Philosophy of Poverty*, elicited from Karl Marx the well-known, much discussed, devastating analysis and criticism, *The Poverty of Philosophy*. This work set the permanent stamp upon the unresolvable opposition of two basic attitudes and two schools of social philosophy. For Proudhon, Marx became the "tapeworm of socialism." In Marx's eyes, Proudhon was another petty-bourgeois, who disguised as Hegelian radical dialectics a scheme that sought to "balance out" oppositions and "reconcile" them, without reference to history and economic reality. The system represented a separation of theory and practice; and its principal and dangerous faults lay in Proudhon's distrust of direct action, even strikes; his disparagement of universal suffrage as a political and social weapon; his personal isolation and extreme individualism; and finally, his narrow viewpoint of the small artisan and small peasant proprietor, altogether inadequate to cope with the vast expansion of modern capitalism and industry. Proudhon, too, like the bourgeois, had fallen for a belief in "absolutes."

> Proudhon does not rise above the bourgeois horizon ... He seeks for a synthesis of their ideas, their equilibrium, and does not see that the only equilibrium possible is the one that exists today. Actually, he does what all good bourgeois do. All of them tell you that competition, monopoly, etc., are, in principle, that is, taken abstractly, the only foundations of life, but that they leave much to be desired in practice. All of them want competition without its fatal consequences. All of them want the impossible, that is, the conditions of bourgeois life, without the necessary consequences of these conditions. All of them do not understand that the bourgeois form of production is a historical and transient phenomenon, just as the feudal form was. This error arises from the fact that the bourgeois man represents to them the only possible basis for society, and they cannot imagine a social order in which the man ceases to be bourgeois.[41]

This was but one of the many acrimonious controversies of the latter 1840s,[42] part of the tremendous turmoil that was very soon to be out-thundered by the giant outbreaks of 1848.

A keen-sighted Russian visiting Paris in those years was impressed by the premonitory ferment:

> The first thing that struck one on encountering the capital of France was, of course, its social movements. Everywhere throughout Europe there already existed parties which were subjecting the conditions and institutions of European life to analysis, and everywhere there had already formed societies for the consideration of measures to halt, change, and redirect the course of contemporary life, but only in Paris did this critical activity enter into, so to speak, the ordinary daily run of things. ... One could not resist feeling drawn into this activity which was made up of shrewd and clever articles from the world of journalism, propaganda in the theater, series of lectures and discussions by professors and nonprofessors. For example, I spent three Sundays in a row listening to A. Comte himself, expatiating, in the hall of a certain arcade, on the basic features of his theory before a crowd of people who could have had no inkling of what that theory would become later on. This activity was supplemented by a huge number of books on social topics, which began the well-known war against official political economy, and also by affiliations of honest, well-read, and well-developed workers who had already taken account of the new socialist positions and had revised them in their own fashion, such as Corbon, a future deputy, who was a watchmaker by trade and whom I also had a chance to see in the shop that served him also as the office of his journal, *L'Atelier*. All these were the flames that preceded the famous Revolution of 1848.[43]

* * *

Je croyais à l'avenir parce que je le faisais moi-même.
I believed in the future because I was myself making it.
—Jules Michelet

Sentinelles héréditaires,
Les fils de la grande cité,
Se sont levés, comme leur pères,
Pour les droits de l'humanité.

Hereditary sentinels, sons of the great city,
Have risen, like their fathers, for the rights of Humanity.
   See! See! Sublime battle! Saintly glory!
People arise! To the proud sons of the future,
Heaven accords victory! The reign of evil is over!
The Earth has conquered Hell! …
—Jean Journet, "Le Triomphe des travailleurs," March 1848.

The French Revolution of 1848 began with banquets and ended in bloodbaths. This was literally true for France; it was symbolically true for the rest of Europe. In France, the banquets inaugurated in 1847, in imitation of the English model favored by William Cobbett during the Corn Law agitations, represented the most successful means of evading the repressive legislation directed against secret societies, meetings, and the press, and the most effective, popular way of giving wide voice to, and notice of, the feelings of the opposition, and rallying them to a common agitation for reform, principally of the unjust electoral system.

In addition to the thousands who paid as gustatory participants, there were many other thousands who came if only to see, hear, and cheer. These banquets were addressed by parliamentary and other notables, and their views ranged from moderate to radical republicanism as well as socialism. They multiplied in popularity and in intensity of feeling and expression. Sometimes even moderate republican speakers, carried away by their own and their audience's enthusiasm, allowed themselves more radical sentiments than they had intended. There was the famed banquet of July 18, 1847, at Macon, when its deputy Alphonse de Lamartine, exquisite poet, author of the recently published *History of the Girondins* (this being the alleged occasion for the celebration), and in his own eyes another Lafayette, potential savior of his country, spoke to almost six thousand listeners. He was predicting the doom of the Louis-Philippe monarchy: "*Elle tombera,*" Lamartine exclaimed, "*cette royauté, non dans son sang…*"

It will fall, this royalty, be sure of that. It will fall, not in its blood, like that of '89, but it will fall in its trap. And after having had the revolutions of freedom and the counter-revolution of glory, you will have the revolution of public conscience and the revolution of contempt.[44]

"*La révolution du mépris!*"

The banquets became more numerous and more animated, the demands for reform more extensive, now even embracing the workers who had hitherto been given little mind in the agitations. Even the moderates of the opposition became frightened—as did the government. It was the attempted cancellation of such a banquet in February 1848, originally planned for the predominantly workers' quarters of the twelfth *arrondissement* on the Left Bank, that set off the demonstrations that within a few days would overthrow a régime that had lasted eighteen years.

The stupidity of astute statesmen and rulers is as proverbial as it is astonishing. There were signs enough to forewarn Guizot; and the King, even if he believed, as it is said, that there was no danger because Parisians never make a revolution in winter, might have been persuaded that when revolutions are brewing the weather is often of little consequence. Had they read the government organ, the *Moniteur* of January 30, they might have become aware of a speech delivered in the Chamber of Deputies the day before, by Alexis de Tocqueville—assuming they had not been present when it was delivered. This is what Tocqueville said:

> I believe that we are at this moment sleeping on a volcano. ... I am told that there is no danger because there are no riots; I am told that, because there is no visible disorder on the surface of society, there is no revolution at hand. ... True, there is no actual disorder; but it has entered deeply into men's minds. See what is preparing itself among the working classes, who, I grant, are at present quiet. No doubt, they are not disturbed by political passions, properly so-called, to the same extent as they have been; but can you not see that their passions, instead of political, have now become social? Do you not see that they are gradually forming opinions and ideas which are destined not only to upset this or that law, ministry, or even form of government, but society itself, until it totters upon the foundations on which it rests today? Do you not listen to what they say to themselves each day? Do you not hear them repeating unceasingly that all that is above them is incapable and unworthy of governing them; that the distribution of goods prevalent until now throughout the world is unjust—that property rests on a foundation which is not an equitable one? And do you not realize that when such opinions take root, when they spread in an almost universal manner, when they sink deeply into the masses, they are bound to bring with them sooner or later, I know not when or how, a most formidable revolution? ... Do you not feel, by some intuitive instinct which is not capable of analysis, but which is undeniable, that the earth is quaking once again in Europe? And do you not feel—what shall I say?—as it were a gale of revolution in the air? ...[45]

Overdramatic?—perhaps.

But the populace, especially of the workers' *arrondissements*, is aroused, furious at the deputies who have so easily yielded to ministerial pressure. Sometimes people and events move faster than their alleged movers suspect. And now the students of the medical and law schools are up in arms, literally. On February 23 crowds come out *en masse*; at various points of the city, Government troops are already on the alert. But the National Guard, bulwark of constitutional monarchy, is for the greater part no longer on the King's side. That of the twelfth *arrondissement* is against him; that of the eighth refuses even to honor the call to arms. As for King and counsellors ... it is too little too late. Guizot is sacrificed, but this is not enough. Not Thiers, nor any one else at this moment, will satisfy the people.

The demonstration moves in front of the Ministry of Foreign Affairs. The army is there. A chance shot—was it panic or was it deliberate? Who knows? The Revolution is on. Fifty are dead.

Barricades go up—over 1500 of them; the fighting spreads to the Chateau d'Eau, then over to the Palais Royal, thereafter to the Hôtel de Ville, which is taken, with its cannon, and then comes the march to the royal palace of the Tuileries. Nothing can assuage the militant crowds, neither the much-hated General Bugeaud, commander of the King's forces, nor the more friendly Odilon Barrot. The cry is up—for a Republic! The King's offer to abdicate in favor of his young grandson and his mother's regency is not acceptable, though Lamartine is not altogether opposed. He had hesitated to proclaim the Republic, but the people are doing it.

At the offices of the *National* and the *Réforme* a provisional government is being formed. Conflicting groups have to be reconciled. The moderates would have liked to exclude the radicals, but the workers protest against it. Louis Blanc and Albert, a working man, are included. Lamartine is there too, and the great astronomer Arago—all, with the exception of Blanc and the working man Albert, moderate republicans of the bourgeois persuasion. The extreme right too has rallied to the Revolution, particularly the Legitimists, rejoicing in the expulsion of the Orléanist pretender, and having gotten over fear for their lives, are assured now also of their vast properties.

For the moment at least, there is for the generality of the people of Paris the dream and the hope. The new government has moved to abolish sweat labor and has fixed the work day to ten and eleven hours. It has proposed to "guarantee work" by establishing "national workshops." It has created a labor commission, the so-called Luxembourg Commission, made Louis Blanc its chairman, and set him to work on a labor program. But it is also suspiciously hurried in setting new elections, following passage of a universal suffrage decree. The electorate will now be enlarged from 250,000 to nine million. The radical groups are ill at ease: is the rest of France, especially the agrarian part, ready for such an election, uninstructed as it is in the ideas of the new régime and its program, and itself so very suspicious of Paris and its revolutionary left?

A multipolar phenomenon now comes into sight. One aspect of it is perhaps best seen in the description by Tocqueville of his experiences during the first days of the February Revolution:

> I spent the whole afternoon in walking about Paris. Two things in particular struck me: the first was, I will not say the mainly, but the uniquely and exclusively, popular character of the revolution that had just taken place; the omnipotence it had given to the people, properly so called—that is to say, the classes who work with their hands—over all others. The second was the comparative absence of malignant passion, or, as a matter of fact, of any keen passion—an absence which at once made it clear that the lower orders had suddenly become the masters of Paris ... The Revolution of July was effected by the people, but the middle class had stirred it up and led it, and secured the principal fruits of it. The Revolution of February, on the contrary, seemed to be made entirely outside the *bourgeoisie* and against it ... Nothing more novel had been known in our annals.[46]

It was this sense of a *new force*—a new motive element of history—that struck even those who were less conscious than Tocqueville of the class conflict now revealed. None was more aware of this new phenomenon than that segment of society, the bourgeoisie, that had with the assistance of the lower orders now come into power and intended to consolidate it. The bourgeois liberals, the moderate republicans, now became the right wing and proceeded to confirm their ascendency by crushing, or at least immobilizing or neutralizing, the more radical of the working-class elements and their leadership. Once in power, they began to segregate Louis Blanc, whom, next to Blanqui, they regarded as their most formidable menace. Isolated in the Luxembourg Commission, he was proposing various plans for worker cooperatives and extensive social services which they in due time could nullify. The newly established national workshops they entrusted to Emile Thomas, a skilful and persuasive organizer. Here workers were either directly supported or assigned work in a paramilitary structure. These too, they imagined, could be used when the time was ripe as an army to crush other recalcitrants or for other purposes. In the meantime they applied themselves to active propaganda in other parts of France where, with the aid of dominant influences in the provinces, they could use the elections to crush the have-nots ...

Louis-Desiré Véron, proprietor of the influential journal the *Constitutionnel*, was perhaps too harsh, but not too far from the truth when he asserted in his memoirs that "the day following the February Revolution, the bourgeois of Paris trembled for his head, and once he was sure of retaining it, he trembled for his purse."[47]

Once beginning to be reassured of his purse, he proceeded to form new coalitions to secure his newly found powers.

> While the Luxembourg sought the philosopher's stone, in the Hôtel de Ville they minted the current coinage.[48]

The Provisional Government proceeded to buy the confidence of the French financiers by paying interest on state loans in advance. It imposed a 45-centime surtax onto the four direct taxes, which fell most heavily on the impoverished peasantry, and thus tried to make them pay for the costs of the February Revolution and at the same time, by arousing their resentment, turn them into the most potent counterrevolutionary element in France. It formed the Mobile Guards, recruited from the Paris *lumpenproletariat*, an army of 24,000, as another counterrevolutionary force. At the same time Lamartine, sensing possible trouble ahead, made provisions for the reenforcement of the regular army, and held it in readiness. The pleas of the radicals for postponement of the elections was disregarded. Demonstrations and counterdemonstrations in March 1848 portended trouble. April 23 and the elections arrived. ...

The measure of popular discontent was full to overflowing. The economy stagnated, and national workshops could not—even if their directors had so desired—fill the needs of the unemployed of Paris and of those who had drifted in from the provinces. The plans of Louis Blanc's Commission remained mostly on paper; and outside of Paris the peasant-farmers, already burdened with heavy taxes, now faced the additional imposts with burning resentment, for in their eyes they were being made to pay for the support of Paris working men and women and for the enrichment of Paris overlords. Thus, both the proletariat of Paris and other cities, and the peasants of France, regarded the government measures as provocations; and it is not at all certain that the government did not so regard them too, and welcomed them as such. The counterrevolutionary alliances that were being welded throughout the country boded ill for liberal and radical republicans. A delegate from Charente and Poitiers reported how the "bourgeois, the nobles, men of money, yesterday separated into several opposed parties, today united to pervert the spirit of the revolution and stop the torrent of reforms ... Nobles, the high clergy ... bankers, and some poor dupes" also joined forces for the same purposes.[49] And when those inveterate enemies the Orléanists and the Legitimists joined forces, it did not require keen ears to hear a doomsday knell in the distance.

The prospects of the election frightened the radical left. George Sand, who had hurried to Paris to place herself at the service of the Revolution, and who became one of the editors of the *Bulletin de la République,* voiced the general fear in its issue of April 14.

> Unless the elections bring about the triumph of social truth, if they are no more than an expression of the interests of one class, wrenched from the loyal and trusting people, then the elections which should be the salvation of the Republic will be its destruction; of that there can be no doubt. Then there will be only one road to salvation for the people who set up the barricades, and that will be to demonstrate their wishes for a second time and put off the decisions taken by the false National Representation.[50]

Alas! Cassandra proved to be right ... The elections returned about three hundred moderate republicans to the Constituent National Assembly, out of nine hundred; two hundred Orléanists; one hundred Legitimists; and a bare seventy-five or eighty radicals and socialists. In Paris, only Armand Barbès and twelve socialists were elected, Louis Blanc among them. Blanqui and Raspail failed of support. For the time being, everyone in the Assembly spoke like a republican, even the most diehard royalists. Republicanism was the fashion.

If it was not yet time to liquidate the republic, it seemed high time to pulverize the radical working class and its leaders. The sharp class-antagonisms that were to rock France and the rest of Europe for years to come were laid bare as never before. Working-class riots that broke out in several cities—in Limoges, in Rouen—were soon suppressed. Tempers in the clubs of Paris boiled over. Barbès, Blanqui, Raspail were not men to sit idly by and watch the Revolution being—as they felt—betrayed. The lines were being drawn—tightly—and the Assembly, looking to Lamartine to lead it, dominated as it was by "notables," that is, men of property and wealth, joined by the petty and middle bourgeoisie, was set to fight the radical menace and eradicate it as soon as feasible. Alongside of them they now had the support and prestige of the Catholic party, headed by Montalambert. The Assembly set to work on May 4 and began proceedings by acclaiming and proclaiming the Republic. *Absit omen!*

There were in their midst many would-be executioners of the newborn republic, eager to prove their skill and exercise their *métier.* There was one absentee, however, who from faraway London watched the historic proceedings in France—from the wings, so to speak—ready to make his appearance at the proper moment—one who was eventually destined to wield the axe with adroitness and expedition. This was Prince Louis-Napoleon, nephew of Napoleon Bonaparte.

The drama of "liquidation" by the hand of the government now moved rapidly toward a *dénouement.* The first step was to attempt to decapitate the leadership of the radical wing of the working classes, and opportunity soon offered itself. On May 15, a mass demonstration of workers and others forced its way into the Assembly in order to compel it to intervene in the interest of Poland against Austria and Russia, as well as to voice its chagrin at the slowing pace of social improvement, now threatened with total paralysis. Blanqui and Barbès at first opposed the demonstration, but its momentum forced them into a reluctant leadership. From the Assembly the masses moved toward the Hôtel de Ville, intent on demanding a new government. The government in power had been waiting for just such a moment, and crushed the movement before it had the chance to spread. Blanqui, Barbès and other leaders were arrested.

Thereupon, the government moved to liquidate whatever remained of its "socialist" program. It rejected Louis Blanc's demands for the establishment of a ministry of labor, and the moderate reforms his Commission had been proposing. Then it proceeded to the more radical (from its point of view) and necessary step of abolishing the expensive and dangerous national workshops that had been established to give relief to the unemployed but had barely been able to minister to a fraction of them. On May 24 it was decided to drop those who had been resident in Paris less than three months, and to send the younger members into the army. Others were to be transferred out of Paris to clear marshes. Thousands were to be left altogether destitute, having before this learned how to starve on the pitiful subsistence handed out to them. Such a provocation would not have been undertaken without the assurance that means were already at hand to meet a crisis of resistance. General Eugène Cavaignac, the severe governor-general of Algeria, was summoned back and entrusted with the prospective tasks: he was to command the troops, the National Guard, and the Mobile Guards.

The tragic tale is soon told—all too soon. But it was to remain engraved in the minds of men and women forever after. The June Days of 1848. . .

* * *

La France est pâle come un lis,
Le front ceint de gris verveines,
Dans le massacre de ses fils,
Son sang a coulé de ses veines . . .
O Niobé des temps passés,
Viens voir la douleur de la France! . . .
Quatre jours pleins et quatre nuits,
L'ange des rouges funérailles,
Ouvrant ses ailes sur Paris,
A soufflé le vent des batailles. . . .

France is pale as a lily,
Her brow circled with grey vervain,
In the massacre of her children,
Her blood flowed from her veins . . .
O Niobe of ancient times,
Come, see the grief of France! . . .
Four days, and through four nights
The angel of bloody destruction
Spreading her wings over Paris,
Fanned the winds of warfare. . . .
—Pierre Dupont, "Les Journées de Juin"—1848

All changed, changed utterly:
A terrible beauty is born.
—William Butler Yeats, "Easter 1916"

Nothing like this had happened before.

"*Du pain, du travaille, ou du plomb!*" "Bread, work, or lead!"—the cry of some of the fifty thousand of the workers who on June 22 massed to protest the actions of the Assembly. It was an uprising of hunger. These were the men and women who only a few months before, in February, had offered—in the words of one of them, a worker—to "put three months of misery at the service of the Republic." Now their sacrifice was being repaid in such words as Minister Marie uttered to a petitioning delegation of workers. "Obey the orders of the Government; the workers do not wish to go to the provinces—we will compel them by force ... by force, do you understand?"[51] Some time earlier they had been told that there was no such thing as the "right to work"—only the "right to assistance." They were to be dispersed, sent to the provinces!

These were the men and women whose leaders had been jailed, who had been deserted by their middle-class and radical allies (Lamartine and Proudhon were standing aside, looking on), who on June 22 faced the combined forces of General Cavaignac—the army, the Mobile Guards, the Paris National Guard, the National Guards that had been brought in from the provinces. Leaderless, they made their own leaders and manned the barricades. There they were—the mechanics from Chapelle; metal workers, carpenters, cabinet makers in the St.-Antoine district; dockers in the Cité; ragpickers and quarry workers in the twelfth *arrondissement* of the Pantheon. There were printers and transport workers, some members of the liberal professions, and shopkeepers.

For the first time, the poet-statesman heard the cry, "*Lamartine à la lanterne!*"—a cry of disenchantment and hunger. Another Lafayette had betrayed them and the Revolution ...

Alexis de Tocqueville, again. ... He is now with the right wing of the Assembly, but he cannot recall the event without astonishment:

> I come at last to the insurrection of June, the most extensive and the most singular that has occurred in our history, and perhaps in any other: the most extensive, because, during four days, more than a hundred thousand men were engaged in it; the most singular, because the insurgents fought without a war-cry, without leaders, without flags, and yet with a marvelous harmony and an amount of military experience that astonished the oldest officers ... A struggle of class against class ... It must also be observed that this formidable insurrection was not the enterprise of a certain number of conspirators, but the revolt of one whole section of the population against another. Women took part in it as well as men. While the latter fought, the former prepared and carried ammunition; and when at last the time had come to surrender, the women were the last to yield. These women went to battle with, as it were, a housewifely ardour; they looked to victory for the comfort of their husbands and the education of their children. ... On the 22nd of June, they marched through Paris in troops, singing in cadence, in a monotonous chant, "We won't be sent away, we won't be sent away." ... On the 23rd, on going to the Assembly, I saw a large number of omnibuses grouped around the Madeleine. This told me

that they were beginning to erect barricades in the streets ... They proceeded in their work with the cunning and regularity of an engineer, not unpaving more stones than were necessary to lay the foundations of a very thick, solid and even neatly-built wall, in which they left generally a small opening by the side of the house to permit ingress and egress ...[52]

Friday, June 23: Barricades. First blood is shed at the Port-Saint-Denis. Government reenforcements begin to pour in from all parts of France. It seemed almost as if all of France was up in arms against Paris. On June 24 the Assembly made General Cavaignac dictator. What a far cry from those days in February when Lamartine was hailing the Revolution with the words, "The Republic is a surprise which has turned into a miracle."

The miracle—if there was any—was now on the barricades. General Cavaignac held off until he could strike with full force. On Sunday, June 25, Corpus Christi Day, the Chapelle sector was stormed and taken; on Monday the Bastille positions. Soon it was all over ... Not quite ... For then followed the reprisals and the massacre of the prisoners. ... Between twelve and fifteen thousand arrested; three thousand or so cut down in cold blood, or shot out of hand.

> Indeed, the National Assembly seemed implacable (writes a modern American historian, partisan of General Cavaignac) as it summarily voted on June 27 to send insurgent "leaders" before courts-martial and to deport all others without a trial. A few radicals pleaded vainly for less stringent penalties, but the Assembly refused even to exempt the aged and minors from the prospective voyage to a tropical prison camp.[53]

George Sand was brokenhearted. "I no longer believe in the existence of a republic which begins by killing the proletariat ... Today, I am ashamed of being French, I who used to be so proud of it."[54]

Others listened and heard the sound of ominous shots that meant more prisoners were being executed. That great Russian, Alexander Herzen, who had managed to leave Russia in order to begin enjoying the blessings of Western freedom, has some memorable pages in which he describes the sanguinary aftermath of the June insurrection and the feelings of desperation he and his friends experienced. He was one of that remarkable group of Russians, the so-called "generation of the '40s"—including men like Bakunin, Belinsky, Ivan Turgenev—all living abroad and destined, each in his own way, to affect history. Herzen had arrived in western Europe in 1847 and had come back from Italy just in time for the Revolution. This was the aftermath of the original exultation:

> On the other side of the river in all the streets and alleys barricades were being built. I can see now those dark figures dragging stones; women and children were helping them. A young Polytechnic student climbed onto one barricade that apparently was finished, hoisted a banner and began singing the "Marseillaise" in a gentle, mournful voice; all those who were working joined in, and the chorus of the grand song resounding from the stones of the barricades laid hold of one's heart ... and the tocsin still rang out. Meanwhile, the artillery thudded over the bridge, and from the bridge General Bédeau scanned the *enemy's* position through a telescope ...

And then on the 26th of June it was all over. ...

On the evening of the 26th of June, after the victory of the *National* over Paris, we heard regular salvos at short intervals ... We glanced at one another and all our faces were green. ... 'They are shooting people," we said with one voice, and turned away from one another. I pressed my forehead against the window-pane. Such moments provoke ten years of hatred, a lifetime of thirst for vengeance: *woe to him who forgives at such moments!*

Herzen's friends were leaving the country one by one; but he resolved to remain, wracked as he was by despair, a despair shared by many others.

Many times in moments of weakness and despair, when the cup of bitterness was too full, when my whole life seemed to me nothing but one prolonged blunder, when I doubted of myself, of "the last thing, all that is left," those words came into my head: "Why did I not take the gun from the workman and stay at the barricade?" Struck down by a sudden bullet, I should have borne two or three beliefs with me to the grave.[55]

History, in presenting us with movement, currents, flux and reflux, often hides from us the individuals who are the actors, and we tend to forget the individual in the mass. That young workman who offered Herzen a gun is part of a drama; Herzen, who did not take it, is part of a drama. Those men and women who built and fortified the barricades had individual heart-blood in them, each craved bread and security, and each was making history in more senses than he realized. What individual and concerted heroism it was to face the disciplined assault of a well-armed soldiery, when your own arms are either nonexistent or in scant supply! One is both alone and together with others. In their massed effort, in the community of their undertaking, in their common acceptance of their roles as heirs of the Great Revolutions, of the risk of defeat and death, or of hopes of victory, in their fused identities they represent movement—the movement of history. Yet each individual felt himself master of his destiny at that moment, the mould of the future in the hand that held rifle, or spade, or other makeshift weapons, and for four days they seemed such. For four days they defied the decree of annihilation issued against them by the other side. They were defeated. Looking back upon the event, History may see it as a tragic illusion, with that condescension which the survivor has toward the dead. Yet who shall deny that that "illusion" was to perpetuate itself not as "illusion," but as a reality that even in its tragic immediacy changed the course of history?

For Karl Marx, as for Alexis de Tocqueville, the event represented a historic "reality" of the first magnitude, a turning point of history, antipodal as were the political and social philosophies of the two men.

The February republic was won by the workers with the passive support of the bourgeoisie ... Just as the February republic, with its socialist concessions, required a battle of the proletariat, united with the bourgeoisie, against monarchy, so a second battle was necessary in order to sever the republic from socialist concessions, in order officially to work out the bourgeois republic as dominant. The bourgeoisie had to refute the demands of the proletariat with arms in its hands. And the real birthplace of the bourgeois republic is not the *February victory; it is the June defeat* ... The workers were left no choice. They had to starve or start to fight. They answered on June 22 with the tremendous insurrection in which the first great battle was fought between the two classes that split modern society. It was a fight for the preservation or annihilation of the *bourgeois order*. The veil that shrouded the republic was torn to pieces.[56]

The French historian and biographer of Blanqui, Gustave Geffroy, has eloquently tried to rescue from the dark pits of oblivion and anonymity the individuality of the participants:

The anonymous mass that fought and succumbed in the shadows, went into battle without leaders and without a program, and the best of those who fought against them, the great poets, Lamartine and Hugo, those indeed who should have mounted high and advanced the future, understood nothing of this arrival of the masses. Everyone believed it to be a revolt of the obscure mob, an irruption of uncomprehending wild animals; not one of them saw that these wretches wanted to come out of the night and that ... with tears, and with invocations to death, they clamored forth their hunger for light and happiness ... No one was in command of this elemental force, that army of fatality, that had already signed a pact with death ... It is with difficulty, searching among these ruins, these débris of history, that one discovers the vague names, already obliterated, of those who assembled the men, sounded the alarm, and gave orders behind the barricades. Le Genissel, club orator, was in the *faubourg* Poissonnière; Benjamin Laroque, man of letters, at the close of St.-Lazare; the shoemaker Voisambert commanded in the rue Planche-Mibray; and the mechanic Barthélemy, in the rue Grange-aux-Belles ... The principal actor in this drama was the nameless mass, as confused and indistinct in life as in their common grave, a lamentable and heroic chorus, going its way in a herd, without goal, without hope. It is they who have emerged into the political world in June, and will never again disappear from the world stage.[57]

Though Victor Hugo—still a monarchist—was not of them, nor that weathervane Lamartine, there were poets to celebrate and mourn the June martyrs. Louis Ménard, a member of the Blanquist club, had been on the barricades in that month. He composed a "Prologue d'une Révolution," in which he paid tribute to the fallen insurrectionists:

> *Puisque vos ennemis couronnent d'immortelles*
> *Le cercueil triomphal où reposent leur morts,*
> *Pendant que, sans honneur, entassés pêle-mêle,*
> *Dans las fosse commune on va jeter vos corps ...*

> With crowns of immortelles your enemies have decked
> The triumphal bier where rest their dead;
> While despoiled of honor, piled in heaps,
> They hurled your bodies into the common ditch;
> Accept this tribute of our silent tears,
> Brothers, we follow alone your sacred remains,
> And in the discreet night, we will venture again
> To the graveyard corner where you found repose.

> But no! behind you we will march without tears,
> For you have fallen in a sacred war,
> Hope in your hearts, arms in your hand,
> We who survive, will weep no more ...

In another poem, he vowed vengeance:

> *Si l'aveugle hasard me donnait la puissance*
> *Pour un jour, je voudrais tenir*
> *La glaive justicier de la sainte vengeance*
> *Et le droit sacré de punir ...*

> If blind chance were to give me the power
> For just one day, I would love to hold
> The retributive sword of holy vengeance
> And the sacred right of punishment. ...

> Vengeance will come; the inevitable day
> Of just expiations
> Will dawn, and sweep a crime-ridden race
> With the wind of revolutions ...

> It will be your turn, no pardon, our masters,
> Neither prayers nor penitent's pleas
> Will save you from kissing the sacred spots
> Drenched by our martyrs' blood. ...[58]

2. Germany

I am forced to make the solemn declaration that there is no power on earth that can ever move me to transform the natural relationship between Prince and his people, made so strong among us through its innermost truth, into a formal, constitutional one. And that not now or ever will I allow a sheet of written paper to intrude between God in Heaven and this land of ours, like a second Providence, to rule over us with its paragraphs, and take the place of our time-honored, sacred sense of loyalty.

—King Frederick William IV of Prussia—April 11, 1847

> *Oui, ma chère, nous sommes morts.*
> Yes, my dear, we are dead.
> —Prince Metternich to his wife, March 1848

The locomotive of history rushed on with headlong speed. Or better, the locomotive of revolution. Its thunders resounded throughout Europe, shaking dynasties, empires, and institutions as never before.

March 1848: the *mensis mirabilis*, the "miracle month" of German revolutions. For in that single month following the upheaval in France, King Ludwig of Bavaria had to abdicate; King Frederick William of Prussia, he who would not yield in 1847, bowed bareheaded before the hearses of those slain by his soldiery in the streets of Berlin, and thereafter paraded through the city, greeting the citizens and bearing the revolutionary colors on his arm. In this month Prince Metternich, barely escaping with his life, left Vienna by a back door to make his way to England; and the Prince of Prussia, the future Emperor William I—brother of Frederick William IV—also sought refuge there ...

It was in March too, on the sixth of that month, that the Hungarian nationalist leader Lajos Kossuth addressed the Diet at Pressburg:

The future of our Fatherland is not assured so long as the system of government in the other provinces [of Austria] is in gross contradiction to all constitutional principles, so long as the State Council which has charge of the common affairs of the Monarchy continues, in its elements, its combination and its tendency, to render homage to absolutism ... From the ossuaries of Vienna's System a pestilential air blows toward us, which numbs our nerves and fetters our spirits ... It is for us to save the dynasty, to attach its future to the brotherhood of the different races in Austria, and for the evil binding force of bayonets and bureaucratic oppression to substitute the firm cement of a free constitution ... We therefore seek to surround the imperial throne with constitutional organizations, and to obtain the grant of a constitution to all countries within the Austrian Empire.[59]

The address reverberates throughout the Austrian monarchy. And in Vienna it is read aloud to the thousands upon thousands who are gathered in protest before the Landhaus, meeting place of the Estates, with their demands for a Constitution and other reforms. This is March 13. The revolution has begun.... The end of Viennese *Gemütlichkeit*. ...

The news of the fall and flight of Metternich sends a lightning thrill throughout the German states. Already fired by wave upon wave of discontent, aroused in meetings fecund in petitions, the agitations mount. Berlin is aflame. Hatred of the military, whose very presence is provocation, leads to the raucous cry, "The soldiers must go!" The petitions are comparatively mild, but they are an affront to the affable father of his country, and unbecoming in hitherto well-behaved children: "Freedom of the Press, convocation of the Diets, withdrawal of troops, arming of the citizens, withdrawal of the ministers, protection of labor."

This time, the constitution that had been time and again promised by Prussian kings since 1815, and with equal regularity denied, could no longer be withheld. The crust of malaise, of apathy, of despair that had settled on the Germans after the defeat of their hopes in the 1830s, was broken. Not since 1815 had paternal despots found mornings so different from the nights before. Would France again undertake a campaign and bring another revolution into all the sacrosanct corners of Europe? True, Lamartine was reassuring the world that France had only peaceful intentions. But who would trust those French? A horrified Prussian king turned to England's Queen Victoria with desperate warnings of perils besetting her country. Failing of consolation here, he would soon welcome the intervention of the Russian giant in the East. In Paris, Heinrich Heine—who had anticipated and forewarned of the impending *débacle* of French royalty, but had incredulously asked, "Will there be a revolution in Germany?"—heard the news from the other side of the Rhine with disbelief. For the last time in his life he walked through the streets of Paris on his own legs. Thereafter, for eight long years until his death in 1856, he would look upon his beloved city only when, carried in the arms of his wife, he was brought to the balcony of his apartment.

Panic-stricken German monarchs hastened to grant concessions—hopeful of repudiating them when the time came. Their difficulties, and those of the "rabble" which was up in arms, stemmed from the fragmentation of the country.

And miracle of miracles! The nation of philosophers, poets, dreamers, thinkers—as well as inveterate coffeehouse debaters—had descended from the ethereal clouds of Ideas onto the barricades of Reality! Celestial dialectics turned into street battles! ....

The lesser German states were not far behind. Fires of revolt flared up everywhere: in Baden, Württemberg, Cologne and other Rhine provinces, thereafter in Saxony, Nassau, Hesse-Darmstadt … The liberalizing spirit was strongest in the south and west of Germany, and it was from these regions that a call resounded for a united Parliament and a General German Assembly. For the moment, diversity and divergence became unity as both constitutionalists and republicans joined forces in preparation for what was to be the momentous Frankfurt Parliament. The liberals were led by Heinrich von Gagern, prime minister of Hesse-Darmstadt; the revolutionary radicals, by Friedrich Hecker and Gustav von Struve. When the assembly finally convened at St. Paul's Church in Frankfurt on May 18, 1848, it was constituted predominantly of the upper and middle classes, most of them "intellectuals"—95 lawyers, 104 professors, 124 bureaucrats, 100 judicial officers, 34 landowners, 13 businessmen, and a microscopic representation of the working-class population, these led by the redoubtable Robert Blum of Leipzig. Heinrich von Gagern presided.

As was to be expected in the presence of so many professionals, an exuberant, unrestrainable oratory seemed at times to take precedence over the need for action. Indeed, this Frankfurt Parliament has often been derided, if not objurgated, as a congregation of chatterboxes. It is therefore not the least remarkable of wonders that for the time being some very positive actions should have been undertaken, and even set in motion, in an atmosphere of violent disputations within the St. Paul's Church, and amid the fierce political and physical clashes outside its walls and in other parts of the German states. The dominant tone of the assembly was conservative and antirevolutionary, and in that spirit it elected Archduke John of Austria as *Reichsverweser*— vicar-general or regent—of what was to be a unified Germany (including, at the moment, Austria), and set about preparing a Constitution and instituting immediately necessary reforms (or at least proposing them), such as freedom of movement, of speech, publication, meetings and assemblies, of thought and religion; of learning and equality before the law; public trials; inviolability of property; protection for national minorities; abolition of the death penalty, etc. But of the rights of labor and the reform of laboring conditions there was nothing at all.

Rarely had such a galactic company of brilliant intellectuals graced a political gathering. "*Welch reicher Himmel!*"—What a rich sky! There were such stars as Jakob Grimm, Ludwig Uhland the poet, writers and historians, Heinrich Laube, Arnold Ruge, Droysen, Duncker, Gervinus; the Viennese poet, Anastasius Grün; the eminent theologian Ignaz Döllinger. What might they not agree and disagree on! It was hardly surprising that uneasy elements should intrude, like German chauvinism and supernationalism; suspicion of non-Germanic minorities; local interests and particularism; bitter antirepublicanism, panic fear of "anarchy," and a dread of the more radical revolutionaries. A constitutional monarchy represented their highest ideal. Their dream: a federal empire under the leadership of Prussia, with Frederick William IV at the head.

The intentions and programs were well-meaning enough, and corresponded in the main with the interests of the predominantly middle-class liberal groups. But how to bring all this into the realm of "actuality"? Or was this Assembly of notables a Frankfurt "never-never-land"—debating, arguing, planning, philosophizing—while all around it the world was in conflagration? An assembly suspected (even despised) by the ruling classes of all the German states, suspected by the lower classes and the radicals—a "government" without a treasury, courts, or an army?

When in 1849 the Frankfurt Assembly finally came up with a constitution—in many ways a fairly liberal one, though without provisions for the improvement of the lot of the working population—and then resolved to offer the crown of "Germany" to King Frederick William IV of Prussia, the tide of revolution had already waned, and reaction had begun to gain the upper hand. The King of Prussia haughtily declined both the Constitution and the honor of heading a yet nonexistent united Germany. He would not, in his own words, besmirch his royal head with a "crown from the gutter." He would accept it only if handed him by the German sovereigns of the several states. "*Gegen Demokraten, helfen nur Soldaten.*" "Against Democrats, he would manage with the aid of his soldiery!" The King's attitude spelled Doomsday for the Assembly. Already split between right and left, it soon disintegrated. A working-class uprising in Frankfurt against it, though quickly suppressed, only sealed its doom. A left-wing rump removed to Stuttgart, where it was soon dispersed by the government. The Assembly's life had run almost concurrently with the course of revolution on the Continent; when it expired, its death was only an ignominious parody of the tragedy of blood and human sacrifice that was being enacted everywhere else.

But before the humbled monarchs would rise again and with reborn insolence reassert their authority, many of them were forced to eat the dust of shame and humiliation. Also to eat their words. The King of Prussia, who vowed never, never to cede, saw Berlin rise up against him in March 1848; stood bareheaded as the procession of those his army had killed wove before his eyes, close to three hundred, practically all of them workers and artisans of the city; promised an assembly, a constitution, a liberal cabinet; and was forced to listen to the monster demonstration that called for universal suffrage, a ministry of labor, a minimum wage, a ten-hour day—a frightful spectacle not only to kings but also to respectable Germans, and not only in Berlin but in the Rhineland as well. One workers' society sprang up after another. In Cologne, the *Neue Rheinische Zeitung* began appearing in June, edited by Karl Marx, now returned from exile ...

No less startling was the news from the south of Europe. In Rome, Pope Pius IX was forced to grant a constitution on March 10; a few days later a Milanese uprising and attack on the Austrians drove the latter back to Verona. In the same month an uprising in Venice resulted in the declaration of a republic; and almost against his will, King Charles Albert of Piedmont was moved to declare war on Austria and was sending his army into Lombardy.

The ice-crust that had congealed so much of Europe's heart booms as it begins to break and rush down in irresistible floes against dikes and barriers, intent on crushing them. And if all the currents had flowed together, there would have been no resisting them. But crosscurrents and countercurrents, national self-interests, national hatreds, local patriotisms and chauvinisms, legitimate national strivings, countered the pressing currents of democratic internationalism; class interests strove against one another. Yet that the situation was desperate in the eyes of the powers is nevertheless proved by the call Austria extended to the Russian Tsar for help in crushing the almost-victorious uprisings in Hungary.

It would be a disservice to historical truth to overlook the fervent sense of internationalism that characterized the revolutions, the feeling that this was truly *one* war against privilege and oppression, though seemingly fragmented and discontinuous. Such a sense of unity is perhaps well symbolized in the action of the Polish soldier General Josef Bem, a veteran of the Polish struggles of the 1830s, who now felt it his duty to come to the aid of the revolutionaries of Vienna, and soon thereafter, of Hungary. It is also symbolized in the figure of Robert Blum, the political leader of Leipzig, a member of the Frankfurt Assembly, who went to Vienna, participated in the insurgent movement there, and was upon its defeat shamefully executed, despite his parliamentary immunity. And it is also symbolized in the irrepressible and omnipresent Mikhail Bakunin, a Russian.

The chronicle of these revolutions may be epitomized as flux and reflux—until the shattering defeats toward the end of 1849. As was to be expected, a great deal of the quixotic was manifested in a number of ill-planned ventures; there were Hotspurs leading the way to disaster, as in the April uprisings in Baden planned by Hecker and the German poet Georg Herwegh. Yet ever and again there rose frequent visions of proximate victory to be salvaged from disasters. Lurid and macabre paradoxes, too, manifest themselves, as when the French government, having crushed the June uprising in Paris, proceeded in July 1849 to destroy the newly established Roman republic and restore the Pope. But here and there, minor epics of resistance were still wrought, as in the battles around Rome; in the heroism of Venice under Daniele Manin against the Austrians. But the bastions of revolution were falling one by one, as Prussian, Russian and Austrian armies ranged far and wide.

3. Austria

But not before at least two extraordinary exploits electrified the world. One was the Hungarian resistance to the Austro-Russian forces; the other, the second uprising of the populace of Vienna in October 1848. The two events were interlaced.

Emperor Franz of Austria had once remarked: "My peoples are strangers to each other, and that is all right. They do not get the same sickness at the same time ... From their antipathy will be born order, and from mutual hatred, general peace."[60] And so it was indeed—at least for a time. That strange miraculous thing—Austria— giant with feet of clay, a clay that seemed imperishably tenacious but was held together in part by the national hatred and rivalries of Germans, Magyars, Slavs, Croats, Serbs, Czechs—an Austria still semifeudal, only a small segment of it industrialized. Its highly bureaucratic machine, centered in Vienna, was headed by an absolute autocrat, the feebleminded Emperor Ferdinand; its authority was vested in the stick that descended with varied degrees of vigor from the Emperor down to the least paterfamilias. What seemed an impenetrable Chinese Wall of censorship and police surveillance sealed off ideas from abroad; fear kept them down internally. But every wall has its chinks, and some of those winds of doctrine and revolution that were howling outside managed to penetrate. The February of Paris became the March of Vienna. And who would have expected it of Vienna? That city was hailed as

> *Stadt der Freude, Stadt der Töne,*
> *Morgenfrohes, stolzes Wien ...*

> City of pleasures, city of music,
> Proud and morning-joyous Vienna,
> Lo! spring-times' happy children
> Are nurturing Freedom's roses![61]

And who would have thought the impoverished intellectual proletariat—the university students—would form the vanguard, and one of the mainstays, of the revolutionary armies?

> Lo, who be these so proud in bearing?
> The bayonets flash, the flags fly free.
> They come with silver trumpets blaring,
> The University![62]

Under the leadership of an inspired professor-priest, Anton Füster, these students sparked the movement of resistance among the workers, tradesmen, and intellectuals. And these in turn sent forth their petitions demanding fundamental reforms. They marched to the Landhaus, meeting place of the Estates, and here a young Jewish doctor, Adolf Fischoff, spoke in the name of all for a free press, a united Empire, and other reforms. Then someone read aloud Kossuth's spirited speech, and shouts arose: "Constitution! Metternich must go!" Misery needs little ideology for a vent—and though the proletariat was scarcely class-conscious, they joined in the common upsurge and demanded the right to bear arms.

When troops were called out, the natural thing happened. There was a clash, arms went off, and a number of protesters were killed. The Revolution was on. Arsenals were ransacked, an Academic Legion came into being, a citizens' National Guard and a Militia. Rifts widened, tempers rose, demands became more forceful, more extensive: for a constitutional convention convened through universal suffrage. Now, worker and servants, previously ignored, were making their voices heard. ...

Emperor Ferdinand fled, along with his camarilla, to the more loyal terrain of Innsbruck. Here they hoped to find time and support for a happier return. His generals were already beginning to retrieve some of their earlier losses: Prince Windischgrätz was liquidating the revolution in Prague; Radetzky was successfully counterattacking in Lombardy; and the Croat leader Joseph Jelačič was secretly conspiring with the Austrians to attack the rebellious Hungarians. Thus Croat and Serb nationalism, repressed by the Hungarians, could now be used in the interests of the common overlord!

Though the uprisings in Vienna had less of socialist consciousness or theory than any other in Europe, their ultimate fate would be determined by the extent to which the middle classes would lend their support. In the earlier stages of the revolution in Vienna, before the demands of the lower classes had become more articulate and emphatic, tradesmen, manufacturers, business people in general, whose interests had been neglected by the Austrian bureaucracy and who had been hampered in their enterprises, naturally sided with the movement for a liberalization of government control and for a share in governmental decisions. But the revolution, as always happens, loosed new forces—in this case laborers and machinists and railroad workers. These in turn represented a fresh menace to the middle groups. And an economic crisis sharpened the differences which had already become manifest.

The return of the Emperor to the capital was therefore hailed by the moderates. It also marked the incipience of a counteroffensive against the radicals. Pitiful subsidies of doles for the unemployed, resented by those who were better off, were now to be reduced if not altogether abolished. Skirmishes between workers and the national guard occurred; there were fatalities. The workers were defeated. Civil war was in the air. With victory over the Italian rebels assured, there were now two goals for the reaction—total defeat of the now established autonomous Hungarian régime directed by Lajos Kossuth; and simultaneously, assault on the Viennese insurgents, and their destruction. Latour, Minister of War, had been deep in the conspiracies directed toward both these end—he was the *bête noire* of liberals and radicals—and it was his action in October that precipitated the last, most dramatic phase of the revolution in Vienna, the October uprising.

Racial and national animosities marked the Viennese Assembly that had been convoked as a result of the elections. For the first time the many varied national groups were represented by their spokesmen, who set about to prepare a Constitution. Yet how sharp the divisions were, and how deeply ingrained, can be gauged from the attitude of the Austrian middle and upper classes as they hailed Radetzky's victories over the Italians. Here nationalist fervor and economic self-interest overlapped, for "Lombardy and Venetia contributed a third of the revenue of the imperial treasury."[63] How much more does it redound to the credit of the radical left that it recognized a kinship with Poles, Hungarians, and Italians in their common aspirations! For it was as much in the cause of Hungarian independence as in their own interest that the students, workers, and other citizens of Vienna organized the October insurrection, thus identifying themselves with the international revolutionary movement of all Europe.

The drama erupted on October 6, 1848. The role of sacrificial goat fell to Minister of War Latour. This pitiful and malevolent official was torn and hanged on a lantern by an infuriated populace. It seemed to the Emperor and his entourage that the appropriate moment had arrived. The Emperor was securely lodged in Bohemian Olmütz, whence he could address his beloved Viennese while thrusting the mighty iron of his armies agains the city.

The drama of counterrevolution had been well prepared. The Croat Jelačič was now commander-in-chief of all troops in Hungary, Transylvania, and Croatia, and also Imperial Commissioner for Hungary.

On October 6, Minister of War Latour had ordered an Austrian battalion to move from Vienna and join Jelačič for an attack on the Hungarians. The Austrian battalion refused to move. An alerted student body, aided by a good portion of the aroused population, joined forces in obstructing the movement of the army. The Assembly was powerless; masses stormed the arsenal and seized arms. Latour had ventured into the streets and was murdered. The Emperor, still in the Hofburg but planning an escape to Olmütz, promised amnesty—in fact, anything. But Jelačič and the Croatians, as well as Windischgrätz and his army, were at the same time moving on Vienna. Soon some 60,000 men surrounded the city.

Vienna prepared for the siege. Influential citizens, Habsburg adherents, the well-to-do, and others, had already fled the city.

It was no highly trained and disciplined army of citizens that was about to face the guns of the enemy. Only the Academic Legion was militarily prepared. There was no trained commander to lead them. Women joined in the defense. A writer, Wenzel Messenhauer, who had some knowledge of army strategy, was placed in command. He was fortunate in having at his side General Josef Bem, commander of the Mobile Guard. Bem was a soldier, and commanded respect. From Frankfurt came Robert Blum and Julius Fröbel. Surely, outside help would be forthcoming. Surely the Hungarians, still undefeated, would soon come to their aid?

Had not the Viennese themselves risen up to help them? And had they not sung on an earlier, happier day, offering to staunch the wounds of their Hungarian comrades?—

> We of you our brothers make,
> And curse who'e'er this bond will break!
> Hail to you! We greet each other;
> Austria'll never desert her brother . . .[64]

Recruits dribbled in—from Brünn, from Graz, from Styria . . .

But what could these avail? The undisciplined Viennese fought as best they could amid rumors and counter-rumors, the most bedeviling being those that spoke of an imminent incursion by Hungarians, who under General Perczel were stationed on the outskirts of the city behind Jelačić, whom they had successfully pursued.

History and historians have since that time debated: guilt or strategy? Had the Hungarians betrayed, or had they merely adhered to a strict legalism? When the Hungarians finally moved, it was too late.

October 31: Vienna's day of doom. The city capitulated, and Jelačić and his victorious armies moved in on November 3. "Ladies . . . were waving their handkerchiefs from every window, and saluting Jelačić, who bowed courteously on every side . . . *Vivat, vivat, vivat!*" Spectators thundered their welcome.[65]

Historians have variously evaluated the actions of the Viennese radicals in defending the city. One very recent scholar writes as follows:

> Nearly all the important people—the influential ones—sided with the Habsburgs. The democrats were the "little people": the students, the lower-middle-class artisans and shopkeepers, and the great proletarian masses. The revolutionary leaders were mostly young people or penniless intellectuals. On the whole, they were people who had nothing to lose but their unhappy lives.[66]

Another historian, writing in 1851, evaluated the Viennese uprising and the nature and objectives of its participants in somewhat different terms:

> We have seen that the Viennese, with all the generosity of a newly-freed people, had risen for a cause which, though ultimately their own, was, in the first instance and above all, that of the Hungarians. Rather than suffer the Austrian troops to march upon Hungary, they would draw their first and most terrible onslaught upon themselves . . . And if

Hungary should even have forgotten that Vienna had fought the first battle of Hungary, she owed it to her own safety not to forget that Vienna was the only outpost of Hungarian independence, and that after the fall of Vienna nothing could meet the advance of the imperial troops against herself ... as a German, we may further be allowed to say, that not for all the showy victories and glorious battles of the Hungarian campaign would we exchange that spontaneous, single-handed rising, and heroic resistance of the people of Vienna, our countrymen, which gave Hungary the time to organize the army that could do such great things.[67]

The chronicle of the aftermath lists among those executed by the victorious Habsburg troops the names of the journalists Julius Becker and Hermann Jellinek, the commander-in-chief Messenhauer, and the deputy to the Frankfurt Parliament Robert Blum. It is not recorded that these had nothing to lose "but their unhappy lives." On the contrary, the measure of their life's quality can be gauged by the way they met their death.

Here are two accounts of eyewitnesses. One concerns the last hours of Becker and Jellinek. In this instance it is an army Major involved in the executions who narrated his experience:

Throughout the whole day the Major had been too agitated to eat, because he had been obliged, early that morning, to superintend the carrying out of two executions, which had made a profound impression upon him. The matter concerned two journalists, who were to be made the targets of the Royal and Imperial riflemen, on the charge of having, through the newspaper *The Radical*, incited the people to revolt against His Majesty the Kaiser, and to offer armed resistance to his Highness, Field-marshal Prince Windischgrätz. One of these accused was Dr. Julius Becker, 45 years old, of the Protestant faith, proprietor and responsible editor of the above paper. The other was his collaborator, Dr. Hermann Jellinek, 25 years old, of the Jewish religion. Dr. Becker. ... walked to his death with a firm step and calm glance, without wasting one word. ... Dr. Jellinek ... tried with the help of lively gestures to make clear to the Major that some error underlay the entire affair ... As soon as he had convinced himself that all further talk was useless, he pulled himself together and cried, stepping back resolutely, "Now, shoot me dead.!"—assuming at the same time a bearing which showed that moral strength did not fail him ...[68]

The other is Robert Blum's last letter, written to his wife:

My treasured, good dear Wife, Farewell! farewell for the time, some call for ever, but that will not be so. Bring up our—now only *your* children to be noble, then they will never bring shame upon their father. Sell our little property with the help of our friends. God and good men will help you. All that I feel is melting into tears, hence once again, Farewell, dear Wife! Consider our child to be a precious bequest to foster and cherish, and thus you will honor your faithful husband. Farewell, farewell! A thousand, thousand last kisses from your Robert. Vienna, November 9, 1848, morning, five o'clock, at six o'clock I shall no longer be. I had forgotten the rings. I press the last kiss for you upon the marriage ring. My seal ring is for Hans, my watch for Richard, the diamond stud for Ida, the chain for Alfred, as keepsakes. Distribute all the other keepsakes according to your judgment. They are coming! Farewell! Farewell![69]

He was shot on November 9, 1848.

He forbade the binding of his eyes, but allowed it when they pointed out that the riflemen would shoot more accurately. With the words, "I die for German freedom, for which I have fought. May the Fatherland keep me in remembrance!"—he offered his breast to the bullets, which laid him low.[70]

4. Failure of the Revolutions

Wenn wir doch knien könnten, wir lägen auf den Knien;
Wenn wir doch beten könnten, wir beteten für Wien!

If only we knew how to kneel, on our knees we would have lain;
If only we knew how to pray, for Vienna we would have prayed! ...[71]

Thus the German poet, Ferdinand Freiligrath, in November 1848, in a desperate and vain plea to his fellow-Germans to come to the aid of the beleaguered revolutionaries of Vienna. But alas! neither knee-bending nor prayers alone could have availed. The Hungarians had failed them; their fellow-Germans had failed them; the peasantry they had helped liberate from feudal obligations and bonds had failed them. The execution of Robert Blum, deputy of the Frankfurt Parliament, was a deliberate and shocking insult to that body, and to all liberal Germany.

The collapse of the October uprising in Vienna, together with that of the preceding June in Paris, marks the actual, though not the immediate, *finis* of these revolutions. The tidal wave is now reversed; the reaction is not only heartened, but feels empowered to proceed with ever bolder steps to the ultimate accounting.

Prussia picked up the cue at once, and the King began taking the offensive against a recalcitrant and frequently insistent Prussian parliament that defied royal prerogatives and agitated for its own constitution as against that "granted" by the ruler. In October a huge demonstration even brought forward demands for Prussian intervention in favor of the Viennese! There was great noise, but little action. The Viennese disaster dismayed the Berlin population, and General Wrangel occupied the city without resistance. Parliament was dissolved. The following year a new electoral law was passed which effectively barred workers from any voice or participation in the government. Once more the propertied classes, the large landowners, and the upper middle classes had proved victorious. Royal authority was fully restored in the new constitution of 1850. The army had proved a decisive factor in the defeat of the revolution.[72]

For the Austrian government the subjugation of Hungary proved a far more difficult and bloody undertaking. Here it met with the brilliant, and for a time, incredible resistance of the Hungarian armies, skilfully led and abetted by the country's unity. High had been the hopes raised in Hungarian hearts by the March revolution. On March 15, 1848, the Parliament at Pressburg voted for the abolition of serfdom. Actually it hoped to eliminate Viennese control, establish an independent state formally united under the person of the Austrian Emperor, who would be King of Hungary, and eventually incorporate Croatia and other Slavonic provinces. Such a Hungarian state would have an independent government, with a ministry responsible to its Parliament. The so-called "March Laws" called for elections to the Lower House by males over twenty, but circumscribed the franchise with considerable property qualifications. For the time being the upper classes acceded to these radical reforms, and, like their coevals in other threatened lands, bided their time. There was a more radical sector in Hungary that even demanded a republic. Sándor Petöfi, the poet, was one of the leaders of this group. Reluctantly, Ferdinand approved of the measures proposed by the Hungarian government. Lajos Kossuth's influence and prestige in the country were too powerful at the moment for resistance by disapproving countrymen. As events became more and more favorable to Austria, the Habsburg camarilla, heartened by the repression of Prague and the victories of Radetzky in Italy, proceeded to annul Ferdinand's reluctant promises. The Emperor repudiated the March Laws, dissolved the Hungarian Parliament, and declared all its decisions invalid. Capitalizing on the strong anti-Hungarian sentiment among the Croats and other non-Magyars, he now made use of Jelačič to undo Hungary.

The final reckoning came with the Vienna débacle, the abdication of Ferdinand, and the accession of Franz Josef. The new Emperor declared Kossuth and his supporters to be traitors. He also counted on the disaffected Magyar magnates, Kossuth's bitter opponents, to rally to the Habsburg cause. What no one, however, had counted on was the miracle of Hungary's resistance, her victories under the leadership of that military genius Artur Görgei, who even threatened a march on Vienna. The victories of March 1849 by soldiers under the indestructible General Bem finally forced Austrian minister Schwarzenberg to turn to Russia for help. Ultimately 360,000 Russians were sent in response. Kossuth appealed in vain to "friendly" nations for help. In addition, he found himself opposed by Görgei, who favored accommodation with the Habsburgs.

On August 13, 1849, Görgei surrendered with his army to the Russians at Világos. A few weeks later, the last of the Hungarian bastions fell, and the war was over. But not the recriminations. Julius von Haynau, Austrian general, who earned the sobriquet of "Hyena of Brescia" for his atrocities in Italy, proved true to his nickname. Kossuth and General Bem managed to escape to Turkey. Sándor Petöfi, Hungary's uncrowned poet-laureate, a soldier in Bem's army, fell on the field of battle. He was twenty-six years old.[73]

⋆   ⋆   ⋆

The critical months of July, August, and September 1849 ring down the curtain on the European Revolutions of 1848 and 1849. In July, the newly established republic of Rome capitulated to the French army. In August, Venice surrendered to the Austrians. August and September mark the expiration of Hungarian resistance to the Russians and Austrians. Some seventeen months before, in April 1848, the British government had dealt Chartism in England a crushing defeat, all without barricade or bloodshed.

The drama of Rome's revolution and Rome's fall, its republican life extinguished after only five months' duration, reveals glaringly how far the tide of reaction had swung. For it was neither a Russian army nor an Austrian force that brought about the surrender, but French soldiery led by a French general. It was the France of General Cavaignac, the France of its new president, Louis-Napoleon, that now joined other European powers in order to shatter the last remains of revolution and republicanism.

It was General Oudinot of the Republic of France who administered the death-stroke to the Republic of Rome!

Yet there had been times when it seemed that the Italians would at last throw off the yoke of Austria, bring about the unification of the country, and realize the apostolic and apocalyptic vision of Giuseppe Mazzini and his "Young Italy" followers. The dream was to create the "Third Rome"—to follow that of the first Rome and that of the Popes—a Rome that would lead the world toward a confederation of nations—even republics! Others hoped for a Rome less radical, a unified Italy that would do away with a medieval past and emerge as a modern, advanced industrial and commercial land. The clogs of autocracy, the burden of sustaining a foreign rule, of contributing manpower and wealth to its support—and not least, the pressures from within the country itself, of a critically poor population also suffering from the international crisis, and the potential danger it posed—all these actuated both the more liberal aristocracy, the landlords, and whatever there was of a bourgeoisie, to agitate for reforms that could only be achieved through a concomitant liberation of the land. The uneasy torpor that had bound the nation's energies was suddenly broken by the news from France, and the March uprising in Vienna made it clear that powerful Austria was also vulnerable. Now seemed to be the moment to realize the dream of an Italian *risorgimento*. But who was to lead? The spiritual leaders were there to press the Italian destiny—Giuseppe Mazzini and the Abbé Gioberti. As for national leadership, the eyes turned upon King Charles Albert of Sardinia, who was coveting the Austrian provinces of Lombardy and Venetia to unite them with his own Piedmont, and who, though he had twice betrayed the cause of liberalism, might perhaps now be impelled by the great upsurge to lead the Italian armies against Austria. Philosophers like Gioberti looked to Pope Pius IX, whose "liberal" aura had not yet been dimmed.

When in the month of March, 1848 Milan rose up, built barricades, and after its "five glorious days" succeeded in driving out the army of the formidable Radetzky, forcing him to retreat, the auguries of success seemed inerrable. Once again, it was the workers, the artisans, who did the fighting, leaving the direction of affairs to the upper and middle-class provisional government. Indecisive King Charles Albert moved and, had he not been Charles Albert, might have successfully overcome the retreating armies of Radetzky and actually destroyed them in the regions to which they had retreated. The chances of doing so were excellent, for a revolution had broken out in adjoining Venetia. Whatever Charles Albert's reasons or fears, it is likely that he dreaded the radical eventualities of a revolution in Milan, as did no doubt a great many of his upper and middle-class supporters. His halfheartedness, his failure to follow up his early successes and those of the Milan revolutionaries, gave the eighty-one year old Radetzky—probably the most gifted soldier of his day—time to reinforce his troops, recoup his losses, and counterattack at the appropriate moment. In spite of, or in the face of, an earlier opposition on the part of his Austrian superiors, he did that very thing. In the end, his successful counteroffensives spelled the doom of Charles Albert's ambitions and all too belated efforts, costing him his crown. Unfortunately, it also blasted Italy's hopes of liberation for years to come.

Those who had believed in Pope Pius IX as the potential leader of a united and free Italy under a liberalized régime, were doomed to bitter disenchantment. In 1846, on his accession, he had been hailed as the coming savior of his country; even in France he was looked upon by many as the lodestar of freedom. The French poet Pierre Dupont had then addressed a plea to him, to save the world from despair,

> *Rends-lui, rends-lui la liberté,*
> *Veux-tu commencer la croisade?*
>
> Give it, give it liberty!
> Do you wish to begin the crusade?[74]

Of course, Italy itself reacted to the accession of the Pope with extravagant expectations. Giuseppe Verdi altered the chorus of his opera *Ernani*, substituting for "*A Carlo Quinto sia gloria e onor,*" "*A Pio Nono …*"

Giuseppe Mazzini's messianic words reechoed throughout the land:

> The destiny of Italy is that of the world … Rome, by design of Providence … is the eternal city, to which is entrusted the mission of disseminating the Word that will unite the world … Nationalism is the share God grants people in the work of mankind. It is that people's mission, the task it must perform on earth, so that God's purpose may be fulfilled, the achievement which gives it the freedom of the City of Mankind, the baptism which endows it with its character and assigns it a place among the peoples, its brothers …[75]

The patriot-poet Goffredo Mameli, Mazzini's devoted follower, soon to die in the defense of Rome, electrified the country with his battle hymn, "*Alla Vittoria.*"

> *Fratelli d'Italia,*
> *L'Italia s' è desta…*

"Italian brothers, Italy is awake. Hitherto despised and derided, because we were not a people, because we were divided,"

> *Uniamoci, amiamoci:*
> *L'unione e l'amore*
> *Rivelano ai popoli*
> *Le vie del Signore …*

"Let us unite, and love; for union and love reveal God's ways to the people. Let us swear to liberate our native soil; united by God, who can conquer us?"[76] Mazzini's words were turned into this battle cry. The incredible, legendary warrior Giuseppe Garibaldi, returned from his works of liberation in South America ready for similar tasks in his native Italy, confessed that he was swept away by the sound of Mameli's lines. Verdi set them to music.

As the fires of 1848 raged throughout the Italian states, even reluctant princelings and other rulers were compelled to join in sending troops for the assault on the Austrians. In due time they were to repent and withdraw them. But now, with all cities astir, Rome and the Papal States too became agitated. Pope Pius IX, who had already been constrained to grant something of a constitution to his people, was pressured to join the "crusade" against Austria and yield to demands for the greater liberalization of his domain. He began to have second thoughts. A month after having granted a constitution, he pronounced an allocution on April 19, 1848:

> Although some persons desire that we, together with other peoples and princes of Italy, make war against the Austrians, we deem it proper to disclose clearly in this solemn meeting of ours, that it is wholly foreign to our intentions, since we, however unworthy, exercise on earth the functions of Him who is the author of peace and lover of charity, and according to the office of our supreme Apostolate we follow and embrace all races, peoples, and nations with equal and paternal love.[77]

He also declined to have any part in a proposal to make Italy a united republic under his presidency (this was Gioberti's program) and urged all Italians to reject such plans and remain loyal to their princes.

In the upheaval that followed, Pellegrino Rossi, one of the Pope's cabinet ministers, was assassinated on November 15, 1848. A violent uprising on the same day, accompanied by emphatic demands for a democratic cabinet and a declaration of war, forced the Pope to yield—outwardly at least. For on November 24, he secretly fled from Rome and took refuge in Gaeta, in the Kingdom of Naples. From his retreat he sent forth appeals to the great powers asking for intervention. In Rome, the elections for a constituent assembly returned a democratic majority; the latter declared the power of the Pope at an end, and on February 9, 1849 proclaimed the Roman Republic. Additionally, it decreed the nationalization of church properties, abolished clerical control of the university, suppressed the Inquisition, abolished censorship, and enacted other measures for the benefit of the poor.

It was not long thereafter that Louis-Napoleon sent his army to bring Rome to her senses and restore the Pope. With Mazzini now in Rome to inspire her citizens, and with Garibaldi ready to engage in daring sorties and forays with his legionnaires, the poorly equipped army under General Pietro Roselli surprised the first contingents of General Oudinot's troops, and even inflicted serious damage upon them. The dedication and courage of the besieged, men and women, proved as heroic as in the end it proved futile. For soon the reinforced French army numbered 30,000 men, and when the final assault began on June 3, it became evident that the city could not long withstand the bombardment. Garibaldi managed to extract his followers, and in typical fashion proceeded to lead them to the succor of the besieged Venetians. Mazzini eventually found his way to London. On July 3, the French occupied Rome. The Pope waited until April 12 of the next year before reassuming his sovereignty. The Restoration was complete.

It remained now to subjugate the stubborn republicans of Venice. ...

Venice too rejoiced at the news of the Vienna uprising of March. Like Milan, she felt that Austrian domination of Italy was, if not at an end, at least badly shaken. Venetians shared in the triumphs of Milan's "five days," as they expelled their Austrian governor and stormed the arsenal. Unfortunately they forgot to secure the naval fleet. They carried the liberated Daniele Manin, formerly prisoner of the Austrians, on their shoulders, and placed this tried republican in leadership. Eagerly they waited for the approach of Charles Albert's army as it swept back Radetzky's forces; like Lombardy, they voted for union with Piedmont under that king, against the hopes and urgings of

Manin. But Charles Albert did not come; he retreated, betraying Venice's fondest hopes. Once more they turned to Manin ...

Then the Austrians blockaded the city, severed it from the mainland, and bided their time through the winter of 1848 and 1849. In March 1849, Radetzky effectively defeated Charles Albert at Novara and forced his abdication in favor of his son Victor Emmanuel II. In the same month the Venetians elected Manin President of their Republic. Then began the bombardment of the city by the Austrians. Led by General Pepe, who had defected from King Ferdinand of Naples, the besieged city did what it could against cannon, famine, and the cholera. With miraculous heroism it held out until August 22. Within a brief period of not quite two months, Venice followed the fate of Rome, of Hungary. The Venetian Republic was over. Manin was allowed to leave.

Under her new Emperor, young Franz Josef, Austria settled back to reestablish the old order. A few placebos, such as mild constitutional sops, were distributed to the awakened national minorities.

In other parts of Europe a few occasional post-mortem flareups betrayed the last mortal agonies of the Revolution. Then the fires died down altogether. ...

Chapter Three

The Lyre and the Sword
Art and Revolution

1. Hungary—July 31, 1849: Sándor Petöfi—The Poet as Warrior

I conned the Book of History, and at the end,
I asked myself, "Is this the chronicle of Man?"
A river of blood, springing from rocks of misty past,
And flowing on, down to our own day …
Oh, do not think its well-heads ever slacken,
For without pause, it rushes toward the sea,
A surge of blood into a bloody ocean!
I see approaching days of untold dread,
Such as no human eye has ever seen,
Will make this day's peace seem the graveyard's quiet,
One moment between the lightning and the thunder's roar.
The veil of future lifts; I see before me
A sight that rends my soul, yet thrills with joy:
I see anew the God of War in armor,
With sword in hand, coursing the wide world,
Calling the people to arms in the last of wars;
I see two nations arrayed against each other:
Here stands the Good—there the Evil one,
And ever-vanquished Good soon to be victor,
A triumph won through seas of untold blood!
No matter! The Day of Judgment's here!
Foretold of prophets in the name of God.
Yes, Day of Judgment—dawn of Life and Bliss—
When Man no longer needs to grasp for Heaven,
For Heaven descends, embracing Man and Earth!
　　—Sándor Petöfi, "The Day of Judgment," 1847

July 31, 1849. This was the day on which Sándor Petöfi, Hungary's uncrowned poet-laureate, was last seen alive. He fell at the battle of Segesvár, a soldier in General Bem's armies, during the disastrous defeat at the hands of the Russians. His body was never recovered. But his cenotaph, aside from the innumerable physical monuments erected to his memory, remains to this day in the indestructible body of his poetry. His life, his work, and his death at the age of twenty-six, enshrined, not only for Hungary but also for the world at large, the full meaning of the Revolutions of 1848 and 1849. It is indeed a strange paradox that the first Hungarian poet to breach the borders of his country and join his name to the great ones of European and world fame, should also have proved the most eloquent voice of those years, and the most vivid personal embodiment of the ideal of poet, citizen, and soldier of the revolution.

Petöfi's participation in Hungary's war of independence was not the result of a momentary whim or caprice. It was the culmination of a rapid maturation that began with the usual personal rebellion of a young boy and was later translated into profounder national and social terms during the intense upheavals of the 1840s. He was a Jacobin even before he was aware of the meaning of the French Revolution, and a republican almost by nature. His rapid intellectual and poetic growth is all the more astonishing considering the economic and political backwardness of Hungary, semifeudal in structure, predominantly agrarian, with only a very small proletarian class and a weak middle class. Yet, the liberalizing winds and storms that swept over the rest of the continent had not left Hungary immune; the intellectual and political structure was visibly shaken. The urgency for change was being manifested in the activities of the more liberal nobility and middle class, particularly in the persons of Count István Széchenyi, a disciple of Jeremy Bentham, and the radical bourgeois lawyer Lajos Kossuth. In the literary field as well as in social and philosophical thought, the revolutionary romanticism of the rest of Europe, especially that of England, Scotland, Germany, and France, was also transforming the horizon. Not even the most stringent surveillance succeeded in keeping out the ideas of the Saint-Simonians and the other French and English utopian socialist thinkers.

Petöfi, too, was profoundly affected by these impulses. Storm was the element most persistent in his life—storms within him and without him. It was no accident that he was so intensely drawn to the life and poetry of Shelley, whose "Ode to the West Wind" might well epitomize the Hungarian poet's feeling and being. His literary banner was also inscribed with the names of Shakespeare, Scott, Byron, Heine, Victor Hugo, Burns, and Béranger, as well as Schiller. He too was the storm-bird of that second wave of Romanticism with its social and political manifestations and its tangible realization as words and deeds. Symbolically, one might say that his death on the battlefield in 1849 marks the death of both Romanticism, particularly its more utopian aspects, and the Revolutions of 1848–1849.

He came of humble parents. He was born Sándor Petrovics (he later Magyarized the name to Petöfi); in Kiskörös, county of Pest, the son of a butcher and a housemaid of the Protestant Evangelical faith. István Petrovics, the father, became comparatively prosperous, but suffered serious reverses in 1838 from which he never recovered. The parents' ambitions for their gifted child knew no bounds; the father in particular promised himself a son who would rise to an honorable and remunerative bourgeois career, bolstered by a good education. Alas! he was to be sadly disenchanted; no school or gymnasium could keep the boy bound, whether at Pest or Aszód! How could his parents have known that they had bred a bird of passage—an eagle, in fact, who was never to find a true resting place?

The boy wanted to be a poet and an actor! An actor above all! While a student at Aszód—he was then only fifteen—the urge to join the theatre proved irresistible, as did a young local actress. Sándor Petöfi requested a release from the gymnasium director, who, as might have been foreseen, immediately notified the boy's father. The poet later recalled the incident most graphically:

> My teacher (God bless him!) felt it incumbent to report my plans directly, before they could be realized, and wrote to a man who possessed the praiseworthy quality, strangely enough, of hating the theatre. This remarkable person was none other than my father, who, like all good fathers, did not wait long before coming to the rescue of a son who was hell-bent for perdition. His paternal counsel, in evidence thereafter for weeks on my back and other portions of my mortal frame, actually dissuaded me from my godless project.[1]

For a time he was locked up in his room, and it was there and then, as he confessed in a poem written in 1847, that he made his first vow: He would have but one goal in life—to war on tyrannical power![2]

During the rest of his life he was never to blunt the sharp edge of that decision, nor to betray his vow.

What could one make of such a character? He turned itinerant actor, vagabond, wandering scholar, and even soldier! And poet, too. His father gave him up, and after a while refused to come to his support. His mother grieved, loved him and forgave him.

His fascination with the theatre remained a lifelong obsession, one which those who have been close to the stage can easily understand. Here an imagined and imaginary world turns life into poetry and romance; The wizardry of stage lights, props, costume, makeup, actors, gossip and intrigues effects a magical transformation the moment the curtain rises. So it appeared to the heated imagination of Sándor Petöfi, even after he had observed and been the victim of its more drab and miserable aspects. Nothing would wean him from the illusion that he was born to be a great actor. Repeated failures rarely daunted him; he tried and tried again, failed and failed again. All this was a portion of that errant search to find himself; and he endured great hardships during the six years in which he wandered about, poor, too often disappointed, sometimes even desperate; finally even volunteering for army service as a private (in the Austrian army no less!), fitted neither spiritually nor physically to endure the torments and humiliations of that military establishment. Fortunately, he had within him another gift that he had begun to cherish, the gift of poetry. Reluctantly, he at last abandoned the Thespian *fata morgana* and, having succeeded in obtaining a discharge because of his physical condition, began seriously considering a career in literature.

Deeply shaken, desperate, and needy, even now he thought of acting as the only salvation. He was already twenty-one.

> I stand on the brink of a frightful abyss [he wrote to his friend, Szeberényi], and I must cross it. In doing so, I may be breaking the hearts of two people (my parents). But I cannot help myself. Dear friend, I must be an actor! There is no other way out for me. ... To become an actor—and for the third time! ... My parents cannot support me. But let us see what fate destines for me ... I need hardly tell you that it is not my aim merely to try to earn my living ... I have a much higher goal, of which I will never lose sight. I burn

with the ambition of being an artist, a poet. For long ago it was predicted of me that I was not born to be a nobody. *Aut Caesar aut nihil.*[3]

He could not have been aware in those years of wandering, as he roamed the Hungarian backlands and towns, the *pusztas*, meeting gypsies and peasants, hobnobbing with impoverished actors and itinerant workmen, what a rich gold store he was mining for his future craft. He absorbed living and inanimate nature; time and again he returned to his homeland—the "Lowlands"—his native regions between the Danube and the Tisza. Meanwhile, even in his most miserable period of military service, he composed poetry.

Often he was despondent; sometimes despairing, but never for a moment did he lose the faith that he was destined for a glorious future. His poems had already begun to appear in various journals. He was making friends among writers and editors; he had established a close relationship with the future novelist (now still nourishing the hope of becoming a painter), Mór Jókai. He had become reconciled with his father, now an impoverished innkeeper, to whom he read his convivial drinking songs, and who still shook his head at the benighted professions his son was following—poetry and acting! His mother needed no greater persuasion than the return of her wandering boy. She had faith in him, no matter what! Had she not, as he was later to write in a beautiful poem, prophesied that a dream of his meant he was destined to a long life? And had he not in the same poem assured her, as he envisioned an early death for himself, that he was destined for the immortality of a poet?[4]

In the winter of 1843–1844 he was in Debrecen, once more engaged by an acting company, and once more achieving exemplary failure. He was ill; a poor woman, the theatre's ticketseller, took care of the penniless actor. His only wealth consisted of sheafs of poems. When he was partially recovered, he made his way to the city of Pest on foot.

> For six years [he wrote] I was abandoned by God and man, a vagabond. For six years I was pursued by two dark shadows, misery and spiritual torments—from the time I was sixteen, till I was twenty-two … It was my last chance. I was overcome with despair. I went to see one of Hungary's greatest men, with all the trepidation of a gambler staking his last coin on a card—Life or Death! And this man, to whom I owe my life, to whom the fatherland must also be grateful if ever I have been or will be of use to it—this man was Vörösmarty.[5]

Mihály Vörösmarty was at that time Hungary's foremost poet. Twenty-three years older than Petöfi, he was in many respects the Victor Hugo of the Hungarian romantic movement. The author of numerous epics and narrative poems, he had been fired, like so many of his European contemporaries, by the events of 1830 in France and elsewhere in Europe. He was revolted by the repressiveness of the atmosphere under the Austrian autocracy. In 1836 he had composed a poem, "The Summons"—"*Szótat*" —which became a second national anthem. In the cause of the Polish struggles he had written a fiery and celebrated ode, "The Living Statue," "*Az elö szobor.*"

Vörösmarty had already before this taken note of Petöfi's gifts, and now he generously bestirred himself in bringing about the publication of his first volume of verse.

Petőfi versek—The Poems of Petőfi—appeared in 1844, and though they did not meet with immediate fanfare or acclaim, they were soon recognized as constituting a turning point in the history of Hungarian letters. The year also became a crucial one in Petőfi's life and creation.

With this volume Petőfi was joining the company of the great Romantics, joining in that massive choral symphony of which Wordsworth and Coleridge, with their *Lyrical Ballads*, Heine with his *Buch der Lieder*, Byron, Leopardi, Shelley, and Robert Burns constituted the eloquent voices. He had many affinities with Burns. Like the Scottish poet he could be an excoriating satirist, at other times a delightful humorist. Like Burns, Petőfi had that ardent love of nature, animals, landscape, and simple people; feelings for the "outcasts" of society, the tippler, the beggar, the horse thief. Both harbored a passionate love of their country and hatred of clerical as well as political and social oppressors. Like Heine, from whom Petőfi had also learned, the Hungarian poet could sing sweetly, laugh bitterly, and compose love poems. Balladry and folk song were a part of him. Like Heine and the tragic Austrian poet Lenau, whose works he admired, he could also write of the soul's self-division. Like Alfred de Musset he expressed something of the *mal du siècle*, but unlike the unhappy French poet, he knew how eventually to transcend it. He was able to fuse all these elements, the individual with the national, the national with the universal, so as indeed to become not only Hungary's national poet, but also the poet of Europe and the world.

Physically he was a slender reed that could be bent but never broken. And his spirit was like that too. We see him as he appears in the painting by his friend Soma Orlai-Petrich in 1844, with that remarkable chiseled face, deep-set eyes, so penetrating and intense, a fine mouth—altogether a striking picture. From a contemporary Hungarian, who was to become one of his early translators into German, we obtain a somewhat heightened, but none the less vivid portrait, two years later. Here is how K. M. Kertbeny saw him in 1846:

> One evening I sat once more in the elegant quarters of the poet Bakody, in the midst of a cloud of smoke through which it was impossible to descry my nearest neighbor. Casually I leafed through a pile of newly published books of our literature, and I chanced on a volume entitled, *Versek. Irta Petőfi Sándor.* Hastily I glanced at the poems, but soon my eyes became fixed on the pages ... "His name is Petőfi?" I asked of a young man sitting near me, who had been introduced to me, but whose name had then escaped me. I was struck by his characteristically noble bearing. He might have been around twenty-three, with a clearly defined, bony, but healthy-looking face, somewhat bronzed, with black, curly hair; he was of slight stature, but of an elastic frame; his hands were fine, but muscular ... He was scrupulously dressed in the national Hungarian style, with a jaunty cap topped by a full-blown rose! I repeated my question, and he spoke: "This little poet is the bad, dissipated son of a decent, honorable father, a master-butcher, in the Lowlands, and Petőfi never came to anything really, whether in trade, or as a young, roving actor, or as a common soldier. And here too, at the university, he will do no better, you may rest assured!" I grew heated, and began berating our Philistine generation for failing to know its true prophets. My interlocutor grew more and more amused as I proceeded, and when I asked scornfully, "Surely *you* don't write this kind of poetry?"—he replied, "I? Unfortunately yes. As a matter of fact I wrote these! I am Sándor Petőfi."[6]

He was like all young romantics; now on the heights of ecstasy; now in the depths of depression. When he exulted, his heart was ready to embrace the world. One winter day, he wrote,

> If my cheer could bring forth seedlings,
> I'd scatter them on snow-decked field,
> And wintry snow-field soon would be
> One single rose-bush.
>
> And if my heart were the sun on high,
> I'd stand it on the heaven's expanse,
> Its rays would surely spread their warmth
> Over all the earth ...[7]

He could not forget the theatrical world, he continued to mourn his departure from it. Bound to a journalistic desk, he remembered the "roses" of those days, which though plucked sometimes at the expense of pain, had no equal in the world—that romantic, beautiful heaven—now lost to him, but not, he prays, forever.[8]

He was also learning a great deal about politics. He became an abstractor of parliamentary debates and addresses in Pressburg, and had occasion to see and hear the outstanding statesmen and leaders of Hungary, including the brilliant and fiery Kossuth. His range of understanding widened; his sense of national humiliation and subjection was exacerbated. He, too, thought back on the heroic days of Hungary's noble liberators, like Árpád and Lehel.

> Oh, torpid age, in which I live,
> What glories can the poet chant?
> And were there such—what would it help?
> When tongue-tied word can scarcely sigh?[9]

Often he turned to his beloved Lowlands, and like Wordsworth in the Lake Country, sought the "tranquillity" and restoration of Nature there. He recognized the turbulence within himself, and rejoiced in it. And how could he have expected, in times like his, to attain placidity of soul?

> Reason proposes [he wrote], and the heart disposes. Just as God is so much more powerful than man, so is the heart mightier than the reason ... It is frightful to observe how my heart ordains and rules over me. It is in truth a despot, or rather a devout, kind-hearted father who can and will counsel, but will not command. I am overjoyed that it is so. A human being like that can be very unhappy, but only such a being can be truly happy.[10]

But now he had at last made his decision. He would live by the pen, no matter what might happen. No poet of Hungary could survive merely by writing poetry; journalism and hackwork would eke out the meager income that verse sometimes brought in. But the world was too full of stir and excitement; history was in the making; he would tolerate no compromises. He had so much to say, so much to give. He was at the full-tide of creation. He wished to thunder to his countrymen, and he did. He wished to sing. The enraged spirit within him lashed out against oppression and tyranny; the censorship inhibited him. Toward the end of 1844 he wrote a savage diatribe in verse against kings. Humanity, he cried, has now grown to maturity. It no longer needs the toys and baubles of kingship. Now is the time for the princelings to descend from their thrones and abjure their crowns. If not—then, the poet warns, we will do it for them! But let them beware that their heads do not accompany their crowns. The thunder that resounded in Paris will soon be heard here too, and then we will be like wild beasts, and with your blood we will write on the canopy of heaven that the world has really come of age!—Needless to say, the poem had to wait some years before seeing the light ...

But he never lost his sense of humor and playfulness. He could caper and disport himself. No sooner was his first volume of poems out, than he set to work on a folk epic of a romantic and semi-comic nature, yet with that strain of seriousness that was always companion of his lighter moments. The poem was *János Vitéz*, a romantic pastoral of the love of shepherd János and the peasant girl Iluska, and their ill-fated separation brought about by the lover's carelessness—for as he was kissing the delicious damsel, he lost a number of his sheep and was driven away by his master. Iluska too suffers from the malignity of a witch-like stepmother. Many are the strange things János encounters, many the strange feats he performs in his wanderings. He rescues the French king's daughter from the Turks and nobly declines to marry her, for he has his own Iluska waiting for him at home. Alas! how should he know that while he was away, she had died? Brokenhearted on his return, he plucks a flower from her grave— and is off again. Finally he reaches the land of the fairies, and there—wonder of wonders!—he is reunited with his love; for as we learn, the flower he has carried with him, when cast into the magic lake, restores her to life! It is a tongue-in-cheek work, humorous and touching at the same time, a glorification of simple love and fidelity—a Hungarian pastoral eclogue.

Before finding his one great love, Petőfi had loved aplenty, and passionately. He had met with rebuffs because of his low estate, and had been thwarted by the death of the one who loved him. Like so many of the romantics, he too loved a very young girl who died (Novalis comes to mind), and whom he mourned in moving verses. At such times he fell into depression, raged at the world, saw its blackness, and regarded mankind as his enemy. He was sensitive almost to a pathological degree, reacted with extreme irritability to a slight or a criticism even from his closest friends, and was all too ready to explode. In one such mood he composed the poem of the "Madman"— "*Az őrült*"—who addresses humanity as follows:

> What's this? Why do you bother me?
> Away with you ...
> I'm set upon a great task,
> I weave a scourge—
> A scourge made of the sun's rays,
> To whip the world with—
> And then I'll laugh—when howl on howl
> I hear—as once you laughed
> When I howled ...
> When the fruit is ripe, it falls to the ground,
> Earth! you are ripe and must fall—

> I'll wait till tomorrow.
> And if by then no doomsday has come,
> I'll dig a hole deep into you,
> And fill it up with gunpowder,
> And wreck the world,
> Till it flies into the air.
> And then I'll laugh! I'll laugh!

He knew himself still self-divided, and compared his state to that of his world. His life, he mourned, was a "battlefield of sorrows and passions," and his Muse sang "half-madly." "And yet," he wrote, "this self-division is not altogether my own fault, rather that of the century. Every nation, every family, yes, every human being, is divided within himself ... Such is the century, and how can I be different?—I, the true son of my century!"[11]

But unlike many of his romantic contemporaries he did not long remain the child of sickly and frustrating despair. Aware of his own inner scissions—those that marked him the poet, the citizen, the lover—and the distinct claims each made with irresistible urgency, he sought to find the cement with which to bind them into a coherent and compact whole.

The times and his own life experiences were to come to his aid. He found the love he had been seeking, and the woman to love and love him, and he married her. And national and international events opened to him, and to his fellow-countrymen, new vistas, a new field of action, breaking the lethargy and the inertia and dejection that had prevailed for so long. ...

* * *

Júlia Szendrey was five years younger than Petőfi. He was then twenty-three. She was the daughter of a prosperous steward of the estates of Count Ludwig Károlyi. Petőfi was already a celebrated poet. They met in the fall of 1846—and fell in love. The poet's distinction counted for little in her parents' eyes: He was poor, his prospects uncertain. She had been brought up in comfort and was the center of an admiring group of well-to-do, upper-class wooers. Though not preeminently beautiful in the traditional sense, Júlia Szendrey was a very sensitive, high-strung and compelling person and, though young, of a determined character. She loved and wrote poetry, read greatly, and was a most passionate devotée of the novels of George Sand. She was equally excited by Petőfi's poetry. The father objected to a son-in-law without a tangible future: though he liked the poet personally, marriage was something else. The girl, under domestic pressures, wavered for a while. Petőfi's moods and feelings responded accordingly. He demanded of the father that he attend to the high claims of love. The girl was courageous, and she was deeply in love. She knew she was entering upon a perilous journey—upon life with a genius driven by extreme passions and impulses. The father would not say yes, but he did not stand in his daughter's way. He refused to attend the wedding, however, which took place in September 1847. Szendrey and Petőfi remained enemies to the end ...

The lovers were ecstatic. Petőfi's poetry soared, along with his emotions. Only the poetry was controlled.

"Why, oh why, Lord, did you make the human breast so narrow?" he wrote. "It cannot contain all my bliss, and I am forced to waste the greater part of it in tears! ..."[12]

Like the hero of his own folk tale, *Mad Stephen—Bolond Istók*, a kind of Hungarian Till Eulenspiegel, the wanderer Petőfi found a home and love at last. Had he also found perfect serenity, he would not have been Sándor Petőfi. The happy couple settled in Pest, in quarters far removed from the spaciousness and luxuries that Júlia had enjoyed in Erdőd. Mór Jókai, the poet's friend, has left us a picture of their home life:

> We had an apartment in common, consisting of three rooms ... one of them mine, the other our common dining room, the last that of the Petőfis—their writing-room, bedroom, and reception—all in one—Helicon and Vaucluse at the same time. The furnishings were simple, the most valuable portion consisting of the library, with precious, engraved editions of Béranger, Victor Hugo, Heine, the history of the Girondists, Shakespeare, Ossian, Byron, Shelley ... On the walls were the outstanding figures of the French Revolution, among them not only Madame Roland, but also Charlotte Corday. That was their only luxury ... Our sole amusement was the theatre. Petőfi and his wife never attended the opera, made almost no visits, nor received any. In their apartment there was no piano, no flowers, no singing bird.[13]

Petőfi's revolutionary pantheon also included Cassius, William Tell, Camille Desmoulins—and he hoped that he might prove himself their worthy heir.[14]

His emotional life was now deepened; he was uplifted by his love and strengthened in his faith in himself as a person, a lover, and poet. He gained greater assurance, spoke more confidently as Hungary's and humanity's poet. The times were soon to provide him with another longed-for vocation—that of warrior.

In 1846, after having overcome a temporary depression, he composed a personal testament of faith, "Fate, Open for Me a Field,"—"*Sors, nyiss nekem tért*"—

> Oh, Fate, grant me a field of action,
> That human bliss I multiply,
> That not in vain this sacred flame
> Within my bosom unused die.
>
> There burns the flame, God's own gift,
> Till every drop—a red-hot glow,
> Oh grant that with each pulsing motion,
> I joy, and hope, and love may sow.
>
> How gladly would I speak in deeds!
> Not with an empty word, that lulls!
> Though my reward be a new cross
> Upon an ever new Field of Skulls!
>
> To perish for the weal of Man,
> What blessed death! What blissful peace!
> Better than all joyful life
> That wilts, and dies in unused ease.

> Fate, please declare: "Yes, you shall die,
> A blessed death!"—And I—
> With my own hands will carve the Cross
> On which to die![15]

More than ever he was also filled with a love of the countryside and his familiar haunts. To his beloved river, Tisza, he dedicated one of his loveliest lyrics. Standing on the shore, he contemplates the winding waters. It is sunset, summer eve ...

> *Nyári napnak alkonyulatánál*
> *Megállék a kanyargó Tiszánál ...*

He stops at the point where the Tur rushes into the Tisza as on to a mother's lap, and the dancing fairy rays on the water's surface sound like the jingle of spurs; the cut swathes spread out like the lines of a book, and a peasant woman is dipping her pitcher in the stream. Motionless he stands, stunned by all this, in a "deep intoxication." To his friends in a tavern he defends the river Tisza. It is so "meek"! But only two days later, storm signals ring out, and the "meek" Tisza has turned into a roaring torrent that threatens to swallow the whole world![16] For was he not himself like the Tisza—now seemingly subdued, but ever and anon ready to break out and overflow the banks and overwhelm all around him? Júlia knew that whoever bound himself to the poet was making a compact to live the unexpected, the storm-tossed, the ever restless ...

She was also aware how deep was the tie that moored her husband to the fate of his country. Had he not already confessed, "*Szabadság, szerelem!*" "Liberty! Love!" It was his impassioned watchword. "These two I need, for my love I will sacrifice life, for liberty I will sacrifice my love." She understood, and accepted the challenge. She did not know how soon she would be put to the test.

The smouldering fires of liberal opposition in the Hungarian parliament soon burst into flames. Like all the rest of Europe, Hungary too underwent a severe economic crisis and experienced serious agricultural failures. In the wake of such European youth movements as "Young Germany," "Young Italy," it was natural that there should also arise a "Young Hungary." Petöfi and his associates organized in 1846 a "Society of Ten," along with János Arany, Mór Jókai, Pál Vasvári, and many university students. In the pages of the journal *Eletképek*, they preached a radicalization of literature and political life more inclusive than that proposed by liberals. Oppositional elements in Parliament issued demands for reforms, such as equality before the law, taxation of the nobility, liberation of serfs, freedom of the press. It might be added that 1847 was the year in which Hungary built her first railroad. Two worlds clashed. Petöfi hailed the advent exultantly.

In January 1847 he addressed an impassioned invocation to his fellow poets to meet their responsibilities to the nation and themselves. Make an end, he pleaded, to personal laments. Do you not know that poets are the pillars of fire ordained by the Lord to lead the people into the promised land of Canaan?

> Forward then, whosoever is a poet,
> Through fire and water let him march,
> And a curse upon him who with poltroon hand

> Flings down the people's banner, or hangs back,
> To rest in coward sloth,
> While others toil and struggle.
> False prophets, they who lure and shout,
> "The Promised Land is here!"
> A lie! …
> When all alike from the bourne of plenty
> Share in the goods the world contains,
> When equals at the table of justice
> Take their place with equals, Then—
> When through the windows of our homes
> The light of Spirit shines on all,
> Then—we can say, "Halt! Here we stay,
> For Canaan's here!"[17]

He had always been haunted by the idea of Death, and it is not surprising that in moments of highest exultation he should be shadowed by Death more than ever. A strange and pitiful cry is wrung from him as he contemplates Love and Death. Not long after his marriage he composed the poem "At the End of September":

> In the valley the garden flowers are still in bloom,
> Before my window the poplar is still green,
> But do you not see the winter-world approaching?
> Snow has already covered mountaintops.
> Yet in my heart young midsummer flames,
> Lush spring is there with its scented flowers,
> But see! Already autumn's grey has tinged my hair,
> And winter's frost has already touched my brow. …

He envisions his own death, and what might happen thereafter …

> And if one day you cast aside the widow's veil,
> Then plant it a dark banner on my tomb,
> And I'll arise at midnight from the shadows,
> And bear it with me down into the grave,
> To dry my scalding tears of pain and sorrow,
> For one forgetful of a deathless faith,
> And bind the searing wounds of steadfast heart,
> That loved, and loves, and will forever love.[18]

But he could not long remain couched in such sombre thoughts. Like his river Tisza, almost overnight all of Europe was swept by the floods of revolution. First, in Italy. It was in January 1848, and Petöfi, in a mood of incredulity and exultation, in a kind of Shelleyan paean, celebrates the passing of winter and the coming of spring— the death of tyranny and the coming of freedom. His heart was now full of Europe, as one by one the countries resounded with the clash of arms. Italy, which had seemed to be crawling in the mud, now witnessed the resurrection of Brutus and no longer bent the knee to "those dwarfs." "Oh God of Freedom," he chanted, "these are your warriors; come, help these men of glory in their need!"[19]

February 1848: Paris! March 1848: Vienna! Berlin! Suddenly, it seemed to him that the "dead letters" of French Revolutionary history had "come to life," within him and in the world outside. "So I waited for the future," he wrote, and,

> It happened! Suddenly the heavens crashed down to earth, and the future became the present! ... In Italy a revolution had broken out!. ... In Paris, Louis-Philippe was driven from the throne, like the money-changers out of the Temple of Jerusalem ... France was a republic! ... *Vive la république!* I cried out, and stood mute and frozen, yet burning like a pillar of fire ... Trembling and out of breath I reached home ... The flames of revolution were now licking Germany, shooting out all around, and finally touched Vienna, yes, Vienna! ... Shall the Revolution begin without me?[20]

No, he could not conceive a Hungarian revolution without his participation! Soon he was in the midst of it. But he also found time for poetry.

> Dear Overlords, Honorable Gentlemen!
> How are you?
> Are your necks twitching a bit?
> Cravats of a new mode are being made for you ...
> Remember, how we prayed to you—
> Look, we said, we are human beings—
> Do not begrudge us the little sunlight—
> So we prayed—but your ears were deaf ...
>
> We were beasts, you thought, and said,
> And now the beast is having his day.
>
> You millions in your huts awake!
> Seize hayforks, spades, scythes! And away!
> A thousand years now cry: "Revenge!". ...
>
> But no! We shall be nobler and better far
> Than you. For "People" is a title high,
> Noble as God—not made for mockery ...
> Come to us, you noble Lords,
> And take our hands, and brothers all,
> Abjure your rank and titles!
> But do not shirk—the time is short—
> And then—may the Lord God
> Be gracious to you![21]

And a portion of the upper classes did indeed participate in the early stages of the Hungarian movement for liberalization and partial independence. They represented an indispensable element in a country still so undeveloped economically and politically as Hungary, with an insufficiently strong or informed middle class, a depressed and degraded, though large, peasantry, and a small proletarian population. That such a coalition could not long continue, in view of the sharpening differences brought about by the momentum of revolution and the radicalization of the masses, was not obvious at first. But the speed of events soon carried Petöfi as well as many others far beyond the limitations, compromises and accommodations eventually proposed, and even achieved, by the more conservative elements.

Now, on March 15, he was in the van. He became one of the leaders of the student and popular movement. He was one of the signers of a proclamation prepared by the oppositional forces, setting forth demands for a free press, a responsible ministry in Budapest, a national guard, legal equality of religion and taxation, the freeing of political prisoners, and the abolition of feudal inequities. With Jókai and other leaders, he commandeered a press and saw to the printing of the Twelve Point Proclamation, as well as his own newly composed National Song. These were ready before thousands of demonstrators, before an assembly of the "people"—such as Petőfi had dreamed of and hoped for—amid thunders of approving shouts and hurrahs. The crowds heard the poet reciting his own lines: *Talpra magyar, hí a haza!*

> Rise Hungarians, for your land
> Calls to you, the hour's at hand ...
> Brighter far than chains, the blade ...
> Where our gravestones stand one day,
> Sons of sons shall kneel and pray. ...

What followed became history. The excited crowds betook themselves from their several gathering places to the city prison to free the courageous writer Táncsics. At last Hungarians had achieved freedom of speech and freedom of the press, both celebrated by Petőfi in appropriate poems.

Threatened on all sides, the panic-stricken Emperor Ferdinand of Austria, King of Hungary, soon yielded and granted in part the demands of the Hungarians. At the same time his camarilla and generals were preparing for a counteroffensive against the revolutions as soon as the time was ripe. In Hungary there was no lack of counterrevolutionary activity on the part of those who sought a compromise or feared the expansion of the revolutionary wave. Petőfi, ever alert and now a political figure, offered himself as a candidate in the parliamentary elections, but was defeated by adroit maneuvers and terrorist tactics of the conservative opposition.

But the world was in flames! "A Mighty Sea Has Risen"—"*Föltámadott a tenger.*" In masterly lines Petőfi celebrated the exhilarating upsurge which to many like him appeared irresistible. "The ocean of mankind," he wrote in that poem, is dancing "a wild reel," roaring out its music, for it is the people "at play!" Ships are driven hither and thither; many are crushed. "Know and write it on the heavens as lessons never to perish: Though the galleys ride the water, the water is master still!"[22]

He was a republican, and he wanted a republic. He viewed with trepidation the compromising activities of the Hungarian Parliament. The situation was becoming more critical every moment. On September 11, 1848, the Croatian leader General Jelačič began the invasion of Hungary. In the face of this threat, the conservative-liberal leader Count Batthyány gave way to the more radical Kossuth. A national army was formed. The murder of the Austrian imperial commissioner Lamberg in Budapest amounted to a declaration of war. The die was cast, and war with Austria was on. On September 29, 1848, Jelačič's forces suffered a decisive defeat at the hands of the Hungarians and were driven back toward Vienna. On October 3, the Austrian government declared war on Hungary. In the same month, the October Revolution broke out in Vienna, soon to be crushed. On the 31st, Vienna surrendered to General Windischgrätz.

During those months of almost unsupportable tension, hopes, dejection, elation and despair, Petöfi never relaxed his activities, political or literary. During June and September 1848 he composed a rhapsodic epic, *The Apostle*, a *confessio fidei* that may well be considered both a culmination and a "recessional" coda to the republican revolutionary poetry of 1848 and 1849. There was something mystical about Petöfi's republicanism, with its touches of Hegelianism.

> I am a republican [he wrote] out of religious feelings. Monarchists do not believe in the development, the progress of the World Spirit, or they wish to stop its course. That is atheism. I, however, believe that the World Spirit unfolds from stage to stage. I see him develop. I see the path he follows. He moves slowly, one step may even take a hundred, sometimes a thousand years. Why should he hurry? He has time enough; eternity is his. And now once more, he is raising his foot, and is taking another step—from monarchy to republic. Shall I stand in his way that he may curse and annihilate me with his reproachful gaze? No! I fall down before him, as he utters his blessing over me. I rise. I take hold of his sacred robe, and I follow in his glorious footsteps.[23]

The Apostle of Petöfi's poem is a modern Prisoner of Chillon—a tormented martyr of Freedom, a visionary whose immediate defeats and despairs never quench his ultimate hopes of salvation. While not autobiographical in its details, it is in its ideational content. Petöfi's hatred of kings and emperors was almost pathological: regicide was close to his heart. Neither his own education, his extensive reading, his own history nor that of his country offered him the full possibilities of understanding the larger issues of social revolution, such as the liberation of the masses through their participation as masses, class-conscious and militant—theories which were then being formulated with greater precision in France, and particularly by German radicals.

But he had a keen, native sense of history and historic urgencies and needs. Where he might have fallen short intellectually, his feelings guided him aright. Through his poetic genius and insight, by virtue of his high notion of the poet's vocation, he proved himself the spokesman for the nation, the people, and the age. He possessed the inestimable capacity of condensing the explosive emotions and thoughts of those around him—and of the "people"—into pregnant lyrical speech, in language at once poetical, pure, and accessible. In the best sense of the word he was Hungary's folk-poet; and many of his poems became folksongs or national hymns. In addition, he stood before his people not only as a man of words (high honor indeed!), but also as a man of deeds, fulfilling like a number of his great contemporaries the role of poet-thinker and poet-doer, the role of Shelley's "unacknowledged legislator" of human history. The nineteenth century was the last of the centuries to raise and duly honor the literary figure as a great moral force, to deem the poet a "hero" of the age, and to furnish preeminent exemplars in writers such as Mickiewicz, Victor Hugo, Tolstoy and, not least, Petöfi.

The tragic-heroic protagonist of *The Apostle* is named Sylvester (that is, New Year's Day)—the day, parenthetically, on which Petöfi himself was born. He is a foundling, a child of nowhere and nobody, raised in circumstances of wretchedness, crime, and beggary until he is "discovered" and set on the high road by a tutor of a genteel family where Sylvester worked as lackey to the young master. Sylvester is an Oliver Twist come to a profound self-consciousness of himself and his vocation. Enabled by the tutor's kindness to go to school and educate himself, he gradually becomes aware of the world around him and the degradation, the oppression, that prevails all about. Like young Petöfi, he makes his vow of dedication to freedom and service, noting, also like his poetic creator, that the World Spirit needs time to come to a full realization of himself, to achieve what Marx was to call a "reform of consciousness" in mankind. Sylvester meditates:

> World history! what wonders in that book!
> Wherein each man may read his own vision.
> One reads of surging Life, another of Death.
> The one she arms with shining sword and says:
> "Go, on to battle! No, it is not in vain
> In battling so, you fight for all mankind!"
> To the other: "It is in vain!
> Doff your armor—and take your rest,
> The world is doomed; misery is its lot.
> It was ever so, and will be so forever."

Sylvester comes to his own conclusion:

> Look at the grape! See what a tiny growth!
> And yet needs all the summer to ripen into fruit.
> And is not our own Earth, a fruit like that,
> Though larger far?
> And what eternities shall suffice
> For it to ripen?
> Ten thousand years, nay, even a million,
> But ripen it will and must in the end.

As the grape needs the sun to bring it to fruition, so

> Our earth too ripens in the light of sun,
> But all those rays are not of the sun,
> But of the human soul.
> Great souls are sunlight's rays ...

And he feels that he too is such a soul, such a ray of light, part of the infinity spreading before him, an iota, but a significant iota, in the advance of humanity.

> Well, now to work!
> My soul, go forth! in doing is your worth!

He pledges himself and will dedicate himself to the happiness and freedom of Humanity. He fulfils his vow. Disappointments beset him; hopes seeming for a moment about to be realized, are dashed. The people acclaim, then abjure him. He is pursued by misfortunes. The great light of his life, however, is the dedication and understanding of a woman—his wife. By means of a secret press he is finally enabled to disseminate his ideas. Apprehended, he is imprisoned for ten years. When finally liberated, he discovers that instead of having freed themselves, his countrymen are groveling before a king. In desperation he undertakes what he believes to be one last symbolic deed for his people—he attempts to kill the king. He fails, and is executed.

Had it all been in vain? No, says the poet:

> The craven generation aged and vanished,
> A new race rose, that blushed with shame
> When speaking of their fathers ...
> A new heroic race that cried, "Revolt!"
> And cast the chains, their parents' shameful heirloom,
> Upon the graves of those had made them theirs,
> So that affrighted by the mighty clamor,
> They too might feel their shame even in their grave!
> In their triumph they hastened to recall
> The Great and Saintly, who themselves enslaved,
> Yet knew to pronounce the word of Freedom,
> And for reward earned obloquy and death. ...
> And with the wreath of names so high and sacred
> They wove the coronals of joy and triumph,
> And hastened their remains to bear
> Into the Pantheon—for glory and for peace.
> But where to seek, and where were they to find them?
> Alas! at gallows' foot their bones had long decayed!

Such is the end of the poem. Here romanticism mingles with realism—the romanticism of the Roman liberator who with his dagger asserts freedom (Sylvester was to use a pistol); the realism of the man who understands the pace of history. And above all, the unquenchable hope that masters despair and dejection.

But not all the poems of the time are solemn chorales or political invocations. Side by side with *The Apostle*, and the numerous paeans to the approaching republic, to revolution, Petőfi also created those extraordinary and beautiful hymeneals, celebrations of the woman he loved, of domestic felicity and the triumphs of love. These call to mind the best of Elizabeth Barrett Browning's *Sonnets from the Portuguese*, and of Victor Hugo's poems. Petőfi writes,

> How shall I name thee,
> When quiet, shadowed with thought,
> My wondering eye perceives
> Your eyes as the evening star,
> As if never seen before ...
> The star,
> Each ray a flood of light and love,
> Streaming into my soul's deep sea—
> How shall I name thee? ...
>
> How shall I name thee?
> When the glowing rubies of your lips
> Touch mine,
> And our souls mingle,

> In flames of kisses,
> As day and night within the morning light,
> Dispersing time and place,
> And floods of immortality
> Bring blisses yet unknown—
> How shall I name thee?[24]

Or, in a similar vein, he seeks to find the birds with which to compare his Júlia, discovering in her the qualities of a goldfinch, a nightingale, and an eagle. Or, when already a soldier in 1848, he allows himself a brief reunion with his wife, who is already with child. He has exchanged, he says, his "lyre" for the sword; the golden star of poetry for the reddening northern lights of war:

> Scarcely had day dawned; and already night is here,
> Scarcely arrived—and already I must part,
> Scarcely "Welcome" had I said to you,
> And parting words were already on my heart;
> Farewell, my own, my soul, my life,
> May God be with you, beloved wife![25]

He was fortunate enough to live to see the first astounding victories of the Hungarians over the Austrians. He lived to see Hungary declared a republic, and the cities of Buda and Pest recaptured from the enemy. Unfortunately he was also destined to see Russian forces, sent by the Tsar at the frantic call of Emperor Franz Joseph, invade his country under the overall command of "butcher" General Haynau. It was apparent that his country was meeting an army twice its strength. He was fortunate, however, in dying before his country's disaster, the shattering of his hopes, and the bloody aftermath of the Revolution.

In 1849, Hungary stood alone. Kossuth issued a call to national resistance. He asked for help of other nations. None came. Petöfi appealed to his own people in the name of the "Liberal Party."

> We have no brother-nation, from whom we can expect help. We stand like the lone tree
> of the *puszta*. We can only rely on our own strength and on God. This will suffice to insure the honor and the life of the Hungarian nation forever.[26]

How proud he was of his father, who, aged and weak, joined the forces as a standard-bearer; and in a touching poem the son proclaimed his admiration for the man, soon to precede him to his grave, who was defending not his possessions, for he had none, but his fatherland!

The son joined the army, and in the very month of October, 1848, when it seemed as if the Viennese would indeed triumph in their revolution, he became captain of a *Honvéd* battalion—the national army—at Debrecen. In December of that year, he put his wife and his newly born son into the safekeeping of close friends. In January 1849, he joined General Bem. This seasoned Polish soldier, veteran of Polish uprisings, of the Vienna revolt, was now on the battlefield once more, unshakable, immovable, as ever dedicated, an inspiration to his troops. Bem knew how to appreciate Petöfi's worth—the worth of the fiery, volatile, temperamental poet and soldier—and Petöfi in turn found in the old soldier another father. Bem tried hard to keep the poet out of the range of guns, but did not always succeed. He employed him as courier and liaison officer with the ministry of war, but the poet's pride and sensitiveness frequently resulted in disciplinary infractions that elicited reprimands from the higher authorities. But Petőfi was a true soldier.

On April 11, 1849, he reported from Mühlbach:

Yesterday Bem distributed the smaller decorations to the best men of his army. I too was honored to be among them. I was rewarded, beyond measure, not by reason of the distinction which I received, but by the manner in which it was conferred. With his own hand he fastened it to my chest, with his left hand, for his right hand was still in a sling. "I fasten this order with my left hand, which is the one nearest to my heart," he said, as he embraced me. All the world knows that I am far from modest, but this, by God, I did not deserve! I replied with such deep feeling, that, in recalling it, my soul shudders: "My General, I owe you more than even to my father. My father gave me life, you have given me honor."[27]

Three years before he had written:

> One thought alone torments me—that I lie
> Upon a featherbed to die!
> Slowly wither, slowly waste away,
> Flower-like; the furtive earth-worm's prey;
> Like a candle, slowly to be spent,
> In an empty, lonely tenement.
> No death like this, oh, Power Divine,
> No death like this, be ever mine!
> Let me be a tree through which the lightning flashes,
> Or tempest plucks by roots and smashes,
> Let me be a rock from mountain rent asunder,
> Hurtled to the gorge, by sky-earth shaking thunder ...
> Grant that I may yield
> Life on the battlefield,
> There let the blood of my youth flow from my heart,
> And when, from my lips, the last paeans start,
> Let them be drowned in the clatter of steel,
> In the roar of guns, in the trumpet's peal;
> And over my stilled corpse
> Let horse after horse
> Gallop ahead to the victory won,
> And I shall lie to be trampled upon.
> There let them gather my scattered bones,
> When once the great day of burial comes,
> With solemn, muffled drums for the dead,
> With sable-shrouded banners ahead,
> One grave for all! who died for thee,
> O sacred name, World Liberty![28]

On July 25, 1849, he was with Bem's forces in the Transylvanian region. Bem had 4,200 men and eight cannons. The Russian general Lüders had 18,000 men and forty-six cannons. At first successful in their onslaughts on the enemy, Bem's forces soon fell into a trap, as concealed Cossacks executed a pincer movement against him. Petöfi was last seen on July 31, 1849. He fell with hundreds of others in the battle of Segesvár. On August 13, the Hungarian armies surrendered at Világos. Days of terror succeeded. On August 15, Heinrich Heine received K. M. Kertbeny's German versions of Petöfi's poems. Petöfi was now speaking to the world.

Of his last days and movements he spoke in a letter to his wife. It was dated Maros-Vásárhely, July 29, 1849:

My dearest, most beloved Julichka! I have just arrived here, after an uninterrupted journey of six days. I am tired. My hand shakes, so that I can hardly hold the pen ... I will describe my journey. We learned that General Bem had advanced his troops toward the Vltava River. We followed ... and found him at Bereck, on his return from the Vltava, where he had brought his fiery proclamation, and had thoroughly thrashed four thousand Russians with only one battalion. In Bereck he learned that our troops had been beaten at Szász-Régen, and frightfully scattered, so he galloped to restore order ... I met him at Bereck. I stopped beside his coach, and greeted him. He looked up, recognized me, and cried out, stretching his arms toward me. I jumped up, and fell on his neck, and we embraced and kissed. "*Mon fils, mon fils, mon fils,*" the old man said with tears. Those who were around asked Gábor Egressy, "Is that the General's son?" And now he is even kinder, more warm-hearted and fatherly toward me than ever. Today he told his other adjutant, "Please report to the Ministry of War, and be sure to use my exact words: 'My adjutant, Major Petöfi, who has resigned because of the shameful conduct of General Klapka, is again restored to the service.'" On the way he told me that he would provide living quarters here, in Maros-Vásárhely, for you, and that I was to bring you here. This is my dearest wish. But I dare not do it so long as we have not secured our position vis-à-vis the Russians, who are in the vicinity. They're only two miles away; our troops have driven them apart during the last couple of days like hens. But as soon as this place is more secure, it is the first thing I'll do, you may be sure. How are you, my dear adored ones! If only I could hear from you! If you could somehow manage to write a word or two, my angel! I'll let no chance go by to write you. Is my son still being breast-fed? Do wean him as soon as possible; teach him to talk, so that I may have a surprise. I kiss your souls, your hearts, a million times, numberless times, and remain your adoring husband, Sándor.[29]

On the last day he wrote what may well be called his own precious epitaph:

> I hear the lark again singing,
> Long forgotten song I hear,
> Sing, oh sing, spring's prophet,
> Sing your song, spring's herald!
> God! how my heart is eased by your song,
> After the battle's din—
> Like a cool mountain brook
> That bathes the searing wound.
> Sing, oh sing, little bird,
> Bring to mind that now a soldier,

A messenger of death,
I am a Poet too.
Memory and hope I see,
Rose trees blooming at the sound of your song,
Bending all their cool greenery,
Over my enraptured soul ...
Sing, lark, sing,
Your sounds awaken flowers,
And my soul and heart—now so bare,
Burst like your song into bloom.[30]

And at the same time, an epitaph for his country, abandoned to her agonies:

Europe is quiet again, quiet,
Stilled is the people's thunder,
Europe is quiet—oh, shame!
And Freedom's undone!. ...

My people: Raise up your head,
You are God's torch to light
All through this darkened night,
While others sleep.

For, if not for our light,
Blazing thoughout the dark,
Heaven might indeed believe,
The world's end had come.

Freedom, look down on us,
See how our people bleed,
Others scarce give their tears,
We—our life's blood.

Say, what more can we give,
Your blessings to deserve?
Remnants, we are the last—
Faithful—in faithless days![31]

2. Russia: Tsar and Serf—Taras Shevchenko

One night I strolled along the Neva's shore,
Lost in my thoughts. When suddenly I mused:
"If only slaves would scorn to bend the knee,
Then all these sorry palaces on Neva's bank,
Would not be standing, and men would look
On other men as brothers. But alas!
Behold the ruler sits enthroned here!
No ruler! For neither God nor demi-God
Now rules this world.

But only kennel-keepers lord it over all.
While we, their politic nobodies, weep,
Lickspittles we, we weep and wail our fate."

Such were my thoughts one night as I
Walked lost in musings along the Neva's bank.
When suddenly I was ware of eyes—two lights
That glared at me from one of Neva's isles!
The prison fortress of Saint Peter and Saint Paul!

Startled, I crossed myself and spat out thrice,
To drive the devil back. And I resumed my thoughts
Thus interrupted. And then went home.[32]

Thus Taras Shevchenko in 1860, three years after his return from a ten years' exile. In 1847 he had gotten to know the inside of the prison of Peter and Paul, its interior even more forbidding than its outside. And if he shuddered now, again a free man, it was with good cause.

He had not changed. Exile had tempered the steel of his character, hardened him, in fact; but had also filed his insights to a greater sharpness and understanding. His body had suffered. Those who saw him now, like the Princess Repnin, were shocked by this forty-three year old man who had aged so prematurely, lost his hair, and walked with the gait of a decrepit ancient ...

In his *Journal* for 1857, he had written in retrospect:

All this unspeakable grief, all kinds of humiliations and insults have passed, as if without touching me ... No part of my inner self has changed ... And from the depth of my heart I thank my Almighty Creator that He did not permit my terrible experience to touch with its iron claw my convictions, my shining child-like beliefs. Some things became brighter, more rounded, assumed more natural dimensions and appearance. But this is the result of the serenely circling old Saturn, and by no means the result of my bitter experience.[33]

Taras Shevchenko was no novice in misfortunes. Attending divinities that minister at the birth of serf-children are scarcely generous, and the privileges with which they endowed him were the normal ones: the doom of a life of suffering, oppression, humiliation, resentments. But fortunately, they made one exception: they also conferred upon him that unpredictable gift—not always the most grateful or happy one—of genius. It was his primal misfortune to be born a serf, the son and grandson of serfs, and to spend the first twenty-four years of his life in bondage. It was his happy fortune that in time his talent proved a juicy bait to tempt his master's greed and thus bring salvation to the young man. As for his servitude, it was neither simple nor single. He was born a Ukrainian or "Little Russian," of a subject nationality, almost a colony, ruled by Great Russia. He spoke Ukrainian, or Ruthenian, a vernacular belonging to the Slavic branch of languages but regarded by the dominant Russians as nothing more than a barbarous jargon. Even the enlightened Belinsky shared this prejudice. Like all oppressed minorities, the Ukrainians too, if they had not sworn total allegiance to the Russian ruler, boasted of an erstwhile independence as a state, boasted of ancient Cossack glories and victories until subjugated in turn by Poles and then Russians, and prayed and hoped for redemption. Now, as a result of numerous Polish and other partitions, one portion of the Ukraine belonged to Russia, the other to Austria. Gogol had romantically described the life of the Cossacks, but had given little thought to the national consciousness of the Ukrainians or their aspirations for independence. Those Ukrainians who were moved by national sentiments regarded "Greater Russia" as inferior in both culture and historic past as compared with their own former centers of civilization, such as Kiev.

Of course, these notions were as yet far from the consciousness of the little serf-boy born on the estates of Count Engelhardt in the tiny village of Morintsi, government of Kiev, two years after the Napoleonic invasion …

On his own body, in his spirit, he came to know the meaning of serfdom—of hard labor, beatings, degradations, hunger and sickness. His early "education" in such a school guarded him, in the future, from any illusions about the happiness and tranquility that surround the bucolic life. Of the so-called benefits that Nature confers upon her denizens he was a qualified witness. That extreme glorification of Nature and Nature's blessings, of which the Romantics were such fervent apostles and which was also, in part, Wordsworth's creed, Shevchenko would have scorned, had he known of it. He could scarcely have understood that poet's lines,

> One impulse from a vernal wood,
> May teach you more of man,
> Of moral evil and of good,
> Than all the sages can …

Wordsworth, of course, was saved from his own exaggerated naiveté by the corrective experiences of the French Revolution, so that he could also add the mournful reflection on "What man has made of man."

If Shevchenko did have an analogue in British literature, it would have been Robert Burns, whose poetry he knew and admired, and whose hard life paralleled his own in many respects, save that Burns was a peasant-farmer, nominally a free man, and Shevchenko but a piece of chattel.

Whatever the secret impulses that Nature through her "vernal woods" dispenses to her inhabitants, impulses that "moralize" the human being, they were hidden from the little serf in Kirilivka, the village to which his family had soon removed. He did not need to "return to Nature" to find truth; he was there to witness it and later to report it. With little flourish he wrote *finis* to the bucolic myth.

In 1850 (still in exile), he composed, like so many romantics, his brief autobiography. It was not the autobiography of a "romantic." Wordworth had his *Prelude: The Growth of a Poet's Mind*, Coleridge his *Biographia Literaria*, Goethe his *Dichtung und Wahrheit*. Shevchenko's Truth and Poetry were one:

> If you but knew, fine gentlemen,
> If you but knew where there are tears,
> You would not write idyllic songs,
> Nor praise the goodness of Heaven in vain,

Making a mock of our bitter dole.
How can you call that hut in the woods,
A tranquil paradise on earth?
Once in that cot I suffered griefs,
There it was I wept first tears,
I ask of God if there exist
In all this world an evil worse
Than in that hut—that Paradise!
No Paradise for me that village hut
Hard by the pond.
Here mother bore and swaddled me,
Sang to me, and wept for me,
And scalded me with her hot tears.
In that small wood, that Paradise,
I lived hell's woes, a bondman's child,
A slave to endless toiling, chained,
Not even time for prayers ...
And there it was my mother died,
Died in her youth of penury and toil.
My father too, amid his brood
(All small and naked)
Could stand his bitter lot no more,
And died a serf; while we, the young,
Like tiny mice dispersed among strangers.
I went to school—a water-carrier;
My brothers too were to slavery yoked,
Until the time when with heads sheared,
They were sent for soldiers.
And sisters, sisters mine,
What unkind fate awaits you, doves?
For sake of whom do you draw breath?
In serfdom your black hair will whiten.
In serfdom you will die![34]

Such was his school. Like other serfs, he might have lived out his life, gone for a soldier, and died worn out by work and sickness. Whatever he had of an education had been at the hands of ignorant and brutal priest-teachers, and of no value. But as a very little boy he had begun to display a talent for drawing and painting. One evening he was caught in the act of copying by candlelight, mercilessly thrashed by his young master (in fear of a fire). It was not his first beating, but none proved so providential. Young Engelhardt, as avaricious as any of his co-brother lords, saw a potential source of income in the young scamp, and set him to work with trained masters. Whatever poetic genius was stirring within him had not as yet become manifest. But there was no doubt he could draw and paint. From the little village of the Ukraine, young Vassily Engelhardt brought Shevchenko to Vilno, and then to Warsaw, to be taught. And then, in fear of the Polish uprising of 1830, the master fled to Saint Petersburg, taking his serf along with him.

For the first time Dame Fortune looked upon Shevchenko almost benignly. Here his talents impressed a number of prominent personalities, among them Karl Briullov, the most celebrated painter of the day, an academician famous for his giant picture of "The Last Days of Pompei," other artists, as well as the poet Zhukovsky. Since serfs were excluded from entering the Academy of Arts, these and other patrons devised a scheme for raising the 2,500 rubles demanded by Engelhardt for his chattel. Briullov would paint a portrait of Zhukovsky, which would then be auctioned off for that amount. On April 22, 1838, seven years after his arrival in the capital, Taras Shevchenko was declared a free man, and qualified for entrance into the Academy. His master Engelhardt was thus enabled to achieve immortality by virtue of his serf and the rubles expended to liberate him. Shevchenko was then twenty-four.

At the Academy of Art, under Briullov, Shevchenko prospered. But even more important than the school was the city itself, its intellectual and moral atmosphere, and the personalities he was thus able to meet, the books he could now obtain, the régime he could observe at first hand. He became a skilful painter, was in demand for portraits, painted classical subjects in keeping with the demand of the times, but also swerved aside to paint things and persons closer to his heart.

In letters, he was his own teacher. His range of self-education was amazing. He knew no foreign languages, but his native intelligence, his penetrating genius, enabled him to absorb and understand whatever he read, even in translations. He read and read: Rousseau, Victor Hugo, Béranger, Schiller, Heine, the Polish poets Mickiewicz and Kraśinski, Byron, Burns, Dante, the Greek classics. The intellectual atmosphere around him, for all its inhibitions, was vibrant with innovation. The 1830s had brought forth Pushkin's poetry and plays, Gogol's "Taras Bulba" and *The Government Inspector*, the works of Lermontov. The following decade proved no less inspiring, but much freer now that the numerous "circles" were playing such an important role in the cultural and political life of Russia. The amazed and ignorant household serf who had arrived in St. Petersburg in 1831 became in time an intellectual, a member of the "intelligentsia"—a serf consorting with members of the nobility, the gentry, the upper middle classes, students and professors!

He never lost his spirit of independence, nor his sense of inner dignity. He never forgot what he had been, nor those with whom he had once lived in common unfreedom and drudgery. He never lost sight of the Ukraine and its people—and he longed to return there. We do not know whether he ever became acquainted with any member of the Petrashevsky group or other revolutionary circles. But the current of new ideas swirled around him, inescapable. If he was not yet a "son" of the Decembrists, he would soon become one. His observant eye noted Tsar and commoner, and his burgeoning poetic talents reserved these for future expression.

Though many knew him for his paintings, few knew that he had also been writing verse; fewer would have predicted that the poet would far outdistance the skilful painter and in time emerge as Ukraine's first national singer.

In the poems he thought of himself as a Ukrainian "minstrel," or *kobzar*, playing upon the *kobza*, the popular stringed instrument. Hence he entitled his first collection of verse *The Kobzar*. The small book was published with the assistance of a well-to-do patron in 1840. As kobzar Shevchenko commenced his poetic career, as kobzar he would end his life.

With the great Romantics he shared the fervor of nationalism that pervaded the Western world, and he too spoke the poetry of national history, national spirit, national pride. But he spoke from the purview of a former serf; hence he sang the sorrows of his people—the peasant, the serf; raged against lord and master, the oppressor; mourned the humiliations and low estate of the Ukraine. Like the great romantic national poets speaking to their own subject peoples, he too endeavored to rouse his countrymen from their sense of hopelessness, of debasement, by recalling their past history and the Cossack glories as revealed in their wars against oppressor Poles and Russians. But the past did not withhold him from the present, which he knew so well. He knew from his own experience the fate of the serf—if male and young, destined to hard labor or endless soldiery; if young woman, to toil, enforced subservience to a male master, seduction, shameful motherhood, and miserable end; if bastard child, to the ignominy and mockery of a whole village. Such occurrences were too common to be "romanticized," and if the poet dwells on them time and again, it was because the sufferers appeared to have been forgotten by God.

His heart glowed with pride when he turned to the past history of the Ukraine, when he recounted, as in the epic poem *The Haidamaks*, the feats, often frightfully bloody, of Ukrainian heroes. Here he felt himself on native terrain. His imagination was fired at the recollection of the great Cossack and peasant uprising of 1768. He defied tradition by using his native Ukrainian, and boasted of it, throwing down the gauntlet to his Russian critics (as well as a number of his snobbish compatriots) who disdained such a barbarous "dialect" for literary uses ... Here he spoke with the accents of Robert Burns.

He was a celebrity. In his poems, readers recognized not only their native tongue, used with mastery, but also their native and popular folk-song and folklore. The verse forms too he had adopted from popular tradition.

"*Et ego in Arcadia fui.*" "*Auch ich war in Arkadien geboren.*" He too could boast of having been born in Arcadia. He too was a poet. He longed to return to his Ukraine, though he knew that it was no romantic Arcadia. After fourteen years of absence, he did go back. His songs and poems were known to many already. And written in their own maligned tongue!

> *Nashcho mieni chorni brovi,*
> *Nashcho kari ochi,*
> *Nashcho lita molodyi,*
> *Veseli, divochi?*
> *Lita moyi molodyi*
> *Marno propadayut,*
> *Ochi plachut, chorni brovi*
> *Od vitru liniayut ...*

Soon composers would set them, and the people would sing them.

> What avail my coal-black brows,
> What my coal-black eyes,
> What avail my maiden years,
> That so gay should be?

Years of youth will pass away,
Passing like the flowers,
Eyes are weeping, and the tresses,
With the winds will fade.
The heart aches. It's tired of life,
Like the captive bird.
What avails my beauty now,
If the joy's all gone? . . . . .[35]

He would sing of such forlorn maidens time and again, each time perhaps with greater tenderness, and later, along with the tenderness, anger and even savagery. Here in the Ukraine he was hailed. With the famous Ukrainian poet, ethnographer, and novelist Panteleimon Kulish, he would explore the historic sites, Cossack burial places and monuments. Here, too, he would be received by Prince Repnin, like himself a Ukrainian patriot, and his sister the Princess Varvara Repnin, somewhat older than himself, but not too old to fall in love. The Prince was once governor of Kiev, now in disfavor. The princess loved Shevchenko's poems, and even the poet himself; had he been a nobleman she might have married him. As it was, she welcomed him to her salon and read his poems, wept over them, or exulted.

He was like Antaeus. He needed the earth to feel his true strength. And the Ukraine exalted him, fired him, and broadened him. More than ever he became aware of the horrors that lay concealed under the outward veneer of the commonplace, everyday life.

In his earlier works he had arraigned the Poles for their past oppression of his countrymen. But now he saw that it was not Poland that deserved his execration, but Tsarist Russia. Yet he had also observed his own Ukrainian landscape more closely, and with wiser eye, and he noted that here it was the Ukrainian landlords themselves who were the worst exploiters of their own people.

The Academy of Art conferred upon him in 1845 the title and diploma of "Free Artist of the Academy." Once more he left St. Petersburg, to accept a commission to explore the ancient monuments of the Ukraine. More than ever he came into close association with men and women who were, like himself, deeply concerned for their country and eager for reform, especially of the condition of the serfs. If he was more fiery than most of his companions, and if, as was true, he was more effervescent, violent, and indiscreet in his onslaught on tsars and on Russia, they attributed it to his poetic temperament, and counseled moderation, at least in public. In private, they read with glee, often aloud, his manuscript poems, with occasional shudders at the poet's temerity; many of them could not forbear cheering. At last their own poet! From hand to hand his poems passed, particularly those the censor, if his eyes ever fell on them, would be sure to suppress and probably call to the attention of the Third Section.

No fear held him back. The three years between 1844 and 1847 proved most productive; he had in fact matured rapidly. But his temper had not cooled, nor had his voice softened. He who had been whipped as a boy and young man was now ready in his turn to scourge. But not out of personal resentment. His view, now enlarged, encompassed a great portion of humanity. He spoke now not only of Ukrainians enslaved; but of Russians enslaved, exiled, silenced; he scourged the oppressors wherever they were. Popular figures derived from folklore and folk poetry—the witch, the gypsy, the village idiot, or the holy madman—become symbolic of the new fervor that penetrates the poet with respect to the trials of common life. But it is in such longer poems as "The Dream," "The Caucasus," and "The Heretic" that the full rhapsodic fury of the rebel-poet erupts in red-hot volcanic lava. Taking such traditional devices as a dream or a vision of mountains or a heroic figure of another day, Shevchenko adapts these to his novel purposes—the indictment of tyranny and evil-doing on the part of the masters of the world. A dream carries him on a flight over the Ukraine, over Siberia, and to St. Petersburg. He is overcome by the beauty of his native countryside, and yet, he asks himself,

> My soul,
> Why are you so sad?
> My soul, in anguish,
> Why do you weep so bitterly?

> *Dushe moya,*
> *Chovo ti sumyesh?*
> *Dushe moya ubogaya,*
> *Chovo marno plachesh.*[36]

> Why do you grieve for things you do not see?
> When you cannot hear the sound of human tears?
> Then look and mark: For I am flying high,
> Above the swiftly-moving clouds.
> No rulers there, nor any penalties condign.
> No sound of laughter reaches, nor the cries of woe.
> But see: in that Eden you have now departed,
> Patched garments are stripped from backs of cripples;
> And so too their hides—for these the lord requires
> To shoe his princelings. And see yon widow on the rack,
> To pay her poll-tax. And her poor son, her only one,
> Her only child—torn from her to be sent for a soldier!

And in bitterness:

> Does God behind the clouds,
> See our ancient tears and anguish?
> Perhaps ... But helps our ills,
> Like the timeless giant mountains,
> That flow with human blood. ...

Once more he pursues his flight. He sights Siberia, hears the clank of chains, and sees emerging from the belly of the earth the exiled prisoners confined to the gold mines. Then on to St. Petersburg ... Looking on the busy and majestic city, the poet recalls the bloody sacrifices exacted by Peter the Great from the thousands of Cossacks brought by force to build the capital, who died of the cruel service. And now he sees the Tsar and the Tsaritsa, and their subjects and lackeys, courtiers, and petitioners, and the humiliations to which the latter are subjected. Here the poem lapses into painful burlesque. Here there is nothing less than *lèse majesté*. The Tsaritsa is a "dry mushroom," a "heron," and both she and her consort are "owls." The Tsar is a "bear" when he is in the presence of his subjects; but his true nature is that of a "kitten." But the full odium of tsarism is expressed in the obloquy heaped upon Peter the Great (and by analogy on all Tsardom) by the dead Cossacks:

> You slaughtered us, you stripped our skins,
> Of them made mantles; and sewed with our sinews
> New robes for your city. Gaze and wonder!
> See your palaces and churches! Savage hangman,
> Accursed forever!

It is doubtful if any other Russian writer had spoken in these terms. Shevchenko was staking his head. His friends, who thrilled to his lines, feared for him, and with justice.

In like manner the majestic heights of the Caucasus elicit not merely wonder and exultation at the beauty of the landscape and the exoticism of its population, but immediately brings to the poet's mind the image of Prometheus chained, of that glorious Titan whose figure had attracted innumerable poets of the age. Pushkin and Lermontov had rejoiced in the Caucasus, loved its strangeness, its otherworldliness, its wildness, its primitiveness. They saw it as a refuge from civilization. Byron had brought similar passion to the Alps, had seen in them an echo of his Promethean defiance of the world.

For Shevchenko, Prometheus, enchained on the Caucasus, gnawed by an insatiable vulture, was, as to Shelley, humanity itself, staunch, resolute, inflexible, suffering. But also humanity as the bearer of some impregnable "Truth" that would in the end be victorious. Shevchenko's Prometheus, though pain-racked, smiles in his mortal agonies. The vital word of God and Truth that is his to utter is the promise of Freedom to mankind. Yet Shevchenko is troubled: Where is God? When will the word of Truth awaken? When will the Lord, the weary One, lie down to rest and give the human spirit leave to live?

For these fantastic Caucasian heights, beautiful as they are, are also blood-drenched. The Russian conqueror has penetrated here, and with fire and sword has subjugated the native populations.

Ognenne morie! Slava! Slava!

"A sea of fire! Glory! Glory! Glory to hounds, and harriers, and trainers!" The Russians say: All we want is "your high mountains—that is all. The rest we have—both land and ocean!"[37]

In the long poem "The Heretic," the Promethean role is now filled by the celebrated historical figure of Jan Hus, the Bohemian reformer and martyr. Though he was burned at the stake, his word too, the word of "Truth" cannot be annihilated. For he too was destined to have a succession of "avenging angels."

There were other fiery poems of similar character, each of which may be characterized as a segment of a Ukrainian *Marseillaise*. In the circles where they were read and recited, they were regarded as such.

There was no doubt now. He was the revolutionary spokesman for the Ukraine. His own "Testament," composed in 1845, became a kind of national anthem.

Yak umru, to pokhovayet
Mene na mogli.
Sered stepu shirokov,
Na Vraini milyi ...

When I am dead, pray place my bones
High on a mound to be my tomb—
Amid the vastness of the steppe,
In my beloved Ukraine!

That I may look on endless fields,
The Dnieper and his craggy shores—
And hear his waters roar.

When far from my beloved land
The Dnieper bears the blood of foes,
I shall arise, leave hills and fields,
And soar to God and pray to him.
And till that day of freedom comes,
I'll own no God!

Bury me thus. And then arise!
Break at last your slavish chains,
And with the blood of enemies
Water the tree of liberty!

And when at last the day arrives,
When as brothers, free you meet,
Then with a gentle, peaceful word,
Recall that I have been.[38]

But Shevchenko's activities were not confined merely to poetry, to archaeological research, or to social gatherings. In 1846, when he settled in Kiev, he made the acquaintance of the prominent historian and Ukrainian nationalist, Mikola Kostomarov, author of the celebrated *Books of the Genesis of the Ukrainian People.* It was this book that formed the ideological basis for the establishment of the Brotherhood of Saints Cyril and Methodius, which he founded along with P. Kulish. The society was to be the means of fostering and developing an understanding of the need for a Pan-Slavic Union of nations and nationalities in a federation founded on the principles of Christian morality and ethics. Each of the states was to have equal status, self-determination and self-rule, and would be republican in character, on the model of the United States of America. Its program included the emancipation of the serfs, a strong and popular educational movement, and special attention to the native language. The society was, of course, secret.

Shevchenko was at home with the ideas of the Brotherhood, and as a matter of fact went far beyond them. Kostomarov reported in his *Autobiography:*

When I told Shevchenko of the existence of the Brotherhood, he immediately expressed his readiness to join it, but he did carry the ideas of the Society to extremes, a circumstance that led to numerous differences of opinion between Shevchenko and myself. He read a number of his unpublished works to me, which held me spellbound. I was especially impressed by his poem, "The Dream," that composition of Shevchenko's which remained unpublished, because the censorship would never have passed it. With genuine enthusiasm I read and reread the poem throughout the night. During the summer evening we sat for hours ... in our garden. There were endless conversations and discussions.[39]

Shevchenko was not really a member, and appeared at the Brotherhood gatherings infrequently; but his poetry and his sentiments were well known there. He was the Society's lyrical inspiration. When away from Kiev, he propagandized with his customary fervor. Perhaps with too great fervor, for he did not altogether approve of the Brotherhood's gentle Christian and peaceful programs for effecting the changes he and its members desired.

The Brotherhood met, talked, sang, and read poetry, and planned for a future confederation of Slavic states. Shevchenko's lines were frequently on their lips. How were they to know that there was a spy, a student, Petrov, who made it his business to eavesdrop on their talk? The inevitable happened. The members of the Brotherhood were arrested. So was Shevchenko, on April 5, 1847. He was sent along with the others to St. Petersburg, and imprisoned in the Peter-Paul Fortress.

So it was that the poems of the "Three Years" (1844–1847) were found on him, to incriminate him, as well as some letters, and additional information lodged against him by another Kiev student, Andruzky.

The subsequent inquiry did not produce evidence of the poet's membership. But the charges against him were heavy, not least that he had slandered the imperial house—so the ominous Count Orlov reported to the Tsar. In addition, he had lamented the enslavement of the Ukraine; insolently forgotten "his conscience and the fear of God," and called for an independent Ukraine! On May 26, he was sentenced to exile, as a "private in the Orenburg Separate Corps." And once again Tsar Nicholas's penchant for graciousness took the form of another prohibition: "under the strictest supervision" he was to be forbidden to write or to sketch.[40]

The members of the Brotherhood were also given severe sentences, ranging from years of solitary confinement in the detested Schlüsselberg prison, to years of exile. Kostomarov, from his prison window, saw on May 30,

Shevchenko being brought into the courtyard in his soldier's uniform. Smiling, he bade his friends farewell. I wept when I saw him. Smiling, he doffed his hat and entered the carriage. His face was peaceful and firm.[41]

The journey into exile was a long one. And finally prisoner and guards reached the distant city of Orsk and its fortress. Ten years of exile! "I was tortured, I was tormented," he wrote later, "but I did not implore pardon."[42]

Though forbidden to write or draw, he wrote and drew in secret. He made for himself tiny notebooks and slipped them into his boots. Here were to be found some of his most magnificent poems. His artistic talent procured him a minor respite from soldiery and torture. He was assigned to accompany an expedition to the distant Aral Sea region. He was to serve as draughtsman. So upon the hardships of the Orsk fortress and the solitude and brutality of the barracks, the attacks of rheumatism and scurvy, followed the no less arduous long journey, in parching heat and tormenting thirst. At least a change. When he returned to Orenburg, comparative relaxation alternated with new excesses of severity, transfer to other fortresses like that of Novopetrovsk on the Caspian Sea. His frequent appeals for relief, for remission of the sentence, addressed through a few of his friends at home, were all useless. Even the accession of the new Tsar Alexander II did not help. The general amnesty extended by the new Emperor omitted Shevchenko. The memory of his insults to majesty had not been extinguished.

When finally freed in 1858 he was already an old man. But he had not been crushed. In fact his indignation burned more fiercely than ever. His heart was heavy. He had been deeply hurt while in exile by the continued silence of his friends, who had not written to him in fear of recriminations. Chastened by his experiences, he was no longer ready to embrace hopes of an immediate political change, and his works now alternate between savage excoriations of tyranny, and rage at his countrymen's apathy and inertness. But he never ceased from a call to arms. On his return to St. Petersburg he came into contact with a new generation of radicals like Chernyshevsky and Dobrolyubov. His friendships grew in number. His reputation was never higher. He was particularly impressed by the theatrical genius of the American black actor, Ira Aldridge, whose interpretations of Shakespeare moved him profoundly. But he remained as indiscreet as ever. On a return journey to the Ukraine in 1859 he was arrested for having written and circulated certain allegedly blasphemous poems. He was ordered to return to the capital. Strangely enough, he was also appointed academician and professor at the Academy, and was allowed to publish his collected poems—with the exclusion of objectionable ones. This collection appeared in 1860, again under the title of *The Kobzar*. His personal life, however, remained empty. The Princess Repnin was estranged from him; she had turned into a religious fanatic. His numerous attempts to find a wife—he sought them not in the upper circles, but among young serf-girls—miscarried time and again. He was doomed to loneliness.

Yet the productions of his last years lose nothing of inspiration, imagination or force. There is no sign that his own physical debilitation, which became more and more deleterious and marked, and which without question resulted from his deprivations during exile, intrudes itself into his creations. Here his energies are at their fullest. Bitterness and exultation, love and hatred, anger and kindness, sympathy and rage are here. His religious fervor has been deepened, but has also grown more heretical. His Christianity has become revolutionary.

Shevchenko's Christianity was anti-institutional; it harked back to earlier traditions of martyrdom and adherence to a militant, radically new ethic. He now speaks as it were with the voice of a Lamennais—but a Lamennais who understands the oppressiveness of a religion that is sister to secular authority, perhaps its handmaiden, and who has seen its baleful influence on the serf population of Russia and the Ukraine. He speaks—if one may carry the analogy farther—with the voice of the English Levellers and Diggers of the Puritan Revolution. Of Lamennais, we are sure, he knew little, if anything; of the Puritans, probably nothing.

Thus he identifies the early Christian martyrs of the days of Nero with the Decembrists of Russia, as prototypes of revolutionaries in the cause of Truth and Justice, as in the epic poem "The Neophytes." In another poem, "Mary," he recreates the story of Jesus and his mother in a naturalistic fashion, with beauty and tenderness, in the style of a folk epic, simply and graphically. The Mother of Christ emerges as a woman of the people, whose love for the angel of the annunciation is told in bucolic style, unconventionally startling in its naturalness and physical elements, with a naïveté that conceals its artistic sophistication.

The Prophets of the Old Testament are with him as he translates their words into corresponding arraignments of his own age and its rulers, and his identification with the lowly. The sacred strains of the original are retained, but heightened to speak the language of Shevchenko's day. So in the poem based on *Isaiah* 35, the poet translates the Hebrew prophet into the speech and needs of his people. Thus Shevchenko:

> And the weary hands are at rest, that have borne the chains,
> And the feeble knees are at rest, that have borne the manacles.
> Be comforted, ye of feeble hearts, and fear not the wonder,
> Come ye who have been ground down, ye who have suffered.
> Avenge ye on the evil ones!

Or,

> Life now fills the steppes and lakes, and not endless highways.
> Ways that are free, ways that are wide, through the land of holiness.
> A highway not for masters. No! Here slaves shall wander freely,
> Without clamor or cries they shall gather for joy and gladness.
> And in the desert wastes once more shall cheerful villages flourish.[43]

Hours of despair are brightened only by a call to arms:

> My heart waits. Suffers. …
> It weeps, and cannot sleep,
> Like a child that cries for food.
> Heart, oh heart, you await
> A time of grim disasters?
> There is nothing good to hope for,
> There is no Freedom—that longed-for good.
> She sleeps. Tsar Nicholas
> Has lulled her. Believe me,
> To waken the languid one,
> We must together, one and all
> Harden the axe-shaft, whet the blade,
> And start to rouse her. …[44]

He was equally incautious in the expression of his religious views. It was these that eventually brought upon him the wrath of the authorities. Such a poem as "Hymn of the Nuns" scandalized and outraged them. The virgin nuns inveigh against the Lord for having denied them the fruits of love and joy.

> Strike thunder, strike this house today,
> This holy mansion where we waste away,
> Lord our God, we lay the blame on thee,
> And bear thee ill and malice, and we sing
>   Hallelujah!. ...[45]

Nor is another poem, "The Idiot," more sparing of the Divinity:

> Oh You, All-seeing Eye, You who from on high
> See fettered slaves herded to Siberian wastes,
> Slaves, blessed and just, chained, racked and hanged!
> And crucified!
>
> And You All-unknowing?
> Or have you seen, and yet not been blinded?
> Oh Eye, Great Eye that surveys all,
> You do not gaze too closely.
> You sleep in gilded tabernacles, while Tsar on Tsar ...
> But why speak of these?
> May the Evil One take them off! ...[46]

And yet, "hope sprang eternal." He was on a steamer on the Volga in 1860, shortly before his death. An emancipated serf was playing snatches of Chopin on his violin, and Shevchenko records his impression:

> Under the impact of these plaintive, sorrow-laden tones of this poor emancipated serf, in the graveyard stillnes of the night, the steamer seemed like a gigantic monster, with its muffled roar, ready with gaping maw to swallow landowners and inquisitors. Oh great Fulton! And you, great Watt! Your child—as yet tender—but growing hourly—will before long gnaw at the cudgels, the thrones, and the crowns, and will swallow diplomats and landowners as an *hors d'oeuvre!* What the French Encyclopedists initiated, your colossal and magnificent offspring will complete on our entire planet. My prophecy will be fulfilled![47]

Shevchenko died on March 10, 1861 in St. Petersburg. Some time later his body was transferred to the Ukraine, and his monument today overlooks the Dnieper—*his* Dnieper.

What Pushkin became for Russia, Mickiewicz for Poland, Petöfi for Hungary, and earlier, Robert Burns for Scotland, Taras Shevchenko became for the Ukraine—not only a national, but also an international poet. For his own and the succeeding generations, he is one link in that golden chain of fraternity that marks a grand community of interests and aspirations such as had never been witnessed before. Shelley in his "Ode to the West Wind" had hoped to send forth the sparks from his "unextinguished hearth"—his "thoughts" to "hasten a new birth." So too Shevchenko—the former serf who had been tied to the soil of the Ukraine, the peasant, the poet, the painter, the voice of all lands and all peoples—sends forth his poems, "his blossoms," as he called them, his thoughts, and like a ploughman prays for a good harvesting in due time. And he sings:

Be thou plowed in low and high lands,
Field so dear to me!
Embrace the seed, beloved meadow,
The seed of liberty!
Spread thy blessing far and wide,
Watered by fair fortune,
Stretch thy bold dimensions—
Rich and fertile meadow!
Be not sown with words alone—
Reason be your seedlings—
Men will come to reap the fruit,
In a joyful season!
Spread, unfold beloved field,
My poor, lowly meadow![48]

3. Siegfried on the Barricades: Richard Wagner in Dresden, May 1849

Yes, the old world is in ruins, And a new world will arise. For the sublime goddess Revolution comes rushing on the wings of the storm ...

—Richard Wagner, "Revolution," 1849

All peoples and all men are full of presentiments. Everyone whose living organs are not paralyzed sees with trembling expectation the approach of the future which will utter the decisive word ... The air is sultry; it is heavy with storms! And therefore we call to our blinded brothers: Repent! Repent! The Kingdom of God is nigh. Let us put our trust in the eternal spirit which destroys and annihilates only because it is the unsearchable and eternally creative source of all life. The passion for destruction is also a creative passion!

—Mikhail Bakunin, "Reaction in Germany," 1842

In a world filled with amazing incongruities, not the least strange was the meeting and associated activities in Dresden, the capital of Saxony, of two antipodal characters: Richard Wagner, Leipzig-born Kapellmeister of the Royal Theatre of that city, and Mikhail Bakunin, apostle of anarchism, Russian-born son of landowning parentage in the province of Tver.

It was as if the irony, and what Hegel called the cunning, of Reason were at work. For while Tsarism was sending its military power to the aid of Austria and Prussia in order to suppress revolution, it was also unwittingly sending forth emissaries not only intent on abetting revolution, but also ardently dedicated to the overthrow of Russian absolutism.

But the internationalism of 1848 and 1849 brought about many astonishing conjunctures and coalesced many otherwise incompatible and dissimilar temperaments and energies. Both actors in the Dresden drama of 1849, shortly to be enacted, were in their thirties: Wagner was thirty-six, Bakunin one year younger. Physically they were as unlike as they were intellectually. Richard Wagner was undersized, still somewhat undernourished; Bakunin was a towering, bearded giant. They were alike however in the possession of supercharged stores of energies, in the explosiveness of their feelings and their passion for change. Their careers were to be spectacularly dissimilar. But both had already attained a measure of ascendency in their respective vocations. Neither of them recognized any obstacles as being insurmountable in the attainment of their objectives, though they had encountered them all too frequently.

In their moral composition they were also far apart. Wagner knew only the "self" which demanded fulfilment at whatever cost; he possessed an overpowering "ego" that needed to make all around him subservient to himself and his goals—the creation of music, of a new art form of such dimensions as to require a revolution in the theatre and the opera. At the age of thirty, in 1843, when he was appointed Royal Kapellmeister at Dresden by King Friedrich August II of Saxony, Wagner already had an impressive though stormy career behind him. He was already known as an extraordinarily daring interpreter of the musical works of other composers, unorthodox but compelling; but he had also composed a surprising number of works in his own right, orchestral, operatic, and dramatic.

When he was not quite eighteen, his Concert Overture in B flat was performed by the Leipzig Gewandhaus Orchestra; when he was twenty, his Symphony in C major, by the same distinguished group. At twenty-one he had completed the opera, *Die Feen—The Fairies*—and was already the conductor of an opera company in Magdeburg. Another opera, *Das Liebesverbot—Love Prohibited*, based on Shakespeare's *Measure for Measure*, was performed in Magdeburg when he was twenty-three. It was in that year, 1836, that he married the lovely actress Minna Planer. By the time he was appointed to Dresden in 1843, Wagner had scored a triumph with the historical opera *Rienzi*, but he failed of success with the subsequent *Flying Dutchman*. In 1845 he completed the score of *Tannhäuser*, and in the fateful month of March 1848, finished scoring *Lohengrin*. He was himself the poet of his operatic texts.

Years before, during his somewhat irregular student days in Leipzig, he too had been swept by the news of the Paris July Revolution of 1830, and had given way to moderate manifestations of enthusiasm. In the following year he became excited by the stream of Polish refugees who were arriving in Saxony after the revolutionary débacle in their country. He saw with his own eyes the heroic generals Bem and Count Tyszkiewicz. He celebrated these events in a "Political Overture," now lost; and in 1836 in another overture, "Polonia." The July days and their repercussions in Leipzig and Dresden were to remain vivid for him. "From this day," he confessed in his autobiography, *My Life*, "the world of history had its commencement for me."[49]

The German literary movement of revolt, the so-called "Young Germany," inspired him to celebrate one of its tenets—the "rehabilitation of the flesh" and "free sensuality"—and to scourge Puritan hypocrisy in *Das Liebesverbot*, an opera which failed dismally when performed in Magdeburg.

He was resilient, irrepressible and self-confident, and even under the most trying circumstances, undefeatable. Toward the end of 1839 he went to Paris, hoping to capture that city, or at least obtain a performance of the hapless *Liebesverbot*. Paris was, after all, *the* city of opera. He was overwhelmed by the magnificence of the performances, especially of the works of Meyerbeer; he was thrilled by the excellence of Parisian orchestras, and for the first time heard Beethoven's *Ninth Symphony* performed in a way that brought the work home to him in its profound greatness. He attended concerts of the works of Berlioz, with whom he was to develop a lifelong rivalry; he met Franz Liszt, not yet aware of the importance that generous and great man was to have for his future career. But he did not succeed in getting his own opera produced. Despite this disappointment, however, he managed to complete the score of *Rienzi*, to write the text of *The Flying Dutchman*, commence its musical setting, and complete the unorchestrated version in seven weeks. He was ever in need of money, borrowed freely, and eked out a desperate existence by doing hackwork for the *Gazette musicale*.

He was never to forgive Paris for neglecting him; and though time and again it drew him like a magnet, that city, and France herself, were forever to remain bitter reminders of defeat.

But he had much to look forward to in his own country: the prospect of a production of *The Flying Dutchman* in Berlin, and even more certainly that of *Rienzi* in Dresden.

The lifetime appointment of Wagner as Kapellmeister in Dresden, in 1843, promised a secure haven. But his was a restless, tumult-ridden spirit. In addition, he was a spendthrift and had sybaritic tastes. He was self-indulgent. He possessed the self-consciousness of a genius to whom the world was always in debt. His was a prehensile temperament, intellectually and physically. He possessed an extraordinary absorptive capacity and powers of assimilation. He had a magnetic personality, and drew to himself passionate admirers among men and women. But he could also make enemies—all too easily. He was unsparing of his own energies in the fulfilment of his artistic objectives, and equally demanding of others who worked with or under him. He was not easily satisfied with the quality of performance or repertory at the Dresden theatre. Nor could his associates, superiors, or audiences at the time fully understand his goals, his radical dreams of reorganizing the entire dramatic and musical domain in an environment that was still strictly bound to older traditions. How could they keep pace with his headlong ideas, and particularly with his lightning development as creator? Hence, their reception of his works alternated between a wild, hectic enthusiasm for *Rienzi*, and a dismal coldness toward *The Flying Dutchman*. And already he was transcending even these creations! But he won farsighted votaries and worshippers—admirers like Franz Liszt, who had come to Dresden for the *Rienzi* production; and among the young, the brilliant conductor Hans von Bülow, in whose later life he was to play so dramatic, even tragic, a role.

His prestige in circumscribed Dresden was mounting; if only he were not so arrogant, so insistent on change, so contemptuous of the court personnel and their interference in matters they understood so little! They had little sympathy for his ideas of reorganization—the creation of a national theatre, of the cooperation and collaboration of dramatist and composer, of a school of theatrical arts—in fact, a theatre that would be equal to and worthy of performing the Wagnerian works he had in mind! They also looked askance upon the spendthrift, whom the Court again and again graciously rescued from the pressure of creditors.

Had they been able to look into that head of his, with its schemes of such vast proportions, ideas of such magnitude and novelty, they would have been even more outraged. How could they understand his projects for a new opera that would no longer be opera in the Meyerbeerian sense, but a recreation in modern terms of what he believed to have been the character of Greek tragedy? or his ambition to restore drama, to coalesce speech, sound, and dance into a unitary creation? How could they understand his dream of bringing back into the theatre the modern equivalents of "myth," which he believed to be the basic elements of human or "folk" experience, enlarged into cosmic meanings? The *Tannhäuser* production of October 1845 failed, not merely because of the public's inability to understand the meaning and intent of the musical drama, but also because of the inadequacies of the two stars, the notable Schröder-Devrient, and the Tannhäuser of the evening, Tichatschek.

Yet it was true that theatre—drama and opera—were sadly in need of revolution. They had sunk to a pathetically low estate. In the German principalities, where it had been kept alive by the various courts, the theatre was tradition-bound and senescent. This was no less true of the theatres of Vienna. England licensed only two theatres in London, where, aside from the classical fare like Shakespeare and Sheridan, the repertory was dismally shallow. Nor was France an exception. Romanticism was dying on its theatrical boards, but was kept spuriously alive in the opera. Theatrical taste was perhaps best exemplified in the highly successful combination of the sensational and cliché-ridden librettos of Eugène Scribe as set to music by the grandiloquent Meyerbeer. In all these instances, it must also be remembered that the theatre was subjected to the tightest control on the part of the state authorities, such as could never be exercised with respect to journalism and the novel. Here and there exceptional dramatic talent, even genius appeared, though doomed to tragic frustration. In Germany, for example, there were Christian Grabbe and Georg Büchner, of the preceding decade; in Vienna, contemporaries like Franz Grillparzer and Friedrich Hebbel were forced to compromise their original gifts in deference to imperial authority. The tragic history of Hector Berlioz, complicated as it was, represents but another instance of original genius at war with ironbound tradition, political and personal machinations, and invidious suspicion of radical artistic innovation.

What is perhaps most paradoxical about the prospective revolution that Wagner was advocating in drama and music is the fact that it begins, continues, and ends as a kind of belated Romanticism. In the very year, 1843, in which he assumed the conductorship at the Dresden theatre, Romanticism may be said to have died in superannuation in France, as it was dying in the rest of Europe. The failure of Victor Hugo's drama *Les Burgraves* in Paris marks its death-knell. It will never fully die out, but like a surviving ghost will appear and reappear throughout the century, devoid of blood and bone but still exercising its own necrophilic magnetism. Even when somewhat later the scope of Wagner's theorizing and practice is enlarged to include social and political—aside from purely aesthetic—elements, it marches under the bondage of Romanticism. And it will continue to do so until the very end. Within the first stages of his theorizing are contained most of the seeds that will determine his life and work, up to his achievement of consummate mastery.

As with other European Romantics, a preoccupation with medievalism was at the root of Wagner's creations. Romanticism, in its many varieties and tendencies, had uncovered vast treasures of literature, art, and thought of the Middle Ages. The "Gothic," once an object of derision and abuse, equated with "barbarism," now acquired a radiance and glory, as fresh understanding and enthusiasm gazed upon the splendors of the Gothic cathedrals, scanned the rediscovered literary treasures of the medieval poets, and conned the myths and folklore of nations. The "romances" of chivalry composed by such poets as Chrétien de Troyes, Gottfried von Strassburg, Wolfram von Eschenbach, the poetry of the troubadours, trouvères, and minnesingers, opened vast worlds of fantasy and dream. The rich storehouses of Arthurian legend, the Round Table and the Holy Grail renewed the poetic imagination of the new age. But there was also another trove that was uncovered, little known till then. This was the Nordic mythology and legend contained in the Icelandic sagas. The rich tapestry of Arthurian lore was now rivaled by the dour, imposing, sombre tales of Odin, Sigurd the Volsung, Balder, and the doom of the world and of the gods.

It was in these treasures that Wagner's imagination reveled. Here were to be found Tristan and Iseult, Parsifal, Siegfried, Wotan, and in a strange commixture, also the medieval Frederick Barbarossa, the long-awaited Emperor-Redeemer of Germany. The mythic world was now enlarged in Wagner's purview to include Jesus of Nazareth.

Wagner came upon Jacob Grimm's epochal *Deutsche Mythologie* in 1843, some eight years after its publication. "A new birth took place within me," he wrote many years later in his autobiography.[50] In these confused, fragmentary Nordic narratives he felt as if he had rediscovered "a long forgotten, long sought-for consciousness."

David Friedrich Strauss's *Life of Jesus*, containing a mythical interpretation of the life of Christ, had appeared almost at the same time as Grimm's seminal work. The concurrent studies of comparative religions, mythology, and folklore, the historic researches in the Old and New Testaments, the explorations in the Near and Far East, were laying the foundations for a comparative study of many cultures, particularly as to their similarities and dissimilarities.

Along with the emergence of national conscience had come an investigation into what might be called the "spirit" of nations, races, and peoples that found its distinctive expression in its culture, particularly poetry and myth. This was the *Volksgeist*. In the manifestations of this "folk-spirit," presumed to create instinctively, spontaneously, even unconsciously, were to be found the true meaning and essence of a people, its thinking and feeling. These "unconscious" creators poured their dreams, visions, images of the world, their understanding of the universe, into their "myths." History presented the sheer facts of a people's existence; "myth" gave its picture in a totality, in an "idealized" form. To understand the spirit of a people it was necessary to dig deeply into the recesses of its mythical life—its true life. Within the triad of "folk," "myth," and the "unconscious," was enclosed the secret of a people—its essence.

Political romanticism wove into that conception of a "folk" and its "mythic life" a fantasy and dream that would somehow succeed in rehabilitating the past to counter a disturbing, distraught, ever-changing and challenging present. Modern psychology would fix medieval "mythic" life permanently into what it calls the "collective unconscious."

The great synthesis Richard Wagner was proposing, to correspond to that in the Greek tragedy and its myths, he believed he could establish through its Germanic counterpart. It would be a discovery of the "mythic element" in an *Urgermanentum* —the primal Germanic soul. Having completed *Tannhäuser* and *Lohengrin*, he was now ready to bring *ur*-Germanic gods and heroes upon his stage. Soon he was at work on the first of these dramas, *Siegfrieds Tod—Siegfried's Death*, completed in 1848. Hindsight may find some symbolism in the fact that the great subject of lust for gold and the doom it carried should have been projected in that fateful period when it seemed, in fact, that an old world was crashing and a new world was in birth ...

Richard Wagner was in the midst of conducting a rehearsal of Flotow's *Martha* when his musical associate and friend August Röckel brought him the electrifying news that King Louis-Philippe had fled Paris and that a republic had been proclaimed in France![51]

Wagner could understand Röckel's delirium. For as a boy, Röckel had been in Paris at the outbreak of the Revolution of 1830; he had lived in England; he was a fervent democrat and radical. At this time he was editor of the local *Volksblätter*, which was agitating for social and political reforms. Like Wagner, he hated court and courtiers, bureaucrats, and absolutism. Both were at one in their hopes and wishes for the regeneration of the arts.

Wagner shared Röckel's excitement. Such a grand upheaval boded well for his plans and his projects. When news arrived of the uprisings in Berlin and Vienna, when a German parliament, convened in Frankfurt, began working on what promised to be a new democratic constitution for the entire country, his enthusiasm knew no bounds. Always ready with counsel, he now hastened to offer advice to that body through the local delegate. He proposed that the parliament assume sole constitutive authority, introduce immediate "folk-arming," and form an offensive and defensive alliance with France.[52]

In honor of the Viennese uprising of March 1848, Wagner wrote highly inflammatory verses in which he assured the insurgents that that city's example would soon be followed by the rest of Germany, and that Germany in her turn would fall on her enemies, aristocrats and others, and do what the French had done. Vienna, he concluded, has taught us that if "anyone should now command us, to our everlasting shame, to return to our past slavery, we will retort with the vow, 'We'll do as they did in Vienna.'"[53] He even undertook a visit to that embattled city to persuade the citizens of Vienna to consider a renovation of the theatre according to his plans.

With typical ardor he proclaimed, "There is a movement sweeping the world—the storm of European revolution. All have a part in it; whoever does not abet it and forward it, strengthens it by opposing it."[54]

In a vehement poem, which does more credit to his sentiments than to his poetical talents, he scourges "egoists" who had closed their eyes to human misery and had thus violated the dignity of nature, of man and woman, even of the Lord God himself. "Need" (also the title of the poem) is addressed as a divinity, whose torch "now burning brightly, proclaims to all villains the end of human suffering ... and the emergence out of the human wreckage of a new humanity that will join Nature, and thus make a unity of the two."[55]

He was not the only musician of distinction swept by the exultation of the day. Franz Liszt recast a revolutionary symphony of 1830, a daring act considering that he was attached to the court of Weimar; Robert Schumann composed a so-called "Barricades March" in 1849; Ludwig Spohr, at the age of seventy, added a note to his completed Sextet, op. 140: "Written in March and April, at the time of the glorious revolution of the peoples for liberty, unity, and the grandeur of Germany." Peter Cornelius fought on the Berlin barricades, for he was an irrepressible republican. Schumann too had declared himself a republican.[56]

The execution of Robert Blum by the Austrian government aroused feelings of horror and exasperation among Saxon citizens. Blum had been the secretary of the Leipzig Theatre, and one of the most outspoken and courageous democratic leaders of the state. An outpouring of thousands of citizens in a memorial service testified to the regard of his fellows as well as to the critical tensions prevailing. The roar and thunder of revolution in other regions finally reached the ears of the King of Saxony; and like the other German autocrats he bowed to these persuasive exigencies—at least for the time being. He dismissed a particularly obnoxious and reactionary minister. A new election sent a predominantly liberal representation to the House of Deputies, among them August Röckel. When the atmosphere became more heated, Röckel was dismissed from his theatrical post.

Plunged into the whirlpool of political agitation and action in 1848, Wagner developed—if that term may be used—a bizarre assortment of political and social ideas. He foresaw the new utopia: a republic, but, amazingly enough, headed by the King of Saxony, "the first and truest republican of all." All aristocratic privileges would of course be abolished. The King would proclaim a republic, and the royal house of Wettin would be established as the heads of state forever. The published article was signed merely, "A Member of the *Vaterlandsverein*" (a notoriously radical organization); but its authorship was not in doubt, for Wagner had delivered it as a speech before an audience of almost three thousand the day before its publication on June 16. Was he shocked, startled, surprised when he was informed that an announced performance of *Rienzi* had been canceled as a result? Or was he too deeply involved in political agitation, or perhaps in the Nibelungen gold-hoard and his sun-god Siegfried? For no matter what the external circumstances around him in which he might be involved, his mind worked and worked—always germinating new plans for new creations.

Was it any wonder that his superiors at the Theatre like the Baron von Lüttichau, and members of that organization, were asking questions about the unpredictable Kapellmeister? Even the Court and the King were looking askance. It was a strong wind that was driving Wagner's imperiled skiff on to tumultuous waters, and it would need a skilful pilot to bring it to safety. . . .

He was intoxicated. The ominous reports of revolutionary setbacks emanating from Prague, from Austria and Italy—the triumphs of Generals Windischgrätz and Haynau—these did not sober him. The world was still aflame, and the Hungarians were still resisting. In Germany, there were outbreaks in many states. Fire-music danced in his brain, as he wrote:

> *Die Fackel, ha! sie brenne helle,*
> *sie brenne tief un breit,*
> *zu Asche brenn'sie Statt und Stelle,*
> *dem Mammondienst geweiht! ...*
>
> *Denn über allen Trümmerstätten*
> *blüht auf des Lebens Glück:*

es blieb die Menschheit frei von Ketten,
und die Natur zurück.
Natur und Mensch—ein Elemente!
vernichtet ist, was je sie trennte!
Der Freiheit Morgenrot—
entzündet hat's—die Not!

"Lo, let the torch of Want burn bright, burn far and wide, and reduce to ashes all that has been dedicated to the God Mammon … And above all these ruins, human happiness now flowers, and liberated Humanity rejoins Nature, and Freedom's dawn is lit by the God of Want."[57]

So he sang, and so he believed, as the year 1848 neared its end. He was there at the meetings of the *Vaterlandsverein*, if not a principal mover, very much to the fore. He was like a charge of dynamite ready to explode. Time and the incendiary torch were near. …

In Wagner's celebrated autobiography, *My Life*, the incidents of the years 1848 and 1849 stand out with special vividness, warmth, and a truthfulness not always sustained on other pages. Though not altogether free of a certain attenuation of his own part in the hectic days of May 1849, they breathe a spirit of contemporaneity. One event and one person Wagner recalled with particular vivacity. On Palm Sunday, April 1, 1849, he was conducting a public rehearsal of Beethoven's *Ninth Symphony*. A strange figure was present.

> Michael Bakunin [Wagner writes] attended this dress rehearsal in secret, unknown to the police. At the end, without hesitating, he came up to me and called out for all to hear, that if all of music were to be destroyed in the long-awaited world-conflagration, it would be our duty to get together, even at the risk of our lives, in order to save this symphony.[58]

He had known Mikhail Bakunin personally for only a brief period, but he had heard and read a great deal about him before that. The above incident remained in his mind probably because Bakunin, though a lover of music, rated this and the other arts as altogether secondary to the realization of world revolution.

Police surveillance, hiding, sudden emergence, had become a part of Bakunin's way of life since he had left Russia and begun engaging in revolutionary activity. Now he was in Dresden, having come from Leipzig, where he was exploring the prospects for an uprising of Slavs. August Röckel housed him for a time, and Bakunin went by the name of "Dr. Schwarz."

In Bakunin, Wagner found that rare phenomenon, a counterpart, an equal, a force to which he, usually so domineering in his own right, was willing to yield sway. Wagner, the very epitome and embodiment of the "self," was confronted by a personality which, if anything, had cast all "self" aside and was ever identifying with that which he was planning or doing, or with those who were so involved—that is, the upheaval of the existing order. And now, in the presence of such a monolithic being, it seemed as if, for the moment, the Wagnerian "self" was abated, and another nature—that of self-giving—was coming to the surface.

This "strange, altogether imposing personality," as Wagner described him in eloquent lines, was "in the full flowering of his thirty-odd years." About him "everything was colossal, yet imprinted with the mark of primitive spontaneity." He overwhelmed not only the young, but all those with whom he came in contact. There were few who were able to contend with his sharp yet persuasive arguments. They reminded one of the "Socratic method." They were the arguments of a Hegelian who had whetted the sharp blade of dialectic to its finest cutting edge. Here was the giant who preached world destruction as preliminary to the emergence of a new birth, and yet was himself a "kind-hearted and affectionate person." Having given up class, rank and possession, he often lived from hand to mouth, yet accepted this as a normal way of living. Wagner confessed that he was torn between "involuntary terror" and "irresistible attraction" in Bakunin's presence. We may be sure that August Röckel, no less a passionate republican and revolutionary, was taken by Bakunin with the same force. There seemed to be no reservations, no self-interest or self-regard, no equivocations, in the man's character. This was Wagner's judgment, and the tribute he paid to Bakunin was such as few others were destined to receive from him.[59]

It must have been with particular entrancement that the company that gathered at Röckel's listened to Bakunin's remarkable life story.

He had left family, country, and a promising army career to go to Berlin in order to study philosophy with Professor Werder, like his countryman Stankievich and so many others of his generation. He immersed himself in Hegel; he had heard and been impressed by the lectures of the philosopher Schelling and the historian Ranke. He had rapidly gone over to the Left Hegelians and had thereupon begun his "vocation of revolt." In Dresden he had met the brilliant journalist Arnold Ruge, who later described that moment in Bakunin's history:

> Bakunin threw himself headlong into the German intellectual movement of the thirties and the forties, after becoming acquainted in Berlin not only with Hegelianism, but also after having appropriated the living dialectic, that creative soul of the universe. He visited me in Dresden, where I was publishing the *Deutsche Jahrbücher*, and concurred with me on the transformation of abstract theory into practice, and on the imminence of the revolution.[60]

For Ruge's *Jahrbücher* Bakunin had written an article signed "Jules Elisard" (a protection against Russian spies and informers), which aroused a great deal of attention. It was entitled "Reaction in Germany," and transformed the Hegelian dialectic with typical Bakunian *sang-froid*. Hegel's thesis and antithesis now represented the warfare of the positive and the negative; but in this case, the positive was the old, the reactionary (say, Schelling's philosophy of revelation), while the negative was the emergent new, in this instance the democratic party and its ideas, still in their incompleteness. In the clash of the two, the negative, in destroying the positive, also destroys itself. Both perish. That which emerges is altogether new—the total transformation of the world. Negation has thus become the necessary self-destroying destroyer of the positive. The whole being of the negative, "its content, [is] ... found in its opposition to the positive, and its vital energy consists in the destruction of the positive."[61]

Such is the way in which the Hegelian dialectic is "transformed" into a warfare in which both contestants are superseded. For Hegel the higher historic form developed out of the conflict of thesis and antithesis, and was contained within them. For

Bakunin the two theses annulled each other, and gave way to the totally new being. The principle of destruction is thus made supreme. "The desire for destruction," Bakunin wrote, "is also a creative desire."

> The positive is negated by the negative; and conversely, the negative by the positive. What then is the common element which transcends both of them? It is the fact of negation, the fact of destruction, the fact of the passionate devouring of the positive.[62]

And in tones of a biblical prophet, Bakunin thundered his admonitions:

> All the peoples, all men, are filled with a certain presentiment, and everyone looks with a certain terrible apprehension toward the future which will pronounce the saving word ... The air is heavy, it forebodes storms. That is why we adjure our bewildered brothers: "Do penance! Do penance! The Kingdom of God is near!"[63]

Such was Bakunin's apocalyptic vision. Destruction was in the nature of things. Do not fear, he was saying, to destroy. Suspected of being the author of the inflammatory appeal, Bakunin fled to Switzerland, where he came in contact with the proletarian socialist Weitling, by whose personality and socialist views he was deeply affected. His notions were further enlarged by the ideas of Ludwig Feuerbach and other Left Hegelians, who were concerned with translating theory into action. Paris completed this stage of his education. For here, in the smithy of revolutions, he met the outstanding figures of Karl Marx and Proudhon. Toward Marx he developed an ambivalent relation that was to persist for the rest of his life—profound admiration and bitter antagonism, the latter of which was to produce a sharp split in the socialist movement. To Proudhon he remained faithful throughout.

Like Marx, he was expelled from France, and like the former he returned to Paris on the outbreak of the February Revolution. He was not one to look on passively. He was on the barricades, hobnobbing with the workers, talking interminably, proselytizing. He was also projecting what was to be his central commitment, the organization of a Pan-Slavic congress that would, he hoped, eventuate in a union of the Slavs and overthrow tsardom. The French government was only too glad to help him on that mission (he had been a thorn in their side!), and Bakunin had gone to Prague, where his project went aground in the internecine rivalries of the Slav groups themselves. When the ill-planned, ill-starred insurrection broke out in the Czech capital, he was once more embattled; when it was easily expunged by the Austrian Windischgrätz, he escaped to Leipzig. Once again, eye-witnesses testified to his coolheadedness, his courage, and his organizational capacities amidst the Prague insurrectionists ...

He never gave up hope. The overthrow of tsardom was his ever-present dream. To him it was imminent. All revolutions anywhere were its presages; but the Slavs would bring it about. German absolutism too would soon meet its doom. ...

He did not boast. If he exaggerated, it was only hopes and prospects. He had a monomaniacal integrity of purpose and character. It was this monolithic force that imposed itself upon and impressed Wagner, whose moral nature was of a more vacillating fibre.

After years of imprisonment August Röckel could still recall the image of Bakunin with warmth. He remembered how, in 1849, Bakunin had come secretly from Leipzig, and remained with me in concealment for a number of days. A man of extraordinary intellectual powers and strength of character, combined with an imposing personality and overpowering eloquence, it had been easy for him not only to inspire youth everywhere, but also to attract more mature persons, particularly since his outlook was free of national limitations and characterized by the noblest, all-embracing humanism.[64]

The anarch in Wagner responded to Bakunin's explosive sentiments, such as

> The age of parliamentary life ... is over. I do not believe in constitutions and in laws; not even the best constitution could ever satisfy me. We need something different: Storm and Life. A new, law-free land—that is, a free land—hence a free world.[65]

Into the rooms of Röckel Bakunin must have brought all his fiery eloquence to bear upon those visions of a united Slav republic, and one could almost hear the crash as Moscow and St. Petersburg collapsed, and "European slavery" was buried "among its ruins." He brought with him the hopes of all those humanitarians whom he had met and seen, Béranger, Louis Blanc, Michelet, Proudhon, George Sand, the Paris societies of the *Ouvriers*; the history of Decembrists gone and still alive; experiences with Belgian radicals, English Chartists, Marx and others; augurs of a future that was bound to break on the morrow. ...

> Soon, perhaps in less than a year, the monstrous Austrian Empire will be destroyed. The liberated Italians will proclaim an Italian republic. The Germans, united into a single great nation, will proclaim a German republic. The Polish democrats after seventeen years in exile will return to their homes. The revolutionary movement will stop only when Europe, the whole of Europe, not excluding Russia, is turned into a federal democratic republic.[66]

In no less emphatic but more realistic terms, Bakunin sketched the decadence of Western Europe, its lack of any true convictions, particularly in the privileged and ruling elements. Egoism was God. Only among the raw, uncultivated masses was there any vigor, freshness, striving, though still inchoate and vague. These manifested themselves as a communism that was "invisible, impalpable, ubiquitous, living in one form or another in all beings without exception ..."[67]

Thus he spoke, and was to speak again and again. Undeterred by setbacks, he was destined ever to come back hopefully, a virtuoso of failure, living this side of greatness—a kind of mythical greatness devoid of success, a tragic Antaeus ...

"We are called upon to destroy, not to build. Others will build, who are better, wiser, and fresher than we are."[68]

* * *

Assured that the tide of revolution in Prussia and in Vienna had been stemmed, certain of Prussian aid when called for, King Friedrich August II of Saxony took steps to reassert absolute authority. Early in February 1849 he dismissed the liberal minister Oberländer and appointed the conservative Count von Beust in his place. Toward the end of April he dissolved the Saxon Diet, which had approved the democratic constitution of the Frankfurt Assembly and had organized a Communal Guard. Parliamentary immunity of the elected delegates was lifted. August Röckel, feeling himself most threatened for his forthright speech and activities, fled to Bohemia. The long-expected moment had arrived for Dresden. King and city faced each other in open enmity.

Days before the planned uprising, which had been set by the *Vaterlandsverein* for May 9, Richard Wagner had been in conferences and meetings with Röckel, the architect Semper, and other members of the Verein. Though not as yet taking a leading part, Bakunin was present at some of these gatherings. Arms were being stored, and it is certain that Wagner himself had a hand in ordering hand grenades, some of them destined for an anticipated rising in Prague.

Wagner was never in the background of these activities. His political ideas were a welter of confusion. Declaring himself an enemy of the State, he advocated a republic ruled by a king; he objurgated the Court and its hirelings while at the same time addressing a poem "To the Princes," in which he implored them to rescue the beleaguered Arts from the hands of "Mercury, the god of the market-place," that is, the benighted bourgeois philistines![69]

In another poem of March 22, 1849, Wagner instructed the Public Prosecutor in the meaning of the "new life" that was burgeoning, to which, obviously, that official was still blind; blinded "by the State—that great egoist, that eternal devourer of all true life."

> Death is dead; and you will never bring it back,
> And what is living, you will never undo;
> Nor can you ever weave the golden threads of life,
> From what is dead and mute.
> And if from Death you cannot wring a pittance,
> Say, what is your guerdon for your diurnal dying?[70]

Wagner was never content with half measures. To feel was to act. Revolution was in the air, and Revolution would bring him and mankind not only a better life, but what was even more important, a new Art, a new Theatre.

An article appeared in the *Volksblätter* of April 8, 1849, entitled *"Die Revolution."* It was unsigned, but everyone knew the author. Wagner had not been listening to Bakunin in vain. The words are Wagner's; the spirit, Bakunin's.

> The old world is in ruins. And a new world will arise. For the sublime goddess Revolution comes rushing on the wings of the storm, her august head radiant with lightnings, a sword in her right hand, a torch in her left; her eyes are dark and punitive, and cold; yet what warmth of the purest love, what fullness of happiness flow from them toward him who dares face her steadily! Rushing on she comes, the ever-rejuvenating mother of mankind; destroying and blessing, she sweeps across the earth; before her the storm is howling; man's handiwork is shaken so violently, that vast clouds of dust darken the air; where her mighty foot steps, all that has been built up for the ages in idle vanity crashes in ruins, and the hem of her robe sweeps away the last remnants. ...

Into the mouth of Revolution, he places these words:

> I am the ever-rejuvenating, ever-creative Life! Where I am not, is Death! I am the dream, the balm, the hope of the suffering. I annihilate that which exists, and wherever I walk, there new life wells forth from the dead rock. I come to you to break all the fetters that oppress you, to redeem you from the embrace of Death, and to pour young life into your

veins. Whatever is must pass away, for such is the eternal law of Nature, such is the condition of Life, and I, the eternal destroyer, fulfil the law and create eternal young Life. I will destroy the order of things from its roots, under which you are living, for it has sprung from sin, and its flower is misery and its fruit is crime. The harvest is ripe and I am the reaper. I will destroy every illusion that has power over men. I will destroy the rule of the one over the many, the dead over the living, matter over spirit. I will break the power of the mighty, of law and of property. Only man's own will shall be master of man, his own desire shall be his only law, his own power shall be his total possession, for only free man is that which is holy, and there is nothing higher than he. ...

I will destroy the present order of things that divides what shall be one mankind into hostile nations, into the powerful and the weak, into the privileged and the outlawed, into rich and poor ... I will destroy the order of things that makes millions the slaves of the few, and makes of these few the slaves of their own power, of their own riches. I will destroy this order of things that saps enjoyment from labor, making labor a burden, and enjoyment a vice, that makes one man miserable through want and another through superfluity. ... that compels hundreds of thousands to devote their vigorous youth in the busy idleness of soldiers, officials, speculators, and money-makers, and to the maintenance of these vile conditions, while the other half must support the whole shameful edifice at the cost of the immeasurable exhaustion of their powers and the sacrifice of all the joys of life. ...

So up, ye peoples of the earth! Up ye mourners, ye oppressed, ye poor! ... Up and follow my steps in all your varied multitudes, for I know no distinction among those who follow me. Two peoples only are there henceforth: the one that follows me, the other that withstands me. The one I lead to happiness; over the other I tread, crushing it under foot, for I am Revolution, I am the ever-creative Life, I am the one God whom all beings acknowledge, who comprises, animates and makes happy all that is![71]

Such is Wagner's manifesto of 1849. Had he seen that other manifesto of Marx and Engels of 1848? Had Bakunin brought it along with him, perhaps? Or had he recited it from memory? Wagner's highstrung appeal is compounded of many elements: there is Feuerbach in it, for does it not conclude with the impassioned words that "I am a Man," also means "Man is become God"? There is the hedonistic socialism of the St.-Simonians and the utopian socialists. And not least, the hurricane fury of Bakunin. ...

Wagner had taken over the management of the *Volksblätter* while Röckel was away in Prague. The latter was soon to discover that the revolution in Bohemia so eloquently anticipated by Bakunin, who had armed the German emissary with letters, was even less than a figment. It was nonexistent. So he must have received Wagner's note of May 2, the day before the Dresden uprising, with some relief.

Everything is in a state of unrest here. All the associations, this afternoon the Communal Guard, and even the Prince Albert regiment, which is stationed here, have declared in the most energetic terms for the German Constitution. So has the Town Council. A decisive conflict is in the offing, if not with the King, at any rate with the Prussian troops. Only one thing is feared—a revolution may break out too soon. ...[72]

The uprising broke out the next day, and upon hearing the news Röckel returned immediately.

May 3, 1849. The King rejected the demands of the democratic party for the Constitution, and proceeded to order the Communal Guard dissolved. Wagner had been attending a meeting of the *Vaterlandsverein*, merely, as he made sure to state later in his autobiography, as a "guest-listener." As he was making his way home,

> Suddenly from the nearby Tower of St. Anne's Church I heard the clang of the storm signal—a sign that the outbreak had begun. . . . . The sound of the bell so close by had a very decided impact on me ... The entire square before me appeared bathed in a dark-yellowish, almost brown light, something I had once experienced in Magdeburg during an eclipse of the sun. At the same time I had the sensation of a vast, indeed extravagant, delight.

The struggle had commenced. A crowd of citizens had attacked the arsenal. Soldiers had fired upon them, and there were numerous casualties.

> The sight excited me beyond measure, and I understood the cries that came from all sides. "To the barricades! To the barricades!" Mechanically I was swept along with the stream toward the City Hall.[73]

He hurried to the printer Römpler and asked him to print a number of placards with the inscription directed to the Saxon troops: "Are you with us against the foreign troops?" For along with others, he had heard that in the Württemberg insurrection, the revolutionaries had been able to win over the army to their side. Had there been better organization and leadership at the beginning of the Dresden uprising, a similar *coup* might have been achieved. But alas! while there was no lack of courage, daring, and will among the population—where were the leaders?

On the night of May 3–4 the King of Saxony fled to the city of Königstein, and in Dresden a provisional government took over. Spirits ran high, for news from other parts of Germany spoke of uprisings in Baden, the Palatinate, and Breslau. In Saxony, a student corps was already on its way to join their brothers in Dresden.

Both Wagner and Bakunin are in general agreement as to the role the latter played at a critical moment of the uprising. His own role Wagner minimized, in keeping with his retrospective revisionary tendency. Bakunin's schooled eye saw at once the dangers and the possibilities in the uprising—the hazards of a disorganized and inexperienced leadership, especially on the military side; the divisions within the ranks of the provisional government consisting of conflicting political factions; the weakness of the opposition due to the paucity of Saxon troops in the city; the possibility of winning the city in an immediate, organized, and unified attack. In the end, Bakunin overcame the national suspicion of some of the leaders and prevailed upon them to engage experienced Polish military men who were available. It was in a moment of crisis that Bakunin always proved most coolheaded and firm. Others in these tense moments might vacillate—as they did; some of the leaders, already weakened, absented themselves from the city or fled to safety. The rank and file of insurrectionists, abandoned by the more conservative elements, fought stubbornly. Reinforcements from surrounding localities kept arriving. Unfortunately, on May 5, the first Prussian troops appeared in Dresden. The critical point had been reached. Recalling those hours, Bakunin wrote:

I spoke a great deal, I gave advice and commands, and became, so to speak, the entire "Provisional Government." I did everything in my power to save the lost and apparently dying Revolution. I did not sleep, eat or drink; I was utterly exhausted, and yet could not for a moment leave the council room of the government, for fear Tzschirner [one of the members of that government] might once more take flight, and leave my dear friend Heubner alone. Several times I convoked the leaders of the barricades, and strove to restore order and to concentrate forces for the imminent attacks.[74]

Concerning Otto Leonhard Heubner, city councillor of Dresden and a member of the provisional government, Bakunin could not speak enough. A moderate republican and democrat, he gave all his energies and spirit to the revolutionary movement, shirking no tasks, firm and dedicated to the last. As Wagner reported,

Heubner recognized the necessity of the most energetic measures, and no longer shrank from any of Bakunin's proposals. . . Bakunin never left the city hall and Heubner in order to issue counsel and information everywhere, doing so with remarkable coolness and self-possession.[75]

Wagner himself, though not in any official or near-official capacity, was no less active. With the arrival of Prussian troops, he was enjoined to serve as lookout, and his point of observation was the Kreuzkirche, the Church of the Holy Cross. His observations he communicated on papers wrapped around stones thrown to sentries below. He was there, and he was everywhere; moving from the church to the town hall, escorting additional reinforcements to the proper mustering places. At night, in the tower, he discussed philosophy and music, and undoubtedly his own artistic plans for the future. He moved around freely, and took occasion to visit his home and reassure Minna as to his safety, and, it seems certain, also to plan possible routes of escape should there be an ultimate collapse. ... But he remained courageous and undaunted, even though the tower of the church soon came under fire from the opposing soldiery.

The issue was not long in being resolved. By May 9, the combined Prussian and Saxon troops began closing in on the Town Hall.

When it became apparent [Bakunin reported] that Dresden could not hold out much longer, I proposed to the "Provisional Government" to blow us all up along with the Town Hall, for I had accumulated plenty of ammunition there. But I was overruled ...[76]

Tragedy is winged. Retreat was proclaimed toward Freiberg and Chemnitz, where it was hoped that the forces could be regrouped and strengthened with reinforcements. For safety, Wagner had gone ahead and deposited Minna in Chemnitz, where his brother-in-law and sister resided. Volunteers streaming toward beleaguered Dresden forced him to return to that city. Here he learned that Röckel had already been captured by the enemy. Wagner was commissioned to set out and rally troops from adjacent districts, and on the way he learned that almost all hope was gone.

Was Richard Wagner the unwitting angel of the doom that fell upon the leaders Bakunin, Heubner, and Martin? Ernest Newman believes he was, and that in the account Wagner gives of these incidents in his autobiography, he

refrains from adding, that, as we learn from Bakunin himself, he too counselled Heubner to keep up the struggle; he described the promising state of affairs in Chemnitz, on the strength of which he advised a march thither, where a call should be made for a Constituent Assembly for all Saxony ... Wagner, in fact, had once more managed to persuade himself that all was not yet lost; Chemnitz and the whole of the Vogtland, he assured his associates, were strong for revolution. Bakunin, at his trial, deposed that "it was Wagner's account of the state of affairs in Chemnitz that determined us to make for there." In a sense, then, the subsequent capture of the other leaders at Chemnitz was the direct result of Wagner's harangues. He was the one man who, in virtue of his recent visit to the town, could presumably speak with assurance of the hopefulness of the conditions there. The others listened to him, and as a consequence went to their doom.[77]

Whatever the ultimate truth, the tragic fact remains that while Wagner was away visiting his wife and relatives in one part of Chemnitz, in another, in a hotel, Bakunin, Heubner, and Martin were seized by the police and arrested.

Richard Wagner escaped. Helped along by friends and relatives and leaving Minna in Chemnitz, he made his way to Weimar, where his friend Liszt was preparing a performance of *Tannhäuser*. Hidden from general view, the political fugitive attended a rehearsal and was overwhelmed by Liszt's production. Stay in the Duchy of Weimar was, however, hazardous. It was not likely that the ruling house of Weimar would grant him asylum.

In the *Dresden Anzeiger* of May 19, 1849, six days after Wagner's arrival in Weimar, appeared a notice:

> The Royal Kapellmeister Richard Wagner, of this place, who is more particularly described below, is wanted for examination on account of his active participation in the recent rising here, but as yet has not been found. The police are therefore instructed to look out for him, and, if he is found, to arrest him and communicate at once with me.

> Dresden, the 16th of May, 1849. Von Oppell, Deputy Town Police.[78]

With a warrant out for him, Wagner managed to make his way to Zurich. Here he obtained a passport for Paris, and thence returned to Zurich once more around June 26, where he was joined by Minna, who had gone back to Dresden ...

* * *

There were no triumphant horn-calls to announce his arrivals now. Relieved that he had not been caught in the widening police net spread out for him and others, his conscience slightly tormented by the fate that awaited his imprisoned associates, there was little of the heroic Siegfried about him. What would he not have given to possess that hero's magic cloak of invisibility, the *Tarnkappe?* For the time being he was comparatively safe. In his traveling bags were numerous finished and unfinished works; in his head innumerable projects, some of vast dimension. Had he not, even under fire in the Kreuzkirche, planned the composition of a dramatic work on the subject of Achilles, with a strongly Feuerbachian ingredient?

He also carried with him—in his mind, of course—Siegfried's sword, Baldung, a dangerously double-edged weapon. It scintillated with the lightnings of "myth," "folk," and "the unconscious." One edge still sparkled Revolution, Feuerbach, Bakunin, and world-reform. When in time this edge dulled, the other was sharpened, and shed strange, new lights ...

For the time being Siegfried is his sun god, victorious over the dark dragon guarding the gold-hoard, and thus possessor of cosmic powers over creation. But already there is an incumbent darkness, for as day succeeds night, so Siegfried too will be doomed. In the eternal iteration, the dragon's heirs will bring about his downfall.

The golden hoard is the metallic entrails of the earth. It is power, it is weaponry, it is the ring that commands. Above all, it is Gold—the fulcrum for dominating the world.[79]

For the children of light as well as of darkness covet it greatly. ...

* * *

It is a strange, conglomerate mythology that Wagner is creating. It associates Siegfried, Jesus Christ and Emperor Frederick Barbarossa in a common enterprise, and endows the primitive Germans with a special mission. As Wagner saw it through Frederick's eyes,

> The most ancient, legitimate race of kings is preserved in the German people. It derives from a Son of God, who is known as Siegfried by his immediate racial succession; but among other peoples of the earth he is known as Christ. For the salvation and happiness of his race, and its succession, the peoples of the earth, he performed the most glorious feat, and suffered death therefor.[80]

Siegfried and Jesus are sun gods, and Frederick Barbarossa was originally the High Priest, King and Guardian of the Hoard, which, as Wagner now states, and thereby previsions things to come, was later transformed into the Holy Grail!

After the destruction of the race of the Nibelungs, the great myth of Siegfried and the Hoard became the property of poetry. The gold itself settled like a precipitate, and was turned into the idea of "real possession or property."

> Though in the most ancient religious representations the hoard appears as the magnificence of the earth disclosed in the light of day, we, of a later generation, see in its poetic formulation, the might-giving booty of the hero, a reward for the most valiant and marvelous deed over a vanquished and terrible foe.[81]

Once upon a time, under the institution of feudalism, in its original purity, the hoard was the guerdon given for services, for deeds performed.

> But from the moment that a fief became hereditary, man, and along with him personal proficiency, his activity and deeds, lost their worth, which was now transferred to possessions. Hereditary possessions, and not the soundness of the individual, endowed heirs with their importance. The ever deeper devaluation of man, compared with the ever-rising valuation of possessions which followed, became ultimately embodied in the most anti-human institutions, like that of primogeniture, from whose perverted nature the later nobles sucked in all sorts of obscurantism and pride, without considering that in deriving their worth only from family possessions, that had grown rigid, they were openly denying human nobility, and rejecting it. ...

> Possession became right, and it was so preserved because thereafter, under more developed systems, all that existed and was deemed valid, was derived from it. Whoever participated in possessions, and knew how to obtain them, was thenceforth considered a natural prop of public power. ...

The "poor people" sang, read, and in time printed the Songs of the Nibelungs, the only heirloom remaining to them of the hoard; their faith in it never ceased; they only knew that it was not to be found in this world, but was once more hidden away in a mountainside, whence Siegfried once wrested it from the Nibelungs. ...[82]

He believed that "the way from desire to satisfaction is Activity,"[83] and he practised what he believed. In the theoretical essays of 1849 to 1852, Wagner set forth the programmatic background for his own dramatic and operatic work that was to culminate in the *Ring der Nibelungen*, as well as a general formulation of the role and nature of Artist, and Man, in particular, as he foresaw him in the future he was delineating.

An incandescent white flame of rebellion against the tendencies of his own time, especially as reflected in Art, fuses these essays into a unity. Entitled "Art and Revolution," "The Artistic Genius of the Future," "Artistic Creation of the Future," "Opera and Drama," they attempt a historic summation of the history of art, most particularly of the drama, in its relation to the historic changes within their times. Sketchy, and frequently faulty in historical accuracy or in matters of interpretation, they nevertheless contain, on the whole, a number of profound statements, acute insights, and valid demands for the restoration of the artist and his art to what Wagner believes to be his rightful place in the world.

The underlying metaphysic, if such it may be called, upon which Wagner relies, is that of Feuerbach and the Young Hegelians, particularly in his rejection of traditional "idealism," whether of the philosophical schools or of Christianity—although the figure of Christ remains ever luminous as humanity's Savior. Nature and the natural world are the bases upon which man builds his world of art and thought, and the highest products of art are achieved in a harmonious understanding between man and nature.

> The free Greek, ... created art out of the joy of man; the Christian, who rejected both Nature and himself, could bring his offerings to his God solely on the altar of renunciation; he could not bring his actions, his labors as an offering; only through abstention from all independent, vigorous creation could he, so he believed, bind himself to God. Art is the loftiest activity of Man, who is sensuously developed, and is in harmony both with himself and with Nature.[84]

As for the human art of the future, that is rooted in the soil of nature, from which it rises to "unapprehended heights."

> Its growth is from that which is below to that which is above; like that of a tree, it rises from the earth to the sky, from man's nature into the farthest spiritual reaches of humanity.[85]

The Greeks could portray and embody their ideal in "the beautiful, strong and free man," because within them the spirit of community was active and powerful. Hence, in the highest achievement of Greek poetry, that is, Tragedy, man could recognize himself in "the noblest part of his being," as "united with the noblest part of the communal being of the whole nation."[86]

With the dissolution of the Attic state, the communal spirit splintered in a thousand directions. With Rome came "materialism," slavery, and the loss of human dignity.

And the fullest expression of this condition could no longer be found in Art, but in Christianity, which, rejecting Man and his Nature, could only make its offerings on the "altar of renunciation." But that too degenerated, and remains degenerate in our own day, for Christianity today has tied itself to political absolutism. Art became subservient to the "ruler." And worst of all, now an even more degraded master, Industry, has come to rule the arts, and his god is Mercury.

> Such then is the art now filling the entire civilized world! Its true nature is Industry, its moral goal and purpose, Money; its aesthetic object, the entertainment of the bored.[87]

Art has become a mechanical handicraft; industry knows no love or purpose and neither does the slave of industry, dishonored in his dignity as a human being. Today, we are all slaves. Greed and egoism are the watchwords of our civilization. That which was once one is now disparate, atomized. Tragedy, which combined the elements of dance, word, and song, has likewise become fragmented. We have forgotten what the Greeks taught us, that "beauty and strength, as the basis of public life, can only achieve a felicitous permanence when they are the property of all human beings."[88]

It was necessary to free Art from the tentacles of Mammon.

> Only the great human Revolution ... can win for us this form of art. The artistic work of the future must embrace the spirit of man free of all national limitation ... We must love all mankind, in order to love ourselves ... We must rise up from the dishonoring yoke of slavery, the universal mechanization, with its pallid Mammon-soul, toward a free artistic humanity with its radiant world soul.[89]

For Art and Revolution have this common goal: "the beautiful Man." Revolution will give him strength, and Art, beauty.

> Hitherto Man has thought himself merely an instrument in the achievement of a purpose lying outside himself. But once Man sees himself as the ultimate end of Man, and understands that he can achieve this goal only in community with other men ... then Social Reason will have become the Holy Father of Humanity.[90]

The splintered communal spirit will thus be integrated into a whole; and Egoism, that bane of mankind, will be annihilated, through the fullest satisfaction of Ego's needs on a universal basis.

> The fullest satisfaction of egoism is reached in Communism—i.e., through the complete negation, annulment of egoism; for a need is satisfied only when it is no longer present.[91]

And addressing himself to sceptical contemporaries:

> Do you believe that with the decline of our present conditions and with the commencement of the new, communistic world-order history and the historic life of man will cease? On the contrary, only then will the true, lucid historic life begin when traditional, so-called historic consistency ceases, founded on fable, tradition, myth and religion, custom and institutions, justification and assumptions which at their utmost rested not upon a historic consciousness, but, for the most part, on mythical, fantastic invention. Take monarchy and hereditary possession as examples.[92]

The State must be destroyed, for it exists solely as a result of the vices of society. Whatever virtues society possesses are the gifts of human individuality. The destruction of the State means "the self-realization of the religious consciousness of society in its purely human essence."[93] Only in a freely self-determined individuality can we find the basis for the social religion of the future.

What of Art? It too must transcend prevalent egoism, which is the essence of its contemporary expression, centering as it does on the "individual" genius. Such transcendence of individuality in the future will make of genius a participant in the "communal genius." For the true "inventor" is always the People, which attains to full consciousness of itself not so much in Science as in Art.[94]

> Who will be the Artist of the Future? The poet, the actor, the musician, the sculptor? Let us put it succinctly: The People. The same People to whom we owe Art in general, the only true art form, that which lives in our memory, and has been subjected by us to imitation and distortion, through our deleterious obsession with possessions and property, and the preservation of what is.

Not the "people" as we see it today, a monstrous distortion of our present civilization, a product of an unnatural culture, in no wise different from those who think only of a profitable gain of five per cent,[95] that which today is called "rabble."

Thus a mystical *Volksgeist*—"folk-spirit"—is tied to a concrete Revolution, both to find their most articulate embodiment in the new synthesis: the Drama of the Future, the "true drama," conceivable only out of the "common impulse of all the arts toward a direct communication with a common public."[96]

For the Theatre is the "most comprehensive, the most influential of cultural institutions," and must be made a public art, freed of the idea of gain. All people must have free entry to the theatre. It is their communal expression, by way of the artist. Drama must become "universal drama," the fullest embodiment of the artistic desire for communication, and demanding communal participation.[97]

Beethoven has paved the way, and his Ninth Symphony is the "salvation of Music from its particularity into the generality of Art." In breaking down the separateness of the various constituents of art, he already anticipates the synthesis of the future.

But not only will the artist be freed from the quotidian concerns of the market, but Man in general, also thus liberated and enabled to gain the greatest joys out of life— he too will be dedicated to making Man an Artist.

> Jesus Christ will have shown us that we are all brothers and equal; Apollo, however, will have set the stamp of strength and beauty upon this great brotherhood; he will have conducted humanity out of doubt as to her own worth to a consciousness of her own highest powers ... So let us build the altar of the future, in life as well as in living Art, to the two sublimest teachers of mankind: Jesus, who suffered for humanity's sake, and Apollo, who raised her to her joyous dignity.[98]

In rhapsodic terms, Wagner apostrophizes "the people," comparing them to the mythical Wieland, the Nordic smith, who though captured and maimed by the evil King Neiding, succeeds in forging his own wings and escapes to his beloved Swanhilde. It is "the people" who are the true creators of this very legend.

Oh sole, magnificent Folk. You yourselves are Wieland! Forge your own wings, and swing aloft![99]

As for the Artist, of all human beings he is the one who is capable of seeing a still unformed world as if already formed. He is

the begetter of the art-work of the future …, who anticipates the life of the future, and desires to be contained within it. Whoever nourishes this longing born of his own capacities is already living in the better life. Only one being is capable of this—the Artist.[100]

It is sad to reflect that as he grew older and more successful, Wagner became inclined to forget his debts to those he had borrowed from, as if to obliterate their memories. *Das Kunstwerk der Zukunft*—"Artistic Creation of the Future," one of his most inspired manifestos of this time, he dedicated in 1850 to Ludwig Feuerbach, from whom he had drawn so many of his philosophical notions. In later republications of that work, he retained the borrowings but omitted the dedication to his creditor, whom he had addressed in "grateful reverence" and to whom he had declared in the dedication that in this particular work he was only returning Feuerbach's property to him. "This work owes its existence to the impression your writings made on me …"[101]

His own "artistic creation of the future" was maturing. In 1851 he wrote:

I propose to present my myth in three complete operas, preceded by a prologue … In a festival dedicated to this end, I propose to present these three dramas and prologue in the course of three days and an evening before. I will have attained the purposes of this presentation fully, if I and my artistic collaborators, the actual performers, succeed in communicating them to the audience there gathered, so that they experience a truly emotional (not critical) understanding.[102]

Thus, during the stormy years between 1848 and 1852 he conceived and carried out the idea of a series of connected dramas that were to form *The Ring of the Nibelungs*. To what extent historical events of which he had been a part in Dresden, the fate of his associates and friends, his own flight, the debacle of the German Revolution—and similar disasters in other countries, particularly France—and finally the Napoleonic *coup d'état*, affected the work in progress, is hard to determine precisely. Eventually he combined the theme of the first completed drama, *The Death of Siegfried*, for which he had already sketched the music in 1850, with that of Wotan and the Doom of the Gods. What had begun as a triumphant paean to a Germano-Hellenic hero, a poem of affirmation, terminated in the grim debacle of Valhalla and the universe. Hero and gods alike perish, direct and indirect victims of the curse on the hoard of gold—a crime that can never be exorcised or atoned for. The redemptive hero cannot save the world through his self-sacrifice, or the tainted gods through a return of the gold.

It might almost seem that the contemporary events of history had at first brightened and then darkened Wagner's horizon, and that Schopenhauer had replaced Feuerbach. Cosmic change—growth, decay and death—were to become world-processes, and the height of wisdom demanded that the will acquiesce in this process. Wotan, in Wagner's words, was to rise to the tragic height of willing his own doom. The curse of the gold stolen from Nature had proved fatal to love, and even its restoration cannot annul the decree of Fatality. …

For the moment, in addition to projecting the Art Forms of the future, he had also defined the Woman of the Future. Actually she was, and was to remain, the idealized vision and image of the women of his own present, in the course of years intensified in an erotic crescendo, to burst into an orgiastic fortissimo in *Tristan and Isolde.* That woman had already appeared in *The Flying Dutchman* and in *Tannhäuser,* as well as in *Lohengrin.*

As an element of the Artistic Creation of the Future, however,

> Music is Woman. The nature of woman is Love; but this very love is a receptive one; and in its receptivity an unreserved self-yielding love. Only at the moment of her surrender does woman achieve full individuality. … Woman loves unconditionally, because she must love.

Already we hear anticipations of Isolde, as her dedication becomes equivalent to a "self-annulment"—for "in order to *do,* a woman need only to be what she is," a spontaneous creature, who "must not *will,* for she can only will one thing—to be Woman!"[103]

In *The Death of Siegfried,* Wagner had already developed the verse form he was to use for his heroic cycle, approximating, as he believed, the prosody of the Icelandic *Eddas.* The lines are generally brief, and emphatically alliterated. This is the celebrated *Stabreim.*

Here is Brünnhilde, anticipating Siegfried's approach:

> *Siegfried! Siegfried ist nah'!*
> *Seinen Gruss sendet er her!—*
> *Verglimme, machtlose Glut!*
> *Ich steh' in stärk' rem Schutz!*

A modern German rendering of the Icelandic *Song of Sigurd,* which approximates the original alliterations, goes as follows (Sigurd is addressing Brynhild):

> *Dräue mir Tod auch, ich denk' nicht an Flucht,*
> *als Zager nicht ward ich erzeugt;*
> *Mein Gluck wird's sein, dich ganz zu besitzen,*
> *solange das Leben mir währt.*[104]

* * *

From the heights of Valhalla and its gods and heroes, we return to terrestrial matters and other grim dooms—those of the participants in the Dresden uprising of 1849.

The leaders were condemned to death, but their sentences were commuted to long-term or life imprisonment. Among those, August Röckel and Mikhail Bakunin were confined to the Saxon fortress-prison of Königstein. Röckel was to remain imprisoned till 1862, adamant and intractable in his refusal to repent and recant. Bakunin's incarcerations were more sensational and international, for he was moved from Saxony to Bohemia and then to Russia.

In the early part of 1850 Wagner was staying in Bordeaux, before returning to and settling in Switzerland. He had not heard of the commutations, and the news of the imminent execution of Röckel and Bakunin circulating in French journals moved him to address a letter to his friends in March 1850, which he hoped would be transmitted to the prisoners by Frau von Lüttichau.

> My dear Friends, Never would I have written to you in order to console you, for I knew you needed no such consolation. Now I am informed that the King of Saxony has confirmed your death-sentences. ... Whether I was awake or asleep, you were always near me; in your strength and in your suffering, you who were both enviable and to be commiserated with. And now, I am writing you when you are preparing to receive the stroke from the hand of that same executioner, for whose humanization you had been fighting. ... We see two heroes before us, who driven by the holy need to love mankind, have grown into joyful heroes. I greet you, my dear ones! You show us what all of us could be. Die then, gladly, in the bliss of your high worth! ... I look freely and calmly toward the future, and thus with renewed and winged strength to do my part and work with all my abilities for that for which you are now giving up your lives. You will live on! Like an ever-widening circle in a pool, your memory will swell and be a gladdening and loving remembrance to coming generations. Die then, envied, admired, and beloved.![105]

The letter never reached the prisoners. Whether its rhetoric would have heartened is doubtful, or whether they would have rejoiced with him in his invitation to die "gladly." At the moment of writing, Wagner no doubt felt that he was actually making a commitment to continue the work of his friends. But he was beset by moral and psychological ambiguities. In June 1849 he had written his friend Liszt, giving him his assurance that he had "learned" his lesson from the Dresden rising.

> It is out of the question that I should ever again take part in a political upheaval. What rejoices me, and what I can swear to, is that I have become entirely an artist.[106]

But to Uhlig he was writing as late as 1851, speaking of the *Ring*, that he could imagine a performance of that work "only after the revolution."

> For the revolution alone can provide me with my artists and my audience. The next revolution must of necessity make an end of the whole of this theatre business of ours; it must and will all come crashing down; that is inevitable. Then I will throw up a theatre on the Rhine and send out invitations to a great dramatic festival. After a year of preparation, I then produce my whole work in the course of four days; and with it I make clear to the men and women the meaning of this revolution in the noblest sense of the word. The public will understand me. The present cannot.[107]

While he was thus communing and communicating, Mikhail Bakunin was undergoing strange experiences. On June 6, 1850, the King of Saxony commuted his death sentence (along with that of two others) to lifelong imprisonment. On the demand of Austria, he was soon yielded up, lodged in the Bohemian prisons of Hradčin and Olomouc. On May 15, 1851, he was found guilty of high treason and condemned to death; but on that same day as a result of Tsarist pressure, he was conveyed to Russia, imprisoned in the Peter-Paul Fortress of ignominious celebrity, and condemned to solitary confinement. In 1854 he was transferred to the other dreaded prison, Schlüsselberg, on Lake Ladoga. Tsar Nicholas time and again rejected Bakunin's pleas to be sent to hard labor in Siberia. Nicholas died in 1855, and Alexander II came to the throne. Many prisoners and exiles were then amnestied, but not Bakunin. Once more Bakunin's appeal fell on deaf ears. Bakunin's old mother pleaded with the new Tsar, but all she received was the answer, "*Sachez, Madame, que tant que votre fils vivra, il ne pourra jamais être libre.*"[108] So it seemed that her son was destined to remain in solitary and die in prison. The Tsar was proved wrong, not because of his graciousness, but because he did not know Bakunin. ...

It was during his confinement in the Peter-Paul Fortress that Bakunin composed the notorious *Confession*. It was not published until after the Bolshevik Revolution, and remained totally unknown, except to the authorities, until 1921. But it was a document that would haunt its author for the rest of his life. Tsar Nicholas transmitted through Count Orlov of the Third Division his request—as, in his words, a "spiritual father" addressing his "spiritual son"—to write out a full account of his life, his activities, and his errors. For was the Tsar not the head both of state and church, and in truth the Father of his people?

With the ominous prospect of a life within four walls, with no one to speak to, and worse, no prospect of any activity; with prevision of mind and body deteriorating, Bakunin composed an abject "recantation." "*Mea culpa, mea culpa,*" he cried. It is a shocking, striking, utterly distressing document. Was it designed as a shrewd piece of strategy, a show of sincerity to cover up a skilful piece of insincerity? For the document is not all of one piece. Alongside the breast-beatings, there are many brilliant and perceptive arguments in justification of his past behavior. He did not altogether abjure his moral being. He did not, as he put it, name those who might be endangered by his confession and who might be within reach of the Tsar or the Third Division or their West-European allies. He gave an astonishingly vivid picture of his own life and the conditions that brought him to revolutionary activity. He presented a graphic image of what he believed to be the decadence of the West and the emergence of Communism. At times one is surprised at his warm candor, as for example in his description of the bearing of French workers during the 1848 Revolution.

> At that time I lived [Bakunin writes] for over a week in a barrack, in the company of workers, two paces from the Luxemburg Palace. . . . . Majesty! I assure your Majesty, within no other class, nowhere else, and at no other time did I find such noble self-sacrifice, such moving and true honesty, so much warm feeling and joy along with such great heroism, as among these kindly, uncultured people, a thousand times better than their leaders![109]

As for his anti-Russian activities,

> Your Majesty, I confess that I proposed to the Slav-Congress the project—the total destruction of the Austrian Monarchy ... My second and principal aim was to discover in the union of the Slavs a point of departure for a broadly planned, revolutionary propaganda in Russia, in order to launch a struggle against You, Your Majesty![110]

In astonishingly frank words, Bakunin went on to depict conditions in Russia, the corruption of officials, the degraded state of the peasants, the reign of fear that prompted him to envision salvation in a revolution—and in a republic. But now, he wrote,

> I believe that in Russia more than anywhere else what is needed is a strong dictatorship, exclusively devoted to the improvement and enlightenment of the masses ... but one

without parliamentary forms …, a strong power thoroughly uncircumscribed or delimited …[111]

And then the apology.

In a word, my crimes against your sacred powers knew no measure or bounds … I confess out of my deepest soul, that I have committed crimes again You, Your Majesty, against Russia, and that they deserve the severest punishment![112]

I am a great criminal and do not deserve mercy. I beg of Your Majesty … do not allow me to rot in eternal bondage … Were the severest punishment of hard labor to be my lot, I would accept it gladly … In solitary confinement one is tormented by uninterrupted, useless memories. Thinking and remembering become unspeakable torture; one lives for a long time, against one's will, and without dying, one dies daily in inactivity and grief … If I had to choose, I believe I would prefer not only death, but even corporal punishment to lifelong imprisonment in the fortress.[113]

The terrifying *Confession* concludes with a request once more to see his family.

Not the least fascinating elements of the *Confession* are the notations from the pen of the Tsar himself, glossing Bakunin's remarks. They range from exclamations of approval of such statements as "the fruit of German Protestantism is Anarchy," to an ironic comment on Bakunin's hope that the Tsar of Russia would place himself at the head of a great revolutionary movement that would unite all the Slavs, as well as to paternal, forgiving sentiments, such as, "the repentance of any sinner can bring him salvation, but only when he speaks with his heart," and to sarcastic and angry ones, as when Bakunin pleads not to be forced to involve others in his Confession, "not to confess the sins of others," as he put it, and Nicholas comments, "With these words he destroys all confidence!"

The Tsar read the *Confession* very carefully. In the end, he agreed with Count Orlov. "He is not to be trusted. I believe he can continue to stay where he is now."

The plea Bakunin addressed to Alexander II in February 1857 was even more self-abasing and sycophantic.

Your Majesty! With what name shall I call my past life? Squandered in chimerical and fruitless efforts, it ended in criminality. But I myself was neither self-seeking nor evil. I harbored a deep love of the good and the true, and was ready to sacrifice myself for it. But false principles, a false attitude and sinful self-love misled me into criminal entanglements, and once I had entered upon a false trail, I believed it to be my duty and honor to persist to the end. I plunged into the abyss from which only the all-powerful and saving hand of Your Majesty can free me. …[114]

This time he succeeded. He was ordered deported to Siberia. Four years later, he did the unforeseeable—he managed to escape. He made his way to Japan, then the U.S.A., and then to England. And one day, toward the end of 1861, he knocked on Alexander Herzen's door in London. …

This is as Herzen saw him:

Bakunin was just the same; he had grown older in body only, his spirit was as young and enthusiastic as in the days of the all-night argument with Khomyakov in Moscow. He was just as devoted to one idea, just as capable of being carried away by it, and seeing in everything the fulfilment of his desires and ideals, and even more ready for every experience, every sacrifice, feeling that he had not so much life before him … As soon as Bakunin had looked about him and settled down in London, that is, had made the acquaintance of all the Poles and Russians who were there, he set to work … His nature was a heroic one, left out of work by the course of history … Is it not in itself a sign of greatness that, wherever he was cast up by fate, as soon as he grasped two or three features of his surroundings, he singled out the revolutionary current and at once set to work it farther, to expand it, making it the burning question of life?[115]

An amazing man, this Mikhail Bakunin! Of course, Herzen knew nothing about the *Confession*, nor of the slavish appeal to Alexander II. But was not all of this a successful stratagem? He had traveled two-thirds of the way around the world to return to his beloved scenes of action. Wherever there was to be revolution, there he must be. In this respect he had not changed.

And soon there would indeed be an insurrection in Poland. He was waiting for that moment. . . .

When August Röckel emerged from his long imprisonment, Wagner, then at his height, came to his aid. There is no evidence that he ever met or saw Bakunin again. . . .

4. Alexander Herzen and the Russian Self-Exiled

"And so farewell, my friends, for a long while. … Give me your hands, your support. For I need both. After that … who knows? What have we not seen of late! It may not be so far away as it may seem, that day when we shall meet in Moscow as of old and shall fearlessly raise our glasses to the toast: 'For Russia and freedom.' … My heart refuses to believe that that day will not come; it sinks at the thought of a parting for ever. … It cannot be! And yet, if it is—then I bequeath my toast to my children, and dying on alien soil, I shall preserve my faith in the future of the Russian people and bless it from the distant land of my voluntary exile."

Thus Alexander Herzen on leaving Russia in 1847.

And his cousin, lifelong friend, and future associate in exile as well as in his political publications, the poet Nikolay Ogarev, voices his feelings on his departure:

> Rejoice with me, for I am free at last!
> Free to set forth to foreign land at will.
> But is it not a dream, deceiving me?
> Not so! Tomorrow come the post-horses,
> And then "*von Ort zu Ort*" I'll gallop on,
> Paying for passports what the price may be …
> With fear and doubt I stand before the gate
> Of Europe. And my heart is full
> Of hope, and troubled shadowy dreams. …[116]

Such, indeed, must have been the sentiments of hundreds of other Russians, but few of them were enabled to make their way west unless aided by personal or family affluence or political influence, their efforts being made extremely difficult if they were suspected of a past liberalism. Alexander Herzen and Ogarev had already passed their apprenticeship in Russian exile; while others, like Mikhail Bakunin, were to pay their tribute of imprisonment and exile at a future time. And still another, the novelist Ivan Turgenev, was to wander back and forth between Russia and Western Europe, until he finally settled for good in the West.

Herzen, Bakunin, and Turgenev became the most celebrated of these Russian self-exiles, and their diverse influence was to play an important role in the diffusion of Russian ideas and knowledge of Russian life in Western Europe; in turn they were to act as important agents in the stir and turmoil of the post-1848 reaction in their mother country.

Alexander Herzen was already thirty-five years old when he saw Paris for the first time (Western Europe in fact) in March 1847. This was the moment he and his wife Natalie had long been waiting for.

> In Paris! ... Of that minute I had been dreaming since my childhood. If I might only see the Hôtel de Ville, the Café Foy in the Palais Royal, where Camille Desmoulins picked a green leaf, stuck it on his hat for a cockade and shouted *"à la Bastille!"*
>
> I could not stay indoors; I dressed and went out to stroll about at random. ... Here was the Rue St-Honoré, the Champs-Elysées—all those names to which I had felt akin for long years ... and here was Bakunin himself ... I met him at a street corner; he was walking with three friends and, just as in Moscow, discoursing to them, continually stopping and waving his cigarette. ... I was beside myself with happiness![117]

Who has not felt the same way on first seeing Paris? Who has not followed its streets, dazzled and dazed at the same time by the familiar names, wondering if this were not really a dream? And now to meet Mikhail Bakunin, an old friend, and one who, having come to Western Europe seven years before, was as familiar with it as with his own Moscow? ... That long-interrupted dialogue of seven years earlier, could it not now be resumed, to continue in the Russian way, unintermittently? ....

Yet how far away Russia seemed in those days!

This was the world that epitomized one half of Herzen's education. The other half—the harsher one—was Russian. It had begun with his birth in the fateful year of 1812, almost under French gunfire and within the very presence of the great Napoleon. Alexander Herzen was the illegitimate son of the well-to-do landowner Ivan Yakovlev and his German "mistress," an unacknowledged "wife" in fact, but one who, with her son, was kept apart as if alien, though allowed every advantage the father's wealth could offer. The father was a removed, moody, and hypochondriacal personality, with cultural sympathies of an eighteenth-century Frenchman. The mother remained in the background, a shadowy character, no doubt a long-suffering one, confined to another part of the house, to another world. She is hardly mentioned in her son's *Memoirs*. "Herzen" was the name given the boy, no doubt in remembrance of his German antecedence; and Alexander was brought up trilingually in German, French, and Russian. He was precocious and quick, the spoiled center of the household; he learned easily. But the most drastic lesson he learned when, at age ten or twelve, he discovered his "false position." It was no accident that somewhat later he was to be drawn so intensely to his cousin Natalie, whom he was to marry, and who, like himself, was an illegitimate offspring.

Alexander Herzen's political education commenced upon his first acquaintance with the history of the Decembrist uprising against the Tsar in 1825. It may be said that for him, as for his distant relative and close friend Ogarev, the martyrdom of its five hanged leaders and the exile of the others became enshrined as an ineradicable portion of his life experience. Especially was this true of the young, ill-fated poet Kondraty Ryleev and the political ideologue Pavel Pestel. Herzen and Ogarev's future London periodicals in Russian, composed for Russia, *The Polar Star* and *The Bell*, may be said to have been the "godchildren" of these heroes, just as both writers had always considered themselves "sons of the Decembrists." Both had become fervent admirers of the works of Friedrich Schiller as young men, and remained such to the end. As youngsters they found in him full aesthetic and political gratification; the cult of the *schöne Seele*, "the beautiful soul," and its idealism. Schiller was the poet of Liberty, the creator of the libertarian figure of Don Carlos. At Moscow University, the brilliant philosopher-scientist Prof. Pavlov, a chemist, brought them a sense of the importance of science and scientific thought, along with the philosophy of Schelling and Oken. And of course there were the discussion groups and dinners, the exuberance of which, tinged with political radicalism, led to government recriminations.

Schelling's philosophy was very much in the air, and the young adherents of the Herzen-Ogarev circle revelled in the pantheistic idealism of that thinker. But for the admirers of Decembrism, such an aloof system would scarcely satisfy. The year 1830 and the Revolution in France, and subsequently the insurrection in Warsaw and its suppression, offered the more concrete elements of a reorientation. The process was such as we have seen in other instances. Saint-Simon became superimposed upon philosophic idealism; the march of history as envisioned in that thinker's program brought enthusiasts to a study of French historians such as Guizot, Thierry, and Michelet. The dialectic of ideas received a hastening momentum from history. Thence to action—even if, at the time, such action would be limited to blazing discussions and argumentation. Lamennais hove into Ogarev's ken; he was taken with the Frenchman's vision of a regenerated Christianity, of a God who is humanity and a humanity which could be Godlike. While Herzen wavered for a time between absolute idealism and scientific materialism, eventually he came over to the latter. It was under the influence of his cousin the "Chemist" (Aleksey Aleksandrovich Yakovlev) that he had chosen the faculty of Physics and Mathematics, and he became convinced that

> Without the natural sciences there is no salvation for modern man. Without that wholesome food, without that strict training of the mind by facts, without that closeness to the life surrounding us, without humility before its independence, the monastic cell remains hidden somewhere in the soul, and in the drop of mysticism which might have flooded the whole understanding with its dark waters.[118]

There was, of course, danger in such thoughts and their expression. A jittery government and its agents were quite aware of them and their propounders. It needed but one or two heedless or overt acts, perhaps innocent in themselves but none the less sufficiently provocative, for the authorities to bear down with all their oppressive might. Suspected even while at the university of one or two anti-government pranks, their authors were now under closer surveillance. An earlier university dereliction, such as, for example, coming to the financial aid of the recently exiled Sungurov, brought down a severe reprimand on Ogarev and his friends. But in 1834 it needed but a spy, a provocateur, and a few suspicious fires in Moscow (how often such fires proved useful to the government!) to bring about a tightening of the net. For example, a drinking party, some rather free singing, an informer; and though neither Herzen nor Ogarev was present, accusing fingers pointed to Ogarev as the prime culprit. He was the author of unpublished political songs; other fingers pointed to Herzen's "incriminating" letters to Ogarev. Benckendorff and his Third Section were ever vigilant; arrests followed. The charges were trivial enough: principally of "freethinking" on the part of the alleged culprits. Had they been willing to plead guilty and ask for mercy, they would have gotten off easily. But they refused, and so they were punished— Herzen with a ten months' imprisonment and five years' exile, first to Viatka, then to Vladimir (the first of these on the fringes of Siberia); Ogarev, with exile to his native province of Penza. Others, like Sokolovsky, were sentenced to confinement in the dreaded Schlüsselberg fortress.

In 1834, Herzen was twenty-two years old, Ogarev twenty-one. When they returned from their exile six years later, they were both matured and better educated, though certainly not in the way the Government could have wished or hoped.

They were both "noblemen," and in prison and in exile they learned how differently those of the upper classes were treated from those below them. If they were both to be classed with the "repentant noblemen," those who "repented" of their class status and abdicated from it, they remained "unrepentant" in what they thought and in what they would henceforth do.

The stages of their further education would proceed even more rapidly.

Alexander Herzen and his wife Natalie (they had been married in 1838) returned to metropolitan life in 1840, ready once more to plunge into the stream of ideas and actions. Herzen had seen much by this time that made for a greater readiness of accessibility. Exile had shown him the full extent of that corruption of authority and administration which Gogol had laughingly held up to his fellow-men, and which now manifested itself to Herzen in all its base and degenerate sordidness. He had seen how the superficial crust of "progress" that the regime of Nicholas had tried to impose upon the provinces concealed a vast enslavement and degradation of the human personality. Gogol might laugh, with his broad near-Rabelaisian laughter; Herzen could not. He was later to summarize his impression of the Russia of Nicholas:

> The serf-owner says to his servant: "Shut up, I won't stand for you to answer me." The head of the department remarks, growing pale, to the functionary who dared a rejoinder: "You forget, you know, *with whom* you are speaking!" The Emperor *for opinions* exiles men to Siberia, *for verses* starves others to death in dungeons, and all three are sooner ready to forgive thievery, bribery, murder and brigandage than the insolence of a sense of human dignity and the audacity of independent speech.[119]

And now the intellectual atmosphere in Moscow and Petersburg was alive with Hegel and Hegelianism. What a contrast to the moral barbarism to which he had so recently been exposed! At first sceptical of the easy verbiage with which Hegel was being expounded, he soon plunged into his own, deeper study of the philosopher. Here were Mikhail Bakunin and Vissarion Belinsky, making strange applications of Hegelian doctrine. There was a quarrel with Belinsky—a momentary one, it is true. Bakunin, though, was beginning to see the true meaning of Hegel. Herzen proceeded on his own:

> In the midst of this intestine strife I saw the necessity *ex ipso fonte bibere* and began studying Hegel in earnest. I even think that a man who has not *lived through* Hegel's *Phenomenology* and Proudhon's *Contradictions of Political Economy*, who has not passed through that furnace and been tempered by it, is not complete, not modern. ... The philosophy of Hegel is the algebra of revolution; it emancipates a man in an unusual way and leaves not one stone upon another of the Christian world, of the world of tradition that has outlived itself ...[120]

This was, of course, written much later than the period of the early 1840s, but it represents Herzen's profound insights even at that period. In June 1842 Ogarev returned from Germany, where he had been studying political economy and medicine, while also imbibing philosophy. He brought with him a copy of Feuerbach's *Essence of Christianity*. Herzen recounts the impact of that book:

> After reading the first pages I leapt up with joy. Down with the trapping of masquerade; away with the stammering allegory! We are free men and not the slaves of Xanthos; there is no need for us to wrap the truth in myth.[121]

This was a far cry from those mystical and religious ruminations and daydreams that Herzen and Natalie had indulged in when corresponding with each other when he was in exile, or in the first year of their marriage.

But Herzen's personal ordeals were not by any means over. Once more he was subjected to one of those incredible acts of the Tsar that combined horror with ludicrousness. Toward the end of 1840, Alexander Herzen in one of his letters to his father had made a slighting remark about the St. Petersburg police. The "slur" came to the attention of the authorities, and although both Benckendorff and Dubelt did their best to intervene, the Tsar himself decided on a more or less severe punishment—a term of exile. Herzen was then working for the Ministry of the Interior, and through the good graces of his superior he was transferred in an official capacity to Novgorod, not far removed from Moscow. It was exile nevertheless, but another stage in his education.

It was here that Ogarev visited him, having returned from Germany, and presented him with a copy of Feuerbach. Many are the unpredictable ways in which a man's mind unfolds. After Feuerbach, Herzen followed with a close study of Hegel's *Phenomenology*. The intoxication of new ideas was upon him; the draught was inebriating but at the same time fortifying. Feuerbach delivered him from a religious mythology, brought him back to Man as the maker of his gods, Man the transplanter of his best ideals onto the divinities of his own creation. About Hegel's work he now wrote to editor Kraevsky:

> Tell Belinsky that I have at last read through, *and read well*, the *Phenomenology* and that henceforth he should berate only the followers ... but that he should not touch the great

shade himself. Towards the end of the book it is as if one were entering a great sea: depth, transparence, and the breath of the spirit carries one along—*lasciate ogni speranza*—the shores disappear, one's sole salvation is within one's breast, but suddenly the cry is heard: *Quid timeas? Caesarem vehis*, fear vanishes, the shore is there before you, the wonderful leaves of fantasy are gone, but the succulent fruits of reality are there ...[122]

A number of philosophical currents now seemed to converge: the Feuerbachian vision of man's self-alienation and its transcendence; the Hegelian dialectic—the cosmos as in eternal motion; the universe in constant struggle and in constant resolution; the preeminence of science as one of the highest manifestations of the march of Reason; and finally, activity as the full realization of life itself. Philosophy and science now were seen not as opponents, but as complementary, one incomplete without the other, like "two Magdeburg hemispheres which seek each other and which, once they are joined, cannot be pulled apart by all the king's horses."[123]

Two essays, "Dilettantism in Science," published in *Notes of the Fatherland* in 1843, and "Letters on the Study of Nature," in the same publication in 1845–1846, constitute paeans to Science, Reason and Man. The latter essay in particular played a very significant part in the philosophic development of Russia. Science, Herzen contended,

> ... has understood, cognized and evolved the truth of reason *as underlying reality*: it has liberated the thought of the world from the phenomenon of the world, all things that exist, from the fortuitous. It has dissolved everything solid and immobile, made transparent everything that is obscure, brought light into darkness; it has revealed the eternal in the transient, the infinite in the finite, and recognized their necessary existence. Finally, it has destroyed the Chinese wall separating the absolute, the true, from man and has hoisted the banner of the autonomy of reason over the ruins.[124]

And as if to underscore this lofty claim, Herzen recounts the achievements of science within his own day:

> What one could hardly dream of at the end of the last century has been accomplished before our very eyes. The small buds of organic chemistry, geology, paleontology, comparative anatomy have grown in our century into huge branches and borne fruit exceeding our wildest hopes. The world of the past, obedient to the mighty voice of science, has left the tomb to bear witness to the upheavals which accompany the evolution of the surface of the globe; the soil on which we live, this tombstone of the past life, is growing transparent, as it were; the stone vaults have opened, the interior of the rocks could not retain their secrets. Not only do the half-decayed, half-petrified vestiges again assume flesh, paleontology also strives to discover the law of the relation between geologic epochs and their complete flora and fauna. Then everything that ever lived will be resurrected in the human mind, will be saved from the sad fate of utter oblivion, and those whose bones have been completely decayed, whose phenomenal existence has been utterly obliterated, will be restored in the bright sanctuary of science where the temporal finds its repose and is perpetuated.

This is poetically beautiful and true. But it is not all. In the realm of biology, and of chemistry, scientists have already begun to investigate life itself, the secrets of organic bodies. But it is not only in the theoretical aspects that astounding progress has been achieved. They have reached outside their studies and laboratories to contribute "to a solution of the most important social problems by the use of machines, by bringing into play unemployed and wasted forces. ... They give us the means for freeing the hands of man from endless backbreaking toil."[125]

The realm of the possible seems infinite. Impossibility disappears.

Impossible for whom [Herzen asks]? When? Why? What is the criterion? Napoleon held that steamships were an impossibility.[126]

And in his diary, he entered, quoting the *Deutsche Jahrbücher:*

"It is necessary to decide once and for all: 'either Christianity and monarchy or science and the republic!'"[127]

What the Tsar, Schelling, and the German idealists had begun, the French now completed. Fourier, Louis Blanc, Proudhon, and again, not least, George Sand—property and capital, the organization of labor, the phalanstery, love and marriage, the role of woman—"socialism" in all its variations—now stood arrayed against the Germans. For Herzen, Proudhon loomed as the equal of Hegel. Only he was more concretely, more fiercely and persistently destructive—of religion, of institutions, of the state.

Herzen ranged himself with other "repentant noblemen." "When I look at the poor peasants," he wrote in 1844 in his diary, "the blood rushes to my heart. I am ashamed of my rights; I am ashamed that I am partly responsible for the misery of their life."[128]

The "repentant noble" was to play a significant role in the thinking both of Russians and of West Europeans; his figure spans the entire century and beyond, from the Decembrists down to Tolstoy and Prince Kropotkin.

The process of emancipation did not stop merely at the renunciation of class privileges, or in an acceptance of "socialism" theoretically, but turned also to the problem of home, love, and marriage. For Belinsky and for Herzen, the novels of George Sand became the new declarations of independence so far as woman and domestic life was concerned. The Saint-Simonian doctrine of the "rehabilitation of the flesh"—the freedom to love—and the liberation from the traditional views of the sanctity of marriage not based on a free union, became crucial elements in the libertarian thinking and reformatory efforts of the Russian liberal intelligentsia. It is out of these currents and the effect of George Sand's own personality and life, that Herzen composed a novel, *Kto vinovat?—Who Is To Blame?*—into which he could now place his own maturing thoughts on the profound social interrelations of personal morality.

Inferior as a work of art, Herzen's novel is still one of the signal contributions of the generation of the forties in its daring and forthright enunciation of radical ideas. Because he was here enabled to weave a great many threads of his own personal experiences and those of his wife, Natalya Alexandrovna Zakharin, Herzen fashioned a formidable subjective and objective projection of a crucial problem. Begun while he was in his second "exile" in Novgorod, the book was completed in 1846 and published in the *Notes of the Fatherland.*

Is it right, Herzen asks, that a human being sacrifice her life in deference to the mandates of a "formal" marriage, as against the claims of passion and love? Such is the case of Lyubov, the heroine of the novel—in many ways a projection of Herzen himself, for she is the illegitimate daughter of General Negrov and a serf woman—a passionate girl living in "two worlds," a product of a decayed social system. Having married her tutor Krutsifersky, a well-meaning but colorless person, she is withering away in the aridity of provincialism. She meets Beltov, like herself a product of two classes, an attractive, worldly figure, a dilettante of culture, a wayward personality without anchor, stability, or goal in life, living in the moment and for the moment. They fall in love, but renounce it. ... He goes abroad, her husband takes to drink, and she falls a prey to a fatal disease.

Who is to blame? Obviously, none of the principal characters. They are destroyed, but are guiltless. They are the innocent products of a gentry background, so far as Lyubov and Beltov are concerned; the more "plebeian" tutor Krutsifersky is its victim. In the drabness and humiliations of provincial life, each suffers in his human dignity, in his or her loss of purpose in life, in some appropriate self-realization. The only exception is the doctor, Krupov, a "scientist," even something of a "materialist," whose clear vision is never blurred by what is around him, and who finds his life fulfilment in service to human beings. Beltov is a "superfluous man," Dr. Krupov is not.

The "superfluous man" is a wraith that wanders through the course of Russian letters in manifold avatars. He is the anti-hero or non-hero of literature, as of life. He is given poetic form in the figures of Eugene Onegin and Lenski in Pushkin's epic poem; he emerges as a demoniac, destructive, and self-destructive element in Lermontov's Pechorin, the "hero" of *A Hero of our Time*, a series of haunting and horrifying episodes. He is a Byron without Greece. Such figures had many descendants, becoming more prosaic, perhaps, and less romantic, but none the less acquiring greater and greater realism and veracity, finally culminating in the classic "anti-heroes" of Turgenev's novels and, consummately, in Goncharov's *Oblomov*. They are the alienated waifs—mostly of the landed classes—who know something of many things, have picked up smatterings of Western letters and philosophy, dabble in science, have little care for their estates, are bored by their dreary neighbors, brood a great deal, and do little. In their mind's eye they see vast plans for this or that reform, but they bring about nothing. Beltov is an exemplification of such a phenomenon, and in that personality Herzen was depicting his own friend Ogarev (only too accurately destined to fulfil Herzen's prediction), as well as Herzen himself at that moment. The danger was there; to escape it was an immediate necessity.[129]

Would he ever really escape it?

In his description of Beltov, T. G. Masaryk has given a masterly epitome of not only this character, but the whole type:

The Russian, who has received a thoroughly European education at the hands of Genevese Frenchmen, astonished the German specialists by his versatility and astonished the French by his profundity, but whereas the Germans and the Frenchmen achieve much, he achieves nothing. He has a positively morbid love of work, but he is unable to secure a practical position in relation to life, incompetent to make contact with an environment wholly foreign to him. He lives only in thoughts and passions, a frigid dreamer, eternally a child. Half his life is spent upon the choice of a profession, and again and again he begins a new career, for he has inherited neither culture nor traditions from his father, nothing but property he does not know how to manage. Thus Beltov's life is the Russian active inactivity, and Beltov is only a generalised human being, a moral Caspar Hauser as it were. ....[130]

To his diary, Herzen confided his more intimate and more daring thoughts:

> Marriage is not the natural result of love, but its Christian result; it brings with it the terrible responsibility of the education of the children, of life in an organized family, etc. ... In the future there will be no marriage; the wife will be freed from slavery; and what sort of word is wife anyway? Woman is so humiliated that, like an animal, she is called by the name of her master. Free relations between the sexes, the public education of children and the organization of property; morality, conscience, public opinion, and not least the police—all this will define the details of relationships. . . . . Why is it that in general woman is rarely able to give herself to living, social interests, but instead leads a purely private life? ... What changes will socialism bring in this respect?. ... In communal life, developed on broad foundations, woman will be more involved in general interests; she will be strengthened morally by education, she will not be so one-sidedly attached to the family. ....[131]

Herzen's dissatisfaction with the Russia of Tsar Nicholas now knew no bounds. What he was later to describe as the "pestilential zone that extended from 1825 to 1855," closed in upon him too. He fought against the constant incompatibility of living in "outward slavery and inward freedom," knowing that such a life meant ultimate disaster. In addition, he was coming into conflict not only with the so-called "Slavophiles," who looked upon all Western thought and movements as destructive of Russia's future, and who would shrink in horror from "socialist" doctrines, but also with his own group of friends, like the historian Granovsky, who were all too ready to compromise, and thought it might be possible to come to terms with autocracy, although they too espoused Western ideas. Herzen was deeply Russian, and Russia was to be the center of his thoughts for the rest of his life. But he could stay no longer. The death of his father in 1846 left him a considerable fortune, and the moment favored departure. He could not have foreseen that had he tarried another two years, his chances of leaving would have disappeared.

So here he was, in 1847, with his wife and children in Western Europe. And here were his Russian countrymen, like Sazanov and Mikhail Bakunin. With the French he found it harder to make friends. He hated hero worship, and resented what he believed to be a certain French superciliousness toward other nationalities, particularly Russians. The Germans in Paris seemed much closer, friendlier, and more communicative. There was Adolf Reichel, the musician; there was Karl Vogt, the biologist, later to be elected to the Frankfurt Parliament; there was the gifted German poet Georg Herwegh. With the last of these (oh, could he but have foreseen!) Herzen's life was to be bound up in tragic convolutions ...

But Paris was astir. This was 1847. Electric currents passed back and forth: forebodings, rumors, talk, publications, meetings, the city itself never resting, never sleeping. It was not only Russians who loved to argue. There was, for example, the talking session between Bakunin and Proudhon, as Herzen describes it:

> ... Until then I had seen very little of Proudhon; I had met him twice at the lodgings of Bakunin, with whom he was very intimate. Bakunin was living at the other side of the

Seine in the Rue de Bourgogne. Proudhon often went there to listen to Reichel's Beethoven and Bakunin's Hegel; the philosophical discussions lasted longer than the symphonies. ... In 1847 Karl Vogt, who also lived in the Rue de Bourgogne, and often visited Reichel and Bakunin, was bored one evening with listening to the endless discussions of phenomenology, and went home to bed. Next morning he went round for Reichel, for they were to go to the Jardin des Plantes together; he was surprised to hear conversation in Bakunin's study at that early hour. He opened the door—Proudhon and Bakunin were sitting in the same place before the burnt-out embers in the fireplace, finishing in a brief summing-up the argument begun overnight.[132]

Very soon it was not to be only talk. The season was pregnant with new fruit; the current of history was swelling. Where would these waters bear them? In many and unpredictable ways, in many strange fashions, lives that had seemed to dwell apart were to be intertwined for good and evil, joy and sorrow, hope and despair, for comradeship and enmity. Disparate and farflung destinies were to be conjoined and severed.

Herzen would never return to his Russia, but remained here in Western Europe to become the bold spokesman for his country, the liberal voice that would resound all over and the writer of one the great memoirs of the century. But his life too will be twisted and interwoven with that of others in tragic ways. And Mikhail Bakunin, the Hegelian? Who would ever have imagined that when the hour struck he would be beside Richard Wagner, his boon-companion and comrade in arms?...

Herzen and his wife were in Italy in February 1848 when the Revolution broke out in France. In May he was in Paris. In June he witnessed the uprisings there, sparked by the closing of the government workshops and the crushing blows administered by the counterrevolutionary forces under Cavaignac, which marked the end of the Revolution and ushered in the days of bitter reaction, recrimination, executions, and deportations. In his *Memoirs* Herzen recalled:

On the evening of the 26th of June ... we heard salvos at short intervals ... We glanced at one another and all our faces were green ... 'They are shooting people,' we said with one voice, and turned away from one another. I pressed my forehead against the window-pane. Such moments provoke ten years of hatred, a lifetime of thirst for vengeance; *woe to him who forgives at such moments!*

He, at any rate, would never forget. He regretted the moment when in one of the barricaded streets a revolutionary, a young man, had offered him a musket. Why had he not mounted the barricade? And now, "I did not die, but it aged me; I am recovering after the days of June as if after a serious illness."[133]

He recovered. To his thinking, the "revolution" was far from over. It would come in the form of an indescribable cataclysm. He, Herzen, was himself a member of the "aristocracy"—he was, after all, a "repentant nobleman," one who had deliberately abjured titles and rights, who recognized, as Herzen wrote in October 1848, that "aristocracy is really a more or less civilized form of cannibalism," as was also true of the "manufacturer who grows rich at the expense of his workmen; a landowner who draws an enormous rent from his estate." "Once the workers no longer want to work for another—that's the end of cannibalism, the point where aristocracy stops." But let the workers and peasants begin to realize their strength and join forces, "then you may bid farewell to your leisure" (Herzen is addressing both aristocrat and bourgeois) "your luxury, your civilization; then the majority can no longer be expended in order to produce a brilliant luxurious life for the minority." And he concluded, "in the realm of ideas, the exploitation of man by man is over, because no one any longer considers the relation to be just."[134]

The upheaval, when it comes, will be violent, terrifying. But such is, and has been, Nature's course. The bitterness within him from the defeated revolution he had just witnessed rankles, and in almost biblical terms he predicts this new "revolution," comparing it to a volcano, or to the march of the early Christians, or to the invasion of the "barbarians": "This lava, these barbarians, this new world, these Nazarenes, who are coming to finish all that is old and impotent and clear the path for the fresh and the new—they are nearer than you think. For it is they, none other, who are dying of hunger, of cold; it is they whose muttering we hear above us, in garrets and in cellars. ..."[135]

He, at least, was not frightened. Time and again he was to be tested. His personal life was not immune from tragic blows (his mother and son would drown in a ship accident); his domestic life was to be marked by agonizing crises—yet he never collapsed. Was he not one of the "sons of the Decembrists"?

And in Paris, he was a marked man. He was known to have collaborated with the Polish poet Adam Mickiewicz in the founding of the radical periodical, *Tribune des peuples*. Foreign emigrés were being constantly watched, and more and more intensely, as the country moved toward a monarchial restoration. In November 1850 he was expelled from Paris, set for another period of wanderings. In 1852 his wife Natalie died, and in that year he finally arrived in England, to begin what was to be another, probably his most fruitful career, as a publicist. His friendships extended far and wide, and in his catalogue of the heroic, he could now join to the names of the Decembrists, contemporaries like Proudhon, Mazzini, Blanqui, and Bakunin, and many, many others. In 1849 he had turned down the Russian government's order to return to that country. The break was final; he was never to return.

There was no denying that Herzen was a deeply wounded spirit. Revolution in Western Europe had been crushed. France, lodestar of revolutions, was now a monarchy, and another "Napoleon"—Louis-Napoleon by name—sat on her throne. And Russia? Herself a most formidable agent in the great debacle, she was entering upon a period of incomparable repression. The period 1848 to 1856, in the words of a Russian historian, "is the darkest hour in the night of Russian obscurantism."[136] Of these dark years, a contemporary wrote as follows:

> One could not move, one could not even dream; it was dangerous to give any sign of thought—of the fact that you were not afraid; on the contrary, you were required to show that you were scared, even when there was no real ground for it—that is what those years have created in the Russian masses.[137]

It was most important to break through this curtain of terror. Tsarist Russia must be apprised that there were forces outside of Russia aware of these conditions, forces of liberalism and hope, to hearten whatever liberal thought was still alive. Tsar Nicholas must not be allowed an absolute triumph. Russia had her own creative forces of resistance: among the peasants, among the middle classes and landowners, even among the aristocracy. And so, in 1853 Herzen established the "Free Russian Press in London," to follow two years later with the Russian Journal *Polnaya zvezda (The Polar Star)*—the name borrowed from the publication edited by the Decembrist Ryleev—and later by a supplement, the *Kolokol (The Bell)*. The papers were immensely successful, and their circulation grew. Smuggled across what might seem impenetrable frontiers and guards, they reached and influenced readers who, Herzen hoped, might in turn influence others, even the peasants. Herzen regarded the peasant-communes of Russia (the *obshchina*) as potential cradles of future revolutionary activity. The abolition of serfdom became a major battle cry; so did the abolition of the Russian censorship. The outbreak of the Crimean War in 1853, and its catastrophic termination for Russia in 1856, were to add additional fuel in Herzen's campaign for reforms. He even appealed to the Russian soldiers stationed in Poland to mutiny. "You are defending the Tsar and the people... By defending him, you will defend all the evils of Russia."[138]

In 1855, while the war was still going on, Tsar Nicholas I died. He was succeeded by Alexander II. And Herzen cried out, "We are drunk, we have gone mad, we have become young again!"[139]

The first issue of the *Polar Star*, edited by Herzen and Ogarev in 1855, carried at its head a poem of the Decembrist Ryleev, written some thirty-two years before and addressed to the then five-year-old grand duke:

> *Bit mozhet, otrok moee, korona*
> *Tebye eeznachena tvortsom ...,*

enjoining him to love the people and honor the rule of Law; learn how to be a good Tsar... and destroy the ignoble spirit of slavery and injustice. Herzen himself addressed the new ruler, recalling for him the Decembrists, "these stout-hearted warriors for peace, these martyrs for their convictions."[140]

In extremely bold words, Herzen addressed the new Tsar: "I am an incorrigible socialist, you are an autocratic emperor; but between your flag and mine there can be one thing in common—love for the people." He asked for free speech, emancipation of the serfs with land.[141]

February 19, 1861 Tsar Alexander II issued his Manifesto freeing the serfs. Herzen celebrated the Manifesto with a banquet. Unfortunately a few days later he learned of fearful and bloody repressions in Poland at Russian hands. Herzen had reached the apogee of his influence by 1863. The Polish revolt of that year, and its repression, the political divisions in Russia and the emergence there of a more radical opposition such as that of "Young Russia" and the revolutionary association, "Land and Freedom"; the opposition of even the older radicals, the intrusion of Marxist socialist ideas, and not least, Herzen's own futile conviction that he could appeal persuasively for reforms by addressing himself to the Tsar and the gentry, and that such reform could emanate from "above"—to which might be added the growing impact of "nihilist" activity—all these succeeded in blunting the effectiveness of Herzen's program. Not least disenchanting for Herzen, no less than for all other Russian liberals and radicals, was the failure of the government to implement the Emancipation Manifesto of

1861, and Ogarev's futile scheme to petition for a national assembly. To many Russians it appeared that Herzen's hopes for a nonviolent revolution in Russia were utterly utopian, like his hope for a revolution arising out of the peasant communes. Herzen was of the generation of the Forties, and the differences between that generation and the more radical one of the Sixties is best epitomized by the reproach addressed to him by the author of "Young Russia":

> His hopes of a gift from Alexander or some other member of the imperial family; his short-sighted reply to the letter of a man who said that the time had come to begin to sound the alarm and summon the people to rise, and not to play the liberal; his complete failure to understand the contemporary situation in Russia, his hope of a peaceful revolution; his aversion from bloody deeds, from extreme measures, the only way by which anything can be achieved—has finally discredited the journal in the eyes of the republican party.[142]

Whatever justice there may be in this indictment, Herzen could never be impugned for lack of irrefragable honesty, unwavering courage, and deep sympathies for the oppressed of the world. His glowing *Memoirs*, touching, illuminating and eloquent, are a masterpiece of Russian prose and an illuminating chronicle of a Russian noble's "education" into world-citizenship. The revolution he was waiting for did come—in 1905—thirty years after he death. It too was suppressed in blood. Another far greater one would follow some thirteen years later, with worldwide repercussions. As a staunch defender of democratic rights, rights for the least privileged members of humanity, Herzen will always be remembered. He left a testament to his son, in a preface to a later edition of his book, *From the Other Shore*, which may well be quoted as a living memorial to himself:

> I do not wish to delude you; I desire that you should know the truth as I know it. This truth shall be yours as a birthright, so that you need not discover it through painful errors, through murderous disillusionments. ... The man of to-day ... does no more than build the bridge, which will be crossed by an unknown in the unknown future. You, perhaps, will catch a glimpse of that unknown ... Do not stay on the old shore. ... It is better to perish than to remain safe in the madhouse of reaction. The religion of the coming social reconstruction is the only religion I bequeath you. In that religion there is no paradise, no recompense, outside the individual consciousness, the personal conscience. When the right hour comes, make your way homeward to our own people to preach to them this gospel; there men once liked to hear me and perchance will recall my name. .
>
> My blessings upon you in the name of human reason, personal liberty, and brotherly love.

Part Four

Swan Song and Elegy
Germany and the Poets

What a shame that we Germans have disowned the flower of the century, with its noblest names, that we have not only attacked and buried the vanquished and the perished, but have also sought to deliver them over to laughter and contempt. We, who began with the year 1870, called the great thoughts of freedom and brotherhood either ridiculous or criminal, and while we excited ourselves over success or money, or—if idealistic—over some literary movement, we derided or flew into a passion at those who had bled on the barricades. We once were the possessor of a heroic youth, which was prepared to die for its gods, and did indeed die. And our generation not only imprisoned, martyrized, and killed them, we dishonored their memory, and dragged their shades in the mire. In our minds, there existed no virtue but to secure our possessions and do homage to the powers that be.
—Ricarda Huch, *Bakunin*, 1923

Courage yet, my brother or my sister!
Keep on—Liberty is to be subserv'd whatever occurs;
There is nothing that is quell'd by one or two failures, or
    any number of failures,
Or by the indifference or ingratitude of the people, or
    by any unfaithfulness,
Or the show of the tushes of power, soldiers, cannon,
    penal statutes.
What we believe in waits latent forever through all the
    continents,
Invites no one, promises nothing, sits in calmness and
    light, is positive and composed, knows no discour-
    agement,
Waiting patiently, waiting its time. . . .
—Walt Whitman, "To a Foil'd European Revolutionnaire"

Rarely had the *Zeitgeist*—the Spirit of the Age—revealed such coherence of feeling and thought, such a sense of participation in momentous historical experiences. That the events of 1848 and 1849 formed a sharp dividing line between past, present, and future seemed apparent to all, whether they shared exultations, fears, hopes, or despairs. Posterity, with the pages of subsequent history clearly before it, can, of course, trace many of the historical phenomena of the post-Revolutionary era to roots embedded in 1848 and 1849. Yet even to contemporaries came intimations of the future. They could not, of course, anticipate it in all its dire harshness. How could the Germans have foreseen that in the defeat of the democratic ideals—or rather in the way they had sacrificed them in the name of German unity—they were watering the roots of the tree that was to become Bismarckian Germany? Nor could many Frenchmen have previsioned that out of the ruins of Revolution would arise a quasi-Napoleonic empire that would find its less heroic Waterloo at Sedan! The bourgeoisie was triumphant: henceforth, in alliance with the still powerful landed aristocracy and the monarchial elements, it was to dominate the century and to a great extent determine its course. Its principal enemy, the proletariat and its allies, though defeated, still presented a menacing possibility. To a few it was given to foresee that out of these defeats, and out of the bitter experiences of the two fateful years which had placed it on the stage of world history as an independent force, a new gathering of resurgent blood and nerve would soon make for a resurrection of a terrifying sort—a specter again come to life!

For literature and the other arts no less than for society, the two years of revolution represented an immense watershed. In her eloquent and angry apostrophe, Ricarda Huch sets forth, from the vantage ground of the following century, the meaning and the consequences for Germany and Austria, and tangentially, by implication, for the rest of the world.* At stake would be not only art, but the very structure and content of a society in all its aspects. The barricades, its defenders and victims, were to impress themselves unforgettably on the consciousness and conscience of the age—whether in horror, joy, or sorrow.

With 1848, Romanticism comes to an end. Not merely that Romanticism which is bound up with letters and the arts, but Romanticism as a way of life, of thought, of action or inaction. In a brilliant prevision, Hegel spoke of the new age approaching as "the prose of the world." He was speaking of the coming fragmentation, of the monadic isolation of the individual, destructive of "that appearance of autonomous and complete vitality and freedom which is the very foundation of the notion of beauty." In another sense, however, which he would not have accepted, the "prose" of this world also produced the "world of prose"—in both a literal and figurative sense. If the "prose of the world" was embodied by the triumphant new order of society— the bourgeoisie—the "world of prose" was to be the dominant expression of its greatest and most perceptive critics, drawing upon the new vistas opened to them by portentous historic events. Glorified by a Macaulay, execrated by a Flaubert, this new "specter" would be as obsessive to them and to others as that other "specter," evoked by Karl Marx, was to be and to remain for the bourgeoisie. The bourgeois specter was

---

* Ed. note: Ricarda Octavia Huch (1864–1947), German historian. Prof. Ewen refers here to her *1848, Die Revolution des 19. Jahrhunderts in Deutschland* (Zurich, 1944). Other relevant studies by her are *Die Romantik: Blütezeit, Ausbreitung und Verfall* (Tübingen 1951) originally published in two volumes (1899, 1901), and *Michael Bakunin und die Anarchie* (Leipzig 1923). Unfortunately these classic works are not available in English translation.

also to haunt the epigonal Romantics of the century—for Romanticism in other forms and disguises still stalked the world—a disembodied ghost with its own grave-yard claims, bearing the same relation to the Romanticism of its forebears as petrified lava to the brilliant original volcanic flames.

Realism is the watchword of the new era, a Realism that transcends the purely artistic manifestations and extends into all realms of life's experiences. It is the stamp of the age, utilizing the age's multiform discoveries and movements, itself an instrument for penetrating into the nature of the world, and for interpreting it. It is a portion and an heir of the age's extraordinary productions, as remarkable as those of any other time. Realism is the child of the Revolutions of 1848 and 1849.

The intellectual, moral and political future of the German lands was sealed with the defeat of the democratic ideals of the two decades preceding 1848. The abandonment of those ideals by the bourgeoisie in the name of German unity, and the harnessing of its most productive forces to the interests of absolutism and despotism, the alliance, in the case of Germany, of bourgeois, Junker, and autocracy in opposition to the betrayed working classes, was, it is true, to produce a truly astonishing phenomenon in modern Europe: the emergence of the nation within a brief period as one of the most highly developed technological and industrial societies, an imperial challenger to other imperial states for world dominance. The fruits of such challenges and counter-challenges were to be harvested eventually in two world wars.

It is in this light that one may examine the great contrasts offered by the intellectual life of the German lands in the pre-March period and thereafter.

Some time before 1848 that philosopher of anarchy, Max Stirner, wrote: "Over the gateway of our times is inscribed not that Apollonian saying, 'Know Thyself,' but the words, 'Realize and utilize yourself!'" It is this adjuration and its attempted effectuation that made those years so significant for German history, a chapter that was to have no subsequent equivalent. First came the years of profound frustration immediately following the debacle of the hopes engendered by the July Revolution in the early thirties. An icy helplessness and isolation beset the fragmented country. A land that had invented the term *Weltschmerz* was only too prone to relapse into that state when the occasion arose. Literature spoke of such hopelessness as the sense of being "epigonal." For example the novelist Karl Immermann, in 1836:

> Alas! poor things that we are! Prematurely ripened, we no longer have either buds or blossoms. For we were born with snow on our brows.[1]

Along with those feelings came a profound self-contempt, as well as contempt for one's fellow Germans. Of the latter attitude, Heinrich Heine is, of course, the prime exemplar. But others were no less vehement. Jakob Venedey spoke the feelings of many other exiles and self-exiles when he wrote in the Parisian journal *Der Geächtete—The Outlawed*:

> I want to speak of Germany! Be still, my beating heart; restrain those tears of rage, those tears of heart-rending woe! ... There was a time once, when one could be proud of being a German, when the name of Germany was pronounced with reverence. Boys read about it in the histories of Rome. But we must not think about it without shame and without anger and anguish ...[2]

Such, indeed, was the *Zerrissenheit*—the self-diremption and self-division that afflicted the generation of the 1830s, and of which it was only too conscious. Poets echoed these sentiments, none more powerfully than August von Platen, Heine's lifelong *bête noire* and satirical target. Platen was a passionate admirer of the Polish heroes of the 1830s, and composed a series of poems (like so many other German poets) on the subject. In an epilogue he bids farewell to Germany (he was to die of the cholera in Italy), excoriating his fellow countrymen for their apathy, their indifference to poetry and poets, and bewailing the impossibility, in view of the strict censorship, of writing honestly. He concludes,

> *Doch gib, o Dichter, dich zufrieden,*
> *Es büsst die Welt nur wenig ein;*
> *Du weisst es längst, man kann hienieden*
> *Nichts schlechteres als ein Deutscher sein.*

> Come, poet, take heart and comfort,
> The world your loss will scarcely mourn,
> Know that on earth there's nothing meaner
> Than to be a German born.[3]

This is one side of the picture. On the other are still audible the voices that despite censorship, imprisonment, and exile dared to speak defiance, courage, hope, and dignity. Succeeding generations aglow with the triumphs and victories of a unified Germany might wish to forget or even bury such spokesmen as un-German enemies. But their memories persisted; and in due time a resurrection would even reveal the presence of true, if forgotten, creative genius.

One such was to be rediscovered in the decade of Germany's greatest military triumph—Sedan—in 1870, more than thirty years after his death, to grow in stature and influence with the succeeding years as a literary pioneer and, even more, as the personification of the heroic tragedy of the 1830s. This was Georg Büchner.

1. Georg Büchner

> *Mein Büchner tot! Ihr habt mein Herz begraben!*
> *Mein Büchner tot, als seine Hand schon offen,*
> *Und als ein Volk schon harrte der Gaben ...*

> My Büchner's dead! My heart lies buried with him,
> My Büchner's dead—just when from his open hand
> A people waited for his generous bounty,
> A Prince struck down by Death's malicious stroke,
> A Leader lost to youth's embattled cause,
> And Time bereft of yet another Spring!. ...

The poet Georg Herwegh read this elegy on Georg Büchner in 1841, four years after the latter's death. The full sense of their loss could not have been known to his audience in Zurich, though the young man who had died in 1837 at the age of twenty-three was already known as a brilliant young university lecturer on anatomy, and as the author of one published drama, *Danton's Death*. They were not aware of how much more there was of him, not to be rediscovered until some forty years later; nor how much of his literary work had been destroyed at the time of his death. Nor could they have foreseen that it would take almost a century before Büchner would emerge at his true worth as a literary pioneer of great genius, and as a profoundly significant influence on the course of both drama and music.

What the poet Herwegh had sensed, however, and perhaps conveyed to his hearers and readers, was that Büchner, tragic figure that he was, was a maverick in his own decade of the 1830s and actually belonged to the generation of the 1840s. It was in that decade that he might have found those congenial stimuli and associations, intellectual, political and moral, that would have made for the recognition of an equal partnership and a favorable atmosphere for the fuller development of his genius.

Georg Büchner was one of those precocious wonder-children who mature with meteoric speed and develop multiform talents. He possessed that rare combination of creative genius: an equal measure of scientific and poetic gifts. In his rapid flight, this Icarus marks the trajectory of the buoyant hopes and despairs of the 1830s, and as a revolutionary, he previsions many of the ideas and actualities of later periods. In him there is something of that unpolluted clarity of spirit that Keats possessed; the social dedication and scientific insights of a Shelley; and an incessant turmoil within that is Byronic.

He was born in 1813 in the small town of Goddelau, near Darmstadt in Hessen, the son of a successful government physician who, not long thereafter, became medical councillor in Darmstadt. His was a family of unusual endowments—the father had served with Napoleon and was all his life a Bonapartist and Francophile, though politically conservative. Thus, the spirit of France was omnipresent in the household. A brother, Ludwig, was later to become celebrated as a philosophical materialist, author of *Kraft und Stoff—Matter and Energy*—and for a time far outshone his sibling. There was also a sister with pronounced literary talent. Young Georg Büchner was destined for a medical career, and after attending the Gymnasium in Darmstadt, left for the University of Strasbourg.

This city was a part of France, and though the population was in great part German, the spirit was French, and for the young student, dangerously French. Here he was able to assimilate and fuse the best of two cultures: the German classical tradition and France's social philosophies, and in addition, obtain an excellent scientific training. After the restricted atmosphere of Hessen, this was a liberation of the spirit. For a time he was free of the oppressive thought of Hessen's Grand Duke Ludwig II and his abhorrent minister Du Thil, and the censorship and political pettiness of all the little Metternichs.

Here, the two sides of France stood revealed. On the one hand the radical and utopian socialist ideals, and in practical life, the societies, such as that of "The Friends of the People," or "The Rights of Man," and the still-staunch republicanism; on the other, the full evidences of the *juste milieu* of Louis-Philippe. On the one hand, the feverish reception by the city of the self-exiled Poles, on the other, the echoes of the brutal repression of the Lyons silk workers in 1831. Such education as young Büchner was receiving both inside and outside the university was to be decisive for his life; though his extracurricular activities and interests would scarcely have been approved of at home. In Strasbourg, he also became secretly betrothed to Minna Jaeglé, daughter of a Protestant pastor. Their love, unforgettably revealed in whatever remains of their letters, was unfortunately never to be fulfilled in marriage. On her part, it was to survive long after his death.

When Büchner returned to Hessen to continue his studies at the University of Giessen, he was already a convinced revolutionary. Residence at this ducal university was a prerequisite for medical practice in the state. Here desolation overcame him as he contemplated the low intellectual calibre of his professors. But his political views now found a fertile field for practical expression. The Grand Duchy was in the midst of a seething conflict between the ruler and the more liberal members of the Diet over constitutional matters. Secret societies were springing up, and Giessen was not far behind. "The Rights of Man" would of course find Büchner at its center.

He was not one to remain aloof from such a world of passionate possibilities. The extent of his political involvement was not known at home, though the rumors that reached Darmstadt were sufficiently disquieting, particularly to his father, to elicit questions about Büchner's alleged behavior and from him a fervent self-defence and a kind of *confessio fidei*, which while not fully explicit, gave them sufficient indication of the sort of person he was. In a letter written in February 1834 is contained, *in ovo*, a good portion of the later man. He is proud, independent, self-respectful, and decisive. It is a personal manifesto; the socialist manifesto was soon to follow.

Already he is a philosophical determinist of a fixed kind. In defending his views, he insists that it is Circumstances that rule all of us, and that there is nothing one can do about them.

> I despise no one [he writes to his family], least of all because of his understanding or education, for it is in no man's power to be neither a blockhead nor a criminal, for like circumstances would make us all alike. Circumstances lie outside our power ... Hate is as permissible as love, and I harbor it to its fullest extent toward those who practise contempt. There are many such, who, because they possess a ridiculous exterior, or the dead trumpery they call learning, sacrifice the great mass of their brothers to their own egoism. Aristocratism is the ignominious contempt of the Holy Ghost in Man; against it I turn its own weapons: Pride against Pride; Scorn against Scorn ...[4]

In the spring of 1834 he met the remarkable pastor of the town of Butzbach, Friedrich Ludwig Weidig. Twenty-odd years older than Büchner, Weidig had undergone an extraordinary intellectual and moral transformation that turned him from monarchist to republican and, after 1832, into an active organizer of secret societies and author and distributor of leaflets and pamphlets, mostly moderate in their expression. Weidig took to Büchner immediately, though he had a hard time attuning fully to the latter's fieriness and radical ardor. The constitutionalist and the revolutionary joined hands and hearts. Out of that association was born Büchner's masterly political and social manifesto *Der Hessische Landbote—The Hessian Courier*, of 1834. What serious consequences this was to have for all who were concerned in it, no one was of course aware at that moment. In his efforts at moderating the tone of this publication, Weidig garbled it, obtruding upon it hortatory preachments and biblical adjuration. But even in its published form, it spoke with the voices of the French Revolution, like Babeuf resurrected. Printed secretly in June 1834, its distribution was seen to by a number of associates. It addressed itself principally to what Büchner and Weidig felt to be the most oppressed of the Hessian population—the farmers and the peasants. They were the hungry of the land, and without idealizing them, Büchner felt hunger would drive them to revolutionary action. He understood well that they had little political interest in parliament or franchise, freedom of the press, and the "rights of man," but that they knew what it was to starve. He felt that they would understand, if it was clearly set forth for them, who it was that was draining their life's blood, parasitically living from their labor. One of the most startling portions of the pamphlet consists of a statistical presentation of the way in which court and state, ruler and bureaucrat, the rich and well-to-do, absorbed the bulk of the financial tribute exacted from the population. Citing the disastrous succession of the French July Revolution, he pours scorn upon mere parliamentarianism and electoral promises. He would have nothing to do with an alliance with liberals, constitutionalists, etc. The peasantry was for him the center of any potential uprising or revolt, with hunger their prime incentive.

Büchner's indignation scorches:

> The Prince is the head of the leech that creeps over you, the Ministers are its teeth, and the officials its tail. The hungry bellies of all the aristocratic gentlemen to whom he has distributed the high places, are the cupping-glasses which he has set on the land. ... The royal robe is the carpet on which the lords and ladies wallow in their lechery. They hide their running sores with orders and ribbons, and their scabby bodies they cover with precious garments. The daughters of the people are their serving-maids and whores, the sons of the people their lackeys and soldiers. Go to Darmstadt and see for yourselves what good times these gentlemen have on your money. ...
>
> The peasant follows his plow, while the aristocrat drives him along with the oxen at the plow; he takes his grain, and leaves the peasant the stubble. The life of the peasant is one long workday. Strangers devour his fields before his very eyes; his body is a welt, and his sweat is the salt on the tables of the aristocrat.[5]

And at the head of the pamphlet were set the French Revolutionary words:

> "Freedom for the Huts! War on the Palaces!"

Such inflammatory appeals would have been enough to alert the authorities to the seriousness of the menace in their midst. There had been a few bloody incidents between Hessian farmers and the soldiery in the past. There were fears of others to come.

The work was itself an unusual combination of clearsightedness and political naiveté born of inexperience. The statistical evidence was compelling and irrefutable; the appeal was to a section that was the most exploited in the Grand Duchy. The excusable error lay in Büchner's belief that he could apply the experiences of the first French Revolution, with its already fairly advanced working-class population and its more sophisticated peasantry, to the politically immature farmers of Hessen. Whether, if time had allowed, he could have offered a serious program of action is doubtful. The blow fell before there was time for that or for anything else.

An informer named Kuhl, one of the members of the group, had apprised the authorities concerning the printing and proposed distribution of *The Hessian Courier*. A number of copies had already found their way into various hands, and a number of farmers turned them over to the police. Minnigerode, one member of the society, was apprehended before he could distribute his quota. An investigation was set afoot, headed by a notoriously sadistic High Court Justice, Konrad Georgi. In the course of time, a number of the other participants were implicated and imprisoned. Among them were August Becker and Gustav Klemm, The latter was eventually to point the finger at Büchner; and Kuhl was some time later to implicate Weidig.

So far as Büchner was concerned, it seemed only a matter of days before he too would be apprehended, as soon as it was discovered that he was the principal author of the pamphlet. Time and again he was summoned for interrogation. He retired to his father's house in Darmstadt, where, kept close, he was to prepare himself for further medical studies. But he knew that he must escape as soon as possible.

It is an extraordinary mark of Büchner's capacity for concentration, that while still on tenterhooks, and preparing for flight, he could command sufficient presence of mind and creative energy not only to pore over medical texts, but also to set down a drama and bring it to completion. It was under such stresses that the play *Danton's Death* was born. Being in need of funds for his departure (his father would never have supplied them!), he sent the play to Karl Gutzkow, the noted leader of the Young Germany school of writers. Gutzkow, who seems at once to have recognized the talents of the correspondent, obtained a publisher for the play and even helped him financially. On March 1, 1835, Büchner left Darmstadt; ten days later he was in Strasbourg again. In April 1835, Becker and Klemm were arrested.

The shock of defeat, bound up also with concern over the fate that awaited his associates, was to unsettle him for a long time. The failure of what he considered a revolutionary action found its profoundest and saddest expression in *Danton's Death*. Here he was translating a recent episode in the light of French experiences of 1794. Yet, despite his troubled state, nothing could paralyze the creative urge and verve within him. He set to work and completed the delightful dramatic fantasy of *Leonce and Lena*, and the brilliant novelette *Lenz*. He also translated two of Victor Hugo's tragedies, and began his own tragedy, *Woyzeck*. Nor were his scientific studies intermitted. On June 13, 1835 a warrant for his arrest was issued in Darmstadt.

> The hereinafter named Georg Büchner, medical student of Darmstadt, has removed himself from the juridical investigation into his proved participation in treasonable activities against the State by leaving the Fatherland. It is therefore requested that the public authorities of the Interior and Exterior apprehend him upon his appearance, and deliver him under guard at the place indicated below.
>
> (Signed): Georgi. Investigating Justice of Upper-Hessen, appointed by the Grand Ducal Court of Justice.

This was followed by a description of the escaped.

In 1836 he completed his doctoral dissertation on the nervous system of the barbel, which he submitted to the University of Zurich, and in September he received his degree. He was fortunate in that the Rector of that university, the celebrated scientist and philosopher Lorenz Oken, himself a refugee from Germany, had taken note of the talented younger man, and invited him to deliver a trial lecture on the subject of cranial nerves. Büchner was in Zurich by the middle of October, delivered his lecture on November 5, and won unanimous approval. He was appointed *Privatdozent* at the university. As was to be expected, he divided his time between science and literature. "During the day," he wrote, "I sit with the scalpel and at night with my books." He now had the prospect of an extablished career, and could indulge in the expectation of marriage.

He had practically completed the play, *Woyzeck*. Another play, *Pietro Aretino*, was in its finished state. In December an epidemic of typhus struck Zurich. Büchner succumbed to it. His highly nervous organism, strained by intellectual and emotional tensions, his physique that had been subject to such incessant and excessive labor, could not hold out against the disease. On February 2, 1837 he fell ill, and on February 19 he died. Minna Jaeglé rushed to his bedside, and had the consolation of loving recognition from the delirious betrothed. In his last days, he was surrounded by devoted friends.

Minna remained faithful to his memory for the rest of her life. She never married. She destroyed a great many letters among Büchner's remains, as well as, among other manuscripts, the play of *Pietro Aretino*, her devout religious sense undoubtedly outraged by that work's atheism.

In his own lifetime, Büchner was destined to see only one of his works, *Danton's Death*, published. *Leonce and Lena* appeared in 1841. The rest was to wait for some forty years before being printed.

As Büchner lay on his deathbed he could not have known that his old associate, Pastor Weidig, was also nearing his end in prison. Arrested in 1836, he had been subjected to torture and humiliations at the hands of Georgi; his mind and body debilitated, he took his own life on February 23, 1837. A surviving letter to his wife, withheld from her by the authorities, reveals his continued firmness in the face of sadistic pressures, despite physical and mental suffering. "I am unchanged," he wrote, "and I reiterate the promises I gave you on leaving Friedberg; I can and do repeat them so long as the breath remains in my body. I ... repeat the request .. that you, as my proxy, will contradict anything that may be said to my disparagement and believe no one but myself and your own heart, for people are fond of lying about others and especially about those who are buried alive ..."[6] This moving document was suppressed for many years for "police reasons of state."

* * *

Büchner's social and philosophical outlook was shaped early, and received its final and permanent stamp after his experiences with the *Hessische Bote*. From beginning to end, he never ceased to be outraged by hunger, poverty, and political oppression. What he wrote in a letter of 1833 as a young man of twenty,

Political conditions would make me raving mad. The poor people patiently drag their chariot on which Princes and Liberals enact their shameful tomfooleries. Every evening I pray for the hempen rope and the lantern ...[7]

was to remain with him when he came to write *Woyzeck*. He was disgusted with the idle talk of liberals and intellectuals for their failure to understand the true source of discontents and to discover that the root of revolution and change lay in the relations of rich and poor. He mocked their dream of reforming society through the agency of the educated. To Karl Gutzkow he wrote:

> The relation of rich and poor is the only revolutionary element in the world. Only Hunger can be the Goddess of Freedom, and only a Moses who would send us the seven Egyptian plagues, could become a Messiah ...[8]

He was no friend of those who harked back to the Middle Ages, whether in their political or their poetical ventures. His eye was fixed on the present. And in this very present he saw clearly what was obscured for others. For example, he understood the true nature of "violence."

> They reproach the younger generation for their use of violence. But isn't it true that we live in an eternal condition of violence? Because we were born in prison, and brought up there, we no longer see that we are stuck in a hole, our hands and feet in chains, and our mouths gagged. What is it that you call a legal situation? A law that makes the great mass of citizens drudging chattel, in order to satisfy the unnatural needs of an insignificant and corrupt minority? And this law, propped by brutal military force and the stupid cunning of its agents—this law is eternal, raw violence, committed against Right and sound Reason, and I will fight against it with word and hand, wherever I can.[9]

If he saw clearly, and even defended the use of violence it was not from hardheartedness. Never for a moment does he lose sight of the poverty that surrounds him.

> I have just come from the Christmas market. Everywhere swarms of ragged, freezing children, standing with eyes agape and sad faces before the splendors made of water and flour, muck and gilded paper. The thought that for most people even the most wretched pleasures and joys are unattainable treasures fills me with bitterness.[10]

His metaphysical system was also formed very early. A student in the Gymnasium, he discussed the problem of suicide and its relation to the question of Freedom versus Determinism. Life, he said, was its own justification; and he scorned the religious notion that it was merely a "proving ground" for an eternal hereafter.

> I believe that Life is its own goal, and that development is the goal of Life. Life is itself an unfolding ...[11]

In the same spirit he was later to speak of Nature, in opposition to those who attributed a teleology to it.

> Nature does not act in accordance with purposes. She does not wear herself out in an infinite series of purposes, in which one is conditioned by the other. But in all her expressions she is directly self-sufficient. All that is, is there for her own sake ...[12]

Like his brother Ludwig, he was a materialist. The basis of his philosophy was a static determinism. In the agonized words he writes to his betrothed early in 1834 is contained his tortured wrestling with a cosmic problem, which is soon to find its expression in *Danton's Death*.

I studied the history of the [French] Revolution. I felt as if I were shattered underneath the monstrous fatality of History. I find in human nature a horrifying sameness, in human relations an inevitable violence vouchsafed to all and none. The individual is only a foam on the wave, greatness merely an accident, the preeminence of genius a puppet play, a laughable contest with an iron law, which it is the highest achievement to recognize, but an impossibility to master … The "Must" is one of the words of damnation with which humanity is baptized …[13]

Such, in fact, was the program for *Danton's Death*, a work composed in fever heat, under the oppression of imminent arrest, and under the still greater burdens of political disaster. Begun early in 1835, it was completed by February of the same year, as if he himself were being spurred by that "Must" he was now to illuminate.

Danton's Death is a dramatic elegy—an elegy on the revolutions of the 1830s and Büchner's personal elegy on his own and his associates' debacle of 1834. Sentiments and events are transposed to the crucial months beginning March 24, 1794 and ending (by intimation, in Büchner's play), with Thermidor, Robespierre's execution, and the victory of reaction on July 27 of the same year. The true protagonists of the tragedy are not the ostensible principals, Danton and Robespierre. The true protagonists are Fatality, garbed as Revolution; and Hunger, in the figures of the nameless masses. Almost unwittingly, Büchner had translated the Hegelian "cunning of Reason" into the fateful cunning of Fatality—not as some force that achieves and realizes itself through an ever-ascendant development, but as something fixed, static, that acting blindly and inexorably makes of human beings and of history what they are—altogether beyond their willing or not willing …

Revolution, as Büchner apprehends it, is Fatality—it is the Maker of events and men's actions. Not the human individual, no matter how great we deem him, determines the course of events, and in this case, the Revolution; it is Revolution that determines it. The Revolution is already in the process of decay as the play opens, and Danton is himself the physical and moral embodiment of that disintegration. The "lava of Revolution" is about to bury him, as it will Robespierre, so different from Danton, so intent on acting and forwarding it. Neither Danton nor Robespierre realizes the direction toward which the Revolution is moving. Not Danton, the once radical firebrand, now the cynical, despairing voluptuary, who has already given up the Revolution and previsions Thermidor; not Robespierre, the ascetic, the puritanical Aristides. For neither can exorcise the specter that stalks outside their quarters—the specter of Hunger. Danton is an apostate from the Revolution, for whom "life is a whore," and "the world is chaos." He is, as he confesses, a "relic." The figurative images that surround him, and the very physical presences, are those of whoredom, decay, decadence; his passivity is an acceptance of Fatality; the sense of the "Must" obsesses him, as also, to use a more modern term, does the "Death-wish." For him all human beings are "epicureans," whether they are the self-denying Robespierres or the self-indulgent Dantons. Significantly, he dallies with the ladies of pleasure while the common people cry for bread. And not far away, another more ominous figure stands and waits and secretly conspires—the bourgeois Mammon, who after defeating the Revolution will give the populace the bread it is crying for.

There are no heroes; there are no villains. The sybaritic pessimist Danton and the puritanical Robespierre are both "lonely" actors in a cosmic drama. "*Wir sind sehr einsam,*" Danton says. And Robespierre to Camille Desmoulins, (whom he will soon send to the scaffold, although he is his dearest friend):

> Truly the Son of Man is crucified in all of us. We all wrestle in bloody agony in Gardens of Gethsemane, but no one redeems the other with his wounds. Oh Camille! They are all leaving me. The world is void and empty. I am alone.[14]

All of hopelessness is visible in Danton's acceptance of Fatality—almost a heroism of passivity. The Committee of Public Safety had just ordered his arrest. Flight is still possible, or some counter-action against Robespierre. To the urgings of Camille Desmoulins, Danton replies:

> I'm tired; even the soles of my feet burn.
> Camille: Where will you go. ... I'm asking seriously: where?
> Danton: For a walk, my friend, for a walk. (He goes out.)[15]

Thus Büchner mirrors the doom that befell France, not so much in 1794 as after 1830 in the triumph of Louis-Philippe and the bankocracy of the *juste milieu.* Thus he mirrors the defeat of Büchner, and his friends Becker, Minnigerode, and Weidig, in 1834. (Weidig was to die; the other two were to face prison and, still unbroken, would find their way to America, where they would participate in the Civil War in the cause of anti-slavery. ...)

Ninety years after its composition, a defeated, truncated Germany, devoid of empire and emperor, would rediscover this tragedy, and in the magnificent productions of Max Reinhardt would once more live through dramas of despairs and hopes; would understand the vividness of its kaleidoscopic movement like the rapid progression of history, and perceive in the play the great forerunner of its own "epic" theatre; it would relish the language, with its obscenities, its colloquialisms, and its beauty—a language even Gutzkow was compelled to bowdlerize for his own day. It would also understand the meaning of those masses of people who move through it, its significant actors; and above all, it would comprehend, perhaps as no previous German generation had, the meaning of one of its principal protagonists, Hunger. ... It would also grasp the meaning of that which one of its imprisoned characters utters anent another of its central themes—the misery of the world—as the "bed-rock of atheism." It is Thomas Paine speaking:

> First do away with the imperfect, and then you can demonstrate God. Spinoza tried it. One can deny evil, but not pain. Only Reason can prove God, feeling rebels against it. ... Why do I suffer? That is the bed-rock of atheism. The slightest quiver of pain, if only in an atom, makes a rent in the Creation from top to bottom.[16]

That this theme was a persistent one with Büchner is shown once more in the short novelette *Lenz,* where the latter says, "But I, were I almighty, almighty, you see, if I were that, I could not tolerate all this suffering. I would help, I would help ..."[17]

* * *

If *Danton's Death* is Büchner's elegy on a dying revolution, *Woyzeck* is the elegiac drama of the "little man." Danton is caught up in the fatality of history and Woyzeck in the fatality of society. Both tragedies are studies of "victims"—in one case of historic figures of great magnitude, in the other, of a "nobody." The play of *Woyzeck* has had its own history, too, and a peculiar one. Rediscovered in a manuscript in 1879, and with difficulty deciphered, it was finally published in a mangled form, and only very recently restored in what might seem an authentic text. It exists in a number of variants and fragments. The plot is based on an actual historic occurrence, the murder in 1821 by a barber of his mistress, in Leipzig, and his eventual beheading in 1824. Woyzeck's became a *cause célèbre*, for it entailed the question of mental sanity, much debated pro and con.

Büchner's Woyzeck is a military barber. He kills Marie, his sweetheart and the mother of his illegitimate child, after he discovers that she has been unfaithful to him with the highly imposing drum major. The bare story gave Büchner the occasion of writing one of the most impressive dramatic works of the nineteenth century, and one having a major influence in the twentieth.

At the head of *Woyzeck*, Büchner might well have set the words he put into Danton's mouth:

> Who will curse the hand which has been cursed by "Must"? Who has spoken that "Must"? Who? What is it in us that lies, whores, murders?[18]

That question the military barber Woyzeck can neither ask nor answer. He is an alienated nullity: the butt of the entire world, the subject of experiments on the part of the Doctor, the object of derision on the part of the Captain, the lover whose sweetheart is seduced by a drum major. He is less than the animals that are publicly exhibited. Yet, he stands forth as the ultimate critic of the world, of God, and of mankind, no less than of society and Fate. His simplicity speaks forth flames of condemnation.

The Captain whom he is shaving reproves him for not being "moral" in having fathered a child "without the blessings of the Church." To which Woyzeck replies:

> Sir, the good Lord is not going to look at the poor worm to see if someone said "Amen" over it before we began making it. The Lord said, "Suffer little children to come unto me."

And as for "virtue," Woyzeck continues,

> Virtue—I haven't got much of that. You see, we common sort we haven't got virtue. All that happens to us is nature. But if I could be a gentleman, and had a hat and a watch and a monocle and could talk refined, I'd want to be virtuous, I would. There must be something very fine about virtue, Sir, but I'm such a poor, common fellow!

The Doctor, on his part, is conducting his scientific experiment on him, and is reproving him for pissing in the street when he was being paid three groschen per diem for supplying urine. Woyzeck pleads Nature as his excuse.

The Doctor shouts back at him,

> Nature, Nature! Haven't I proved to you that the *musculus constrictor vesicae* is subject to the will? Nature! Woyzeck, Man is free; in Man Individuality transfigures itself into Freedom. ...

What of Marie? Is she to be blamed for succumbing to the magnificent physique and uniform of the drum major? He gives her such a good time, and such lovely earrings! Would she understand the meaning of "Freedom"?

Woyzeck has visions—hallucinations. To the Doctor his is a wonderful case of *aberratio mentalis partialis* of a secondary sort. What a beautiful instance of the *idée fixe* to observe and study! And he raises Woyzeck's wages ... Poor Woyzeck becomes more obsessed than ever. He hears voices calling on him to stab, stab ... And he kills Marie with a knife ...

Like Danton and Robespierre, Woyzeck is a "lonely" man. People in the play speak not so much with or to each other, but past each other, "*aneinander vorbei*", as the Germans put it. Each expresses his social status, the morality of his class: the Captain, the pedantic Doctor, Woyzeck. But Woyzeck is spiritually and economically naked. He is the "little man" on whom everyone else tramples. He is the nobody who is constantly preached to and lectured at by "moralists," who would have him be virtuous, have him recognize that he is a "morally free" individual. But Woyzeck knows better. Has he not seen that virtue and freedom mean money? Has he not seen the only truly deep relationship he has developed with a woman destroyed by the superior allurements his rival can offer? On every side he is badgered, used, and so he becomes a driven man, maddened to the point of murder. A free man? A virtuous man? A man at all?

The swiftly moving scenes are the hammer beats of an inexorable Fate. The racy, often obscene speech is colloquial and local; the discourses are often disconnected and wild; all of this has the quality of something inevitable, of a nightmare too deeply rooted in reality to be mere fantasy. The post-World-War I era would assimilate this play too into what was to be called "Expressionist" doctrine. It would serve as the text for one of the most impressive musical works of the twentieth century, Alban Berg's *Wozzeck*. Across the hundred or so years, Büchner could look upon a rich posterity, not the least of his heirs being Bertolt Brecht. Thus, by a strange historic paradox, Büchner would join the great company of the theatre's renovators, from Ibsen and Strindberg, to Wedekind, down to the present.

Though deeply in the grip of a "static determinism," which he certainly would have modified had he lived into the exciting philosophical revolution of the following decade, and which would have basically altered his interpretation of the force of Circumstance, inflexible and unalterable, in the life of individuals and society; and though touched with a profound, humane pessimism; he never lapsed into that hapless and hopeless cynicism that is the death-rattle of frustrated Romanticism. He was saved by a pervasive sense of confraternity with human beings, especially with the least of them—the atomized nullities, if one may excuse this paradox—and a compassion that was neither factitious nor fictitious. He was not of those pessimists who, like the greatest of them, Arthur Schopenhauer, could urge cosmic compassion for the victims of the transcendental Will, while at the same time watch with the *sang-froid* of a Metternich, and even with some glee, the shooting down of Frankfurt revolutionaries by the soldiery, even lending them his spyglass for greater accuracy. Büchner had failed to understand a great many things, true; but he never abandoned one principle in life, which he embodied in an immortal sentence:

Weisst du auch, Valerio, dass selbst der Geringste unter den Menschen so gross ist, dass das Leben noch viel zu kurz ist, um ihn lieben zu kennen?

It is one of his characters, Leonce, speaking:

Do you know, Valerio, that the least among human beings is yet so great, that life is too short for us adequately to love him?[19]

It is such a testament a twenty-three year old young man left to posterity for eternal remembrance.

And through his character, Lenz, he enunciates his theory of art, his conception of a true realism:

I demand in all things that it be Life, and the possibility that it exist; that's the thing. We then have no need to ask whether it is beautiful or ugly. ... Idealism is the most shameful of insults to human nature. Let them try just once to immerse themselves in the life of the most humble and reproduce it again in all its palpitations, intimations, in the whole of its subtle, scarcely perceptible play of expression ... The organs of feeling are the same in almost all human beings, only the crust is more or less thick through which it must break. ... One must love mankind in order to penetrate into the peculiar essence of each; no one must be too common, too ugly. Only then can they be understood ...[20]

2. Georg Herwegh

The icy crust of defeatism and lethargy that marked German intellectual life in the 1830s shivered and cracked in the following decade. The "lightning of ideas" that was bringing philosophy down from the skyey heights of Hegelianism into the arena of quotidian battles, struck poetry too, and in turn made it the companion of both the new philosophy and the immediate political and social problems of the day. In an unprecedented brotherhood, poets and philosophers joined hands to associate themselves with others of like mind in the common battle against absolutism, and in demanding radical changes. Such a sense of marching with the forward movement of history would not be characteristic of philosophy and letters in the German lands for many years to come.

It was heralded by Georg Herwegh, the poet who had recognized Büchner's place among the advance-guard, and whose volume of poems, *Gedichte eines Lebendigen—Poems of One Alive*—which appeared in 1841, broke the ten years' sleep. The near hysterical reception of these poems and their author, and the book's astonishing sales, reveal the hunger that had prevailed and which now promised to be stilled. The very title of the volume was a call to resurrection. It was to be but the first of many such counterparts as succeeding years in ever fuller measure spoke of this new sense of revival.

"One morning, as I lay in bed, I opened and read the first volume of Herwegh's poems ... The new ringing tones gripped me like a trumpet-blast that suddenly rouses a vast camp of nations to arms." Thus Gottfried Keller, a young Swiss poet and painter, destined to become one of the greatest of novelists of German-speaking lands, pays his tribute and follows with a fiery sonnet:

> *Schäum brausend auf!—Wir haben lang gedürstet,*
> *Du Goldpokal, nach einem jungen Wein. …*

> O foaming draught! Long have we thirsted sore,
> Thou cup of gold, to taste a strong, new wine;
> In thy red heart we saw a vintage shine.
> Oh how we drank, and, drinking, called for more!. …
> Our age is dead, for dead men's bones a shrine;
> The sleepers bide the last dread trumpet's sign;
> But thou, to wake us, prince-like come'st before. …[21]

He was only one of thousands to hail the appearance of Herwegh's poems. Franz Liszt was taken with them, and set a number of them. The book was issued in Zurich, for Herwegh too was a refugee, having escaped military service, to which he had been sentenced for having insulted an officer in Stuttgart, his native town. He had early become inspired by the *Zeitgeist*—which he was to call the "Madonna of poets"—the spirit of a time that called writers to arms. "Literature is politics," he asserted, and it is "the Muse of History that composed the first pages of our new literature." "The Principle of the new literature is … that of Democracy." Among his guiding stars were Börne and Heine as well as Robert Burns and Shelley. The Frenchman Béranger he lauded as the "nightingale with the eagle's claws."[22]

His was to be a tempestuous career, initially marked by triumphs reserved for few poets, then checkered with dramatic alternations including both serious and comic elements, pathos, heroism and unheroics, a military engagement, meetings with Karl Marx and King Friedrich Wilhelm IV, and association with such other diverse figures as Wilhelm Weitling the "communist," Richard Wagner, and Alexander Herzen—sometimes with very significant consequences.

For the time being there was triumph. There was fire in those poems of "one who was alive," meant to inflame others to action. There was bombast, but also inspired invocation. There were calls to freedom, and also a nationalistic note on keeping the Rhine "German." Here one found Poland's battles of liberation once more celebrated, and the German censor excoriated. He offers Béranger a "sword decked with roses" as a tribute to the warrior-poet, for steel and flowers are conjoined in these new German poets of liberation. In a moving sonnet he offers a memorable tribute to Shelley.

These were clarion calls to which readers responded, sometimes shrill, sometimes truly inspired. The lark that Shelley had sung becomes in Herwegh's transfiguration the augur of freedom.

> *Die Lerche war's, nicht die Nachtigall,*
> *Die eben am Himmel geschlagen:*
> *Schon schwingt er sich auf, der Sonnenball,*
> *Vom Winde des Morgens getragen.*
> *Der Tag, der Tag ist erwacht!. …*
> *Heraus wer ans ewige Licht noch glaubt!*
> *Ihr Schläfer, die Rosen der Liebe vom Haupt,*
> *Und ein flammendes Schwert um die Lenden!*

It was the lark, not the nightingale,
  Has poured her song from the skies,
And the sun's burning orb in a crimson veil
On the wind of the morning lies.
  The day, the day is bright! . . . . .
Up! up! whosoever in Light puts his trust,
Sleepers awake! tread love's roses in dust,
  And gird flaming swords on your thighs! ...[23]

This is Herwegh, "the iron lark," as Heinrich Heine called him in a celebrated poem. Iron and steel are more apparent in another poem, "*Aufruf*"—"The Summons."

Reisst die Kreuze aus der Erden!
Alle sollen Schwerter werden ...

Cross from tomb and temple tear!
Beat to blades that men may bear!
  God in Heaven will allow.
Truce to song! Let all the singing
Iron be on anvil ringing!
  Steel be your Redeemer now! ...[24]

This was daring speech, and it thrilled. The poems circulated in the German states, even in Prussia, where the honeymoon of pious expectation of more liberal days was still in full flower following the accession of the new king. Herwegh too imagined that new times were coming, and he addressed a poetic appeal to Friedrich Willhelm IV, inviting him to become a true "shepherd" of his people and to heed the call of the young for leadership in deeds of heroism, even war!

Herwegh's successes went to his head. Particularly so when on returning to Germany and embarking on a triumphal tour, he was everywhere hailed as the poet-prophet. He now imagined himself to be another Marquis Posa, who like the hero of Schiller's tragedy *Don Carlos*, could plead a people's cause of freedom before a monarch. Alas! the King was gracious enough to receive Herwegh in audience and exchange a few kindly words as an honest antagonist, and—if we are to trust Herwegh's version—to wish the poet a speedy reformation, *à la* Damascus. Here, in the palace, was at least one person who had not been converted by the *Poems of One Alive!*

But if the king did not swoon over these poems, there was a woman who did. This was Emma Siegmund, the daughter of a wealthy businessman of Berlin. She fell in love with the poet and they became engaged. The occasion was marred by a slight indiscretion on Herwegh's part, a letter addressed to the King of Prussia anent the suppression in the kingdom of something he had written in Switzerland. The procession of triumph was cut short, for Herwegh was ordered to leave the country. He returned to Switzerland, where he was to celebrate his nuptials. Among those who witnessed the ceremony was Mikhail Bakunin. But the political atmosphere in Switzerland in the year 1843 was no less sultry than that of Prussia, and Herwegh was invited to leave. Husband and wife departed for Paris.

Herwegh's political education was being rounded out. Already in 1842 he had met Marx in Cologne, where the latter was editing the *Rheinische Zeitung.* Arnold Ruge and Bruno Bauer drew him into their liberal circle, *Die Freien*. His own personal experiences had added materially to his development. In Paris he was to meet old acquaintances, also exiles, and to make new ones, in an atmosphere that was charged with political dynamite. And what a company of men and women! Herwegh, an attractive man and celebrated poet, was welcomed. Soon he met them all: George Sand, the Comtesse d'Agoult, Béranger, Victor Hugo; Heinrich Heine, Marx, Ruge, and Bakunin; the scientist Karl Vogt also, in whose company and that of Bakunin he undertook the study of "nature" at St.-Malô. In Paris he prepared the second volume of his poems, and voiced his resentment of the King of Prussia with full-throated violence. ...

He wrote:

> Forbidden books fly through the air and what the people wants to read it will read despite all government decrees. Your Majesty's ministers forbade my poems fifteen months ago, and I am now in the happy position of seeing a fifth edition of them through the press. Your Majesty's ministers have ordered the confiscation of books that appeared dangerous, and on my journey through Germany I have been able to see for myself that they are in everybody's hands.[25]

In a long, mordant verse-diatribe against the King, which he launched from Paris, Herwegh mingled reprobation with prophecy; sounded a note of sorrow that the King had not hearkened to the Poet. But what could one expect of this royal master who behaves like another Saul facing a David? (Herwegh was never too modest in his selection of archetypes!) Wait, he concluded, wait and see—but take warning. For a day is coming,

> When the ship with all its inept crew,
> And you, and your hapless throne,
> Will be shivered against a mighty rock!
> For know—The Sphinx of Revolution lives! ...[26]

Well, that day did dawn. February 1848 of Paris had its March in Berlin and Vienna. Karl Marx hastened back from Brussels, and the poet Ferdinand Freiligrath from his exile in London. German hearts in Paris rejoiced as, in Herwegh's words, they gloried in the "three days that sufficed the children of Paris to bury the old, rotting world with all its prejudices, and privileges ... and to forge the blessed bond uniting all nations."[27]

Thousands of them hastened to make their protestations of fraternity to the Provisional Government, in processions marked by songs and headed by a poet—Herwegh. What a joy to present two intertwined banners, that of France and Germany, and to hear heartwarming words of one of the members of the provisional government, Crémieux, declare that Germany, "the seat of philosophy and science ... knew well the meaning of freedom, and would know how to win it without outside help ..."[28]

In the wake of such enthusiasm arose the idea of organizing a German legion to abet the revolutionary movement, particularly in Baden and Württemberg. With Herwegh in the lead, some five hundred Germans were gathered together. Enthusiasm outran wisdom. The forces gathered in Paris were eventually to join those being gathered in the south by Struve and Hecker. There were voices that warned against so hurried a project, with all its fanfare. Karl Marx was opposed to a venture intended to revolutionize a country from the outside, especially by a hastily organized, poorly directed and inexperienced army. Against the disciplined military of Baden and Württemberg such campaigns were doomed. Emma, Herwegh's wife, a brave if somewhat romantic person, stood by her husband's side throughout the battles; whatever was left of the routed forces fled across the border into Switzerland. Thus April 1848 proved a disaster. Though badly scarred by the defeat of his dreams, and never destined to equal the success of his early verses, Herwegh in Switzerland remained unshaken as the poet of the opposition to the reaction that was soon to triumph in Germany.

He saw what he called "the old night" settling once more over all of Europe—Austria the "spider" spinning her web of despotism ever more tightly as the "barbarians enter the Milan Cathedral"—and heard the cries of mortal agony of the Czechs, the Poles, and the Italians.[29]

He followed the course of Germany's history, and particularly the rise of a new working-class movement, with deep interest. For Ferdinand Lassalle's Workingmen's Association he adapted Shelley's "Song to the Men of England" as a "Song of Confederation"—the *Bundeslied*. He dedicated verses to the International Working Men's Association led by Marx and Engels. He watched Germany's rise to world power under Bismarck and Wilhelm I with trepidation; he spoke of Prussian and German "arrogant striving for world domination." In the Franco-Prussian War of 1870–1871 he was one of a few Germans to excoriate that spirit; and to those intoxicated with the victories he called out: "Unity is a vain thing, unless it is unity with the Good; yours is not the Unity baptized in Freedom, but by the Devil!"[30] He prophesied the resurrection of Garibaldi's Italy; he reprehended the German annexation of Alsace-Lorraine. And two years before his death in 1875, he recalled with fervor the glories of 1848 and the "Eighteenth of March":

> *Achtzenhundert vierzig und acht,*
> *Als im Lenze der Eis gekracht. ...*
>
> *Achtzehnhundert siebzig und drei,*
> *Reich der Reichen, da stehst du, juchhei! ...*

and the great contrast between 1873 and 1848, when the workers of Berlin forced the "German Caesar" to do homage to them. But now,

> Eighteen hundred and seventy-three!
> Land of the Rich, there you stand, Hurrah!
> But we the Poor, the sold and betrayed,
> Remember the deeds of our brothers that day,
> No! Not all the March days are gone away,
> Eighteen hundred and seventy-three![31]

And to Count Zeppelin he wrote:

I will never set foot in Alsace, now that it has become German. But let my son go there in my stead. He will see what a Germany drunk with blood and glory is capable of and may he remember it for ever.[32]

3. Ferdinand Freiligrath

Awareness of change within oneself is perhaps one of the outstanding characteristics of the writers of the forties. It is but another of those links that brought them closer to one another in Germany and Austria, and beyond these countries, to writers in more distant lands. In the poet Ferdinand Freiligrath, seven years Herwegh's senior, the stages of radical change are even more clearly demarcated.

In 1844 he published a collection of poems (not his first) that created something of a sensation. It was called *Glaubensbekenntnis—Confession of Faith*—and contained a preface with the following words, intended to explain to his readers why the contents of that volume differed so radically from those he had previously published:

> All the schooling which I as an individual have acquired in full view of the nation is, after all, the same which the nation, in striving for a political consciousness and political education, has collectively acquired and is still acquiring. The worst that I can be charged with, in the final analysis, is that I have descended from the "higher watchtower" to the "ramparts of a Party." This I admit is true. Firm and unshakable, I join the side of those who set their hearts and souls against Reaction. Not for me a life without Freedom! Whatever lot be in store for me or my book, so long as the oppression under which I see my Fatherland groaning exists, my heart will bleed and rebel. May my tongue and my arms never weary in doing all in my power to help bring about better times. May the Lord God and the confidence of my people abet me in this task. I turn my face toward the Future.[33]

This from a poet whose earlier works, beginning with 1838, had won him the favor of the King of Prussia and a sizable annual stipend that relieved him of onerous commercial occupations, was enough to startle the world—and in fact constituted a challenge and a personal declaration of political independence.

Freiligrath was already an acknowledged poet when Friedrich Engels, ten years his junior, saw him in Barmen in 1838. Freiligrath, too, like the more affluent Engels but for much more pressing and immediate reasons, was forced into accepting a post in a commercial establishment. The pressure came not only from an insistent parent, but also from need. Thus both men were brought into contact with the world of commerce and industry. And both faced their clerical occupations with reluctance, more inclined to adore the poetic Muse than a prosaic Mammon. Neither could have foreseen how close would be their dedication in friendship and collaboration in years to come, nor on what common political roads they were to travel for a long time ...

For Freiligrath's early poetry scarcely suggests the fervent involvements in which he was soon to engage. All the cliché themes of a belated romanticism are here: America of the vast plains, the mysterious East, Greece, the wild ocean, the Negro as alien abroad, brigands, pirates. Byron is there, and even more forcefully Victor Hugo of the *Orientales*. But the German generation of the 1830s still relished such post-romantic fare, delighting to wander afield in imagination when it could not move in fact. Young Engels, too, commenced his poetic career with exotic dreams ...

Politically conservative Freiligrath regarded the poet as standing "above the battle." Impartial and Olympian, he is as just to the heroic Napoleon as he is to the latter's murdered victim, the Duke d'Enghien. So he affirmed even in 1841, the year in which Herwegh produced his *Poems of One Alive*.

In a poem dedicated to the memory of the arch-conservative Spanish General Diego de León, whose unsuccessful conspiracy to restore the Regent Queen Maria Cristina to the throne of Spain ended in his execution at the hands of the liberal leader Espartero, Freiligrath had written,

> The Poet stands upon a loftier tower
> Than a Party's ramparts and battlements.
> He bends the knee before the hero Bonaparte,
> And outraged hears d'Enghien's mortal cry ...
>
> *Der Dichter steht auf einer höhern Warte,*
> *Als auf den Zinnen der Partei. ...*

—lines which were to be carried from lip to lip.[34]

In 1842 he received the royal stipend that was intended to enable him to devote himself to poetry. In the same year, Herwegh addressed a reply to Freiligrath *à propos* of those verses.

> Party! who is there who can stand aloof?
> Party is Mother of all victories.
> How can the poet scorn this mighty word?. ...
> Have not the gods themselves descended from Olympus
> To do battle in an earth-born Cause?[35]

Freiligrath, bridling at this challenge, took his revenge a year later in a brightly satirical though malicious "Letter" in verse, making sport of Herwegh's tour through Germany, his interview with the King, and his ultimate fiasco. In more brilliant fashion, Heinrich Heine too was to pour his wit over poor Herwegh. How could Freiligrath himself have foreseen that before long he himself would hasten to descend from Olympus, hearken to the call of "Party," and then rival Herwegh in his political and social commitment?

Yet by 1844 he was a changed man. In that year he published a collection of poems, *Ein Glaubensbekenntnis—A Confession of Faith*, the same year in which Heinrich Heine issued his *Neue Gedichte*. Freiligrath's volume sold over eight thousand copies in its first year. Once more, *Zeitgeist*, the Spirit of the Age, was speaking out directly, unequivocally—and finding response. Here was another challenge to Prussian authority. For the poet had already had several severe brushes with the censor. A number of the poems he was now giving the public had in fact been barred from publication in one or the other of the journals. None of the poems now appearing were revolutionary. But they were liberal enough to warrant, in the eyes of the authorities, prohibition, and for the author, worse. Freiligrath was venturing his pension; he was venturing his personal freedom. Like his hero Ulrich von Hutten, he was saying, "*Ich hab's gewagt. Jacta est aulea!*" "I have dared it! The die is cast!" He was affirming what liberalism in the German states was expressing more and more articulately. Freedom and Right are twin sisters! Freedom through Right! He was lauding those who had suffered and were suffering persecution, and asserting, Freedom is not dead![36] Like so many other poets, Heine not least, he was expressing outrage at the oppression and starvation of the Silesian weavers. He was celebrating the "Tree of Humanity" in its constant cycles of renewal that nothing can stop; the everlasting blooming and rebirth that brings life from death, and will do the same for Poland and Spain. "*Immer Früh-ling, immer Freiheit träumend*," "Always dreaming Spring, always dreaming Freedom."[37] He was inviting the poet Hoffmann von Fallersleben, who had been deprived of his Breslau professorship, to leave the sultry climate of Prussia and enjoy the freer atmos-phere of the Rhine, to hurry before the "sword of his own poetry" had driven Freiligrath "westward." He was offering translations of the radical English Corn Law Rhymer Ebenezer Elliot, of Robert Burns's "For A' That." And not least, that challenge to Germany that was to become his most celebrated poem—"Hamlet."

> *Deutschland ist Hamlet! Ernst und stumm*
> *In seinen Toren jede Nacht*
> *Geht die begrabne Freiheit um …*

"Germany is Hamlet," and buried freedom, solemn and mute, haunts her gates, up-braiding the dilatory Prince for delaying his vengeance. But Hamlet is not stirring!

> He sits too much beside the fire,
> He lies and reads too long in bed,
> His sluggish blood is thick with mire.
> He's scant of breath and too well fed.
> 'Tis learned oakum all he picks
> With little work and too much thinking,
> Too long in Wittenberg he sticks,
> Frequenting lecture-halls, and drinking …

Such is our German Hamlet. Four acts have gone, now for the fifth; let it not follow Shakespeare's scheme! "Now is the moment … There still is time …" The way is free!

> Think of thy oath and play thy part,
> Revenge our buried freedom's wrong.
> Yet the dear dreamer shall I blame,
> Because he waits and shilly-shallies:
> In my heart am I not the same?
> A creature that delays and dallies?[38]

No, Freiligrath was no such German Hamlet. He did not hesitate. He renounced his royal pension, and in anticipation of prosecution, he left Germany and made his way to Brussels. There he met other refugees, among them Karl Marx, "a nice fellow," as Freiligrath described him, "interesting and modest in his attitude."[39]

Brussels could not hold him, and he soon went to Switzerland. But his head and heart were afire with new poems that far outdistanced those he had written before, and soon in 1846 he published a small volume of them with the title taken from the French revolutionary chant, *Ça ira!* Here in Switzerland the atmosphere was freer and more receptive. Here he found German refugees like himself, many of them more or less radical socialists. Here he met Franz Liszt and Gottfried Keller. Here too a struggle between the old and the new, the Liberals and the Catholics, was taking place, soon to erupt in a civil war. Freiligrath moved quickly, for the *Ça ira* was his own "*Marseillaise.*"

It is hard to specify the influences that had played upon him, or were playing upon him—the atmosphere around him was thick with social doctrines of varying kinds and forcefulness. Freiligrath was a wide reader; he knew English and French perfectly, and he was to become a consummate translator from both languages. He was deep in the poets of the times, and no doubt drew inspiration also from the more theoretical writings of the day. His was not a philosophical mind. What he read and thought through, he converted to deeply felt sentiment.

The first poem of the little collection is in fact set to the music of the "*Marseillaise.*" It is an invitation to a voyage, toward a discovery of a new America. For the name of the ship is "Revolution"!

> Oh black fire-ship! Hurl your rockets
> Into the canting churches' yachts,
> Against the silver fleets of masters,
> Bravely point the cannons' mouth.
> In the deep sea's teeming bottom,
> Let Greed's rich treasures rot!
> Ahoy then! Ahoy! the vessel well-manned!
> Set sail! Set sail! Beyond is new land![40]

This was incendiary enough. But even more so was the poem "*Freie Presse*"—"A Free Press"—in which the master and his printing mates are turning type into an "arrogant morning paper"—that is, bullets. Thereafter will the bullets once more be recast into type. ... "*Von unten oben,*"—"Up from Below," is the most daring of these poems. It casts defiance at the King of Prussia. The King and the Queen, visiting their castle on the Rhine, are aboard the Rhine steamer. The trip is delightful, the company gay; King and Queen are pleased up on deck! But down below in the boiler room, amid the grime and the heat, there is one who makes the boat move. For a moment he comes up on deck and views the joyful gathering from his opened hatch. In his hand a glowing iron, his face and arms reddened, he reflects: How like a state is this ship! You, King, in the light up above; you in the light; I, down below, in the darkness—stoking, and stirring the volcanic fires. It is in my hands that I hold both your fate and the fate of the ship, and were I so minded I could blow you both up in the air. Not yet! But the time will come—the ground will burst, the fires will rise from the depths; and we, those below, we will ascend from the pits of fire into the light.

> For we are Power! With youthful strength
> We shatter the rotting state!
> We, who work below, we are God's rage![41]

Such is Freiligrath's first forthright proletarian poem. At the same time he wrote:

I am no communist, at least not a fanatical one, but I believe that this new dogma, even if regarded merely as a form of transition, is yet an essential step forward, and that because of its humanitarian basis it can do more to inspire, promote, and effect a decisive change than can any one-sided political doctrine. Surely we have passed beyond the illusions of German constitutionalism—petty or large! Communism will have a future! All its dreams will not be realized, but if like Columbus it fail to land in India, it will yet discover an America.[42]

His life, as he put it in one of his poems, was like a chessboard, and he like a knight, ready to jump, though he was not as yet sure where. He was not afraid of the future. He could not hope to survive by poetry alone. He would have to reconcile himself once more to some commercial or banking post. Would it be in America? He decided for England, and in July 1846, left for London—an emigrant once more, with family responsibilities, embarking on a peripatetic existence—something taken for granted by his generation.

In London Freiligrath found a commercial position through friends and settled down to a modest if still precarious life. Longfellow, whom he had met some years before, was urging him to be his guest in America. But he hesitated. He had gotten to know a number of congenial people; among British men of letters he became acquainted with Tennyson, Barry Cornwall, Monckton-Milnes, and Bulwer. He was busy translating English poetry, especially that of Thomas Hood. He was renewing relations with Karl Marx, and soon would meet Engels on a firmer footing. The inclusive influence of these men was to widen his political and social horizon and sharpen his political verse as well as his thinking.

And then one day in February 1848, when he had finally made up his mind to cross the Atlantic, startling news arrived from across the Channel. Gone was the thought of emigration. Here, here was his America; here that battleship of Revolution which he had sung, and here its booming salvoes!

How could one record the feelings of those hours—his own and those of his friends? On February 25, Freiligrath composed a poem, "*Im Hochland fiel der erste Schuss*"—"In the Highlands the first shot rang," celebrating the Swiss triumph over the *Sonderbund*; the events in Italy, and France.

> My eyes are dimmed with tears,
> My heart is forever singing:
> "*Mourir pour la Patrie!*"
> Blessings, blessing glorious year,
> Blessings happy month!
> "*Allons enfants! Mourir, mourir,
> Mourir pour la Patrie!*"

What about the Rhine and the Elbe? he was asking himself. March came, and with it the days of Berlin and Vienna. For the Berliners he composed a strong poem, warning them not relax from the battle, to remain true to the fallen revolutionaries. It was, he said, "People or Crown!" "*Volk heisst es oder Krone!*" Do not, he begged, let the dead heroes stem the floods of Freedom, let them be the stepping stones toward a new future! Be on your guard lest you exchange the struggle for Freedom solely for that of German unity.

> For we too have been thirsting long,
> For a nation One and Free:

> One—only when she's free,
> And free without her lords.
>
> And now our bags our fully packed,
> And we are on our way!
> Now, holy Freedom, comfort bring
> To Mother, Bride, and Child
> Of him who fell. And to our own
> If steel should mow us down.[43]

Freiligrath was as good as his word. In May he was back in Düsseldorf. He took part in the meetings of the Frankfurt Assembly. His association with Karl Marx, who was now in Cologne, deepened into friendship and close cooperation. Aghast, they watched the ring of reaction closing tightly around the country, while the German Hamlet scarcely moved. Freiligrath's poems now took on a sharper edge. He turned Burns's "For A' That" into a scorching arraignment of the Germans' acquiescence in their own disarming. "So fill the mortar's maw," he wrote, "with iron, lead, and a' that, and we'll hold our ground for a' that." This poem was circulated in thousands as a leaflet, as was the even more searing, *"Die Toten an die Lebenden"*—"The Dead to the Living," of which nine thousand copies were sold. In the latter, he was once more reminding his fellow-countrymen of the hundred and eighty-seven victims of the Berlin barricades of March 18. Such reminders were badly needed. Freiligrath is speaking with the voices of the perished:

> *Die Kugel mitten in der Brust, die Stirne breit gespalten,*
> *So habt ihr uns auf blut'gem Brett hoch in die Luft gehalten!*
> *Hoch in die Luft mit wildem Schrei, dass unsre Schmerzgebärde*
> *Dem, der zu töten uns befahl, ein Fluch auf ewig werden!*
>
> Each with a bullet in his heart, and forehead gaping wide,
> You raised us on our blood-stained boards above the human tide,
> High in the air with wild uproar, that each set face of pain
> Might prove an everlasting curse to him that had us slain!. ...
>
> We thought high was the price, but good the cause for which we bled
> And stretched us quietly to rest, each on his narrow bed.
> Out on you! Were we not deceived? Four moons their course scarce run,
> Your coward hands have fooled away what was so stoutly won. ...

We, who humbled the King, and forced him to come "reeling to our bed" and doff his royal hat, were made to watch the subsequent shaming of our ideal, the betrayal of Poland, the return of the cowardly Prussian Prince ...[44]

In Cologne, Karl Marx was reconstituting his former newspaper into the *Neue Rheinische Zeitung*. Once again it became a formidable and fearless organ of the opposition, and a sharp thorn in the flesh of Prussian reaction. Freiligrath joined its editorial staff in the fall of 1848. Soon he was to join the League of Communists. Yet even before these associations took place, he felt the oppressive weight of the government. Amid popular outrage, he was brought to trial for the poem, "The Dead to the Living," but was ultimately exonerated. Far from being deterred, he now began to appear in the pages of the *Neue Rheinische Zeitung*, where his poetry contributed the crystal-lized emotional and aesthetic impact, a coadjutor of the other editors' polemical articles, a brilliant flame that illumined a significant moment of history. Here, in November 1848, he published his lines on "Vienna" with their desperate plea to Germans to come to that city's help. Here, too, he dedicated a moving hymn to the memory of the executed Robert Blum, when his native city, Cologne, paid him a memorial honor. Here Freiligrath celebrated the signal resistance of the Hungarians.

In 1849 only Hungary was still holding out. Barricade after barricade had fallen. The Prussian king was in the saddle once more. Prussian troops acted as the vanguard executioners of revolution all over the land. And now Louis-Napoleon was elected President of the French Republic. In the Rhineland the harassment suffered by the *Rheinische Zeitung* and its principal editor became more blatant and overt. On March 11, 1849, Marx was ordered expelled from Prussian territory. The fate of the *Neue Rheinische Zeitung* was sealed. Its last number appeared on May 19, 1849, and carried a "Farewell" to its readers from the hand of Freiligrath. "Though a stricken corpse," the poem said, "I remain undaunted, and with my last breath I cry defiance and call to arms." And it promised to return:

> *Wenn die letzte Krone wie Glas zerbricht*
> *In des Kampfes Wettern und Flammen ...*

> When the last royal diadem has splintered like glass,
> In battles' fierce turmoil and roar,
> When the People has thundered its last "Guilty!" doom,
> I will stand by your side once more.

> With word and with deed, by Danube and Rhine,
> Amid gunsmoke and shattering alarms,
> When the last of thrones has crashed to the dust,
> I'll be there—your comrade-at-arms![45]

Karl Marx had gone to Paris, where the French government made it known that he was unwelcome. So once more he took his *Wanderstab*—and in September 1849 he arrived in London, where he was soon joined by his wife. Impecunious and troubled, he began, upon arrival, to plan publication of a *Neue Rheinische Revue*. In the Rhineland he had left, the full force of repression was soon to fall on many of his political associates. Eventually it culminated in the notorious Cologne anti-Communist trial, which in 1852 resulted in severe prison sentences for seven of those tried. Freiligrath, who was not implicated, remained in the field to settle the affairs of the defunct journal, and to raise funds for the relief of the accused and their families. His devotion, his loyalty, and his courage knew no compromises. Wherever he was needed, there he was. He himself did not know how long he would be free, or how long he would remain. ...

In 1851 appeared the second volume of his *Neuere politische und soziale Gedichte*, which with the previously published first part contained the fulminant poems of the preceding years. Freiligrath was still hopeful of a resurgence of revolution. But now prosecution threatened him. In May 1851 he left for London. Here he was to live for sixteen years. Once again he returned to the counting-house ...

His poetic career was practically over. He needed the intense situation of battle to fire him to his most eloquent utterances. Not that emigrant elements in London — French, German, Italian, Hungarian, Polish, Russian—lacked matter over which to quarrel. In many of their hearts still lurked a vision of another imminent revolution on the Continent, decried as vain illusion by the more hard-headed. For a number of years Freiligrath remained a devoted friend of Marx and Engels, always ready to assist Marx when the latter needed him. In time he drifted away from political activity, devoting himself to his commercial duties, and to translations and journalism. He became a notable intermediary connecting French, British and American letters with Germany; and, in the London *Athenaeum*, a significant interpreter of German literature to England. He was among the first to make Walt Whitman known in Germany; he translated the poetry of William Cullen Bryant and Longfellow. He composed consummate versions of Hugo's poetry. But the spark that had fired the verses of his "Confession of Faith" and his "New Political and Social Poems" was out. In 1858 he became a naturalized British citizen, and three years later he rejected the political amnesty extended by Wilhelm I. With age, the longing to return to Germany became irresistible, and when, in the economic crisis of 1866, the Swiss banking firm in whose London branch he had been employed for years suffered reverses, he found himself unemployed and in straits. In Germany a movement to raise a national subscription on his behalf found many supporters, and he received the sum of 60,000 Thalers. On June 24, 1868, he returned to Germany, where he would die in 1874. Unlike Georg Herwegh, he became a fervent supporter of his country in the Franco-German War, and composed a number of patriotic lyrics. His revolutionary poetry was practically forgotten in the Bismarckian and Wilhelminian era, until it was momentarily and paradoxically revived with the collapse of Germany in the First World War. On June 24, 1923, in one of the darkest moments of German history, on the anniversary of the assassination of Walther Rathenau, Hugo Preuss rose in the Reichstag and recited Freiligrath's revolutionary verses, "*Trotz alledem*," "For A' That!" In one of those macabre and anomalous transpositions of meaning, he turned Freiligrath's fiery words of defiance against the oppressors of German humanity, the monarchs, the Junkers, the bourgeois, into a defiance of the victors, of the world! Freiligrath had cried, "*Wir sind das Volk, die Menschheit wir*" . . .

> We are the people, humanity we,
> For a' that and for a' that!
> We dare you come! for a' that!
> You can constrain—but not compel—
> Ours is the world, for a' that![46]

O, ominous and prophetic realm of ambiguities!

4. Georg Weerth and Adolf Glassbrenner

Brussels, July 19, 1845

Dear Mother,

. . . For the rest, it is likely that in the future I shall be doing many things which will be contrary to your wishes and ideas. I must ask you, once and for all, to let me go my own way. You may be certain that everything I do will be with the purest of motives. I belong to the "Rag-Tag Communists," who are now being pelted with mud, and whose sole crime has been to fight for the poor and oppressed in a life and death struggle. Let the gentlemen of property beware; the mighty arms of the people are on our side, and the best minds of all nations will come over by and by. There is my dearest friend from Barmen, Friedrich Engels, who has written a book in favor of the English workers, and has lashed out furiously at the manufacturers, and with perfect justice. His own father has factories in England and Germany.

Now he's had a terrible quarrel with his family, who think him godless and wicked, and his rich father does not give him a penny for his support. I, however, know the son to be a supremely good human being, of extraordinary intelligence and vision, who fights for the good of the working classes with all his might, night and day ....[47]

So the twenty-three year old Georg Weerth to his mother, widow of a very substantial clergyman, senior minister in Detmold, whose house adjoined that of the Freiligrath family.

The mother had reason to be disturbed. Her son was embarked, it seemed, on a successful commercial career, an important agent for a cotton concern in Bradford, to which town he had moved in 1843 after an apprenticeship in Elberfeld and Cologne. The year following his arrival there he had begun cultivating the friendship of Friedrich Engels, who was employed in nearby Manchester. The following year he had gone to Brussels on business, where he had met Marx and was drawn into the latter's political circle. The fact that young Georg Weerth was giving undue attention to poetry and journalism, and was contributing political articles to newspapers in Cologne, must have been equally disturbing.

What could not have been clear to his mother and the rest of his family, however, was the rapidity with which Weerth had been assimilating new knowledge and ideas. Like Engels, like Freiligrath, Weerth too had looked out the windows of a commercial or manufacturing establishment in the industrial section of the Wupperthal and seen startling things, men and machines, machines and men, women and children. In each of them the sight had awakened a strange and new sensation. Education had begun ... books and friends and additional personal experiences rounded out such studies as no university could have offered at that time.

It was a small world still upon which they had looked. Barmen, Elberfeld, the Cologne region, throbbing and thriving as they seemed, were but small particles in the larger, pulsating world of Industry. To go to England was to transfer from a small parochial school to a cosmic university. Here Industry was the world.

Young Georg Weerth was appalled, amazed, excited and outraged by what he saw in England. Nowhere in the world was there a city like London for imposing beauty and horrifying drabness, for bustle and trade, for multitudes ever filling the streets, for the turmoil of the dockyards and the innumerable ships that daily plied between the city and all parts of the world—contrasting so violently with the provincialism of what he had hitherto known.

Here was the heartbeat, the pulse, the nerve center of the present and the future. Combined with the industrial north, with Manchester, Liverpool, Bradford—here was

England! He loved London, as he detested Bradford—one represented a buoyant life; the other work, work, and more work. No amusements, no libraries, no social distractions. Like Heine, he felt this was no land for a poet, yet the country stimulated him, as nothing had done before, to his best poetic creations.

> *Du Mann im schlechten blauen Kittel,*
> *Arbeite! Schaffe Salz und Brot!*
> *Arbeit! Arbeit ist ein Mittel,*
> *Probat für Pestilenz und Not.*

> You, Man in your shabby blue smock,
> Work! Work for your salt and bread!
> Work, for Work is the steel that will arm you
> Agains the Plague, against Need![48]

He did not require many masters to shape him and direct him. In poetry, he took Heinrich Heine—for simplicity, directness, humor, and controversy. His philosophy was shaped by Feuerbach, Engels and Marx. To these he added his life's experiences, and his contacts with the working population around him, German, English, Irish. He felt not only for them; he spoke as one who was of them. He translated Engels into poetry, over which the genius of Heine also presided. But he had an advantage over other German revolutionary poets that could be obtained only through a close association with the workers he was describing and for whom he was writing.

Like so many other seekers of that and succeeding generations throughout Europe, Weerth found in Ludwig Feuerbach the key to some problems of existence. Feuerbach brought him back to earth from his wide-ranging romantic flights, from that *Schmerz* that wished, as he put it, to "outrace" the stars, and pile Ossa on Pelion. Feuerbach saved him from religious superstitions and returned to him the gift of life and of the senses.

> One day, your words, great Feuerbach,
> From my inmost heart wrested my last doubts,
> And I plucked the fairest flowers of Knowledge,
> And was free of gods and devils.[49]

His other good masters completed his "education"—not least among them England herself:

This cradle of trade and politics, this England, has quickly given me such opportunities to accumulate knowledge and make observations which I would have sought in vain elsewhere. I believe that at this moment England is the true school for a young person: for this cold, canting people, from the Prime Minister down to the common tradesman, commits all possible vileness under the mask of religion; yet, at the same time, stands at the head of all beneficent world movements, and at one stroke opens the prospect of abysmal infamy and magnificent, purely human activity. In addition, England appears to be the terrain of the next Revolution—for nowhere else are poverty and discontent so rife as here. The leaders of the popular opposition make good use of this ... for they direct the full fury of their attack on the very nerve of contemporary society, that is, Money and Property ...[50]

He confessed that, despite Bradford, he had come to "love England." England, he added, because life there, being "more serious," had made him more serious too.[51]

Brussels, Marx, and the Communist League completed Weerth's education. He admired Marx greatly, and could not get over the man's inexhaustible energy. "Marx is working at his History of National Economy like one possessed. This man has for some years now been sleeping no more than four hours the night." He marveled at his "truly Jovian head, his marble brow, and wild black hair."[52]

His wide travels on business, his range of acquaintanceship, his own experiences, enabled him to become an international spokesman for the working-class movements. He knew the foremost Chartist leaders, Irish and English, wrote and spoke both about them and in their name. In 1847, in Brussels, he could stand up before an international congress called to consider Free Trade, which, he saw, had failed to raise the question of the working classes, and in a fiery address delivered in French, expose the emptiness of the pretensions that Free Trade worked in the cause of the laboring classes. "The workers," he said, "are tired of being repaid for their suffering with drafts not accepted even by the celestial bank of the good Lord ... When, in 1830, they fought for you in the streets of Paris or of Brussels, they were hailed, fêted, embraced; but when, a little later, they were dying of hunger and were begging for bread—they were shot down! ..." Free trade would not do them any good, and, speaking in the name of the British, the working people there knew this very well.[53]

As was to be expected, February 1848 found Weerth in Paris. He wrote to his mother:

> I cannot describe what I have seen and heard in the last two weeks. Such thing cannot be retold; one must have been there to understand how a person can weep in the streets without shame. One of the most beautiful nations in the world in three days has reconquered her freedom ... From morning till night I took part in everything ... We issued a call to all Germans living in Paris to gather for a great demonstration in favor of the republic ... Herwegh, the poet, was elected President, others of us to a Committee ... Wednesday we gathered along with all German democrats at the Place Caroussel—seven thousand of us—and four by four we marched with the black-red-gold flag and the tricolor to the Hôtel de Ville to transmit an address to the Provisional Government. Five hundred members of a chorus at the head of our procession sang French and German songs ... Herwegh read our address, and Crémieux responded ... Read the newspapers carefully ... This Revolution will change the face of the world, and this is as it should be! *Vive la République!*[54]

When he visited the Tuileries and, in the royal chambers, surrounded by paintings of kings and nobles, saw the many cots with the wounded upon them, "the heroes of February 24," he was overcome.[55]

It was time to return to Germany. Here, like Freiligrath somewhat later, Weerth joined Marx and the *Neue Rheinische Zeitung*, a steady source of literary and political articles and satires. Here he published, using the brilliant vein of Heine, his devastating satire on Prince Lichnowsky, *The Life and Deeds of the Renowned Knight Schnapphahnski*—the name roughly translated and de-Polonized would be "Highway Robber"—actually a searing portrait of the whole tribe of feudal Junkers. Weerth was somewhat later to pay for this daring act, after the actual prototype for the book was killed during a brief Frankfurt uprising.

Like the others, Weerth watched the vicissitudes of the revolutionary movements with exultation, then with trepidation, and finally with despair. Not the least shattering blow was the collapse of the Chartist movement, of which he was a witness in London. Against the advice of his friends, he returned to Germany and, in order to preserve his citizenship, accepted three months' imprisonment on charges of libelling the late Prince Lichnowsky. With the fading of the Revolution, his own spirits fell, but not his sharpness of observation. He returned to his commercial occupations, wandering far and wide, particularly to the New World of the Caribbean and of South America and Mexico. He had become *Europa-müde*—weary of Europe—but he did not recover his creative talents abroad. He died of a tropical fever in Havana in July 1856.

Weerth's disgust at the way the Chartist leadership, particularly Feargus O'Connor, had first disarmed, castrated, and then betrayed the English working classes, knew no bounds. From Hamburg, in one of his last letter to Marx, he said farewell to his literary career:

> During the last day I have written all sorts of things, but finished none, for I see no purpose or goal in literary work. When *you* write about national economy, there is some sense or reason in it. But for *me*? … My literary activity came to an end with the *Neue Rheinische Zeitung* … I must admit I am sorry to have lost the last three years for nothing; as sorry, as I am happy when I think of our association in Cologne. We have *not* compromised ourselves. That is the principal thing. Since the days of Frederick the Great no one has scourged our German riffraff like the *Neue Rheinische Zeitung*. I will not say that this was my merit; but I was there …[56]

He had little to reproach himself with. He departed with clean hands and a clear heart, leaving behind him a small body of precious poetry, a brilliant satirical work, an unfinished novel, and a number of keen, incisive articles on social and political conditions. A profound analyst of the current historical scene, also gifted with fine foresight, he estimated with accuracy the nature of the post-1848 prosperity, that, for a time at least, meant the quietus of revolution.

> The English are at work again in all the mines, smithies, spinning industries, harbors, not because a Prince Windischgrätz is having Viennese shot summarily—no, they are working because the markets of Canton, of New York, and St. Petersburg must be provided with manufactured goods, because in California a seemingly inexhaustible field for speculation has been opened, because the poor harvests of 1845 and 1846 were followed by two good harvests in 1847 and 1848, because they have shelved railway speculation, and because moneys are now returning to their regular channels. And they will work until a new economic crisis arises.[57]

For him, Germany was a doomed land, altogether incapable of taking part in the new competitive economic wars which were emerging. (His foresight failed him here!) To Heinrich Heine he wrote:

> Yes, while we Germans are moving towards the graveyard, the great nations around us are engaged in ever new enterprises, in ever greater achievements. While we bring to our

markets the dead and the crazy, in London the whole world lies open, with the most magnificent of its products. Across the Atlantic, the British and the Americans are racing to see who can reach New York or Liverpool in ten days, or nine days and so many hours. In California a new empire has risen within two years. The products of the Australian coast have risen so greatly within the last few years that the wool of the Antipodes threatens to drive the production of our noble Saxon and Silesian sheep breeders to the ground. ... Then begins the great war—not the war between Christianity and Paganism, of the Guelfs against the Ghibellines, the Whigs against the Tories—no! It will be the war between the gold of the Urals and the gold of California; the wheat of America, of Russia; Australia's wool against Germany's; cotton versus flax; West Indian colonies against the German beet-root. In this concussion, this great migration, not of Cimbri, or Goths, or Huns, no—of sacks of corn, coffee and wool, yes—in this hitherto unheard-of competition between the products of the virgin lands—the ancient empires of the Franks and the Germans will be sucked dry down to the very dregs, made debtors head over ears, and struggle in vain to assert themselves through their lands, their science and new institutions ... Then we shall surely be defeated and destroyed in this great war of competition, so that for years perhaps nothing will remain of Germany but the Hegelian philosophy and a volume of your poems. This is the sole comfort I can extend to you. ...[58]

His most genuine feelings came to the fore in his poems, *Songs from Lancashire* and *Workmen's Songs*—*Lieder aus Lancashire* and *Handwerkburschenlieder*. In these poems he joined in close handshakes the workers of Germany, of England, and of Ireland. Their masterly sparseness reminds one of Heine, but their sentiments touch more closely on the personal as well as the social. The Lancashire operatives hear of the brave though hopeless resistance of their Silesian weaver-brothers, and they join in their fate.

> They clenched their fists, they swung their caps,
> They stormed a fierce "Hurrah!"
> So that wood and field sent echoes back,
> "Hats off! Hail brave Silesia!"[59]

Once more, as he along with other Germans is crossing the Irish Sea on the way to Ireland, all of them recall their homeland with yearning; but also their Silesian brethren:

> And all fell silent; the sea sounded hollow and dull,
> Their German hearts filled with sadness,
> But came the morrow—and the darkness sped,
> As jubilant shouts joined in gladness!
> For there—as the morning rose over the sea,
> On the waves—lo!—an emerald green!
> Like Hope's own unfading, luminous image,
> O'Connell's sweet island—green Erin![60]

In a more savage mood, the poem *"Gericht"*—"Court"—calls for a second trial of those imprisoned: the criminal, the thief, the prostitute, the political prisoner, and also those already dead, calling for a day and a generation that will at least redeem for their progeny the debt owed.

Amid other glistening flags and other liveries,
Rage, dauntless racer, stamps impatient for the fray;
And before the gaping portals of the Future,
The thund'ring Present stands in battle-array.

Und vor der Zukunft weit erschlossnen Pforten
Lärmt kampfgerüstet schon die Gegenwart.

Once more, as in the case of Büchner, it took many generations to rediscover their first great proletarian poet, and to utilize the great traditions of 1848. Bertolt Brecht was one such in whom the poetry of Weerth and Büchner found a responsive ear of genius. For a few of Weerth's poems might well have come out of the 1920s and the later 1930s. Such as the song about the cannon founder, for example, who had toiled all his life long, and in old age had been cast adrift:

He went—his breast full of anguished wrath,
His wrath he could barely hold,
It thundered like all the mortars he'd
From the roaring furnace rolled!

Accursed wretch! You just wait!
Thus spoke the poor, old founder,
Soon we'll be pouring for *our own sport*,
A four-and-twenty-pounder![61]

Or the "Song of the Poor Tailor,"

There was once a poor tailor,
His needles he would ply,
He'd sewed for well nigh thirty years,
Although he knew not why.

And when a Saturday came round again,
And another week flew by,
The tailor began to weep,
Although he knew not why.

And then he took the shining needle,
And the scissors he had plied,
He broke the needle, the scissors too,
Although he knew not why.

He fastened many a strong thread,
To the ceiling's beam on high,
And twisted them around his neck,
Although he knew not why.

He knew not why—the evening bells,
Sent forth their hum and sigh.
The tailor died at half past seven,
And no one could tell why.[62]

He was of Heine's tribe. For that poet Weerth's admiration never waned. He corresponded with the sick poet, conveying to him his pleasure, when, visiting Hamburg and the bookstore of Heine's publisher Campe, he noted the excitement created by the appearance of Heine's *Romanzero*.

> Other poets, Weerth wrote, age. You grow younger with the days. Yes, I understand the secret of your illness. Already years ago, Death wished to get hold of you, but in the fateful moment, he shrank back in fright at seeing such youthfulness. His sickle froze in the air as he raised it, and you live on. ...[63]

Both poets died in 1856.

* * *

Revolution had its pungent humor too. There was Weerth's *Schnapphahnski*; there was Heinrich Heine, of course preeminent. Theirs was highly sophisticated humor, addressed to the politically instructed, the culturally advanced. But the sharp, bitter, lusty humor that could speak to the populace at large in their own idiom found its most brilliant expression in the Berlin writer Adolf Glassbrenner, initiator of a long line of homely, acidulous, and popular humorous journals in Germany and Austria. A Berlin lover through and through, he was a master of its dialect, capable of translating sophisticated political and social ideas into racy popular idiom. His vignettes of the city paralleled those of Dickens in his *Sketches by Boz*.

Forthright in character and thought, he did not conceal his contempt for the *gemütliche* German bourgeois and philistine. He addressed himself directly to the populace—the people of the workshops, of the streets, to the ordinary citizen. He was a gadfly, but an irrepressible and indestructible one. He stung hard at the subservient German *Bürger*, at the aristocracy, at the bureaucracy. Before the outbreak of the March Revolution he had lashed out at their indecisiveness in verses that for their skilful alliteration defy translation:

> *Die Zwitter und die Zitterer,*
> *Die zischelten zusammen,*
> *Ob's an der Zeit, die Despotie*
> *Aus Deutschland zu verbannen.*
> *Der Erste sagte: es müsse gehn;*
> *Der Zweite sprach: es macht sich;*
> *Der Dritte setzt die Brille auf*
> *Und hat er noch bedacht sich;*
> *Der Fünfte sprach: 's noch nicht Zeit,*
> *Die Fürsten sind dagegen!. ...*

> The twitterers and the quiverers,
> Were whispering man to man,
> If it really weren't time
> Despotism to ban.
> The first one said: "It must go!"
> The second: "It'll go by and by!"
> The third one put on spectacles,
> In thought he seemed engrossed—

> The fifth one said: "It's not yet time!
> The Princes are opposed!"

He thus defined a whole era of irresolution, and the illusion of "revolution from above." He propounded his conception of the writer's function in a serio-comic dedication to Apollo with which he prefaced his collection of local sketches, *Berliner Volksleben*, with its "live figures of the people."

> We are separated [he wrote] from the people by everything; by distorted custom and education, by money, by our speech, by our clothes and by that phantom of "honor" which leads the elect by the nose. Till we writers join hands with the people and come to an understanding with them no true freedom is possible … Not the despot and reactionary alone are to blame for the people's ignorance. No, those also are to blame who think that literature is for a caste, who seek the fulness of life in scrutinizing a worn-out copper coin for an obliterated date, while a wealth of uncoined gold is lying at their feet; who live and move and have their being in the mouldy atmosphere of the past, and turn their backs on the present and the future.[64]

His literary career was a constant clash with censor and police. He was irrefragable. No sooner was one of his humorous journals suppressed than he commenced another. He never intermitted his criticism of despotism and injustice, continuing right up to his death in 1876. He hated war, and in the Franco-German collision of 1870 he wrote: "Our good angels show sympathy neither for Germany nor France. It's for the wary they weep." "This is a glorious one for us, but—a war! While one is proud to be a German, one is ashamed to be a Man."[65]

His supreme achievement in satire was the creation of the *Guckkästner*—the "Peep-show Man," Glassbrenner's spokesman. He used him with delicious and superb success in 1848. One of his dramatic sketches is entitled "The New Europe." It was written on the morrow of the Berlin March Revolution. We are in the streets of Berlin, more specifically Unter den Linden, and it is nine o'clock in the evening. The Peep-show Man is singing:

> I am a German. Do you know my colors?
> Black, red and gold—here, see, they're displayed;
> Witnesses bold, these colors wave before me,
> Of German Freedom, for which my brothers died.
> Now I proclaim, and proudly do I shout it,
> Proud am I to take my stand:
> The night is gone, and the sun of Freedom,
> Has risen over all our German land.

He looks around him. Can this be the same Berlin I used to know? Come one, come all, he cries out. "It's all in my peep-show! See the great battles for Europe's freedom!" Customers come, they pay and peep. First pictures: Paris, France, Lamartine! Not that that drama is over yet. He sings them a song about Louis-Philippe, the Revolution and Lamartine. Whom, he asks, did the French people choose to represent them? A numbskull? A dolt? No! A Poet! Lamartine! Hail that man who chanted Freedom, Equality, Brotherhood, Work for All, Joy and Peace! but

> On these heaps of sinfulness,
> As Lamartine seeks,
> To build a Kingdom of the Just
> Takes more than a couple of weeks!

The Peep-show Man proceeds to unroll the full drama of the Revolutions—even of those still to come. There are Ludwig of Bavaria and Lola Montez. "Poor fellow," the tailor who is peeping whispers; to which the Peep-show Man replies, "Yes, we Germans are very kindhearted, even when we're treated like dogs." He shows the Spanish Revolution "which hasn't taken place yet," and then Vienna and Metternich. And in the Berlin dialect he sings:

> *Aufjing die Sonne der Freiheit*
> *Durch Oesterreichs lange Nacht;*
> *Die licht, joldene Neiheit,*
> *Hat Wien confus jemacht …*
> *Bald tobt's mit wildem Schalle,*
> *Bald herzen, küssen sie Alle:*
> *Durchlaucht von Metternich!*

> Up rose the sun of Freedom,
> And scattered Austria's night,
> So new, so free this Freedom—
> For Vienna quite a sight!
> Your Highness, Mr. Metternich,
> How quickly you've disappeared,
> For you—there are only curses!
> For you—there are no tears!. …

Again, a tailor-spectator commiserates with Metternich—after all, he had great sympathy with us Germans! But the Peep-show Man replies:

> Sympathy? Yes, indeed. Censorship, tortures, prisons,
> darkness, treason—that's the kind of sympathy he had!

He invites the audience to view the Berlin scenes of the March days, and sings them a song adjuring them to remember, always remember:

> *Das ist das Lied vom Monat März!*
> *Vergiss es nicht Berliner Herz!*
> *Sing's alle Dage wieder,*
> *Denn sonst—ju'n Nacht, ihr Brüder!*

No other pictures? someone asks. Not yet—they're not ready. "I'm working on an Italian Republic. Come tomorrow and you'll see the new German Emperor. Six groschen entrance." "Too dear," a young man says, and "anyway, if you hear that I've been elected Emperor, tell them I decline. My father says the main thing is to secure a piece of bread and earn an honest living. Learn a trade."

The tailor reproves the Peep-show Man for his bold speech. Peep-show Man yawns, closes the show and goes off, while the young man is heard singing an ironic song:

Forgive us, Policeman and Soldier,
Forgive us our Revolutions,
We promise never, never again,
To trouble prince or lordling.
Oh, we'll be just, we'll be devout—
If not, send us Russian Nich'las with his knout!

5. *Heinrich Heine*

Beat the drum, and do not fear,
Kiss the lovely sutler dame,
That is all you need to know,
That is wisdom's highest aim.

Drum the sleepers from their sleep,
Drum Reveille with youthful glow,
Forward, forward! Drum ahead!
That is all you need to know.

That's the sum of Hegel's teaching,
All the wisdom books can spell,
I have grasped it, for I am clever,
And a lusty drummer as well!
            —Heinrich Heine, "*Doktrin*"

The master of them all for satire, irony, wit and insight—Heinrich Heine—whom Théophile Gautier had once called the German Apollo—marked the Revolution of 1848 by walking through the streets of Paris for the last time in May 1848.[66] Thereafter, for eight long years, on his "mattress grave"—his sickbed in the rue d'Amsterdam, and later in the avenue Matignon—he lay, immobilized. But he remained no less alert, no less the inquisitive and eager spectator of portentous historic events. He had been sick a long time now, his eyes were going, as was his body—gradually dissolving from the ravages of the disease he had contracted as a very young man. His faithful wife Mathilde would from now on carry him, shrunk almost to a boy's size, in her arms, to the balcony overlooking the city he loved, the Paris he had made his home. A world-famous poet now, he had many visitors. Friends brought him news of the outside world—not least, of the unsuccessful June uprising of 1848; later, of the election of Louis-Napoleon to the Presidency of France, and thereafter, of his assumption of the crown of Emperor by a *coup d'état*.

Yet his mind's brilliance never faded, nor his inspiration or creativeness. As a matter of fact, the more Heine's body decayed, the more, luminous and glowing became his poetic art. His thoughts deepened, and his wit remained, as ever, incandescent.

For him, too, the year 1848 marked a sharp division between past and future. For him, too, the forties had initiated a new stage of thinking and creation. He could look back to 1844 and the publication of his *Neue Gedichte*, to the year before, when he completed that scintillating beast-satire *Atta Troll*, and not long thereafter to that remarkable commentary on Germany in brilliant quatrains, the long poem *Deutschland: Ein Wintermärchen—Germany: A Winter's Tale*. After thirteen years' absence he had once more gone back to Hamburg, to revisit the city, his country, and, not least, to see his mother. He had come back quickened to that new creation, which along with other, shorter poems of the same period, made a significant contribution to the literature on the political and social problems of the day. He had before that already established himself, in prose and verse, as a spokesman of the future. He had weighed and absorbed the various social theories afloat in Paris and elsewhere. But now, toward the end of 1843, he came into contact with the radical wing of the Young Hegelians, and particularly with Karl Marx and Arnold Ruge. The latter two were editing the *Deutsch-Französische Jahrbücher*. And Marx was one of the more significant contributors to the journal *Vorwärts*, the socialist publication also appearing in Paris.

At this moment, Heine could turn from a passionate and profound seriousness to fireworks of wit and scathing satire. Like other German writers he was roused by the revolt of the Silesian textile workers; but the lyric he wrote for the *Vorwärts* is the most inspired of all—fury and prophecy mastered by his poetic genius and controlled in a scorching incandescent flame. He fuses the outraged words he puts into the mouths of the weavers with a searing requiem for Germany; that is, to the accompanying refrain of "We weave, we weave!" Cursing the God that had betrayed them, the King—"King of the rich"—cursing the fatherland, worm-eaten and rotten, they conclude their anathemas:

> Das Schifflein fliegt, der Webstuhl kracht,
> Wir weben emsig Tag und Nacht—
> Altdeutschland, wir weben dein Leichentuch,
> Wir weben heinein den dreifachen Fluch,
>   Wir weben, wir weben!

> The loom is creaking, the shuttle flies;
> Nor night nor day do we close our eyes.
> Old Germany, your shroud's on our loom,
> And in it we weave the threefold doom;
>   We weave; we weave![67]

Great-hearted William Blake, who died in 1827, had he been alive, would have approved these prophecies. For had he himself not written in his "Auguries of Innocence":

> One Mite wrung from the Lab'rer's hands
> Shall buy and sell the Miser's Lands
> Or if protected from on high
> Does that whole Nation sell and buy ...

> The Harlot's cry from Street to Street
> Shall weave Old England's winding Sheet ...?

At kings and other oppressors Heine aimed his lightning shafts of venom and scorn—at the tippling, muddle-brained King of Prussia, Friedrich Wilhelm IV, whose self-portrait he drew: "I'm not bad; and I'm not good," not "dumb" and not "too bright," "today I move a few steps forward; tomorrow backwards"—a King who reconciled Bacchus with Jesus—"both divine extremes." Now he is celebrated as the "Emperor of China," now as the "new Alexander."[68]

Poor Ludwig I of Bavaria fared no better in the devastating "Hymns of Praise."[69]

Nor did he spare his fellow Germans, those "bearskin sluggards." It was no accident that around 1841, when he had gone to the Pyrenees for a cure, he came upon the idea of making a bear the hero of a tragicomic epic. From times past animals had been made spokesmen for or against Man, against injustice, against oppression. Heine's bear is a philosophical animal, and a rebel, who is made to pay for his temporary freedom. In the legendary region of the Pyrenees, redolent of the deeds of Roland, the land of Ronceval, there it is that the poet encounters the bear, Atta Troll, and his bear-wife, Mumma—both dancing bears—and their master, Laskaro. Against the romantic background of the rugged, forbidding mountains and crags (and how could Heine, that old Romantic, fail to respond?) is performed the realistic drama of a bear hunt. For Atta Troll escapes, leaving his wife behind; and Laskaro, his keeper, accompanied by the poet, enters upon a pursuit.

Back in his lair, alongside his brood but bereft of wife, Atta Troll reflects aloud on the nature of the world and of Man, as well as of animals. For, mind you, Atta Troll is no common bear. He may not have read Hegel and the Young Hegelians, but he knew his Proudhon very well indeed. He expatiates on the brutalities of human beings: how once upon a time they sacrificed human life to their gods, but alas! in these more enlightened times they shed blood only out of greed, everyone robbing for his own good. "Property is theft!"

> Yes, our common heritage,
> Inheritance of all of us,
> Become the booty of one man,
> Who boldly claims "possessor's rights!"
>
> Property! Possessors' rights!
> O such thievery—saucy lies!
> Mingling such of cunning, nonsense,
> As only Man could have invented.
>
> Nature never made possessions,
> All of us are naked born,
> When we come into the world,
> There are no pockets in our skins.
>
> Only man, that smooth-skinned being.
> Dressed in garments not his own,
> Only man with dreadful cunning
> Knew to make himself these pockets …[70]

And he vows death and destruction to these "pickpockets." But alas! philosophical reflections are no armor against man's wiles. Laskaro obtains the aid of his mother, a witch, who with her arts imitates the call of Mumma. Poor Atta Troll is lured from his hiding place and shot. In due time his skin is converted into a bear rug for the dainty feet of the poet's Juliette. ... Was this poem, as Heine wrote, "perhaps Romanticism's last woodland song, lost in today's warring noises ..."?

He now turned to "trumpets stern."

He needed the sharp fillip that his visit to Germany and his return had given him, to set about the most ambitious of his poems to date, *Germany: A Winter's Tale*. He loved and hated the country at the same time; and to see once again those sites and sights that had in the past given him so much joy and pain, to witness its present malaise, had awakened within him all those ambivalences that demanded resolution. He felt himself indeed the "son" of Aristophanes as his wit played with a juggler's supreme skill, as he tossed and caught the flaming torches of wit and seriousness. He will sing, he says, "a new song," not one of transterrestrial joys, of renunciation, but a "marriage hymnal."

> A new song, and a better song,
> Oh friends, I'll sing for you.
> Here on earth we mean to make
> Our Paradise come true. ...
>
> Young Europe's betrothed to Liberty,
> That genius of beauty and grace,
> They lie in each other's passionate arms,
> They feast on their first embrace.[71]

And thus he revisits many towns: Aachen, the burial place of Charlemagne, a town of obscurantists, where the peaked helmets of the soldiery fill him with horror and indignation; and Cologne, with its imposing unfinished cathedral, for whose restoration moneys are being collected, and where Franz Liszt is performing on the piano. And here in Cologne he becomes aware of an uneasy feeling—the presence near him of a "familiar spirit." He turns out to be someone who has been following the poet for a long time. It is an executioner with an axe! Challenged by the poet, the dire companion explains himself:

"*Ich bin die Tat von deinen Gedanken.*" "I am the deed of your thoughts."

> And even though the years go by,
> I find no satisfaction
> Till thought becomes reality;
> You think, and I take action.
>
> You are the judge; the headsman am I,
> Who stands and awaits your will;
> And whether your judgment be right or wrong,
> Obediently I kill ...[72]

He falls asleep and dreams—German featherbeds are particularly conducive to dreams—and who loves to dream more than the German?

> The French and the Russians rule the land;
> The British rule the sea;
> But in the realms of dream we own,
> Unchallenged mastery.

> Here we become one mighty state,
> Here, in dreams we are crowned—
> While other peoples build their realms,
> Upon the level ground ...[73]

At the Kyffhäuser, Emperor Frederick Barbarossa is sleeping, along with his mighty retinue, waiting for the call to awaken and redeem the land. Just as Richard Wagner was dreaming. In a nocturnal vision, Heine sees this Kaiser waiting and waiting ... How long? Frederick, in a colloquy with the poet, inquires about past figures, and learns with horror that an instrument recently invented was used to cut off the heads that once wore crowns. He is outraged. So is the poet outraged and disgusted with Redbeard. Stay where you are, he cries in anger—which he soon regrets. Very well, come back, and use whatever instrument of execution you wish; bring back your medievalism, but save us from that hybrid monster which our contemporaries are dishing up as the true Middle Ages, and which they wish to restore!

And at last, Hamburg, and his overjoyed mother, plying him with delicacies and ticklish questions; his publisher Campe, also a genial host; and finally, a crucial meeting with the imposing divinity of Hamburg—the city's tutelary goddess—Hammonia. The poet and the goddess engage in an intimate conversation; she invites him to her chambers, generously serving tea and rum. He is overcome with a German *Heimweh.* "Germany is really not so bad," she assures him. "Come, and I will show you something of her future." She takes him toward a close-stool and begs him to bend over for a Sybilline communication. Alas! the smells that rise from that region rob the poet of his senses. ... What sights! What mephitic fumes!

The scatological and scurrilous ending, funny as it may be, robs the poem of a satisfactory conclusion. It is not redeemed by the epilogue in which Heine adjures the German monarch to beware of the ire of poets; for it is in their power to consign him and his ilk to an eternal, unredeemable hell. *Vide* Dante.

> Do not offend the living bards;
> They've weapons and conflagrations
> More dreadful than all the lightnings of Jove
> —Which were only a poet's creations ...
>
> Have you not heard of Dante's Hell,
> The tercets that flamed from his pen?
> He whom the poet imprisons there
> Can never go free again—
>
> No God, no Saviour, can free him from
> This conflagration of rhyme!
> Beware, lest we hold you in such a Hell
> Until the end of time![74]

Dear, dear Heine! Did he really believe that poets had such power? Perhaps he thought that other poets too had their familiar spirit—an executioner with an axe?

He knew that the poem would arouse furious indignation among most Germans. For this work, as he said in a letter, is "not merely radical, revolutionary, but also antinational, and I'll have the whole pack of journalists on my back."[75]

He would be regarded as the enemy of his country, a traitorous Francophile. In the Preface to the published poem he defended himself vigorously and eloquently. Addressing himself to Germans, he wrote:

> I will regard and respect your colors when they deserve it, when they are no longer merely an idle and servile pastime. Plant the black, red, and gold banner on the heights of German thought, and I will offer my dearest heart's blood for it. Do not fear. I love the Fatherland as deeply as you ... When we complete what the French have begun, when we outstrip them in action, as we already have in thought; when we ascend to the very ultimate consequences of such thought, and destroy servitude everywhere, even in its last stronghold, Heaven; when we redeem the God who dwells on earth in man from debasement; when we become the saviours of God, restore the poor, a people disinherited of happiness, to dignity; and scorned and derided genius, and outraged beauty—as our great masters have said and sung, and as we, their disciples, wish it—yes, then not only Alsace and Lorraine, but all of France, all of Europe, the whole world will become ours—the whole world will become German! It is of this mission and universal sovereignty of Germany that I often dream as I wander under oak-trees. That is *my* patriotism.[76]

This was a kind of "Pan-Germanism" few could understand or appreciate. For it implied a universalism that would eventually dissolve all nationalisms in a cosmic world community.

As the revolutionary wave in Europe waned, then ended with the defeat of the Hungarians, Heine wrote its requiem, and forever thereafter bade farewell to politics. Germany, he wrote in the poem "October 1849," has settled back and is preparing for Christmas festivities, while Hungarians are bleeding to death.

> When someone speaks of Hungary
> My German vest becomes too small;
> A mighty tide swells up in me—
> I hear the challenge of the bugle-call.
> The myth of heroes, hushed so long,
> Once more goes crashing through my soul:
> The iron-savage hero-song
> That tells us of the Nibelungen's fall ...

The bestial forces have won; the heroes have perished. ... The pain, especially when he thinks of Germany's fate, is too great to bear.

> Poet be still; your anguish grows—
> You are so sick, 'twere wiser not to speak.

There is a howling, a grunting, a barking of the victors ...

> *Doch still, Poet, das greift dich an—*
> *Du bist so krank, und schweigen wäre klüger.*[77]

He wrote of himself as the "*enfant perdu*" of the battles for Freedom, having fallen on the field of battle, unvanquished, weapons not broken. "*Nur mein Herz zerbrach.*" "Only my heart was broken."[78]

His body might be shrunk, his eyesight gone, the pain almost incessant—but, miracle of miracles, his imagination, his fantasy, his inventive powers if anything grew in scope and depth. His wit was no less scintillating, though not without a certain poignancy. Between those years, 1850 and 1856, he produced many of his most memorable and moving poems. With the publication in 1851 of the collection, *Romanzero*, truly the crown of crowns of his poetic career, he proved that his creative vein had never been so rich, so various—so original. For any other poet it would have counted as a masterpiece; for the prisoner on his "mattress grave," it was an incomparable triumph of spirit over body. At night he composed, and in the morning his secretary set down his nocturnal creations. His virtuosity as poetic craftsman and master was equalled only by the new range of subjects out of which his poems were distilled. Here in the *Romanzero* he wandered far and wide, into many, for him hitherto undiscovered, regions. Here were new ballads about historical figures such as Charles I of England, Marie Antoinette, King David, the Persian poet Firdusi, the troubadour Geoffrey Rudel, Cortez the Conquistador, subtly modern in their psychology, rendered with the simplicity of supreme sophistication.

He had been Apollo. And now he was Job. For here too are those poems, entitled "Lazarus" in which the sick man speaks his personal laments, his litany of sorrows. Was he not like Lazarus, "a certain beggar ... which was laid at the gate of a rich man, full of sores, and desiring to be fed with the crumbs that fell from the rich man's table. Moreoever, the dogs came and licked his wounds"? He was Lazarus-Poet, and had he not been contemned for it by his rich uncle Solomon Heine in Hamburg, scorned and rejected? He was Job too, but a jesting Job, reproving God for the seven years' slow death. He chides the Lord for his illogic in creating the "merriest of poets" and depriving him of his good humor!

> The pain it dampens my happy mood,
> And makes me melancholy,
> If this merry jest is not soon done,
> I may even turn Catholic.
>
> And then I'll howl into your ears,
> Like other pious Christians,
> O Miserere! And you will have lost,
> The best of humorists![79]

He had climbed Mount Olympus once and had communed with and embraced gods and goddesses; like his own Tannhäuser he had sported with Dame Venus in her luxuriant mountain. He had hobnobbed with Hegel and Hegelian philosophy, soared with Hegelian ungodly Reason.

Now he climbed Mount Horeb, Israel's holy heights, to commune with Moses and his posterity, and rediscovered himself. Born a Jew, he had found Protestantism—like so many of his coevals—a handy "passport into society." And now he again conned the Holy Book, history, the poets of Israel—and found in them unexpected treasures. And he reshaped what he now knew into those incomparable "Hebrew Melodies"— poems like "Princess Sabbath" and the even nobler one about "Jehuda Halevi," greatest of medieval Hebrew poets. But he was no fanatic, as he revealed in the highly satirical "Disputation" between the Spanish Capucin and the Jewish Rabbi on the subject, "Which is the true God?" All these and more are to be found in the *Romanzero* of 1851. ...

How slowly Time, the frightful snail,
Crawls to the corner that I lie in;
While I, who cannot move at all,
Watch from the place that I must die in.

Here in my darkened cell no hope
Enters and breaks the gloom asunder;
I know I shall not leave this room
Except for one that's six feet under.

Perhaps I have been dead some time;
Perhaps my bright and whirling fancies
Are only ghosts that, in my head,
Keep up their wild, nocturnal dances.

They well might be a pack of ghosts,
Some sort of pagan gods or devils;
And a dead poet's skull is just
The place they'd choose to have their revels!

Those orgies, furious and sweet,
Come suddenly, without a warning ...
And then the poet's cold, dead hand
Attempts to write them down next morning.[80]

Into that "cell," as to some shrine, came many visitors from near and afar; his cousin Therese, whom he had been in love with, as he had been with her older sister Amalie Heine; new women to love; people of name and fame, and some without either. But they found no heavy solemnity there, though the figure of the shrunken poet would have been enough to break any heart. They found here all the wit for which he was famed, as sprightly as ever; they found the same live curiosity. ...

And the ever-present ambiguity. For he was many things at once—brilliantly, but often unreconciled. He was a Romantic, and an anti-Romantic; in the great tradition of German classical poetry, and a rebel against it; pagan and believer; Hellenic and Hebraic; ironic and sentimental. Politically he was radical, revolutionary even, and also monarchist. He feared and yet also welcomed revolution. He feared and loved the people; yet he trembled at what would happen to art and the artist should the people triumph.

He had lightning flashes of prevision, which amaze us today even more than they could have his contemporaries. He foresaw a good portion of Germany's future. He marks the end of a literary era, and was its last giant.

Torn as he was, his aristocratic mind did not in the end keep him from accepting the consequences of that "terrible syllogism," as he looked forth upon a world that was still ripe for revolution, and particularly a revolution of the masses: What would happen to the artist and his art?

A terrible syllogism holds me in its grasp, and if I am unable to refute the premise, "that every man has the right to eat," then I am forced to submit to all its consequences. From much thinking about it I am on the verge of losing my reason. I see all the demons of truth dancing triumphantly around me, and at length the generosity of despair takes possession of my heart and I cry: "For long this old society has been judged and condemned. Let justice be done! Let this old world be smashed, in which innocence is long since dead, where egoism prospers, and man battens on man! Let these whited sepulchres be destroyed from top to bottom, these caverns of falsehood and iniquity. And blessed be the grocer who shall one day use the pages of my poems as paper bags for the coffee and snuff of poor old women, who in this present world of injustice often have to go without that solace. *Fiat justitia, pereat mundus.*"[81]

He died on February 17, 1856.

Part Five

England
Crystal Palace and Bleak House

Chapter One

The March of Empire and the Victorian Conscience

Look around you and see what is the characteristic of
your country and of your generation at this moment.
What a yearning, what an expectation, amid infinite
falsehoods and confusions, of some nobler, more chivalrous, more god-like state! Your very costermonger trolls
out his belief that "there's a good time coming," and the
hearts of *gamins*, as well as millenarians, answer, "True!"
… And for flesh, what new materials are springing up
among you every month … railroads, electric telegraphs
… chemical agriculture, a matchless school of inductive
science, and equally matchless school of naturalist
painters—and all this in the very workshop of the world!
—Charles Kingsley, *Yeast*, 1851

There it stood—unreal, yet true—the unbelievable, the mighty structure of steel and
glass, spreading its gigantic majesty over Hyde Park: England's Great Exhibition Hall,
soon to be named Crystal Palace. On May 1, 1851 it was officially opened by the Queen,
the Prince Consort in attendance. Actually it was the latter's project brought to life; he
had fostered it, helped in its planning and in its fulfilment. Its creation was the work
of that fabulous gardener's son, Joseph Paxton. Two thousand feet long, four hundred
feet wide, sixty-six high—glass, buttressed by iron, many of its parts prefabricated!
Prophecy and fortress of reassurance and pride, its transepts rose over one hundred
feet. The architects had taken care to protect the ecological beauties of Hyde Park, for
the building enclosed its finest elms.

What was probably the first World's Fair brought together thirteen thousand ex-
hibitors from many parts of the world, with their numerous products—handicrafts as
well as machinery. One half of the exhibits were of England's or her colonies' manufacture; among foreigners, French and German products stood out. Here was the
world's plenty—reaping machines from America, the Jacquard loom, the electric telegraph, agricultural implements—a physical compendium of modern technology. And
not least, the building itself, another superb example of modern architecture—a fit
monitory counterpart and answer to the prevailing taste for Gothic architecture,

so graceful, so delicate, so airy, that its translucent beauty remains graven on my memory, wrote Lord Redesdale … No mere human hand and hammers and builders' tools
could have wrought such a miracle.[1]

Not even Coleridge's "magic dome," that fantasy that his Kubla Khan had raised, could compete with this tribute to the modern spirit ...

Thomas Babington Macaulay rejoiced,

> ... A most gorgeous sight; vast, graceful; beyond the dreams of Arabian romances ...[2]

And lest all this seem of the ancient past, the modern reader will rejoice to learn that the refreshments, including non-alcoholic beverages (*de rigueur*, of course) were provided by the firm of Schweppes ...

That such a vast enterprise should have been completed within six months was merely another mark of England's prepotency, underlined by the exhibition of her steam engines—"the trophies of her bloodless war."

It was, of course, particularly fitting that the ceremonies and visits to Crystal Palace be accompanied by due thanks to the Lord Almighty in various houses of worship, not excluding St. Paul's and Westminster Abbey. Thus was the Holy Gospel joined to those other no less sacred ones, the gospels of work, of peace, and Free Trade ... a tribute to the "working bees of the world's hive." And the six million visitors who streamed into those magnificent halls might have been reassured by the words of the very eminent William Whewell, D.D., Master of Trinity College, Cambridge, who proclaimed that

> ... Here, the man who is powerful in the weapons of peace, capital and machinery, uses them to give comfort and enjoyment to the public whose servant he is, and thus becomes rich while he enriches others with his goods ...[3]

If anything else were needed to underline the "grandeur" and meaning of the Crystal Palace, it was there too—if not immediately in Hyde Park, then in the north of England. What was symbol here was reality there: the vast factories and mines, with their chimneys belching black smoke, with their machines roaring, with their thousands of men, women, and children, underground and above ground, laboring like "bees"—sweating, panting, scurrying to affirm England's greatness ...

England's most popular poet—a master of catchy jingles—Martin Tupper, exulted:

> We travel quicker now than Isthmians might,
>   In books we quaff the veriest Hebe's chalice;
> All wonders of the world gladden the sight
>   In that world's wonder-house, the Crystal Palace;
> And everywhere is Might enslaved to Right.

Queen Victoria rejoiced:

> This day is one of the greatest & most glorious of our lives, with which, to my pride and joy the name of my dearly beloved Albert is forever associated! It is a day which makes my heart swell with thankfulness.[4]

Prince Albert too was happy, for he saw in the Crystal Palace and the attendant ceremonies a celebration of Peace, all signs pointing to the eventual realization of the "unity of mankind."

Was the nightmare of the "Hungry '40s" done with once and for all? Were the terror and panic of 1848 and 1849, the contagion of the revolutions on the Continent, and the fright at the Chartist uprising and demonstrations of 1848 exorcised, never to return? Was the marriage of Order and Change to be realized?

So it seemed. For Britain was entering upon a period of prosperity unprecedented in her history. Yet amid all the Hosannahs to Peace and Progress and Wealth, there were mingled expressions of concern, such as that of Prince Albert himself:

> We are entering upon most dangerous times in which Military Despotism and Red Republicanism will for some time be the only Powers on the Continent, to both of which the Constitutional Monarch of England will be equally hateful. That the calm influence of our institutions, however, should succeed in assuaging the contest abroad must be the anxious wish of every Englishman.[5]

* * *

> The greatest and most highly civilized people that ever the world saw, have spread their dominion over every quarter of the globe ..., have created a maritime power which would annihilate in a quarter of an hour the navies of Tyre, Athens, Carthage, Venice, and Genoa together, have carried the science of healing, the means of locomotion and correspondence, every mechanical art, every manufacture, every thing that promotes the convenience of life, to a perfection which our ancestors would have thought magical. ... The history of England is emphatically the history of progress ..."
> —T. B. Macaulay, "Sir James Mackintosh," 1835

It was no secret: God was English. Else why should He have showered so many of his benefactions upon Britain? Did He not, in Carlyle's words, appear to have conferred upon that land the "grand industrial task of conquering some half or more of the Terraqueous Planet for the use of man"? And did we not have the Rev. Charles Kingsley's word, that

> as it has pleased God that ... the father of inductive science, Bacon Lord Verulam, should have been an Englishman, so it has pleased Him, that we, Lord Bacon's countrymen, should improve that precious heirloom of science, inventing, producing, exporting, importing, till it seems as if the whole human race, and every land from the equator to the pole must henceforth bear the indelible impress and sign manual of English science ...[6]

And for reassurance, there is Lord Shaftesbury's affirmation that "the safety of the English people is the special care of Providence"?[7]

There could be no doubt: Great Britain was the European power of indisputable preeminence. Her imperial sway extended to South Africa, Australia, New Zealand, and India. She was first in world commerce and industry. And between 1849 and 1870 she enjoyed almost uninterrupted prosperity. Until 1870 she was unrivaled as a world power. Was it any wonder she could boast dazzling statistics such as the growth of population in her industrial cities, where between 1801 and 1850 Manchester showed an increase of roughly 400%; Leeds and Sheffield, 300%; Bradford, 900%, and so on? ... In 1850 her coal output was 56 million tons a year; pig iron 2 million tons. In her close to two thousand cotton factories there were over three hundred thousand workers. There were five thousand miles of railroads. And she possessed 60% of the world's ocean tonnage.[8]

The market value of British exports quadrupled between 1842 and 1870; and the gross national income, over half a billion pounds in 1851, was to be doubled by 1881.[9] By 1871 close to five hundred thousand worked in cotton mills ...

World's workshop, banker, shipbuilder, clearing house ... such triumphs rejoiced the heart of manufacturer, banker, and shipbuilder. Nor were the Tory landowners any the less content. "At the beginning of the Victorian era, no aristocratic landowner possessed less than 10,000 acres; by 1883 twenty-eight noblemen owned estates of 100,000 acres each."[10]

If God, who had so favored that country, was English, surely he was a Protestant God, not the Roman One. So once again hear the Rev. Charles Kingsley, bitter anti-Papist, fervent in his adoration of England's progress:

> When your party compare sneeringly Romish Sanctity and English Civilization, I say, "Take you the Sanctity, and give me Civilization! ... Give me the political economist, the sanitary reformer, the engineer; and take your saints and virgins, relics and miracles. The spinning jenny and the railroad, Cunard's liners and the electric telegraph, are to me, if not to you, signs that we are, on some point at least, in harmony with the universe, and that there is a mighty spirit working among us, who cannot be your anarchist and de-stroying Devil, and therefore must be the Ordering and Creating God."[11]

And other equally pious souls would echo their, "He hath not done so with any people."[12]

All evidence proved it, all voices proclaimed it. Thomas Babington Macaulay, the most persuasive and eloquent of the moderate liberals, enshrined it in his brilliant *History of England*, seeing in his age the fulfilment of the promise announced in the English "Glorious Revolution" of 1688. As Carlyle's *French Revolution* had been the voice of warning, so Macaulay's was the voice of gratulation. We have had our Revolution. Period. Only ours is a conservative Revolution, and Whiggism is its highest manifestation. The Reform of 1832 proved the triumph of a "liberal" conservatism, giving the vote to those who most deserved it—the middle classes.[13]

From the seats of the mighty, Lord Palmerston affirmed it:

> We have shown the example of a nation in which every class of society accepts with cheerfulness that lot which Providence has assigned to it, while at the same time each individual of each class is constantly trying to raise himself in the social scale—not by injustice and wrong, not by violence and illegality—but by persevering good conduct, and by the steady and energetic exertion of the moral and intellectual faculties with which the Creator has endowed him.[14]

The Gospel of Work assumed a new authority and fervor. Carlyle had cried, "Pro-duce! Produce!" and from his Italian retreats, Robert Browning was communicating a message direct from Heaven, "All service ranks the same with God." And in England, Samuel Smiles had composed that new bible, *Self-Help*. ...

The Irish Famine and the hunger of the 1840s had in 1846 forced a repeal of the Corn Laws which had so favored the landowner; and bread was now cheaper. Peel's wish that "we must make this country a cheap country for living," was more hopeful than realizable at the moment,[15] but there was cause for contentment now. In the marketplaces, the exchanges, and the manor houses of landlord and manufacturer an inaudible Requiem was celebrated, and the Revolution that had threatened in 1848 was, so it seemed, quietly buried. The lips whispered, "*Requiescat*," anxiety added, "*Nec resurgat!*"

It was not only the Tory landlord of Tennyson's poem "Walking to the Mail" that was frightened, recalling past lower-class uprisings:

> I once was near him, when his bailiff brought
> A Chartist pike. You should have seen him wince
> As from a venomous thing: he thought himself
> A mark for all, and shuddered, lest a cry
> Should break his sleep by night, and his nice eyes
> Should see the raw mechanic's bloody thumbs
> Sweat on his blazon'd chairs; but, sir, you know
> That these two parties still divide the world—
> Of those that want, and those that have: and still
> The same old sore breaks out from age to age
> With much the same result ...

Even the formidable Duke of Wellington, England's staunchest Tory and hero, could not forbear certain doubts. Shortly before his death in 1852 he attended "a social gathering at which a local clergyman led the assembly in this traditional song: 'God bless the squire and all his relations—And keep us poor people in our proper stations.'" "'By all means,' murmured the old warrior under his breath, 'if it can be done.'"[16]

* * *

> High hopes that burned like Stars sublime
> Go down i' the Heaven of Freedom,
> And true hearts perish in the time
> We bitterliest need 'em;
> But never sit we down and say
> There's nothing left but sorrow;
> We walk the Wilderness To-day,
> The Promised Land To-morrow.

So wrote the Chartist poet Gerald Massey after the defeat of the great Chartist demonstration of April 10, 1848.[17]

It was a day that few of the thousands who flocked to the Crystal Palace in 1851 and 1852 were likely to forget—some with relief at the outcome, others with deep regret or even heartbreak. It was the last echo of the vast revolutionary wave that had swept over their limited world, the closing act of a great drama. For the Chartists it was a shattering tragedy.

For April 10 and the Great Charter were but the culmination of a seething anger that had been gathering during the "Hungry '40s"—a reflection of the Great Famine, of the disenchantment of the lower classes with the Reform Act of 1832 and its betrayals—a "reform" that had benefited them not at all, but which had merely strengthened their masters, the manufacturing class; disenchantment with the minimal fruits of the Corn Law repeal; a reaction to the poor crops and hunger. Finding new life, Chartism once more renewed its agitation for parliamentary reform and universal franchise. An explosive Ireland contributed both a partial leadership and additional momentum to the movement.

It needed but the news from Paris to bring about an eruption ...

Louis-Philippe's abdication and the proclamation of a French republic—such was the word that was brought to a meeting of the Fraternal Democrats at the "White Hart" tavern in Drury Lane:

> The effect was electrical. Frenchmen, Germans, Poles, Magyars sprang to their feet, embraced, shouted, and gesticulated in the wildest enthusiasm. Snatches of oratory were delivered in excited tones, and flags were caught from walls, to be waved exultantly, amidst cries of "*Hoch! Eljen! Vive la République!*" Then the doors were opened, and the whole assemblage ... with linked arms and colours flying, marched to the meeting place of the Westminster Chartists in Dean Street, Soho. There another enthusiastic fraternization took place, and great was the clinking of glasses that night in and around Soho and Leicester Square.[18]

The illustrious Duke of Wellington had been advising intense preparation for a war with France; the income tax was raised from 7d. to one shilling in the pound to defray the expenses of preparedness; while the royal house was welcoming the escaped Louis-Philippe, who, as the scarcely pseudonymous "Mr. Smith," touched the soil of England with the words: "I have always felt pleasure in coming to England. Thank God I am in England once more."[19]

Unfortunately for him, it was not to be the short visit he had anticipated. He could not know, of course, that his royal successor Louis-Napoleon, then also in England, was waiting to fill the empty throne of France ...

While delegations of liberal and radical Englishmen and Irishmen went to Paris to hail the Provisional Government of France, serious riots broke out in many parts of England and Scotland—Manchester, Glasgow, Aberdeen, Edinburgh, and elsewhere. London witnessed a demonstration that drew over 15,000. In Glasgow the cry resounded, "Bread or Revolution!" And Chartist posters proclaimed, "The Republic for France and Chartism for England." In Paris, international solidarity was celebrated by the representatives of many nations, its extent perhaps symbolized by the friendly exchange between the Chartist leader, George Julian Harney, and the Russian Mikhail Bakunin.

April was the month of decision. Under the veteran leadership of such men as Harney, Bronterre O'Brien, Feargus O'Connor and Ernest Jones, a national convention launched the Third Petition, with millions of signatories. It was to be presented to Parliament on April 10, and a mass meeting was planned for Kennington Common, to be followed by a procession to Westminster. Once more the Charter called for universal manhood suffrage, annual Parliaments, equal electoral districts, the removal of property qualifications for members of Parliament, and payment to them.

Almost as if it welcomed the confrontation, the Government proceeded to act so as to quell and destroy the movement, prevent the procession, and demonstrate who was master of England.

Never before had internationalism seemed so greatly effective; what was happening in the rest of Europe now appeared to bear fruit in England. The dream of an international working-class movement and alliance that had been toasted and launched with the Fraternal Democrats at a November 1847 banquet in the presence of Marx, Engels, Harney, and representatives of other nations, would now be realized, and political reform of a radical nature would be brought to fruition.

And this demonstration—would it be allowed to march on Parliament? Was not that an incitement to Revolution? Of course, the demonstrators were well behaved and good-natured—altogether unarmed and peaceful. But one had to take care. For London (and the rest of Britain) from the tradesman up to the Queen showed alarm. The example of France was ever before them. France appeared to be moving toward socialism; and who could warrant that the infection—like a cholera—would not touch these shores? For it was also notorious that among the leaders of Chartism there were a few who advocated "physical force" should the demonstration fail of persuading the Government. Formerly the allies of the lower orders, the middle classes, having achieved a moderate Reform that favored them, were at one with the Tories (now called Conservatives) in their terror of the masses.

Such, certainly, was the fear expressed by young Matthew Arnold as he watched the heightening of the crisis.

> What agitates me, he wrote to his sister ... is this, if the new state of things succeeds in France, social changes are *inevitable* here and elsewhere, for no one looks on seeing his neighbour mending without asking himself if he cannot mend the same way; but without waiting for the result, the spectacle of France is likely to breed great agitation here, and such is the state of our masses that their movements now *can* only be be brutal, plundering and destroying. ... You must by this time begin to see what people mean by placing France *politically* in the van of Europe; it is the *intelligence* of their *idea-moved masses* which makes them, politically, as far superior to the *insensible masses* of England as to the Russian serfs. ...[20]

London was not Paris. And this demonstration was not an uprising. These men and women who came from the industrial regions in the North had no armed civil guard to back them with guns, nor had they arms of their own; there were no barricades to enable them to resist a suppression. They had trudged from afar; many of them came from their domestic hand looms, in a last protest against their displacement by the machine. (By 1854 there would be only about 30,000 of them left of the more than five hundred thousand of fifteen years before.) Yet they were met as if they were a revolutionary army bent on overthrowing the existing régime! Nor had they, like the French, poets, journalists, men and women of note to speak for them—no Lamennais, no George Sand, not even a Lamartine.

And against them ranged the whole force that the Government could muster—the Home Secretary Lord Grey prepared the yeomanry and special constables; troops were concentrated at critical points; the telegraph was seized, and local meetings forbidden in many places. Nine thousand soldiers and marines, four batteries, 150,000 special constables, including none other than Louis-Napoleon himself on horseback! All under the direction of the Iron Duke of Wellington ... Indeed "all the King's horses and all the King's men" were commandeered to seal off the bridges leading from the south side of the Thames. Though allowing the meeting at Kennington Common, they were there to prevent any movement toward Parliament. In the face of such a show of force, Feargus O'Connor lost heart, cancelled the procession, and agreed to a dispersal of the demonstration. The Petition itself, like a funeral cortège, was brought to Parliament in three carriages, where, as one historian remarked, "the day of terror ended in shouts of laughter that greeted its arrival in the House of Commons."[21] Though the scrutiny of the Petition discovered some falsifications, two million signatures were found to be authentic—no mean number, that!

Yet demonstrations continued in other localities—in Sheffield, in Liverpool, in Dublin—while the Government proceeded to enact legislation such as the repressive "Crown and Government Security Act," to root out further chances of agitation. The so-called "Gagging Act" followed, with arrests and transportations. Ernest Jones was sentenced along with others to imprisonment, some to transportation for life. But Chartism was defeated as much from within as from without—internecine warfare of the leadership, divided counsels (force or moral suasion? alliance with middle-class radicalism or independent action?). One is reminded of the pregnant words of General Charles Napier on the occasion of another Chartist demonstration in 1842:

> Poor people! They will suffer ... We have the physical force, not they ... What would their 100,000 men do with my hundred rockets wriggling their fiery tails among them, roaring, scorching, tearing, smashing all they came near?[22]

Ireland was the special victim of English persecution, when her most articulate spokesman in Commons, Smith O'Brien, member for Limerick, was transported to Tasmania.

> The French Revolution of 1848 saved the English middle class. The Socialistic pronunciamentos of the victorious French workmen frightened the small middle class of England and disorganized the narrower, but more matter-of-fact movement of the English working class. At the very moment when Chartism was bound to assert itself in its full strength, it collapsed internally before it collapsed externally on the 10 of April, 1848. The action of the working class was thrust into the background. The capitalist class triumphed along the whole line.[23]

Queen Victoria was relieved. On April 11 she wrote to King Leopold of Belgium:

> Thank God, the Chartist meeting & Procession had turned out a complete failure; the loyalty of the people at large has been very striking & their indignation at their peace being interfered with by such wanton and worthless men—immense.[24]

Yet, for all the setbacks the British working classes suffered in 1848 and 1849, the Charter of 1848 was to triumph in the end, though it would take many years. New ways and methods would have to be found to direct and organize their strength anew, fresh energies to be directed toward the creation of an international working-class movement. Difficult and slow labor! Eventually it was the Communist Manifesto of 1848 that was destined to supersede the Chartist Petition of the same year....

As in the rest of Europe, the collapse of the insurgent movement in England marks the end of an era and the beginning of an altogether different one. In the wake of the European debacles of 1849, numerous refugees sought safety in London. Among them was Karl Marx, who arrived in August 1849, soon followed by Friedrich Engels. It was not these refugees that were on the mind of Queen Victoria when she contemplated what the new Republic of France was doing to royal and ducal houses as a result of what she called "the great calamity":

> The Queen fears (indeed knows), she wrote, that the poor Duc and Duchesse of Nemours are in sad want of all means; and she knows the poor Duchesse of Orleans is equally so.—It is very lamentable and the Queen feels much for them, for it is a position which, if one reflects on it, requires great courage and resignation to submit to. It would be infamous if the Republic gave them nothing. …[25]

✳ ✳ ✳

> The spirit of the country is quiet but reasonable, indisposed to sweeping innovations, and equally indisposed to keeping in the old Tory ways, everything which is because it is. The moderate members of both parties represent this spirit fairly. At a recent election a poor voter is reported to have said that both candidates were very nice gentlemen, but that for his part he could not see much difference between them; and this is the simple truth.
> —Walter Bagehot, *The English Constitution*, 1867

"Chartism is dead!" the noted philanthropist the Earl of Shaftesbury wrote from Manchester to the liberal manufacturer John Bright in 1851.[26] Thus both aristocracy and the well-to-do bourgeoisie expressed their relief over the fact that the danger of "revolution" was over. In another way, the two symbolized the triumph of what was to be called "Victorianism"—the happy union of their two powerful classes and their reassurance that the governance of the British Isles was in secure hands. The term "Victorian" came into being in 1851. The Queen had been on the throne now for fourteen years, and she was to reign till the turn of the century. But the years from 1848 to 1873, the latter the year of a commencing world depression, marked the high point of her sway as sovereign of a dominant world power.

"Victorianism" is not an abstraction. Despite its multifarious facets and aspects, it describes an astounding phenomenon of the century—the penetration, within those twenty years, into British life—spiritual, moral, philosophical, social, political, and cultural—of what may be termed the "bourgeois spirit."

Such a triumph could not have been achieved save by the reciprocal concessions of the two dominant powers, the landed interests and the "commercial" classes—the latter by their willingness to turn over the reins of government to the former, the aristocracy and the landed gentry; the former by being assured that their property rights in the land and in power, in no way truly infringed by the Reform of 1832, would be secured against the challenges of the "lower" classes. Minor concessions and minor reforms would be granted whenever necessary; and when the threat became more serious, as in the late sixties, even major ones, such as the Reform Bill of 1867 with its radical extension of the franchise. The Chartist defeat of 1848 had temporarily disarmed the working classes; their middle-class allies, whom they had helped achieve the repeal of the Corn Laws and other victories, had now deserted them. In the wake of the disorganization that followed, and while the working-class efforts were being redirected into a strengthening of the trade-union movement, its more advanced and skilled sectors would be wooed as a "labor aristocracy" to become allies rather than enemies, perhaps even appendages of the more liberal elements within the middle classes. Was it not the British statesman John Chamberlain, who shocked Queen Victoria by describing Reform as "the ransom which society must pay for its security"?[27]

The confidence in the eventual success of such an alliance could not have existed without the major economic phenomenon of the advancing century—namely, the full development of world capitalism, and Britain's world domination of its markets.

It was not difficult to translate the more prosaic and stark "commercial spirit" into a religious gospel, to speak of its missionary duty to advance world civilization. The extraordinary advances in the sciences and in technology only served to underscore such a credo. Thus Richard Cobden could write,

> Commerce is the grand panacea, which like a beneficent medical discovery, will serve to inoculate with the healthy and saving taste for civilization all the nations of the world. Not a bale of merchandise leaves our shores, but it bears the seeds of intelligence and fruitful thought to the members of some less enlightened community; not a merchant visits our seats of manufacturing industry, but he returns to his own country the missionary of freedom, peace, and good government—while our steam boats, that now visit every port of Europe, our miraculous railroads, that are the talk of all nations, are advertisements and vouchers for the value of our enlightened institutions.[28]

The practice of entrusting the conduct of government to a ruling oligarchy was not peculiar to Britain in the nineteenth century. The bourgeoisie of France was about to do the same in installing a dictatorship under Louis-Napoleon, and in 1870, a united Germany would place itself under the leadership of a Prussian Junker-led autocracy. The British pattern of a cabinet filled by aristocrats prevailed until the end of the century, with only two marked exceptions under Gladstone.

The Victorian alliance of landowner and manufacturer, while not free of restive moments and conflicts, directed its efforts at defining and delimiting the disjunctive forces at work in a highly dynamic society, and at achieving a cohesiveness that would obviate revolutionary movements. It proclaimed the principle of the "reconciliation" of the various interests, while at the same time safeguarding its own. To achieve this, it brought into play various instruments of propaganda and policy, and the organs at its command. Here the vast power that resided in the landowning section was of major influence.

For it must be remembered that of the twenty or so millions that constituted the population of England and Wales, nearly nine million lived on the land. Here the power structure of one section of English society is glaringly revealed. As late as 1875 it was estimated that of the total acreage of England and Wales, more than forty-one per cent was owned by only some 1,700 "great" landlords. The Duke of Sutherland owned close to a million and a half acres; the Marquess of Lansdowne almost 150,000; Sir John Ramsden owned most of Huddersfield; the Marquess of Bute owned Cardiff and Glamorganshire.[29]

The Reform Bill of 1832 had barely scratched the aristocratic proprietary hold on the House of Commons.

> At the core of Parliament of 1865 there was a "cousinhood" of landed families, which included well over half the members. The House of Commons remained very closely attached socially to the House of Lords.[30]

A contemporary observer and analyst forcefully summed up the nature of landed power:

> The Parliamentary frame is kneaded together almost out of one class; it has the strength of a giant and the compactness of a dwarf. ... So vast is their traditional power, so broadly does it sit over the land, so deep and ancient are its roots, so multiplied and ramified everywhere are its tendrils, and creepers, and feelers, that the danger is never lest they should have too little, but always lest they should have too much power, and so, even involuntarily, check down the possibilities of new life from below ...[31]

The "cousinhood" of landed families was indeed a close one, as four-fifths of the land belonged to only seven thousand families. Caste distinctions were rigorously observed. The aristocracy of land looked with condescension mingled with contempt on the "money-grubbing" tradesmen and manufacturers. "I don't like the middle classes," Lord Melbourne confessed. "The higher and the lower classes, there's some good in them, but the middle classes are all affectation and conceit and pretense and concealment."[32] And Earl Russell was reported to have shocked upper-class society in 1866 when he invited the distinguished John Bright, a public figure but also a middle-class manufacturer, to dinner![33]

But such contempt for the rich but crude middle classes did not keep the aristocratic landowner from lending a willing ear to the lure of land speculation, from investing in urban land-development in London and other cities, or from drawing sizable profits from railroads and mining. Mammon was no longer Mammon when he boasted a coat of arms ...

The influence and power of this class were sustained by moral, social, as well as economic pressures. The Established Church was to a great extent its province, for it controlled clerical "patronage." Bishops were either of aristocratic or gentry background. The landed class controlled the upper echelons of the army, and the colonial empire was its preserve—in James Mill's words, "a vast system of outdoor relief for the upper classes."[34]

Locally, the tenant farmer was at the landlord's mercy, though, it must be admitted, frequently submitting of his own free will. It was expected that he would send to Parliament the Tory candidate favored by the master; and in persuading him to do so, the local cleric might bring a few urgent words. Separated from the turmoils and conflicts of industrialism, isolated from the violent winds of doctrine that swept the country, little given to reading (assuming he could read), he was all the more ready to accept the word of his betters, as he thought them; looking to them to defend him, when such occasions arose, from the depredations or rick-burnings of the starving agricultural workers.

But no less helpful, and less savoring of pressure, was the British "habit of authority" and the principle of deference. The celebrated statesman George Canning had once stated that if democracy were to arrive in England, it must do so only "inlaid with a Peerage and topped with a Crown."[35] A less gentle critic, George Eliot, spoke of the "safeguard of spontaneous servility."[36] Spontaneous or compelled, it was there, not only in the countryside but also in the city. It was preached; and it was sung to the little ones, as in Miss Humphrey's *Hymns for Little Children*, which appeared in 1848:

> The rich man in his castle,
> The poor man at his gate,
> God made them, high and lowly,
> And ordered their estate.[37]

It was this attitude that made Richard Cobden explode:

> We are a servile, aristocracy-loving, lord-ridden people, who regard the land with as much reverence as we still do the peerage and the baronetage. Not only have not nineteen-twentieth of us any share in the soil, but we have not presumed to think that we are worthy to possess a few acres of mother earth.[38]

Confirmed in their possession by the law of primogeniture, and in their influence by possession of the clerical offices, frequently assigned to a younger son, and their hold on the two universities and their elite, they could allow a certain upward mobility of the "commercial" class, no less aspiring to rise to a higher station. For degree, rank and caste permeated all of society down to the smallest parish and the lowest orders. It was this element that made Charles Dickens so terribly ashamed of his past in the blacking-shop, and George Meredith conceal for a long time his descent from master-tailors.

As for the poor agricultural laborer, who was without a vote and was preached at in the local church or chapel, adjured to repentance for his sinful life and also promised a piece of restful eternity if he behaved properly—how should he resist the conviction that "the one thing needful in this life is to do our duty in the station we are called to fill"?[39]

Nor was it surprising that landlord–tenant relations, especially in the North of England, should have retained their semifeudal character, or that at an annual banquet given by the duke of Northumberland in 1859, his assembled dependents should have been singing:

> Those relics of the feudal yoke
> Still in the north remain unbroke:
> That social yoke, with one accord,
> That binds the Peasant to his Lord ...
> And liberty, that idle vaunt,
> Is not the comfort that we want;
> It only serves to turn the head,
> But gives to none their daily bread.
> We want community of feeling,
> And landlords kindly in their dealing.[40]

* * *

Miserable children in rags ... like young rats, slunk and hid, fed on offal, huddled together for warmth, and were hunted about (look to the rats young and old, all ye Barnacles, for before God they are eating away our foundations, and will bring the roofs on our heads!).

—Charles Dickens, *Little Dorrit*

If England was now the world's workshop, banker, broker, shipper and colonial lord, she was no less a laboratory of the social sciences for the rest of the world. Where else could one study, in so concentrated an area, the social conditions of the populations? It was here that foreigners found not only such wonders as displayed in the Crystal Palace, and to the North the boom and bustle and roar of machinery—but also the less to be wondered at, sometimes the less admirable, effects of all this great business. For not very far from the Crystal Palace was Hungerford Market, and here as well as in other parts of London, there stretched a panorama to shock the onlooker and frighten away the queasy.

Almost at the same time as engineers and builders were raising up the mighty steel in Hyde Park, there appeared in the *Morning Chronicle* a series of descriptive articles on "London Labour and the London Poor," by the journalist Henry Mayhew.

Sensitive souls were outraged, shocked, and profoundly moved. For what was true of London was no less true of Manchester or Liverpool, and, though more deftly concealed, of the cottages in the agricultural areas.

> Do you read the *Morning Chronicle*? [wrote Douglas Jerrold, father-in-law of Mayhew, and himself a notable journalist and playwright]. Do you devour those marvellous revelations of the inferno of misery, of wretchedness, that is smouldering under our feet? We live in a mockery of Christianity that, with the thought of this hypocrisy, makes me sick. We know nothing of the terrible life that is about us—us, in our smug respectability. To read of the sufferings of one class, and of the avarice, the tyranny, the pocket cannibalism of the other, makes one almost wonder that the world should go on, that the misery and wretchedness of the earth, are not, by an Almighty fiat, ended. And when we see the spires of pleasant churches pointing to Heaven, and are told—paying thousands to Bishops for the glad intelligence—that we are Christians! The cant of this country is enough to poison the atmosphere.[41]

Yes, it was true, as the French social student Eugène Buret observed in 1840, England was "the prime country for social studies, the country from which we had more to learn than from the whole of the rest of the world."[42]

Yes, they could learn much—about the burdens of overpopulation, about the Malthusian theories, about the way poor-relief was administered so as not to hurt the manufacturing interests; about how to obviate threats to the "common weal."

They could also learn that in the great year 1851 one Englishman out of seven was a pauper. What new dangers might not be lurking in the back streets and alleys of the cities! While celebrating England's dazzling achievements, another writer, in the year 1851, issued a stern warning:

> Sparta had 300,000 slaves to 30,000 freemen; does not our situation in some sort resemble hers? ... Already, we have a revolution, slumbering, but gathering power in all our cities, and still we pursue our way with intrepid stupidity, dreaming of Eden in the very midst of a reign of terror.[43]

An enterprising stranger, or a more intrepid middle-class Londoner, who dared penetrate the purlieus behind the Crystal Palace, say, into some of the markets and less fashionable districts of London, would no doubt have been struck by the mephitic odors that prevailed, as well as by the scavengers who were gathering up decaying shrimp and other castoffs, and by the hundreds of street vendors.

But not all the odors emanated from the streets and alleys. The Thames itself, that noble river, extolled by such Renaissance poets as Edmund Spenser, ("sweet Thames," he had chanted, "run softly till I end my song"), assailed, if not the ears, certainly the nostrils and tastebuds of Victorian London. As noxious as any pestilence, it strengthened its maleficence with the concurrent emanations of the city's cesspools and manure heaps, the latter a source of income to the householder as a commodity for the farmer. A modern reader will respond sympathetically to descriptions contained in contemporary medical reports. One such, compiled in 1858, relates,

> Never, perhaps, in the annals of mankind has such a thing been known before, as that the whole stream of a large river for a distance of seven miles should be in a state of putrid fermentation. The cause is the hot water acting upon 90 millions of gallons of sewage which discharge themselves daily into the Thames. By sewage must be understood not merely house and land drainage, but also drainage from bone-boilers, soap-boilers, chemical works, breweries, gas factories—the last most filthy of all ...[44]

The so-called drinking water was thus conducted in open channels, and after receiving the bestowals described above, "on their arrival in the metropolis (after a short subsidence in reservoirs, which themselves are not unobjectionable) are distributed, without filtration, to the public."[45]

One may very well imagine, without great difficulty, the combined effect of these phenomena upon the household—the poor man's, with his private dunghill; the rich home, majestically above its own cesspool; the traditional suspicion of fresh air and the preference for closed windows (remember, there was also a tax on windows!). In 1846 there were some two hundred thousand undrained cesspools in London. ...

Now add to that the overcrowding of the slum areas—"rookeries," as they were then called—examples of which in London as well as other industrial cities are truly appalling. In Liverpool, for example, in the 1860s, there were over sixty thousand human beings squeezed into every square mile; in Manchester, somewhat earlier, between forty and fifty thousand lived in cellars. "Lived" is scarcely the word: some ten years before Crystal Palace the death rate in the slums was reported as rising to sixty in the thousand. What cholera failed to effect, consumption, typhoid and typhus did, abetting exhaustion and the inadequate diet.[46]

London became the gauge by which poverty and destitution were measured in other countries. It was not in the spirit of national chauvinism that Flora Tristan, that remarkable Frenchwoman, visited England, and in 1840 published *Promenades dans Londres*. She was no less harsh and critical in her description of the poor of Paris and Lyons. London, which she called the "monstrous" city, fascinated her. She penetrated into many quarters, the slums inhabited by the Irish and the Jews; those inhabited by the English. She visited prisons. She observed the northern factories and their operatives. She admired the new machinery, but was horrified by the conditions under which human beings were living. She was no less appalled by the extent of prostitution in London, and estimated the number of prostitutes at between eighty and a hundred thousand. A strong defender of woman's rights, she wrote: "So long as she is subject to the yoke of man or of prejudice, so long as she does not receive a professional training, and is deprived of civil rights, there can be no hope of her becoming 'moral.'" "In France, and in all other countries that pride themselves on some measure of civility, the being most honored is woman; in England—it is a horse."[47]

That which she saw in London in 1839, Mayhew saw in 1850. What she witnessed in the industrial part of England was only in a very small measure different from what other visitors beheld ten or twenty years later.

Conditions in the industrial regions had indeed changed very little. The much-embattled Ten Hours Law, passed in 1847 and more often breached than observed, applied only to the textile industry. The Coal Mines Act of 1842, while it did indeed prohibit the employment of women, permitted the employment of boys over ten. In an occupation which had until the beginning of the century been kept in actual feudal bondage (the colliers and their children were, in Scotland, the property of the coal master), this represented a minor advance. But as late as 1862 a Children's Employment Commission found children working in various industries at the age of nine, earning between one shilling and eighteen pence a week; in the potteries the age was eight. In the millinery industry in Manchester boys and girls worked between fourteen and fifteen hours a day; in the firebricks industry girls aged twelve worked up to sixteen hours. This was in the Birmingham district. In the Lancashire mills boys could attain at thirteen the status of full-time operatives if approved by a local doctor. For such and others of the factory,

> Every morning the factory-bell rings at half-past five o'clock, and work commences at six ... Half an hour is allowed for breakfast .. The dinner hour is ... curtailed considerably when the Government inspector is thought to be out of the way. The day's work ceases at six p.m.[48]

For males, the weekly wage in industry varied from the ten and a half shillings in cotton, up to eighteen shillings in the iron trades. Women received lower wages.

So far as employment of women is concerned, over one million of them were in domestic service. Housemaids earned between ten to fifteen pounds a year and generally worked from six in the morning till ten in the evening.

The plight of the agricultural worker was, if anything, worse. Generally hired as members of a gang under the "gangman," and moving from place to place, the men, women, boys and girls were subject to double exploitation, on the part of the farmer who hired them as a gang, and the "gangman" who controlled their wages. In addition, they sometimes had to trudge from five to seven miles to work. The brutalizing effect of their life can be gleaned from a Commission Report on the number of pregnancies that occurred, often in the case of girls not older than thirteen. In seasons of good harvest, there was work, and a passable existence. When harvests were bad and bread became dear, they lived next door to starvation. When they rebelled and turned to "rick-burning," they were brought before the local magistrate, generally a landowner, who had them deported to a penal colony.

The Novel and the Crisis of Conscience
The Brontës—The Caged Rebels of Haworth

I wish you would not think me a woman. I wish all reviewers believed "Currer Bell" to be a man; they would
be more just to him. You will, I know, keep measuring
me by some standard of what you deem becoming to my
sex; where I am not what you consider graceful, you will
condemn me … Come what will, I cannot, when I write,
think always of myself and of what is elegant and charming in femininity; it is not on those terms, or with such
ideas, I ever took pen in hand; and if it is only on such
terms my writing will be tolerated, I shall pass away from
the public and trouble it no more. Out of obscurity I
came, to obscurity I can easily return.

—Charlotte Brontë to G. H. Lewes, 1849

The village of Haworth, in Yorkshire, was in the early nineteenth century—to use the words of one of its visitors—a "dreary, black-looking village," defying, through a steep ascent of its roadway, the footing of a visitor. The street leading to the top was paved with flagstones, so placed that pedestrians, horses, and carriages would not slip back. Past uninviting stone dwellings, one clambers till one comes to the church, the church-yard, and finally the Haworth parsonage. Today, hundreds upon hundreds of pilgrims make their way as to some shrine of a "saint" or "martyr," once the home of the three Brontë sisters; and the modest parsonage ranks second in popularity only to that other "shrine" at Stratford on Avon. Many come to Haworth to honor literary genius; others, heroic womanhood.

Such posthumous celebrity would have astounded no one more than a certain vis-itor, who, in the fall of 1853, two years before Charlotte Brontë's death, made her way to the home of the last surviving of the three sisters. This was Mrs. Elizabeth Gaskell, her future biographer, herself a novelist of some distinction. She had met Charlotte Brontë a few years before and had been deeply impressed by her personality, perhaps even more than by her celebrity as the author of *Jane Eyre*.

This was Mrs. Gaskell's first view of Haworth. Standing at the front door of the parsonage, she reflected on the loneliness of the spot. "Moors everywhere, beyond and above," she wrote. "Oh! those high, wild, desolate moors, up above the whole world, and the very realms of silence!"[1]

These realms of silence also included the churchyard, with its time- and weather-stained tombstones lying flat, stretching far and wide. Here lay buried many members of the Brontë family—the mother, three daughters, and a son. Another daughter, Anne, had been laid to rest in Scarborough.

And now, since 1849, the parsonage was emptied out: only Charlotte and her father were there, along with their lifelong servant Tabby, now ninety years old.

It was hard to believe that at one time not very long ago, despite the sombreness of the surroundings, the inclemencies of the weather and the isolation, the house had been bright, ringing with noises, even the laughter of young people. Once there had been five daughters and a son; and an aunt who had replaced the mother, deceased when the children were very young.

But here are Charlotte Brontë now, and her father the Rev. Patrick Brontë, to receive the guest. Miss Brontë is thirty-seven years old, and an "old maid," or "spinster" in the customary parlance of the day. Her figure is diminutive, almost childlike. She is "very plain," a source of distress throughout her life; though her plainness is redeemed by beautiful, though very near-sighted, eyes, a shy manner, and a sweet voice. From her behavior one would not conceive that she is one of the famed writers of the day. Beside her looms the stately, forbidding form of her father, now in his seventy-sixth year, for thirty years now perpetual curate at Haworth—a dominating patriarchal figure encased in a white neckcloth, aloof and retiring.

At last Mrs. Gaskell has Charlotte Brontë all to herself.

"We talked over the old times of her childhood," she wrote later. The story as it was to unfold at that time, and more elaborately after Charlotte's death, was one that might well entrance a novelist. It may have been that at that moment the idea of eventually writing her biography was born in Mrs. Gaskell's mind. It was a fascinating story, sad and exciting, even tragic at times—a chronicle of light and darkness.

Light—as in the year the family arrived at Haworth. Mr. Brontë was to take over the curacy. There were then five daughters and a son—the youngest, Anne, a babe in arms. The mother was ailing. Between 1813 and 1819 she had produced a child practically every year. Two years after their arrival in Haworth she died. An aunt, Elizabeth Branwell, arrived from Penzance to take over as surrogate mother.

Such were the beginnings at Haworth.

Darkness—four of the children, Maria, Elizabeth, Charlotte and Anne are sent to a school at Cowan Bridge, an institution for needy clergymen's daughters. Here the two older girls, aged ten and eleven, contract a noisome fever—is it typhus or perhaps typhoid?—then epidemic—that sweeps the institution, and die soon after being removed. Charlotte and Emily too are brought back home.

Whatever might have been the children's predisposition to disease, particularly tuberculosis, their susceptibility was without doubt aggravated by the general unsanitary conditions that prevailed at school, in Haworth, and sad to say, all over the country. Perhaps Haworth may be said to have outdone other localities. The water supply was polluted, in part by the seepage from the graveyard. The barbarous absence of any adequate sewage disposal and the limited outhouse facilities contributed to the frequency of epidemics, whether pulmonary or intestinal. Even in the 1850s, at the time of Mrs. Gaskell's visit, conditions were little different from what they had been in the

'20s. A health inspection undertaken in 1850 found that at Haworth 516 houses shared 69 privies; that an open channel ran down the main street. "Fastidious villagers walked half a mile to the Head Well to draw their water, which nevertheless was scanty and occasionally so green and putrid that cattle refused to drink it. The (Haworth) parsonage boasted a pump in the kitchen—the well sunk in the ground just yards away from the cemetery."[2] Is it any wonder that between 1838 and 1849, 41.6 percent of the population of Haworth died before reaching the age of six? In the country at large the normal life expectancy, especially among the lower classes, was around 26![3] Let the encomiasts of "merry old England" consider some of the common afflictions that beset Victorian life—measles, croup, whooping cough, scarlet fever, enteric fever, typhoid and typhus, tuberculosis, and not least, frequent epidemics of cholera. And oh! the "sweet Thames" thus celebrated by the Elizabethan poet, Edmund Spenser, did in the days of Victoria smell to such high heavens, that it even reached the Houses of Parliament!. ...

* * *

The Brontës' was a religious household, with regular prayers during the day, and, of course, with services at the church on Sundays. Its religious intensity varied from the more strict near-Calvinism of Aunt Branwell, deeply impregnated with the sense of original sin, election, reprobation and eternal damnation, to the more moderate faith of Patrick Brontë, in whose creed there was still a possibility of redeeming the sinner if repentant and reformed, but also of a horrible fate if unregenerate. Given to poetry and narrative prose, Patrick wrote,

> With horrible din,
> Afflictions may swell,—
> They cleanse me from sin,
> They save me from hell:
> They're all but the rod
> Of Jesus, in love,
> They lead me to God,
> And blessings above ...

He also warned,

> Both rich and poor, who serve not God,
> But live in sin, averse to good,
> Rejecting Christ's atoning blood,
> Midst hellish shoals,
> Shall welter in that fiery flood,
> Which hissing rolls ...[4]

How could the young children avoid the sense, the ever-present sense, of mortality? Inside the house they had witnessed the passing of their mother and two sisters. Outside there was that eternal *memento mori*, the graveyard with its innumerable tombstones. Death and the preparation for death, the weaknesses of the flesh, "the burning lakes of hell"—and on the other side, the blisses of eternal life—these were to seep into their consciousness and remain there for a long time ...

At the Cowan Bridge school were sown the seeds of that rebellion which was to be the earmark of their thinking and one of the sources of their imaginative creations. Here Charlotte and Emily witnessed the physical and moral ravages visited upon the inmates: the tyranny and cruelty of some of the mistresses, even down to the physical punishments; the insufficient and often revolting diet; the exposure to cold weather during the long marches to church on Sundays; and not least, the bigotry and hypocrisy in the person of one of the most influential of the school's patrons—in fact, its founder—the Rev. Carus Wilson, whose addresses to the young were spicily sprinkled with mortuary and charnel-house visions. Here were born many of the figures of *Jane Eyre*, particularly that of the Rev. Mr. Brocklehurst—an unmistakable Mr. Wilson. Here too was born that revulsion from what Charlotte was to call the "doctrine of endurance"—the doctrine of docile acceptance of pain and suffering and abuse—that self-abnegation which she had seen embodied in her sister Maria, and later, when she came to write *Jane Eyre*, in the unforgettable figure of Helen Burns.

Liberated from school, Charlotte and Emily rejoined the Haworth household, and now, in conjunction with sister Anne, they began to lead that double life—one public, the other secret—which in a way was to determine their future. The public life consisted of household duties, under the supervision of Aunt Branwell and Tabby the maid. The other was a collusive, private life. They were all of them, Charlotte, Emily, Anne—and in a lesser sense their brother, Branwell—"born writers." They were also astonishingly precocious, and already voracious readers. They began building their own world, a world of fantasy, which they set down in writing—in what they called "plays," and in stories. Here they were to find that freedom which was denied them in daily life. Branwell alone was excepted, for he was a boy. He was free to roam.

Of this "secret" life their father was scarcely aware. Secluded in his study much of the time, he emerged for breakfast, prayers, and tea. He almost always dined alone. He could scarcely have suspected what a dangerous brood he had spawned, nor what a direct agent he was in spurring these literary activities when he bought Branwell a box of toy soldiers. Had he known, he might have shaken his head in kindly condescension. Writing was a fitting avocation for girls who were growing up. For the boy, however, he harbored lofty ambitions. Branwell was "destined" for a glorious career. As for the women, he would like to keep them home forever—he was extremely possessive—or he would wait until some respectable and well-to-do suitor might appear and take them off. He was not ready to yield any of them to some neighboring curate, even if it were one of his own assistants—some poor devil earning no more than £90 a year. His own means were scant enough, £200 or so, and there was little or nothing left of that to set aside for a dowry! How could he be blamed for having such thoughts? He had himself led a hard life. The son of a poor Irish Protestant farmer, one of ten children, he had by dint of his persistent ambition and force of character succeeded in making something of himself. He had been able to attend Oxford and attain to clerical orders. Ambitious, proud, intelligent, and endowed with an irrefragable will, he was also something of a writer. He must have had attractive qualities to win the life-long devotion and near-worship of a wife whose touching letters during their courtship reveal a woman of deep feelings. Her last agonized illness and her untimely death at the age of thirty-eight scarred him deeply.

He believed in having educated children, and he made sure they had instruction in music, drawing, and French. He himself took charge of Branwell's education, teaching him, among other subjects, Latin and Greek. The boy showed some talents, especially in art—in fact he had enough talent in other departments to make him a passable mediocrity. What would the father have made of the notion that it was not his son, but his daughters who were to make him immortal!

It was not an utterly secluded world in which the young Brontës lived. There was a library at home, and a more copious one in nearby Keightley. "Nearby" must not be construed in modern terms: it meant trudging ten miles or so. After 1831, when Charlotte attended Miss Wooler's school at Roe Head and had made what were to be lifelong friendships with Ellen Nussey and Mary Taylor, there were the books in the Taylor household which she would borrow. The collection was rich in French and English books, for Mr. Joshua Taylor, a well-to-do manufacturer and banker, was a man of the world, a genuine lover of art and letters, and a person of strong liberal political views, slightly to the left of the Whigs. He was a staunch Republican, and it was probably from his library that Charlotte was able to obtain the works of modern French writers like Balzac and George Sand. He and his daughter were later to be immortalized in Charlotte's novels.

At any rate, while still in their early teens the Brontës read widely. Of course, they could not escape the current mania for the so-called "Gothic" novels, those tales of terror and mystery, thrillers of which *Frankenstein* by Mary Shelley is still remembered today. There were hundreds of such "shockers" produced by experts like Mrs. Anne Radcliffe and Matthew Gregory Lewis, whose highly scurrilous and strongly anti-Catholic *Monk* proved among the most popular. There was also, on a more serious level, the great Sir Walter Scott, the most successful novelist of that time both at home and abroad. But not least, there was the inescapable, magnetic and entrancing poet George Gordon Lord Byron, the much reviled and attractive leader of the so-called "Satanic School," whose notorious poems and plays such as *Childe Harold, Cain, Manfred* and *Don Juan* were read by all—even if only privately.

Here is Charlotte Brontë at the ripe age of thirteen, writing of a day's doings:

… While I write this I am in the kitchen of the Parsonage, Haworth; Tabby, the servant, is washing up the breakfast things, and Anne, my youngest sister (Maria was my oldest), is kneeling on a chair, looking at some cakes which Tabby is baking for us. Emily is in the parlour, brushing the carpet. Papa and Branwell are gone to Keightly. Aunt is up-stairs in her room, and I am sitting by the table writing this in the kitchen. Keightly is a small town four miles from here. Papa and Branwell are gone for the newspaper, the "Leeds Intelligencer," a most excellent Tory newspaper, edited by Mr. Wood, and the proprietor, Mr. Henneman. We take two and see three newspapers a week. We take the "Leeds Intelligencer," Tory, and the "Leeds Mercury," Whig, edited by Mr. Baines, and his brother, son-in-law, and his two sons, Edward and Talbot. We see the "John Bull"; it is a high Tory, very violent. Dr. Driver lends us it as likewise "Blackwood's Magazine," the most able periodical there is. …[5]

So that even as children they were exposed to politics and political discussions. The name of the Duke of Wellington was a household word—the hero of heroes.

They were "prolific authors." By the time Charlotte was thirteen, she drew up with all the seriousness of a mature professional a "catalogue of my books," with the periods of their composition—all in all "making in the whole twenty-two volumes." The father's gift of the wooden soldiers had become the source of their most fertile fantasies, each of the children selecting his or her own for hero. Charlotte's soldier was the Duke of Wellington; Branwell's, the more martial Bonaparte. The others followed suit. Charlotte and Branwell between them created the kingdom or realm of Angria and peopled it with heroes and villains, rulers and subjects. They built magnificent cities; and they spawned intrigues, adventures, loves both licit and illicit, conspiracies, and irresistible men whom all women adored, and whom they regularly betrayed; Branwell supplied the military campaigns, not at all sparing of human blood and wholesale slaughters. In Charlotte's tales a sultry eroticism pervaded the action. Emily and Anne created their own imaginative world which they named Gondal. Unfortunately the prose version of these tales has disappeared, leaving us only the intercalated poems—some of Emily's best.

They bound these productions in over a hundred little "books" in wrapping papers; they were written in that minuscule hand of Charlotte's which defies reading without magnifying glasses.

It is impossible to describe the hold these fantasies had on the growing youthful authors. A hothouse fever pervaded their activities, which lasted, at least in Charlotte's case, till she was twenty-three. She lived more closely with these creations of her imagination than with the human beings surrounding her, whether these were her young charges or her employers', the Misses Wooler. Emily, at Haworth, no doubt continued in the same vein. While Charlotte was away, Branwell continued the narratives, and she lived in imagination with her Byronic dark-browed hero Zamorna and his entourage of women, defying all the laws of accepted morality—cruel Zamorna! beautiful as ever![6]

Thus armed, in their own special enclave, the young Brontës became the denizens of a special world. Here their "genii," as they called themselves, could create and uncreate; here they could destroy and undo destruction; here they could mete out death and restore to life. Here Eros could have free play, and Thanatos could be shackled. Outside servitudes, whether as pupils at school or as governess-teachers, gave way to freedom. Or so they imagined. ...

And beyond the parsonage stretched the moors, their own domain in Nature, voicing their own inner feelings, at times magnetic, inviting, at others hostile and defiant, like themselves—sometimes even terrifying. They could remember as little children, when Branwell and Anne were out with their maids, how the moors literally exploded with volcanic violence—probably as a result of the gathered subterranean gases—and the "peaty subsoil roared down ... hurtling boulders into the valleys." But there were also seasons of enchantment, when the moors burgeoned with the purple heath and flowers, and the air was filled with the noises of larks, throstles and blackbirds. Then the ravines and the brooks proved inviting, and there was enough beauty and enchantment to make one of Charlotte's later novelistic characters exclaim: "Our England is a bonny island ... and Yorkshire is one of her bonniest nooks."[7]

Recalling what they thought were magic years, Charlotte celebrated them in a poem:

We wove a web in childhood,
   A web of sunny air;
We dug a spring in infancy
   Of water pure and fair.

We sowed in youth a mustard seed;
   We cut an almond rod.
We now are grown to riper age:
   Are they withered in the sod?

Are they blighted, failed, and faded?
   Are they mouldered back to clay?
For life is darkly shaded,
   And its joys fleet fast away.

Faded! the web is still of air,
   But how its folds are spread!
And from its tints of crimson clear,
   How deep a glow is shed!
The light of an Italian sky,
Where clouds of sunset lingering lie;
   Is not more ruby red.

But the spring was under a mossy stone,
   Its jet may gush no more.
Hark, skeptic, bid thy doubts be gone:
   Is that a feeble roar
Rushing around thee? Lo! the tide
Of waves where armed fleets may ride,
Sinking and swelling frowns and smiles,
An ocean with a thousand isles
   And scarce a glimpse of shore.

The mustard seed in distant land
   Bends down a mighty tree,
The dry, unbudding almond wand
   Has touched eternity.[8]

Did they in fact realize that in weaving and continuing to weave those fairy webs they were in fact seeking some magic charm that would enable them to retain their childhood forever—perhaps some elixir which would save them from the outside world? That they were actually reluctant to grow up? That in them lay a false freedom that might bear within itself infinite dangers? That fantasy is only one element in the process of growing?

*   *   *

But soon Necessity intruded. They would have to venture out of the magic enclave. To eke out the family income, it would be necessary to find work. And what work was there for a woman like Charlotte, aged nineteen? The field was narrow: teaching or being a governess. In their fantasies they had been the "genii," masters of fate—now a stark reality faced them. Charlotte announced the news to her friend Ellen Nussey in a letter written in 1835. "Emily is going to school, Branwell is going to London, and I am going to be a governess."[9]

Branwell, the favored child, was to be sent to London to apply to the Royal Academy of Art. He had shown some talent for painting. He had also displayed a modest talent for writing. The talents had been magnified at home and in his imagination to the point of megalomania. Fantasy had taken over completely. To anticipate somewhat: instead of reporting to the Academy, Branwell went a-roaming, to museums at times, and, much more frequently, into London pubs, his favorite haunts. Already he was exhibiting a profound instability and insecurity. Thereafter he would return home to Haworth, to commence one career after another, all marked eventually by failure …

Charlotte was to be a teacher-governess. She was going back to Miss Wooler's school at Roe Head. What was it like to be a governess? As late as 1890, the comic journal *Punch* described that profession, which must have been even more arduous and unsupportable sixty years earlier:

> Poor Miss Harker went to Stockton, to Stockton on the Tees,
> But not to make her fortune, or to loll at home at ease;
> She went to be a governess, and hoped, it would appear,
> To board and lodge and dress herself on £15 a-year.

> So all day long with urchins three Miss Harker toiled in chains,
> And she poured the oil of learning well upon their rusty brains,
> And she practised them in music, and she polished up their sense
> With the adverbs and the adjectives, and verbs in mood and tense.

> And they said, "She's doing nicely, we will give her something more
> (Not of money, but of labour) ere we show her to the door,
> Why, we've got two baby children, it is really only fair
> That Miss Harker should look after them and wash and dress the pair."
> Etc. Etc. . .

So it was scarcely the road to freedom upon which they were entering. For they were leaving a sanctuary and entering upon the outer world unarmed, literally and figuratively orphans. All through life they would carry on the battle against strangers, with that pathological shyness in the presence of others, that withdrawal, which would be imbedded in Emily throughout her life and would characterize Charlotte even in the days of her celebrity when she had become a cynosure in London. An even heavier burden was theirs—a sense of their moral imperfection, a burden of putative sinfulness, an inheritance no doubt from their Aunt Branwell. "If Christian perfection be necessary to Salvation," Charlotte wrote to Ellen Nussey, "I shall never be saved. … I abhor myself, I despise myself—if the doctrine of Calvinism be true, I am already an outcast."[10] Not the least disadvantage under which they were to labor was their total ignorance of how to deal with children, which was to make for an additional hardship when they entered into the lives of strangers. Emily, who was with Charlotte at Miss Wooler's as a free pupil, could not stand what she considered imprisonment. Three months sufficed and she returned to Haworth. Anne replaced her; Charlotte remained. She too felt a heavy bondage, more mental than physical. The hauntings that she was a sinful creature would not abate, she felt "unreconciled to God," wretched and hopeless as ever. She asks her friend to pray along with her, and sends her own "polluted petitions" along with with Ellen's "own pure requests." Was it flippancy, flightiness, thoughtlessness to have engaged in those writing enterprises? Wasn't it a sin to rebel? The monotony of her present life became unbearable. She had no sympathy for her charges. "Teach, teach, teach," she writes. There was no relief in sight. Her anger was even directed against Heaven! "You cannot imagine how hard, rebellious and intractable all my feelings are. When I begin to study the subject, I almost grow blasphemous, atheistical in my sentiments."[11] "The thought came over me: Am I to spend the best part of of my life in this wretched bondage?"[12]

Her home was not here, in Roe Head. Her home was ever that imagined Angria she and her brother had constructed and which by that time had become a constant obsession. How deep, one can judge from her journals of that time, her confessions. What was happening in that kingdom of theirs, of which her brother had possession? What was happening to that satanic Zamorna, hero and sinner? What was happening in the city of their own creation, Verdopolis? Everything around her faded. She listens to the howling wind outside. Surely that wind is heard in Haworth!

> I fulfil my duties strictly and well [she writes in her Journal] ... As God was not in the fire nor the wind nor the earthquake, so neither is my heart in the task, the theme, or the exercise. It is the still small voice always that comes to me at eventide ... It is that which engrosses all my living feelings, all my energies which are not merely mechanical ...[13]

Inspired by that almost divine voice, at that moment she feels that she could write a narrative "better at least than anything" she had ever produced. But alas! just then a "dolt came up with a lesson."[14]

She was possessed.

> Never shall I, Charlotte Brontë, forget what a voice of wild and wailing music now came thrillingly to my mind's, almost my body's ear, nor how distinctly I, sitting in the school-room at Roe Head, saw the Duke of Zamorna leaning against that obelisk ... I was quite gone. I had really, utterly forgot where I was and all the gloom and cheerlessness of my situation. I felt myself breathing quick and short as I beheld the Duke lifting up his sable crest ... "Miss Brontë what are you thinking about?" said a voice that dissipated all the charm ...[15]

The "web spun in childhood" had become a dangerous snare.

And quite as suddenly she became terrified. "I had had enough of morbidly vivid realizations. Every advantage has its corresponding disadvantage. Tea's real. Miss Wooler is impatient."[16]

A momentous event. This was a prelude to a "Farewell to Angria." It would take time, but in that moment of panic Charlotte Brontë the novelist was born. She left Miss Wooler's school in 1839, and in the following year she went forth once more as a governess to the family of the Sidgwicks. A few months before, her sister Anne had gone to work for family in Mirfield. Emily's attempt at teaching three years earlier had proved a failure, and she left after six months, totally weakened. Branwell continued his career of failures—in turn as a portrait painter, a railway clerk, and finally as a tutor. There were other trials as governesses for both Charlotte and Anne. But each new experiment brought on nervous distresses. It was obvious, as Mrs. Gaskell remarked, that "the hieroglyphics of childhood were an unknown language to them."[17] It cannot be said that the three of them had not tried hard to fill the place of governess in the various families. But the status of that occupation was such that it left its occupants without status. Recruited mostly from middle-class families with limited means, governesses found themselves, when employed, in that sea of indefiniteness, floating somewhere between the position of servant and an undefined member of the family—in "no woman's land." Typically deprived of authority, they were incapable of handling the problems of discipline, faced as they were with an unsympathetic attitude on the part of the mistress of the household. They were overworked, miserably underpaid, with neither privacy nor leisure. Often high-strung, nervous, sensitive, and—as in the case of the Brontës—gifted, governesses were frequently brought to the verge of nervous collapse by these tensions.

Such was their situation, then, made particularly difficult because they had literary talent and ambition. But they were poor and must suffer. Freedom seemed as far off as ever. Charlotte cried out in one of her letters to Ellen, expressing "a strong wish for wings ... wings such as wealth can furnish," envying her friend Mary Taylor who was traveling on the continent and was visiting galleries and cathedrals. There was so much in this world still to absorb and so much yet to learn! And as for writing. ...

In 1837, while still with Miss Wooler, she had sent a poem enclosed in a very humble letter to Robert Southey, the poet laureate and former associate of Wordsworth and Coleridge. The poem, it must be admitted, was mediocre. Southey's reply was kind, for he granted that she had talent for verse, but at the same time warned her not to indulge in daydreams, thus unfitting herself for "the ordinary uses of the world." "Literature," he added, "cannot be the business of a woman's life, and it ought not to be. The more she is engaged in her proper duties, the less leisure will she have for it even as an accomplishment and a recreation."[18] She replied with gratitude and humility, citing her own devotion to home and parent and giving a short picture of her life. Yes, she would give up her ambition to see her name in print, and if "the wish should arise," she wrote, "I'll look at Southey's letter and suppress it."[19] Southey graciously acknowledged the missive, and added an invitation to visit him at Keswick in the Lake Region. That, however, was out of the question. There was no money for such a trip.

But the decision to leave the imaginary Angria for other regions closer to home had not been abandoned. Charlotte had been saddened and set back by Southey's counsel. But she knew that she had to write. No one would be able to dissuade her. Addressing an imaginary reader, she bids Angria farewell; it was with a heavy heart and some apprehension.

> I have now written a great many books and for a long time have dwelt on the same characters and scenes and subjects. ... My readers have been habituated to one set of features ... but we must change, for the eye is tired of the picture so often recurring and now so familiar.
>
> Yet do not urge me too fast, reader; it is no easy theme to dismiss from my imagination the images which have filled it so long; they were my friends and my intimate acquaintances.

... When I depart from these I feel almost as if I stood on the threshold of a home and were bidding farewell to its inmates. When I strive to conjure up new inmates I feel as if I had got into a distant country where every face was unknown and the character of all the population an enigma which it would take much study to comprehend and much talent to expound. Still I long to quit for a while that burning clime where we have sojourned too long ... and turn now to a cooler region where the dawn breaks grey and sober ... and the coming day for a time at least is subdued by clouds.[20]

Charlotte Brontë was now twenty-three years old. She had had, and was still to have, many bitter experiences in her life. She was reluctantly leaving what she would later call "Elfland" for the "shores of Reality."[21] She was about to leave childhood—not forever; indeed, no one ever does—but against those unreal worlds, the real world she was now experiencing, and had experienced since childhood, began making its own urgent claims. If she was to be a writer, she would have to write for readers of this and not the Angrian world. The need that had forced the Brontës out of Haworth and into activity—the need, in brief, for some measure of economic independence—represented but the first step in the development of their artistic consciousness. If Charlotte wished to reach a public, she must write for the public. Of course, the fantasies of the past would not be totally abandoned. They were too deeply ingrained, and in some cases even of importance to the future writer. They would have to be recast and eventually fused into the new matter. The transition would be difficult, but it could not be evaded. It is the great "leap" that every artist who is maturing must ultimately make—the leap from a dependence into an independence—what Stendhal has called the "crystallization." It would take some five years and important events before the hot metal of creativity turned into the ingot.

* * *

Reader, perhaps you were never in Belgium? Haply you don't know the physiognomy of the country? You have not its lineaments defined upon your memory, as I have them on mine? ... Belgium! name unromantic and unpoetic, yet name that whenever uttered has in my ear a sound, in my heart an echo, such as no other assemblage of syllables, however, sweet or classic, can produce. Belgium! I repeat the word, now as I sit alone near midnight. It stirs my world of the past like a summons to resurrection; the graves unclose, the dead are raised; thoughts, feelings, memories that slept, are seen by me ascending from the clods—haloed most of them—but while I gaze on their vapoury forms, and strive to ascertain definitely their outline, the sound which awakened them dies, and they sink, each and all, like the light wreath of mist, absorbed in the mould, recalled to urns, resealed in monuments. Farewell, luminous phantoms!

Thus Charlotte, through the lips of one of the characters in her first novel *The Professor*, composed in 1846 for publication but not published until after her death. Some time late in 1841 the three Brontë sisters, still in search of security, decided to open a school of their own. In preparation for that enterprise, and in order to improve their French and German, Charlotte and Emily lighted on Brussels and the *pensionnat* of M. and Madam Heger as the most suitable place. Aunt Branwell generously supported the plan, and in February of 1842, accompanied by their father, they left Haworth. Until this time they had never been very far from the parsonage, and for the first time they saw London. For the first time they were on the Continent. For the first time, too, the sisters were literally alone.

Except for a few scattered English friends in Brussels, they were among total strangers, speaking a totally foreign language. They were also surrounded by Catholics. Charlotte was constitutionally hostile to Catholics and Catholicism, and no amount of experience was to temper that antagonism. Nor was she or Emily at ease among their fellow students. M. and Madame Heger were kind and considerate and did their best at first to mitigate the anguish of isolation.

For Charlotte, the Brussels experience would become perhaps the most vital, though not the happiest, of her entire life. Both sisters proved very good students: Charlotte meek and diligent, and very bright; Emily, very bright as always, but proud, stubborn, and rebellious. M. Heger was their master in French.

Charlotte's first description of M. Heger is highly interesting. She writes to Ellen Nussey of her first reactions:

> There is an individual of whom I have not yet spoken, M. Heger, the husband of Madame. He is professor of rhetoric, a man of power as to mind, but very choleric and irritable in temperament; a little black being, with a face that varies in expression. Sometimes he borrows the lineaments of an insane tom-cat, sometimes those of a delirious hyena; occasionally, but very seldom, he discards these perilous attractions and assumes an air not above 100 degrees removed from mild and gentlemanlike...[22]

Two years before coming to Brussels, Charlotte had lectured her friend Ellen on the matter of Love:

> ... No young lady should fall in love, till the offer has been made, accepted—the marriage ceremony performed and the first half year of wedded life has passed away—a woman may then begin to love, but with great precaution—very coolly—very modestly—very rationally—if she ever love so much that a harsh word or cold look from her husband cuts her to the heart—she is a fool.[23]

She was twenty-four when she wrote those lines. Now twenty-six, she fell in love with her master, M. Heger. Despite a number of proposals from an assorted number of curates, she had never had any profound emotional attachments. Now she fell in love with a married man eight years older than herself and the father of a family. In October 1842, Aunt Branwell died, and Charlotte and Emily returned to Haworth. Charlotte had been invited by the Hegers to come back as teacher of English, in return for instruction in French. Emily refused to go back. She preferred to stay home and pursue her own secret inner life (how rich that was to be eventually!)—and bake bread. Charlotte would remain in Brussels until January 1844.

M. Heger was no doubt attracted by this eager, now worshipful, student. How much more he felt, we do not know. She in turn was passionately in love for the first time in her life—unequivocally, irretrievably. What she expected of that love was far beyond anyone's fathoming. Though there was of course no physical relation, and though M. Heger must have reacted with sobriety if not aloofness, all her passion, hitherto repressed, went out to him. And in that way, never to another...

Today, we would describe it as a "sticky" situation. In May 1843, Charlotte writes to Ellen: "Of late days M. and Mde. Heger rarely speak to me ... I am convinced she does not like me ..." As for M. Heger, she continues, "he is wonderfully influenced by madame ..."[24] And on August 6, a pathetic cry: "Alas, I can hardly write, I have such a dreary weight at my heart; and I do so wish to go home..."[25]

Now more than ever alone, distraught, overwhelmed, she wanders through the city, visits the cemetery lying outside the town, returns to the rue d'Isabelle, where the *pensionnat* was located, and finds herself opposite the church of Ste. Gudule. The letter to Emily is dated September 2nd, 1843. "The bell, whose voice you know, began to toll for the evening *salut*. I went in." ... "In two confessionals I saw a priest. ... When people are by themselves they have singular fancies ... I took a fancy to change myself into a Catholic and go and make a real confession to see what it was like ... I approached ... I actually did confess—a real confession."[26] She continues:

> When I had done he told me his address, and said that every morning I was to go to the rue du Parc—to his house—and he would reason with me and try to convince me of the error and enormity of being a Protestant! I promised faithfully to go. Of course, however, the adventure stops there, and I hope I shall never see the priest again. I think you had better not tell papa of this. He will not understand that it was only a freak, and will perhaps think I am going to turn Catholic...[27]

Charlotte returned home, broken in spirit—heartbroken. On January 2, 1844, she was in Haworth once more. What Mrs. Gaskell was to say about her in connection with another episode proved true now. "Brave heart, ready to die in harness. She went back to work."[28] Circulars were issued announcing the new school, but no pupils appeared. Another failure.

The memories of Brussels could not be expunged. What she felt now she expressed in a poem, and in those few of the letters she kept on sending to M. Heger that have been preserved. His have probably been destroyed. The poem is entitled "Reason." Its date is uncertain; probably it was written sometime in 1843.

> Unloved I love, unwept I weep,
> Grief I restrain, hope I repress,
> Vain is this anguish fixed and deep,
> Vainer desires or means of bliss...
>
> Devoid of charm how could I dream
> My unasked love would e'er return?
> What fate, what influence, lit the flame
> I still feel inly, deeply, burn?

She calls to her aid "Reason, Science, Learning, Thought"—and comforts herself: "Doubt not I shall be strong to-morrow."[29]

The surviving letters to M. Heger were written between July 1844 and the latter part of 1845. They are all in French, with one paragraph in English. We cite a few passages here.

She is, she writes him, keeping up with her French studies "*car je suis bien persuadée que je vous reverrai un jour—je ne sais pas comment ni quand—mais cela doit être puisque je le désire tant ...*"* She cannot overcome her lethargy, and can no longer

---

* "For I am well persuaded that I shall see you again one day—I know not how or when—but it must be, for I want to so much ..."

do her writing. Besides, her eyesight is failing. "Otherwise do you know what I should do, Monsieur? I should write a book and I should dedicate it to my literature-master—the only master I ever had—to you Monsieur ... The career of letters is closed to me—only that of teaching is open." ... And in another letter: "As soon as I shall have earned enough money to go to Brussels I shall go there—and I shall see you again if only for a moment. ..." When she receives no reply to her letters, she writes: "Day and night I find neither rest nor peace. If I sleep I am disturbed by tormenting dreams in which I see you, always severe, always grave, always incensed against me. ... You will say once more that I am hysterical—that I have black thoughts. ... All I know is, that I cannot, that I will not resign myself to lose wholly the friendship of my master ..." "Monsieur, the poor have not need of much to sustain them—they ask only for the crumbs that fall from the rich man's table. But if they are refused the crumbs, they die of hunger. Nor do I, either, need much affection from those I love. I should not know what to do with a friendship entire and complete—I am not used to it. But you showed me of yore a *little* interest, when I was your pupil in Brussels, and I hold on to the maintenance of that *little* interest—I hold on to it as I would hold on to life. ..." And in the last surviving letter: "May I write to you next May? I would rather wait a year, but it is impossible—it is too long. C. Brontë." The editor of the letter adds: "It is on the edge of this letter that Professor Heger made some commonplace notes in pencil—one of them the name and address of a shoemaker."[30]

The Brussels experience was to be one of the major determinants of her future creative career. It sets the stage, or is directly or indirectly implicated, in all her novels, whether the inchoate work entitled *The Professor*, or the mature *Jane Eyre*, or *Shirley*. It is the core and very soul of the last—and in many ways the most personal—of her confessional books, *Villette*.

* * *

She returned to Haworth and a household that was soon to take on the character of an infirmary. Emily and Anne were in constant ill health; Branwell was rapidly deteriorating after having been dismissed as tutor from the family in which Anne had served as governess. He had imagined himself in love with the master's wife, and her in love with him, and was hopeful of marrying her once she attained widowhood. He was a shattered human being—addicted more than ever to alcohol and opium—a specter haunting the parsonage. And not least, there was the father, going blind and soon in need of an operation for cataracts. Though the small legacy Aunt Branwell had left them was helpful, the needs of the household had increased.

Charlotte felt herself growing old, for she was approaching thirty. "One day resembles another," she wrote in March 1845, "and all have lifeless physiognomies—Sunday baking and Saturday are the only ones that bear the slightest distinctive marks ... I feel as if we were all buried here—I long to travel—to work—to live a life of action ..."[31] And in January 1846: "Something in me which used to be enthusiasm is tamed down and broken. I have few illusions."[32]

Who, in reading these words, would imagine that just the preceding autumn Charlotte Brontë had made a discovery that was to change not only her own life, but also that of Emily and Anne?

She had one day unexpectedly come upon Emily's poetry. The story is well known, and needs only a brief recounting here. Let Charlotte tell it:

> One day, in the autumn of 1845, I accidentally lighted on a MS. volume of verse in my sister's handwriting. Of course, I was not surprised, knowing that she could and did write verse: I looked it over, and something more than surprise seized me,—a deep conviction that these were not common effusions, nor at all like the poetry women generally write. I thought them condensed and terse, vigorous and genuine. To my ear they had also a peculiar music—wild, melancholy, and elevating.[33]

It took some persuading to convince Emily to agree to publication. Anne had written poetry too, and she was amenable. So was Charlotte. Under the pseudonyms of Currer, Ellis, and Acton Bell—and at their own expense—they had the *Poems* published in 1846. As for using masculine names, Charlotte explained:

> We had a vague impression that authoresses are liable to be looked on with prejudice; we had noticed how critics sometimes use for their chastisement the weapon of personality, and for their reward, a flattery, which is not true praise.[34]

They had, of course, the celebrated example of George Sand to guide them.

In addition, they confessed to their publisher that they had in preparation for the press a work of fiction consisting of three distinct and unconnected tales. The "tales" were Charlotte's *Professor*, Emily's *Wuthering Heights*, and Anne's *Agnes Grey*.

The Professor was rejected by the publisher. The other two tales were accepted on payment of expenses of publication. *The Professor* went the rounds of many publishers, until at last it landed on the desks of Smith, Elder and Company, a highly respected firm. It was rejected, but with an accompanying letter which suggested that it had impressed, and added that if the writer had a three-volume work (the so-called "three-decker") they would welcome examining it. The writer answered Yes, and sent *Jane Eyre*. It was accepted at once, and issued in October 1847. In the same year, the publisher of the *Poems*, again on payment, brought out *Wuthering Heights* and *Agnes Grey*. Let us remember that Charlotte began writing *Jane Eyre* in Manchester in August 1846 while her father was recovering from his cataract operation. Branwell, at home, was going downhill at a disastrous pace. We need more than astonishment to measure adequately the inner strength that was a part of Charlotte's genius. ...

> "I have to live, perhaps, till seventy years. As far as I know, I have good health. Half a century of existence may lie before me. How am I to occupy it? What am I to do to fill the interval of time which spreads between me and the grave? ... What was I created for I wonder. Where is my place in the world?"
>
> —Charlotte Brontë, *Shirley*

Such are the thoughts of one of Charlotte Brontë's later heroines, Caroline Helstone. She has reached the age of eighteen. She is at the crossroads of her life. In one of those clearly autobiographical passages of that book the author speaks of the two worlds of the young woman, the one she is leaving and the other she is about to enter:

> ... At eighteen drawing near the confines of the illusive, void dreams, Elf-land lies behind us, the shores of Reality rise in front ... Before that time our world is heroic; its inhabitants

half-divine or semi-demon … What a moon we gaze on before that time! How the trembling of ours at her aspect bears witness to its unalterable beauty! As to our sun,—it is a burning heaven—the world of gods…

But now, we reach the "shores of Reality."

Could we but reach this land we think to hunger and thirst no more! whereas many a wilderness and often the flood of Death, or some stream of sorrow as cold and almost as black as Death, is to be crossed ere true bliss can be tasted …, the heart's blood must gem with red beads of the combatant before the wreath of victory rustles over it …[35]

"From Elfland" to "the shores of Reality." Such, indeed had been the experience of the three Brontë sisters and their brother, the urgent need to leave the claustral security of the rectory and their life of fantasy and to engage in a life of reality, to come to grips with the problems of a livelihood, the economics of existence.

The challenge had now been met. The sisters had been writing in secrecy, sometimes, as we have seen, even concealing their productions from one another. Now, sparked by Charlotte's discovery of Emily's poetry and the prospect of the publication of their poetic work, they seemed ready to expose themselves to the public eye, even if only pseudonymously. Emily Brontë had already completed a novel, *Wuthering Heights*; Anne had one also ready, *Agnes Grey*. Charlotte was completing *The Professor* early in 1846; undismayed by the publisher's rejection, she set about writing *Jane Eyre* in August of that year.

The Professor was not to be published until two years after Charlotte's death. The "leap" from that novel to *Jane Eyre* represents an astonishing advance, rare in literary history considering the near-simultaneity of their production. It is as if by some strange chance the "inhibitions" so evident in the earlier work has been lifted, enabling Charlotte to risk greater self-revelation and candor. Biographers have speculated that the trauma of discovering the depth and force of Emily's iconoclasm in both the poems and the novel might have acted as the catalyst of her sister's creative growth.

The Brussels experience lies at the center of both works, as do the themes of the orphan-outsider, the rebellious young woman, the quest for understanding and love, for independence and self-realization.

But whereas in the later novels the major protagonists would be women, in *The Professor* it is a man, William Crimsworth, who is also the narrator. At first he appears as the "outsider," what the Russian writers called a "superfluous" man. He has no true vocation. An orphan, descended from a well-to-do family, Crimsworth refuses to acquiesce in his relatives' determination that he enter the Church, or in his uncles' contempt for his father's profession as tradesman. Though himself a contemner of the "counting-house" and commerce, he joins his brother's manufacturing establishment, but finds this equally intolerable, as he is subjected to cruelty and humiliations.

The predicament of an "outsider" like William Crimsworth is sharply described by another character, the radical Whig manufacturer Yorke Hunsdon (modeled on Joshua Taylor, Mary Taylor's father, who was to appear in greater detail as Hiram Yorke in *Shirley*), in a conversation with Crimsworth:

Now if you'd only an estate and a mansion, and a park, and a title, how you could play the exclusive, maintain the rights of your class, train your tenantry in habits of respect to the peerage, oppose at every step the advancing power of the people, support your order, and be ready for its sake to wade knee-deep in churls' blood; as it is, you've no power; you can do nothing; you're wrecked and stranded on the shores of commerce; forced into collision with practical men, with whom you cannot cope, for *you'll never be* a tradesman.[36]

Crimsworth is persuaded by Hunsdon to go to the Continent, and with the help of an introduction from the latter, is enabled to obtain a position as a teacher of English in Mlle. Reuter's establishment. This is the only truly positive measure that Crimsworth takes in his search for an independent career. In all other respects he is a passive figure, moved by chance, accident, happy coincidence, or the help of kind intermediaries. To his credit, he is not too snobbish to fall in love with a person of the lower classes, or to accept teaching as a worthy profession. The young woman, Frances Evans Henri, a lacemaker, is the protype of all the "orphan-outsiders" of the future novels. Of Swiss descent, she is alone in an alien world and has come to school to learn English, for she is an admirer of England and English institutions, and hopes to migrate to that country and become a governess there.

In making Crimsworth rather than Frances the narrator and chief protagonist, Charlotte Brontë hoped to veil the intrinsic and auguishing experience of Brussels— still in the spring of 1846 all too fresh in her mind and heart—or at least attenuate it. Herein lay the central blunder, for she was then in a much better position to assess and assay the feelings of a woman than those of a man, those of a pupil than those of a master. Crimsworth is scarcely an adequately equipped spokesman for the complex emotions which either he himself or Frances were to experience and express. He is neither emotionally nor psychological able to attain to the freedom that would be central to the women characters of her later work. Too fearful of passion, he is rarely "natural" in the sense in which Charlotte was to employ that term. Violence of feelings, even if only incipient velleities, alarms him.

An example or two will suffice: Frances, unable to bear the jealousy of the directress Mlle Reuter, has fled the *pensionnat* where she was teaching lacemaking, and after a great deal of trouble Crimsworth finds her in the Protestant cemetery before the tombstone of her lately deceased aunt. On seeing him, Frances cannot control herself, and exclaims, "*Mon maître! mon maître!*" Crimsworth recounts his reactions:

I knew how quietly and how deeply the well bubbled in her heart; I knew how the more dangerous flame burned safely under the eyes of reason; I had seen when the fire shot up a moment high and vivid, when the accelerated heat troubled life's current in its channels; I had seen reason reduce the rebel, and humble its blaze to embers. I had confidence in Frances Evans …[37]

And here is Crimsworth's account of his proposal of marriage to Frances and its acceptance:

"Will my pupil consent to pass her life with me? Speak English now, Frances." Some moments were taken for reflection; the answer pronounced slowly ran thus:

"You have always made me happy; I like to hear you speak; I like to see you; I like to be near you; I believe you are very good, and very superior; I know you are stern to those who are careless and idle, but you are kind to the attentive and industrious, even if they are not clever. Master, I should be *glad* to live with you always," and she made a sort of movement, as if she would have clung to me, but restraining herself she only added with earnest emphasis—"Master, I consent to pass my life with you."

"Very well, Frances."

I drew her a little nearer to my heart; I took a first kiss from her lips, thereby sealing the compact, now framed between us; afterwards she and I were silent, nor was our silence brief ...[38]

Such a conversation suggests nothing so much as what would be entered into if Frances were applying for a job as lacemaker and Crimsworth were in an employing mood. It also belies a later passage in which Frances proves far from the passive, prissy betrothed, and is already a foreshadowing of Charlotte's later heroines like Jane Eyre. Here is Frances as recorded by her future husband:

... "Monsieur, I wished merely to say, that I should like, of course, to retain my employment of teaching. You will teach, I suppose, Monsieur?"

"Oh, Yes! It is all I have to depend on."

"*Bon*—I mean good. Thus we shall have both the same profession, I like that; and my efforts to get on will be as unrestrained as yours—will they not, Monsieur?"

"You are laying plans to be independent of me," said I.

"Yes, Monsieur; I must be no incumbrance to you—no burden in any way." ...

"Think of my marrying you to be kept by you, Monsieur! I could not do it; and how dull my days would be! You would be away teaching in close, noisy schoolrooms, from morning till evening, and I should be lingering at home, unemployed and solitary; I should get depressed and sullen, and you would soon tire of me ..."

A declaration of independence such as would have, without doubt, sent either shudders of panic or thrills (certainly in much rarer instances) down the spines of lady readers, and throbs of alarm down those of their male counterparts!

In *The Professor* she had gone far beyond the limits of her talents in allotting the burden of narration to a man, yet asking him to speak in the name of both man and woman. To be true to her own dictates of honesty and reality, she would have to overcome her timidity and give herself wholeheartedly as a woman to the task of translating those experiences she had had as a woman, or with which she could identify as only a woman could. It was a triumph for her to recognize that to be true to her genius she would have to "dare," within the limits of her own profound experiences internal and external, to speak out in the name of the feminine "I." Where she failed to do so and wandered into strange territories of factitious or still insufficient knowledge, she would slip into falsifications that might prove disastrous. To be true to her own avowed program, the "I" of the woman must stand unambiguous. She sped to the new task with the assurance of a master craftswoman. The new coin rang true, and *Jane Eyre* emerged.

Her new heroine was unlike Frances of *The Professor*. Charlotte Brontë, stooping to the fashion of the times, had made her an attractive heroine, bound to draw Crimsworth's heart. But Jane Eyre was of a different mould. She was to be "plain, small, unattractive." No magnet here to rivet all eyes and cause all speech to stop. Plain and ordinary-looking as Charlotte Brontë was herself—and throughout her life knew herself to be, painful as was the admission—Jane Eyre lacked one of the prime assets of a marketable commodity in the Victorian world. Add to that disadvantage another: she was poor. Whatever notable assets she possessed did not lie on the surface for easy assessment and appraisal ...

The editors of the London firm of Smith, Elder & Co., William Smith Williams and the partner, George Smith—be it said to their credit—bestowed on the book an enthusiasm rarely shown new writers. (They were not aware that the author, "Currer Bell" was a woman.) Before the year 1847 was out, a second printing became necessary. Charlotte Brontë earned £500 on the book. ...

The very first sentence of *Jane Eyre* (with its near-Tolstoyan ring) sets the tone: "There was no possibility of taking a walk that day." It is Jane Eyre, the narrator, sounding forth what is the central theme, the theme of "exclusion"—the theme of the "outsider." The ten-year-old orphan, Jane Eyre, is living in the hostile world of the Reed family, the unwanted, the to-be-rejected. The seeds of rebellion are already being sown as she responds with violence to the physical and verbal abuses of the younger members of the family and the unsympathetic and tyrannical attitude of their mother, her aunt. The ultimate outrage is inflicted upon the child when she is shut up in the "red room" and exposed to the terrors of aloneness and superstition, for this is the room in which the elder Mr. Reed, her kindly uncle, had died.

Prison and rebellion. One might say that these mark the various stages of Jane Eyre's "progress" through life as she embarks on her pilgrimage toward maturity, toward full womanhood and the full flowering of consciousness and self-consciousness. In the prison of the "red room" she becomes cognizant of the world's injustices and of herself as the victim. "Unjust, unjust!" her reason cries out. "And all my heart in insurrection." The description of Jane's mounting terror, frustration and rage, ending in a hysterical seizure, are unequalled in contemporary Victorian literature. In this way she obtains partial freedom, only to be now subjected to new servitudes. She is sent off to a poor clergyman's daughters' school, the "Lowood Institution."

In the Reed family she had been made well aware of her dependent economic position, being assured on the one hand by young John Reed, "You are a dependant, mama says; you have no money," and on the other by the servant Bessie, "You are less than a servant, for you do nothing for your keep."

Jane Eyre had brought to school with her a heart that was in "insurrection" against any show of tyranny, injustice, or brutality. Here, however, she encounters the total obverse of her own attitude in the person of young Helen Burns, also an orphan charge, slightly older than herself. Helen, unlike Jane, is no rebel. She is the congenital martyr, passive, humble, all-suffering, who accepts even physical punishment, unjustly meted out by a sadistic teacher, with incredible submission and passiveness. Jane is outraged. "I could not comprehend the doctrine of endurance." She expostulates with her young fellow-student:

> "If people were always kind and obedient to those who are cruel and unjust, the wicked people would have it all their own way: they would never feel afraid, and so they would

never alter, but would grow worse and worse. When we are struck at without a reason, we should strike back again very hard; I am sure we should—as to teach the person who struck us never to do it again."[39]

Helen dies in the school, a victim of tuberculosis, her death hastened by an outbreak of an epidemic at the institution. In writing of Helen, Charlotte Brontë had her adored oldest sister Maria in mind, who, similar in spirit to Helen, had been carried off by a pestilential outbreak of "low fever" at Cowan Bridge and died at the age of twelve.

Already Jane is no partisan or upholder of the Victorian doctrine of "suffer and be still" applied to womanhood. Life, she has already learned, is warfare. Passivity is self-imprisonment.

Activity is the essence of life—is life itself. That is what she learns in her eight-year residence at the school, where she ends up as one of the teachers. Here, too, she feels the walls of a prison-house beginning to close in upon her. She is now a grown woman. The combat must take new forms. The wide world outside beckons. What is she to do? Until now she had been sheltered. The orphan had found at least one person in Lowood who stood her "in the stead of mother, governess, and latterly companion." That had been Miss Temple, the superintendent of the school, an extraordinary personality, at once sympathetic and understanding—a person of feeling. But she leaves to be married. Once more, Jane is alone. And the departure precipitates an internal revolution in Jane's mind, a new stage in the process of her growth, in the process of her liberation as a woman and as a person. A new element of self-understanding has entered, which she is able to clarify for herself:

> … Another discovery dawned on me, namely that in the interval I had undergone a transforming process; that my mind had put off all it had borrowed from Miss Temple— or rather that she had taken with her the serene atmosphere I had been breathing in her vicinity—and that now I was left in my natural element … the reason for tranquillity was no more. My world had for some years been in Lowood: my experience had been of its rules and systems; now I remembered that the real world was wide, and that a varied field of hopes and fears, of sensations and excitements, awaited those who had the courage to go forth into its expanse, to seek real knowledge of life amidst its perils …

All within the boundaries of Lowood "seemed prison-ground, and exile limits."

> I desire liberty; for liberty I gasped; for liberty I uttered a prayer; it seemed scattered on the wind then faintly blowing. I abandoned it and framed a humbler supplication; for change, stimulus: that petition, too, seemed swept off into vague space: "Then," I cried, half desperate, "grant me at least a new servitude!"[40]

From passivity to activity: she takes the step of advertising for the position of governess …

This marks the end of the first act of the drama of *Jane Eyre*. Actually, the novel falls almost naturally into the dramatic form, in which the second act might be entitled Love and Loss, and the third Triumph of the Self. Each of the two last acts is marked by a highly intensive Crisis (which might be called the Testing of Self). As a matter of fact, Jane Eyre herself speaks of her life at the beginning of the second phase as a new chapter in a novel being "something like a new scene in a play,"[41] and about drawing up the curtain.

She is now governess at Thornfield, Mr. Rochester's estate, in charge of a young girl, Adèle Varens. When she arrives, Mr. Rochester is absent, and while waiting for his return, she once more becomes fretful in the somewhat "vault-like" atmosphere of the manor and its air of antiquity. She is still restless. For she is much alone, the unknown master being away. Will Thornfield prove another prison, chaining her into passivity and inertness? She longs for the "busy world, towns, regions full of life," she has heard about. Once again, her reflections mark her ever-expanding maturity, as she considers the plight of women in general and her own in particular:

> It is in vain to say human beings ought to be satisfied with tranquillity: they must have action; and they will make it if they cannot find it. Millions are condemned to a stiller doom than mine, and millions are in silent revolt against their lot. Nobody knows how many rebellions besides political rebellions ferment in the masses of life which people the earth. Women are supposed to be very calm generally: but women feel just as men feel; the need of exercise for their faculties, and a field for their efforts as much as their brothers do; they suffer from too rigid a restraint, too absolute a stagnation, precisely as men would suffer; and it is narrow-minded in their more privileged fellow-creatures to say that they ought to confine themselves to making puddings and knitting stockings, to playing on the piano and embroidering bags. It is thoughtless to condemn them or laugh at them, if they seek to do more or learn more than custom has pronounced necessary for their sex.[42]

How could Jane have foreseen at that moment that her prayer would be answered in ways altogether unimaginable, and very soon at that? And that a life of "activity" was preparing for her?

For as she is returning one day from a walk to post a letter, she encounters a horseman and his dog. As they approach, the horse shies and the rider is thrown and injured. She helps him remount his horse. She does not know that this is Mr. Rochester, her new employer. This act of hers is revelatory, symbolic and real, and she recognizes its true import:

> The incident had occurred and was gone for me: it *was* an incident of no moment, no romance, no interest in a sense; yet it marked with change one single hour of a monotonous life. My help had been needed and claimed; I had given it: I was pleased to have done something; trivial, transitory though the deed was, it was yet an active thing, and I was weary of an existence all passive ...[43]

It has fulfilled for the moment the need to be needed, to be of use to someone; the need to *do*.

The new life she had been longing for does not require removal to other, strange places. The transformation takes place at Thornfield. It takes place within her. It embodies the emancipation of her own inner self—the emancipation of feelings. She falls in love with Mr. Rochester and for the first time enters upon those new realms of ecstasy and terror, hopes and fears, joys and pangs that accompany that mystery. Concentration on the secondary and ancillary elements of the novel, such as the so-called "Gothic" elements of horror and mystery that Charlotte Brontë employs, has frequently obscured for her critics' eyes the subtleties which the author has utilized in depicting the evolution of love in a young woman. Thornfield is haunted; not, it is true, by a "ghost" out of the novels of terror that had also infatuated the young Brontë household, but by a living threat, constant and inescapable, "a foul German specter—a Vampyre," in the form of the madwoman in the garret, Rochester's mad wife. That is the "terror" upon which the flourishing love and hopes of the young woman threaten to be wrecked. The other and more significant "terror" resides in the person of the demonic, Byronic Mr. Rochester himself—typically burdened with a guilty "past," an enigma difficult for Jane to unravel. The child in Jane is affrighted, the woman in her is challenged. The subtleties that work a change in Jane as she becomes overpowered by her love are no less apparent in the changes wrought in the character of Rochester, as the two interrelate and interplay. The pupil becomes the teacher and the teacher, the pupil.

For Jane immediately brings into the household the element of genuineness, a candor that startles. Already at the beginning of her service Rochester becomes aware of it. To her he had at first appeared by turns stern and gloomy, smiling and grim, with his "granite-hewn features and his great, dark eyes."

> "You examine me, Miss Eyre," said he: "do you think me handsome?" I should, if I had deliberated, have replied to this question by something conventionally vague and polite; but the answer somehow slipped from my tongue before I was aware.—"No sir."
> "Ah! By my word! there is something singular about you," said he. ...[44]

Free of sham, she in time makes him aware of the sham of the life he had been living, as well as that of the aristocratic and wealthy Ingram family, of whose daughter he is a pretended suitor.

What she was to call the "fire of her nature," which had been kept low and repressed, now bursts into full flame as she becomes aware of tenderness on his part—the first expression of which he openly manifests after she has been instrumental in saving his life from a fire set by the strange woman of the garret. He had called her "My cherished preserver." Jane records her feelings:

> I regained my couch, but never thought of sleep. Till morning dawned I was tossed on a buoyant but unquiet sea, where billows of trouble rolled under surges of joy. I thought sometimes I saw beyond its wild waters a shore, sweet as the hills of Beulah; and now and then a freshening gale, wakened by hopes, bore my spirit triumphantly towards the bourne; but I could not reach it, even in fancy—a counteracting breeze blew off land, and continually drove me back. Sense would resist delirium: judgment would warn passion. Too feverish to rest, I rose as soon as day dawned.[45]

Her "self" is still weak. She compares herself unfavorably with the attractive Miss Ingram, and in imagination draws two portraits, of herself and of the woman she deems her rival. "You," she reflects in an interior monologue, "a favourite with Mr. Rochester ...?" Hers was the portrait of a "a Governess, disconnected, poor, and plain." What had Mr. Rochester to do with this "indigent and insignificant plebeian"? Very soon thereafter, she does sketch the two portraits, and thus believes she has reconciled herself to her fate ... Reason had triumphed ...

After a brief absence Mr. Rochester returns, and all her rational resolutions collapse. In the variegated company present, she is able to compare herself with the others, Miss Ingram among them, and realizes that Rochester is "not of their kind." Not beautiful in the accepted sense of beauty, he is "more than beautiful to her"—with his "colorless, olive face, square, massive brow, broad jetty eyebrows, deep eyes"—"all energy, decision, will." "I had not intended to love him" ... and now, at the first renewed view of him, the sparks of love are rekindled. "He made me love him without looking at me ..." and even if she is sure that they are "for ever sundered ..." "yet while I breathe and think I must love him."[46]

With the growth of her love and of her own sense of selfhood, she becomes more daring, less affrighted by the complexities of Rochester's character. His volcanic temper, sometimes appearing so sinister, now challenges her to deeper explorations of his true nature. "Instead of wishing to shun, I longed only to dare—to divine it."[47] She believes herself even capable of understanding Rochester's and Miss Ingram's ideas of marriage as an arrangement "for interest and connections," as very much an aspect of their class upbringing. And she brings the same feeling of self-confidence to bear upon her relations to her aunt Mrs. Reed, whom she had left in such a turmoil of resentment when she was sent to Lowood. Now Mrs. Reed is on her deathbed, and in a repentant mood has summoned her niece. As Jane approaches Gateshead, she is conscious of her change of feelings:

> The same hostile roof now again arose before me: my prospects were doubtful yet; and I had yet an aching heart. I still felt as a wanderer on the face of the earth; but I experienced firmer trust in myself and my own powers, and less withering dread of oppression. The gaping wound of my wrongs, too, was now quite healed; and the flame of resentment extinguished.[48]

But in reality she knew she had a home—Thornfield; and the prospect of leaving it, in view of what she believed to be the impending union of Rochester and Ingram, is terrifying. Thornfield had given her what she had yearned for: she had not been, as she put it, trampled, buried with inferior minds, excluded from communion with other spirits. With Miss Ingram established as the new mistress of Thornfield, she cannot possibly stay. But Rochester is not about to marry Miss Ingram, and with near-sadistic strains plays upon Jane's feelings, at the same time having concealed his own, now full-grown, love for her. He evokes from her that highly explosive and eloquent declaration which is one of the climactic scenes of the book. Rochester is urging Jane to remain on after the presumed marriage. And Jane flares up:

> "I tell you I must go!" I retorted, roused to something like passion. "Do you think I can stay to become nothing to you? Do you think I am an automaton?—a machine without feelings? and can bear to have my morsel of bread snatched from my lips, and my drop of living water dashed from my cup? Do you think, because I am poor, obscure, plain, and little, I am soulless and heartless? You think wrong!—I have as much soul as you,—and full as much heart! And if God had gifted me with some beauty, and much wealth, I should have made it as hard for you to leave me, as it is now for me to leave you. I am not talking to you now through the medium of custom, conventionalities, or even of mortal flesh:—it is my spirit that addresses your spirit; just as if both had passed through the grave, and we stood at God's feet, equal—as we are!"[49]

She asserts her moral superiority over him, for she would have scorned the kind of union he is about to enter, a union of convenience and not of love. "Therefore I am better than you—let me go!"

It is then that he proposes to her: "My bride is here ... because my equal is here, and my likeness ... You—poor and obscure, and small and plain as you are—I entreat to accept me as a husband."

She accepts him, but her acceptance is that very night accompanied by a serious storm, and the next morning she is told that "the great horse-chestnut at the bottom of the orchard had been struck by lightning ... and half of it split away."[50]

For Jane lives a life also full of fantasies, omens, and dreams; and the very world of Thornfield she is living in is conducive to anxieties. Now, particularly, that she is on the eve of her emotional fulfilment, there are presages that sometimes darken the blue crystal of her blue heaven. Storms in particular are frightening, for they are evocative of the deep eroticism that has been submerged; love has sharpened her sensibilities, her sensitiveness, and expanded her emotional capacities and sensual reactions, naturally plunging her into a vortex of contradictory emotional experiences. Her dream-life is one major aspect of that awakening—filled as it is with visions of infants—now laughing, now wailing. She interprets one such dream as premonitory of death, and in fact it proves to be such, for she is soon informed of the impending demise of her aunt Mrs. Reed. But such dreams will continue, though she will scarcely recognize that the child in the dream is often her own self—the outsider, the orphan, the wanderer, subjected to threats ... And so too, the horsechestnut in the orchard becomes a symbol, as we shall see, both for evil and for good. As a child, she had wanted nothing so much as to be loved, as she confessed to Helen Burns; now she was loved, and she could give her own love full sway. She was no longer the "unworthy" reject. She could fully assert her "selfhood."

Now she can exact a "charter" of equality from her beloved. She will not be a "kept" woman, like the French mother of Adèle, her ward. "I shall continue to act as Adèle's governess; by that I shall earn my board and lodging, and thirty pounds a year besides. I'll furnish my own wardrobe out of that money, and you shall give me nothing but—" "Well, but what?" "Your regard; and if I give you mine in return, that debt will be quit."[51]

> My future husband was becoming to me my whole world; and more than the world: almost my hope of heaven. He stood between me and every thought of religion, as an eclipse between man and the broad sun. I could not, in those days see God for his creature: of whom I had made an idol.[52]

She had as yet no clue as to the identity of the inhabitant of the upper story, though a horrifying experience preceding the wedding ceremony apprises her of her true physical existence. Her dreams acquire more and more terrifying intensity, now once more featuring a child, and herself in great anxiety; now presenting her with a vivid picture of a ruined Thornfield Hall. But the climactic fulfilment of her dread is still to come, and to bring tragedy with it. The wedding ceremony which is to join her to Rochester is dramatically disrupted by the arrival of the brother of the madwoman in the attic—who is now revealed as being Bertha Mason, the legal wife of Rochester. A succeeding episode, a visit to the attic, in which Jane participates, discloses the "clothed hyena"—the madwoman turned into a near-beast. There is nothing now for Jane to do—she decides she cannot remain at Thornfield, and resisting Rochester's plea that she remain as his beloved, she makes her escape. Heartbroken, Rochester has in her eyes lost "the attribute of stainless truth." But she is still in love with him.

What follows constitutes the last "act" of the novel-drama, which we may call Triumph of the Self—perhaps also Resurrection. Not knowing where she is heading, with very few possessions (which she loses on the way), Jane wanders for two days and two nights, until one evening she sinks, exhausted and thoroughly famished, at the door of the Rivers family—consisting of two sisters and their brother St. John Rivers, parson of a neighboring parish. Here she finds a cordial sympathy, and is persuaded by the Rev. St. John to undertake charge of a newly-established girls' school, attended mostly by poor farmers' children. A new element enters her life, and new conflicts ensue. In the course of time, she is pressed by the cleric to become his wife.

For in the Rev. St. John Rivers she is faced with a personality of seemingly monolithic power and determination. And she in turn lays bare her own ambiguities—her own drive to submit as a child, warring with the drive of insurrection. She is attracted by power, and St. John draws her and at the same time repels her. His singleness of purpose and mind seem almost irresistible. Almost—but not entirely. She stands in admiration of his monomaniacal decision to sacrifice himself in the cause of the Church by a martyrdom as missionary to India. But he is no hypocrite, no mealy-mouthed tyrant. His tyranny is toward himself, a need to subjugate within himself all earthly passions. Jane Eyre, however, is clearsighted enough to perceive that that self-same dedication was in truth a passion for mastery and domination, which might as easily have turned him into an army general, a ruler of nations, an autocratic leader. She even senses his strong erotic nature, which he is sublimating in those other drives. She is aware that he is in fact incapable of love—whether of a woman or of humanity at large. He speaks of mankind as "worms." Yet, she is almost swayed by his strength into joining him in his crusade to convert infidels. She will go, she says finally, not as his wife, but as his sister, his curate, his adjutant, for that is what he needs. But he is intractable. ...

* * *

And yet, ever present beside the powerful figure of St. John, stood the other figure—that of Rochester. Nothing could obliterate the latter's presence in her mind and, even more significantly, in her dreams. Here a potent erotic element makes its demands:

> ... I used to rush into strange dreams at night: dreams many-coloured, agitated, full of the ideal, the stirring, the stormy—dreams where amidst unusual scenes, charged with adventure, with agitating risk and romantic chance, I still again and again met Mr. Rochester, always at some exciting crisis; and then the sense of being in his arms, hearing his voice, meeting his eye, touching his hand and cheek, loving him, being loved by him—the hope of passing a lifetime at his side, would be renewed, with all its first force and fire. Then I awoke. Then I recalled where I was, and how situated. Then I rose up on my curtainless bed, trembling and quivering; and then the still, dark night witnessed the convulsion of despair, and heard the burst of passion. By nine o'clock the next morning

I was punctually opening the school; tranquil, settled, prepared for the steady duties of the day.[53]

So, torn between dreams of true love, impossible to realize, and the insistent, immediate presence of St. John, immense in his singleness, Jane almost breaks. What she calls an "iron shroud" seems more and more to be constricting her. St. John appears to be engrossing her own "liberty of mind." She is almost magnetized into admiration at his dedication to Him, whom he calls his "king ... lawgiver ... captain ... the All-perfect."[54] Under that influence, she abandons her study of German and begins to study, at his side, Hindustani. She feels that he prizes her "as a soldier would," as "a good weapon." Yet she is also aware that within him rages a struggle, a constant warfare to down the "human" side of himself, and that her imprisonment, should she yield, would mean the death of her feelings. She would always be forced "to keep the fire of her nature continually low, to compel it to burn inwardly and never utter a cry, though the imprisoned flame consumed vital after vital. *This* would be unendurable."

She is finally brought to a climactic explosion—her vision having become clearer and clearer—with a psychological insight that had not yet appeared in any of the Victorian novels. When she again refuses to marry him, she adds that the reason for her refusal was "Formerly ... because you did not love me; now, I reply, because you almost hate me. It I were to marry you, you would kill me. You are killing me now."[55] There is one more effort on his part, as he refuses to give her up "to perdition" and "the lake which burneth with fire and brimstone," and warns her away from being sinfully misled by "the good things in life."

Who could resist such persistence, such strength, such self-assurance and such self-dedication? Life in death, or life itself is the choice. She had told him before that "God did not give me my life to throw away."

And at the point of yielding, when she and St. John are alone, she has that extraordinary experience that determines her for life.

> ... The one candle was dying out: the room was full of moonlight. My heart beat fast and thick: I heard its throb. Suddenly it stood still to an inexpressible feeling that thrilled it through, and passed at once to my head and extremities. The feeling was not like an electric shock; but it was quite as sharp, as strange, as startling: it acted on my sense as if their utmost activity hitherto had been but torpor; from which they were now summoned, and forced to wake. They rose expectant: eye and ear waited, while the flesh quivered on my bones.
>   "What have you heard: What do you see?" asked St. John. I saw nothing: but I heard a voice somewhere cry—"Jane! Jane! Jane!" nothing more. "Oh God! what is it?" I gasped.[56]

She finds Rochester again, but not at Thornfield Hall. Thornfield Hall is wrecked, burnt down as a result of a fire set by the madwoman, Bertha Mason. Bertha Mason is dead; and Rochester himself is blinded and crippled. Jane Eyre becomes his strong arm, and his eyes.

"Reader, I married him." The line became celebrated.

She had found both love and the right to be useful. Once upon a time he was sole "giver and protector." Now she is in a position to give, to give wholeheartedly. She is in a position to act. This, she assures her future husband, is no sacrifice.

"Sacrifice! What do I sacrifice: Famine for food, expectation for content. To be privileged to put my arms round what I value—to press my lips to what I love—to repose on what I trust: is that to make a sacrifice? If so, then certainly I delight in sacrifice."

And when he compares himself to the old lightning-struck chestnut tree in the Thornfield orchard, she counters

"You are no ruin, sir—no lightning-struck tree: you are green and vigorous. Plants will grow about your roots, whether you ask them or not because they take delight in your bountiful shade; and as they grow they will lean towards you, and wind round you, because your strength offers them a safe prop."[57]

Almost without being aware of it, she finds herself replying: "I am coming! Where are you?" And it seems to her that she hears the answering cry: "Where are you?"

She has her answer, no doubt in the making for a long time, even when she had been under constant siege, an answer that was to speak of her own growth as an individual. Whether this is to be accounted an extrasensory experience or not, matters little. And she herself comments,

"Down superstition!" I commented. ... "It is the work of nature. She was roused and did—no miracle—but her best."

Nature had once more reasserted herself, in no equivocal accents. Once more, Jane had been recalled from the torpor of death, loosed from the "iron shroud," the prison of submission, and recalled to an acceptance of Life: living, feeling, and love.

In his despair he had called to her and had heard her reply, "I am coming, wait for me." She makes no effort to enlighten him about this telepathic miracle and her own part in it, for she would not further darken his mind. After telling his story, he utters a devout prayer of thanks to the Lord. Though blinded, he had been restored to a newer "seeing."

Then he stretched his hand out to be led. I took that dear hand, held it a moment to my lips, then let it pass round my shoulder: being so much lower of stature than he, I served both for his prop and guide. We entered the wood, and wended homeward. ...

Reader, I married him ...

After so much that is truly motivated and convincing, the conclusion of *Jane Eyre* must strike the reader as mechanical and somewhat contrived. Rochester's conversion from an avowed "atheism" to a firm belief in God appears factitious. Setting aside these and other minor lapses, the book stands out as a superbly moving study of the struggle toward humanization of two characters, self-recognition, and recognition of other selves, of the worth of the human being, especially of a woman, and the value of the struggle to achieve that sense of worth.

* * *

A year ago—had a prophet warned me how I should stand in June 1849—how stripped and bereaved—had he foretold the autumn, the winter, the spring of sickness and suffering to be gone through—I should have thought—this can never be endured. It is over. Branwell—Emily—Anne are gone like dreams—gone as Maria and Elizabeth went twenty years ago. One by one I have watched them fall asleep on my arm—and closed

their glazed eyes—I have seen them buried one by one—and—thus far—God has up-
held me. From my heart I thank Him.
                    —Charlotte Brontë to William S. Williams, June 13, 1849

"The book is now finished (thank God).
                    —August 29, 1849

It might seem as if a tidal wave of calamities had broken loose upon the Haworth
household, and for a while it appeared as if Charlotte, too, might be overborne. Between the end of September 1848 and the end of May 1849 she lost her brother and her
two sisters, and was left alone to support a heartbroken father—she, in her own
words, "the weakest, puniest, the least promising of his six children."[58] The Reverend
Patrick Brontë had regarded his son Branwell as the jewel of the family, the ever-
bright hope and heir, and had, like the others, watched with grief his unremitting
moral and physical deterioration.

Had it not been for these afflictions, Charlotte would have had good reason to feel
satisfaction, perhaps the greatest of her life. In April 1848, *Jane Eyre* had gone into a
third printing, and she had earned altogether £500, a not inconsiderable sum. There
had been the brackish taste of a few savage reviews, but there were more that had been
vociferous in their appreciation and enthusiasm. In July she had gone to London,
along with Anne, to visit her publishers and clear her name; for the unscrupulous
publisher of Emily's and Anne's novels, capitalizing on the success of *Jane Eyre*, was
proclaiming one of Anne's works as being by "Currer Bell." In London, Charlotte
Brontë became something of a reluctant lioness, honored by the eminent of the day.
Such triumphs could not mitigate the apprehensions with which she returned to the
parsonage. Branwell died in September; Emily in December, 1848. In the following
year Anne, too, was gone.

Sometimes she was near despair. "There must be a Heaven," she wrote to her pub-
lisher-friend William S. Williams, soon after Anne's death, "or we must despair—for
life seems bitter, brief—blank."[59]

Who, besides her ailing father, was there to share her many griefs?

She had, however, one refuge—what she called "the faculty of imagination." She
had a talent to safeguard and to exercise. "It is for me a part of my religion to defend
this gift and profit by its possession."[60] She had her work; and with customary re-
silience she rose to the occasion. Interrupted as she had been, and was, time and
again, she had managed to complete her second major novel, *Shirley*. It was published
in October 1849.

* * *

If the year 1848 was an anguished one in the Haworth vicarage, it was no less tumultuous and disruptive in the wide world outside. It was a year of revolutions which,
commencing in France in February, soon spread over all of Europe. An inveterate
Francophobe, Charlotte Brontë had little sympathy with the insurrectionary movement in France.

... Every struggle any nation makes in the cause of Freedom and Truth has something
noble in it—something that makes me wish it success; but I cannot believe that

France—or at least Paris—will ever be the battle-ground of Liberty, or the scene of its real triumphs ... Has Paris the materials within her for thorough reform?[61]

And in a letter to her old friend, Miss Wooler, in March of the same year:

... Convulsive revolutions put back the world in all that is good, check civilisation, bring the dregs of society to its surface—in short, it appears to me that insurrections and battles are the acute diseases of nations and that their tendency is to exhaust by their violence the vital energies of the countries where they occur. That England may be spared the spasms, cramps, and frenzy-fits now contorting the Continent and threatening Ireland, I earnestly pray! With the French and Irish I have no sympathy. With the Germans and Italians I think the case is different—as different as the love of freedom is from lust of license. ...[62]

Alas! England was not destined to be spared upheavals and violence. Charlotte Brontë undoubtedly remembered the stormy days in the 1830s when the working population of the country, depressed and aroused by a serious economic crisis, and in utter disenchantment with the Reform Bill of 1832 that left their great body utterly unfranchised, fashioned their so-called Chartist Petition for the Reform Bill and marched in thousands on Parliament. Now, once again, heartened by the events on the Continent, and once more in the midst of another economic depression that brought down their wages and increased unemployment, they began recovering from the defeats of the preceding decade. They pressed for their Charter, asking not only their rightful vote, but also a decisive role in determining their working condition and their life's destinies.

In setting about writing *Shirley*, Charlote Brontë took as her subject, locale and time, not the present upheavals or those of the eighteen-thirties, but rather the disturbances that had erupted in Nottinghamshire and Yorkshire in the years between 1811 and 1823.

Chartism had not yet been born then, nor had the rapid expansion of workers' organizations yet occurred. The industrial revolution was still in its incipient stages, although advanced enough to arouse serious discontents. New machines, steam-driven or driven by hand, had begun to make their way, and the displacement of the domestic weaving and spinning industry by the factory had already begun. Europe was in a state of war, and the reciprocal blockades were working havoc with the clothing industry. Those were years of extreme hardship, even hunger. Wages were being depressed. The domestic weaver, apprehensive of his doom, began agitating with ever greater violence against the factories and the new machinery. Under the legendary leadership of Capt. Nedd Ludd, the new "Robin Hood" of the weavers, and with his name on their lips, they banded together to redress their grievances, first in Nottinghamshire, then in the Yorkshire West Riding. Far from being the murderous mobs imagined by the panic-stricken citizens, the weavers worked in disciplined contingents. They had their printed appeals, songs, and broadsheets, such as proclaimed

Chant no more your old rhymes about Robin Hood,
His feats I but little admire.
I will sing the Achievements of General Ludd,
Now the Hero of Nottinghamshire. ...[63]

Or,

> Come all you cotton weavers, your looms you may pull down;
> You must get employ'd in factories, in country or in town.
> For our cotton-masters have found out a wonderful new scheme,
> These calico goods now wove by hand they're going to weave by steam.[64]

Such were the "Luddites," the so-called "machine-wreckers." They discriminated, records show, between the "good" and the "bad" masters, and they had numerous supporters in towns and villages, whose inhabitants often refused to reveal their identities. The equally depressed and aroused farmworkers vented their despair in the so-called "rick-burning" on farms and estates.

Charlotte Brontë was not unaware of the difficulties she faced in entering upon so complex a subject with what she herself recognized as insufficient knowledge.

As she wrote to her publisher W. S. Williams in January 1848,

> … Though I must limit my sympathies; though my observations cannot penetrate where the very deepest political and social truths are to be learnt … though I must guess and calculate and grope my way in the dark … yet with every disadvantage, I mean still, in my own contracted way, to do my best. Imperfect my best will be, and poor, as compared with the works of the true masters . .[65]

For the history of the Luddite struggle she used the contemporary accounts available in the *Leeds Mercury*, which she could obtain in the neighboring Keightly Library, as well as the oral recollections of her father, Miss Wooler, and various other witnesses, and her neighbors in the immediate surroundings.

The narrative centers on the Luddite uprising in April 1812. The woollen mill owned by William Cartwright at Rasfolds in the Spen Valley was attacked by 150 insurgents in an attempt to destroy the new shearing frames he had recently introduced into his factory. The attackers were foiled, there were a number of casualties, and William Cartwright became a kind of "hero" to the neighboring manufacturers and the local squirearchy. In pursuit of the rioters, the Rev. Hammond Robertson distinguished himself for his unremitting zeal in hounding out what he called the "vermin." In the novel he appears as the Rev. Matthewson Helstone, and Cartwright as Robert Gerard Moore. The remaining characters are drawn from Charlotte Brontë's immediate knowledge and vicinity. The Whig "radical" Taylor family became the Yorkes. Her own sisters are drawn upon in the principal female personalities.

Yet in another way she was embarking on a revolutionary change in her own writing. Hitherto, her novels had been "autobiographical"; the principal characters had been the narrators, and the personal "I" dominated the scenes. Such had been the case with *The Professor* and *Jane Eyre*. In *Shirley*, however, Charlotte Brontë is the omniscient authorial narrator, observer, and commentator. The canvas is broadened; the characters can be seen from the "outside" as well as from the "inside"; the viewpoints are multiple. In content, too, themes are multiplied and broadened to include the sociopolitical, the familial, and the clerical landscapes. Not that Charlotte's personal "self" completely disappears from the scene, for her own experiences in Brussels reappear, albeit in an utterly disguised manner. In addition, both her sisters, Anne and

Emily, emerge as the principal protagonists, highly idealized, as Caroline Helstone and Shirley Keeldar, respectively.

The style of the novel, too, shows an extraordinary diversification. The novel ranges all the way from the "satiric" and realistic to the poetical and lyrical, and even to what we might call the "mythical." Dialogue frequently alternates with "interior" monologue.

If the "drama" of *Shirley* is set in a distant 1812, a time of convulsions, the ideas are those of the Charlotte Brontë of 1848, and applicable, so far as she was concerned, to her own time. The multiple points of view allow her to enlarge the canvas; the world now is seen through the eyes of three principals, all women: Caroline Helstone, a young woman of 18; Shirley Keeldar, 21; and the author herself, through her own authorial comment.

Once more the usual polarities are established: polarities of characters, as in Caroline Helstone, impecunious niece of her uncle the Rev. Helstone, the embodiment of the "passive" but rebellious young woman, longing to escape from the "gray" Rectory; and Shirley, the "active" personality, now come of age and full heiress of a considerable estate that includes the factory owned by Robert Moore. The other polarities are those of clerical import, the "good" and the "black" shepherds and their service or neglect of service to their flocks; and not least important, the polarities now of immediate and urgent history: the conflict of the "mercantile" and the "landed" interests in a time of war and serious economic crisis, social upheaval and rioting.

Once again we find Nature and the "natural" human being at war with social convention, rigid conformity, blind authority; human individuality as against oppressive rigidity; feelings against repression. The book is in essence a vindication of the worth of the human being, the individual personality, and the need to safeguard its inner values against erosion and annihilation. The Rectory thus becomes symbolic of the prison, as is the matrimonial market that sets status, wealth, and social position above the heart's inclinations and needs. At the center stands the woman, and that is only natural; for she is the "natural" victim and "prisoner" in Victorian society.

The personal crisis and dilemma of Victorian womanhood may be said to be most sharply crystallized in the utterances of Caroline Helstone: "What was I created for? … What is my place in the world? … Does Virtue lie in abnegation of self? … I do not *live*. I endure existence …"

They are also expressed in the defense of Life, and one's personality, by youthful Rose Yorke, daughter of the Whig radical Hiram Yorke, the recollected image of Charlotte Brontë's friend Mary Taylor: "I am resolved that my life shall be a life, not a black trance like the toad's, buried in marble, nor a long slow death like yours in Briarfield Rectory." (This to Caroline.) And to her mother, who had observed that "solid satisfaction is only to be realized by doing one's duty," Rose objects:

> Right, mother! And if my Master has given me ten talents, my duty is to trade with them, and make then ten talents more. Not in the dust of household drawers shall the coin be interred. I will *not* deposit it in a broken-spouted teapot, and shut up in a china-closet among tea-things. I will *not* commit it to your work-table to be smothered in piles of woollen hose. I will *not* prison it in the linen-press to find shrouds among the sheets; and least of all, mother … least of all will I hide it in a tureen of cold potatoes, to be ranged with bread, butter, pastry and ham on the shelves of the larder … Mother, the

Lord who gave each of us our talents will come home some day, and will demand from all an account ... Suffer your daughters, at least, to put the money to the exchangers, that they may be enabled at the Master's coming to pay Him His own with usury.[66]

The real Mary Taylor acted upon her own injunction and went off to New Zealand.

The children of the Yorke family are fortunate that, save for their mother, they find responsive sympathy and hearing from their father, the well-to-do Yorkshire industrialist with radical Whig proclivities. But Caroline Helstone, one of the two chief protagonists of the novel, has no such fortunate court of appeal. Her uncle the Rev. Helstone is a hidebound Tory and a good exemplar of extreme Victorian male chauvinism. He has no understanding of the young woman who is sensitive and thoughtful, of her yearning for some sort of self-fulfilment, whether emotional or intellectual. He is a "man of bronze" who has no respect for women as such, or for their "weak female minds." He would have been (and this is not the first time such a clerical character is so characterized in Charlotte's novels) a soldier, or a huntsman.

> He thought, so long as a woman was silent, nothing ailed her, and she wanted nothing. If she did not complain of solitude, solitude, however continued, could not be irksome to her. If she did not talk, and put herself forward, express a partiality for this, and aversion to that, she had no partialities or aversions, and it was useless to consult her tastes. He made no pretence of comprehending women, or comparing them with men: they were a different, probably a very inferior, order of existence; a wife could not be her husband's companion, much less his confidant, much less his stay. ...[67]

Caroline's hesitant wish to become a governess offends his genteel, status-conscious soul. "While I live, you shall not turn out as a governess, Caroline. I will not have it said that my niece is a governess."

Barring marriage, what prospect lies before her? Spinsterhood and loneliness. As for marriage, dowerless as she is, there is not much hope. ... unless ... unless ... She is young, and beautiful, and very much in love with her cousin Robert Moore, owner of the adjacent woollen mill. At first hopeful, she soon despairs as she sets herself beside the wealthy young heiress Shirley. Her uncle's advice is scarcely a comfort:

> Stick to the needle—learn shirt-making, and gown-making, and pie-crust making, and you'll be a clever woman some day. Go to bed, now; I'm busy with a pamphlet here. ... Put all crotchets out of your head, and run away and amuse yourself."[68]

With Helstone's "air of a veteran officer," the author remarks, "Gospel mildness, apostolic benignity, never seemed to have breathed their influence over that keen brown visage."[69] He views marriage as a capital aberration.

Caroline is a devout Christian, and under such circumstances she cannot but feel she had been abandoned by God as doomed to eternal reprobation. She cannot believe that life's fulfilment can lie in abnegation of the self, that life's sole purposes can be satisfied in doing good to others and annihilating oneself.

Hers is a rebellion against Death and desiccation. Hers is an affirmation of the sacredness of Life and a purposeful existence.

> Is there not, she asks, a terrible hollowness, mockery, want, craving, in that existence which is given away to others for want of something of your own to bestow it on? I suspect there is. Does virtue lie in abnegation of self? I do not believe it.[70]

Was she merely a "poor doomed mortal" asking in vain why she was born and to what end she was living? Measuring time at the Rectory, not really living but "enduring" existence, what was there in this enclosed prison to satisfy "a famished heart"?

She addresses herself to the "Men of England" in tones that almost echo those of John Milton's *Areopagitica:*

> Men of England, look at your poor girls, many of them fading around you, dropping off in consumption or decline; or, what is worse, degenerating to sour old maids—envious, backbiting, wretched, because life is a desert to them ... Look at the numerous families of girls in this neighbourhood. ... The brothers of these girls are every one in business or in professions: they have something to do. Their sisters have no earthly employment, but household work and sewing, no earthly pleasure but an unprofitable visiting, and no hope, in all their life to come, of anything better. This stagnant state of things makes them decline in health; they are never well, and their minds and views shrink to wondrous narrowness ... What do they expect them to do at home? If you ask, they would answer, sew and cook ... as if they had not germs of faculties for anything else ... Could men live so themselves? ... God surely did not create us, and cause us to live with the sole end of wishing always to die. I believe in my heart we were intended to prize life and enjoy it, so long as we retain it. ...[71]

Caroline is Nature—embodiment of the "natural" woman, advocate of spontaneity, feeling, of the Self. "Untaught, intuitive, fitful, she is revolted by any denigration of Love, the blaspheming of what she calls the "living fire, seraph-brought from a Divine altar," and she is horrified by any denigration of marriage.[72]

If Caroline Helstone is the exemplification of "Nature" and what might paradoxically be called "passive" rebellion, Shirley Keeldar is "Nature" as an active element. Caroline is the imprisoned victim, incapable of realizing her potentialities, incapable of achieving the freedom she longs for, fettered as she is by both family ties and her economic dependence. The best she can hope for is the "freedom" of a subordinate governess. But even that is denied her by her status-conscious uncle. Where, then, is her emancipation to come from? There is only one person around her who would understand her true feelings and her plight. That is Shirley. In Shirley's company she find herself as an equal.

Shirley stands for power. She has the capacities generally attributed to men. Her name is in fact masculine, for her parents had hoped for a son, and instead . . . . She is twenty-one, and has come into her estate. She is, as she says, "landed proprietor and lord of the manor." She alludes to herself as a "gentleman," and she even whistles! She is fearless and independent. But she, too, in spite of all her advantages, is seeking to find meaning to her existence. And like Caroline she is a rebel—against constrictions, against the falseness of conventional life, against the repression of feelings and thought.

Louis Moore, a brother of the manufacturer, and her former tutor, thus describes her to herself:

> There is not a shoulder in England on which you would rest your hand for support—far less a bosom which you would permit to pillow your head. Of course, you must live alone.[73]

But above all, she rebels against the dominant conception of womanhood entertained by society, the derogation of woman, and particularly the traditional vilification of our first Mother, Eve. Bitterly, she reproaches the poet John Milton for the role he assigns the first of created woman in *Paradise Lost*. In a highly poetic, often rhapsodic apostrophe, she places Eve among the Titans: The passage is one of the most eloquent, and indeed one of the boldest that Charlotte Brontë ever wrote. The Sunday church bells are summoning both Caroline and Shirley to church, but Shirley insists on remaining in the open, and to Caroline's dismay, declaims a paean to Nature instead. Her devotion will be of a different strain:

> … Here I must stay. … Nature is now at her evening prayers; she is kneeling before those red hills. I see her prostrate on the great steps of her altar, praying for a fair night for mariners at sea, for travellers in deserts, for lambs on moors, and unfledged birds in woods. Caroline, I see her, and will tell you what she is like: she is like what Eve was when she and Adam stood alone on earth.

As Caroline interposes: "And that is not Milton's Eve, Shirley."

> Milton's Eve! Milton's Eve, I repeat! No, by the pure Mother of God, she is not! Cary, we are alone: we may speak what we think. Milton was great; but was he good? His brain was right; how was his heart? … Milton tried to see the first woman; but, Cary, he saw her not … It was his cook that he saw … I would beg to remind him that the first men of the earth were Titans, and that Eve was their mother: from her sprang Saturn, Hyperion, Oceanus; she bore Prometheus … I say there were giants on the earth in those days— giants that strove to scale heaven. The first woman's breast that heaved with life on this world yielded the daring which could contend with Omnipotence … The first woman was heaven-born. Vast was the heart whence gushed the well-spring of the blood of nations; and grand the undegenerate head where rested the consort-crown of creation … That Eve is Jehovah's daughter, as Adam was His son.

And in response to Caroline's insistence that they go into the Church:

> Caroline, I will not; I will stay here with my mother Eve, in these days called Nature … Heaven may have faded from her brow when she fell in Paradise, but all that is glorious on earth shines there still …

Such was Shirley's "Titan vision," and one does not wonder that Caroline dubs her a "Pagan."[74]

Her vision is indeed "Pagan"—a worship of Nature as primal goddess—and Eve as a primal deity, none other than grand Nature herself. At a far remove from Milton's "snare,"[75] Eve is here rehabilitated womanhood.

The unrest within them is paralleled by the turbulence of their outside world. Far and wide the Luddite agitation is threatening the mills and their masters. The new shears and frames that were being transported for Robert Moore's factory have been waylaid and destroyed, and soon his very mill is threatened with attack. Both Caroline Helstone and Shirley are involved in Moore's fortunes: Caroline because she is in love with her cousin, and Shirley as proprietor of the land on which the factory is built. Both witness from a distance the attack and the resistance, each with her own emotional reference and emotional investment.

For Caroline the struggle is a heroic contest between good and evil, a knightly tilting against maleficent forces, a combat seen through a haze:

A crash—smash—shiver— ... A simultaneously hurled volley of stones had saluted the broad front of the mill, with all its windows; and now every pane of every lattice lay in shattered and pounded fragments. A yell followed this demonstration—a rioters' yell—a North-of-England—a Yorkshire—a West-Riding—a West-Riding-clothing-district-of-Yorkshire rioters' yell. You never heard that sound, perhaps, reader? So much the better for your ears—perhaps for your heart; since, if it rends the air in hate to yourself, or to the men or principles you approve, the interests to which you wish well. Wrath wakens to the cry of Hate; the Lion shakes his mane, and rises to the howl of the Hyena: Caste stands up, ireful against Caste; and the indignant, wronged spirit of the Middle Rank bears down in zeal and scorn on the famished and furious mass of the Operative class. It is difficult to be tolerant—difficult to be just—in such moments.[76]

Caroline is ready to go to Robert Moore's aid. "I would help him," she says to Shirley, and the latter, more levelheaded and less sentimental:

"How? By inspiring him with heroism? Pooh! These are not the days of chivalry: it is not a tilt at a tournament we are going to behold, but a struggle about money, and food, and life."

"It is natural that I should be at his side."

"As queen of his heart? His mill is his lady-love, Cary! Backed by his factory and his frames, he has all the encouragement he wants or can know. It is not for love or beauty, but for the ledger and broad-cloth, he is going to break a spear. Don't be sentimental; Robert is not so."[77]

The attack is repelled; there is gunfire, and six of the assailants are injured, one fatally. None of the defenders suffers appreciable harm ...

The true implications of the Luddite clashes, that incipient class-struggle that the poet Shelley had understood so clearly and that in time would have such a determining influence on English society, escapes Shirley, as it did the author herself. But they do understand the nature of the economic crisis besetting the country, the way in which England's war against Napoleon and the consequent blockades are damaging the interests of the commercial and industrial classes, represented by the Whig opposition, that desired an end of the war and sought a change of government. They also sought the abolition of the restrictive Corn Laws that worked in favor of the agricultural squirearchy by keeping up prices, raising the cost of bread. The fall of wages, unemployment and even hunger, the introduction of more efficient machinery into the factories, were the sparks that finally flamed into violent response on the part of the lower orders.

The failure to penetrate into the meaning of the struggles is reflected in Shirley's (and Charlotte Brontë's) attribution of the insurgence to a few rabblerousers, to a disreputable and degenerate leadership, and to their misunderstanding of the organization of the various groups of agitators and insurgents. Thus the spokesman for the local Luddites, Moses Barraclaugh, is a one-legged tailor, a "Methodee," a crapulous and ranting "hypocrite"; another agitator, Michael Hartley (the man who later shoots Moore), is a "half-crazed weaver ... a frantic Antinomian in religion, and a mad leveller in politics."[78] That the insurrectionists were moved by moral as well as social and economic considerations, that many of them were devout dissenters with considerable understanding of the issues, is completely overlooked.

Shirley lectures the radical Whig manufacturer, who is anti-government, anti-Church hierarchy, and a near-republican, on his extremism:

> All ridiculous, irrational crying up of one class, whether the same be aristocrat or democrat—all howling down of another class, whether clerical or military—all exacting injustice to individuals, whether monarch or mendicant—is really sickening to me: all arraying of ranks against ranks, all party hatred, all tyrannies disguised as liberties, I reject and wash my hands of ... *You* think you are a philanthropist; *you* think you are an advocate of liberty; but I will tell you this—Mr. Hall, the parson of Nunnely, is a better friend both of man and freedom than Hiram Yorke, the Reformer of Briarfield.[79]

Shirley is forthright and honest in her consciousness of her own class-interests as an aristocrat, landowner, and factory owner. She is generous, and has aided the mill owner Moore through this hard period. She is benevolent in recognizing the plight of the suffering poor and unemployed. She is charitable, and believes that benevolence and philanthropy are the ultimate cure for the evils generated by the incipient industrial system. But she will not stand for "ruffian defiance," and she will resist it with all her power. Her ideal "working-man" is William Farren, who has lost his factory job:

> He had the aspect of a man who had not known what it was to live in comfort and plenty for weeks, perhaps months past: and yet there was no ferocity, no malignity, in his countenance: it was worn, dejected, austere, but still patient.[80]

Yet this was the man who just a while before had been brusquely rebuffed by manufacturer Moore, with whom he had pleaded to go slow on the replacement of machinery; this was the man whose family was starving! ... And Shirley's favorite clergyman, the Rev. Mr. Hall, who is all sympathy for Farren and his family, and offers him some financial help, has no better counsel for the unemployed man and his plight that to say, "Sad times ... And they last long. It is the will of God: His will be done! But He tries us to the utmost."

Charlotte Brontë, we may guess, had little knowledge of what went on in the factories, and it is with a certain startling surprise at her naïveté that we read her description of the children's morning procession to work in Mr. Moore's plant. Remember, it is six o'clock in the morning:

> ... The mill windows were alight, the bell still rung loud, and now the little children came running in, in too great a hurry, let us hope, to feel very much nipped by the inclement air. And, indeed, by contrast, perhaps the morning appeared rather favourable to them, than otherwise, for they had often come to work that winter through snowstorms, through heavy rains, through hoarfrost."[81]

Charlotte Brontë might have overlooked that she was describing a situation that was occurring before the 1830s, that is, before the passage of a law that restricted children's employment to 48 hours a week; those above 13, to 68 hours! And that it was not until 1850 that a ten-hour law affecting women and young persons was passed! And that the little ones in 1811 and 1812, whether they worked in their home cottages or in the mills, were kept from early dawn to sunset and beyond. She feels satisfied that "neither Mr. Moore nor his overseer ever struck a child in their mill. ... The novelist may be excused from sullying his page" with a record of the deeds of "child-torturers, slave-masters and drivers" ...

> It was eight o'clock; the children released for half an hour from toil, betook themselves to the little cans which held their coffee, and to the small baskets which contained their allowance of bread. Let us hope they have enough to eat; it would be a pity otherwise.

It is not that either Shirley or her author is in favor of the machine industry or its masters. Both of them are violent in their feelings about the new industrialism as well as the "mercantile spirit" which has taken hold of their country.

Here is Charlotte Brontë speaking in her own voice:

> All men, taken singly, are more or less selfish, and taken in bodies they are intensely so. The British merchant is no exception to this rule; the mercantile classes illustrate it strikingly. These classes certainly think too exclusively of making money; they are too oblivious of every national consideration but that of extending England's (*i.e.*, their own) commerce. Chivalrous feeling, disinterestedness, pride in honour, is too dead in their hearts. A land ruled by them alone would too often make ignominious submission—not at all from the motives Christ teaches, but rather from those Mammon instills ... Whoever is not in trade is accused of eating the bread of idleness, of passing a useless existence. Long may it be ere England really becomes a nation of shopkeepers![82]

And her heroine, Shirley, has her own bitter experience at the hand of the "mercantile" Robert Moore, whom she admires, and whom she has helped financially. Hard-headed and cool in the advancement of his threatened establishment, he sues for the hand of the wealthy Shirley, frankly professing his objective. She, who is fond of him though not in love, is horrified:

> "You have made a strange proposal—strange from *you*; and if you knew how strangely you worded it, and looked it, you would be startled at yourself. You spoke like a brigand who demanded my purse, rather than like a lover who asked my heart ... You want to make a speculation of me! you would immolate me to that mill—your Moloch![83]

Shopkeepers, Mammon and Moloch! Incipient industrialism and the mercantile establishment have rarely been so upbraided!

Shirley is a Tory, yet a rebel. Now, having come of age, she can declare her independence of the taboos and proscriptions of her class. In that respect she offers defiance to her own class, particularly in the matter of marriage. She will not marry for rank, status or greater wealth. Like Caroline she affirms the mandates of the heart, the sanctity of Love. Defying her uncle and former guardian Mr. Sympson, she rejects the proposal that she make a "brilliant" match with the aristocratic Sir Philip Nunnely. Her ideal of marriage is shockingly different from his:

> I walk, she says, by another creed, light, faith, and hope than you ... an infidel to your religion; an atheist to your god. Your god, sir, is the World. In my eyes, you too, if not an infidel, are an idolater ... Sir, your god, your great Bel, your fish-tailed Dagon rises before me as a demon ... Behold how hideously he governs! See him busied at the work he likes best—making marriages. He binds the young to the old, the strong to the imbecile ... He

fetters the dead to the living … Your god is a masked Death! … My heart, my conscience shall dispose of my hand—*they only* …[84]

Pursuant to her feelings—her heart—she accepts the indigent former tutor of the Sympson household as her betrothed, and later as husband. The outraged Sympsons break all ties with her. The tutor is none other than Louis Moore, a brother of Robert Moore, whose confession of love for Shirley, with all its prior uncertainties, hopes, and despairs, is contained in a series of notebooks, unmailed letters, and interior monologs in which he fights out his inner emotional battles. Thus, once again, Charlotte Brontë's unforgettable Brussels love for M. Heger, that tenacious obsession, is recapitulated—but, as in *The Professor*, with a reversal of roles. If it is the man Louis Moore who is writing, it is Charlotte Brontë the woman who is guiding his pen, with all her affection, diffidence, and doubts. This time, fantasy ordains success for her imaginary characters …

If Shirley is affirmative womanhood, Nature and Eve, assertive Nature and Freedom, brave in her acceptance of the lowly tutor as betrothed and bridegroom, she is also the embodiment of Power—a power derived from wealth, which enables her to engage in an active life and exercise her philanthropies toward the less fortunate of her neighbors. Through humane benevolence and charity she hopes to mitigate the injustices of her society. She is Power because she has Money, just as Caroline is helpless because she lacks it. Yet for all her affirmation of the Titanism of Mother Eve, and her manifesto of emancipation from traditional detraction, Shirley stops short of complete self-emancipation, of the assertion of woman's equality with man. Even the superior woman needs a "master." In an exchange with her hidebound uncle, she describes the kind of man she would choose—one that would be her "master."

> I will accept no hand which cannot hold me in check … Did I not say I prefer a *master*? One in whose presence I shall feel obliged and disposed to be good. One whose control my impatient temper must acknowledge. A man whose approbation can reward—whose displeasure punish me. A man I shall feel it impossible not to love, and very possible to fear.[85]

Untamed Shirley is referred to repeatedly in Louis Moore's "little blank book"—his confessional—as a "leopardess," "pantheress," "lioness"—a wild and beautiful animal, perverse, unpredictable, capricious. But she will eventually bow to her "keeper." In condescending to her tutor, she is indeed "rising." She is willing to be tamed by a stronger, wiser hand. The relationship hitherto existing between pupil and master is thus symbolically and actually now extended, as each of them achieves "freedom." He abjures his tutorship, and she, her rank and wealth:

> "Mr. Moore," said she, looking up with a sweet, open, earnest countenance [the reader must remember it is Louis Moore who is recording the incident], "teach me and help me to be good … Be my companion through life; be my guide where I am ignorant; be my master where I am faulty; be my friend always."

Charlotte Brontë's authorial benevolence brings the novel to a fortunate close. Despite the Rev. Helstone's cynical warnings about marriage, Caroline weds Robert Moore. In defiance of her uncle, Shirley marries a tutor. Robert Moore, reformed mill-owner, learns charity, and plans to build new factories in the region and replace rural beauty and greenness with cottages for laborers, and with mills and their mill stacks (much to the annoyance of the author of the book). Troubled times fade into the background. The personal element triumphs over the social, as a number of rioters are either transported overseas or hanged. ...

Yet in spite of these accommodations, the novel did not escape serious censure. Both the publishers and a number of reviewers (the *Times* being preeminent) asserted that "Currer Bell" had been uncommonly brash, if not utterly blasphemous, in his treatment of the clerical establishment, particularly in his satirical and quite impious treatment of the local curates. That practically the author's whole life had been spent in the vicinity of those worthies, and that she knew them as few of the critics did, did not matter. That each of of the personalities so sharply delineated in the book had his prototype in reality—that, too, did not matter.

It is true, the poor curates got short shrift at Charlotte Brontë's hand. They are described as "shuffling"; they exploit the hospitality of their hosts, come to tea and dinner in droves, frequently even unannounced; they are demanding and, worst of all, indulge in backbiting, are intolerant of other sects, and disparage one another.

As Shirley remarks to Hiram Yorke,

> When I hear Messrs. Malone and Donne chatter about the authority of the Church, the dignity and claims of the priesthood, the deference due to them as clergymen; when I hear the outbreaks of their small spite against Dissenters; when I witness their silly, narrow jealousies and assumptions; when their palaver about forms, and traditions, and superstitions is sounding in my ear; when I behold their insolent carriage to the poor, their often base servility to the rich, I think the Establishment is indeed in a poor way, and both she and her sons appear in the utmost need of reformation."[86]

But they are not all of them a bad lot! There are the devoted shepherds like Mr. Hall and others like him, but for whom the Church of England would be in a sad state indeed. "Britain would miss her Church if that Church fell. God save it! God also reform it!"[87]

To her critics, Charlotte Brontë responded with courage.

To her friendly publishers, who had remonstrated with her that her critical attitude toward the Church might offend many readers, not to mention the Church establishment itself, she replied:

> ... What you say with reference to the first chapter shall be duly weighed. At present I feel reluctant to withdraw it, because, as I formerly said of the Lowood part of *Jane Eyre*, *it is true*. ... I should like you to explain to me more fully the ground of your objections. Is it because you think this chapter will render the work liable to severe handling by the press? Is it because knowing as you now do the identity of "Currer Bell," this scene strikes you as unfeminine? Is it because it is intrinsically defective and inferior? I am afraid the two first reasons would not weigh with me—the last would ...[88]

She will write, she insists time and again, without considering "what is elegant and charming in femininity."—"I must have my own way in the matter of writing."[89]

How could they understand that writing had been her salvation during the years of indescribable distress and grief; her affirmation of independence from Time and

Death; in fact her transformation of Death into Life—the life of Caroline and Shirley—both of them transfigurations and heightened reinvocations of her sisters Anne and Emily; her way of saying Aye to Life itself, in the zestful, humor she lavished along with satire on the curates; her rebellion and wrath against the Rev. Helstone and the high-handed and low-minded family of the Sympsons; and her own frustrated affective life sublimated in the ultimately happy union of Caroline with Robert Moore, and of Shirley with Louis Moore? She had built happy monuments for her two sisters, without mawkishness or bathos, and enshrined courageous and outspoken womanhood as titanic Eve.

Shirley as a work of art is obviously flawed—flawed, in the first place, because the canvas is too large and too broad; too immense for the "parochialism" of its author to master. The world is viewed from the narrow vantage grounds upon which both Caroline Helstone and Shirley Keeldar stand—the self-occlusive, the personal. They are both protesters against the enslavement of woman, but neither (and that includes Charlotte Brontë herself) can see that such enslavement is bound up with the society which includes not only the dominant male, but also the Luddite incursion into the life of Yorkshire. Thus, resolutions are entirely individual and personal: Caroline's problem is revolved by marriage; Shirley's larger concerns, by both marriage and philanthropy. Shirley is able to "act" where the less opulent Caroline moves "passively," because Shirley has money and Caroline does not. Louis Moore, the poor tutor who is in love with "freedom"—as he so fervently proclaims—attains to it by marrying into wealth, so that he too can turn from the "passive" into the "active." Robert Moore, now reformed, and with the economic crisis over, will convert the countryside into ideal factories, ideal housing for the operatives; he will put "justice" above self-interest ...

As for the "woman" question, Charlotte Brontë has perhaps given us the clearest of her views in one of her letters, redolent of a quietism, if not utter pessimism, for which she was sharply reprimanded by her militant friend Mary Taylor, who was making a new life for herself in New Zealand:

Here is Charlotte Brontë to her publisher, W.S. Williams:

> I often wish to say something about the "condition of women" question, but it is one respecting which so much "cant" has been talked, that one feels a sort of repugnance to approach it. It is true enough that the present market for female labour is quite overstocked, but where or how could another be opened? Many say that the professions now filled only by men should be open to women also; but are not their present occupants and candidates more than enough to answer every demand? Is there any room for female lawyers, female doctors, female engravers, for more female artists, more authoresses? One can see where the evil lies, but who can point out the remedy? When a woman has a family to rear and educate and a household to conduct, her hands are full, her vocation is evident; when her destiny isolates her, I suppose she must do what she can, complain as little, bear as much, work as well as possible ... At the same time, I conceived that when patience has done its utmost and industry its best, whether in the case of women or operatives, and when both are baffled, and pain and want triumph, the sufferer is free, is entitled, at last to send up to Heaven any piercing cry of relief, if by that cry he can hope to obtain succour.[90]

* * *

> So stood I, in Heaven's glorious sun
> And in the glare of Hell—
> My Spirit drank a mingled tone
>   Of seraph's song and demon's moan—
>   What my soul bore my soul alone
>   Within itself could tell.
>
>   —Emily Brontë

It seems almost incredible that a household like that of the Brontës, with all the intimacy that bound its members together, should still have been marked by secrecy and mystery. As sisters and brother had once been secret collaborators on the juvenile *Angria* narratives, so too in their maturity they harbored their own secrets. These included nothing less than their creative works. Thus the father, the Rev. Patrick Brontë, was not aware that he had major novelists and poets in his house, whose works had achieved publication—until he was so informed. And it was only by sheer accident that Charlotte Brontë discovered that her sister Emily had been composing numerous poems. In 1845 Charlotte set about getting these published, along with poetry by herself and her sister Anne. They appeared in 1846 under the pseudonyms of "Currer," "Ellis," and "Acton Bell." And in 1847 there was cause for rejoicing when novels by the three sisters saw the light: *Jane Eyre* by Charlotte, *Wuthering Heights* by Emily, and *Agnes Gray* by Anne, all of them under their assumed names. But whatever their joys, and their reclusive father's total surprise, during the following years these were to be heavily paid for, almost as if some malignant spirit was hovering over the rectory and demanding retribution. The father was losing his sight. The brother, Branwell, was living through a self-inflicted decline in both body and mind, a hapless victim of alcohol and opium. Death struck three times: between September 1848 and January 1849, Branwell, Emily, and Anne died. After attending Branwell's interment on October 1, 1848, Emily caught cold, and on December 19, she died. Anne died early the following year. At their deaths Branwell was thirty-one years old, Anne was twenty-nine, and Emily thirty.

The "secret" of Emily Brontë's interior life will probably never be resolved. Whatever documentary material existed at one time has, with very few exceptions, disappeared, or was destroyed by Charlotte herself. In Emily's case we unfortunately do not have letters that might have supplied us with a partial key, as do those of Charlotte. The few scraps of self-revelation we have from Emily only tease us into sad reflection on how much we are indeed missing. Left to surmises, we must turn, for even a partial comprehension, to her poetry, to *Wuthering Heights*, and here and there to Charlotte herself.

"Bleak solitudes" (Emily own words) might be said to describe Emily's self-enclosed existence. Within that solitude she lived a strangely tormented and excited life—a life of the imagination. Whatever her living experiences of the outer world, such as her brief tenure as governess or teacher or her stay in Brussels as a student; whatever she was able to gather in the talk of the Haworth household, servants' tales or gossip, and not least, from reading; could only form a small element in her life of imagination. Such life was expansive and daring. It supplied the needed surrogates for her creative activity, her poetry and her novel. Here it was that she could tread strange and even dangerous paths—paths that no doubt startled, alarmed, and perhaps even appalled Charlotte.

When Emily spoke of the "mingled tone of seraph's song and demon's moan," she revealed a dualism, a dichotomy, which seems to have haunted her throughout life. When still very young, she gave evidence of heterodox thinking about the universe. While at school in Brussels, she wrote a French essay on butterflies which, we may be sure, must have startled M. Héger, her Catholic master.

The essay was entitled "*Le Papillon*"—"The Butterfly." Actually it is a kind of confession of faith, the full meaning of which is conveyed in its conclusion, when she addresses the butterfly directly: "*Mais pourquoi m'adresser à toi seul?*" she asks.

> Why do I address myself to you alone? All of creation is equally unfeeling. The flies above the brook, the swallows and fish diminish their number every minute; and they in turn become the prey of some tyrant of the air or of water. And man for his amusement or his necessities kills their murderers. Nature is an inexplicable problem. She exists on the principle of destruction: either all beings become an indefatigable instrument of death of others; or they cease to live themselves. And yet we celebrate our day of birth, and we praise the Lord for allowing us to come into the world. ... I am almost in doubt as to the goodness of God, for not having destroyed man on the day of his creation. ... However, a voice within me speaks: Let no human creature judge His Creation; for just as the caterpillar is the origin of a splendid butterfly, so is the globe the embryo of a new heaven and a new earth, whose least beauty will exceed the human imagination. ... God is the God of justice and mercy.[91]

Thus she tries to escape from a profound pessimism, taking refuge in the assurance of some ultimate divine justice that would somehow resolve the world's and nature's unending warfare.

Like Goethe's Faust, she nurtured "two souls" within her breast, one striving upward, the other drawn downward. Within Emily, there was this warping sense of inner "corruption" that threatened perdition and doom (undoubtedly an inheritance from her Calvinist aunt Branwell); the other, the rebel soul, revolted by such doctrine. Already, in an earlier poem she had spoken unmistakably of her inner feeling and especially her sense of isolation:

> I am the only being whose doom
> No tongue would ask, no eye would mourn;
> I never caused a thought of gloom,
> A smile of joy, since I was born.
>
> In secret pleasure, secret tears,
> This changeful life has slipped away,
> As friendless after eighteen years,
> As lone as on my natal day.

And she concludes:

> And then experience told me truth
> In mortal bosoms never grew.

> 'Twas grief enough to think mankind
> All hollow, servile, insincere;
> But worse to trust to my own mind,
> And find the same corruption there.[92]

She had always been something of a stranger even in her own family, a kind of resident "outsider," even though she took part in the household duties and actually enjoyed them. Stubborn, proud, fearless yet morbidly timid, she was rarely seen in the streets of Haworth, and its inhabitants scarcely knew that she existed.

Her vision of the world darkened with the years. As she looked up at the heaven of "glorious spheres ... rolling on its course of light in eternal bliss," she expressed the hope that at least on high there might exist a world where Love and Virtue were not besmirched and betrayed, where Truth did not war in vain against Treachery, where Life was not a "labour void and brief," ruled by Death, "despot of the whole." Perhaps there, too, was a realm where humankind was not the victim of an inexorable, merciless Fatality, holding sway through "relentless laws that disallow virtue and true joy down below."[93]

Like Charlotte, she recoiled from their aunt's rigid Calvinism, with its dread of eternal damnation for the many, the doom of reprobation, and its proclaimed salvation for the "few."

> And say not that my early tomb
> Will give me to a darker doom:
> Shall these long, agonising years
> Be punished by eternal tears?
>
> No; *that* I feel can never be;
> A God of *hate* could hardly bear
> To watch through all eternity
> His own creations' dread despair. ...
>
> If I have sinned, long, long ago
> That sin was purified by woe.[94]

Such then her world! a theatre of woe, with Death an ever-present reality. As she looked out of the windows of the parsonage, there it was, engraved on the gravestones in endless rows. In 1841 she wrote a death-haunted poem, in some ways her most touching:

> I see around me tombstones grey,
> Stretching their shadows far away. ...

And, reflecting on the "torments, and madness, and tears and sin" that lay buried there, she contends that Heaven itself, and its fortunate children, those blessed ones, could never understand the sufferings that bow down mortal man and woman. And even more daringly, in near-pagan tones, she insists that it is only Earth, mother of us here, who alone understands and compassionates them fully. Earth has no wish for any one else to share her misery. And she addresses her:

> Indeed, no dazzling land above
> Can cheat thee of thy children's love. ...

> We would not leave our native home
> For *any* world beyond the Tomb;
> No—rather on thy kindly breast
> Let us be laid in lasting rest;
> Or waken but to share with thee
> A mutual immortality.[95]

Exultantly, defiantly, she cries out,

> I know our souls are all divine:
> I know that when we die,
> What seems the vilest, even like thine
> A part of God himself shall shine
> In perfect purity. ...[96]

What havens of refuge then for herself? And what solace for a world so woefully afflicted?

For herself there were two havens: the Mind or Imagination; and Nature. There was also a third—Death; and the death wish was often with her:

> O for the time when I shall sleep
> Without identity,
> And never care how rain may steep
> Or snow may cover me.[97]

For the living Emily, it was the Mind, the Imagination—her Mind, and her Imagination—that formed the sacred retreats where she found the Freedom she was seeking. Here she could create her own world, a world of vividness and reality. Here she could revel in all the exaltations of self-knowledge and creation. And the other refuge, Nature, too, was a secure habitation. Here, like some pagan deity, she could roam. The moors were her pastures of freedom.

Imagination is her "God of Visions." It is her "slave ... comrade and King." And she speaks to that "god":

> So hopeless is the world without,
> The world within I doubly prize ...
> Where thou and I and Liberty
> Have undisputed sovereignty.[98]
>
> And am I wrong to worship where
> Faith cannot doubt nor Hope despair,
> Since my own soul can grant my prayer:
> Speak, God of Visions, plead for me
> And tell why I have chosen thee![99]

As for Nature,

> I'll walk where my own nature would be leading:
> It vexes me to choose another guide:
> Where the grey flocks in ferny glens are feeding;
> Where the wild wind blows on the mountain side.

> What have these lonely mountains worth revealing?
> More glory and more grief than I can tell:
> The *earth* that wakes *one* human heart to feeling
> Can centre both the worlds of Heaven and Hell.[100]

Such, too, Emily's "secret." The poems offer the best clues to her novel *Wuthering Heights.*

* * *

After Emily's death, Charlotte Brontë wrote a preface to the reissued edition of *Wuthering Heights.* What emerged was more an apologia than an illumination. Charlotte was nonplussed by what she termed the "rough utterance, the harsh manifested passions, the unbridled inversions, the headlong partialities of unlettered hinds and rugged moorland squires." What would readers make of this "horror of great darkness" that broods over so much of *Wuthering Heights?* She was baffled by the character of Heathcliff. "Whether it is right or advisable to create beings like Heathcliff, I do not know," she wrote. "I scarcely think it is." In her eyes he appeared like some "magnate of the infernal world."

Dismayed, Charlotte sought to explain Emily's creation as the product of some unconscious or subconscious driving force that her sister could not control—a sort of demonic presence that took possession, breaking through all rational restraints—and that propelled the central characters, in the novel, Catherine Earnshaw and Heathcliff, toward each other, and toward Death. How often, in her own life, had not Charlotte herself called upon Reason to restrain and curb her own dangerous feelings! In her sister's novel she found an insupportable glorification of Passion as a redemptive power. Where, she wondered, could this maelstrom have come from? It was scarcely surprising that a number of reviewers of the book viewed it as a product of a wild, barbarous imagination.

Scholars have tried to trace the literary sources of *Wuthering Heights* in Emily's far-ranging reading, say, of Byron, George Sand, Sir Walter Scott, and the very popular contemporary novels of "terror"—the so-called "Gothic" romances of such writers as Mrs. Ann Radcliffe, Matthew Gregory Lewis, author of the notorious *Monk*, or the tales of the German writer E. T. A. Hoffmann.

Setting aside all these possible derivations, *Wuthering Heights* is a consciously developed, original entity, the product of a thoughtful mind and a rich imagination, embodying the writer's emotional and metaphysical outlook in a superbly constructed action containing all the elements and inevitability of true tragedy. Critics have remarked how carefully Emily Brontë ordered the chronology of events, and with what precision she treated such details as land tenure and inheritance.[101]

What was no doubt to shock early readers of the novel, and is striking even today, is the element of violence that dominates the narrative from its beginning almost to its very end, a violence that is set against the physical background of the rugged Yorkshire moors. *Wuthering Heights* is well named, the local term "wuthering" being suggestive of storm and tumult. The very first scene sets the ultimate tone of the novel: strangeness, gruffness, and disorder. The narrative has a double structure: an outer "scrim," which serves to frame the inner retrospect or flashback that is the central core of the book. We begin in the year 1801, that is, when what we like to call the "drama" is over. The action really commences in 1771. In 1801, Mr. Lockwood, the new tenant of Thrushcross Grange, visits its owner, Mr. Heathcliff of Wuthering Heights. Thereafter we move back to 1771, through the second "scrim," as the story unfolds through the narration of the principal *raisonneur*, Nelly Dean, the housekeeper. Nelly Dean has the great advantage of having lived long enough to be a member of two households. From childhood to the very end she has been an eyewitness of all significant happenings.

At the opening, Mr. Lockwood meets the raw and powerful figure of Heathcliff; his daughter-in-law, the younger Catherine Heathcliff, née Linton; and the strange wild young Hareton Earnshaw, son of Hindley Earnshaw, once owner of Wuthering Heights. Mr. Lockwood encounters a weird and disorderly household.

Forced by a snowstorm to remain overnight, Mr. Lockwood, through a perusal of her handwritten notes in books and in an Old Testament, becomes aware of another Catherine. While asleep, he has a nightmare vision: the long-dead Catherine Linton, née Earnshaw, appears at the window, pitifully pleads for admittance, and is brutally shut out by the dreamer. When on the following morning Heathcliff is told of this experience, he gives way to a frenzied outbreak. Such is our prologue to the entire story which, a short time later, Mr. Lockwood is enabled to obtain in full from the lips of Nelly Dean, a simple woman, housekeeper at Thrushcross. Not only has she been both participant and onlooker, but she is endowed with a somewhat startling memory. She is levelheaded, though superstitious and full of premonitions. The full import of what has happend is beyond her. This is wisely left to the reader.

The novel has, as we have suggested, all the elements of a classical tragedy. It has a "tragic error" with all its unfailing consequences, and moves toward a *dénouement* and a final restoration—"all passion spent." The drama is staged against the self-enclosed world of Yorkshire. The outside world exists physically only as if by hearsay. We live for a time in an enclave of thoughts, feeling and actions, segregated like Emily Brontë's own world, yet always aware of wider implications—almost cosmic in character. It is a little world full of wide contentions, physical, psychological, and even social.

* * *

What is central to *Wuthering Heights* is warfare, manifesting itself in the spiritual as well as the material realm—a war between Nature and Social Convention; a war between the "natural" in man or woman against the conventional social order; a war between the "non-possessor" and the "possessor." It is a war between Power and Weakness, of Life against Death, and in the moral order, Integrity of the Heart against Corruption. In the fierceness of the combat there is something that suggests an element of the "demonic" in the participating characters.

The struggle begins when Mr. Earnshaw, head of a farming family, on returning from a business trip to Liverpool, brings back with him a young boy, a "waif"—nameless, homeless, emaciated—whom he found wandering in the streets of the city. He had been moved by compassion for the "swarthy" child, who seemed to belong to another race. The boy is given the single name of Heathcliff and no Christian first name, as if to underline his role in life—the unpossessed and the unpossessing outsider. More ominously, he is seen by Mr. Earnshaw and, more insistently, by Nelly

Dean, as harboring within him something of the demonic. The one-year-old Catherine Earnshaw is drawn to this outsider in a kind of conspiracy of identities. For she too is something of an outsider in the family, already a rebel, insubordinate, wayward, capricious, and capable of both cruelty and sympathy. Catherine is a mystery to her father and to those around her. She is as complex as she is beautiful. In the household, Catherine and Heathcliff have two enemies: the sanctimonious servant Joseph, and Catherine's older brother Hindley, who resents the intruder and "usurper" and perpetrates various acts of cruelty against him; surreptitiously while the father is alive, and outrageously and inhumanly when he falls heir to Wuthering Heights. Nelly Dean is and remains ambivalent, suspicious and premonitory, as she watches Cathy, who in her eyes "was too much fond of Heathcliff."[102] Now and then she is inclined to sympathize with Heathcliff when she sees him humiliated, abused, and eventually reduced to the status of a servant. But on the whole she perceives in him an element of the diabolic.[103] Her commonplace mind cannot, of course, gauge the true natures of Catherine and Heathcliff or penetrate into the mystery of their reciprocal attraction. Nor can she perceive the "demonic" element in Catherine herself. They are both "children of Nature" akin to the Yorkshire moors, which have become their true homes. Here they roam like wild native creatures, sharing nature's wildness and terrors, as well as her beauty.

It is on one of those wandering expeditions that Catherine and Heathcliff stumble upon the home of the Lintons, a gentry family. Peering through their windows, they become aware of another world, one of opulence and comfort—an adventure which is to become a crucial turning point in both their lives. Their intrusion is soon discovered—Catherine is bitten by the watchdog. She is admitted into the household, and her identity is soon disclosed. Heathcliff is driven away—another such humiliation as he will add to his catalogue of abuses, never to be forgotten or forgiven. But even more tragically for him, Catherine is taken up by the Lintons. Edgar Linton eventually becomes a suitor for her hand, and will marry her.

Here, one may say, is the first part of the "tragedy." Here lies Catherine's "tragic guilt": in her betrayal of her own nature, and of Nature herself, by yielding to the allurements of status and wealth. She has done so deliberately, consciously.

Her "error"—or her "tragic guilt"—is only too evident to herself, as she confesses to Nelly Dean in a memorable and moving scene. Catherine is nearing sixteen. During all her years she has been witness to the outrages perpetrated against Heathcliff and has seen him finally reduced to service in field and stable. She recounts a dream to Nelly in which she saw herself in heaven. Yet, she adds,

> Heaven did not seem to be my home; and I broke my heart with weeping to come back to earth, and the angels were so angry they flung me out into the middle of the heath on top of Wuthering Heights; where I woke sobbing for joy. ... I've no more business to marry Edgar Linton than I have to be in heaven; and if the wicked man in there (i.e. her brother) had not brought Heathcliff so low, I shouldn't have thought of it. It would degrade me to marry Heathcliff now; so he shall never know how I love him; and that, not because he's handsome, but because he's more myself than I am ...

Catherine is not aware that, while she is speaking, Heathcliff is not far from her, and remains listening long enough to hear her say that it would degrade her to marry him. Infuriated, he slips away, and does not hear her declaration of love, nor the passionate words that followed:

> What were the use of my creation, if I were entirely contained here: My great miseries in this world have been Heathcliff's miseries, and I watched and I watched and felt each from the beginning: my great thought in living is himself. If all else perished and *he* remained, *I* should still continue to be; and if all else remained, and he were annihilated, the universe would turn to a mighty stranger: I should not seem a part of it. ... Nelly, I *am* Heathcliff! He's always, always in my mind: not as a pleasure, any more than I am always a pleasure to myself, but as my own being.[104]

After an absence of three years, Heathcliff returns, thoroughly transformed. Where he has been, what he has been doing during that time is as mysterious as his own origins. Now he is a wealthy man, and as Nelly describes him, "grown tall, athletic, well-formed." His face shows no mark of his former degradation.

With his reappearance Catherine's obsession flares up, now to its fullest intensity. Nor has Heathcliff's passion for Catherine been diminished. But now it is conjoined with the seething fury of vengeance, first directed again Hindley Earnshaw, his former foe, but now also again the Linton household. Nor has he forgiven Catherine her betrayal and her marriage to Linton. His malice now achieves something of a Satanic grandeur, as he skilfully weaves his net around his victims. Once himself expropriated, Heathcliff becomes the insatiable expropriator. Once a humiliated servant, he prepares to tread down his former masters and oppressors. Like an anarchic world-destroyer he sets about his work. In his rage against Linton, he abducts the latter's sister, marries her, and after she and their son both die, becomes heir to the Thrushcross estate. In like manner, by playing on Hindley Earnshaw's weaknesses and dissipations, he becomes possessor of Wuthering Heights.

But Catherine, his beloved, is dying. While Edgar Linton is away, Heathcliff obtains entry into Catherine's death chamber. Nelly Dean records their last meeting:

> An instant they held asunder, and then how they met I hardly saw, but Catherine made a spring, and he caught her, and they were locked in an embrace from which I thought my mistress would never be released alive; in fact, in my eyes, she seemed directly insensible. ... She put up her hand to clasp his neck, and bring her cheek to his as he held her; while, he, in return, covering her with frantic caresses, said wildly—"You teach me how cruel you've been—cruel and false. *Why* did you despise me? *Why* did you betray your own heart, Cathy? I have not one word of comfort. You deserve this. You have killed yourself. Yes, you may kiss me, and cry; and wring out my kisses and tears: they'll blight you—they'll damn you. You loved me—then what right had you to leave me?. ... Because misery and degradation, and death, and nothing that God or Satan could inflict would have parted us; *you*, of your will did it. I have not broken your heart—you have broken it; and in breaking it, you have broken mine. ..."

And Nelly continues:

> ... About twelve o'clock that night was born the Catherine you saw at Wuthering Heights. ... A puny, seven months' child; and two hours after, the mother died.[105]

For a moment, then, this chaotic world is relieved by the human and emotional outpouring that sweeps over both characters. For Catherine there is nothing but death; for Heathcliff, a life in death. Heathcliff has attained through his power the vengeance he has sought, but at what price! At the price of utter dehumanization, which, in the end, he recognizes bitterly. Now, it is as if the graveyard has taken possession of him. A pathological, morbid hallucination surrounds him—the presence of Catherine. In a near-necrophilic derangement he even uncovers her grave, sees her still unmarred face, and feels that she is present at his side.

Yet there are two creatures living with him at Wuthering Heights to remind him of the past and recall him to the present. There is young Hareton Earnshaw, son of Hindley, Heathcliff's former tormentor and victim, who is dead; and there is young Catherine, widow of Heathcliff's deceased son. She is now eighteen, and Hareton, twenty-three. When Heathcliff looks at their eyes, he believes he is seeing Catherine. He is himself near death, for his will to live is gone. When he dies he will be buried by the side of her who had never been his, and yet had never left him. He insists that he be buried without the benefit of a Christian service.

He has left behind him earnests for the future. Catherine and Hareton are to be married and will live at Thrushgrove Grange. Wuthering Heights will be inhabited by the superstitious old servant Joseph.

And here the retrospective portion of the story ends.

We are again at the beginning. Lockwood is listening to Nelly's long tale. As they sit there, the garden gate swings open. Catherine and Hareton are returning from their walk. Mr. Lockwood reflects: "*They* are afraid of nothing. ... Together they would brave Satan and all his legions."

The "tragedy" of *Wuthering Heights* is over. As in all tragedy, we end with a restoration of Order. In young Catherine and young Hareton there will be the new birth. Hitherto uncouth and almost savage, Hareton (another Heathcliff, only younger) will be humanized by Love. For Catherine is the young Eve, leading Adam; she is guide, teacher, and mate. The elder Catherine's "tragic guilt"—her violation and betrayal of the heart—have been sufficiently atoned for. Love, the redemptive power of true Passion, has been justified. One can almost hear Emily herself whispering, "It is the only redemptive force of Nature that justifies itself."

* * *

The metaphysical universe that Emily Brontë appears to be constructing postulates a dualism in which the forces of good and evil, light and darkness, are in a constant state of war. The two principal characters of the novel are in fact "anarchs" in defiance of such a universe: Catherine the "anarch" within the social system; Heathcliff, outside it. She is a "rebel," without understanding the nature or grounds of her rebellion, a source of constant grief to her domineering father; Heathcliff's rebellion is the revolt of the "outcast," the nameless and propertyless foundling. There is a demonic element in both these figures that drives them toward one another in an almost half-conscious instinctual recognition of their identity. They fuse and complement each other, forced toward one another by a natural passion that is its own justification. When Catherine affirms that she *is* Heathcliff, she is also affirming the demon within herself. It is her betrayal of that element in herself that makes for Heathcliff's destruction, and turns him into a debased Lucifer—a demonical Nemesis. For in a nihilistic world the only redemption lies in Passion, Love, and the Imagination. It is Emily Brontë's rebellion against a constrictive universe, a rebellion against a constrictive life, against oppression, against a denial of Nature. It is the rebellion of the biblical Eve when she submits to the fatal temptation which, while "unparadising" her, will also bring her the ambiguous paradise of knowledge, sex, and love.

Is it any wonder that Charlotte Brontë was abashed when she read *Wuthering Heights*, at its depicted world: on the one hand bounded by the Haworth graveyard, Death; on the other by the wild moors, eternal Nature herself!

Emily Brontë died as she had lived, defiant even when near death. Not until the very last hours would she agree to have one of what she called the "poisoning doctors" attend her. Charlotte had spoken of Emily as possessing an "upright heretical and English spirit." How heretical, Charlotte would not admit even to herself. ...

As the old, bereaved father and his two surviving children, Charlotte and Anne, followed the coffin to the grave, they were joined by Keeper, Emily's fierce, faithful bulldog. He walked alongside of the mourners, and into the church, and stayed quietly there all the time that the burial service was being read. When he came home, he lay down in Emily's chamber door, and howled pitifully for many days ...[106]

Part Six

Woman of Valor

George Eliot and the Victorians

Were it not a pleasant thing
    To fall asleep with all one's friends;
To pass with all our social ties
    To silence from the paths of men;
And every hundred years to rise
    And learn the world, and sleep again;
To sleep through terms of mighty wars,
    And wake on science grown to more,
On secrets of the brain, the stars,
    As well as aught of fairy lore;
And all that else the years will show,
    The Poet-forms of stronger hours,
The vast Republic that may grow,
    The Federations and the Powers;
Titanic forces taking birth
    In divers seasons, divers climes;
For we are Ancients of the earth,
    And in the morning of the times.
                                        —"L'Envoi"

So Tennyson dreams in his early poetic career in the 1830s. If we, today, are the unfulfilled inheritors of those dreams, the heirs of those "titanic forces" as well as of untold anxieties and questings, it may, perhaps, do us good to look back, instead of forward—at least for the moment—say, a hundred years or so, into an age which has done so much to shape our own, to trace back to the roots of our own being and thinking, listen again to the roar of progress, the excitements of discoveries, the hopes, promises, and even despairs, as well as achievements and questionings, not very much unlike ours—though, to the historic eye and perspective, simplified in comparison— as the past so often is to the more sophisticated present. We think of our age as one of incomparable upheaval (which it is), of rebellion and discontent, and we envy what we believe to have been the placidity of the Victorians, and especially of Victorian womanhood.

Let us then turn back to a letter written a century and a quarter ago;

My dear Father, As all my efforts in conversation have hitherto failed in making you aware of my real nature of my sentiments, I am induced to try if I can express myself more clearly on paper so that both I in writing and you in reading may have our judgements unobstructed by feeling, which can hardly be when we are together. I wish entirely to re-move from your mind the false notion that I am inclined visibly to united myself with any Christian community, or that I have any affinity in opinion with Unitarians more than with other classes of believers in the Divine authority of the books comprising the Jewish and Christian Scriptures. I regard these writings as histories consisting of min-gled truth and fiction, and while I admire and cherish much of what I believe to have been the moral teaching of Jesus himself, I consider the system of doctrines built upon the facts of his life and drawn as to its materials from Jewish notions to be most dishon-orable to God and most pernicious in its influence on individual and social happiness ... Such being my very strong convictions, it cannot be a question with any mind of strict integrity, whatever judgement may be passed on their truth, that I could not without vile hypocrisy and a miserable truckling to the smile of the world for the sake of my sup-posed interests, profess to join in worship which I wholly disapprove. This and *this alone* I will not do even for your sake—anything else however painful I would cheerfully brave to give you a moment's joy.

I do not hope to convince any other member of our family and probably not yourself that I am really sincere ... But the prospect of contempt and rejection shall not make me swerve from my determination so much as a hair's breadth until I feel that I *ought* to do so. ... I fear nothing but voluntarily leaving you. I can cheerfully do it if you desire it and shall go with deep gratitude for all the tenderness and rich kindness you have never been tired of shewing me. So far from complaining I shall joyfully submit if as a proper pun-ishment for the pain I have most unintentionally given you, you determine to appropriate any provision you have intended to make for my future support to your other children whom you may consider more deserving. As a last vindication of herself from one who has no one to speak for her I may be permitted to say that if I ever loved you I do so now, if ever I sought to obey the laws of my Creator and to follow duty wherever it may lead me I have that determination now and the consciousness of this will support me though every being on earth were to frown upon me. Your affectionate Daughter Mary Ann.[1]

The girl, Mary Ann Evans, was then twenty-two years old, and whatever future might have been predicted for her (who could then have known that she would be George Eliot?), one thing was sure: She would never swerve from the paths of in-tegrity she had marked out for herself.

Her father was pained; her family outraged. What had come over the girl? In a provincial community of Warwickshire, in the town of Coventry and the surrounding country, where her father Robert Evans had an established reputation as a land agent and general factotum of an aristocratic landowning family, and was financially suc-cessful and secure—such dereliction was almost unpardonable. It was with pain that the poor man had noted in his Journal for January: "Went to Trinity Church in the forenoon ... Mary Ann did not go."[2] He was not a fanatic, but he was a believer and a respecter of authority and convention. Revolutionary doctrines were taught by "fools and scoundrels." George Eliot would recall later, but not with rancor, how he would

utter the word 'Government' in a tone that charged it with awe, and made it part of my effective religion, in contrast with the word "rebel," which seemed to carry the stamp of evil in its syllables, and, lit by the fact that Satan was the first rebel, made an argument dispensing with more detailed inquiry.[3]

Her brother Isaac, practical man that he was, was upset that she would now have no chance of "getting the one thing needful—a husband and a settlement." What was she doing associating with "Chartists and Radicals," for only such would fall in love with her if she did not belong to the Church. It was fortunate that their mother was no longer alive. To avoid a total break, Mary Ann yielded on one point: She would attend services; but she would not pray. Nor change her mind.

What had in fact happened to that shy, withdrawn, awkward girl, who had hitherto displayed religious fervor? Under the influence of one of her teachers, she had early been attracted to the teachings of the Evangelicals, had taken to a "gloomy Calvinism," and had read and wept over *The Imitation of Christ* and John Keble's *Christian Year*. Her youthful mind, only too susceptible to a morbid religiosity and otherworldliness, had been filled with thoughts of sin, repentance, eternal damnation and salvation. She had thrilled to such hymnal lines as

> Lord have mercy, and remove us
> Early to thy place of rest. ...

carefully copied out in her own hand and preserved. She had been in turn horrified and thrilled by visions of hell and damnation. She had read widely in religious books on Christian dogma and history. She had even tried her hand at religious poetry, and had one of her poems printed in *The Christian Observer* in 1840. It was dedicated to Death:

> As o'er the fields by evening's light I stray,
> I hear a still, small whisper—Come away!
> Thou must to this bright, lovely world soon say
> > Farewell!
> The mandate I'd obey, my lamp prepare,
> Gird up my garments, give my soul to pray'r
> And say to earth and all that breathe earth's air
> > Farewell![4]

She was then already almost twenty. Visions of sainthood, of becoming another St. Paul, floated across her perfervid horizon. "May I be sanctified wholly," she prayed.[5]

But alongside of her reading of religious literature, other books began intruding—for she was omnivorous—strange companions like Byron, Shelley, Schiller, and soon Carlyle.

Then, toward the beginning of 1841, a momentous event occurred. Her father turned over his responsibilities at Griff, where they had been living, to his son Isaac, and took a new house at Foleshill near Coventry. Mary Ann went to live with him. A new and crucial chapter opened in her life ...

* * *

She arrived at her new home, Bird-Grove, just one mile from Coventry, still an Evangelical. She was acknowledged an unusually bright woman; how many women (not to mention men!) could read French, German, Latin, a little Greek? How many had read Carlyle with such understanding? And Goethe's works, and Schiller's? How many could argue so effectively, and with such learning, sometimes complex theological questions? Coventry was an industrial town, particularly famous for its ribbon manu-facture; and not far off were the coal mines, startlingly filled with Methodists and—so many believed—immorality! But Coventry also contained notable groups of bright intellects, male and female. There were the Brays, Charles and Caroline. Charles Bray, well-to-do ribbon manufacturer, had just published the first volume of a *Philosophy of Necessity*, an exposition of determinism in Nature and human life. Caroline's brother, Charles Christian Hennell, had three years earlier issued a radical *Inquiry into the Origins of Christianity*, which, in Mary Ann's later description, produced "the convic-tion that [Christ] was an enthusiast and a revolutionist, no less than a reformer and a moral and religious teacher."[6]

Mary Ann Evans, shy, and lonely, and frequently depressed, with few friends to whom she could open her heart, or who might share her intellectual interests, was soon drawn into these circles. Nor was she behindhand in acquainting herself with Bray's and Hennell's books. At Rosehill, the hospitable home of the Brays, she found the discussion lively and provocative, and the exchange of new ideas about new books a deliverance from her previous isolation. Strange names began cropping up, and titles of momentous books. For example, David Friedrich Strauss, and his *Life of Jesus*. Dr. Herbert Brabant, an eminent physician whose daughter was being wooed by Charles Hennell, had even studied in Germany and personally associated with the great theologian Paulus, and with Strauss himself. Mary Ann Evans no doubt felt as if she was rapidly being projected into the future. She had been introduced to that circle by a rather conservative sponsor who hoped that Mary Ann, "the superior young lady of Evangelical principles might be beneficial to the heretical minds of its members." But the "superior young lady" was soon writing to her Evangelical teacher and friend Maria Lewis, after reading Hennell's *Inquiry*,

> My whole soul has been engrossed in the most interesting of all enquiries for the last few days, and to what results my thoughts may lead I know not—possibly to one that will startle you.[7]

Maria Lewis was more than startled. For had she not been one of the principal influences in Mary Ann's religious education?

The storm broke early in 1842, and all efforts to reconvert the young woman—even by bringing in the heavy battery of a noted theologian—failed. What was one to do with a person who was armed with replies based on sure knowledge and who came to the conclusion, which she expressed to the Professor of Theology at Birmingham, that "the awful anticipations entailed by a reception of all the dogmas in the New Testa-ment, operate unfavourably on moral beauty by disturbing that spontaneity, that choice of good for its own sake, that answers my ideal"?[8]

That well-to-do manufacturers and other professionals should be so intensely in-volved in religious controversy, and so eager to support liberal re-examination of reli-gious history and dogma, may at first surprise the modern student of the nineteenth century. From the early 1830s, and particularly during the period of the first Reform agitation, the question of Church and State had been of paramount importance. The so-called Oxford Movement had been, in greater part, a reply to the triumph of the first Reform Bill, which appeared to threaten a greater involvement of Parliament in the affairs of the Established Church. It will be remembered that the Bishops voted almost unanimously in the House of Lords against passage of the Bill. The vast control exercised by the church establishment over appointments to clerical posts; the stupendous incomes of the hierarchy, and pluralism; and, perhaps most important, the laxity or indifference in office, had led to a kind of inner revolution for the spiritual purification of the church, to bring it back to its apostolic heritage and high ceremonial as well as total dedication, while at the same time emphasizing the supremacy of the religious over the secular authority. It was also an effort to counter the liberalizing tendencies within Protestantism itself, such as emanated from the German theologians and their "Higher Criticism" of the Old and New Testaments. For the liberal manufacturer, mostly either Dissenter or Unitarian, or at best a mild adherent of the Establishment, liberal theology was a way of strengthening his own economic and social position in the country and in Parliament. He could not, of course, anticipate how far such a movement would go and in what way it might eventually affect the thinking and actions of the "lower classes." But the criticism of religion thus became an important element, a precondition for the liberalization of the political structure.

Once Mary Ann had opened herself to all these new influences, a world of unlimited possibilities and practical activities lay before her. It was not long before her exceptional talents were to be put to use. She knew German well. Would she be willing to undertake a translation from that language? Dr. Brabant's daughter had been approached to render Strauss's *Life of Jesus* into English; had in fact begun it, but, being married now (to Charles Hennell) had found it difficult to continue. Joseph Parkes, liberal reformer, stood sponsor to the undertaking. It was a stupendous endeavor, and it took Mary Ann Evans two years to complete it. She labored at the mighty tome, with its innumerable references and quotations in many languages; at times hating it—for she found herself disagreeing with many of its ideas—but also learning a great deal. Yet the book, which had had a shattering impact in Germany and abroad when first published in 1835, opened another window on an ever-expanding horizon. Under Strauss's critical pen, the historical figure of Christ disappeared as a person, or rather was dissolved into a Straussian "Myth."* And Myth was the "creation of a fact out of ideas." It was the expression of a people's search to discover the origins of its institutions, which were hidden in "oblivion." For Myth was the expression not of an individual consciousness, but of a people's collective unconscious, a spontaneous product of the imagination. The myth of Jesus embodied not the vision of an individual Savior, but a Savior who stood for Humanity, for the species. This Godhead was not One—not a Jesus of Nazareth—but the Godhead of Humanity.

If not many of Strauss's metaphysical and Hegelian constructions appealed to the English translator, it is nevertheless likely that the idea of a God-man as personified Humanity struck her, for it was a theme that she would ponder in years to come and elaborate into a secular religion of humanity. ...

She completed the arduous task in August of 1845, and the book appeared the following June.

---

* On David Friedrich Strauss, see above, pp. 170–175.

How far she had travelled from that part of her past life that had been marred by the "slough and crust of sin" (to use Tennyson's phrase)! And the ever couchant terror of guilt and retribution!

For now she had many auxiliars, new friends, new books, new ideas. Her widening mind could dwell on mundane matters too. She was translating Spinoza's *Tractatus* and fell under the spell of Pantheism. But she was also reaching out to other areas, closer to home—to the relations of human beings. For the first time in her life she felt that she belonged, that she was being understood and appreciated, that her intellectual life (still in process of developing), was beginning to coalesce with her emotional needs, until that time so thoroughly hampered in the home environment. By nature she was a passionate woman, and part of her growth was in the recognition of that fact. She sought expression for the natural spontaneities of life and feeling. Uncertain of herself as a woman, as an intellectual, she was becoming aware of the immense potentialities within her. Feelings now stood at the center of her life, and she found them fed by two great teachers, one long dead, another still alive but in another country: Rousseau and George Sand. She worshipped both, not in blind adoration nor without certain reservations; yet as she confessed, Rousseau had awakened her to new perceptions, had so quickened her faculties that she was able now, as she put it, to "shape more definitely" ideals that had previously dwelt as dim "intimations" in her soul, allowing her to make new combinations.

New combinations! The process is particularly important to note. She was one of those creators who needed to round out a philosophy of life, achieve a rounded theory, before she could essay the practice, whether in art or in her own personal actions. In George Sand she found another liberating force, even mightier than Rousseau, for George Sand was alive and very much a part of the expanding history of the times. In European and Russian thought she had been a force of great magnitude. That is what Mary Ann Evans felt:

> I cannot read six pages of hers without feeling that it is given to her to delineate human passion and its results ...—some of the moral instincts and their tendencies—with such truthfulness, such nicety of discrimination, such tragic power, and withal such loving gentle humour, that one might live in a century with nothing but one's own dull faculties and not know so much as those six pages will suggest ...[9]

Here was a woman who thought, lived, and acted in accordance with her own vision. And that was Mary Ann Evans's hope too—to be able to transmute ideas into actions.

She was in that state of emotional and intellectual glow when she heard of the outbreak of the 1848 Revolution in France. A letter to a friend of hers, John Sibree, Jr., is an autobiographical document of extraordinary importance, not only revealing her political leanings, but also representing the high point of her emotional participation in an important revolutionary event.

> Write and tell you that I join you in your happiness about the French Revolution? Very fine, my good friend. If I made you wait for a letter as long as you do me, our little *échantillon* of a Milennium would be over, Satan would be let loose again, and I should have to share your humiliation instead of your triumph ... You and Carlyle (have you seen his article in last week's *Examiner?*) are the only two people who feel just as I would

have them—who can glory in what is actually great and beautiful without putting forth any cold reservations and incredulities to save their credit for wisdom. I am all the more delighted with your enthusiasm because I didn't expect it. I feared that you lacked revolutionary ardour. But no—you are just as sansculottish and rash as I would have you. You are not one of those sages whose reason keeps so tight a rein on their emotion that they are too constantly occupied in calculating consequences to rejoice in any great manifestation of the forces that underlie our everyday existence. ... I thought we had fallen on such evil days that we were to see no really great movement—that ours was what St. Simon calls a purely *critical* epoch, not at all an organic one—but I begin to be glad of my date. I would consent, however, to have a year clipt off my life for the sake of witnessing such a scene as that of the men of the barricade bowing to the image of Christ "who first taught fraternity to men." ... I have little patience with people who find time to pity Louis Philippe and his moustachioed sons. Certainly our decayed monarchs should be pensioned off: we should have a hospital for them, a sort of Zoological Garden, where these worn-out humbugs may be preserved ...

Her comments on England are particularly significant:

I should have no hope of good from any imitative movement at home. Our working classes are eminently inferior to the mass of the French people. In France, the *mind* of the people is highly electrified—they are full of ideas on social subjects—they really desire social *reform*—not merely on acting out of Sancho Panza's favourite proverb "Yesterday for you, to-day for me." .. Here there is so much larger a proportion of selfish radicalism and unsatisfied, brute sensuality (in the agricultural and mining districts especially) than of perception or desire of justice, that a revolutionary movement would be simply destructive—not constructive. Besides, it would be put down. Our military have no notions of "fraternizing." They have the same sort of inveteracy as dogs have for the ill-drest canaille. They are as mere brute force as a battering ram and the aristocracy have got firm hold of them. Our little humbug of a queen is more endurable than the rest of her race because she calls forth a chivalrous feeling, and there is nothing in our constitution to obstruct the slow progress of *political* reform. This is all we are fit for at present. ...[10]

The reference to Queen Victoria is particularly interesting, for it was excised in the first official biography of George Eliot prepared by her husband John Cross.

She commiserated the failure of the Revolution in France, as well as the corruption of her own times:

the loathsome fawning, the transparent hypocrisy, the systematic giving as little as possible for as much as possible, that one meets with here at every turn. I feel that society is training men and women for hell ... Paris, poor Paris, alas! alas![11]

She was soon at another turning point in her life, or rather, she would soon be plunged into a whirlpool in which she would revolve at a breakneck speed before arriving at a center of rest which would determine the rest of her life. Coventry would not hold her for long. She was already known as the translator of Strauss (though the book had been published anonymously), and as a writer of brilliant reviews in the local journal. She knew she must go to London if she was ever to fulfil herself. And the opportunity arose soon. The young publisher John Chapman had acquired the very influential liberal periodical *The Westminster Review*, founded in 1824 by Jeremy Bentham, and since then a notable rival of the powerful *Quarterly* and *Edinburgh Reviews*. Not the least eminent of its editors (1836–1840) had been John Stuart Mill. Chapman had met Mary Ann in 1846, and now, five years later, he sought her out as a possible associate. John Chapman was young, enterprising, handsome—and very seductive. He loved women, and women fell in love with him. His house, 142 Strand, was his office, his residence, and upstairs contained rooms for paying guests. In October 1850, he arrived at Rosehill. Would she do a review of an important book by a disciple of Strauss—on *The Progress of the Intellect* by Robert William Mackay? She would. And she would also try London.

Her father had died the year before, to the last the object of her undiminished devotion and care. Her ties to the other members of her family had loosened. Her father had left her a legacy which, while not large, would with her own writing assure a modest independence. So to London she went, and took quarters at 142 Strand.

The top began spinning—or to improve the figure, one might say that the wine of life became heady, perhaps sometimes too dizzying. The drama of Mary Ann—she now began calling herself Marian—had three simultaneous acts: there was the act which brought on the stage John Chapman, his wife some fourteen years older, and another habitant of the house, the lovely Miss Elisabeth Tilley: *ménage à trois* such as rarely appears in the annals—that is, the public annals—of Victorianism, nor, of course, in novels of the times. With the appearance of Marian Evans the triangle turned quadrilateral. Editorial labors (and Marian was a tireless worker) brought her together with John Chapman—heads and hearts, one might say, and perhaps bodies. It was a situation that could be bothersome ... Naturally there were jealousies and quarrels. But Marian was invaluable. She prepared the prospectus for the rejuvenated *Westminster*. She was soon practically editor of the journal. She was happy. She was in love. How long would act one last?

The next act was also heady: for 142 Strand was the meeting ground of the most eminent writers and thinkers of the day. Where else could she have met and spoken with the scientists T. H. Huxley and David Brewster; Pierre Leroux and Louis Blanc, French émigrés; Mazzini; the Americans Horace Greeley and William Cullen Bryant; the Swedish feminist celebrity Fredrika Bremer; the famous Harriet Martineau; J. S. Mill and Herbert Spencer?

Act Three began with the entrance of a new character, as yet in 1851 not of very great import in her life—but as in so many dramas, the third was the crucial act. This was George Henry Lewes, brilliant drama critic, journalist, scientific thinker, and a committed follower of the Positivist philosopher Auguste Comte—and Marian, too, considered herself a Comtean, agreeing with the French philosopher that, of his celebrated three stages in the progression of mankind, "theological and metaphysical speculation"

> have reached their limit, and that the only hope of extending man's sources of knowledge and happiness is to be found in positive science, and in the universal application of its principles ... Thinkers who are in the van of human progress should devote themselves to the actual rather than to the retrospective.[12]

The air was tingling with scientific speculation, and around her she had some formidable exponents of the new science and philosophy. Science and religion, science and the Bible, the role of evolutionary theory (evolution was much in the air), all these fused with the idea of progress, particularly as defined by Auguste Comte. At times she felt as if civilization were perched on a Mount Pisgah from which could be viewed the promised land.

She was entering upon the last stage of her intellectual education, and almost ready for a descent from her own Mount Pisgah. So far as her emotional development was concerned, that too underwent some extraordinary changes between 1851 and 1853. Emotionally, she was discovering that G. H. Lewes, whom she had in 1851 dubbed, with some condescension, "a sort of miniature Mirabeau," possessed qualities that drew her to him. He was kind and helpful, with something of an encyclopedic mind. But what was more important, he was "a man of heart and conscience wearing a mask of flippancy."[13]

Moreover, he was very unhappy in his marriage, and her sympathies went out to him. He was also readying a major biography of Goethe. And she, almost prepared not merely to descend from the mountain, but to essay a bold leap into the valley of decision, had now also discovered a new secular bible. She was translating and absorbing another epochal work of a German neo-Hegelian, Ludwig Feuerbach's *Das Wesen des Christentums—The Essence of Christianity*.

Anguish commingled with exhilaration. But to whom could she confide the feelings of pain that she felt, when she saw herself forced into rivalry with a woman so much more beautiful than herself? How could she counter with her superiority of soul and mind, involved as she was with the "frail bark" of a man, flighty and exploitative? More and more she became aware of the plight of womanhood in a society of even the most advanced and liberal men. But how much worse was woman's lot than hers, when she looked at the many families around her! She, at least, had the world of intellect open to her. In France, she remarked in a review, things were different:

> Women became superior in France by being admitted to a common fund of ideas, to common objects of interest with men; and this must ever be the essential condition at once of true womanly culture and true social well-being ... Let the whole field of reality be laid open to woman as well as man, and then, that which is peculiar in her mental modification, instead of being, as it is now, a source of discord and repulsion between the sexes, will be found to be a necessary complement to the truth and beauty of life. Then we shall have that marriage of minds which alone can blend all the hues of thought and feeling in one lovely rainbow of promise for the harvest of human happiness.[14]

✳ ✳ ✳

And I advise you, speculative theologians and philosophers: free yourselves from the concepts and presuppositions of existing speculative philosophy if you want to get at things differently, as they are: that is to say, if you want to come to the Truth. And there is no other road for you to Truth and Freedom than through the stream of fire—Feuerbach. Feuerbach is the purgatory of the present.[15]

Marian Evans never saw the above passage (written in 1842), nor was she likely ever to come across it. It was also most unlikely that she had ever spoken to, perhaps even seen the author, though he sometimes stopped at Chapman's quarters in the Strand to collect some mail from his friend in Manchester, Frederick Engels. He was another refugee from Germany named Karl Marx, then occupied with a book, *Contribution to the Critique of Political Economy*, and working in the British Museum.

But she would have understood its meaning perfectly. She too was passing through purgatory, through many a stream of fire, to reach another shore. Nor could she have known that she was the embodiment of an important stage in the progress of the modern mind as defined by the same Karl Marx, who had said that "for Germany, the critique of religion has been essentially completed, and the critique of religion is the premise of all critiques." And was not all of England at that time engaged, from different bastions and fortifications, in parallel battles?

In *The Essence of Christianity* she found the bridge that would carry her from a transcendental spiritualism toward a Naturalism—from God to Man. And it was with a premonitory sense of the crucial that she set about translating a work that was destined to be intricately bound up with her life and work.

In a memorable scene in *The Mill on the Floss*, George Eliot described how, at a critical moment of her early life, the heroine Maggie Tulliver reads Thomas à Kempis's *Imitation of Christ*, and as a result becomes converted to a doctrine of renunciation. In a similar scene many, many years later, Thomas Mann described how the older Buddenbrook comes upon Schopenhauer's *World as Will and Idea* and becomes reconciled to Fatality. If only we had more than the very fragmentary comments to tell us what Marian Evans felt while reading *The Essence of Christianity!* That she agreed "everywhere" with Feuerbach's ideas we know from her letters.[16]

For it is inescapable that for her, as for so many others at the time, Feuerbach served as certification, confirmation, and further clarification of her inner feelings, inchoate at one time, but germinally there. Like Maggie, like Buddenbrook, she read a seminal book at a critical time. Let us, like one of her own omniscient authors, lean over her shoulder as she turns the pages. She reads about marriage:

> Marriage—we mean, of course, marriage as the free bond of love—is sacred in itself, by the very nature of the union which is therein effected. That alone is a religious marriage, which is a true marriage, which corresponds to the essence of marriage—love … Yes, only as the free bond of love; for a marriage the bond of which is merely an external restriction, not the voluntary, contented self-restriction of love, in short, a marriage which is not spontaneously concluded, spontaneously willed, self-suffering, is not a true marriage, and therefore not a truly moral marriage.[17]

Here, perhaps for the first time, she comes to a true apprehension of the meaning of "I" and "Thou." Let us follow her:

> The other is my *thou*—the relation being reciprocal, my *alter ego*, man objective to me, the revelation of my own nature, the eye seeing itself. In another I first have the consciousness of humanity; through him I first learn, I first feel, that I am a man; in my love for him it is first clear to me that he belongs to me and I to him, that we two cannot be without each other, that only community constitutes humanity. …[18]

And with startling force:

> The *ego* … attains to consciousness of the world through consciousness of the *thou*.
> Thus man is the God of man (*Homo homini Deus*). That he is, he has to thank Nature;
> that he is man, he has to thank man … Only where man suns and warms himself in the
> proximity of man arise feeling and imagination. Love, which requires mutuality, is the
> spring of poetry; and only where man communicates with man, only in speech, a social
> act, awakes reason …[19]

And finally,

> The divine being is nothing else than the human being, or, rather the human nature
> purified, freed from the limits of the individual man, made objective—*i.e.*, contemplated
> and revered as another, a distinct being. All the attributes of the divine nature are, there-
> fore, attributes of the human nature … What man withdraws from himself, what he re-
> nounces in himself, he only enjoys in an incomparably higher and fuller measure in God
> … To enrich God, man must become poor; that God may be all, man must be nothing
> … He who makes God act humanly, declares human activity to be divine; he says, A god
> who is not active, and not morally or humanly active, is no god; and thus he makes the
> idea of the Godhead dependent on the idea of activity, that is, of human activity, for a
> higher he knows not.[20]

How the words of Feuerbach, "God is Man's relinquished self" must have rung in
her ears! God is the objectification of the best in man. Religion is Anthropology. Man
realizes himself only in the Species. …

The apprenticeship, to use Goethe's term concerning Wilhelm Meister, was now
practically over. The succeeding *Wanderjahre* and homecoming were to be the realizations of everything that had been germinating within her for years. Fearless as ever,
she was not afraid of giving up the idea of immortality, the soul; she was not afraid to
declare the sacredness of Matter and of the flesh. The man she loved had suffered
much. He was married, the father of children, and separated from his family. His wife
had borne two illegitimate children, and Lewes had acknowledged them as his own,
thus forfeiting his right to a legal divorce. (After his meeting with Marian, his wife
would bear two more illegitimate children.) Lewes had continued to support her, and
the children, legitimate and illegitimate. It would take a great heart and great courage
to join one's fortunes to such a fragile vessel. But she knew the greatness that was in
him, and she dared—dared the world, dared what she called all "the chartered re-
spectabilities"—because she understood that the little, unprepossessing, witty, learned
man could give her more than anyone else; and because for the first time in her life
she was loved as much as she loved. In 1853 she moved to her own lodgings in Cambridge Street. In 1854 *The Essence of Christianity* appeared.

July 20, 1854, she entered in her Journal:

> I said farewell to Cambridge Street … and found myself on board the Ravensbourne,
> bound for Antwerp. The day was glorious, and our passage perfect …

and to the Brays:

> Dear friends, all three—I have only time to say good-bye, and God bless you. *Poste
> Restante*, Weimar, for the next six weeks, and afterwards Berlin. Ever your loving and
> grateful Marian.[21]

And thus was born George Eliot.

* * *

"How is it that the poets have said so many fine things about our first love, so few about our later love? Are their first poems their best? or are not those the best which come from their fuller thought, their larger experience, their deeper-rooted affections? The boy's flute-like voice has its own spring charm; but the man should yield a richer, deeper music."[22]

Marian Evans had imagined herself in love before—with John Chapman, flighty Don Juan of the Strand, and for a short while even with that virginal vestal, Herbert Spencer. Neither of them could have afforded her that wholeness of a relationship that could do justice to her own depths of feeling and her intellectual strivings. With Lewes she found a reciprocal respect, devotion, and understanding, and, perhaps of even greater importance in her development, a stimulus to creation, of revolutionary importance to both her career and the world of letters. It is one of the more lurid paradoxes of the Victorian era that the man and the woman who were to be exposed soon to the cannibalistic obloquies of their English contemporaries should have achieved a relationship that was to stand in a glaring contrast to the infelicitous marital and sexual experiences of Dickens, Ruskin, Meredith, J.S. Mill and even the Carlyles.

That vituperative genius Thomas Carlyle had called G.H. Lewes an "ape." And truth to tell, he was not a good-looking man. Nor was he a genius. But he was a man of many and varied talents, of a wide-ranging mind and with scientific interests that were to make his researches in physiology of prime importance in the life of Ivan Pavlov, and of profound interest to Dostoevsky.

Though unequal to Marian Evans in genius, he was her equal in learning. He was able to enlarge her store of knowledge—for he was at home in German and French letters as well as in science, a student of Comte and, as an editor of the liberal weekly *The Leader*, in touch with French and German refugees and their ideas, particularly French socialists. He was also a supporter of Kossuth, Mazzini and the movements of Italian liberation—and, like Marian Evans herself, a dedicated admirer of George Sand.

And not least, he was a man of deep feelings and boundless generosity. The moment of their union was also the moment of their reciprocal liberation: for him the release from what he called the "dreary and wasted period"—for her, from loneliness and a still unrealized selfhood as woman and writer, waiting, waiting for the "dark seed-growths of consciousness" to come to fruition. Now they were both open to the actuality of happiness. He brought to her the vast possibilities that lay within Science in determining the future of mankind, and in offering her a coherent view of life and art. He made her aware of the great medical contributions of Bichat and Raspail, and she was to follow with eagerness his researches in marine biology and physiology, his microscopic studies and dissections.

But he was also to be her shield against the many unpleasantnesses that were to attend their lives when they returned to England to face a world that would look on both of them, if not with overt hostility, at least with a piercing curiosity. ...

And she brought him understanding such as his complicated personality badly needed; and to his sons she brought a motherly care and affection that helped in a measure to untangle their warped lives.

In August 1854 they were in Weimar. The German "Athens" appeared somewhat provincial to them—but what memories were associated with that ducal town: Goethe, Schiller, Herder, and how many others! Lewes was at work on what would become the first comprehensive life of Goethe in English, and here there was matter enough and personalities to enrich that volume. They both basked in the atmosphere of the past while not neglecting the present. For here in Weimar was Franz Liszt, and there was no disenchantment when they came to meet and speak with him. And what exhilaration when he played for them! Marian was somewhat disappointed in the appearance of the Princess Sayn-Wittgenstein, Liszt's companion, having imagined a more stately and glamorous personality, but she was won by the kindness and geniality of the lady, who occupied an equivocal position similar to her own, though not fraught with such menaces. Here too they met the young prodigy arrived from Russia, Anton Rubinstein, and at the theatre, over which Liszt ruled, they heard the "music of the future"—Wagner's *Tannhäuser, The Flying Dutchman,* and *Lohengrin.* Lewes was bored by the last, as was Marian; but she loved the *Flying Dutchman* and was impressed by *Tannhäuser.* And at the Princess's residence they listened to the piano playing of "a melancholy, interesting creature"—none other than Clara Schumann, "whose husband," Marian Evans wrote, "went mad a year ago, and she has to support eight children."[23]

From Weimar they went to Berlin, and here too life was exciting, though without the aura of a Weimar. Lewes met with some of the more notable scientists; both were guests at a number of the "salons," among them that of the von Enses; Marian was at work on a translation of Spinoza, and there were the great art galleries. How quickly the eight months had passed! Not without a certain trepidation, they left the Continent on March 11, 1855.

For rumors had reached them in Weimar and Berlin that Mrs. Grundy had been more than active while they had been away. Marian's conduct and that of Lewes had shaken up the the moral structure of England. She had shocked the Carlyles; the phrenological Dr. George Combe, a friend of the family, who could only diagnose her act as "insanity"—and began inquiring after a family pathology; she shocked Mr. John Chapman!—and the otherwise freethinking Harriet Martineau, who was never to forgive her … It was whispered, not too softly, that Lewes had run away from his "wife," lured by that "strong-minded" siren, a writer for the *Westminster Review.* Carlyle, who missed no chance of derogation, wrote to his brother:

> Lewes has cast away his wife—who indeed deserved it of him, having openly produced those dirty sooty skinned children which have Thornton Hunt for father, and being ready for a third; Lewes to pay the whole account, even the money part of it.[24]

One of England's most popular sculptors, Thomas Woolner, informed his fellow-artist (a former friend of Lewes's) of the succulent scandal:

> … Blackguard Lewes has bolted with a————and is living in Germany with her. I believe it is dangerous to write facts of anyone nowadays so I will not any further lift the mantle and display the filthy contamination of these hideous satyrs and smirking moralists. …[25]

But the worst, perhaps, was that her own family had rejected her. The rumors had come to them while she was in Weimar, basking in the "genius, benevolence, and tenderness" of Franz Liszt, not believing that she was really sitting "*tête-à-tête* with him for an hour ... and telling him my ideas and feelings."[26] What was equally painful was that some of the aspersions were cast upon the man she loved and honored.

She was equal to the trial, and again stood up bravely and with dignity. From Weimar she wrote to John Chapman:

> ... I do not wish to take the ground of ignoring what is unconventional in my position. I have counted the cost of the step that I have taken and am prepared to bear, without irritation or bitterness, renunciation by all my friends. I am not mistaken in the person to whom I have attached myself. He is worthy of the sacrifice I have incurred, and my only anxiety is that he should be rightly judged.[27]

No, she was not unaware of the hostility she was about to encounter, or of the hurts she was bound to feel. But her fibre of resistance had hardened, without producing in her a venomous bitterness. Perhaps her immersion in Spinoza's *Ethics,* which she was translating, and the contemplation of the philosopher's hardships, gave her additional strength. Her translation of Feuerbach had aroused the *Spectator,* and the book was branded as "rank atheism." Even her friend John Chapman's *Westminster Review* had been unfavorable to Feuerbach. In the eyes of the part of the world that John Stuart Mill had called "this canting England," she was the very embodiment of atheism and immorality.

She insisted that she would and must be known as Mrs. Lewes. If ostracism was the price she must pay, she would pay it.

> For myself I prefer excommunication. I have no earthly thing that I care for, to gain by being brought within the pale of people's personal attention, and I have many things to care for that I should lose—my freedom from petty worldly torments, commonly called pleasures, and that isolation which really keeps my charity warm instead of chilling it, as much contact with frivolous women would do.[28]

What she would have to put up with is revealed in a letter written in 1857 by one "Christian Socialist," Charles Kingsley, to another, the Rev. Frederick Denison Maurice:

> I do hope you will not bother your soul about two Westminster essays. The woman who used to insult you therein—who I suppose does so now—is none other than Miss Evans, the infidel esprit forte, who is now G. H. Lewes' concubine. ...[29]

Sentiments such as this, though distressing, did not keep her from her vocation as a writer. She published a number of important essays, among them a first major evaluation of Heinrich Heine, a truly sympathetic presentation of that genius in his manifold aspects.* But there were greater and more crucial projects in the offing. The beginnings of them lay in a particularly significant event that had occurred while Lewes and Marian Evans were in Berlin.

She was thirty-seven years old—a time in life when artists are usually well on their way toward the peak of creation, or have already attained it. Yet the moment of creation was now so powerful that it carried her with astonishing rapdity from the tentative beginnings of *Scenes from Clerical Life* to the rich complexities of *Middlemarch.* In the course of her abundant creativeness she almost seemed to recapitulate her own

---

* On Heine, see above, pp. 363–371.

life history as she moved from a bucolic reconstruction of the past and the Warwick-shire countryside in the *Scenes* and in *Adam Bede*, with their preoccupation with the religious life of the time; on towards the concentrated and dramatic reconstruction of the childhood and growth of a girl in her struggle for self-realization, and her tragic failure—as in *The Mill on the Floss*—her second stage; and finally, to the vastly enlarged canvases of *Felix Holt, Middlemarch*, and *Daniel Deronda*.

That she would in her first attempts gravitate toward the parish house or the vic-arage of localities so familiar to her, and actual characters she had known more or less intimately, is to be expected. She was a child of her own past, and she would never fully overcome those memories or extinguish them, though she would be able more and more to objectify them. Even in those first efforts, preliminary as they might be, that genius of reconstructing and transcending is already in evidence, as well as her ability to elicit special and extraordinary aspects with her now-matured understand-ing. But one thing was sure—she would not follow conventional ways. And above all she would be truthful. These were already parts of her own history. But who would have predicted the powers of keen observation—observations caught, and stored, and brought back to life in her pages; and who would have given her credit for that sharp humor that lay hidden in the serious girl and woman, crackling, poignant, even acidulous?

⋆ ⋆ ⋆

The story is well known, but bears repetition, for it marks an era in literature and remained for Marian Evans (by that time already famous as "George Eliot") an in-eradicable recollection. The major turning points in the life of an artist are never mere accidents; they are in the making for a long time before, but require the propi-tious incendiary moment to light the flame of realization. Such a moment occurred when they were in Berlin. Among her papers, Marian Evans recovered the introduc-tory chapter of a story written years before, and, in her own words,

> … One evening in Berlin something led me to read it to George. He was struck with it as a bit of concrete description, and it suggested to him the possibility of my being able to write a novel, though he distrusted—indeed disbelieved in—my possession of any dra-matic power. Still, he began to think that I might as well try some time what I could do in fiction. …

Back in England, they were spending some time in Tenby, Wales, Lewes busy explor-ing the seacoast, but also now urging her on to try her hand at a novel.

> … One morning as I was thinking what should be the subject of my first story, my thoughts merged themselves into a dreamy doze, and I imagined myself writing a story, of which the title was "The Sad Fortunes of the Reverend Amos Barton."[30]

Back in their home in Richmond, Marian noted in her Journal for September 23, 1856:

> Began to write "The Sad Fortunes of the Reverend Amos Barton", which I hope to make one of a series called "Scenes of Clerical Life."[31]

Even before setting to work on "Amos Barton," the first of the *Clerical Life* sketches, she had already formulated her aesthetic:

Art is the nearest thing to life; it is a mode of amplifying and extending our contact with our fellow-men beyond the bounds of our personal lot. All the more sacred is the task of the artist when he undertakes to paint the life of the people. Falsification here is far more pernicious than in the more artificial aspects of life. It is not so very serious that we should have false ideas about evanescent fashions, about the manners and conversations of beaux and duchesses; but *it is* serious that our sympathy with the perennial joys and struggles, the toil, the tragedy, and the humour in the life of the more heavily-laden fellow-men, should be perverted, turned towards a false object instead of the true one. ... We want to be taught to feel, not for the heroic artisan or the sentimental peasant, but for the peasant in all his coarse apathy, and the artisan in all his suspicious selfishness.[32]

She believed in "realism"—such as that advocated by John Ruskin in his *Modern Painters*, what she called the "humble and faithful study of nature"—"definite, substantial reality"—an acceptance of which doctrine, she felt, would remould life and make its teacher a "prophet for his generation".[33]

It was perhaps with this in mind that she dealt, in the three stories that constitute the *Scenes of Clerical Life*, with what might be called "broken lives," and ordinary clerics—eccentric, tragic, or regenerated—looked at askance or with suspicion by the community, even as objects of derision. Nor was it an accident that in each of the three stories, women are victims either of an inordinately hard life, of betrayal, or of bestial male brutality.

She evokes what she calls the "pathos" of insignificance as she scans the indigent and exploited curate Amos Barton, who must support a wife and numerous children on eighty pounds a year, the portion allotted him by his superior, himself the possessor of a number of livings on which he thrives. A middling, somewhat ridiculous person, Amos Barton was in his very faults "middling—he was not *very* ungrammatical. It was not in his nature to be superlative in anything; unless, indeed, he was superlatively middling, the quintessential extract of mediocrity." On the part of many of the formidable, pretentious and none-too-kind villagers, he is the subject of ridicule, spite, and malicious gossip. His wife, a poor loyal woman, wears out her life in the innumerable duties of the household, and dies. And Barton himself is forced out by an ambitious rival. In another story, "Janet's Repentance," the dissenting parson, Mr. Tryan, is likewise the object of persecution on the part of the villagers; one of those figures, to reappear in other of George Eliot's stories, whose own sad life has taught him kindliness, forgiveness, and understanding of other people's sufferings, and makes it possible for him to bring relief to the desperate Janet, the demoralized victim of a brutal marriage.

The quality of translating the "ordinary" into an experience in which the reader could participate in humane terms must have been a striking one to the first readers of "Amos Barton" when it appeared in January 1857 in the dignified pages of *Blackwood's Magazine*—as was customary then, without any avowed authorship. Those living in the vicinity of the locales of the story (and of those stories published subsequently) recognized characters and incidents, though at a loss to understand who might have had such a thorough acquaintance as to bring them in such vivid form out of the past into the present. G. H. Lewes had sent the first story to John Blackwood as coming from a "clerical friend," knowing that coming from a man it stood a better chance of attracting attention than if it came from a woman, even an anonymous one. The example of the Brontës, who had adopted male pseudonyms—not to mention the better known pseudonym "George Sand"—was sufficiently monitory of the disadvantage under which women labored in making public appearances. The additional fact of the ambiguous moral position occupied by the writer would certainly have influenced the acceptance and impact of the literary product.

The first part of "Amos Barton," appeared in January 1857, and John Blackwood was enthusiastic. "I am delighted," he wrote to the "author"—who in February assumed the name of "George Eliot,"—"to be able to tell you that Amos seems fairly to have taken with the public."[34] It was not until the following year, when the three stories of the *Scenes*—"Amos Barton," "Mr. Gilfil's Love Story," and "Janet's Repentance"—had appeared in a two-volume edition, and she had already embarked on *Adam Bede*, that Blackwood was informed of the true identity of George Eliot. Such disclosure was made additionally mandatory by the fact that spurious claimants began to assert their authorship of the stories.

Despite an obvious awkwardness in the handling of the materials of the *Scenes* and a tendency, which she would never quite overcome, to moralize, these stories are germinal for the George Eliot to come. There are elements in them of what would come to be called a "revolt from the village"—a realistic portrayal of provincial life in its pathos as well as in its sordidness—such as shocked John Blackwood, and which elicited a strong response from the author. Speaking of "Janet's Repentance" and the characters in it, especially the tyrannical lawyer Dempster, she wrote:

> The collision in the drama is not at all between "bigotted churchmanship" and evangelicalism, but between *ir*religion and religion. ... The real town was more vicious than my Milby; the real Dempster was far more disgusting than mine; the real Janet alas! had a far sadder end than mine, who will melt away from the reader's sight in purity, happiness and beauty.[35]

She was less interested, however, in portraying the less agreeable aspects of such life (though far from evading them) than in depicting

> the poetry and pathos, the tragedy and comedy, lying in the experience of a human soul that looks out through dull grey eyes, and speaks in a voice of quite ordinary tones ...[36]

Amos Barton was just a "grey" character, a "Shlemiel" of the countryside, shuffling along in all the ripeness of his incapacities, trying to do his job as curate as well as he could, contrasting, in his naive but honest "mediocrity," with the stuffy pretentiousness of the more "refined" provincial society. George Eliot was more interested in men such as he, or the Rev. Mr. Tryan, the strong evangelical, who spoke to his neighbors out of what Eliot called an "initiation of suffering," He was one of those who insisted on "caring for individuals," and refused to "adopt the quantitative view of human anguish" in which the human individual becomes only a cipher in a statistical report. Since so much of life revolved around the parish house, she has no use for the buckram-stiff traditional incumbents more interested in preaching incomprehensible and pretentiously learned theological dogma than in responding to the needs of the ordinary parishioner. Their parchment heart knows too little of feeling to be able to enter into the hunger and anguish of their "inferiors."

She was too secure in her own naturalistic ethics to need to become crudely anti-religious. What she demanded was a freedom from fanaticism, dogma, intolerance, and inhumanity in the preachers of the Gospel, an ability to communicate with the ordinary human being. "The first condition of human goodness is something to love; the second something to reverence," she wrote in "Janet's Repentance." She was too devoted a disciple of Feuerbach not to identify the love and reverence as the inter-action of the "I" and the "Thou." And thus she echoed and paraphrased that German thinker in redefining the idea of God as a moral influence, in that it cherished "all that is best and loveliest in man." That there were such qualities in human beings, and that they deserved to be shown, remained the central theme of all her books. Her religion lay in a belief in the "possibilities of human nature."[37]

Her own moral credo, which rejected the idea of immortality as necessary to the good life, she expounded about the same time:

> I am just and honest, not because I expect to live in another world, but because, having felt the pain of injustice and dishonesty towards myself, I have a fellow feeling with other men, who would suffer the same pain if I were unjust or dishonest towards them ... I am honest, because I don't like to inflict evil on others in this life, not because I am afraid of evil to myself in another ... It is a pang to me to witness the sufferings of a fellow-being, and I feel his suffering the more acutely because he is *mortal*—because his life is short, and I would have it, if possible filled with happiness and not misery. Through my union and fellowship with men and women I *have* seen, I feel a like, though a fainter, sympathy with those I have *not* seen; and I am able so to live in imagination with the generations to come, that their good is not alien to me, and is a stimulus to me to labour for ends which may not benefit myself, but will benefit them ... And I should say that if you feel no motive to common morality but your fear of a criminal in heaven, you are decidedly a man for the police on earth to keep their eye upon, since it is a matter of world-old ex-perience that fear of distant consequences is a very insufficient barrier against the rush of immediate desire.[38]

Standing upon the bedrock of her own moral certitudes, she could even depict sympathetically such a figure as the Methodist preacher Dinah Morris in *Adam Bede*, who firmly believed in the "visible manifestation of Jesus," and of course in the im-mortality of the soul, but could communicate her faith in word and practice in an age of almost bankrupt Christianity. That she is at the same time a factory worker in an adjoining town brings her closer to the level of the people she is addressing than is the case with the local establishment rector, Mr. Irwine, who though a good and tolerant fellow, something of an epicurean, practices a tolerance touched with too much ac-commodation, *bonhommie*, and theological *laissez-faire*. Fanatical as Dinah Morris may be, her fervor is preferable to the lustreless Christianity that pervades the community.

Even before the *Scenes of Clerical Life* appeared in book form in January 1858, Mar-ian had already begun working on her first full novel, *Adam Bede*. "George Eliot" was deemed a man, an impressive author, and was on the way to fame. Dickens was one of the few to suspect the author's sex, and so wrote to her, saying that if the *Scenes* "originated with no woman, I believe that no man ever before had the art of making himself, mentally, so like a woman, since the world began ..."[39] He was charmed by the "exquisite truth and delicacy" of the stories.

At the end of 1857 George Eliot had every reason to look back upon the immediate past with great satisfaction. In her Journal she wrote:

The last night of 1857. The dear old year is gone with all its *Weben* and *Streben*. Yet not gone, either; for what I have suffered and enjoyed in it remains to me an everlasting possession while my soul's life remains. This time last year. ... I was writing the Introduction to Mr. Gilfil's Love Story. What a world of thought and feelings since then! My life has deepened unspeakably during the last year: I feel a greater capacity for moral and intellectual enjoyment, a more acute sense of my deficiencies in the past, a more solemn desire to be faithful to coming duties, than I remember at any former period of my life. And my happiness has deepened too: the blessings of a perfect love and union grows daily. I have had some severe suffering this year from anxiety about my sister and what will probably be a final separation from her—there has been no other real trouble. Few women, I fear, have had such reasons as I have to think the long sad years of youth worth living for the sake of middle age ... So goodbye, dear 1857! May I be able to look back on 1858 with equal consciousness of advancement in work and in heart.[40]

It was as if her probationary existence had come to an end. She had been tried, and had tried herself, and she had come through. With confidence in the new novel now in hand, and with Lewes' *Physiology of Common Life* off the press, they betook themselves to the Continent once more. Such journeys were always to form the relaxing moment after great strains, not the least being the escape from ostracism and gossip. To Germany once more, where Lewes could confer with Justus von Liebig, the greatest of German chemical geniuses; and where George Eliot, still at work on *Adam Bede*, could also frequent the excellent museums and indulge herself in the marvelous collections of Dutch art. In Munich she also met once more with David Friedrich Strauss. In Zurich Lewes looked up the physiologist and materialist Moleschott. There can be little question but that, no less that the "realism" of the Dutch painters, these contacts with foreign scientists of an experimental and materialist school, and subsequent discussions with Lewes, had a profound effect on George Eliot's own intellectual direction.

* * *

They returned to England in September 1858, and *Adam Bede* reached completion in November. Blackwood was highly pleased by the chapters he had been reading, and the entire book appeared in February in the typical Victorian three-volume—"three-decker"—format. The author received £1,200 for the work and, now firmly established, Lewes and George Eliot settled in Holly Lodge, Wandsworth. By October 1859, *Adam Bede* had reached its seventh edition!

Like the *Scenes of Clerical Life, Adam Bede* too goes back to a "bucolic" past in England's provincial life. And this represents one of the most striking of the paradoxes in George Eliot's creative world. Her philosophy of life and art was deeply grounded in the present, absorbing much from the scientific thought which Lewes made so available to her now, the evolutionary theories very much in the air, and culminating in the year 1859 in the publication of Charles Darwin's *The Origin of Species*. The overwhelming vista revealing the manifold interrelatedness of Nature and Man, the whole process of evolution—the idea of progress—the amazing discoveries in human physiology associated with Bichat and that even greater genius Claude Bernard—all these tended to confirm and solidify her naturalistic view of the world. Perhaps the immensity that confronted her as well as other Victorians, the vast panoramas that the past and the present were opening to the view of mankind, might have proved somewhat unsettling. But the hold of the past was too strong to shake off. And perhaps that was one of the reasons—aside from its literary merits—for the astonishing popular success of *Adam Bede*.*

How open George Eliot was to new ideas is illustrated by her reaction to Darwin's epochal work: "We are reading Darwin's Book on Species," she wrote in her letters of November and December 1859,

> just come out, after long expectation. It is an elaborate exposition of the evidence in favour of the Development Theory, and so makes an epoch ... So the world gets on step by step toward brave clearness and honesty. But to me the Development theory and all other explanations of processes by which things came to be, produce a feeble impression compared with the mystery that lies under the processes.[41]

An innovator herself, and deep in the stream of these new ideas, she yet looked back with a pained nostalgia on the preindustrial countryside, the elemental rural world in which, it seemed to her, man was so much a part of the nature that surrounded him, living in an ordered, well-established universe that appeared unchangeable. She was doing what in her own words she called letting "the imagination do a little Toryism on the sly"—"revelling in that dear, old, brown crumbling inefficiency," contrasting so markedly with our "new-varnished efficiency," with its endless diagrams, plans, elevations, sections, but alas! no picture."[42] *Adam Bede* takes place at such a time, in fact at the beginning of the century, during the Napoleonic wars, when the village of Hayslope was scarcely aware of the great goings-on elsewhere, except for the price of victuals and goods, and the occasional departure of some of the villagers for the army. It was a time when there were still homes of "unmarketable beauty," clean little market towns without much manufacture, for industry had not yet spread its greedy tentacles into the region nor darkened it with its smoky fumes. And also a time, George Eliot notes significantly, when "the rick-burners had not found their way hither"—a statement of profound significance. For George Eliot, like many of her contemporaries, had not forgotten a later day, when the hungry, miserable agricultural laborers had terrified the hitherto settled countryside with their demands for bread, had set many a hayrick on fire, and had been seized, tried, and either hanged or deported. For this was still a time when you were severely punished for poaching on

---

* A hastily typed note, headed "Addendum: George Eliot," found with the manuscript of this section, indicates that the author intended to expand on this point. [Ed.]:

The Naturalism of G. H. Lewes and George Eliot—It is of course not possible to determine exactly the extent of G. H. Lewes's influence on George Eliot's development and work—but it stands to reason that much of his thinking interpenetrated with hers—and the correspondences that exist between his ideas of literature—particularly realism—and hers—are more than mere accidents. Nor can it be an accident that so much of her own interest in science and scientific research, especially in biology and physiology, derived from him. Actually, there is evidence of a number of suggestions for plot and incident that she adopted—as she herself stated—but the overall influence of science and aesthetic theory of which he was a proponent. ... etc. ... [See Shuttleworth, 1984, under "Further Reading."– Ed.]

the landlord's estate, and hanged for stealing sheep. The fires that had burned so fiercely in her letters of 1848 were now down to a steady glow, and order had become an important element in her life and thought, as it was in the minds of most of the articulate Victorians. Order within Change. ...

It is therefore within Hayslope and the adjoining communities that we find this kind of settled society, where the solar system, to use her own words, was the parish, the parsonage and the manor, and the leading figures were the squire and the priest. Though not sharply divided, the community is conscious of rank, station, and deference. A patriarchal hangover from feudal days prevails.

That even in its simplification this is an idealized world is, perhaps unconsciously, shown by the author herself. Or rather, it is for the moment a dead world, characterized by a torpor which pervades the life and the religion of its inhabitants. That is, until two separate elements enter to precipitate out a serious dislocation. One is the presence of the zealous Methodist preacher, Dinah Morris, whose passionate evangel produces an emotional convulsion among many of her hearers, hungry for words of comfort and hope that will stir them from a sterile void. She is the human bearer of human words, the embodiment of enthusiasm and feeling as against the aridity of conventionalized Christianity. She gives them the assurance of heaven and a living Christ to compensate for the depressed conditions of life. In idealizing her and turning her fanaticism into a saintliness, George Eliot was unwittingly underlining the role that Methodism and Evangelicalism were playing in neutralizing political activity, deterring insurgence, and anaestheticizing discontents. Dinah Morris, who is magnificently drawn, modifies her rigoristic Methodism in the end by falling in love with Adam Bede. But this scarcely negates the above considerations. She acts in keeping with George Eliot's beliefs that feelings transcend dogma and doctrine.

The other disturbing element in the book, as well as in the village life it portrays, is seen in the treatment of Hetty Sorrel, the simple country lass and servant maid in the Poyser household, with whom Adam Bede is in love. She is seduced by the grandson of the local squire, Captain Arthur Donnithorne. The girl is very young, vain, naive, and very, very attractive. That she should fall for the handsome young captain and imagine for herself a life as wife of a landed country squire, with all the finery and affluence thus far denied her, is not altogether too fantastic an occurrence. Betrothed to Adam Bede but already pregnant by young Donnithorne, she runs away to find her seducer, who is on his way to join his regiment in Ireland. Frustrated and utterly distraught, she does away with the baby by exposing it, is apprehended and brought to trial. If it does happen to be *eine alte Geschichte*—an old story—the simple country girl falling a prey to the upper-class seducer, it is amazing that she takes her place in George Eliot's imagination and pages exactly as she would appear to the villagers themselves. That the seduction and Donnithorne's entire conduct reflect a hangover of feudal relationships between lord and servant appears to have escaped her understanding. Class differences of course preclude the possibility of a legal union. The girl is a lower-class commodity, to be used and cast off at pleasure. It is surprising that the novelist, who is given to a great many didactic and moralizing asides, has not been able to spare one for Hetty's poor self. Nor is the persistence Dinah Morris exercises in bringing the imprisoned girl to a confession of her guilt any less horrifying. Hetty's psychic and physical suffering passes without extended comment, except for those moving pages that describe her wanderings.

The strength of the book lies of course in its own vivid, often humorous, but thoroughly absorbing depiction of simple folk in their everyday activities. Among them, and even in comparison with those higher up, Adam Bede stand forth as the embodiment and symbolic representative of rustic virtue. A carpenter, he bring to his work not only a supreme competence and skill, but also an integrity, a passion for work, and a respect for his vocation and for himself—an all-around integrity marred only by pride. In physical build and in personality he is a powerful figure, a heroic non-hero. The only character in the book who truly undergoes change, Adam Bede illustrates George Eliot's doctrine of education through suffering.

> Deep, unspeakable suffering, says George Eliot, may well be called a baptism, a regeneration, the initiation into a new state ... All the intense emotions which had filled the days and nights of the past week, and were compressing themselves again like an eager crowd into the hours of this single morning, made Adam look back on all the previous years as if they had been a dim sleepy existence, and he had only now awaked to full consciousness.[43]

Yet, that new consciousness does not yield revolt, but rather compassion—anger gives way to general forgiveness. Thus a bucolic equilibrium is restored: Hetty, instead of being hanged, is deported, through young Donnithorne's intercession; Donnithorne, now reigning squire, and Adam Bede are reconciled in a general moral conversion—unfortunately the extent of Donnithorne's new understanding can be gauged by his reply to Adam's self-accusation of excessive harshness in the past:

> "Adam," Arthur said, impelled to full confession now, "it would never have happened if I'd known you loved her. That would have helped to save me from it. ..." Their hands were clasped once more, and Adam left the Hermitage, feeling that sorrow was more bearable now hatred was gone. ...[44]

To this general amnesty, the Rev. Irwine is a vigorous accessory, though at first violently opposed by Adam Bede himself, before he is finally convinced.

> "You have no right," says the Rev. Mr. Irwine, "to say that the guilt of her crime lies with him, and that he ought to bear the punishment. It is not for us men to apportion the share of moral guilt and retribution. We find it impossible to avoid mistakes even in determining who had committed a single criminal act, and the problem how far a man is to be held responsible for the unforeseen consequences of his own deed, is one that might well make us tremble to look into it ...[45]

It is the remarkable Mrs. Poyser—a character that might well have come out of Dickens—who is strong enough of mind and tongue to offer resistance when she sees wrong being done, in this case by the old squire, who attempts to work an exchange of land (the Poysers are his tenant-farmers) which would, in Mrs. Poyser's opinion, work to their disadvantage. While the meek Mr. Poyser sits in partial acquiescence, Mrs. Poyser bursts out to old Squire Donnithorne:

> "I know," she says, "there's them as is born t' own the land, and them as is born to sweat on 't"—here Mrs. Poyser paused to gasp a little—"and I know it's christened folks's duty to submit to their betters as fur as flesh and blood 'ull bear it; but I'll not make a martyr

o'myself, and wear myself to skin and bone, and worret myself as if I was a churn wi' butter a-coming in't, for no landlord in England, not if he was King George himself."

And as old Donnithorne beats a hasty retreat:

"You may run away from my words, sir, and you may go spinnin' underhand ways o' doing us mischief, for you've got Old Harry to your friend, though nobody else is, but I tell you for once as we're not dumb creaturs to be abused and made money on by them as ha' got the lash i' their hands, for want o' knowing how t' undo the tackle. An' if I'm th' only one as speaks my mind, there's plenty o' the same way o' thinking i' this parish and the nest to 't, for your name's no better than a brimstone match in everybody's nose ...

"Thee'st done it now," said Mr. Poyser, a little alarmed and uneasy, but not without some triumphant amusement at his wife's outbreak.

"Yis, I know I've done it," said Mrs. Poyser; "but I've had my say out, and I shall be th' easier for't all my life. There's no pleasure i' living, if you're to be corked up for iver, and only dribble your mind out by the sly, like a leaky barrel. ...[46]

Such overt rebellions were rare indeed in the village before steam triumphed, bringing railroads and factories. Nor was George Eliot much concerned at the moment with acts of revolt and sentiments of social discontent. Aside from the nostalgia for things past, she was deeply preoccupied with the moral consciousness of her characters, the motivations—conscious and unconscious—of actions and deeds, and the determinism, the causal nexus, that binds an act to its frequently unforeseen consequence, not only for the actor, but for those around him. Already in *Adam Bede* she was aware of the presence of elements within the human being unrevealed to the consciousness, and playing a formidable part in determining an act. Still unable to deal with it in its fullest complexity, she attempts to sound the unconscious motivations in young Donnithorne's personality and his behavior toward Hetty. There is a point before the catastrophe when he is about to open his heart to the Rev. Irwine but is diverted from his intent, and changes his mind. George Eliot asks:

Was there a motive at work under this strange reluctance of Arthur's which had a sort of backstairs influence, not admitted to himself? Our mental business is carried on much in the same way as the business of the State: a great deal of hard work is done by agents who are not acknowledged. In a piece of machinery, too, I believe there is often a small unnoticeable wheel which has a great deal to do with the motion of the large obvious ones. Possibly there was some such unrecognized agent secretly busy in Arthur's mind at this moment—possibly it was the fear lest he might hereafter find the fact of having made a confession to the Rector a serious annoyance, in case he should *not* be able to carry out his good resolutions: I dare not assert that it was not so. The human soul is a very complex thing.[47]

Adam Bede produced an astonishing impact on its readership. Mrs. Carlyle, who could not induce her husband to read more than a few pages of the book (he had nothing but contempt for novels), wrote to the pseudonymous author that the book was "as good as going to the country for one's health ... The newspapers have decided that you are a clergyman."[48] It was soon translated into German, Dutch, Hungarian, French. Count Leo Tolstoy read it in Russian, and found in it "the highest art."

George Eliot had succeeded in conveying to her readers what she termed the "beauty of the commonplace." She had brought them close to the common life of the villagers, she had drawn them into the lives of Dinah Morris and Adam Bede and Hetty Sorrel. She had appealed to the Victorian religious and moralizing needs, their humane sentiments. Dinah Morris, the missionary, preached God to the cotton workers of Snowfield, to the "lonely, bare stone houses, where there's nothing to give comfort"; she showed them "the hatefulness of sin," and the way of salvation from their "guilt, their wild darkness, and their state of disobedience to God." She bore the consoling word to Hetty Sorrel on the eve of her trial, and brought her to confess her "crime." Adam Bede was shown in his simple grandeur, almost one of Nature's noblemen, great in his sorrow as he goes in search of his unfortunate betrothed, and impressive and moving in his gradual understanding of suffering and grief in the growth of a human being. For George Eliot had tried to show how regeneration of the human heart can be born out of these trials, and that a rebirth of the inner self is the prerequisite to all other changes within human relations.

There is nothing so exhilarating as success. And George Eliot was successful. She had praise and acceptance not only from the general public, which either bought the book (costing over three pounds!) or, more likely, hurried to Mudie's circulating library to rent a copy; but also from the cognoscenti, like Charles Dickens. Such growth of reputation mitigated somewhat the unpleasantness associated with anonymity, the claims made by others to authorship of the book, and the necessity for self-revelation as the true creator of the *Scenes* and of *Adam Bede*. The risk was not minor, for the aura surrounding the unknown author and her works could not but be dimmed by the knowledge that she was Marian Evans, unwedded "wife" of George Henry Lewes, himself a somewhat "tarnished" character. Respectability remained aloof, but also read her novels; and she, for her part, doubly armed now by character and fame, was strong enough to outface scoffers and gossips. It no doubt hurt that Carlyle was utterly indifferent to her and her works, for he had been and remained for a long time her moral ideal; but she was somewhat compensated by Mrs. Carlyle's enthusiasm, and even more by an invitation from Charles Dickens to contribute to his newly established magazine *All the Year Round*—an offer she nevertheless declined. Carlyle might scoff at the woman who presumed to write about a carpenter and carpentering, but who would not be delighted to receive such words from the author of *David Copperfield* as these?—"*Adam Bede* has taken its place among the actual experiences and endurances of my life … I laid the book down fifty times, to shut my eyes and think about it."[49]

Few writers of her time possessed her intellectual passions and voracity. And few could have assimilated that knowledge not only into their own experiences, but crystallized it and integrated it into their creative productions with such consummate mastery. It was not only that she lived in a period of intense intellectual expansion—not since the Renaissance had there been such a scientific revolution as was now taking place—but the various domains of science and technology were being interrelated not only with each other, but also with the problems of individual man and his society. Could the study of society become a "science" such as physics and chemistry, and now biology, physiology, and psychology? Like John Stuart Mill, she and others were asking whether moral and social phenomena are really exceptions to the general certainty and uniformity of the course of nature; and how far the methods, by which so many of the laws of the physical world have been numbered among truths irrevocably acquired and universally assented to, can be made instrumental to the formation of a similar body of received doctrine in moral and political science ...[50]

Her own answer was Yes, for she sided with Comte, and spoke of the "natural history of social bodies," and the need for statesmen, politician and social reformers to study the peculiar characteristics of their society, "of the nation, the province, the class," with the same care and precision hitherto utilized in the natural sciences.

If any man of sufficient moral and intellectual breadth, whose observations would not be vitiated by a foregone conclusion, or by a professional point of view, would devote himself to studying the natural history of our social classes, especially of the small shop-keepers, artisans, and peasantry,—the degree in which they are influenced by local conditions, their maxims and habits, the points of view from which they regard their religious teachers, and the degree in which they are influence by religious doctrines, the interactions of the various classes on each other, and what are the tendencies in their position towards disintegration or towards development, and if, after all this study, he would give us the result of his observations in a book well nourished with specific facts, his work would be a valuable aid to the social and political reformer.[51]

"And to the writer too," she might have added, for it was in part these very observations that she herself was making, though in a limited area. In France, Balzac had already shown the way to the new novel with his magnificent *Human Comedy*. Great as was George Eliot's admiration for Balzac, she was also ambivalent toward him, more by virtue of her own limitations than by that master's fault. In sexual matters she was, like so many of her contemporaries, altogether a Puritan, bound to reticence by that myopia which was to prove so deleterious to the full efflorescence of her own work. Balzac's great failing was the moral one, she believed.

Balzac, she wrote, perhaps the most wonderful writer of fiction the world has ever seen, has in many of his novels overstepped this limit. He drags us by his magic force through scene after scene of unmitigated vice, till the effect of walking among this human carrion is a moral nausea.[52]

She had perhaps forgotten that even Goethe, now truly enthroned in Lewes' book, had been the object of similar accusations.

Yet she was opposed to the traditional idealization of the peasantry, and demanded a greater truthfulness of the artist, who should render them as they really are in all their coarseness and vulgarity.

... No one, she wrote, who has seen much of actual ploughmen thinks them jocund; no one who is well acquainted with the English peasantry can pronounce them merry ... Observe a company of haymakers ... Approach nearer, and you will certainly find that haymaking time is a time for joking, especially if there are women among the laborers; but the coarse laugh that bursts out every now and then, and expresses the triumphant taunt, is as far as possible from your conception of idyllic merriment. That delicious effervescence of the mind, which we call fun, has no equivalent for the northern peasant, except his tipsy revelry; the only realm of fancy and imagination for the English clown exists at the bottom of the third quart pot.[53]

Balzac's novel *The Peasants* would have supplied an excellent example of her desired treatment, but would have revolted her. What she might have said of Zola's *La Terre*, had she lived long enough to read it, would have been easy to predict. Yet it is interesting to note that, just as Zola was describing his own theory as that of the "Experimental Novel," George Eliot too spoke of her own writing as "simply a set of experiments in life—an endeavour to see what our thought and emotion may be capable of—what stores of motive, actual or hinted as possible, give promise of a better after which we may strive ..."[54]

That "experiment in life" she now set in motion with greater assurance and skill when in January 1859 she began work on her next novel, which was to be called *The Mill on the Floss*.

* * *

Feuerbach had said:

> The heart is the source, the centre of all suffering. A being without suffering is a being without a heart. The mystery of the suffering God is the mystery of feeling, sensibility. A suffering God is a feeling, sensitive God. But the proposition: God is a feeling Being is only the religious periphrase of the proposition: feeling is absolute, divine in its nature.[55]

The principal characters of her stories up to this time had all gone through baptisms of suffering and regeneration: Adam Bede, Amos Barton, the Rev. Tryan, the Rev. Gilfil, but that was in "another age," an Arcadian time and place, and the stories had been founded on either distant memories or transformed hearsay. In such a bucolic, almost immobile landscape, where the conflicts were mild, often concealed, but rare, and ancient sanctities of order and rank almost undisturbed, mutual tolerance, forgiveness and reconciliation might be seen as their remedies, restorative of an equilibrium. Life such as this was viewed through the prism of innocence.

But the scene now is changed. We move into the age of steam. Soon the thunder of the locomotive and the railroad cars will change the face of the countryside and the lives of its inhabitants. This is what Mr. Deane explains to young Tom Tulliver, Maggie Tulliver's brother, in *The Mill on the Floss*:

> You see, Tom, ... the world goes on at a smarter pace now than it did when I was a young fellow. Why, sir, forty years ago, when I was much such a strapping youngster as you, a man expected to pull between the shafts the best part of his life before he got the whip in his hands. The looms went slowish, and fashions didn't alter quite so fast; I'd a best suit that lasted me six years. Everything was on a lower scale, sir—in point of expenditure, I mean. It's this steam, you see, that has made the difference; it drives on every wheel double pace, and the wheel of fortune along with 'em ... I don't find fault with the change as some people do. Trade, sir, opens a man's eyes ... Somebody has said it's a fine thing to make two ears of corn grow where only one grew before; but, sir, it's a fine thing to further the exchange of commodities and bring the grains of corn to the mouths that are hungry ...[56]

An autobiographical novel is a stark confrontation of a writer's two selves: the self displayed and the self concealed; the self that is and the self that it would like to become; the self idealized and the self as reality. In George Eliot, it would seem, such a book as *The Mill on the Floss* fulfilled the necessary catharsis that her past life demanded, and was something of a redemptive act, a prerequisite ladder of ascension from her own involvement in her past life and family into an objectification of it, and hence a transcendence. The novel's importance does not of course lie in its correspondence to the facts of her existence, or in their transformation as materials of a moving fictional narrative, but in its masterful interpretation and reinvocation of the struggles of a girl to achieve an independent personality in the face of many adverse elements and factors both within her own self and in the world outside her. Artistically it was also a prelude to her own restoration and a preparation for that enlargement that was to take on the epic breadth of her three last major works. Personally it was her testament, as she confessed many a time speaking of herself, though not of the book—a coming back into life from a death of self-doubt.

A letter written in 1861 gives us a special insight into that aspect of her past life:

> I often think of my dreams when I was four or five and twenty. I thought then how happy fame would make me. I feel no regret that the fame, as such, brings no pleasure; but it *is* a grief to me that I do not constantly feel strong in thankfulness that my past life has vindicated its uses, and given me reason for gladness that such an unpromising woman-child was born into the world ...[57]

For into the conflicts and struggles she had written more than merely a chronicle of a young girl's experiences, but actually an epitome of Victorian womanhood, struggling for a suitable outlet for her emotions and intelligence, for what might be called the freedom to *become* herself.

"I cling strongly to kith and kin, even though they reject me," she wrote around 1866. And the poem, "Brother and Sister," three years later only confirms that sentiment. She was already thirty years old when she ceased tending her father, following his death; what her brother Isaac felt about her we have already seen. He remained her implacable critic practically to the end. She, on her side, never forgot her early association with and love for that brother, the depth of which, had she properly understood it, would no doubt have horrified her had she had a Freudian clue to it. The poem, a series of eleven sonnets, begins:

> I cannot choose but think upon the time
> When our two lives grew like two buds that kiss
> At lightest thrill from the bee's swinging chime,
> Because the one so near the other is ...

It recounts the childhood experiences which she had embodied in the novel, and concludes with,

> ... We had been natives of one happy clime,
> And its dear accent to our utterance clung,
> Till the dire years whose awful name is Change

Had grasped our souls still yearning in divorce,
And pitiless shaped them in two forms that range
Two elements which sever their life's course.

But were another childhood-world my share,
I would be born a little sister there.

The remarkable fact remains that, despite such thoroughly unhealthy personal involvement, she was able in the novel sufficiently to objectify her experiences so as to
render the individual instance with such profound psychological and social insights,
and such deep identification and feeling, that except for the conclusion, we obtain a
typical picture of a complex life and feelings unable to extricate themselves from the
tangled skein of deleterious personal and social influences.

Here, in the characters of Maggie Tulliver and her family, she was enabled success-
fuly and for the first time to exhibit the interaction of the individual with his social
environment, define that environment with its typical social strata and mores, and explore hereditary and family pressures as well as those of individual psychology. But
the preeminent fact is that this is a study of a woman in a masculine society, or better,
perhaps, of women as they reflect the masculine society and either adapt or rebel, a
society that now for the first time exhibits the great changes that were taking place in
the world outside, and in a minor way mirrors them in its preoccupation with the role
of money and status. It is also a study of how a sensitive, highly emotional, and intelligent character can under these circumstances be deformed, and eventually destroyed.

The distortion of such a character begins almost at birth—for she is a girl, hence a
second-class citizen of the family. The boy Tom gets the preferential treatment, at least
from their mother; Mr. Tulliver favors the girl. He is destined for a career—and she?
Somewhat homely, careless of her appearance and already overemotional and defiant,
"this small mistake of nature," as the author calls her, "gifted with the superior power of
misery," finds sustenance in her big brother's company and boyhood exploits, while at
the same time forced to feed her imagination on a fantasy life—her "opium"—and miscellaneous reading; and on the wide range of feeling and affection in her attachment to
father and brother. Her high-strung sensitivity finds an outlet in a "tenderness for deformed things." Her childhood is bound up with the native surroundings, the country,
the mill, the river—the impulses that come from the native woods, so exquisitely celebrated by Wordsworth as having a permanent influence in the formation of character.
She is also a product of two genetic strains, the Dodson, and the Tulliver; Mr. Tulliver
had married above him, and the superior Dodsons make no bones about manifesting
their superiority of wisdom and possessions, their sympathy for the aberrant Mrs. Tulliver, and their condescension to her husband. It is in these relationships that Maggie
first comes into a knowledge of status and class, and early in life begins to display a
spirit of rebellion directed against the tyranny and superiority that speak through her
hated aunt Mrs. Glegg—the most articulate of the Dodsons—and through the equally
humiliating submissiveness of her own mother. Maggie's hopelessly unruly hair is symbolic of her nonconformity; and her rebellion breaks out in a surgical operation on her
curls. In her mother's eyes she is incorrigible, for in her pride and stubbornness she
takes after her father. She is a "Tulliver," and Tom, obviously, more of a "Dodson."

The Mill on the Floss is a tragedy, but it is a tragedy of both the inner and the outer world. It is a tragedy in which the inner weaknesses of the woman collaborate with the outer compulsions of society to bring about an unavoidable disaster. It may even be said that in this instance the outer world of habit, respectability, order and convention aggravates but is not ultimately responsible for the catastrophe. All tragedy is concerned with the problem of freedom, and Maggie Tulliver is bound by chains that are as much self-imposed as they are imposed by her milieu.

In Maggie Tulliver the life-principle is strong; she is a person of deep feelings and passions in search of an emphatic way of life and faith to counter the "dead level" of feeling, belief, and actions of provincial society. Hers is a battle for integrity. This quality is also characteristic of her father, whose pride and stubbornness lead him into quarrels and lawsuits that eventually bring about his downfall, the loss of his mill, and death. Tom, stolid and domineering as he is, has a sense of uprightness that imposes upon him the duty of making good his father's debts and restoring the mill. But neither of them can fully understand the secret needs of Maggie—her yearning for self-fulfilment and a place in the world, her need of affection and support. In this respect Tom is the worst offender, for he never forgives. Bound by familial ties, Maggie ultimately renounces the life-principle and with it her own life's demands, vowing herself to a penitential existence of self-denial. Her rebellions are sporadic and lead to no inner growth that might result in total liberation. Her two most significant moments of self-affirmation and affirmation of passion are annulled through self-denials: in the first case her passive surrender to familial pressure in her relation to Philip Wakem, the crippled but highly gifted son of Mr. Tulliver's enemy, a reaching out on her part, if not of love, then at least of tender understanding and sympathy; and in the second instance, her intensely passionate reaction to Stephen Guest, her first opportunity for emotional fulfilment. Here too she is led to a renunciation, prompted by her sense of "duty" to her cousin, to whom Stephen is betrothed. But she is sufficiently compromised by her innocent escapade, and the community turns its odium on her, as does her own brother. The love between her and Stephen, its gradual awakening and growth, represent in some respects the height of George Eliot's artistry, and a degree of intensity she would never again allow herself to approach. Maggie, having lost all, estranged from her community, friends, and brother, turns to the sympathetic clergyman, and so strong is the wave of hostility, that calumny touches even him. ...

So Maggie is buffeted by fortune, her own propensities, and her environment; a stricken deer, suffering the deadly wound of utter rejection by Tom. She is the passive toy of circumstance, without the will or force to assert her own independence. Her brother is all in all to her, and it is perfectly appropriate that only in death can they be reunited. The rains come, the river overflows, and in her final gesture of love—the attempt to rescue her brother—both of them perish in the waters. The life-force that had never come to fruition is finally extinguished, and the union with her brother consummated.

Yet the tragedy of a stunted life, though it is the center of the book, does not exhaust its full content. For *The Mill on the Floss* has a great richness of humor, satire, irony; of profound social and psychological insights and comments; and of extraordinary character drawing. One of its most solid artistic achievements is the effective and graphic depiction of the environment in which Maggie and Tom grew up, especially the actual and symbolic role occupied by the Dodsons. And the Dodsons, though they are by no means the most affluent or socially prestigious members of St. Ogg's society (that station is occupied Mr. Guest, mill owner, shipping lord and banker), are in their numerous counterparts suggestive of that coming dominance, with its attendant mores and pressures, that will soon pervade a good part of the land. They are the incarnations of Carlyle's "cash-nexus."* It is money that eventually determines the fate of the Tullivers. In the eyes of the Dodsons the successful acquisition of that commodity reveals the hand of God, as failure shows God's judgment. They know and mark out the paths that lead to success, and fashion the human character according to their prescriptions. They possess one "emphatic belief"—money. All other adherences, religious or moral, savor of indifferentism, are matters of habit rather than conviction. They suspect "enthusiasm," any fervent attachment to a cause or credo or strong feeling, as a violation of their legislated decorum. That is the "good" society. It has

> its claret and its velvet-carpets, its dinner engagements six weeks deep, its opera and its faery ball-rooms; … gets its science done by Faraday and its religion by the superior clergy who are to be met within the best houses …

How then, George Eliot asks, "should it have time or need for belief or emphasis"?

Somewhat uncertainly, she proceeds to try to grasp the social structure that makes for that group's "ideology."

> But good society [she continues] … is of very expensive production, requiring nothing less than a wide and arduous national life condensed in unfragrant deafening factories, cramping itself in mines, sweating at furnaces, grinding, hammering, weaving under more or less oppression of carbonic acid—or else, spread over sheepwalks and scattered in lonely houses and huts on the clayey or chalky corn-lands where the rainy days look dreary … Under such circumstances there are many among its myriads of souls who have absolutely needed an emphatic belief: life in this unpleasurable shape demanding some solution even to unspeculative minds …[58]

Some, she continues, find their "emphatic belief" in alcohol, "but the rest require something that good society calls 'enthusiasm.'" Such is Maggie's need, and "without the aid of established authorities and appointed guides," she made out "a faith for herself" through a reading of the Bible, Thomas à Kempis's *Imitation of Christ*, and John Keble's *The Christian Year*. It was from these works that she derived her philosophy of renunciation, and won "happiness."

> "I've been a great deal happier" [she tells Philip Wakem] "since I have given up thinking about what is easy and pleasant, and being discontented because I couldn't have my own will. Our life is determined for us—and it makes the mind very free when we give up wishing and only think of bearing what is laid upon us and doing what is given us to do."[59]

Of course nothing could be more welcome to the "good society" than such "enthusiasm" for total passiveness. This is Maggie's secular Calvinism. It is a fatalistic determinism. Nor could Maggie understand Philip's warnings that she was only seeking "safety in negations," and "committing suicide."

---

* See above, pp. 38–40.

When she directs her attention to the Dodson clan, George Eliot brings an uncanny skill and insight into her analyses. Here irony, satire, and humor, as well as sharp criticism, are the instruments which help smartly to characterize the way in which that class converts human beings into things while at the same time humanizing and even apotheosizing the things they possess. In the characters of Mrs. Glegg, Mrs. Pullet, and Mrs, Tulliver she exposes the way this "fetishism" of things and personalizing of elements of private property become dominating factors in their lives, in establishing their rights to status. Linens, tableware, utensils, bonnets, become human; death itself is made a conduit of personal prestige, and legacies acquire the force of natural laws. What I have is more vital than what I am—or better, perhaps, what I am is what I have. What the Dodsons call the "Dodson spirit" has penetrated into the possessions and transubstantiated them. Death is the marketplace for their most conspicuous ostentation.

Take for example poor, pathetic Mrs. Tulliver, on the lower rung of the Dodson ladder. Her personality has transmigrated into crockery and linens. She is speaking to her husband: Second-best linens are good enough for a visiting guest.

> … As for them best Holland sheets, I should repent buying 'em, only they'll do to lay us out in. An' if you was to die tomorrow, Mr. Tulliver, they're mangled beautiful, an' all ready, an' smell o' lavender as it 'ud be a pleasure to lay 'em out; an' they lie at the left-hand corner o' the big oak linen-chest at the back, not as I should trust anybody to look 'em out but myself.[60]

As for the much more affluent Dodson, Mrs. Glegg,

> … Though, as she often observed, no woman had better clothes, it was not her way to wear her new things out before her old ones. Other women, if they liked, might have their best threadlace in every wash, but when Mrs. Glegg died, it would be found that she had better lace laid by in the right-hand drawer of her wardrobe, in the Spotted Chamber, than ever Mrs. Wooll of St. Ogg's had bought in her life, although Mrs. Wooll wore her lace before it was paid for.[61]

And Mrs. Pullet, another Dodson, exhibits her new bonnet to Mrs. Tulliver. The scene is evocative enough to allow for a longer quotation.

> "Pullet pays for it; he said I was to have the best bonnet at Garum Church, let the next best be whose it would."
>
> She began slowly to adjust the trimmings in preparation for returning it to its place in the wardrobe, and her thought seemed to have taken a melancholy turn, for she shook her head.
>
> "Ah," she said at last, "I may never wear it twice, sister; who knows?"
>
> "Don't talk o' that, sister," answered Mrs. Tulliver. "I hope you'll have your health this summer."
>
> "Ah! But there may come a death in the family, as there did soon after I had my green-satin bonnet. Cousin Abbot may go, and we can't think o' wearing crape less nor half a year for him."
>
> "That *would* be unlucky," said Mrs. Tulliver, entering thoroughly into the possibility of an inopportune decease. "There's never so much pleasure i' wearing a bonnet the second year, especially when the crowns are so chancy—never two summers alike."

"Ah, it's the way i' this world," said Mrs. Pullet, returning the bonnet to the wardrobe and locking it up. She maintained a silence characterized by head-shaking until they had all issued from the solemn chamber and were in her own room again. Then, beginning to cry, she said, "Sister, if you should never see that bonnet again till I'm dead and gone, you'll remember I showed it you this day."[62]

Alas for poor relations! How they must cling to their more prosperous sisters and brothers-in-law, converted into mortuary parchments in which it is hoped (as by Mrs. Tulliver) they will show some signs of "testamentary tenderness"!

Perhaps the most macabre exemple of this substitution of things for persons and feeling is exhibited when the unfortunate sale of the Tulliver household is taking place, and the Dodsons congregate not only, in at least one case, to complacently acknowledge God's hand in that misfortune (suitable punishment for the Tulliver spirit!) but also to consider which of the goods being sold they would need for their own households and which they could forego. And Mrs. Tulliver sits by, lamenting this or that particular object's acquisition by others and bewailing the lot that had brought her such a state. Upstairs Mr. Tulliver lies paralyzed by a stroke.

Respectability, order, and propriety, habitual conduct and decorum—these are the mainstays of that society. Snobbery rules, pervading the various social strata from the highest, the Guest household—especially the daughters—down to the Dodsons; and down, down as far as it can go. So the "good society" is shocked on hearing that Maggie, in one of her few acts of independence, has "gone into service" as a teacher!

Not the least deleterious aspect of this social scene is the attitude toward women. Stephen Guest breaks the traditional chains of social behavior by falling in love with Maggie; but the disgrace that follows falls not upon him but upon the girl. Brilliant as she is, certainly in comparison with her brother, she is made aware from her earliest day that, as her father remarks, Maggie is

... too 'cute for a woman ... It's no mischief much while she's a little un, but an over-'cute woman's no better nor a long-tailed sheep—she'll fetch none the bigger price for that."[63]

That opinion finds further confirmation when Maggie visits Tom at his tutor's and, challenged by her brother, asks,

"Mr. Stelling . ., couldn't I do Euclid, and all Tom's lessons, if you were to teach me instead of him?"

"No; you couldn't," said Tom indignantly. "Girls can't do Euclid, can they, sir?"

"They can pick up a little of everything, I dare say," said Mr. Stelling. "They've a great deal of superficial cleverness, but they couldn't go far into anything. They're quick and shallow." ...

"Ha, ha! Miss Maggie!" said Tom when they were alone. "You see, it's not such a fine thing to be quick. You'll never go far into anything, you know."

And Maggie was so oppressed by this dreadful destiny that she had no spirit for a retort.[64]

"No spirit for retort." For that spirit was to be crushed out of her, she herself a coadjutor in its destruction. "The child is father of the man," Wordsworth had chanted. That the influences in childhood are paramount in determining future development, George Eliot was fully conscious. Nature plays its part; Nature—"the mother tongue of the imagination." But she went beyond Wordsworth in seeking out other forces that, added to the internal ones of the personality, are equally formative. These are universal, affecting both high and low. She justified her particular preoccupation with the Dodson family by the necessity of making the reader "feel" and "understand" how its "oppressive narrowness" "acted on the lives of Tom and Maggie, how it has acted on young natures in many generations ..."

> The suffering, whether of martyr or victim, which belongs to every historical advance of mankind is represented in this way in every town and by hundreds of obscure hearths; and we need not shrink from this comparison of small things with great, for does not science tell us that its highest striving is after the ascertainment of a unity which shall bind the smallest with the greatest?[65]

Henry James, a devoted admirer of both the author and her work, remarked on the Balzacian quality of George Eliot's "attempt to classify the Dodsons socially in a scientific manner," but he objected strenuously to the way she had handled the dénouement. It seemed to him that nothing in the story had prepared for it, and as if it were a "tardy expedient for the solution of Maggie's difficulties." While having no objections to floods and earthquakes, he continues, he would have preferred if Maggie had been left to her own devices, even though "a lonely spinsterhood" would seem a "dismal consummation of her generous life."[66] While it is true that the narrative seems somewhat hurried toward the end, as George Eliot herself later acknowledged, James is somewhat off course. Certainly the *dénouement* is anticipated in Mrs. Tulliver's worry that little Maggie's waywardness might lead to a drowning, and the river is an ever-present motif in the story. But if one of its principal themes is what may be called a "death of the heart," Maggie had already committed herself to an extinction. A distorted personality of potential grandeur, she was one of those trees of which George Eliot said that "if you lop off their finest branches ..., the wounds will be healed over with some rough boss, some odd excrescence; and what might have been a grand tree expanding into liberal shade, is but a whimsical trunk."[67]

The Mill on the Floss proved highly successful, and George Eliot's income grew considerably. Not all reviewers had reacted favorably; as a matter of fact, a number of them were highly critical of the book's morality and religious tone. Might these have been the reasons, as well as her own equivocal status, for a certain reserve with respect to love and passion that crept into her succeeding novels?[68] *The Mill on the Floss* was certainly daring, judged by Victorian standards. George Eliot never duplicated the beautiful love scene between Stephen Guest and Maggie, nor celebrated the "solemnity belonging to all human passion" with the same fervor. She was to widen her horizon immensely in her future works, and explore the problem of freedom and society with greater penetration. But she was never to write a more personal book.

Tolstoy undoubtedly knew *The Mill on the Floss*, and is it not most likely that the celebrated opening sentence of *Anna Karenina*, "All happy families resemble one another, each unhappy family is unhappy in its own way," echoes George Eliot's "the happiest women, like the happiest nations, have no history"?

* * *

With the publication of *The Mill on the Floss* in 1860, and the last of her "bucolic" narratives, *Silas Marner*, the following year, George Eliot became one of the highest-paid writers of the day. The temptation of obtaining ever larger payments—abetted by Lewes—was irresistible, and led her to abandon her time-honored publisher, Blackwood, and yield to George Smith, owner of the *Cornhill Magazine*, in which her historical novel *Romola* was to be serialized on most attractive terms. Though the story proved to be a failure with readers, John Blackwood generously received her back into his fold.

Yet with *Romola*, George Eliot was now embarking on the vaster enterprises which were to take epic form and, with greater success, culminate in her masterpiece *Middlemarch*. Her failure with *Romola* and triumph with *Middlemarch* are both indicative of her true strengths as well as some very significant limitations. She was masterly in depicting the life she knew, either at first hand or through vivid recollection and tradition. Provincial life, especially of the Midlands, was her domain. It is from that center that she was able to radiate into ever larger circles of ideas and experiences. Here she was supreme in being able to translate thought into the vivid reality of life. But in *Romola*, deep and wide as was the scholarship she expended, her historic imagination was not sufficient to transport her into the complicated arena of Renaissance society, its politics, its religious conflicts, into the minds so far removed from her own experience. She had no understanding of the sweep of historical movements of the time, nor a philosophy of history that she could apply to expose the determining influences in the lives of her characters—particularly the central figure of Savonarola. For the great revolution in historiography which distinguishes the nineteenth century had also affected the reinterpretation of the Renaissance in Italy, as well as elsewhere in Europe, thanks to the labors of Jacob Burckhardt, Michelet, Gobineau, John Addington Symonds, and Walter Pater—to name but a few. All historical novels are in the end projections of the writers' current historical understanding. As Tolstoy, the greatest of all historical novelists, put it, "the first germ of interest in history arises out of contemporary events."[69] He might have added that without such understanding of contemporary events, as well as the philosophical ideas of the age, great historical novel-writing is impossible. And great as she was in so many other respects, George Eliot had no profound understanding of the historical movements of her own day. This fault, especially evident in *Felix Holt*, will be explored in greater detail below.

Not that she was unaware of the exigencies of her own times—the 1860s were filled with political and social agitation. The Chartists, seemingly defunct, triumphed posthumously in the second great Reform Bill of 1867. The agitation which preceded that great "concession" by Tory and Whig, had been sparked by another of those periodic economic crises that were to become chronic after 1870. The American Civil War had wide economic and political repercussion throughout the world, but preeminently in England. The victory of Prussian arms against Austria and her German allies at Sadowa in 1866 was a dire omen for the future of the world. Victorian England was shaken.

George Eliot could not escape history. The three major works of her late and most mature period are proof and fruit of it. The triad of epic novels begins with *Felix Holt* in 1866, continues with *Middlemarch*, 1871–1872, and ends with *Daniel Deronda* in 1876. The last two appeared at the time of Napoleon III's fall, the defeat of France, the period of the Commune, the unification of Germany, and the creation of the German Empire.

If the last of these novels, *Daniel Deronda*, is the only one with a contemporary setting, the other two, *Felix Holt* and *Middlemarch*, though they hark back to the first Reform Bill agitations from 1829 to 1832, are singularly pointed reflections of current happenings. So George Eliot too brings her reactions to contemporary events to play upon another period. In that sense, all three novels are addressed to the present.

If we look at these three works in the aggregate, we are struck by the expanse and richness, the multiplicity of characters of various classes, and the skilful handling of the interrelations and interplay among them. There is greater depth and wider resonance. Sometimes details seem to weigh down the central narrative line, but one never loses the sense that a maturer intelligence is at work and is presenting us with new insights and experiences. In that respect, *Middlemarch* stands like a formidable and masterly central fortress, flanked by the less formidable, though very powerful outworks. And if one were to seek a central thread that unites all three it would be found in the struggle to attain freedom and the "transmutation of the self." What we have called the "reform of consciousness" lies at the focal point, brought about by regenerative experiences and the presence of galvanic personality. And the result is the emergence of the ego from a self-contained egotism into a "corporate existence"— and a vision of an "organic part in social life."

G. H. Lewes had taught her that "Life is inseparably linked with Change," and that "every arrest is Death."[70] Their common interest in natural history, their preoccupation with "development" and evolution—the whole prospect of Nature—had confirmed them in the view that Change was the sure constant in the cosmos, change not only in physical nature or in the body of the human being, but within the human being himself—and particularly his mental processes. But a change in the mind is meaningless unless it is accompanied by action. Maggie Tulliver had never changed. At the time of her death she was one with the Maggie of her childhood. And it was no accident that Death should terminate an absence of growth. True, she was rebellious at times—but rebellion, to bear fruit must be, as George Eliot said, a "constructive rebellion." It must have direction, goal. Maggie had drifted at the behest of whatever wind. Now, George Eliot could say, "Drifting depends on something besides the currents, when the sails have been set beforehand."[71] She was in search of that inner compass that would make it possible to set the sails once the right direction had been determined. But which is the right direction? And alas! how many deflections are possible—if we waver, give way to doubt, or let some inner weakness take over! Freedom is not easily achieved in the face of the retarding "friction of circumstance."

At the head of one of the chapters of *Middlemarch*, George Eliot placed an epigraph of her own making:

> First Gent: Our deeds are fetters that we forge ourselves.
> Second Gent: Ay, truly: but I think it is the world that brings the irons.[72]

Deeds have at times irreversible consequences:

> .. Our deeds are like children that are born to us; they live and act apart from our will.
> Nay, children may be strangled, but deeds never. They have an indestructible life both in
> us and out of our consciousness.[73]

And they often cry out for retributive vengeance. ...

* * *

The three novels are stories of quests for the right direction, for the right goals. A high, inexorable tribunal sits in judgment, for this is the court of conscience. Various and insidious are the tugs that pull us one way or another to deflect us from our goals of integrity, many the illusions we harbor that will fall afoul of reality, many a dream that will have to be abandoned, painfully, reluctantly, many a claim that will have to be denied while another is asserted. The novels are set in times of actual or potential disorder. Divergent interests are embroiled in battles. An old order is threatened, or is in the process of decay, or appears to be so. Habitual practices, morals, ethical values, religious ideals are challenged. Issues are polarized as the new faces the old. New values are espoused.

Disintegration and reconstruction—such indeed is the basis of the three "micro-cosms" in which the principal characters of the three novels find themselves. "There is no private life which has not been determined by a wider public life," George Eliot wrote.[74] And it is the interrelationships of the private and the public lives—the individual and his society—that is mirrored in each of the three books. The contrasts are sharp—Felix Holt the radical and Mrs. Transome the aristocrat; Daniel Deronda the visionary and Grandcourt; Ladislaw the maverick—the "artistic" nature—versus Rev. Casaubon. And central to each of these contrasts, a woman in whom the "dark seed-growth of consciousness" comes to fruition. And in each of these novels there is domestic drama, sometimes tragedy, of far-reaching import. Mrs. Transome in *Felix Holt* is the mother of the illegitimate Harold Transome; in *Middlemarch*, matrimonial infe-licities surround the lives of Dorothea Brooke and her husband Casaubon as well as of Lydgate and his wife Rosamond. The marriage of Gwendolen Harleth and Grand-court in *Daniel Deronda* is especially harrowing. Again, each domestic drama or tragedy is envisaged in its larger issues—moral and ethical, or economic and social—and fitted into the broader canvas of the social whole. In each of these novels politics, or a political philosophy, plays a crucial role. Money, status, snobbery, social differ-ences, fanaticism, true and false religious sentiment, hypocrisy, greed, marital tyranny, social aspirations, self-dedication, selfishness and selflessness—all these present an al-most Balzacian spectrum. And on the other hand decency, moral responsibility, devo-tion and humaneness, generosity and understanding, and compassion ...

But above all, the quest for truth, and for a truthful existence for oneself and for others, the struggle to break the shackles of a false convention and a false existence, and discover freedom and one own soul's worth. Such is the story of *Middlemarch* in one of its grand themes. The other, more tragic, is the story of Lydgate and his mar-riage, the betrayal of one's integrity in the name of success, and of one's true vocation for the sake of comfort. In both cases these are studies of failed marriages, Dorothea

Brooke's with the Rev. Casaubon, and Doctor Lydgate's with Rosamond Vincy—in the one case leading toward a greater insight on the part of the woman, in the other, to failure.

The story takes place against the background of 1829 to 1832—the agitation for Reform in the Midlands. Dorothea Brooke, niece of the local landowner-squire Mr. Brooke, a young girl with visions of "sainthood" and a longing for some lofty vocation and some fervent dedication, believes she has found her Pascal in the much older Rev. Casaubon, the beneficed clergyman and rector, also a well-to-do landowner. He is engaged in an encyclopedic enterprise, no less that writing a Key to all Mythologies, and she is ready to devote herself to him and his enterprise. That would certainly seem like doing what she had prayed for, that is, doing "nobly Christian things." She would also do philanthropic work, like building good cottages for the tenant farmers. She has been practicing an asceticism extending to a denial of such pleasures as jewelry, and a horror of her uncle's paintings with their Renaissance "nudities." All this to the sometimes amused disapproval of her more levelheaded sister, Celia. "She likes giving up," the sister says of Dorothea. All the feelings of Dorothea will now go out to her husband, and her ideal of being like another St. Theresa be realized. Unfortunately, the Rev. Casaubon is no Pascal, nor a Bossuet, nor saintly, but a very pedantic, unimaginative, grubbing and unemotional half-scholar, whose object of reconstructing "a past world with a view to the highest purposes of truth," is as illusory as Dorothea's vision of him as another Christian philosopher and thinker. She is in need of love and warmth, and he of more notes for his masterwork. She desires a husband; he, a woman of devotion and subservience to his grander purposes. She desires affection, and he, a good amanuensis.

Soon the "education" of Dorothea has begun. Pathetic creature that he is—and George Eliot has drawn Casaubon with sympathy and understanding—he cannot meet the requirements or dreams of a young, healthy, romantic "idealist" who has come fresh from the customary ladies' schooling into the blisses of a marital union. Victorian tact keeps George Eliot from revealing the extent or even existence of such blisses, just as Victorian girls' schooling has kept Dorothea from any knowledge of what the world is like. Casaubon is not given to frivolities; he does not approve of music, and the wedding journey to Rome cannot remove him from his mountainous accumulations of mythologic facts. Here, in the Eternal City, she experiences her first intimations that there was something wrong. ... She sees Rome, with its historic ruins, and something within her gives way; she returns to her hotel room and weeps and weeps. ... She does not know why. ... Her Protestant soul had rebelled at the glut of statuary forms, yet they had somehow taken possession of her ... And she weeps.

How was she to recognize that something within her had moved "with the secret motion of a watchhand," indicating a change in her "wifely" relations to Mr. Casaubon? The first stage of her education had come. How could he, burrowing in the Vatican library, know what was taking place? How was he to know that she had anticipated "large vistas and wide fresh air" in his mind? Or that she was now perched on an icy slope, and that she would any moment be in danger of sliding down—down? She had looked for a sea—and was now finding an "enclosed basin."

With a subtlety and penetration unequalled by any of her Victorian counterparts, George Eliot traces the awakening of Dorothea's consciousness to the tragedy into which she had so briskly capered. With equal penetration and sympathy she enters into Casaubon's at first uncomprehending mind as he watches Dorothea's growing disenchantment—as it penetrates into his own secret misgivings about himself and his work. It makes a tragedy of two people—mismated, and misunderstanding. One need scarcely go to the end, as the rift widens and as Dorothea understands how futile is her husband's work, so utterly out of touch with the latest historical science and knowledge; and as Casaubon himself reveals his secret hopelessness to himself. He is the "lifeless embalmment of knowledge," a frigid, dulled, dead soul, made even more pathetic by the pathos of self-discovery. Dead during his life, he is alive in his death, as his hand reaches out from the grave to try to enslave her to his work, and to enslave her body and soul by a testamentary prohibition against marrying the man, Ladislaw, Casaubon's second cousin, who had opened for Dorothea new vistas of possible happiness.

Against tradition, convention, the habits and sanctities professed by her relatives and the community, Dorothea asserts her freedom by renouncing her inheritance and insisting on making her own free choice. Such is the consummation of her education as a human being and as a woman.

The parallel drama—or rather, tragedy—of the young physician Tertius Lydgate and his wife Rosamond, is the story of bright ambition, hope, and talents brought to nought through various entanglements. For Lydgate begins his career in Middlemarch burning with the zeal of a true scientist, to bring his new knowledge, acquired abroad, to the community. He builds his hopes on the newly-established hospital built with the bounty of the wealthy banker and evangelical fanatic Bulstrode. Lydgate is a disciple of the great physiologist Bichat, and of the celebrated Paris physician Raspail. He would carry forward the experimental work of these men, particularly in his researches on body tissues. Wishing to combine "intellectual conquest with social good," he regards medicine as the loftiest of vocations. As a young intruder with new theories, he finds himself in conflict not only with the local practitioners of varying capacities but also with the prevalent superstitions, prejudices, and traditional practices. Step by step he is led to compromise his integrity, first in deference to Bulstrode's wishes as to the appointment of a favored chaplain to the infirmary, thereafter in an injudicious marriage to a beautiful but vain young woman with social aspirations, in an indulgence to his own taste for fineries and, in the end, by capitulating to his wife's insistence that he be a "somebody," relinquish his scientific ambitions and become a fashionable physician in London and in exclusive spas. A product of her environment, Rosamond cannot understand her husband's devotion to his vocation, so far removed from her notions of social status.

These two major dramas are acted out against a background of, and in relation to, all the complex elements of Middlemarch society, running the gamut of social castes, caste prejudices and ambitions, as well as conflicting political interests.

A new age is dawning. Reform is in the air, and Mr. Brooke will stand for Parliament. He is a bumbling, drivelling, good-natured chap, who means well in his own indefinable way but, understanding little of politics, meets his Waterloo. The railroads are coming. And money is very much in evidence as a force in the community. Old Mr. Featherstone, who owns land and is now nothing but "a remnant of vices," is nearing his grave, and like a character out of Dickens or Balzac, enjoys the sight of the "Christian carnivora" who surround him in expectation of a legacy. The banker Bulstrode (who has a questionable past) combines the tyranny of money with the terrors of religion. Mrs. Cadwallader, a rector's wife who has married beneath her station and whose household is supported by that feudal relic, the tithes paid by parishioners, looks down on money-grubbing merchants, traders, and manufacturers, just as Rosamond's father Mr. Vincy, the merchant, looks down on the still impecunious Lydgate. Such is the decay of communal spirit and feeling, manifesting itself throughout: in the Rev. Casaubon's futilities and distance from people; in the failing gentry—Mr. Brooke's vacuous politics; in the dehumanized relations of the others. It is against these influences that Lydgate carries on his hopeless struggle; it is against them that Dorothea Brooke succeeds in affirming the humane values of personality. Such too is the affirmation of the dissenting vicar the Rev. Farebrother, who has missed his true vocation of entomologist but can lavish love and understanding on his neighbors, his family, and his flock. Such too is Caleb Garth, who sets a higher price on skilled work well done than on market values, and who brings to his labors a dedication and honesty that become a kind of theology.

But at the center of all these dramas stands Dorothea Brooke—probably the most subtly drawn character in all of Victorian literature. She is a luminous spirit, a heroic figure without the blatancy of heroism, symbolic of all womanhood, but beyond that also of all humankind, in her efforts toward the attainment of a personal clarity that would lead to creative freedom. Hers is a domestic drama that, as George Eliot put it, is a part of "all ordinary life." Unlike so many Victorian women, she had not been forced into marriage by economic or social pressure; a pre-Victorian, she had brought to it the full treasures of ignorance and of romance. Shall one take the consequences for granted and merely shake one's head at yet another unfortunate union? "We do not," George Eliot writes,

> "expect people to be deeply moved by what is not unusual. The element of tragedy which lies in the very fact of frequency has not yet wrought itself into the coarse emotion of mankind, and perhaps our frames could hardly bear much of it. If we had a keen vision and feeling of all ordinary human life, it would be like hearing the grass grow and the squirrel's heart beat, and we should die of that roar which lies on the other side of silence. ...."[75]

"The roar which lies on the other side of silence." What a magnificent way of setting forth the drama, the tragedy that is so often unspoken and unnoticed, and taken for granted if observed! The drama—the conflict within Dorothea—of humane feeling toward her husband, and her duties toward herself, particularly as he is mortally ill, is heightened by the fact that Mr. Casaubon is not a straw man, a foil to be set against Dorothea's more potent emotional character. He is a human being, limited, not deep-feeling, pedantic, somewhat authoritative, traditional in his views of woman and her duties, but himself involved in an internal struggle (also a life and death matter) to cling to an illusion which is fast disappearing, so that he will be left with nothing but innumerable slips of paper and notes that will never coalesce into a significant life's realization. His failed marriage is only a counterpart to the dissipation of his personality into a nothingness. It is doubly tragic that such revelation comes not only from within himself, but must be a portion of the more "public" life of his household. Thus weighted with a double burden, toward herself and toward her dying husband, she heroically accepts the pressure of the "dead hand" when he demands that she continue, after his death, the work that he had begun. It is only when his testamentary codicil reveals how tight a hold the "dead hand" could have, in foreclosing her right to her inheritance should she marry Ladislaw, that she feels the utter crushing blow to her personal dignity. Once more it is Death commanding Life to die—and she affirms Life. Lydgate, in failing to bring to his vocation of scientist and social human being that same honesty, and to his familial life a scientist's integrity, must die—even if only a living death of hapless non-realization.

Middlemarch is George Eliot's highest triumph as a novelist, as it is one of the peaks of Victorian fiction. It is useless to dwell on some of its shortcomings—the multiplicity of plots, details, its obtrusive sensationalism (Bulstrode's criminal past, and his relation to Ladislaw). But there is little doubt that she failed in sufficiently defining the character of Will Ladislaw, Casaubon's second cousin and, for Dorothea and for the novel as a whole, the embodiment of potential regeneration. He is a dilettante—something of a painter, part journalist, a maverick—vaguely standing for the other side of asceticism—the sensuous life-force that will for the first time fully evoke and respond to Dorothea's emotional needs. Beside Lydgate, Casaubon, and even Mr. Brooke, not to mention Dorothea, he stands as a somewhat shadowy being. That after his marriage to Dorothea he is to engage in some sort of parliamentary activity as his contribution to "public life," is scarcely satisfying to the reader who solicits a greater measure of concreteness. What sort of public life? And what ideas and ideals?

Closely akin to this defect is another, perhaps more vital. The action of the novel takes place against the background of the 1829–1832 Reform agitation. The passions that attended that movement were sufficiently strong to stir all of Britain (as we have seen),[*] and represent an index of the importance (exaggerated perhaps) attached to it at the time. Social and political forces stood marshalled against each other as Tory and Whig battled for or against passage of the Reform Bill. In the wider "public life" of which Middlemarch itself is a part, the electioneering is treated in a cavalier fashion as another piece of local violence or hysteria, and Mr. Brooke and the other candidates are given almost comic roles. Such deprecation of political activity is not an accidental aspect of George Eliot's thought, and in the light of the fundamental experiences of political England between 1832 and 1867 and the tremendous changes taking place both politically and socially, marks the limits of her social vision, and exhibits the glaring contrast between her moral and ethical radicalism and her social and political conservatism.

Such then is the paradox of George Eliot—morally an optimist, socially and politically, a pessimist. The years during which *Middlemarch* was appearing, from December 1871 to December 1872, were years of violent convulsions on the Continent. They

---

* Above, pp. 5–7, 26–28, 418.

were also the years in which, it may be said, the heyday of Victorianism came to an end. The sky was darkening. Yet, the fears that had spread far and wide following the Reform Bill, that the lower orders of British society would take over Parliament and the land, were not realized. In the same year, 1866, as George Eliot's *Felix Holt: The Radical* was published, Robert Lowe had warned the House of Commons:

> Once give working men the votes, and the machinery is ready to launch those votes in one compact mass upon the institutions and property of this country.

And Matthew Arnold, shocked by the outbreaks of 1866 and the tearing down of Hyde Park railings, thought it was essential "to compel our future masters to learn their letters."[76]

"The future masters" did not take over the country. They sent very respectable people to Parliament, content to be represented by their "betters." Yet fear of the masses, and of potential violence, was deeply ingrained in the Victorian middle-class and upper-class mind, and George Eliot was not immune to it. Furthermore, both Lewes and she, as disciples of Auguste Comte, had been imbued with the French thinker's belief that the majority of men and women were intellectually mediocre even under ideal circumstances, and that the "innate selfishness of human beings would remain potent factors in political and social life." He had also insisted that an intellectual and moral reorganization of society must precede and direct the political. "Love is our principle; Order our basis; and Progress our end." Indifferent to the constitutional experiments of his century, Comte regarded politics as a matter for experts.[77]

George Eliot criticized Dickens (without naming him) for the "unreality" with which he surrounded his description of social relations.

> One great novelist who is gifted with the utmost power of rendering the external traits of our town population; and if he could give us their psychological character—their conceptions of life, and their emotions—with the same truth as their idiom and manners, his books would be the greatest contribution Art has ever made to the awakening of social sympathies. But ... he scarcely ever passes from the humourous and external to the emotional and tragic, without becoming as transcendent in his unreality as he was a moment before in his artistic truthfulness ... But for the precious salt of his humour. . his preternaturally virtuous poor children and artisans ... would be as noxious as Eugène Sue's idealized proletaires in encouraging the miserable fallacy that high morality and refined sentiment can grow out of harsh social relations, ignorance and want; or that the working-classes are in a condition to enter at once into a millennial state of *altruism*, wherein everyone is caring for everyone else, and no one for himself.[78]

She had never gotten over the brutal sights she had witnessed while still living near Coventry; but the other side of the life of the lower classes—their mutual sympathies and kindnesses, their courage, even heroism and martyrdoms, their penalization and prosecutions—these had completely escaped her.

So that, having found public life corrupting, and the harsh realities of lower class life brutalizing, she felt little sympathy for constitutional or parliamentary reforms. She deprecated the tendency to "believe that all social questions are merged in economical science." (*ibid.*)

It is for this reason that the two novels, *Felix Holt*, which preceded *Middlemarch*, and *Daniel Deronda*, which followed, are so disconcerting to the modern reader. Each has its measure of greatness, of beauty and insights; each has an equal measure of unreality and vagueness. George Eliot was grappling with artistic and intellectual problems the difficulties of which she could hardly have been aware of.

Middlemarch contained the marvelous center, wherein the social and political elements were in a great measure implicated in the domestic dramas and brilliantly reflective of the milieu. In the other two works, the great, broad issues of contemporary life (though in one case the setting may be in the past) are given particular consideration in the overt actions and speeches of the protagonist. Felix Holt is a "radical" and a proletarian. Daniel Deronda is a visionary and a prophet. Each has his antipode or antipodes within the society, and each of them speaks for some generalized human and social values that are meant to transcend the limited moral and social values prevalent. Each bears the message of a new "order."

The designs are extraordinarily ambitious. Their scope is broader than that of *Middlemarch*. For the first time, in *Daniel Deronda*, George Eliot has taken the contemporary world as her subject. In *Felix Holt*, for the first time, she has taken a working man and self-declared proletarian as a hero. She thus encompasses in the two novels past and present, and even looks to the future. In each of the novels there is a "transmutation of the self," in one case a "reform of consciousness," in the other, a "regeneration." In both instances, it must be noted, it is a woman who is thus "transmuted" through the agency of a man.

Both novels open in a masterly way, in fact suggestive of those unforgettable openings of Tolstoy's novels. It is September, "in the memorable year 1832," and "some one was expected at Transome Court." Such is the opening of *Felix Holt*. And in the decaying manor estate, aging Mrs. Transome is awaiting the return of her son Harold Transome after years of absence in the Near East. She is nervous and upset, and worried. In an adjoining room her half-witted husband is toying with his collection of dried insects. What will this son be like after all these years? Will he be loving or cold? Will he be able to rehabilitate the disintegrating fortunes of the Transomes?

And in *Daniel Deronda* we are immediately transported to the German spa Leubrunn, and the gambling tables. It is also a September day, but some time in the 1860s.

> Was she beautiful or not beautiful? and what was the secret of form or expression which gave the dynamic quality to her glance? Was the good or the evil genius dominant in those beams?. ...

Such are the questions that occupy Daniel Deronda as he watches the beautiful unknown, Gwendolen Harleth, in her passionate preoccupation at the gambling table. They exchange glances, but do not meet—as yet. For she is called home by a letter from her mother advising her that the family is ruined owing to a commercial failure, and they are now reduced to live on their uncle Gascoigne's charity. On the chance of recouping her losses, Gwendolen makes one more try, and sells her precious necklace to a jeweler. Mysteriously, the necklace is returned to her. Suspecting the donor, and in anger, she decides to return home at once. Immediately we have been brought face to face with the two principal characters of the book, whose subsequent interrelation will prove one of the more crucial elements of the story.

At the center of each of the two novels lies the problem of polarization. Society was changing rapidly, and divisions were sharpening ominously. George Eliot could not overcome her nostalgia for a simpler past—though she recognized, sadly, that it could never be reconstituted. It is with that feeling that she introduces *Felix Holt* with a reminiscent prologue, which she calls "Author's Introduction," conceived as an imaginary stagecoach journey to the past, a time when the country shepherd's "solar system" was the parish, when there were still homes of "unmarketable beauty"—a land of "protuberant optimists." Alas! the landscape soon changes, and we are in the country of coal pits and handloom noises. ...

The contradictions are there already. The year is 1832. We are once again in the Midlands, in the village of Little Treby, an appendage of the larger town of Treby Magna. At one end of the social spectrum stands Transome Court, and Mrs. Transome. She is a member now of the poorer gentry, but her outlook is aristocratic, if narrow; she is quite intent on seeing "the existing arrangement of English society ... unshaken." In her world, Christianity now

> went hand in hand with civilization, and the providential government of the world, though a little confused and entangled in foreign countries, in our favoured land was clearly seen to be carried forward on Tory and Church of England principles, sustained by the succession of the House of Brunswick, and by sound English divines.[79]

"She had no ultimate analysis of things that went beyond blood and family." She is a remnant, living "in the midst of desecrated sanctities."[80]

She is a pitiful creature, and the writer's heart goes out to her. She is a portion of the decay that seems to be attending the old social order, living with a frayed past, alongside the faded family heraldry. She carries the burden of an estate in declension, a half-wit husband, a dead ne'er-do-well son, and a frightful guilt—for Harold Transome is illegitimate, the son of her bailiff Jermyn, and the only fruit of her unfulfilled love-longings. A frightened woman, she looks with hope upon him to sustain her, the family, and her society. Alas! Harold Transome is cold, calculating, too worldly-wise. He is in the swing of things ... He will stand not as the Tory candidate, but as a "Radical." Not of course in the current meaning of "radical"—for in the Near East he had been banker and merchant, and now is heir and prospective lord of the manor. His radicalism is calculated "to retard the national ruin ... and take the inevitable process of changing everything out of the hand of the beggarly demagogues and purse-proud tradesmen." His slogan will be to "root out abuses," and his uncle, a Tory clergyman seconds him enthusiastically:

> "That's the word I wanted, my lad!" said the Vicar, slapping Harold's knee. "That's a spool to wind a speech on. Abuses is the very word."[81]

Thus Mrs. Transome becomes a thoroughly alienated figure, isolated spiritually, morally, psychologically from the present—a living wraith, fearful of her opportunist son, fearful of the exposure of her past, fearful of an imminent conflict between her son and the bailiff over the management of the estate. A truly tragic figure, she is magnificently delineated by the author.

The hero-protagonist of the novel is Felix Holt, in George Eliot's view a true "radical." It is a remarkable portrait she draws of him. He is the representative of the moral conscience. He is a rebellious son, for he cannot tolerate that his mother, a widow, should continue his father's business of selling patent medicines he knows to be fraudulent. Abandoning the prospect of a middle-class career, he becomes an apprentice to a watchmaker. He is the "class-conscious" proletarian. He feels himself destined for leadership, but its nature is still somewhat vague to him. At times he speaks with a sound and practical eloquence as he looks to the future. To Esther Lyon, the putative daughter of the dissenting minister, the Rev. Rufus Lyon, he opens his heart.

> ... I will never be rich. I don't count that as any peculiar virtue. Some men do well to accept riches, but that is not my inward vocation: I have no fellow-feeling with the rich as a class; the habits of their lives are odious to me ... Whatever the hopes for the world may be,—whether great or small—I am a man of this generation; I will try to make life less bitter for a few within my reach. It is held reasonable enough to toil for the fortunes of a family, though it may turn to imbecility in the third generation. I choose a family with more chances in it.[82]

This is nobly spoken. He recognizes the price one must pay to participate in the scramble for "money and position," and the success that attends it "in the long-run." "I care," he says, "for the people who live now and will not be living when the long-run comes. As it is, I prefer going shares with the unlucky." To the Rev. Lyon, who is in favor of universal franchise, he says, admitting he is a "Radical,"—"Yes; but I want to go to some roots a good deal lower down than the franchise." And he adds significantly, "While Caliban is Caliban"—that is, the masses of men—"though you multiply him by a million, he'll worship every Trinculo that carries a bottle."

At the preliminary polling which takes place in Treby Magna, amidst the noises and discussions, and other turmoils, Felix Holt becomes aware of one voice speaking with effect. The speaker is a working man with "bare and muscular arms" and a pallid complexion that betrays his labors at a furnace. He is obviously a Chartist, for he presents the Chartist program. He attacks "monopolists" and their greed, as well as their counsel to workers to let politics alone, for they are ignorant.

> But I tell them this: the greatest question in the world is, how to give every man a man's share in what goes on in life ...

He calls the Reform Bill a "trick"—"nothing but the swearing-in of special constables to keep the aristocrats safe in their monopoly." He indicts the religious establishment:

> Why do they build churches and endow them that their sons may get well paid for preaching a Saviour, and making themselves as little like Him as can be? ... And what's a Bishop? A bishop's a parson dressed up, who sits in the House of Lords to help and throw out Reform Bills. ... But we'll offer to change with 'em. We'll give them back some of their heaven, and take it out in something for us and our children in this world. ... We must get the suffrage, we must get the votes, that we may send men to parliament who will do our work for us; and we must have parliament dissolved every year, that we may change our man if he doesn't do what we want him to do; and we must have the country divided so that the little kings of the counties can't do as they like, but must be shaken up in one bag with us. I say, if we working men are ever to get a man's share, we must

have universal suffrage, and annual parliaments, and the vote by ballot, and electoral districts.[83]

Felix Holt is aroused. "No!—something before all that," he cries out. Asked to reply, he at once impresses his audience. For his face bears the "peculiar stamp of culture," worthy to be called "the human face divine."

"I want the working man to have power," he says, but "of another sort." Votes, he continues, cannot give political power, "worth having while things are as they are." Nor will they mend the condition of working people, for out of a hundred workers, suppose thirty were sober and sensible, and able to choose rightly, what of the other seventy who are given to drinking, or were too ignorant, or even bribable?

> Now, all the schemes about voting, and districts, and annual parliaments, and the rest, are engines, and the water or steam—the force that is to work them—must come out of human nature—out of men's passions, feelings, desires ... I'll tell you what's the greatest power under heaven ..., and that is public opinion—the ruling belief in society about what is right and what is wrong, what is honourable and what is shameful ...

Election day comes. The crowds are excited, inflamed, and some of them even inebriated. A melée breaks out, and the crowd, out of control, begins by hunting down a scapegoat. Felix Holt is accidentally drawn into the scuffle, and in his efforts to save the victim and divert the crowd, he intervenes and accidentally injures a constable, who eventually dies. He is presumed the leader of a "mob," apprehended, tried, and sentenced to imprisonment.

It is scarcely necessary to enter into the more numerous by-plots, convolutions, and mysteries, without which no Victorian novel would be complete. But it is important to dwell on one or two of the book's interwoven strands.

One of them involves Esther Lyon. Reputed to be the daughter of the Rev. Rufus Lyon, she is only adoptive, the offspring of the foreign woman Lyon had married and who died shortly thereafter. Esther turns out to be the rightful heiress of the Transome estates, owing to a series of legal procedures and inheritance laws too complicated to state. She is a spoiled child, indulged by the kindly and generous father, himself none too affluent. Rufus Lyon is one of those clergymen whose sympathies are wide, whose heart is warm toward those who need his counsel, and who is given, now and then, to long but well-meaning speeches. He is drawn to Felix Holt, and the latter soon becomes a frequent visitor. Under Felix Holt's tutelage, Esther undergoes a spiritual conversion, and they fall in love. At first delighted with her change of fortunes, as she is taken into the Transome household she gradually becomes aware of the emptiness of their lives. She is in love with Felix Holt and renounces her rights to the Transome properties. When Felix Holt is released, they marry and move to another town. And their son Felix, when he grows up, will in the true Comtean tradition become a scientist. ...

As against the solidity—moral and spiritual—of Esther and Felix Holt, we are faced with the tottering domain of the Transomes, held in possession by falsehood, if not fraud, the object of interminable machinations on the part of others, and cankered by an inner disease that momentarily threatens even Esther's integrity as she is courted by both mother and son. Harold Transome's discovery of his parentage is a shattering blow to him; and its revelation another crushing defeat for his mother. The Transomes epitomize a total alienation.

Why then is *Felix Holt: the Radical* an artistic failure? Why is it that one feels a sense of life, of identification with a number of other characters—particularly Mrs. Transome, the Rev. Rufus Tryon, in part even with Esther Lyon and Harold Transome, and a few of the lesser ones, but very little with Felix Holt himself? The answer, it seems, is simple: Felix Holt is not rooted in any reality. He is a "principle"—a noble principle if you wish—but a "principle" more deeply encrusted with an "idea" than with a body and soul. The tragic person of Mrs. Transome has deep roots, even if those be of the tarnished past; Mr. Lyon emerges as a human being, whose feelings, person, and speech constitute a unity. Harold Transome, representing the new, calculating, self-seeking personality of the times, is human. Felix Holt is not. And he is not because he is not truly a working-class figure, nor likely to be a working-class leader. Unlike the other characters, he has no true base of operations—he works in a vacuum. He wishes to get to the "root" of things, be a true "radical," but he cannot get beyond a voluble moralistic set of principles. He has no contact with working people, seems totally ignorant of his Chartist contemporaries and their history, and never gets to the heart of the working-class problems. He is an unreal counterpart—a secular counterpart—of the truly human, religious Mr. Lyon. For a leader, he brings no true sympathy (except in words) to the plight of the lower classes. He is a kind of abstract teacher, standing high above his classroom, raising a monitory finger and preaching good conduct. We are never told of his later activities or ideas, or of his relation to the times. He is George Eliot frightened by 1867.

Hence that logical sequel to the novel, which took the form of an "Address to Working Men, by Felix Holt," written at the suggestion of John Blackwood, as a reply to Disraeli's "address to the working men." When the new Reform Bill comes into operation," Blackwood wrote to George Eliot, "the working man will be on his trial, and if he misconducts himself it will go hard with the country."[84]

George Eliot's "Address" is a composite statement, part of which might have been written by Carlyle and another by Matthew Arnold. She is concerned for the preservation of "Culture," and its bearers. Society can be steadily improved

> not by any attempt to do away directly with the actually existing class distinctions and advantages …, but by turning of Class Interests into Class Functions or duties … Changes can only be good in proportion … as they put knowledge in the place of ignorance, and fellow-feeling in the place of selfishness …

She speaks of the need to preserve the treasures of "knowledge, science, poetry, refinement of thought, feeling and manners", the security of which demands "the preservation of order," but also a certain patience "with many institutions … especially touching the accumulation of wealth." The problem, of course, is to "get the chief power into the hands of the wisest."

> We have all to see to it that we do not help to rouse what I may call the savage beast in the breasts of our generation.

Haunted by that panic, what else could she adjure her workers to but to warn them against debasing the life of the nation?

> Do anything which will throw the classes who hold the treasures of knowledge—nay, I may say, the treasure of refined needs—into the background, cause them to withdraw from public affairs, stop too suddenly any of the sources by which their leisure and ease are furnished, rob them of the chances by which they may be influential and pre-eminent, and you do something as shortsighted as the acts of France and Spain when in jealousy and wrath, not altogether unprovoked, they drove from among them races and classes that held the traditions of handicraft and agriculture.

She is thinking no doubt of the expulsions of the Huguenots from France, and possibly the Jews from Spain.

Which brings us to the last of her "epic" novels, *Daniel Deronda;* a work of great design, written out of an admirable courage, and out of a vastly troubled mind. If it has a slightly schizoid character, if it seems as if she were writing two novels in one, it is not because there is no connection between the two major portions—that dealing with Gwendolen Harleth, and the other dealing with Daniel Deronda. It is rather that George Eliot was looking in two directions for the light to illuminate both the present and the future.

That one of England's major novelists at the peak of her successful career should venture to make a Jew the prophetic visionary of a new message and pilgrimage, was in itself a daring act. Disraeli had ventured this, but he was of Jewish descent. The lifting of Jewish disabilities had scarcely dispersed the persistent aura of overt or tacit antisemitism, or the traditional image of the Jew as Shylock, old-clothes tradesman, pedlar, broker, or as in the case of a Rothschild, Mammon's offspring. Dickens had failed miserably in trying to atone for Fagin.[85]

George Eliot knew she was defying convention, tradition, and public opinion. With that flexibility so characteristic of her, she was even able to transcend her own earlier prejudices. In 1848 she had no very high opinion of Jews, and resented Disraeli's messianic Jewish novels.

> My Gentile nature, she wrote in 1848, kicks most resolutely against any assumption of superiority in the Jews and is almost ready to echo Voltaire's vituperation. I bow to the supremacy of Hebrew poetry, but much of their early mythology and almost all their history is utterly revolting. Their stock has produced a Moses and a Jesus, but Moses was impregnated with Egyptian philosophy and Jesus is venerated and adored by us only for that wherein he transcended or resisted Judaism. The very exaltation of their idea of a national deity into a spiritual monotheism seems to have been borrowed from the other oriental tribes. Everything *specifically* Jewish is low grade …[86]

It is only too easy to see how profoundly ignorant she was at that time of Jews, Jewish history, and Jewish scholarship. That ignorance she shared with many others. The remarkable thing is that she changed, and brought her usual curiosity and assiduity to the research required for her reorientation. She sought out Jewish scholars, immersed herself in Jewish history and Jewish lore, read the epochal works of Zunz and Graetz, visited synagogues and Jewish temples, and even studied Hebrew. No other English writer had attempted that much in preparation of a work, nor a work of such scope, whose intent it was to fit the present into the past, and the past into the present, re-evaluate the role and conditions of Jewry, and relate the wretchedness of Whitechapel and Petticoat Lane to a broad highroad of triumphs and sorrows.

This was not to be a "Jewish" novel. Rather it was projected to mirror an epoch and its relation to the individual and to world history. The Jew and the Jewish problem were to be vehicles for the conveyance of a central ideological theme. The period—the hectic and precipitate historical events—provided sufficient food for anxiety and concern. With the rest of Europe in turmoil, with England, too, beset by economic and social problems, and amid the conflicting choruses of litanies and prophecies and distressing new poetic voices—it seemed as if the old world was near breakup. Was she not also a "Victorian sage" among other sages? She must bring her own moral voice to bear upon crying needs of the day. How to find a common bond that will once more fill one with a sense of community—not only within England itself—between England and the rest of the world? The personal "I" and "Thou" must be given a wider meaning. Or perhaps a new "organic center" must be discovered. *Daniel Deronda* was to exemplify that search, that need of a passionate quest.

Once more antipodal characters and issues are set one against the other, in sharp opposition. Such a clash of opposites is embodied in Gwendolen Harleth. She is Selfness. Daniel Deronda is the transcendence of the Self, the attainment of a view of life, that of the passionate organic center. Since a profound moral transformation— Change itself—is at issue, George Eliot's moral searchlight, her psychological probing, is directed preeminently upon the transformation of a character under the impact of superior forces. Gwendolen is that character.

She is a haughty beauty, the proud and spoiled daughter of a twice-widowed mother. She returns to England after her strange experience at the gambling tables of Leubrunn, where she had been held momentarily by the eyes of a stranger, Daniel Deronda, whom she does not as yet get to know. The financial crashes which had beset England mark a critical turn in her life. She must go back with bleak prospects for her own and her family's future.

Always a rebel without knowing why, Gwendolen was now such by virtue of perceptible circumstances. She was a rebel *déclassée*. She believed herself strong-willed enough to bend everyone and everything around her, and now she would be truly tested.

She had left home for the Continent in an access of aggrieved rage. For she discovered that the aristocratic Grandcourt, to whom she was virtually betrothed, had abandoned Mrs. Glasher, with whom he had been living and who had borne him two children. Had the alliance been legitimized, the boy born of this union would be the natural heir of the Grandcourt estates. She had met Mrs. Glasher, had been moved by her plight, and had immediately left England. Grandcourt, who had followed her, could not overtake her, but at Leubronn he met his uncle Sir Hugo Mallinger and, for the first time, Daniel Deronda, Sir Hugo's ward. Since Sir Hugo had no son, Grandcourt was the heir next in line.

The courtship of Grandcourt and Gwendolen Harleth had been a strange one. There had been no talk of love; rather it was a situation in which two strong-minded characters with something demonic but calculating about them had set about to engage in a psychological duel. And, indeed, George Eliot here provides a penetrating study of two highly complex and pathological psyches. Grandcourt is intrigued by this handsome, self-possessed, cool young woman, the like of whom he had never met. There is a sense of something subtly provocative about her—not aggressive strength, but something subtly challenging. She in turn finds Grandcourt tantalizing in his aristocratic aloofness, coolness, superiority—an enigmatic personality against whom she would like to pit her own strength. To him she is a spirited colt that it would be pleasant to tame; for her he is someone to dominate. A dash of piquancy is added by the fact that she is not dazzled by his station in life.

Yet there were recesses in Gwendolen's soul no sense of mastery or pride could light up. There were times when she had been beset by an indescribable and unfathomable anxiety—a panic, sometimes associated with a superstitious fear. The carapace of enclosed selfness conceals the anxiety of isolation—a fear of the world and of other human beings. Guilt intensifies both anger and fear. Whatever safety she had hitherto enjoyed is now shattered as she is forced out into the world with the need to make her living and help support her family, now more than ever dependent upon their uncle the Rev. Gascoigne.

The prospects are limited and shattering: the choices are that of becoming a governess or a teacher—humiliating and dreary and arduous occupations. The Brontë sisters had already given most vivid and distressing personal pictures of that kind of "fate."*

The only other route of escape is—marriage. When Grandcourt presents himself once more, she accepts him. This despite the gnawing feeling that she is now betraying Mrs. Glasher and the children, betraying herself—for there is no love in her—and not least, entrusting herself to a man who will prove more than a match for her. However, there will be compensations: status, glamour, luxury (if Mr. Grandcourt can solve the problem of his debts), and no doubt a sizable settlement on her and support for her dependents. ...

If George Eliot did not at that time have the full range of psychological terminology, at her command, she had the almost instinctive insights which, strange to note, modern psychiatrists do not sufficiently possess. Already a divided personality, Gwendolen is further riven by the social pressures of the times. She is also a dependent, a luxurious piece of ornamental bric-à-brac that Grandcourt will be proud to exhibit and parade. She has become a piece of property.

And Grandcourt is now master. Furthermore, he is what Gwendolen is not—monolithic. A psychopathic personality who, like Gwendolen, is utterly devoid of love, he is nevertheless inwardly undivided. They are both fond of horses, only in this case he will be the tamer of the bridling colt, will break her to harness. Already implicated in the guilt of having betrayed Mrs. Glasher, she receives its visible and public token in the form of the jewels which Grandcourt had retrieved from his former mistress, and which the latter returns to Gwendolen with an ominous curse.

Grandcourt is an aristocrat of an almost feudal cast.

> Grandcourt's importance as a subject of this realm was of the grandly passive kind which consists in the inheritance of land. Political and social movements touched him only through the wire of his rental, and his most careful biographer need not have read up on Schleswig-Holstein, the policy of Bismarck, trade-unions, household suffrage, or

---

* See pp. 397–399.

even the last commercial panic. He glanced over the best newspaper columns of these topics, and his views on them can hardly be said to have wanted breadth, since he embraced all Germans, all commercial men, and all voters liable to use the wrong kind of soap, under the general epithet of "brutes"; but he took no action on these much agitated questions beyond looking from under his eyelids at any man who mentioned them, and retaining a silence which served to shake the opinions of timid thinkers.[87]

His social sense coalesces with his psychological and moral character—total selfhood of a class amoral and autocratic. That selfhood is fed by the subservience, deference, and almost religious veneration of those below him. The passion to ascend in the social scale transcends all other social and human values. See how the Rev. Gascoigne regards the prospective marriage of Gwendolen and Grandcourt, and you have a piece of that world.

> This match with Grandcourt presented itself to him as a sort of public affair; perhaps there were ways in which it might even strengthen the Establishment. To the Rector, whose father (nobody would have suspected it, and nobody was told) has risen to be a provincial corn-dealer, aristocratic heirship resembled regal heirship in excepting its possessor from the ordinary standard of moral judgments. Grandcourt, the almost certain baronet, the probable peer, was to be ranged with public personages, and was a match to be accepted on broad general grounds national and ecclesiastical ...[88]

Great is the outrage in the family of the Arrowpoints, gentry of *arriviste* character, at their daughter's presumption in falling in love and marrying an artist—in this case a highly gifted Jew, the composer Klesmer. For the musician is here regarded, as was Lydgate by some ladies in *Middlemarch*, as a higher sort of footman. The offense is compounded by the fact that Klesmer is an alien and a Jew. Such, then, is one aspect of the struggle between ossified Old and the dissolvent New.

Much sharper is the conflict between Grandcourt and Gwendolen. The sadistic impulse to destroy, in Grandcourt, and in Gwendolen a gradually developing masochism along with the possibility of a regenerative process, are symbolized by jewelry: the anathema that rests upon Mrs. Glasher's jewels, which brought on a hysteria when Grandcourt demanded that Gwendolen wear them; and the necklace that Daniel Deronda had redeemed for her. Against Gwendolen are lined up all the coercive forces of society—she is a woman and a wife, she is without independent means, and she is actually alone. She has sold herself, and the bargain must be kept. To regain inner freedom, and perhaps external freedom as well, she must undergo a revolution from within, recognize her dependence upon others, and other values than those of her society.

She was to travel far from that moment when, in accepting Grandcourt, she had answered yes to his proposal "as if she had been answering to her name in a court of justice"—calculation prevailing over love—and when she was shown the two horses of Grancourt's, one for him and one for her,

> ... the beautiful creatures, in their fine grooming, sent a thrill of exultation through Gwendolen. They were the symbols of command and luxury, in delightful contrast with the ugliness and humiliation at which she had lately been looking close.[89]

Far from that moment in life, when like a true Victorian girl, ignorant and innocent of the meaning of sex, she had asked her mother whether men generally have children before they are married. "No dear, no," said Mrs. Davilow. "Why do you ask such a question?" How was Gwendolen to know that a great deal of her anxiety and occasional hysteria were occasioned by her fear of life and her fear of sex? And all these bound up with the repression of all feeling? And that the first need of the human being is to discover himself as a feeling being? And that non-feeling is death?

But the marriage mart knows nothing of feelings. Hence for Gwendolen the ultimate awareness consisted in the realization that she had entered a "penitentiary."

How to attain freedom?—the problem that had beset Maggie Tulliver as well as Dorothea Brooke. Nausea and revulsion are not enough—and these she began to feel. The stimulating impulses must come from without. Klesmer the artist had enlightened and set her back when he explained how difficult is the road toward artistic fulfilment, whether in music or theatre ... That was before her marriage. Thus at least one of her illusions had been dispelled. But the primary force for the "reform" of her consciousness was to be another "outsider" and Jew—Daniel Deronda.

For a long time Daniel Deronda believes himself to be the illegitimate son of Sir Hugo. He is therefore also among the disinherited. And since Grandcourt is the immediate heir, Gwendolen finds herself now under the burden of a double guilt feeling. He is like Shelley, an "idealist," but unlike Shelley, is in search of a true center for his existence. He has vague aspirations to do good to humankind, but does not, for a long time, know how. It is his discovery that he is a Jew that prompts a critical reevaluation of himself and lays the basis for a revolution of his consciousness. He saves a beautiful young Jewish girl, Mirah, from drowning herself in the Thames, and in this way is brought close to the Jewish community of London, when he begins searching for members of her family. His search brings him in contact with Mirah's brother Mordecai, and with that a whole new world of ideas and experiences, into the controversial field of national and religious aspirations, to a revision of his previously held conceptions of Jews and Judaism, and, upon discovery of his own descent, to an identification with a mystical national ideal of a Jewish restoration in Palestine. His lifelong yearning to become "an organic part of social life" now finds its fulfilment not only in his own self-realization as a personality, but also in his conviction that this will also be a self-fulfilment for the dispersed, unrooted, and hitherto despised wandering tribes. His hitherto diffused humanitarianism has now found its crystallized center.

It is this sense of the "enlargement of life" that he is able to bring to bear upon Gwendolen Harleth as she becomes more and more conscious of entering upon a critical moment in her relations to Grandcourt. Animal figurations intrude themselves upon her imaginations—Grandcourt had already appeared as a "lizard," and "torpedo"—and his will like that of a "crab" or "boa-constrictor." Numbed in will but unable to numb her own conscience, she begins finding in Deronda the voice of a new set of values—but first of all sympathy, then understanding. She recognizes in him some "unknown standard," which gives her a "new footing" in life, redeems her from the welter of selfishness and anxieties, self-reproaches and guilts which could only lead to her utter demoralization and eventual destruction. He becomes a part of her conscience, a secular "priest"—to help her see how she can create something productive out of her reproaches and self-torments by recognizing the necessity of possible amendment. She is, as a matter of fact, a much keener analyst of her own troubles and condition than Deronda can possibly be as counsellor, though he does become the active, spiritual yeast in her self-recognition; and his presence near Gwendolen, though free from any suggestion of attraction at first, is sufficiently recognized by Grandcourt as a threat to his mastery, that it necessitates a removal from Deronda's influence. He takes her on a yachting cruise off the Italian coast. Here are Gwendolen's reflections as George Eliot interprets them:

> But now enter into the soul of this young creature as she found herself, with the blue Mediterranean dividing her from the world, on the tiny plank-island of a yacht, the domain of the husband to whom she felt that she had sold herself, and had been paid the strict price—nay, paid more than she had dared to ask in the handsome maintenance of her mother:—the husband to whom she had sold her truthfulness and sense of justice, so that he held them throttled into silence, collared and dragged behind him to witness what he would without remonstrance ... But ... what sort of Moslem paradise would quiet the terrible fury of moral repulsion and cowed resistance?. ... While Gwendolen, throned on her cushions at evening, and beholding the glory of sea and sky softening as if with boundless love around her, was hoping that Grandcourt in his march up and down was not going to look at her or speak to her, some woman under a smoky sky, obliged to consider the price of eggs in arranging her dinner, was listening for the music of a footstep that would remove all from her foretaste of joy. ...[90]

It is a terrible contrast—the price of eggs and the price of a soul. First perceptions of existences outside her own narrow self allowed to love and be loved.

Of course, she cannot and never will fully understand Deronda's visionary plans, purposes, and final actions. Having discovered Mordecai, Mirah's brother, and fired by Mordecai's "enthusiasm"—that is, missionary and prophetical fervor—even when Deronda is still ignorant of his own Jewish descent, Deronda, too, changes. He has had a mystical sense of consanguinity before this. Under Mordecai's influence he will become the active agent of Jewish regeneration. He listens to Mordecai's fervent words:

> Revive the organic centre; let the unity of Israel which has made the growth and form of its religion be an outward reality. Looking towards a land and a polity, our dispersed people in all ends of the earth may share the dignity of a national life which has a voice among the peoples of the East and West ... The degraded and scorned of our race will learn to think of their sacred land, not as a place for saintly beggary to await death in loathsome idleness, but as a republic where the Jewish spirit manifests itself in a new order found on the old, purified, enriched by the experience our greatest sons have gathered from the life of the ages. A new Judaea poised between East and West—a covenant of reconciliation ...[91]

Mordecai dies. But Deronda, having married Mirah, is ready to bring that vision into realization. To Gwendolen he confides his plan, both of his impending marriage and his imminent departure:

> "I am going to the East ... The idea that I am possessed with is that of restoring a political existence to my people, making them a nation again, giving them a national centre, such as the English have, though they too are scattered over the face of the globe ... I am

resolved to devote my life to it. At the least, I may awaken a movement in other minds, such as has been awakened in my own."[92]

Gwendolen is of course traumatized. She is to be abandoned. This at a time when she feels herself more totally alone than ever, for George Eliot, having come to another of her *culs de sac*, has had Grandcourt drown just off Genoa, adding to Gwendolen's sense of guilt, for she had been praying for his death. World history, in the form of Deronda's enterprise, has entered her uncomprehending life and mind. For Gwendolen, as for George Eliot now, there was this confounding element of dislodgment; not, perhaps, from Gwendolen's "supremacy in her own world," but from a clear comprehension of the relation of the individual to world history. The years 1865 and 1866, succeeded by the new Reform Bill, with all the events in England and on the Continent—economic depression, political agitations, even threats of violence in London and elsewhere—had challenged the stability of the society at Diplow and Offendene in Wessex, the society of Grandcourt, the Rev. Gascoigne, Sir Hugo, the Arrowpoints, and the lesser crew, though little of that appears in the novel except as perfunctory reference to Sadowa, the Prussian ascendency, and the Civil War in America. If Deronda's vision is meant also to cover the crisis, or at least the dilemmas, at home, it is not made obvious how. His enterprise may be a noble one, but it scarcely answers the pressing needs of the hour, aside from the tragedy of European Jewry. That the individual is a part of a larger political and social whole, and cannot live in isolation is stated throughout the book. Gwendolen is in fact symbolic of such an individual. That she does not and cannot emerge out of her isolation is perhaps also indicative of George Eliot's own dilemma. She has tried to solve a profound and inclusive problem solely in humanistic moral terms. In 1872 that was no longer possible. Hence, like Gwendolen, England too stood bereft of guidance.

> The world seemed getting larger round poor Gwendolen, and she more solitary and helpless in the midst. The thought that he might come back after going to the East, sank before the bewildering vision of these wide-stretching purposes in which she felt herself reduced to a mere speck. There comes a terrible moment to many souls when the great movements of the world, the larger destinies of mankind, which have lain aloof in newspapers and other neglected reading, enter like an earthquake into their own lives. ...[93]

Where was the "organic centre" of England that would bring the nation out of its self-division, out of those very aspects of desolation, philistinism, benign complacence, mild or ferocious selfishness and egotism which she had just been describing? Gwendolen's panic in the face of her isolation, despite her widened "consciousness" under Deronda's tutelage, is the panic of one who does not as yet know where to turn. Was that George Eliot's anxiety too in the face of the complexities, and a retreat into salvation through reform of the moral conscience? She was growing ever more cautious in the face of her public. What Henry James called "the fatality of British decorum," and no doubt her own upbringing, had kept her from penetrating deeply into the sexual life and relations of her characters, and in *Daniel Deronda*, from clarifying the perverseness of both Grandcourt and Gwendolen. She had placed a quotation from Walt Whitman at the head of one of her chapters in that book, but withdrew it in a later edition because of a public outcry against that "nasty" man. Her Comtean conscience rebelled at the prospect of John Stuart Mill's candidacy for a seat in Commons—unbefitting political activity in so prominent an intellectual. She objected to his advocacy of a franchise for women. She no longer felt it feasible to support a fund for Mazzini. That sharp clarity she could bring into her descriptions of the Wessex groups failed her when she turned to Deronda and his associations. Her deep and courageous sympathy with the plight of the Jews, her earnestness in the depiction of the "messianic" element in Mordecai, her understanding of some of the controversies involved in the attempted solutions of the "Jewish problem," cannot obscure the fact that a cloud of mysticism hangs over this part of her extraordinary treatment of the theme of the "wandering Jew." The glorification of the artist in the figure of Klesmer, the composer, and his insistence on the artist's role as a ruler of nations and maker of an age—forceful enough in opposition to the Philistines whom he is addressing—sounds odd in an age where the artist was battling and fighting a rear-guard action against what the elite could call "barbarism." All this bears the marks of a kind of epigonal Romanticism, in contrast to the clearsighted and penetrating observation elsewhere.

Yet even in the political field, it would be unjust not to recognize George Eliot's contribution to liberalism in her advocacy of the Jewish cause. For *Daniel Deronda* proved a significant weapon in what was to become the struggle against political anti-semitism that was soon to sweep over the Continent, and of which the Dreyfus case in France, and the anti-Jewish persecutions in Germany, Austria, and particularly in Russia, were to be such horrifying examples before they were surpassed in our twentieth century.

In one of her very last essays, written shortly before her death, she came back to the question of Jewish persecution throughout the ages:

> On the whole, she wrote, one of the most remarkable phenomena in the history of this scattered people, made for ages "a scorn and a hissing," is, that after being subjected to this process, which might have been expected to be in every sense deteriorating and vitiating, they have come out of it (in any estimate which allows for numerical proportion) rivalling the nations of European countries in healthiness and beauty of physique, in practical ability, in scientific and artistic aptitude, and in some forms of ethical value …[94]

George Eliot was now the high-priestess of English letters. From far and wide she received homages and adulation, gradually even succeeding in a minor way in breaking the *cordon sanitaire* that society had drawn around her. Queen Victoria was one of her devout readers; and one of her daughters, the German princess, broke the barrier by inviting her presence. Men, of course, flocked around her. American literati sought her out, not the least among them Harriet Beecher Stowe and Henry James. Emily Dickinson was enchanted with *Middlemarch*. Young Henry James became one of her most devout worshippers and most perceptive critics, and has left us a portrait of her upon their first meeting. He was writing to his father in May 1869.

> To begin with she is magnificently ugly—deliciously hideous. She has a low forehead, a dull grey eye, a vast pendulous nose, a huge mouth, full of uneven teeth, and a chin and jaw-bone *qui n'en finissent pas* … Now in this vast ugliness resides a most powerful

beauty, which, in a very few minutes steals forth and charms the mind, so that you end as I ended in falling in love with her.

He continues his rhapsody, noting her rich and soft voice, her sagacity and sweetness, dignity, and "a broad hint of a great underlying world of reserve, knowledge, pride and power …" "Altogether, she has a larger circumference than any woman I have ever seen."[95]

That straitlaced American Brahmin, Harvard professor Charles Eliot Norton, came with his straiter-laced wife. While she stayed away for a while, he paid his visit and thought George Eliot a "good woman," admired by many, though he could not condone her conduct, which, as he had heard, set a bad example to others. With the enlightened world at her feet, she was now immune to such minor shocks. Anyway, Lewes was an effective barrier against the more obtrusive or violent criticism of herself and her work. They both prospered and allowed themselves the luxury of a country home. Unfortunately, his health began to fail, and he died of cancer in 1878.

She was shattered. "I am a bruised creature," she confessed, and secluded herself. Soon, however, she set herself to completing one of Lewes' unfinished manuscripts. The blow was all the greater as she had been so dependent on him, emotionally, intellectually, physically. He had been her counsellor and her buffer, her critic and one of her principal inspirations. He had been her teacher in science, and even in aesthetics. Few lives had been so thoroughly intertwined. She had always needed someone to lean on—that was her own psychic and emotional bent (weakness, if you will). She was herself none too well, and felt herself terribly weakened by the great loss. As she began recovering her spirits, she found the sympathy, and indeed the love of the much younger John Cross a sustaining force. She had known him since her Roman days, in 1869, and he had been a loyal friend to both Lewes and herself. Whatever the elements that attracted him to the celebrated woman—he was himself a complex personality—there was no question about his devotion. She in turn felt deeply for him, and they married in 1880. Their happiness was short-lived, for she died in that same year. … They had scarcely had time to settle in their new London home, 4 Cheyne Walk.

Ten years before her death she had written in a letter to a friend:

> … For nearly a year death seems to me my most intimate daily companion. I mingle the thought of it with every other, not sadly, but as one mingles the thought of some one who is nearest in love and duty with all one's motives. I try to delight in the sunshine that will be when I shall never see it any more …[96]

For posterity she had written a testament and a hope, which succeeding times have fully confirmed:

> Oh may I join the choir invisible
> Of those immortal dead who live again
> In minds made better by their presence: live
> In pulses stirred to generosity,
> In deeds of daring rectitude, in scorn
> For miserable aims that end with self,
> In thought sublime that pierce the night like stars,
> And with their mild persistence urge man's search
> To vaster issues. …

Notes

Notes to the Editor's Introduction

1. For full citations of these and other relevant writings, see "Further Reading" at the end of this volume.

2. The Brooklyn College materials, in four archival boxes, were later returned to the Kurz Foundation when negotiations fell through. By the time they were recovered, the rest of the papers had already been accepted by NYU. At the present time, these "Brooklyn College" boxes are in the possession of the Solidarity Foundation (NY); it is expected that in the near future they will be deposited along with the rest of the Ewen papers in the Tamiment Collection, New York University.

3. For example, on proof p. 456, beginning of part three, chapter 3, "The Lyre and the Sword," Kramer's marginal annotation: "Bad writing throughout this section" i.e., msp.458–468, (cf. Kramer, proof p.478: "clichés increase"; 487: "clichés").

Notes to Part One, Chapter One

1. E. J. Hobsbawm, *The Age of Revolution*, 150.

2. Alexis de Tocqueville, *Journeys to England and Ireland*, ed. J. P. Mayer, 107–108; cited in Hobsbawm, *op. cit.*, 27.

3. Cited in Hobsbawm, 298.

4. Friedrich Engels, *The Condition of the Working Class in England*, 296.

5. *The Political Register*, August 3, 1830, cited in Elie Halévy, *The Triumph of Reform*, 8.

6. Cited in E. P. Thompson, *The Making of the English Working Class*, 250.

7. Halévy, *op. cit.*, 18.

8. T. B. Macaulay, *Prose and Poetry*, Selected by G. M. Young, 675–676.

9. Arthur P. Stanley, *Life and Correspondence of Thomas Arnold*, D. D., I, 290.

10. Lord Greville, *Memoirs*, June 16, 1837, cited in Halévy, 298–299.

11. Andrew Ure, *Philosophy of Manufacture* (1836), cited in Halévy, 283.

12. Hetherington's *The Poor Man's Guardian*, October 15, 1832, cited in E. P. Thompson, *The Making of the English Working Class*, 893.

13. "Report of the Proceedings of the Great Public Meeting," cited in Thompson, 909.

14. Thompson, 912.

15. *Ibid.*, 912, 913.

16. Cited in Harold Perkin, *Origins of Modern English Society 1780–1880*, 173.

17. Cited in Owen Rattenbury, *Flame of Freedom*, 188.

18. See the studies of Patricia Hollis, *The Pauper Press*, and E. P. Thompson, *The Making of the English Working Class*.

19. *The Cosmopolite*, March 10, 1832, cited in Hollis, 15.

20. *The Poor Man's Guardian*, July 26, 1834, cited in Hollis, 222–223.

21. Cited in Neff, *Carlyle and Mill*, 142.

22. Elizabeth Longford, *Queen Victoria*, 180.

23. *The Edinburgh Review*, July 1834, cited in Hollis, 247.

24. Fried and Sanders, *Socialist Thought. A Documentary History*, 187–191.

25. Cited in Briggs (ed.), *Chartist Studies*, 373.

Notes to Part One, Chapter Two

1. "An Address delivered to the inhabitants of New Lanark … on the first of January, 1816; "Appendix C," *The Life of Robert Owen*, 351.

2. *Ibid.*, 351.

3. Robert Owen, *A New View of Society*, cited in Derry, The *Radical Tradition*, 137.

4. Cited in Thompson, *The Making of the English Working Class*, 867.

5. Cited in G.D.H. Cole, *The British Common People*, 265.

6. J. S. Mill, "Bentham," reprinted in Bhiku Parekh, *Jeremy Bentham: Ten Critical Essays*, 3.

7. Bentham, *Introduction to the Principles of Morals and Legislation*, cited in Neff, *Carlyle and Mill*, 92.

8. John Stuart Mill, *Utilitarianism*, Everyman's Library Edition, 6.

9. Quoted in Derry, *The Radical Tradition*, 110.

10. James Mill, *Essay on Government*, cited in Mazlish, *James and John Stuart Mill*, 88.

11. Cited in Mazlish, 102.

12. Thomas Carlyle, *Sartor Resartus*, Bk. III, ch. 5.

13. *Blackwood's Magazine* XVII (1825), 22, 24; cited in Harold Perkin, *Origins of Modern English Society*, 229.

Notes to Part One, Chapter Three

1. William Allingham's *Diary*, cited in Wilson, *Carlyle till Marriage*, 147.

2. Carlyle, "Goethe," 1828.

3. See Frederic Ewen, *The Prestige of Schiller in England*, passim.

4. *The Letters of Thomas Carlyle to His Brother Alexander*, 177–178.

5. Wilson, *op. cit.*, 221–222.

6. Goethe, *Wilhelm Meisters Lehrjahre*, Book V, ch. 3.

7. *Ibid.*, Book VII, ch 3.

8. Goethe, *Wilhelm Meisters Wanderjahre*, Bk. II, chaps 1 and 2.

9. *Ibid.*, Bk. V, ch. 9.

10. *Early Letters of Thomas Carlyle*, II, 219, 223.

11. See Susanne Howe, *Wilhelm Meister and His English Kinsmen*, and Jerome Buckley, *Season of Youth: The Bildungsroman from Dickens to Golding*.

12. Froude, *Carlyle: The First Forty Years*, II, 179.

13. From *Two Note Books* (February 7, 1831), cited in Shine, *Carlyle and the Saint-Simonians*, 65.

14. "Signs of the Times," *Edinburgh Review*, No. 98, 1831, 486–487.

15. Froude, *op. cit.*, II, 67.

16. Cited in Shine, *op. cit.*, 54–55.

17. Carlyle, "Characteristics" (1831).

18. *Ibid.*

19. *Sartor Resartus*, Bk. III, ch. 11.

20. *Ibid.*, Bk. II, ch 7: "The Everlasting No."

21. *Ibid.*, Bk. II, ch. 9, "The Everlasting Yea."

22. *Ibid.*, Bk. III, ch. 5.

23. *Ibid.*, Bk. II, ch. 8.

24. *Letters of Thomas Carlyle 1826–1836*, ed. by Charles Eliot Norton, 498–499; see also Thomas Carlyle, *Reminiscences*, section on Jane Welsh Carlyle.

25. Froude, *Carlyle in London*, I, 93.

26. Carlyle, *The French Revolution: A History*, Part I, Bk. II, chaps. 2, 3, 4, 7; Bk. IV, chaps 2, 3.

27. *Ibid.*, Bk. IV, ch. 4.

28. *Ibid.*, Part II, Bk. VI, ch. 2.

29. *Ibid.*, Part III, Bk. VII, ch. 6.

30. *Ibid.*, ch. 7.

31. Edmund Burke, *Reflections on the Revolution in France*; Hippolyte Taine, *Les Origines de la France contemporaine* (1876), I, 18, 53–54, cited in George Rudé, *The Crowd in the French Revolution*, 2.

32. Cited in Hedva Ben-Israel, *English Historians on the French Revolution*, 161.

33. Carlyle, *Past and Present*, Bk. III, ch. 8 (1843).

34. *Ibid.*, Bk. III, ch. 9.

35. *Past and Present.*

36. *Chartism*, chaps. 8, 6 (1839).

37. Carlyle, "Parliament."

38. To wit, Philip Rosenberg, in his book *The Seventh Hero: Thomas Carlyle and the Theory of Radical Activism*, 1974.

39. Froude, *Carlyle: The First Forty Years*, I, 346.

40. *New Letters and Memorials of Jane Welsh Carlyle*, II, 67.

41. *Autobiography*, I, p. 387. Similarly in Martineau, Craik & Knight, *History of the Peace*, 607: "Whatever place we assign him, and by whatever name we call him, Thomas Carlyle appears to be the man who has most essentially modified the mind of his time." [Ed.]

42. Letter to Carlyle, dated Weimar, 19 October 1854. Quoted in full in Haight, "The Carlyles and the Leweses," 100–101. [Ed.]

Notes to Part One, Chapter Four

1. Quoted in Cole and Postgate, *The British Common People*, 261.

2. *The Pickwick Papers*, chaps. 2, 10.

3. *Ibid.*, ch. 15.

4. *Ibid.*, ch. 45.

5. *Ibid.*, ch. 20.

6. *Ibid.*, ch. 67.

7. Cited in Thompson, *The Making of the English Working Class*, 295.

8. *Oliver Twist*, ch. 7.

9. *Nicholas Nickleby*, ch. 5.

10. *Dombey and Son*, ch. 8.

11. Quoted in Humphrey House, *The Dickens World*, 41.

12. *Nicholas Nickleby*, ch. 53.

13. To Edward Fitzgerald, cited in Edgar Johnson, *Charles Dickens*, I, 225.

14. Cited in Forster, *The Life of Charles Dickens* I, 164–165.

15. Humphry House, *The Dickens World*, 35.

16. *The Old Curiosity Shop*, ch. 45.

17. *Barnaby Rudge*, ch. 72.

18. *Nicholas Nickleby*, ch. 30.

19. T. B. Macaulay, *Miscellaneous Works* V, 158; cited in Russell Kirk, *The Conservative Mind*, 166.

20. Cited in Christopher Hibbert, *King Mob*, 181.

21. Forster, *op. cit.*, I, 185.

22. *Ibid.*, 184.

23. *Ibid.*, 194.

24. To Macready, March 22, 1842, cited in Johnson I, 404–405.

25. *Martin Chuzzlewit*, ch. 4.

26. *Ibid.*, ch 3.

27. *Ibid.*, ch. 19.

28. *Dombey and Son*, ch 15.

29. *Ibid.*, ch 1.

30. *Ibid.*, ch. 8.

31. *Ibid.*, ch. 16.

32. *Ibid.*, ch. 1.

33. *Ibid.*, ch. 27.

34. *Ibid.*, ch. 47.

35. Forster, *Life of Charles Dickens*, cited in Buckley, *Seasons of Youth*, 31–32.

36. *Dombey and Son*, ch. 20.

37. Cited in Jack Lindsay, *Charles Dickens*, 277.

38. *David Copperfield*, ch. 52.

Notes to Part One, Chapter Five

1. Michael St. John Packe, *The Life of John Stuart Mill*, 22.

2. To Sir Samuel Bentham, July 30, 1819; *Earlier Letters*, ed. Mineka, I, 7.

3. *Early Draft of John Stuart Mill's Autobiography*, ed. Jack Stillinger, 75; 86.

4. *Lettres inédites de John Stuart Mill à Auguste Comte*, 94. See also J.S. Mill, *John Mill's Boyhood in France*, ed. Anna Jean Mill.

5. Packe, *op. cit.*, 74.

6. *The Early Draft of John Stuart Mill's Autobiography*, ed. Stillinger, 181–185.

7. *Autobiography*, ch. 5.

8. *Ibid.*, ch. 5.

9. *Ibid.*

10. *Ibid.*

11. Auguste Comte, *Cours de Philosophie Positive*, I, 14–27, (1830).

12. To d'Eichthal, March 11, 1829; *Earlier Letters* I, 26–28; 31–34.

13. To John Sterling, April 15, 1829; *Earlier Letters* I, 28–30.

14. To James Mill, Paris, August 20, 1830; *Earlier Letters* I, 55–56.

15. To James Mill, August 18, 1830; *ibid.*, 54–55.

16. To John Sterling, October 20–22, 1831; *Earlier Letters* I, 74–88.

17. "The Spirit of the Age," *The Examiner*, January 6–May 19 1831; Mill, *Essays on Politics and Culture*, ed. Gertrude Himmelfarb, 20.

18. *Ibid.*, 19.

19. Thomas Carlyle to Dr. John Carlyle, Froude II, 430.

20. To the same; *ibid.*, II, 441.

21. *New Letters and Memorials of Jane Welsh Carlyle* I, 49.

22. See the psychohistory of Bruce Mazlish, *James and John Stuart Mill*; as well as Gertrude

Himmelfarb's "The Two Mills" in the *New Leader*, May 10, 1965. The full story of the relationship is told in the important work of F. A. Hayek, *John Stuart Mill and Harriet Taylor*.

23. Hayek, 275; 76–77.

24. *Ibid.*, 82.

25. "Enfranchisement of Women," *Westminster Review* LV (1851), 289–311.

26. *The Early Draft of John Stuart Mill's Autobiography* (Rejected Leaves), 195–196.

27. John Mill, "England and Ireland," *The Examiner*, May 13, 1848; Carlyle, "The Repeal of the Union," *Examiner*, April 19, 1848: cited in Robson, *The Improvement of Mankind*, 91 n. 2.

28. John Stuart Mill, "The Negro Question," *Fraser's Magazine* XLI (1850), 25–31.

29. *Earlier Letters* I, 184; 206–207.

30. Alexis de Tocqueville, *Democracy in America*, translated by Henry Reeve, edited by Henry Steele Commager, 6–7.

31. *Ibid.*, 147, "Advantages from Democratic Government."

32. *Ibid.*, 164, "Unlimited Power of the Majority."

33. *Ibid.*, 169.

34. *Ibid.*, 489–491, Part II, "The Influence of Democratic Opinions and Sentiments."

35. *Ibid.*, 506–507.

36. May 11, 1840; *Earlier Letters* II, 433–434.

37. "Tocqueville on Democracy in America," Mill, *Essays on Politics and Culture*, 218–219.

38. *Ibid.*, 240–241; 278 (1840).

39. *Ibid.*, 226.

40. *Lettres inédites de John Stuart Mill à Auguste Comte*, June 15, 1843, 208.

41. *Ibid.*, 237–240; July, August, and October, 1843.

42. Hayek, 115; Mueller, *John Stuart Mill and French Thought*, 123–124.

43. To John Pringle Nichol, Sept. 30, 1848; *Earlier Letters* II, 739.

44. Auguste Comte, *The Positive Philosophy*, tr. by Harriet Martineau; cited in Zeitlin, *Ideology and the Development of Sociological Theory*, 74–75.

45. J. S. Mill, "Coleridge," in the *London and Westminster Review*, March 1840; *Essays on Politics and Culture*, 157.

46. J.S. Mill, "Bentham," in the *London and Westminster Review*, August 1838; *Politics and Culture*, 85–131.

47. J.S. Mill, "Reorganization of the Reform Party," *London and Westminster Review*, April 1839; *Essays on Politics and Culture*, 304–314.

48. *Ibid.*, 314.

49. To John Austin, April 13, 1847; *Earlier Letters* II, 713–714.

50. To Henry S. Chapman, February 29, 1848; *Earlier Letters* II, 731–732.

51. J. S. Mill, "The French Revolution of 1848 and Its Assailants," *Westminster and Foreign Quarterly Review* LI (April 1849), 1–47.

52. *Principles of Political Economy*, 7th edition, Bk. II, ch. 1, par. 3.

53. "Thoughts on Parliamentary Reform" (1859), *Essays on Politics and Culture*, 339–341.

54. *The Subjection of Women*, ch. 4.

55. *Ibid.*, ch. 4.

56. *Ibid.*

57. "On Liberty," ch. 2.

58. *Ibid.*, ch. 3.

59. *Ibid.*

60. *Ibid.*, ch. 5.

Notes to Part Two, Chapter One

1. *The Diary of a Russian Censor: Aleksandr Nikitenko*, abridged, edited & translated by Helen Saltz Jacobson, 64.

2. Gogol to the actor Shchepkin, May 11, 1836, cited in Magarshack, *Gogol*, 132.

3. Vasiliii Gippius, ed., *N.V. Gogol—v pismakh i vospominnaniiakh*, 122.

4. *Ibid.*, 71–72.

5. October 19, 1835; cited in Gogol, ed. Gippius, 118.

6. Ad. Stender-Petersen, "Gogol und Kotzebue," *Zeitschrift für slavische Philologie* XII (1935), 16–53.

7. Nikitenko's *Diary*, 61.

8. Gogol: "After the Play," cited in Magarshack, 145.

9. Cited in Driessen, *Gogol as a Short-Story Writer*, 43; Gippius, 53 (November 14, 1831).

10. Tatiana Wolff, *Pushkin on Literature*, 299; Gogol, ed. Gippius, 48–49.

11. In *The Contemporary*, (first issue) 1836; Wolff, 381.

12. *Dikanka*, "Christmas Eve," "St. John's Eve," "May Night," "A Terrible Vengeance."

13. *Dikanka*, Part Two, "Ivan Fyodorovich Shponka and His Aunt."

14. Cited in Setchkarev, *Gogol*, 41.

15. Gogol, ed. Gippius, 136–137.

16. June 28, 1826; Gogol, ed. Gippius, 149.

17. To Countess ***, *Selected Passages from Correspondence*, Letter XXVI.

18. Magarshack, 163; Gogol, ed. Gippius, 166–167 (Rome, October 30, 1837).

19. To Pletnev, January 19, 1842; Gogol, ed. Gippius, 216–217; Magarshack, 294–205.

20. Magarshack, 128; Gogol, ed. Gippius, 118 (St. Petersburg, October 19, 1835).

21. *Dead Souls*, ch. I.

22. *Dead Souls*, ch. VII.

23. Gogol, ed. Gippius, 164; Magarshack 154.

24. *Dead Souls*, XI.

25. See Simon Karlinsky, *The Sexual Labyrinth of Nikolai Gogol*, 135–144.

26. *Dead Souls*, ch. XI.

27. Gogol, ed. Gippius, 259; Gogol, *Selected Passages from Correspondence*, Letter XVIII.

28. Alexander Herzen, *Du Développement des idées révolutionnaires en Russie*, cited in Lavrin, *Gogol: A Centenary Survey*, 117.

29. V. G. Belinsky, "A View of Russian Literature in 1847," *Selected Philosophical Works*, 414.

30. See Simon Karlinsky, *The Sexual Labyrinth of Nikolai Gogol*.

31. Setchkarev 54, 66.

32. Gogol, ed. Gippius, 301.

33. Magarshack, 130–231.

34. Gogol, "An Interpretation of *The Government Inspector*."

35. Dimitri Chizhevski, "Gogol Studien," in *Forum Slavicum* X (1966), 116–117.

36. Vladimir Nabokov, *Gogol*, 73. See also James B. Woodward, *Gogol's Dead Souls*.

37. *Selected Passages*, Letter VIII, "A Few Words Concerning our Church …"

38. *Ibid.*, Letter XXII, "The Russian Landowner."

39. *Ibid.*, Letter XXVIII.

40. *Ibid.*, Letter XIV, "Four Letters on *Dead Souls*."

41. Letter to Zhukovsky, March 18, 1847, cited in Magarshack, 141.

42. Lavrin, *op. cit.*, 141.

43. Cited in Gogol, *Sämmtliche Werke*, VIII, 3–9: Letter to Arkady Ossipovich Rossetti, Naples, 1847.

44. Vissarion Belinsky, "Letter to N. V. Gogol, July 3, 1847," *Selected Philosophical Works*, 502 ff.

45. *Ibid.*, 529–530.

46. Cited in Lavrin, 65.

47. Cited in Boris de Schloezer, *Gogol*, 210.

48. Related by Pogodin; Gogol, ed. Gippius, 452–453.

49. Ivan Turgenev, *Literary Reminiscences*, 167–170.

Notes to Part Two, Chapter Two

1. *My Past and Thoughts: The Memoirs of Alexander Herzen*, II, 952–954.

2. See Jesse D. Clarkson, *A History of Russia*, ch. 16; T. G. Masaryk, *The Spirit of Russia*, I, 120ff.

3. Cited in V. Myakotin, in *The History of Russia*, ed. by Paul Miliukov, II, 265.

4. Sidney Monas, *The Third Section*, 154.

5. *Ibid.*, 169.

6. Raymond T. McNally, *The Major Works of Peter Chaadaev*, 27–40; Seton-Watson, *The Russian Empire 1801–1917*, 257–258.

7. Cited in Franco Venturi, *Roots of Revolution*, 41.

8. P. Annenkov, *The Extraordinary Decade*, 77, 142; for Feuerbach, see below, "The Lightning of Ideas," 176–186.

9. Cited in Herbert E. Bowman, *Vissarion Belinski*, 146.

10. Cited in Venturi, 9.

11. Herzen, *Memoirs*, II, 603.

12. To Ivanov, August 7, 1847; cited in Bowman, *Belinski*, 95–96.

13. Bowman, *Belinski*, 96.

14. Masaryk, I, 386.

15. Bowman, 143.

16. *Ibid.*, 145.

17. *Ibid.*, 147.

18. Vissarion Belinsky, *Selected Philosophical Works*, 159–165. Letter to V. P. Botkin, September 8, 1841.

19. Ivan Turgenev, *Literary Reminiscences*, 120–123.

20. Annenkov, 150.

21. Dostoevsky, *Poor Folk*, translated by Lev Navrozov; Makar Devushkin's letter to Varvara, September 9, 180–186.

22. Cited in Ronald Hingley, *The Undiscovered Dostoyevsky*, 5–6.

23. Grigorovich, *Reminiscences*, cited in *Letters of Fyodor Dostoevsky*, translated by Ethel Colburn Mayne, 252–253.

24. *Poor People*, 168.

25. Dostoevsky, *The Diary of a Writer* (1877), translated by Boris Brasol, II, 587–588.

26. Dominique Arban, *Les Années d'apprentissage de Fiodor Dostoievski*, 32–33.

27. *Diary of a Writer*, II, 588.

28. Cited in Konstantin Mochulsky, *Dostoevsky*, 17.

29. *Ibid.*, 17.

30. Cited in Proctor, *Dostoevskij and the Belinskij School of Literary Criticism*, 58.

31. Dostoevsky, "Mr. Prokharchin."

32. Dostoevsky, "White Nights."

33. In addition to the works already cited, the following will be of interest: *Netochka Nezvanova* (the only two completed parts, and the notes thereto); "The Landlady," "Polzunkov," "A Christmas Tree Party and a Wedding."

34. Cited in Proctor, 61.

35. Venturi, 82.

36. Nicholas V. Riasanovsky, "Fourierism in Russia: An Estimate of the Petraševcy," *American Slavic and East European Review* XII (1953), 294.

37. Mochulsky, 116.

38. Cited Riasanovsky, 301, n.30.

39. *Ibid.*, 300–301.

40. *Ibid.*, 294.

41. Cited in Arban, *Correspondance de Dostoievski*, I, xvii.

42. D. D. Akhsharumov, cited in Monas, 255–256.

43. Droz, *Europe between Revolutions*, 184.

44. Dostoyevski, *The Diary of a Writer*, I, 7–9 (1873).

45. Eugene Kamenka, *The Philosophy of Ludwig Feuerbach*, 16; 154, n. 9. See also Venturi, *passim*, and Mochulsky, 130ff.

46. Mochulsky, 131.

47. Mochulsky, 126.

48. Yarmolinsky, *Dostoyevski*, 72.

49. Riasanovsky, 298.

50. Mochulsky, 132.

51. Mochulsky, 119–120.

52. Cited by V. Myakotin, in Miliukov, *History of Russia*, II, 287–288.

53. Monas, 251.

54. Cited in Hofmann, *Les Grands romanciers russes*, 114.

55. For Belinsky's Letter, see above, pp. 119–121.

56. Mochulsky, 122–123.

57. Troyat, 118.

58. *Ibid.*, 120.

59. Mochulsky, 133.

60. Mochulsky, 141–142.

Notes to Part Three, Chapter One

1. Richard Rothe to his father, from Heidelberg, August 16, 1818; cited in Günther Nicolin, *Hegel in Berichten seiner Zeitgenossen*, 176–177.

2. Heinrich Gustav Hotho, *Vorstudien über Leben und Kunst* (1835); cited in Nicolin, 248.

3. Hegel, *The Science of Logic*, translated by W. H. Johnston and L. G. Struthers, I, 142, 146.

4. *Ibid.*, I, 65.

5. Preface to the *Phenomenology of Mind*, Loewenberg, *Hegel*, 15.

6. Hegel, *The Philosophy of History*, Introduction, translated by J. Sibree, 75–77.

7. *Ibid.*, 73.

8. *Ibid.*, 26–27.

9. *Ibid.*, 57.

10. *Ibid.*, 17–18.

11. Herbert Marcuse, *Reason and Revolution*, 245.

12. Hegel, *The Philosophy of History*, 416–417.

13. Marcuse, 96.

14. Hegel, *The Philosophy of Right*, paragraph 333; Marcuse, 222.

15. Hegel, Preface to the *Philosophy of Right*.

16. Hegel, *Theologische Jugendschriften*, cited in Löwith, *From Hegel to Nietzsche*, 168.

17. Hegel, *Philosophy of History*, 324.

18. G. Asverus, May 5, 1819; Nicolin, 194.

19. Friedrich Engels, *Anti-Dühring*,

20. Eduard Gans, *Vermischte Schriften* (1834), 251ff.; cited in David McLellan, *The Young Hegelians and Karl Marx*, 1.

21. Hegel, *Philosophy of Right*, Preface xxviii–xxix.

22. David Friedrich Strauss to Christian Märklin; Nicolin, 466–468.

23. D. F. Strauss, *Märklin*, in his *Gesammelte Schriften* X, 224.

24. W. T. Stace, *The Philosophy of Hegel*, 514.

25. David Friedrich Strauss, *The Life of Jesus. Critically Examined*, I, 42.

26. *Ibid.*, "Concluding Dissertation: The Last Dilemma," III, 437–439.

27. *Ibid.*, 439.

28. *Ibid.*, 437.

29. R. Haym, *Aus meinem Leben*, 195; cited in McLellan, *The Young Hegelians*, 3.

30. Strauss, *Die christliche Glaubenslehre* (1840), I, 68; cited in Hook, *From Hegel to Marx*, 87. See also A. Lévy, *David Friedrich Strauss*, 55, 61, 94.

31. Friedrich Engels to Wilhelm Graeber, October 8, 1839; *Zwischen 18 und 25: Jugendbriefe von Friedrich Engels*, 122.

32. Ludwig Prantl, "Feuerbach," in *Allgemeine deutsche Biographie*; McLellan, *The Young Hegelians*, 85.

33. Nicolin, 269; 292.

34. To Arnold Ruge (March 1843), cited in Kamenka, *The Philosophy of Ludwig Feuerbach*, 28.

35. *Ibid.*, 114.

36. *Ibid.*, 35.

37. *The Essence of Christianity*, Preface, xxxix.

38. *Philosophical Fragments*, cited in Kamenka, 35.

39. *Grundsätze der Philosophie der Zukunft*, pars. 32, 37; Marcuse, 271.

40. Cited in Kamenka, 80.

41. Cited in Hook, *From Hegel to Marx*, 261.

42. *The Essence of Christianity*, ch. 1, Introduction, 2–11. The translation is by George Eliot.

43. *Ibid.*, 14–18.

44. *Ibid.*, 21–25.

45. *Ibid.*, 26.

46. *Ibid.*, 47.

47. *Ibid.*, 48.

48. *Ibid.*, 50.

49. *Ibid.*, 67.

50. *Ibid.*, 73.

51. *Ibid.*, 83.

52. *Ibid.*, 87.

53. *Ibid.*, 171.

54. *Ibid.*, 271, 178.

55. David Friedrich Strauss, *Ausgewählte Briefe*, 184.

56. Friedrich Engels, *Ludwig Feuerbach and the Outcome of Classical German Philosophy*, in Karl Marx, *Selected Works*, I, 428.

57. Cited in McLellan, *The Young Hegelians*, 97. The obvious pun is on Feuerbach's name, "brook of fire." Cf. below, p. 449.

58. Karl Marx, *Zur Kritik der Hegelschen Rechtsphilosophie, Der historische Materialismus*, I, 272.

59. George Herwegh, "Seinem Ludwig Feuerbach, den 13 September 1872."

60. Ludwig Feuerbach, *Die Unsterblichkeitsfrage* (1846)—*The Problem of Immortality*, 28.

61. Karl Marx, Friedrich Engels, *Werke, Ergänzungsband* I, 3.

62. Marx and Engels, *Gesamtausgabe* I, I:2, 260–261.

63. *Briefwechsel*, edited by W. Schuffenhauer, 177; cited in Avineri, 134.

64. Letter to Arnold Ruge, *Karl Marx: Der historische Materialismus*, I, 226–227.

65. *Ibid.*, 224.

66. *A Critique of Hegel's Philosophy of Right* I, Marx, *Der historische Materialismus* I, 263–264; Bottomore, *Karl Marx: Early Writings*, 43–44; McLellan, *Karl Marx: Early Texts*, 115–116.

67. Ibid., I, 278; Bottomore, 58; McLellan, 127–128.

68. Marcuse, 260–261; Avineri, 106 ff.

69. Marcuse, 261.

70. Z.A. Jordan, *The Evolution of Dialectical Materialism*, 61.

71. N. Rotenstreich, *Basic Problems of Marx's Philosophy*, 38–39.

72. Marx and Engels, *The German Ideology (Deutsche Ideologie)*, in *Der historische Materialismus*, II, 458 (1845–1846).

73. Notes on James Mill's *Elements of Political Economy*, Marx-Engels, *Werke*, Ergänzungsband I, 462–463; McLellan, *Marx before Marxism*, 178–179.

74. *Werke*, Ergbd. I, 536; Bottomore, *Early Writings*, 155.

75. Gustav Mayer, *Engels* I, 42.

76. *Ibid.*, I, 34.

77. Engels, "Schelling und die Offenbarung," *ibid.*, I, 78–79.

78. Engels, "History of the Communist League," Karl Marx, *Selected Works* II, 11.

79. "Briefe aus London an den Schweizerischen Republikaner" (1843), in Engels, *Schriften der Frühzeit*, I, 264.

80. Engels, "Die Lage Englands: Past and Present by Thomas Carlyle," *Werke I*, 525–549.

81. Engels, "Die Lage Englands," in *Vorwärts*, September, October, 1844; cited in Cornu III, 193.

82. "Outlines of a Critique of National Economy," cited in G. Mayer, *Engels* I, 170.

83. *Deutsche Ideologie*: "Feuerbach," *Der historische Materialismus* II, 13.

84. *Ibid.*, 11.

85. *Ibid.*, 37–38.

86. Cornu IV, 205.

87. Struik, *Birth of the Communist Manifesto*, 58.

88. Cited in Struik, 66.

89. *Ibid.*

90. *The Communist Manifesto*, II, "Proletarians and Communists."

Notes to Part Three, Chapter Two

1. Cited in William L. Langer, *Political and Social Upheaval*, 323.

2. T. A. Jackson, *Ireland Her Own*, 244.

3. Karl Marx, *Class Struggles in France*, in *Selected Works* II, 198.

4. Cited in Woodham-Smith, *The Great Hunger*, 162–163.

5. March 23, 1846; cited *ibid.*, 72.

6. *Of Democracy in Modern Society*, London, 1838, 32; cited in Talmon, 326–327.

7. Tocqueville, *Recollections*, cited in Droz, *Europe between Revolutions*, 262, Karl Marx, *Selected Works II (Class Struggles in France)*, 195–196.

8. Heinrich Heine, *Lutezia*, in *Sämtliche Werke* IX, 211.

9. Hobsbawm, 200.

10. Cited in Evans, *Social Romanticism in France*, 32–33.

11. Cited in Mougin, *Pierre Leroux*, 47.

12. Cited in Droz, *Europe between Revolutions*, 91.

13. *Lutezia*, December 4, 1842, *Sämtliche Werke*, IX, 260–261.

14. *Ibid.*, 233.

15. Edgar Quinet, *Promethée* (1838), Part III, scene iv, Prologue.

16. *Democracy in America*, Part II, sect. 6.

17. Tocqueville, *Journey to America*, cited in Zetterbaum, *Tocqueville and the Problem of Democracy*, 152.

18. Tocqueville, *L'ancien régime et la Révolution française*; cited in Raymond Aron, *Main Currents in Sociological Thought*, I, 216–217.

19. *Recollections*, 2–3.

20. *Ibid.*, 12–13.

21. Cited in Edmund Wilson, *To the Finland Station*, 17.

22. Michelet, *Le Peuple*, xviii, 151.

23. Roland Barthes, *Michelet par lui-même*, 54–55.

24. Michelet, *Histoire de France*, I, Préface.

25. Louis Blanc, *Organization of Labor*, in Fried, *Socialist Thought*, 231–236.

26. Louis Blanc, *Histoire de dix ans*, II, 311.

27. Cited in Loubère, *Louis Blanc*, 43.

28. Cited in Maurice Dommanget, *Auguste Blanqui: Des origines à la Révolution de 1848*, 7, 9.

29. Heinrich Heine, *Französische Zustände*, Paris, February 10, 1832, *Sämtliche Werke* VI, 126–128.

30. Dommanget, 97–99.

31. *Ibid.*, 103–106 (January 12, 1832).

32. *Ibid.*, 148–151.

33. Auguste Blanqui, "The Man Who Makes the Soup Should Get to Eat It," in Fried, *Socialist Thought*, 194.

34. *Recollections*, 138–139.

35. *De l'Utilité et de la Célébration du Dimanche*, cited in Bowle, *Politics and Opinion in the Nineteenth Century*, 156.

36. *What is Property?*, passim.

37. Cited in Woodcock, *Pierre-Joseph Proudhon*, 92–93.

38. From the "Carnets" for 1843, cited in Woodcock, "The Solitary Revolutionary," *Encounter* 51.

39. *Ibid.*, 51.

40. *Ibid.*, 52.

41. Karl Marx, Letter to Pavel Annenkov, December 18, 1846, *Werke* IV, 55.

42. See in particular Armand Cuvillier, *Hommes et idéologies de 1840*.

43. P. V. Annenkov, *The Extraordinary Decade*, 165.

44. Daniel Stern (Mme. d'Agoult), *Histoire de la révolution de 1848*, I, 21.

45. Tocqueville, *Recollections*, 12–13.

46. *Ibid.*, 78.

47. Cited in Roger Price, *The French Second Republic*, 99.

48. Karl Marx, *Class Struggles in France*, 202.

49. Cited in Price, 130.

50. Albert Fournier, "George Sand en 1848," *Europe* XXVI (1948), 140–150.

51. Price, 157.

52. Tocqueville, *Recollections*, 160–163.

53. Frederick A. De Luna, *The French Republic under Cavaignac*, 219.

54. Letter to Mme. Marliani, July 1848, cited in Fournier, "George Sand en 1848," *Europe* XXVI (1948), 148.

55. Alexander Herzen, *My Past and Thoughts*, II, 842–847.

56. Karl Marx, *The Class Struggles in France*, 216–217.

57. Gustave Geffroy, *L'Enfermé* I, 203–204.

58. Cited in Paul Jamati, "Un Poète et un historien de 48: Louis Ménard," *Europe* XXVI (1948), 183–184.

59. Cited in J. G. Legge, *Rhyme and Revolution in Germany*, 262–263.

60. Priscilla Robertson, *Revolutions of 1848*, 193.

61. Gottfried Keller, "Wien 1848."

62. Ludwig August Frankl, "Die Universität," translated in J. G. Legge, *Rhyme and Revolution in Germany*, 271–172.

63. Robertson, 232.

64. Cited in R. John Rath, *The Viennese Revolution of 1848*, 151–152.

65. Berthold Auerbach's eyewitness report in *Tagebuch aus Wien*, cited in Legge, 493.

66. R. John Rath, *The Viennese Revolution of 1848*, 337.

67. Friedrich Engels, *Germany: Revolution and Counter-Revolution*, in Karl Marx, *Selected Works*, II, 108, 111 (in collaboration with Karl Marx).

68. Franz Bodenstedt, *Aus meinem Leben* II, cited in Legge, 497; Tim Klein, 402–403.

69. Legge, 498–499; Tim Klein, 400.

70. E. Sparfeld, *Das Buch von Robert Blum*, 1849, cited in Legge 499, Tim Klein, 401.

71. Ferdinand Freiligrath, "Wien," *Werke* II, 41–42.

72. Langer, *Political and Social Upheaval*, 476–482.

73. For Petöfi, see below, pp. 256–274.

74. Pierre Dupont, "La France à Pie IX," *Muse populaire*, 133.

75. Cited in Langer, 252; Droz, *Europe between Revolutions*, 165.

76. Goffredo Mameli, "Alla Vittoria." [The correct title is "Il Canto degli Italiani," more commonly called "L'Inno di Mameli" (Mameli's Hymn). Set to music by Michele Novaro, it was adopted as the Italian national anthem.—Ed.]

77. Cited in George Martin, *Verdi*, 227.

Notes to Part Three, Chapter Three

1. Gerhard Steiner, *Petöfi, ein Lesebuch für unsere Zeit*, 10–11.

2. "Else esküm" ("My First Oath") (1847).

3. Alexander Fischer, *Petöfis Leben und Werke*, 173.

4. "Jövendölés" ("Prophecy") (1843).

5. Steiner, 16.

6. Cited in J. Turóczi-Trostler, "Petöfis Eintritt in die Weltliteratur," *Acta Litteraria*, Hungarian Academy of Sciences, IV (1961), 37–38.

7. "Egri hangok" ("Voices from Eger") (1844).

8. ("Farewell to the Stage") (1844).

9. ("Woe to me, I was not born …") (1844).

10. Petöfi, *Prosaische Schriften*, 179–180.

11. Preface to the *Collected Poems* of 1847; Steiner, 29.

12. "Ilyen óriást, mint …" ("Such a Giant I Am") (1847).

13. Fischer, 457–458.

14. "Halhatatlan a lélek, hiszam" ("True, the Soul is Immortal") (1846).

15. "Sors, nyiss nekem tért" ("Fate Open for Me a Field") (1846).

16. "A Tisza" ("To the Tisza") (1847).

17. "A XIX. század költöi" ("To the Poets of the 19th Century") (1847).

18. "Szeptember végén" ("At the End of September") (1847).

19. "Olaszország" ("Italy") (1848).

20. Steiner, 306–307; Fischer, 475–476.

21. "March 11, 1848" (1848).

22. "Föltámadott a tenger" ("The Sea is Risen") (1848).

23. Fischer, 492–494.

24. "Minek nevezzelek?" ("How Shall I Name Thee?") (1848).

25. "Bucsú" ("The Parting") (1848).

26. Fischer, 513–517.

27. *Ibid.*, 541–542.

28. "Egy gondolat bánt engemet" ("One Thought Alone") (1846). Translated by Eugénie Bayard Pierce and Emil Delmár, in *Sixty Poems by Alexander Petöfi*, Budapest, 1948, revised by F. E.

29. Steiner, 451–452.

30. "Pacsírtaszót hallok megint!" ("I Hear Again the Lark Singing") (1849).

31. "Európa csendes, újra csendes" ("Europe is Quiet Again") (1849).

32. "Yakos-to iduchy unochi." (1860), *Tvori* I, 654–655.

33. Cited in Jurij Bojko, "Taras Shevchenko and West European Literature," *SIEEuR* XXXIV (1955–1956), 81.

34. "Yakbi vi znaly, panichi" ("If you but knew"), *Tvori* I, 552–554.

35. "Dumka: Nascho mieni chorni brovi," *Tvori* I, 58–59.

36. "Son" ("The Dream"), *Tvori* I, 218–231.

37. "Kavkaz," ("Caucasus") (1845), *Tvori* I, 303–306.

38. "Yak umru, to pokhovayte," (1845), *Tvori* I, 331–332.

39. M. I. Kostomarov, *Avtobiografiia*, Bojko and Koschmieder, *Taras Shevchenko*, 142.

40. Clarence A. Manning, *Taras Shevchenko*, 23.

41. Bojko and Koschmieder, 145.

42. Guillevic, Rilsky, Deitch, *Tarass Shevchenko*, 52.

43. "Isaiah. Hlava 36," *Tvori* I, 599–600, (1850).

44. "Ya ne nezduzhayu, nivroku," ("I am not ill …"), (1858), *Tvori* I, 596–597.

45. "Hymn chernychyi," (1860), *Tvori* I, 638–639.

46. "Yurodivyi," ("The Idiot") (1857), *Tvori* I, 590–592.

47. Bojko and Koschmieder, 38.

48. "Ne narikayu ya no Boha," ("I do not chide the Lord") (1860), *Tvori* I, 644–645.

49. Richard Wagner, *Mein Leben*, *Sämtliche Schriften* XIII, 54.

50. *Ibid.*, XIV, 58–59.

51. *Ibid.*, 191–192.

52. Newman, *Wagner* II, 7.

53. Richard Wagner, "Gruss aus Sachsen an die Wiener," *Sämtl. Schriften* XII, 358–361.

54. *Sämtl. Schriften* XII, 278.

55. "Die Not" ("Need"), *Sämtl. Schriften* XII, 361–365.

56. Newman, *Wagner* I, 491 f.

57. "Die Not."

58. *Mein Leben, Sämtl. Schriften* XIV, 223–224.

59. *Ibid.,* 223–230.

60. Cited in Arvon, *Bakounine,* 31.

61. T. G. Masaryk, *The Spirit of Russia* I, 488.

62. Cited Arvon, 36.

63. *Ibid.,* 36.

64. Cited in *Michael Bakunins Beichte,* 112–113, n. 210.

65. Bakunin, Letter to Georg Herwegh (1848), cited *ibid.,* 111, n. 94.

66. Mikhail Bakunin, in *La Réforme,* March 13, 1848, cited E. H. Carr, *Bakunin,* 150.

67. Bakunin, *Beichte (Confession),* 7–8.

68. *Ibid.,* 48.

69. "An die Fürsten," *Sämtl. Schriften* XII, 366.

70. "An einen Staatsanwalt," ("To a Public Prosecutor"), *ibid.,* 365–366.

71. "Die Revolution," *Sämtl. Schriften* XII, 245–251.

72. Wagner, *Letters,* ed. Altmann, translated by Bozman, I, 144; Newman, *Wagner,* II, 64–65.

73. *Mein Leben, Sämtl. Schriften* XIV, 232 ff.

74. Bakunin, *Beichte (Confession),* 89.

75. *Mein Leben, Sämtl. Schriften,* XIV, 242.

76. *Beichte,* 90.

77. Newman, *Wagner* II, 95–96.

78. *Ibid.,* 111.

79. Richard Wagner, "Die Nibelungen," (1848), *Sämtl. Schriften* II, 119, 130–134.

80. *Ibid.,* 146.

81. *Ibid.,* 153.

82. *Ibid.,* 154–155.

83. "Aphorismen zu den Kunstschriften der Jahre 1839–1851," *Sämtl. Schriften* XII, 276.

84. Wagner, *Die Kunst und die Revolution (Art and Revolution), Sämtl. Schriften* III, 15.

85. *Ibid.,* rejected passages, *Sämtl. Schriften* XII, 253.

86. *Ibid., Sämtl. Schriften* III, 12.

87. *Ibid.,* 19.

88. *Ibid.,* 26.

89. *Ibid.,* 29–30.

90. *Ibid.,* 32.

91. *Das Künstlertum der Zukunft, (The Artistic Genius of the Future), Sämtl. Schriften* XII, 256–257.

92. *Ibid.,* 255.

93. *Oper und Drama (Opera and Drama), Sämtl. Schriften* IV, 72–73.

94. *Das Künstlertum der Zukunft,* 258–264.

95. *Das Kunstwerk der Zukunft (The Artistic Creation of the Future), Sämtl. Schriften* III, 173.

96. *Ibid.,* 150.

97. *Ibid.,* 96.

98. *Kunst und Revolution, Sämtl. Schriften* III, 41.

99. *Das Kunstwerk der Zukunft,* 177.

100. *Oper und Drama, Sämtl. Schriften* IV, 229.

101. *Das Kunstwerk der Zukunft,* "Zur Widmung" ("Dedication"), *Sämtl. Schriften* XII, 284–285.

102. *Eine Mitteilung an meine Freunde (A Communication to My Friends),* 1851, *Sämtl. Schriften* IV, 343.

103. *Oper und Drama, Sämtl. Schriften* III, 316–320.

104. Richard Wagner, *Siegfrieds Tod*, act I, sc. 3. "Das Lied von Sigrdrifa," translated by Hugo Gering, *Die Edda*, 216.

105. Richard Wagner, *Gesammelte Briefe* II, 436–438.

106. Cited in Newman, *Wagner* II, 59 n. 6.

107. Cited *ibid.*, II, 282.

108. Mikhail Bakunin, *Beichte*, Introduction ix.

109. *Ibid.*, 19.

110. *Ibid.*, 36.

111. *Ibid.*, 46–47.

112. *Ibid.*, 49–50.

113. *Ibid.*, 91.

114. *Ibid.*, 95.

115. Alexander Herzen, *My Past and Thoughts*, III, 1351 ff.

116. Alexander Herzen, *From the Other Shore*, 16–17, 275; Nikolay Ogarev, in Alexander Herzen, *My Past and Thoughts*, II, 598, translated by Juliet M. Soskice.

117. Herzen *My Past and Thoughts*, II, 646.

118. *Ibid.*, I, 102.

119. Cited in Malia, *Herzen*, 148.

120. Herzen, *Memoirs* II, 402–403.

121. *Ibid.*, II, 407.

122. Cited in Malia, 227.

123. Alexander Herzen, "Letters on the Study of Nature," *Selected Philosophical Works*, 104.

124. "Dilettantism in Science," *ibid.*, 72.

125. "Letters on the Study of Nature," *ibid.*, 99–100.

126. *Ibid.*, 101, footnote.

127. Malia, 254.

128. *Ibid.*, 333.

129. See Frank Friedeberg Seely, "The Heyday of the 'Superfluous Man,' in Russia," *SlEEurR* XXXI (1952–1953), 92–112.

130. T. G. Masaryk, *The Spirit of Russia*, I, 428.

131. Cited in Malia, 267–268; 274–275.

132. Herzen, *My Past and Thoughts* II, 812.

133. Herzen, *Memoirs* II, 842, 843.

134. Herzen, *From the Other Shore*, 64.

135. *Ibid.*, 66–67.

136. Isaiah Berlin, "Russia and 1848," *Slavonic and East-European Review*, XXVI (April 1948), 353.

137. Gleb Ouspensky, cited in Berlin, 353–354.

138. Cited in Venturi, 95.

139. *Ibid.*, 96.

140. Patrick O'Meara, *K. F. Ryleev*. Princeton University Press, 1984, 323.

141. Acton, *Alexander Herzen*, 126.

142. Quoted in Acton, *Alexander Herzen*, 177.

Notes to Part Four

1. Karl Immermann, *Epigonen*.

2. Jakob Venedey, "O Deutschland! Armes Deutschland," in Jürgen Moeller, *Deutsche beschimpfen Deutsche*, 201–204.

3. August von Platen, "Epilog, aus den Polenlieder," *Werke* I, 318.

4. *Georg Büchners Sämtliche Werke* (ed. Meinerts), 396–397.

5. "Der Hessische Landbote," *Werke* (ed. Meinerts), 354, 358.

6. Legge, 116–117.

7. *Werke* (ed. Meinerts), 42–43 (Letter to August Stöber, Dec. 9, 1833).

8. *Ibid.*, 425–426.

9. *Ibid.*, 381–382 (April 5, 1833, to his Family).

10. *Ibid.*, 448 (January 1, 1836).

11. Cited in Hans Mayer, *Büchner*, 44.

12. "Uber Schädelnerven" ("Concerning Cranial Nerves"), 1836, *Werke* (ed. Meinerts), 456.

13. *Werke*, 390–391.

14. *Dantons Tod*, Act I, sc. 6.

15. *Ibid.*, Act II, sc. 3.

16. *Ibid.*, Act III, sc. 1.

17. "Lenz," *Werke* (ed. Meinerts, 135).

18. *Dantons Tod*, Act II, sc. 3.

19. *Leonce und Lena*, *Werke* (ed. Meinerts), Act III, sc. 1.

20. *Lenz, Werke* (ed. Meinerts), 121–122.

21. Gottfried Keller, "Herwegh," translated in Legge, 204.

22. Georg Herwegh, *Werke*, Teil III, 135, and Liptzin, *Lyric Pioneers of Modern Germany*, 55.

23. "Morgenruf" ("Reveille"), translation in Legge, 212 (revised).

24. "Aufruf" ("The Summons"), *ibid.*, 209 (revised).

25. Cited in Prawer, *Heine*, 105.

26. "Auch dies gehört dem König" ("This Too is the King's"),

27. Herwegh, *Werke*, Introd., lxviii.

28. *Ibid.*, lxix.

29. "Huldigung" ("Homage"), *Neue Gedichte*, *Werke* Teil III, 31–34.

30. *Ibid.*, 130, 133–134.

31. "Achtzehnter März" ("The Eighteenth of March").

32. *Werke*, "Introduction", c.

33. Ferdinand Freiligrath, *Werke* I, 260–261.

34. "Aus Spanien" ("From Spain") (1841).

35. Georg Herwegh, "An Ferdinand Freiligrath" (1842).

36. "Die Freiheit! Das Recht!" ("Freedom! Right!") (1843).

37. "Der Baum der Menschheit," ("The Tree of Humanity") (1844).

38. "Hamlet," translation in Legge, 146–147 (revised).

39. Mehring, *Marx*, 175.

40. "Vor der Fahrt."

41. "Von unten auf!" (Up from Below!).

42. Letter to Karl Büchner, *Werke* I, Introduction, 53; Liptzin, *Lyric Pioneers*, 137.

43. "Berlin."

44. "Die Toten an die Lebenden," translated in Legge, 317–319.

45. "Abschiedswort der *Neuen Rheinischen Zeitung*."

46. Liptzin, *Lyric Pioneers*, 143–144.

47. Georg Weerth, *Sämtliche Werke* V, 171–172 (July 19, 1845).

48. Weerth, "Arbeite!" *ibid.*, I, 196.

49. "Erinnerungen" ("Remembrances"), *ibid.*, 155.

50. Cited in the Introduction to *Fragment eines Romans*, ed. Unseld, 9–10.

51. Letter to his Mother, August 23, 1845, *Werke* V, 177.

52. *Ibid.,* 239, 244.

53. Letter to his brother, Wilhelm, September 26, 1847, *ibid.,* 273–274.

54. *Ibid.,* 279–281 (March 11, 1848).

55. "A Visit to the Tuileries" (*Kölnische Zeitung,* March 1848), *Werke* IV, 22–23.

56. *Werke* V, 403 (April 28, 1851).

57. *Werke* IV, 179–180.

58. *Werke* V, 412–414 (June 10, 1861.

59. "Sie sassen auf den Bänken" ("They sat on the benches").

60. "Ein Sonntagsabend auf dem Meere" ("Sunday Eve on the Sea").

61. "Der Kanonegiesser."

62. "Es war ein armer Schneider."

63. *Werke,* V, 421 (October 4, 1851).

64. Translated in Legge, 221–223.

65. *Ibid.,* 231.

66. For Heine's earlier career see Frederic Ewen, *Heroic Imagination.*

67. "Die schlesischen Weber," translated by Aaron Kramer, in Ewen, *The Poetry and Prose of Heinrich Heine,* 244.

68. "Der Kaiser von China," "Der neue Alexander."

69. "Lobgesang auf König Ludwig."

70. *Atta Troll,* Canto X.

71. *Deutschland: Ein Wintermärchen,* I; translated by A. Kramer, in Ewen, 182.

72. *Ibid.,* VI; Ewen, 194.

73. *Ibid.,* VII, 195.

74. *Ibid.,* XXVII, 239–240.

75. Letter to Detmold, *Werke* II, 434.

76. *Werke* II, 276–277.

77. "Im Oktober 1849," translated by A. Kramer, Ewen, 252–254.

78. "Enfant perdu."

79. "Die Söhne des Glückes beneide ich nicht."

80. "Wie langsam kriechen sie dahin," translated by A. Kramer; Ewen, 158–159.

81. Ewen, 50.

Notes to Part Five, Chapter One

1. Cited in Priestley, *Victoria's Heyday,* 74.

2. *Ibid.,* 78.

3. Cited in Buckley, *The Victorian Temper,* 125.

4. *Journal,* May 1, 1851; cited in Woodham-Smith, *Queen Victoria,* 320.

5. Cited in Briggs, *Victorian People,* 50.

6. Charles Kingsley, *Scientific Lectures and Essays,* 309; cited in Houghton, *The Victorian Frame of Mind,* 44–45.

7. Houghton, 45.

8. Briggs, *The Age of Improvement,* 395.

9. Altick, *Victorian People,* 12–13.

10. *Ibid.,* 20.

11. Charles Kingsley, *Yeast,* ch. 5.

12. Edwin Paxton Hood, in his *The Age and its Architects* (1851), cited in Briggs, *The Age of Improvement,* 446.

13. A. O. J. Cockshut, "Victorian Thought," in *The Victorians* (ed. Arthur Pollard, 27–29).

14. Cited in Briggs, *Victorian People*, 98.

15. R. J. Evans, *The Victorian Age*, 96.

16. Walter L. Arnstein, "The Survival of Victorian Aristocracy," in Jaher, *The Rich, the Well Born, and the Powerful*, 245.

17. Gerald Massey, "To-Day and To-Morrow," in "Cries of 'Forty-Eight," in *My Lyrical Life*, 281.

18. John Frost, *Forty Years Recollections*, 127–128, cited in Schoyen, *The Chartist Challenge*, 157.

19. Hugh Ross Williamson, "1848 in England," in Woodcock, *A Hundred Years of Revolution*, 135.

20. Matthew Arnold, *Letters* I, 6 (March 10, 1848).

21. Mark Hovell, *The Chartist Movement*, 288.

22. Cited in Elizabeth Longford, *Wellington—Pillar of State*, 333.

23. Friedrich Engels, Preface to the English edition of *The Condition of the Working Class*, in *Marx and Engels on Britain*, 24.

24. Cited in Woodham-Smith, *Queen Victoria*, 293.

25. Brian Connell, ed., *Regina vs. Palmerston*, 91.

26. Cited in J. T. Ward, *Popular Movements*, Introd., 8.

27. Cited in Cruikshank, *Roaring Century*, 174.

28. Cited in David Thomson, *England in the Nineteenth Century*, 32.

29. W. L. Burn, *The Age of Equipoise*, 306, drawing on John Bateman's *The Aristocracy of England* (1876) and *The Great Landowners of Great Britain and Ireland* (1879).

30. Briggs, *The Age of Improvement*, 406–407.

31. Bernard Cracroft, "The Analysis of the House of Commons," cited in Burn, *Equipoise*, 313–314; Briggs, *Age of Improvement*, 406–407.

32. Walter L. Arnstein, "The Survival of Victorian Aristocracy," in Jaher, *The Rich, the Well Born, and the Powerful*, 215.

33. *Ibid.*, 232.

34. *Ibid.*, 238–240.

35. Cited in A. P. Thornton, *The Habit of Authority*, 190.

36. *Felix Holt*, ch. 20.

37. Arnstein, *loc. cit.*, 248.

38. Letter to John Bright (1840), cited in T. J. Ward, *Popular Movements*, 5.

39. Geraldine Jewsbury, *The History of an Adopted Child* (1853).

40. Arnstein, 247.

41. Douglas Jerrold to Mrs. Cowden Clark, February 22, 1850, cited in Gordon N. Ray, *Thackeray: The Uses of Adversity*, 367.

42. Eugène Buret, Preface to *De la misère des classes laborieuses en Angleterre et en France* (1840), cited in Louis Chevalier, *Laboring Classes and Dangerous Classes*, 134.

43. Edwin Paxton Hood, *The Age and Its Architects* (1851), cited in Briggs, *Age of Improvement*, 448–449.

44. Cited in Arthur A. Hayward, *The Days of Dickens*, 103.

45. Dr. John Simon's City Medical Report, 1850, cited in Pike, *Golden Times*, 281.

46. See George Rosen, "Disease, Debility, and Death," in *The Victorian City*, ed., Dyos and Wolff, II, 628 ff.

47. Flora Tristan, *Promenades dans Londres* (1840), 112, 236.

48. W. A. Abram, "Social Conditions … of the Lancashire workers," (1868), cited in Pike, *Golden Times*, 76.

Notes to Part Five, Chapter Two

1. *The Letters of Mrs. Gaskell*, ed. Chapple and Pollard, 248.
2. Cited in Robert Keefe, *Charlotte Brontë's World of Death*, 191–192.
3. Cited in Tom Winfrith, *The Brontës and Their Background*, 32.
4. Cited in Winfrith, 36, 37.
5. Gaskell, *Charlotte Brontë* (Penguin ed.), 116–117; (March 12, 1829).
6. See Charlotte Brontë, *Legends of Angria*, ed. Ratchford and DeVane; and Ratchford, *The Brontës' Web of Childhood*.
7. *Shirley*, ch. 12.
8. Ratchford, *The Legends of Angria*, xxxiii–xxxvi.
9. Gaskell, *Brontë* (Penguin), 156.
10. Gérin, *Charlotte Brontë*, 34.
11. Ratchford, *Angria*, 107.
12. Roe Head Journal, August 11, 1836; *Angria*, 109–110.
13. *Angria*, xxxix.
14. *Ibid.*, xxx.
15. Ratchford, *Web*, 111.
16. Ratchford, *Angria*, xxix–xxx; xxxiii–xxxvi.
17. Gaskell, *Charlotte Brontë* (Penguin), 184.
18. *Ibid.*, 172–173.
19. *Ibid.*, 174–175.
20. Ratchford, *Angria*, 149 (1839).
21. *Shirley*, ch. 7.
22. Gérin, *Charlotte Brontë*, 204.
23. *Ibid.*, 167 (Nov. 22, 1840).
24. Shorter I, 269.
25. *Ibid.*, 269.
26. *Ibid.*, 270–271.
27. *Ibid.*, I, 271.
28. Gaskell, *Brontë*, 3d ed., 134.
29. Unpublished. *Transactions of the Brontë Society*, V, pt. 24 (1924), 56–57.
30. *Ibid.*, 56–75.
31. Shorter, I, 291–292.
32. Cited in Moglen, 74.
33. "Biographical Notice of Ellis, Acton Bell," Preface to 2d edition of *Wuthering Heights*.
34. *Ibid.*
35. Charlotte Brontë, *Shirley*, ch. 7.
36. Charlotte Brontë, *The Professor*, ch. 4.
37. *Ibid.*, ch. 18.
38. *Ibid.*, ch. 23.
39. *Jane Eyre*, ch. 6.
40. *Ibid.*, ch. 10.
41. *Ibid.*, ch. 11.
42. *Ibid.*, ch. 12.
43. *Ibid.*, ch. 12.
44. *Ibid.*, ch. 14.
45. *Ibid.*, ch. 15.
46. *Ibid.*, ch. 17.

47. *Ibid.*, ch. 18.

48. *Ibid.*, ch. 21.

49. *Ibid.*, ch. 23.

50. *Ibid.*, ch. 23.

51. *Ibid.*, ch. 24.

52. *Ibid.*, ch. 24.

53. *Ibid.*, ch. 32.

54. *Ibid.*, ch. 34.

55. *Ibid.*, ch. 35.

56. *Ibid.*, ch. 35.

57. *Ibid.*, ch. 37.

58. Gérin, *Charlotte Brontë*, 383.

59. *Ibid.*, 384.

60. To William S. William, Sept. 21, 1849, cited in Keefe, *Charlotte Brontë's World of Death*, 35.

61. To W. S. Williams, February 25, 1848; Shorter, I, 397.

62. *Ibid.*, I, 406–407.

63. Cited in E. P. Thompson, *The Making of the English Working Class*, 598.

64. Cited in Martha Vicinus, *The Industrial Muse*, 45.

65. Shorter I, 391.

66. Charlotte Brontë, *Shirley*, chaps. 22, 23, 10, 21.

67. *Ibid.*, ch. 4.

68. *Ibid.*, chaps. 7, 11.

69. *Ibid.*, ch. 1.

70. *Ibid.*, ch. 10.

71. *Ibid.*, ch. 22.

72. *Ibid.*, ch. 18.

73. *Ibid.*, ch. 28.

74. *Ibid.*, ch. 18.

75. *Paradise Lost*, Bk. XI.

76. *Shirley*, ch. 19.

77. *Ibid.*, ch. 19.

78. *Ibid.*, ch. 37; ch. 22.

79. *Ibid.*, ch. 21.

80. *Ibid.*, ch. 8.

81. *Ibid.*, ch. 5.

82. *Ibid.*, ch. 10.

83. *Ibid.*, ch. 30.

84. *Ibid.*, ch. 31.

85. *Ibid.*, ch. 31.

86. *Ibid.*, ch. 21.

87. *Ibid.*, ch. 16.

88. Shorter II, 31.

89. To G. H. Lewes, and to her editor Williams, Shorter II, 71, 80.

90. To W. S. Williams, (May 12, 1848), Shorter I, 418–419.

91. Cited in Winifrid Gérin, *Emily Brontë. A Biography*, Oxford 1971, 271–272.

92. *The Complete Poems of Emily Brontë*, ed. C. W. Hatfield No. 11, p. 36.

93. *Ibid.*, no. 157, pp. 184–185 (April 1843).

94. *Ibid.*, no. 133, pp. 137–138 (Jan. 6, 1840).

95. *Ibid.*, no. 149, pp. 166–167 (July 1841).

96. *Ibid.*, no. 137, p. 143 (1840, 1843).

97. *Ibid.*, no. 181, p. 220 (February 1845).

98. "To Imagination," no. 174, pp. 205–206 (Sept. 3, 1844).

99. *Ibid.*, no. 176, p. 209.

100. *Ibid.*, p. 256.

101. See in particular C. P. Sanger, "The Structure of *Wuthering Heights*," in *Twentieth Century Interpretations of Wuthering Heights*, ed. by Thomas A. Vogler.

102. *Wuthering Heights*, ch. 5.

103. For the various and continuous "diabolic" epithets affixed to Heathcliff, see chaps. 4, 7, 10, 11, 13, 17, 34.

104. *Ibid.*, ch. 9.

105. *Ibid.*, chaps. 15, 16.

106. Gaskell, 358.

Notes to Part Six

1. *The George Eliot Letters*, ed. Gordon S. Haight, I, 128–130 (Foleshill, February 28, 1842).

2. *Ibid.*, I, 124.

3. *Impressions of Theophrastus Such*, "Looking Backward."

4. Gordon S. Haight, *George Eliot*, 25–26.

5. Cross, *George Eliot's Life* I, 33.

6. Cited *Ibid.*, 75, from George Eliot's summation in the Analytical Catalogue of Chapman's Publications.

7. Haight, *George Eliot*, 39.

8. *The George Eliot Letters* I, 136.

9. *Ibid.*, 277–278. On George Sand see also Ewen, *Heroic Imagination*, pp. 518–549.

10. *Ibid.*, I, 252–255 (Foleshill, 8 March 1848).

11. Cross I, 143–144 (To Charles Bray, June 8, 1848).

12. "William Mackay's *Progress of the Intellect*, *Westminster Review* LIV (January 1851), reprinted in *Essays of George Eliot*, ed. Pinney, 28

13. Cross I, 197, 232–233.

14. "Woman in France: Madame de Sable," *Westminster Review* LXII (October 1854), reprinted in *Essays of George Eliot*, ed. Thomas Pinney, 80–81.

15. "Luther als Schiedensrichter," *Marx–Engels Gesamtausgabe* (MEGA), I, 26–27. See above, p. 185.

16. *The George Eliot Letters II*, 153; VI, 98.

17. *The Essence of Christianity*, 271.

18. *Ibid.*, 158.

19. *Ibid.*, 83.

20. *Ibid.*, 14, 26, 29.

21. Cross I, 252, 245.

22. George Eliot, *Adam Bede*, ch. 51.

23. Haight, *George Eliot*, 156–157.

24. Cited *ibid.*, 163.

25. To William Bell Scott, October 4, 1854, cited in the *Letters of George Eliot* (ed. Haight), II, 175–176.

26. *Letters* II, 170–171.

27. Cited in Haight, *George Eliot*, 162.

28. *Letters* III, 366–367.

29. Cited in Robert Bernard Martin, *The Dust of Combat: The Life of Charles Kingsley*, 181.

30. Cross I, 313–315.

31. Haight, *George Eliot*, 210.

32. Review of *The Natural History of German Life* (1856), *Works* VI, 419–420.

33. "Consideration of Ruskin: *Modern Painters*," (1856), cited in Haight, *George Eliot*, 183–184.

34. Haight, *George Eliot*, 293.

35. *Letters* II, 347 (June 11, 1857).

36. "Amos Barton."

37. "Evangelical Teaching, Dr. Cumming," *Works* VI, 307.

38. "Worldliness and Other-Worldliness: The Poet Young," *Works* VI, 247–249.

39. *Letters* II, 423.

40. Haight, *George Eliot*, 247.

41. To Charles Bray and Mme Eugene Bodichon, *Letters* III, 214, 227.

42. "Amos Barton."

43. *Adam Bede*, ch. 42.

44. *Ibid.*, ch. 48.

45. *Ibid.*, ch. 46.

46. *Ibid.*, ch. 32.

47. *Ibid.*, ch. 16.

48. *Letters* III, 17.

49. Cited in the *Letters of George Eliot* III, 114.

50. J. S. Mill, *A System of Logic*, p. v, cited in Paris, *Experiments in Life*, 28.

51. George Eliot, Review of "The Natural History of German Life," *Works* VI, 421–422.

52. "The Morality of Wilhelm Meister," (1855), *Essays of George Eliot*, ed. Pinney, 146.

53. "The Natural History of German Life," *Works* VI, 416–417.

54. *The Letters of George Eliot* VI, 216–217 (1876).

55. *The Essence of Christianity* (George Eliot's translation), 62–63.

56. *The Mill on the Floss*, Bk VI, ch. 5.

57. To Mrs. Charles Bray, *Letters* III, 170.

58. *The Mill on the Floss*, Bk. IV, ch 2.

59. *Ibid.*, Bk. IV, ch.2.

60. *The Mill on the Floss*, Bk. I, ch. 2.

61. *Ibid.*, Bk, I, ch. 7.

62. *Ibid.*, Bk. I, ch. 9.

63. *Ibid.*, Bk. I, ch. 3.

64. *Ibid.*, Bk. II, ch. 1.

65. *Ibid.*, Bk. IV, ch. 1.

66. Henry James, "The Novels of George Eliot," in *Views and Reviews*.

67. "Mr. Gilfil's Love Story."

68. See Mathilde Parlett, "The Influence of Contemporary Criticism on George Eliot," *SP* XXX (1933), 102–132.

69. Cited in Aylmer Maude, *The Life of Tolstoy*, I, 265.

70. G. H. Lewes, "Physiology of Common Life," cited in Hilda M Hulme, "*Middlemarch* as Science Fiction," *Novel: a Forum of Fiction*, II (1968), 39.

71. *Daniel Deronda*, ch. 27.

72. *Middlemarch*, Bk. I, ch. 4.

73. *Romola*, ch. 16.

74. *Middlemarch*, Bk I. ch. 4.

75. *Ibid.*, ch. 20.

76. Cited in Arnold Kettle, "Felix Holt the Radical," in *Critical Essays on George Eliot*, ed. Barbara Hardy, 100.

77. See William Myers, "George Eliot: Politics and Personality," in *Literature and Politics in the Nineteenth Century*, ed. John Lucas.

78. "The Natural History of German Life," *Essays*, ed. Pinney, 172–173.

79. *Felix Holt*, ch. 1.

80. *Ibid.*, ch. 40.

81. *Ibid.*, ch. 2.

82. *Ibid.*, ch. 27.

83. *Ibid.*, ch. 30.

84. *Felix Holt*, ed. Peter Coveney, 607.

85. See above, section "Dickens II: The Cracked Mirror." [Ed. note: The author's cross-reference here applies to an earlier version of this work, one of a number of signs that he never revised Part 6. On Fagin, see above, p. 50.]

86. To John Sibree, February 11, 1848, *Letters* I, 246–247.

87. *Daniel Deronda*, Bk. VI, ch. 48.

88. *Ibid.*, Bk. II, ch. 13.

89. *Ibid.*, Bk. III, ch. 27.

90. *Ibid.*, Bk. VII, ch. 54.

91. *Ibid.*, Bk. VI, ch. 42.

92. *Ibid.*, Bk. VIII, ch. 69.

93. *Ibid.*

94. "The Modern Hep! Hep! Hep!," in *Impressions of Theophrastus Such*, XVIII.

95. Cited in Haight, *George Eliot*, 417.

96. *Letters* V, 107 (To the Hon. Mrs. Robert Lytton, July 8, 1870).

Bibliography

Editor's Note

The following bibliography of works cited in the text was reconstructed from Ewen's reference notes. The notes appear in this volume as he left them, except for the correction of obvious errors. All works cited by Ewen are in the bibliographies, but the notes often fail to specify the edition used. For the most part, it has been possible to determine the edition (or a close equivalent), but in some cases more accessible reprints have been listed, or (in the case of some classics), recent critical editions.

Several works cited by Ewen exist in so many editions, both old and new, that only the title is given in the bibliography, without any particular edition being cited. This applies to the novels of Dickens—*Oliver Twist, Nicholas Nickleby, Dombey and Son, The Old Curiosity Shop, Barnaby Rudge, David Copperfield, Little Dorrit,* and *Martin Chuzzlewit.* (Only the last has been listed in a particular edition, that is, the one found in Ewen's personal library.) It also applies to Goethe's *Wilhelm Meisters Lehrjahre* and *Wilhelm Meisters Wanderjahre,* as well as to Marx and Engels' *Communist Manifesto,* John Milton's *Paradise Lost,* and Walt Whitman's *Leaves of Grass.*

Entries preceded by an asterisk (*) are editions known to have been in the author's library.

Primary Sources

Arban. See Dostoevsky, *Correspondance.*

Arnold, Matthew. *Letters of Matthew Arnold 1848–1888.* Ed. by George William Erskine Russell. New York and London, Macmillan and Co., 1900.

Bakunin, Mikhail Aleksandrovich, *Michael Bakunins Beichte aus der Peter-Pauls-Festung an Zar Nikolaus I; gefunden im Geheimschrank des Chefs der III. Abteilung der Kanzlei der früheren Zaren zu Leningrad.* Ed. by Viachislav Polonskii, Kurt Kersten, and others. Berlin, Deutsche Verlagsgesellschaft für Politik und Geschichte, 1926.

Belinsky, Vissarion Grigorievich. *Selected Philosophical Works.* Moscow, Foreign Languages Publishing House, 1956.

Bottomore, T.B. See Marx, Karl. *Early Writings.*

Brontë, Charlotte [under pseudonym Currer Bell]. "Biographical Notice of Ellis and Acton Bell." Preface to the 2nd ed. of Emily Brontë's *Wuthering Heights,* 1850. Reprinted in E. Brontë (1998), 319–323.

———. Charlotte Brontë's Letters to M. Heger. *Transactions of the Brontë Society* V, 28, part 24 (1924), pp. 56–75. = *The Letters of Charlotte Brontë: With a Selection of Letters by Family and Friends: 1829–47.* Ed. by Margaret Smith. Vol. 1. Oxford, Clarendon Press, 1995.

Brontë, Charlotte. *Jane Eyre, a Norton Critical Edition*. Ed. by Richard J. Dunn. 2nd edition. New York, Norton, 1987 (3d ed., 2001).

——. *Legends of Angria*. Ed. by Fannie Elizabeth Ratchford and William C. DeVane. New Haven, Yale University Press; London, H. Milford, Oxford University Press, 1933.

——. A Poem (unpublished), 1843. *Transactions of the Brontë Society* V, pt. 24 (1924), 56–57.

——. *The Professor*. Ed. by Heather Glen. London, Penguin Books, 1989.

——. *Roe Head Journal* (14 Oct. 1836). "All This Day I Have Been in a Dream." Ed. by Christine Alexander. In Richard J. Dunn, ed., *Jane Eyre, a Norton Critical Edition*. 2nd edition. New York, Norton, 1987, p. 413 (= 3d ed., 2001, 403–404.).

——. *Shirley*. Ed. by Herbert Rosengarten and Margaret Smith. Oxford, Clarendon Press; New York, Oxford University Press, 1979.

Brontë, Emily. *Wuthering Heights*. Ed. by Ian Jack, introd. and notes by Patsy Stoneman. London, Oxford University Press, 1998.

——. *The Complete Poems of Emily Jane Brontë*. Ed. by Charles William Hatfield. New York, Columbia University Press, 1941.

Büchner, Georg. *Sämtliche Werke: nebst Briefen und anderen Dokumenten*, Hrsg. von Hans Jürgen Meinerts. 3. Aufl. Gütersloh, S. Mohn, 1965.

Burke, Edmund. *Reflections on the Revolution in France*. New York, Liberal Arts Press, 1955.

Carlyle, Thomas. *Characteristics*. (Published with John Stuart Mill, *Autobiography* and *Essay on Liberty*.) The Harvard Classics, 25. New York: Collier, 1909.

——. *Chartism* (1839). The Works of Thomas Carlyle. Ed. by H.D. Traill. 30 vols. London, Chapman and Hall, 1896–1899, vol. 29, pp. 118–204.

——. *Early Letters of Thomas Carlyle*. Ed. by Charles Eliot Norton. London and New York, Macmillan, 1886.

*——. *The French Revolution; a history*. 2 vols. London, Oxford University Press, 1921.

——. "Goethe" (1828). In *The Works of Thomas Carlyle*. Ed. by H.D. Traill. 30 vols. London, Chapman and Hall, 1896–1899, vol. 26, pp. 198–257.

——. *Letters of Thomas Carlyle*. Ed. by Charles Eliot Norton. London, New York, Macmillan, 1889.

——. *The Letters of Thomas Carlyle to His Brother Alexander, with related family letters*. Ed. by Edwin W. Marrs. Cambridge, Belknap Press of Harvard University Press, 1968.

*——. *The Life of Friedrich Schiller: comprehending an examination of his works*. Ed. by H.D. Traill. New York, C. Scribner's Sons, 1899.

——. "Parliaments" (1850). In his *Latter-Day Pamphlets*. Ed. by Michael K. Goldberg and Jules P. Seigel. Ottawa, Canadian Federation for the Humanities, 1983.

*——. *Past and Present*. New York, Scribners, 1843.

*——. *Reminiscences*. Ed. by James Anthony Froude. New York, C. Scribner's Sons, 1881.

*——. *Sartor Resartus. On heroes, hero-worship and the heroic in history*. London, J.M. Dent; New York, E.P. Dutton, 1918.

——. *Signs of the Times. = Last words of Thomas Carlyle: On Trades-Unions, Promoterism, and the Signs of the Times*. Edinburgh, William Paterson, 1882.

——. *The Works of Thomas Carlyle*. Century Edition. New York, Scribners, 1898–1901. 30 vols.

Carlyle, Jane Welsh. *New Letters and Memorials of Jane Welsh Carlyle; annotated by Thomas Carlyle and ed. by Alexander Carlyle, with an introduction by Sir James Crichton-Browne … with sixteen illustrations*. London, 2 vols. New York, John Lane, 1903.

Chaadaev, Peter Iakovlevich. *The Major Works of P. Chaadaev: a translation and commentary*. Ed. and transl. By Raymond T McNally. Notre Dame and London, University of Notre Dame Press, 1969.

Cross, J.W. See Eliot, *George Eliot's Life*.

Dickens, Charles. *Barnaby Rudge* (See Editor's Note at top of Bibliography.).

——. *David Copperfield* (See Editor's Note at top of Bibliography.).

——. *Dombey and Son* (See Editor's Note at top of Bibliography.).

——. *Little Dorrit* (See Editor's Note at top of Bibliography.).

*——. Martin Chuzzlewit. London, Dent & New York, Dutton, 1950.

——. *Nicholas Nickleby* (See Editor's Note at top of Bibliography.).

——. *The Old Curiosity Shop* (See Editor's Note at top of Bibliography.).

——. *Oliver Twist* (See Editor's Note at top of Bibliography.).

Dostoevsky, Fyodor. *Correspondance de Dostoievski. Première traduction intégrale et conforme au texte russe.* Introduction et notes de Dominique Arban. Paris, Calmann-Lévy, 1949.

——. *The Diary of a Writer.* Transl. by Boris Brasol. 2 vols. New York, C. Scribner's Sons, 1949.

——. *Letters of Fyodor Michailovitch Dostoevsky to his Family and Friends,* Ed. by Alexander Eliasberg and Ethel Colburn Mayne. New York, Macmillan, 1914.

——. *Poor Folk.* Translated from the Russian by Lev Navrozov. Classics of Russian Literature. Moscow, Foreign Languages Publishing House, 1956.

Eliot, George. *Essays of George Eliot.* Ed. by Thomas Pinney. New York, Columbia University Press, 1963.

——. "Evangelical Teaching: Dr. Cumming." In *Essays and Leaves from a Note-book. = The Works of George Eliot,* vol. 6. Standard Edition. Edinburgh, William Blackwood and Sons, 1890.

——. *Felix Holt, the Radical.* Edited by Peter Coveney. Penguin English Library. Harmondsworth, Penguin, 1972.

——. *The George Eliot Letters.* Ed. by Gordon Sherman Haight. 9 vols. New Haven, Yale University Press, 1954–1978.

——. *George Eliot's Life as Related in her Letters and Journals.* Ed. by J. W. Cross. New York, London, Harper, 1903.

——. *The Impressions of Theophrastus Such.* Ed. by D. J. Enright. London, Everyman Paperback Classics, 1995.

——. "The Modern Hep! Hep! Hep!" (*Impressions of Theophrastus Such,* Essay xviii.) See Eliot, ed. Enright (1995).

——. "The Natural History of German Life: Riehl." In *Essays and Leaves from a Note-book. = The Works of George Eliot,* vol. 6. Standard Edition. Edinburgh, William Blackwood and Sons, 1890.

——. "Worldliness and Other-worldliness." In *Essays and Leaves from a Note-book. = The Works of George Eliot,* vol. 6. Standard Edition. Edinburgh, William Blackwood and Sons, 1890.

——. (translator). Ludwig Feuerbach, *The Essence of Christianity.* Translated from the German by George Eliot. Introductory essay by Karl Barth. Foreword by H. Richard Niebuhr. The Library of Religion and Culture. Harper Torchbooks, 11. New York, Harper, 1957.

——. (translator). David Friedrich Strauss, *The Life of Jesus: critically examined.* Translated from the German by George Eliot. 3 vols. London, Chapman, Brothers, 1846.

Engels, Friedrich. *Anti-Duhring: Herr Eugen Duhring's revolution in science.* Trans. Emile Burns. In *Karl Marx—Frederick Engels Collected Works,* vol. 25. Moscow, Progress Publishers, 1987.

——. "Briefe aus London an den schweizerischen Republikaner" (1843). In Engels, Friedrich. *Schriften der Frühzeit: Aufsätze, Korrespondenzen, Briefe, Dichtungen aus den Jahren 1838–1844 nebst einigen Karikaturen und einem unbekannten Jugendbildnis des Verfassers.* Ed. by Gustav Meyer. Berlin, Springer, 1920.

——. *The Condition of the Working Class in England.* Ed. by V.G. Kiernan. London, Penguin Books, 1987.

Engels, Friedrich. Germany: Revolution and Counter-Revolution. In Marx, Karl, Engels, Friedrich, *Karl Marx and Frederick Engels: Selected Works*, vol. 2. Moscow, Foreign Languages Publishing House, 1951.

———. *History of the Communist League.* In Marx & Engels, *Selected Works*, vol. 2 (1951).

———. "Die Lage Englands: Past and Present by Thomas Carlyle." In Marx, Karl & Friedrich Engels, *Werke* I, 525–549. Berlin, Dietz, 1956.

———. "Ludwig Feuerbach and the Outcome of Classical German Philosophy." In Marx & Engels, *Selected Works*, vol. 1 (1951).

———. Preface to the English edition of *The Condition of the Working Class.* In Marx, Karl, Engels, Friedrich. *Karl Marx and Frederick Engels on Britain.* Ed. by Institut Marksa-Engel'sa-Lenina. Moscow, Foreign Languages Publishing House, 1953.

———. *Zwischen 18 und 25. Jugendbriefe.* Hrsg. Hannes Skambraks. Berlin, Dietz, 1965.

Feuerbach, Ludwig. *The Essence of Christianity.* Translated from the German by George Eliot. Introductory essay by Karl Barth. Foreword by H. Richard Niebuhr. The Library of Religion and Culture, Harper Torchbooks, 11. New York, Harper, 1957.

———. *Grundsätze der Philosophie der Zukunft. Kritische Ausgabe.* Hrsg. von Gerhart Schmidt. Frankfurt am Main, V. Klostermann, 1967.

———. *Die Unsterblichkeitsfrage: vom Standpunkt der Anthropologie.* Hrsg. von Kurt Leese. Stuttgart, Alfred Kröner Verlag, 1938.

Freiligrath, Ferdinand. *Werke.* Hrsg. J. Schwering. Hildesheim, G. Olms, 1974 [1909].

Gaskell, Elizabeth Cleghorn. *The Letters of Mrs. Gaskell.* Ed. by J.A. Chapple, and Arthur Pollard. Cambridge, Harvard University Press, 1967 [1966].

———. *The Life of Charlotte Brontë.* Ed. A. Shelston. Harmondsworth, Penguin, 1975.

Goethe, Johann Wolfgang von. See Editor's Note at the top of the Bibliography.

Gogol, Nikolai. "An Interpretation of The Government Inspector." = Nikolai Gogol, "The Denouement of The Government Inspector," (1846). In *The Theater of Nikolay Gogol.* Ed. by Milton Ehre. Chicago, University of Chicago Press, 1980.

———. *N.V. Gogol' v pis'makh i vospominaniiakh.* Ed. by Vasilii Vasilevich Gogol, ed. gippius. Moscow, Federatsiia, 1931.

———. *Sämmtliche Werke.* Hrsg. von Otto Buek. 8 vols. München, G. Müller, 1909–1914.

———. *Selected Passages from Correspondence with Friends.* Trans. J. Zeldin. Vanderbilt U.P., 1969.

Hegel, Georg Wilhelm Friedrich. *Hegel Selections.* Ed. by Jacob Loewenberg. New York: Charles Scribner's Sons, 1929.

———. *Hegel's Science of Logic.* Tr. W.H. Johnston, L. G. Struthers. London, Allen & Unwin, 1966.

———. *The Philosophy of History.* Translated by John Sibree. New York, Dover Publications, 1956.

———. *The Philosophy of Right.* Translated by Thomas Malcolm Knox and John Sibree. Chicago, Encyclopedia Britannica 1955 [1952].

Heine, Heinrich. *Heinrich Heine's sämmtliche Werke.* 22 v. Hamburg, Hoffmann & Campe, 1876.

———. *The Poetry and Prose of Heinrich Heine.* Edited and translated by Frederic Ewen. New York, Citadel Press 1959.

Herwegh, Georg. *Herweghs Werke in drei Teilen.* Hrsg. Hermann Tardel. 3 vols. in 1. Berlin, Bong & Co., 1909.

Herzen, Aleksandr. *From the Other Shore, and The Russian People and Socialism, an Open Letter to Jules Michelet.* Introduction by Isaiah Berlin. 1st American ed. Library of Ideas. New York, G. Braziller, 1956.

———. *My Past and Thoughts; the memoirs of Alexander Herzen.* Translated by Constance Black Garnett and Humphrey Higgens. 4 vols. New York, Knopf, 1968 [1908].

Herzen, Aleksandr. *Selected Philosophical Works*. Translated from the Russian by L. Navrozov. Moscow, Foreign Languages Publishing House, 1956.

Immermann, Karl Leberecht. *Die Epigonen: Familienmemoiren in neun Büchern 1823–1835*. Textvarianten, Kommentar, Zeittafel und Nachwort herausgegeben von Peter Hasubek. Winkler Dünndruck Ausgabe. Munich, Winkler, 1981.

Keller, Gottfried. "Wien 1848." In *Gesammelte Gedichte von Gottfried Keller*. Hrsg. von Jonas Fränkel. Bern und Leipzig, Benteli, 1931. Bd. I, sect. vi: *Rhein- und Naturlieder*.

Klein, Tim, ed. *1848: der Vorkampf deutscher Einheit und Freiheit: Erinnerungen, Urkunden, Berichte, Briefe*. Munich, Ebenhausen, Leipzig, W. Langewiesche-Brandt, 1914.

Kostomarov, Nikolai Ivanovich. *Avtobiografiia N.I. Kostomarova*. Pod redaktsiei V. Kotel'nikova. Biblioteka memuarov. Moskva, Zadruga, 1922.

Macaulay, Thomas Babington. *Prose and Poetry*. Selected by G.M. Young. The Reynard Library. Cambridge, Harvard University Press, 1952.

——. "Sir James Mackintosh" (1835). In *Critical and Historical Essays*, vol. 1. Ed. by Alexander James Grieve. London, J.M. Dent. & Sons; New York, E.P. Dutton, 1907.

Martineau, Harriet. *Harriet Martineau's Autobiography*. New introduction by Gaby Weiner. London, Virago Press, 1983. 2 vols. [Reprinted from 3d edition, Smith, Elder & Co, 1877.].

Martineau, Harriet, George Lillie Craik & Charles Knight. *History of the Peace: being a history of England from 1816 to 1854*. Boston, Walker, Wise & Co., 1864–1866.

Marx, Karl. "Class Struggles in France." In Marx, Karl and Friedrich Engels, *Selected Works*. vol. 2. Moscow, Foreign Languages Pub. House, 2 vols. 1951.

——. *Early Texts*. Selected & edited by David McLellan. New York, Barnes & Noble, 1971.

——. *Karl Marx: Early Writings*. Ed. by T.B. Bottomore. New York, McGraw-Hill, 1964.

——. "Notes in James Mill's Elements of Political Economy." In Marx, Karl, Friedrich Engels, *Werke*. Ergänzungsband. 1. Aufl., 2 vols. Berlin, Dietz, 1967–1968.

——. *Zur Kritik der Hegelschen Rechtsphilosophie*. Ed. by Martina Thom, 1. Aufl. Reclams Universal-Bibliothek, Bd. 1135: Philosophie, Geschichte, Kulturgeschichte. Leipzig, P. Reclam, 1986.

—— & Engels, Friedrich. *Karl Marx, Friedrich Engels Gesamtausgabe* (MEGA). 1. Aufl. Hrsg. vom Institut für Marxismus-Leninismus beim Zentralkomitee der Kommunistischen Partei der Sowjetunion und vom Institut für Marxismus-Leninismus beim Zentralkomitee der Sozialistischen Einheitspartei Deutschlands. Berlin, Dietz, 1972.

——. *The Communist Manifesto*. See Editor's Note at top of bibliography.

——. *The German Ideology (Deutsche Ideologie)*. In Marx, Karl, *Der historische Materialismus; die Frühschriften*, Ed. by Siegfried Landshut and J.P. Mayer. 2 vols. Leipzig, A. Kröner, 1952 [1932].

Massey, Gerald. *My Lyrical Life; poems old and new*. Boston, Colby, 1889.

McLellan, David. See Marx, Karl, *Early Texts*.

MacNally, Raymond T. See Chaadaev, Peter, *Major Works*.

Mill, Harriet Taylor. "Enfranchisement of Women." In *The Complete Works of Harriet Taylor Mill*. Ed. by Jo Ellen Jacob and Paula Harms Payne. Bloomington, Indiana University Press, 1998.

Mill, John Stuart. *Autobiography*. Ed. by Jack Stillinger. Boston, Houghton Mifflin, 1969.

——. *The Early Draft of John Stuart Mill's Autobiography*. Edited by Jack Stillinger, Urbana, University of Illinois Press, 1961.

——. *The Earlier Letters of John Stuart Mill, 1812–1848*. Edited by Francis E. Mineka. Collected works of John Stuart Mill, vols. 12–13. Toronto, University of Toronto Press; London: Routledge & Kegan Paul, 1963.

Mill, John Stuart. *Essays on Politics and Culture.* Ed. and with an introd. by Gertrude Himmel-farb. Garden City, N.Y., Doubleday, 1962.

——. "Enfranchisement of Women." See Mill, Harriet Taylor.

——. "The French Revolution of 1848 and Its Assailants." *Westminster and Foreign Quarterly Review* 51, April 1849, 1–47. Reprinted in Mill, *Dissertations and Discussions,* vol. 2, pp. 335–410. London, G. Routledge (= The Collected Works of John Stuart Mill, ed. J. M. Robson. Toronto, University of Toronto Press, 19).

——. *John Mill's Boyhood Visit to France: being a journal and notebook.* Edited by Anna Jean Mill. Toronto, University of Toronto Press, 1992 [1960].

——. Auguste Comte. *Lettres inédites de John Stuart Mill à Auguste Comte.* Ed. by Lucien Lévy-Bruhl. Bibliothèque de philosophie contemporaine. Paris, F. Alcan, 1899.

——. "The Negro Question." In *Collected Works,* vol. 21: Essays on Equality, Law, and Education. Toronto, University of Toronto Press, 1984.

——. On Liberty. In *The Spirit Of The Age; On Liberty; The Subjection Of Women.* Norton Critical Edition. Ed. by Alan Ryan. New York, W.W. Norton, 1996.

——. *Principles of Political Economy with some of their Applications to Social Philosophy.* Ed. by William J. Ashley. Seventh edition. London, Longmans, Green, 1909 [1871].

——. John Stuart. The Spirit of the Age. In *The Spirit Of The Age; On Liberty; The Subjection Of Women.* Norton Critical Edition. Ed. by Alan Ryan. New York, W.W. Norton, 1996.

——. *The Subjection of Women.* Introd. by Wendell Robert Carr. Cambridge, M.I.T. Press 1970.

Milton, John. *Paradise Lost.* (See Editor's Note at top of Bibliography.).

Owen, Robert. *The Life of Robert Owen.* Reprints of Economic Classics. New York, A.M. Kelley Publishers. 2 vols., 1967 [1857].

Petöfi, Sándor. *Petofi: ein Lesebuch für unsere Zeit.* Hrsg. von Gerhard Steiner in Gemeinschaft mit Josef Turóczi-Trostler und Endre Gáspár. Weimar, Thüringer Volksverlag, 1955.

——. *Prosaische Schriften von Alexander Petöfi.* Aus dem Magyarischen von Adolph Kohut. Reclams Universal-Bibliothek. Leipzig, Philipp Reclam, jun., 1895.

——. *Sixty Poems.* Transl. into English verse by Eugénie Bayard Pierce and Emil Delmár. Introd. by Joseph Reményi. Published under the auspices of the Petöfi Society of Budapest. Budapest, 1948.

Platen, August, Graf von. *Platens Werke.* Hrsg. von G.A. Wolff und V. Schweizer. Kritisch durchgesehene und erläuterte Ausgabe. Meyers Klassiker-Ausgaben. Leipzig und Wien, Bibliographisches Institut. 2 vols., 1895.

Proudhon, Pierre-Joseph, *What is Property? an enquiry into the principle of right and of government.* With a biographical essay by J.A. Langlois. Translated from the French by Benjamin R. Tucker. New York, H. Fertig, 1966.

Pushkin, Aleksandr Sergeevich. *Pushkin on Literature.* Ed. by Tatiana Wolff. London, Methuen, 1971.

Quinet, Edgar. *Prométhée. Les esclaves.* Paris, Hachette, 1895.

Shevchenko, Taras. *Taras Shevchenko, the poet of Ukraine; selected poems.* Ed. by Clarence Augustus Manning. Jersey City, N.J., Ukrainian National Association, 1945.

——. *Tvori.* 3 vols. Winnipeg, Ukrainian pub. Co. [n.d.].

Shorter, Clement King, ed. *The Bront's; life and letters. Being an attempt to present a full and final record of the lives of the three sisters, Charlotte, Emily and Anne Bront' from the biographies of Mrs. Gaskell and others, and from numerous hitherto unpublished manuscripts and letters.* 2 vols. London, Hodder and Stoughton, 1908.

Steiner. See Petöfi, Sándor, *Lesebuch.*

Strauss, David Friedrich. *Ausgewählte Briefe von David Friedrich Strauss*. Hrsg. Von Eduard Zeller. Bonn, E. Strauss, 1895.

——. *Christian Märklin*. In seine *Gesammelte Schriften*, Band 10. Hrsg. von Schubart, Christian Friedrich Daniel, Eduard Zeller, Bonn, E. Strauss, 1876–1878.

——. *The Life of Jesus: critically examined*. Transl. from the 4th German edition by George Eliot. 3 vols. London, Chapman, Brothers, 1846.

Tocqueville, Alexis de. *Democracy in America, an abridgment*. Translated by Henry Reeve, edited by Henry Steele Commager. The World's Classics. Galaxy Edition, 3. New York, Oxford University Press, 1947.

——. *Journeys to England and Ireland*. Transl. by George Lawrence and K. P. Mayer. Ed. by J. P. Mayer. New Haven, Yale University Press, 1958.

Tristan, Flora. *Flora Tristan's London Journal, 1840 = Promenades dans Londres*. Translated from the French by Dennis Palmer and Giselle Pincetl. Boston, Charles River Books, 1980.

Turgenev, Ivan Sergeevich. *Literary Reminiscences and Autobiographical Fragments*. Translated with an introd. by David Magarshack, and an essay on Turgenev by Edmund Wilson. New York, Farrar, Straus and Cudahy, 1958.

Victoria, Queen of Great Britain and Henry John Temple Palmerston. *Regina vs. Palmerston; the correspondence between Queen Victoria and her Foreign and Prime Minister, 1837–1865*. Ed. by Brian Connell. Garden City, N.Y., Doubleday, 1961.

Wagner, Richard. *Letters of Richard Wagner*. Ed. by Wilhelm Altmann, transl. by Mildred Mary Bozman. Dent's International Library of Books on Music. London & Toronto, J.M. Dent & Sons Ltd.; New York, E.P. Dutton & Co. 1927, 2 vols.

——. *Sämtliche Briefe*. Hrsg. von Gertrud Strobel, Werner Wolf, Werner Breig, Klaus Burmeister, Johannes Forner, Leipzig, Deutscher Verlag für Musik VEB, 14 vols. 1967.

——. *Sämtliche Schriften und Dichtungen*. Hrsg. von Richard Sternfeld und Hans von Wolzogen, Volksausgabe. 6. auflage … Leipzig, Breitkopf & Härtel 1912–1914, 16 vols.

——. "Aphorismen," in *Sämtliche Schriften*, vol. 12.

——. "Die Kunst und die Revolution," in *Sämtliche Schriften*, vol. 3.

——. "Das Künstlertum des Zukunft," in *Sämtliche Schriften*, vol. 12.

——. *Mein Leben*, in *Sämtliche Schriften*. vols. 12, 13, 14.

——. "Eine Mitteilung an meine Freunde," in *Sämtliche Schriften*, vol. 4.

——. "Die Niebelungen," in *Sämtliche Schriften*, vol. 2.

——. "Oper und Drama," in *Sämtliche Schriften*, vols. 3, 4.

——. Rejected Passages, in *Sämtliche Schriften*, vol. 12.

Weerth, Georg. *Fragment eines Romans*. Ed. by Siegfried, Unseld. Frankfurt a.M., Insel-Verlag, 1965.

——. *Sämtliche Werke*. Berlin, Aufbau-Verlag, 5 vols. 1956–1957.

Whitman, Walt. "To a Foil'd European Revolutionaire." In *Leaves of Grass*, 1855, (See Editor's Note at top of Bibliography.).

Secondary Sources

Acton, Edward. *Alexander Herzen and the Role of the Intellectual Revolutionary*. Cambridge and New York, Cambridge University Press, 1979.

Altick, Richard Daniel. *Victorian People and Ideas; a companion for the modern reader of Victorian literature*. New York, Norton 1973.

Annenkov, P.V. and Arthur P. Mendel. *The Extraordinary Decade: literary memoirs*. Ann Arbor, University of Michigan Press, 1968.

Arnstein, Walter L. "The Survival of Victorian Aristocracy." In *The Rich, the Well Born, and the*

Powerful; elites and upper classes in history, pp. 203–257. Ed. by Frederic Cople Jaher. Urbana, University of Illinois Press, 1973.

Aron, Raymond. *Main Currents in Sociological Thought*. 2 vols. Garden City, N.Y., Anchor Books, 1968–1970.

Arvon, Henri. See Bakunin, M. *Michel Bakounine ou La vie contre la science.*

Arvon, Henri, and Malcolm Patterson. *Bakounine: absolu et revolution*. Paris, Éditions du Cerf, 1972.

Avineri, Shlomo. *The Social and Political Thought of Karl Marx*. Cambridge Studies in the History and Theory of Politics. London, Cambridge University Press, 1968.

Bagehot, Walter. *The English Constitution*. Introd. by R.H.S. Crossman. Ithaca, N.Y., Cornell University Press, 1966 [1867].

Bakunin, Mikhail Aleksandrovich. *Michel Bakounine ou La vie contre la science*. Ed. by Henri Arvon. [Paris], Seghers, 1966.

Barthes, Roland. See Michelet, J. *Michelet par lui-même.*

Ben-Israel Kidron, Hedva. *English Historians on the French Revolution*. Cambridge, England; New York, Cambridge University Press, 2002 [1968].

Berlin, Isaiah. "Russia and 1848." *Slavonic and East European Review*, 26 (April 1948), pp. 341–360.

Blanc, Louis. *Révolution française: histoire de dix ans, 1830–1840*. Paris, G. Baillière, 12. ed., 5 vols., 1877–1883. [Vol. 1: 12. éd. augm. de nouveaux documents diplomatiques, 1877; vols. 2–5: Nouv. éd. augm. de nouveaux documents diplomatiques, 1883.].

———. *The Organization of Labour* London, H.G. Clarke, 1848.

Bojko, Jurij. "Taras Shevchenko and West European Literature." *Slavic and East-European Review* 34 (1956), pp. 77–98. Reprinted in Manning, ed., *Europe's Freedom Fighter*, pp.18–26.

Boiko, Iurii and Erwin Koschmieder. *Taras Sevcenko; sein Leben und sein Werk*. Wiesbaden, Otto Harrassowitz, 1965.

Bowle, John. *Politics and Opinion in the Nineteenth Century; an historical introduction*. London, J. Cape, 1966.

Bowman, Herbert Eugene, *Vissarion Belinski, 1811–1848; a study in the origins of social criticism in Russia*. New York, Russell & Russell, 1969.

Briggs, Asa. *Victorian People; a reassessment of persons and themes, 1851–67*. [Chicago], University of Chicago Press, 1973.

———.1921– *The Age of Iimprovement, 1783–1867*. Harlow, England; New York, Longman, 2000.

———. *Chartist Studies*. London: Macmillan, 1977.

Buckley, Jerome Hamilton. *Season of Youth: the Bildungsroman from Dickens to Golding*. Cambridge, Mass., Harvard University Press, 1974.

———. *The Victorian Temper: a study in literary culture*. Cambridge, Cambridge University Press, 1981.

Burn, W. L. *The Age of Equipoise: a Study of the Mid-Victorian Generation*. Aldershot, Gregg Revivals, 1993.

Carr, Edward Hallett, *Michael Bakunin*. London, Macmillan, 1975 [1937].

Chevalier, Louis, *Laboring Classes and Dangerous Classes in Paris during the First Half of the Nineteenth Century*. Princeton, N.J., Princeton University Press, 1981 [1973].

Chizhevski, Dimitri. "Gogol Studien." *Forum Slavicum* 10 (1966). Reprinted in Tschizevskij, Dmitri, ed., *Gogol, Turgenev, Dostoevskij, Tolstoj: zur russischen Literatur des neunzehnten Jahrhunderts*, pp. 57–126. Munich, Fink.

Clarkson, Jesse Dunsmore. *A History of Russia, from the Ninth Century*. London, Longmans, 1962.

Cockshut, A.O.J. "Victorian Thought." In *The Victorians (The New History of Literature)*, pp. 13–40. Ed. by Arthur Pollard. New York, Peter Bedrick Books, 1987.

Cole, G. D. H. and Raymond William Postgate, *The British Common People, 1746–1938*. New York, A.A. Knopf, 1939.

Connell, Brian, ed. See Primary Source bibliography: Victoria, Queen of Great Britain.

Cornu, Auguste. *Karl Marx et Friedrich Engels; leur vie et leur oeuvre*. 1. éd. Paris, Presses Universitaires de France, 1955, 2 vols.

——. *Karl Marx et Friedrich Engels: Leur vie et leur oeuvre*. Tome 3: *Marx à Paris*. Paris, Presses Universitaires de France, 1962.

——. *Karl Marx et Friedrich Engels: leur vie et leur oeuvre*. Tome 4: *La formation du matérialisme historique (1845–1846)*. Paris: Presses Universitaires de France, 1970.

Cruikshank, Robert James. *Roaring Century, 1846–1946*. London, H. Hamilton 1946.

Cuvillier, Armand and Georges Bourgin. *Hommes et idéologies de 1840*. Paris, Librairie M. Rivière, 1956.

De Luna, Frederick A. *The French Republic under Cavaignac, 1848*. Princeton, N.J., Princeton University Press, 1969.

Derry, John W. *The Radical Tradition: Tom Paine to Lloyd George*. London, Melbourne [etc.], Macmillan; New York, St. Martin's Press, 1967.

Dommanget, Maurice. *Auguste Blanqui et la révolution de 1848*. Par's: La Haye, Mouton, 1972.

Driessen, Frederik Christoffel. *Gogol as a Short-story Writer; a study of his technique of composition*. The Hague, Mouton, 1965.

Droz, Jacques. *Europe between Revolutions, 1815–1848*. Ithaca, N.Y., Cornell University Press, 1980, [1967].

Dupont, Pierre. "La France—à Pie IX." *Muse Populaire. Chants et poésies*. Paris, 2me éd. 1851.

Evans, David Owen. *Social Romanticism in France, 1830–1848; with a selective critical bibliography*. New York, Octagon Books, 1969 [1951].

Evans, Robert Jocelyn. *The Victorian Age 1815–1914*. 2nd ed. London, Edward Arnold, 1968.

Ewen, Frederic. *Heroic Imagination: the creative genius of Europe from Waterloo (1815) to the Revolution of 1848*. New York, New York University Press, 2004 [1984].

——. *The Prestige of Schiller in England, 1788–1859*. New York, AMS Press, 1973 [1932].

Fischer, Alexander. *Petöfi's Leben und Werke. Eingeführt von Maurus J-kai*. Leipzig, W. Friedrich, 1889.

Forster, John. *The Life of Charles Dickens; in 2 volumes*. London, Dent; New York, Dutton, 1969.

Fournier, Albert. "George Sand en 1848." *Europe* 26 (1948), pp. 140–150.

Fried, Albert and Ronald Sanders, eds. *Socialist Thought: a documentary history*. Garden City, N.Y., Anchor Books, 1964.

Froude, James Anthony. *Thomas Carlyle: a history of the first forty years of his life, 1795–1835*. American edition. New York, C. Scribner's Sons, 2 vols., 1897.

——. *Thomas Carlyle: a history of his life in London, 1834–1881*, 2 vols., London, Longmans, Green, 1897.

Gaskell, Elizabeth Cleghorn. *The Life of Charlotte Bront'*. Ed. by Alan Sheldon. Harmondsworth, Penguin, 1975.

Geffroy, Gustave. *L'enfermé*. Éd. revue et augmentée par l'auteur. Bibliothéque de l'Académie Goncourt. 2 vols. Paris, George Crès, 1926.

Gérin, Winifred. *Emily Bront': a biography*. Oxford; New York, Oxford University Press, 1971.

Gérin, Winifred. *Charlotte Bront': the evolution of genius*. Oxford, Clarendon Press, 1967.

Gering, Hugo, ed. *Die Edda: die Lieder der Sogenannten älteren Edda: nebst einem Anhang, Die mythischen und heroischen Erzählungen der Snorra Edda.* Leipzig, Wien, Bibliographisches Institut, 1896.

Guillevic, E. See Rilsky, Maxime, Alexander Deitch, & Eugène Guillevic.

Haight, Gordon Sherman. *George Eliot: a biography.* London, Clarendon Press, 1968.

——. "The Carlyles and the Leweses." In his *George Eliot's Originals and Contemporaries: essays in Victorian literary history and biography,* pp. 91–116. Ann Arbor, University of Michigan Press, 1992.

Halévy, Elie. *The Triumph of Reform 1830–1841.* History of the English People in the Nineteenth Century, 3. London, Benn, 1961.

Hayek, Friedrich A von. *John Stuart Mill and Harriet Taylor: their friendship and subsequent marriage.* London, Routledge & Kegan Paul, 1969 [1951].

Hayward, Arthur Lawrence. *The Days of Dickens: a glance at some aspects of early Victorian life in London.* New York, E.P. Dutton; London, G. Routledge & Sons, 1926.

Hibbert, Christopher. *King Mob: the story of Lord George Gordon and the riots of 1780.* London, New York: Longmans, Green, 1958.

Himmelfarb, Gertrude. "The Two Mills." *The New Leader,* May 10, 1965, pp. 26–29.

Hingley, Ronald. *The Undiscovered Dostoyevsky.* London, H. Hamilton, 1962.

Hobsbawm, E. J. *The Age of Revolution: Europe 1789–1848* New York, Praeger, 1969 [1962].

Hofmann, Michel Rostislav. *Les grands romanciers russes.* Paris, P. Waleffe, 1967.

Hollis, Patricia. *The Pauper Press: a study in working-class radicalism of the 1830s.* London, Oxford University Press, 1970.

Hook, Sidney. *From Hegel to Marx; studies in the intellectual development of Karl Marx.* Ann Arbor, University of Michigan Press, 1962.

Houghton, Walter Edwards. *The Victorian Frame of Mind, 1830–1870.* New Haven, for Wellesley College by Yale University Press, 1985.

House, Humphry. *The Dickens World.* London, New York, Oxford University Press, 1971.

Hovell, Mark. *The Chartist Movement.* Ed. by T.F. Tout. 3d edition. Manchester, Manchester University Press, 1970.

Howe, Susanne. *Wilhelm Meister and his English Kinsmen; apprentices to life,* New York, Columbia University Press, 1930.

Huch, Ricarda Octavia. *Michael Bakunin und die Anarchie.* Leipzig, Insel-Verlag, 1923.

——. *1848; die Revolution des 19. Jahrhunderts in Deutschland.* Zürich, Atlantis Verlag 1944.

——. *Die Romantik; Ausbreitung, Blütezeit und Verfall.* Tübingen, R. Wunderlich, 1951.

Hulme, Hilda M. "Middlemarch as Science-Fiction: Notes on Language and Imagery." *Novel: a Forum of Fiction* 2 (1968), pp. 36–45.

Jackson, T. A. *Ireland her own; an outline history of the Irish struggle for national freedom and independence.* New York, International Publishers, 1970.

Jamati, Paul. "Un poète et un historien de '48: Louis Ménard." *Europe* 26 (Fevrier 1948), pp. 175–194.

James, Henry. *Views and Reviews.* Introd. by LeRoy Phillips. Freeport, N.Y., Books for Libraries, 1968 [1908].

Jewsbury, Geraldine Endsor. *The History of an Adopted Child.* New York: Harper & Brothers, 1853.

Johnson, Edgar. *Charles Dickens, His Tragedy and Triumph.* 2 vols. Boston, Little, Brown, 1965 [1952].

Jordan, Zbigniew A. *The Evolution of Dialectical Materialism: a philosophical and sociological analysis.* London, Melbourne [etc.] Macmillan; New York, St. Martin's Press, 1967.

Kamenka, Eugene. *Philosophy of Ludwig Feuerbach.* New York, Praeger, 1969.

Karlinsky, Simon. *The Sexual Labyrinth of Nikolai Gogol.* Cambridge, Harvard University Press, 1976.

Keefe, Robert. *Charlotte Bront"s World of Death.* Austin, University of Texas Press, 1979.

Kettle, Arnold. "Felix Holt the Radical." In *Critical Essays on George Eliot.* Edited by Barbara Nathan Hardy. London, Routledge & Kegan Paul, 1970.

Kingsley, Charles. *Yeast; a problem.* (The Life and Works of Charles Kingsley, vol. 15.) London, New York, Macmillan, 1902. [A reissue of the fourth edition of 1859, which contains an extra preface not in the first edition. cf. p. v–xii.].

Kirk, Russell. *The Conservative Mind, from Burke to Eliot.* 3d, revised ed. Chicago, H. Regnery Co., 1960.

Klein, Tim. See Primary Source bibliography.

Lavrin, Janko. *Nikolai Gogol, 1809–1852; a centenary survey.* New York, Russell & Russell, 1968 [1951].

Legge, J. G. *Rhyme and Revolution in Germany: a study in German history, life, literature and character, 1813–1850.* New York, Brentano, 1919.

Lévy, Albert. *David-Frédéric Strauss, la vie et l'oeuvre.* Paris, F. Alcan, 1910.

Lindsay, Jack. *Charles Dickens; a biographical and critical study.* London, Dakers, 1950.

Liptzin, Solomon. *Lyric Pioneers of Modern Germany; studies in German social poetry.* New York, Columbia University Press, 1928.

Loewenberg, Jacob, ed. See Hegel, G.W.F. *Hegel Selections*, in Primary Source bibliography.

Löwith, Karl. *From Hegel to Nietzsche: the revolution in nineteenth-century thought.* Garden City, N.Y., Doubleday, 1967 [1964].

Longford, Elizabeth Harman Pakenham, Countess of. *Queen Victoria: born to succeed.* New York, Harper & Row 1965 [1964].

———. *Wellington: pillar of state.* New York, Harper, 1972.

Loubère, Leo A. *Louis Blanc: his life and his contribution to the rise of French Jacobin-socialism.* Evanston, Ill., Northwestern University Press, 1961.

Magarshack, David. *Gogol, a Life.* London, Faber and Faber, 1957.

Malia, Martin E. *Alexander Herzen and the Birth of Russian Socialism, 1812–1855.* Cambridge, Harvard University Press, 1961.

Manning, Clarence Augustus. *Europe's Freedom Fighter: Taras Shevchenko, 1814–1861; a documentary biography of Ukraine's poet laureate and national hero.* Washington, U.S. Govt. Print. Office, 1960.

Marcuse, Herbert. *Reason and revolution: Hegel and the rise of social theory.* Atlantic Highlands, N.J., Humanities Press, 1989 [1941].

Martin, George Whitney. *Verdi: his music, life, and times.* New York, Dodd, Mead, 1983 [1963].

Martin, Robert Bernard. *The Dust of Combat, a Life of Charles Kingsley.* 1st American ed. New York, Norton, 1960.

Masaryk, T.G. *The Spirit of Russia; studies in history, literature and philosophy.* **2d ed.** London, G. Allen & Unwin; New York, Macmillan, 1955.

Maude, Aylmer. *The Life of Tolstoy.* New York, Dodd, Mead. 2 vols., 1910.

Mayer, Gustav. *Friedrich Engels: eine Biographie.* 2., verbreitete Auflage. 2 vols. Haag, Martinus Nijhoff, 1934.

———. *Friedrich Engels; a biography.* New York, H. Fertig, 1969, [1936].

Mazlish, Bruce. *James and John Stuart Mill: father and son in the nineteenth century* New York, Basic Books, 1975.

McLellan, David. *Marx before Marxism.* New York, Harper & Row, 1970.

McLellan, David. *The Young Hegelians and Karl Marx.* New York, F.A. Praeger, 1969.

Mehring, Franz. *Karl Marx, the Story of His Life*. Ann Arbor, University of Michigan Press, 1962.

Michelet, Jules. *Michelet par lui-même*. Ed. by Roland Barthes. Paris, Editions du Seuil, 1965.

——. *Histoire de France*. Nouvelle edition, revue et augmentée. Paris, C. Marpon et E. Flammarion, 19 vols., 1879–1884.

——. *Le peuple*. Ed. by Lucien Refort. Edition originale, Paris, M. Didier, 1947. [English transl. Michelet, Jules. *The People*. Urbana, University of Illinois Press, 1973.]

Mochulskii, Konstantin. *Dostoevsky: his life and work*. Princeton, N.J., Princeton University Press, 1971 [1967].

Möller, Jürgen, comp. *Deutsche beschimpfen Deutsche: vierhundert Jahre Schelt- und Schmähreden*. Hamburg, Claassen Verlag, 1968.

Moglen, Helene. *Charlotte Bront': the self conceived*. Madison, University of Wisconsin Press, 1984 [1976].

Monas, Sidney. *The Third Section; police and society in Russia under Nicholas I*. Cambridge, Harvard University Press, 1961.

Mougin, Henri. *Pierre Leroux*. Paris, Éditions sociales internationales, 1938.

Mueller, Iris Wessel. *John Stuart Mill and French Thought*. Urbana, University of Illinois Press, 1956.

Myakotin, V. "Nicholas I (1825–1855): The Early Years." In *The History of Russia, vol. 2: The Successors of Peter the Great from Catherine I to the Reign of Nicholas I*, pp. 218–263. Ed. by Paul Miliukov, Charles Seignobos & Louis Eisenmann. Transl. by Charles Lam Markmann. New York, Funk and Wagnalls, 1968–1969.

Myers, William. "George Eliot: Politics and Personality," In *Literature and Politics in the Nineteenth Century*, pp. 105–129. Edited by John Lucas. London, Methuen, 1971.

Nabokov, Vladimir. *Nikolai Gogol*, Norfolk, Conn., New Directions Books, 1944.

Neff, Emery Edward. *Carlyle and Mill; an introduction to Victorian thought*, New York, Columbia University Press, 1926.

Newman, Ernest. *The Life of Richard Wagner*. New York, A.A. Knopf. 4 vols, 1933–1946.

Nicolin, Günther, ed. *Hegel in Berichten seiner Zeitgenossen*. Hamburg, F. Meine, 1970.

Nikitenko, A. *The Diary of a Russian Censor*. Abridged, ed. & transl. by Helen Saltz Jacobson. Amherst: University of Massachusetts Press, 1975.

O'Meara, Patrick. *K. F. Ryleev: a political biography of the Decembrist poet*. Princeton, N.J., Princeton University Press, 1984.

Packe, Michael St. John. *The Life of John Stuart Mill*. New York, Macmillan, 1954.

Parekh, Bhikhu C., ed. *Jeremy Bentham: ten critical essays*. London, Cass 1974.

Paris, Bernard J. *Experiments in Life; George Eliot's quest for values*. Detroit, Wayne State University Press, 1965.

Parlett, M. "Influence of Contemporary Criticism on Eliot." *Studies in Philology* 30 (1933), 102–132.

Perkin, Harold James. *The Origins of Modern English Society 1780–1880*. London, Routledge & Kegan Paul; Toronto, University of Toronto Press, 1969.

Pike, Royston. *Golden Times; human documents of the Victorian age*. New York, Praeger, 1967.

Prantl, Ludwig. "Feuerbach." *Allgemeine deutsche Biographie*. Bd.6, S. 742–753. Leipzig, Duncker & Humblot, 1875–1912.

Prawer, Siegbert Salomon. *Heine, the Tragic Satirist; a study of the later poetry, 1827–1856*. Cambridge, University Press, 1961.

Price, Roger, *The French Second Republic; a social history*. Ithaca, N.Y., Cornell University Press, 1972.

Priestley, J. B. *Victoria's Heyday*. New York, Harper & Row, 1972.

Proctor, Thelwall. *Dostoevskij and the Belinskij School of Literary Criticism.* The Hague, Paris, Mouton, 1969.

Ratchford, Fannie Elizabeth. *The Bront's' Web of Childhood.* New York, Russell & Russell, 1964 [1941].

Rath, Reuben John. *The Viennese Revolution of 1848.* Austin, University of Texas Press, 1957.

Rattenbury, Owen. *Flame of Freedom: the romantic story of the Tolpuddle Martyrs.* With foreword by Arthur Henderson and new preface. 2nd ed. London, Epworth Press, 1933.

Ray, Gordon Norton. *Thackeray: the uses of adversity, 1811–1846.* New York, McGraw-Hill, 1955.

Riasanovsky, Nicholas Valentine. "Fourierism in Russia: an Estimate of the Petraševcy." *American Slavic and East European Review* 12 (1953), pp. 289–302.

Rilsky, Maxime. Alexandre Deitch, & Eugène Guillevic, *Tarass Chevtchenko.* Paris, Seghers, 1964.

Robertson, Priscilla Smith. *Revolutions of 1848, a Social History.* Princeton, Princeton University Press, 1952.

Robson, John M. *The Improvement of Mankind; the social and political thought of John Stuart Mill.* Toronto, University of Toronto Press; [London] Routledge and Kegan Paul, 1968.

Rosen, George. "Disease, Debility, and Death." In *The Victorian City; images and realities,* pp. 625–667. Ed. by H.J. Dyos and Michael Wolff. London, Boston, Routledge & Kegan Paul, 1973.

Rosenberg, Philip. *The Seventh Hero; Thomas Carlyle and the theory of radical activism.* Cambridge, Mass., Harvard University Press, 1974.

Rotenstreich, Nathan. *Basic Problems of Marx's Philosophy.* Indianapolis, Bobbs-Merrill, 1965.

Rudé, George F. E. *The Crowd in the French Revolution.* Oxford, Clarendon Press, 1959.

Sanger, Charles Percy. "The Structure of Wuthering Heights." In *Twentieth Century Interpretations of Wuthering Heights; a collection of critical essays.* Ed. by Thomas A. Vogler. Englewood Cliffs, N.J., Prentice-Hall, 1968.

Schloezer, Boris de. *Gogol.* Paris, Librairie Plon, 1932 [In French: *Gogol.* Paris, J.B. Janin, 1946.].

Schoyen, Albert Robert. *The Chartist Challenge; a portrait of George Julian Harney.* London, Heinemann, 1958.

Seely, Frank Friedeberg. "The Heyday of the 'Superfluous Man' in Russia." *Slavic and East European Review* 31 (1952–1953), pp. 92–112.

Seton-Watson, Hugh. *The Russian Empire.* Oxford, Clarendon Press, 1967.

Setchkarev, Vsevolod. *Gogol: His Life and Works,* New York: New York University Press, 1965. [In German: *N. V. Gogol, Leben und Schaffen.* Berlin, In Kommission bei O. Harrassowitz, 1953.].

Shine, Hill. *Carlyle and the Saint-Simonians; the concept of historical periodicity.* New York, Octagon Books, 1971 [1941].

Stace, W. T. *The Philosophy of Hegel; a systematic exposition,* New York, Dover Publications 1955.

Stanley, Arthur Penrhyn. *The Life and Correspondence of Thomas Arnold, D.D., Late Headmaster of Rugby School and Regius Professor of Modern History in the University of Oxford,* 2 vols. in 1, 1892. New York, C. Scribner's Sons.

Steiner, Gerhard. See Petöfi, Sándor, *Lesebuch.* in Primary Source bibliography.

Stender-Petersen, Adolf. "Gogol und Kotzebue." *Zeitschrift für slavische Philologie* 12 (1935), pp. 16–53.

Stern, Daniel, [pen name of Marie, Comtesse d'Agoult]. *Histoire de la révolution de 1848.* Avant-propos de Dominique Desanti. Paris, Balland, 1985 [1850–1853].

Struik, Dirk Jan. *Birth of the Communist Manifesto, with full text of the Manifesto, all prefaces by Marx and Engels, early drafts by Engels and other supplementary material.* New York, International Publishers, 1971.

Talmon, J.L. *Political Messianism: the Romantic phase*. London, Secker & Warburg, 1960.

Thompson, E. P. *The Making of the English Working Class*. New York, Pantheon Books, 1964 [1963].

Thomson, David. *England in the Nineteenth Century, 1815–1914*. Baltimore, Penguin Books, 1950.

Thornton, A. P. *The Habit of Authority: paternalism in British history*. London, Allen & Unwin, 1966.

Troyat, Henri and Norbert Guterman. *Firebrand; the life of Dostoevsky*. New York, Roy Publishers, 1946.

Turóczi-Trostler, József. "Petöfis Eintritt in die Weltliteratur." *Acta Litteraria* [Hungarian Academy of Sciences], 4 (1961), pp. 217–220.

Venturi, Franco. *Roots of Revolution; a history of the populist and socialist movements in nineteenth-century Russia*. New York, Knopf, 1960.

Vicinus, Martha. *The Industrial Muse: a study of nineteenth century British working-class literature*. New York, Barnes & Noble Books, 1975.

Ward, J. T. *Popular Movements, c. 1830–1850*. London, Macmillan; New York, St. Martin's Press, 197?.

Wilson, Edmund. *To the Finland Station; a study in the writing and acting of history*. Garden City, N.Y., Doubleday, 1953 [1940].

Wilson, David Alec. *Carlyle till Marriage (1795–1826)*. London, Kegan Paul, Trench, Trubner, 1923.

Williamson, Hugh Ross. "1848 in England." In *A Hundred Years of Revolution, 1848 and after [a collection of essays and documents]*. Ed. by George Woodcock. London, Porcupine Press, 1948.

Winnifrith, Tom. *The Brontës and Their Background: romance and reality*. New York, Barnes & Noble Books, 1973.

Wolff, Tatiana, ed. *Pushkin on Literature*. London, Methuen, 1971.

Woodcock, George. "The Solitary Revolutionary." *Encounter*, no. 33, Sept. 1969, pp. 46–55.

——. *Pierre-Joseph Proudhon, a biography*. London, Routledge & Paul, 1956.

Woodcock, George, ed. *A Hundred Years of Revolution, 1848 and After (a collection of essays and documents)*. London, Porcupine Press, 1948.

Woodham Smith, Cecil Blanche Fitz Gerald. *The Great Hunger: Ireland 1845–1849*. New York, Harper & Row, 1962.

——. *Queen Victoria, from Her Birth to the Death of the Prince Consort*. New York, Knopf [distributed by Random House], 1972.

Woodward, James B. *Gogol's Dead Souls*. Princeton, N.J., Princeton University Press, 1978.

Yarmolinsky, Avrahm. *Dostoevsky: his life and art*. 2d ed., completely revised and enlarged. New York, S.G. Phillips, 1957.

Zeitlin, Irving M. *Ideology and the Development of Sociological Theory*. Englewood Cliffs, N.J., Prentice-Hall, 1968.

Zetterbaum, Marvin. *Tocqueville and the Problem of Democracy*. Stanford, Calif., Stanford University Press, 1967.

Heroic Imagination *and* A Half-Century of Greatness: *Further Reading*

Abrams, M.H. *Natural Supernaturalism: tradition and revolution in romantic literature*. New York, Norton, 1971.

——. "Revolutionary Romanticism." *Bucknell Review* 36, no. 1 (1992), 19–34.

Alexander, Christine & Margaret Smith, eds. *The Oxford Companion to the Brontës.* Oxford & New York, Oxford University Press, 2003.

Barghoorn, Frederick C. "Russian Radicals and the West European Revolutions of 1848." *The Review of Politics* 11, no. 3 (July 1949), 338–354.

Berman, Marshall. *Adventures in Marxism.* London, Verso, 1999.

Davis, Michael T., ed. *Radicalism and Revolution in Britain, 1775–1848. Essays in Honour of Malcolm I. Thomis.* New York, St. Martin's Press, 2000.

Davis, Philip. *The Oxford English Literary History, vol. 8: 1830–1880: The Victorians.* Oxford University Press, 2002.

Fletcher, Pauline and John Murphy, Eds. *Wordsworth in Context.* Lewisburg, Pa., Bucknell University Press; London, Associated University Presses, 1992.

Hoppen, K. Theodore. *The Mid-Victorian Generation, 1846–1886.* Oxford, Clarendon Press, 1998.

Löwy, Michael. "The Romantic and the Marxist Critique of Modern Civilization." *Theory and Society* 16, no. 1 (November 1987), 891–904.

———. "Naphta or Settembrini? Lukács and Romantic Anticapitalism." *New German Critique* 42 (1987), 17–31.

——— & Robert Sayre. *Romanticism against the Tide of Modernity.* Transl. by Catherine Porter. Durham, NC, Duke University Press, 2001.

Lukacs, George. *The Theory of the Novel. A historico-philosophical essay on the forms of great epic literature.* Translated from the German by Anna Bostock. London, Merlin Press, 2003. (See especially the 1962 Preface.).

Murray, Christopher John, ed. *Encyclopedia of the Romantic Era, 1760–1850.* 2 vols. New York: Fitzroy Dearborn (Routledge), 2004.

Sayre, Robert and Michael Löwy. "Figures of Romantic Anti-capitalism." *New German Critique* 32 (Spring 1984), pp. 42–92. Reprinted in *Spirits of Fire: English Romantic Writers and Contemporary Historical Methods.* Ed. by G.A. Rosso and Daniel P. Watkins. Rutherford, NJ, Fairleigh Dickinson University Press, 1990.

———. "Romanticism and Capitalism." In *A Companion to European Romanticism.* Ed. by Michael Ferber. Oxford, Blackwell, 2005.

Schenck, Hans George Artur Victor. *The Mind of the European Romantics: an essay in cultural history.* Oxford & London, Oxford University Press, 1979 [1966].

Shuttleworth, Sally. *George Eliot and Nineteenth-century Science.* Cambridge, Cambridge University Press, 1984.

Sperber, Jonathan. *The European Revolutions, 1848–1851.* New York & Cambridge, Cambridge University Press, 1994.

Strandmann, H. Pogge von, and Robert J.W. Evans. *The Revolutions in Europe, 1848–1849: from reform to reaction.* Oxford & New York, Oxford University Press, 2000.

Thomis, Malcolm and Peter Holt. *Threats of Revolution in Britain, 1789–1848.* London, Macmillan, 1977.

Thompson, E.P. *The Romantics: England in a Revolutionary Age.* New York, New Press, 1997.

Wolin, Richard. *Walter Benjamin: an aesthetic of redemption.* With a new introd. by the author. Berkeley & Los Angeles, University of California Press, 1994, pp. 13–28.

Index